*Oxford in India Readings*
*in Sociology and*
*Social Anthropology*

*General Editor*
T. N. MADAN

# SOCIAL CONFLICT

# SOCIAL CONFLICT

*Edited by*

## N. JAYARAM

*and*

## SATISH SABERWAL

DELHI
OXFORD UNIVERSITY PRESS
BOMBAY CALCUTTA MADRAS
1996

Oxford University Press, Walton Street, Oxford OX2 6DP

Oxford   New York
Athens   Auckland   Bangkok   Bombay
Calcutta   Cape Town   Dar es Salaam   Delhi
Florence   Hong Kong   Istanbul   Karachi
Kuala Lumpur   Madras   Madrid   Melbourne
Mexico City   Nairobi   Paris   Singapore
Taipei   Tokyo   Toronto
and associates in
Berlin   Ibadan

ISBN 0 19 563690 2

Typeset by Rastrixi, New Delhi 110070
Printed in India at Rekha Printers Pvt. Ltd., New Delhi 110020
and published by Neil O'Brien, Oxford University Press
YMCA Library Building, Jai Singh Road, New Delhi 110001

*for André Béteille and Triloki Nath Madan*
*who have set the pace for a generation of sociologists in India*

# The Series

Published work on Indian society has grown enormously in recent years. Such writings are not however always readily available. Suitable books of Readings would go a long way in meeting the needs of students, teachers and the general readers, but not many of them exist.

Oxford University Press has therefore decided to bring out a series of Readings in sociology and social anthropology in order to fill this gap. The volumes in this Series cover a wide range of themes. Some, such as social stratification, kinship, religion and politics are of crucial significance in defining the distinctiveness of society and culture in India. Others, such as population, socio-economic development and environment highlight contemporary concerns.

The Series does not try to provide an exhaustive guide to the literature on the discipline. It does however strive to introduce the subject to the interested reader, capturing nuances of theoretical debate and diversities of approach in each area of study.

# *Preface*

Contemporary India is host to an unrivalled density of social conflicts, varied in their levels, scales, and intensities. Over the past generation, numerous scholars have studied conflicts political, agrarian, and industrial; yet the social sciences curricula have not recognized conflict as a focus for designing courses. This volume builds on an established tradition of research to consider the phenomenon in the round, in the hope that it will be a useful resource for students and teachers, and also the general reader.

Four sections assemble studies in the areas of family, of ethnic and cultural issues, of politics, and of agrarian and industrial work, and a fifth in modes of resolving conflict, including panchayats and the modern court system. The editors 'introduce' each section, and provide two substantial essays, an 'Introduction' and an 'Epilogue', besides. These latter review a wide range of perspectives on conflict, including its possible biological bases, functionalism, Marxism, and systems analysis; and also the implications of India's historical experiences for the present profusion of conflicts. These essays offer an introduction to the tradition of studying conflicts, not merely to the Readings. A good deal more could have been said but for limitations of space.

We are pleased to carry two original papers, by Bjorn Alm and Saurabh Dube, and several others which would not be readily accessible. The authors of our selections, and their original publishers, have been generous in granting requests for reprinting; and we are most grateful.

The editorial axe has fallen heavily on footnotes, more heavily in some cases than in others. The editing has addressed the needs of the student more than those of the scholar. A reader curious, for example, about the authorities for a statement will often have to go to the original publication, indicated at the beginning of each selection.

The primary responsibility for the Introduction and Sections 1, 3, and 4 lies with Jayaram; that for Sections 2 and 5 and the

Epilogue, with Saberwal who compiled the bibliography too. Throughout the editorial process, we have had a good deal of give and take, and we accept overall responsibility equally.

We owe much to sage counsel from Karmeshu, Rajiv Lochan, M.N. Panini, and Patricia Uberoi. T.N. Madan advised on the selections, commented on editorial material in detail, and gave the project strong support at every step. Professor J.K. Mittal of Indian Law Institute, New Delhi, facilitated access to its library; and we have drawn upon several other libraries in Bangalore and Delhi. Majid Siddiqi provided bibliographic aid.

We wish particularly to thank the Indian Post Office which carried for us dozens of packets between our two cities speedily, inexpensively, and unfailingly.

Finally, our two families: they appear in this volume in more ways than the reader will ever suspect.

12 April 1995                          N. Jayaram
                                       Satish Saberwal

*Editorial Conventions*

For cross-references to readings in the volume, the author's name appears within brackets, sometimes with page references.

Transcription of words from Indian languages: we have allowed the authors' originals to stand even where it meant some variation, as between Madan's *chulah* and Rizvi's *choolah*.

Some of the sources from which we exerpted our texts had been proofread carelessly in the earlier versions. We have taken the liberty of minor changes in spelling and punctuation without marking each tediously, though anything more substantial is indicated in square brackets.

# Contents

. . . society is impossible without conflict. But society is worse than impossible without control of conflict.

Paul Bohannon (1967: xii)

# Introduction

N. JAYARAM AND SATISH SABERWAL

## THE SETTING

Peace and harmony are ardently sought everywhere, bearing testimony to the pervasive, persistent reality of conflict. Since its quality, frequency, and intensity profoundly affect the structure of any society, and the life of human beings in it, every society evolves ways of limiting conflicts. A minimum of realism about conflict is a prerequisite for any society to survive.

The analysis of society from the viewpoint of its typical conflicts has a long past.[1] The conceptual sources of such analyses may be traced to the scholarly tomes of the ancient world—of Heraclitus (c. 544–484 BC) in Greece, Kautilya (c. 300 BC) in India, Han Fei Tse (c. 220 BC) in China, and Polybius (c. 205–125 BC) in Rome. The preoccupation with issues of social strife is reflected in ancient social thought and informs the development in social philosophy in the eighteenth and nineteenth centuries.

Sociology was born at a time when the phenomenon of conflict was high on Europe's intellectual agenda. The crux of philosophical thought then revolved around the fundamental problems of order and consensus, change and conflict. But the early sociologists' preoccupation with 'order' relegated interest in 'conflict' to the background.[2] This preoccupation nourished the

---

[1] Martindale (1961: 127–207) provides an excellent account of the origin and development of 'conflict theory'.

[2] Marx was the notable exception. His sociology was phrased in terms of class conflict; but he was concerned principally with a particular type of society

structural-functional paradigm, which equated organization with consensus, and consensus, in turn, with integration and equilibrium. Conflict, which was thus viewed negatively, was dismissed as being incongruous with structure.[3]

Following the Second World War, a variety of conflicts, some of which had for long remained dormant, partly owing to colonial conditions, began to resurface with a vigour and tenacity that commanded attention. Sociologists, unless blinkered by ideology, had to recognize the 'reality' of conflict and to grapple with it. A core of concepts and ideas have developed since then which illuminates certain neglected features of society and enables us to explain events which lay beyond the pale for the earlier theoretical enterprise (see Chambliss 1973; Collins 1975; and Rex 1981). We may or may not agree with Chambliss (1973: ix), that this is 'the best perspective we have for explaining social phenomena'; yet its value for analytic insight into contemporary society is beyond dispute.

Sociological curricula in India have tended to bypass 'conflict' as a focus of study in its own right; and we have yet to define the nature and scope of a 'sociology of conflict' here. This is somewhat surprising. There is no scarcity of conflicts in South Asia. Indeed it could be suggested that the region offers them in unparalleled variety and profusion: a fit setting, therefore, for producing significant contributions to this theme.[4] While the study of particular cases of conflict is commonplace in several disciplines in India, conflicts have not been grasped as a category for inquiry and understanding in a unified manner.[5] Sociologists have had

---

(bourgeois) with a specific type of socioeconomic formation (capitalism). The key concept in his analysis was that of 'contradiction', which he saw as expressed in 'class conflict', both of which would terminate with the establishment of Communism.

[3] Lewis Coser, who confirms this, was the first sociologist to explicitly analyze the positive functions of conflict. He rephrased Simmel's propositions on conflict (original in German, 1908; English translation, 1955) in the language of functionalism. Coser's work appeared only in 1956.

[4] The reader would recall that, early in the 1960s, a young Indian scholar, Andre Beteille, recognized that India provided a particularly appropriate base for the study of inequality. His work has since received worldwide attention. Notable work on conflict too is beginning to come from Indian scholars—who appear in this volume in strength.

[5] At least some academic circles in India display—or, until recently, used to

difficulty in moving their analytic focus from the relatively orderly worlds of village, caste, 'development' and the like to the much more disorderly world of conflicts.

The present Reader seeks to offer conflict as a vantage point for understanding society in India.[6] The fact that 'conflict' is still marginal to sociological curricula has had implications for this volume. First, we have to make an attempt to define the field of 'conflict' in our milieu; and we do so in a manner that emphasizes the specific historical experiences, including the counterposing of complex social, religious, and political traditions (see Epilogue, for a brief discussion). In other regions, the field may have different emphasis. In industrialized societies, large corporations and organizations occupy sizable parts of the social space; and the structures of monitoring and control within them provide the frameworks within which conflicts proceed—or are obviated. Consequently, formulations such as those by Dahrendorf (1959) would loom large in their sociology of conflict. These have not proved to be fertile in Indian studies of this phenomenon.

This Introduction seeks to outline the scope of a sociology of conflict in India. The epilogue projects further perspectives for the field. It includes a general conception of societies, their patterns of differentiation and integration, and a discussion of how conflicts in some measure can be expected to flow from the imperatives of social existence. The intervening selections present a diverse array of significant studies on conflict in India. We do not attempt an encyclopedic review of conflicts, or even of types of such conflicts. Our selections seek only to sensitize the reader

---

display—rather strong tendencies to glorify the spontaneous and the rebellious on one side and, on the other, to scoff at orderliness and any form of 'repression'. This may be a collective reaction to the all-too-recent regimes of hierarchy and conformity. The reaction may have a reason; yet no society may ignore the perils of unrestrained conflict.

Since the sociology of conflict is yet to be recognized by the Indian academic establishments as a subfield by itself, there has been very little documentationof the studies on conflict. Neither of the two surveys of research in sociology and social anthropology, commissioned by the Indian Council of Social Science Research, has a separate chapter on the sociology of conflict.

[6] Our intention was to present material covering all South Asia; but the range of work available to us concentrated on India so heavily that we could have covered other countries only in a very small way. We chose, then, to limit it to India alone.

to the substantive areas, theoretical orientations[7] and methodological perspectives, and to the wide range of options available for analysis and interpretation in the field.

Conflicts belong to the full complexity of social existence; their domain is as vast and varied as life itself. One cannot reasonably expect to be able to analyse and interpret, in any reasonable depth, any large variety of conflicts with only a few simple concepts. We draw, therefore, on work done in various specialized disciplines: anthropology, sociology, history, political science, and psychoanalysis. We do not seek to promote a special concept or analytic form but a wide variety of situations and analytic forms and styles. Taken together, these emphasize the importance of an interdisciplinary view for comprehending the complexities of conflicts adequately. By the same token we expect a wide audience for this volume.

On the other hand, we do not expect the reader to read this Introduction, let alone the whole volume, from beginning to end at one go. Rather, the reader may find it advantageous to follow his inclinations in moving back and forth, between one or another section of the Introduction and particular readings; plentiful cross-references, in the selections as well as the Introduction and the Epilogue, will help him make these interconnections.

## CONFLICT: CONCEPTUAL CLARIFICATION

In popular parlance the word conflict is used both as a noun, to mean a fight, struggle, collision, or clashing (of opposed principles, etc.), and as an intransitive verb: to come into disagreement, struggle, clash, or incompatibility. On the basis of these connotations, sociologists have defined conflict in different ways.[8] It is

---

[7] When 'theory' enters a discussion of our endemic conflicts in India at all, it has tended to find inspiration in the Marxian tradition. In some strands of that tradition, the analyst sees his job as done when he can point his finger to an economic element in the grounds for conflict. This volume does not accord economic interests such primacy. We see them as being part of a complex field of elements; our perspective is open to that complexity.

[8] The terms used in the sociological study of conflict are commonly words in everyday language. Many of them have meanings which are neither identical nor entirely distinct, but are overlapping. Moreover, while every language has everyday words for conflicts, all languages do not map conflicts in the same

fruitless to ask for a consensus on the meaning of 'conflict'. We begin, rather, with a working definition and contrast it with related, cognate terms.

Lewis Coser (1956: 8) suggests that social conflict may be taken to mean 'a struggle over values and claims to scarce status, power and resources in which the aims of the opponents are to neutralize, injure or eliminate their rivals'. Defined thus, conflict is a comprehensive category, encompassing a variety of phenomena, from brawls in the bazaar to wars between nations.

However, not all episodes of conflict, are equally significant from a sociological perspective. Sociologically viewed, 'conflict does not mean random disorder'; rather it refers to 'meaningful action in pursuit of goals' (Rex 1981: 104, 119). It is a particular kind of sociation (Simmel 1955: 13) or social relationship (Weber 1964: 132); it entails the formation of collectivities and has implications for interconnected institutions.

Given the emphasis on the relational nature of conflict, it is some times used synonymously with competition; but it is necessary to distinguish between the two. Fink (1968) has listed fourteen more or less discrete pairs of variables which have been used separately and in combination to differentiate competition from conflict. But there appear to be two key criteria: one is that competition is organized in the sense that it has rules and regulations whose observance is supervised; conflict is not so organized. In fact, conflict may start when a sense of shared 'rules of the game' is missing or begins to be flouted. The other is that conscious reference to the striving of others is not necessary in competition, but is central to conflict.

The relational concept of conflict has also to be distinguished from the dialectical concept of contradiction, which is central to Marxism. It is held that the opposition entailed in contradiction cannot be absorbed by the system, whereas that entailed in conflict can be so absorbed. For example, Marx (1963: 67f) identified the opposition between 'the forces of production' and 'the relations of production' as the prime contradiction of any socio–economic

---

way. For the speakers of any language, its map of conflicts—and the conceptualization of the experience of conflicts—reflects their historical experiences in this domain. The hazards of translating, from one language to another, hold equally for the domain of conflict.

formation, which can only be resolved by the destruction of that formation. On the other hand, the opposition arising from a supervisor–worker confrontation can be resolved without destroying the relationship between them.

There is a tendency in Marxism to view all 'significant' conflicts as a reflection of the basic contradictions of society, and to ignore other conflicts as surviving aberrations of a decadent socio–economic formation (Duncan 1973: 55–207). Contradiction, however, is essentially a logical concept, devoid of substantive empirical referents. Placing it at the centre of social analysis can result in reifying, and oversimplifying, one's conceptions of reality.

Psychological concepts like hostility, aggressive impulses, or antagonistic sentiments do bear on conflict, yet refer only to predispositions of individuals and groups to engage in behaviour of a certain kind. Whether or not feelings of hostility result in conflict depends on certain conditions, which are empirically variable. However, conflict always involves a relationship in which such impulses and sentiments find expression.

Rapaport (1960: 8) has proposed a threefold classification of conflicts: fights, game, and debates. Their distinguishing criteria are: how the opponent is viewed, the intent of the parties, and the rational content of the situation. In a fight, the opponent is viewed as a nuisance, the intent is to harm him, and the situation is devoid of rationality. In a game, the opponent is viewed as essentially like oneself, the intent is to outwit him, and the situation is completely rational. And in a debate, the opponent is viewed as essential but of a different sort, the intent is to convince him, and the situation is presumably rational.

We may also consider a set of process concepts such as resistance, protest, rebellion, revolt and revolution in relation to conflict. These processes are associated with relations of dominance. Integral to such relations are questions of power and authority—and therefore, also, the possibilities of conflict. It is possible to posit a continuum of rising conflict. At one end, those subordinated may accept their situation without question, especially if it has strong ideological support (Liddle and Joshi 1986). Further along the continuum, the subordinated may practise silent, yet determined, everyday resistance (see Dirks). Articulated resistance may be called protest. At the other end of the continuum, the subordinated, rejecting the relationship of dominance, may rise in open rebellion, revolt, or revolution (Dhanagare 1983).[9]

Finally, we may notice another dimension on which conflicts vary: in the boundedness of those who may be caught in the conflict. Those who are locked in adversary relationships may or may not be organized in clearly definable, stable groups, and we may speak of a continuum here again: At one end, communal conflict, with its relatively sharply bounded religious or other categories.[10] Somewhat more open would be factions such as described by Pettigrew (1975 ), these groupings are still rather well bounded, though one may exercise choice and shift factions if necessary. At the other end of the continuum, we may think, for example, of those who are involved in different forms of production: the interests of the owners, and possibly the workers, in a hi-tech factory may be pitted against those of low-tech artisans. Their battles may not be fought directly with each other, but indirectly, by way of influencing what third parties, their customers, choose in the market.[11]

## ANALYSIS OF CONFLICT: THE KEY DIMENSIONS

### CAUSES AND CONTENT OF CONFLICT

There can be many causes of conflict, and the content of conflict will vary accordingly. The causes of conflict may be interrelated. Even when it begins in a clear issue, the dispute, once generated, may be transformed by secondary issues. We outline below some

[9] In these distinctions, the viewpoint is that of the subordinated. Other angles are possible: illustratively, that of the dominant groups, striving for decisive authority; that of rival, more or less equivalent, persons or groups seeking the upper hand in relation to each other; or that of the observer, assessing conflict for its costs and benefits.

[10] Yet communal boundaries too are human artifacts, available for rearrangement in response to changing interests and perceptions (Barth & Cohen, 1974) has a particularly cogent statement on this reciprocal determination of interests and identities.

[11] Our discussion of these several terms stays close to surface usages. Riches 1991 outlines a sensitive procedure for exploring such terms, their connotations and implications, in lay and theoretical usages both.

of the major causes of conflict and their varying content: economic, social, political, symbolic, psychological, and multiple.

In his seminal analysis of the evolution, structure and functioning of the capitalist socio-economic formation, Marx (1963: 186–209) located the prime cause of social conflict in the skewed relations of production (between the employer and the employee) and the resultant unequal distribution of wealth and resources. Conflicts in the work sphere with an economic content are generally subsumed under the term class conflict. The selections in Section IV focus on such conflicts, Béteille and Oommen analyse conflicts in the agrarian sector; Ramaswamy and van Wersch in the industrial sphere. These selections emphasize the importance of the nature of the ideology justifying, or challenging, the inequalities prevailing in a society, the impact of market forces, and the presence or otherwise of efficient machinery for resolving conflicts as crucial to an understanding of conflict in the economic/work sphere.

The analysis of class conflict in the Marxian tradition has tended to locate the principal springs to human action in the actor's location in the world of material interests. Without ignoring such interests, analysts in the Weberian tradition have looked at the actor's fuller context, her or his values, and the manner in which s/he perceives and comprehends a situation. These values, and modes of perception and comprehension, have turned out to vary along the several dimensions of stratification (which Weber distinguished in terms of wealth, status, and power) more closely than with material interests alone. Consequently, sociologists have often discerned a close connection between stratification and conflict.

Sociologists distinguish broadly between two systems of stratification, and two corresponding types of society. The first is the fluid system of stratification or the *open society*, in which there is greater scope for movement up and down the hierarchy (that is, social mobility); and such movement actually takes place. The second is the rigid system of stratification or the closed society, in which the boundaries of various strata are rigid; movement between strata is extremely difficult, if not impossible. In reality societies lean one way or the other, depending upon certain socio-economic and cultural conditions.

Social mobility, an integral aspect of social stratification, has significant implications for understanding conflict. Rigidly organized societies with only minimum mobility, as in the traditional caste order, may display very little overt conflict; the increased conflicts in India of the past fifty years have been associated rather with somewhat increased mobility (Gupta 1991: Section IV). On the other hand, societies with high rates of mobility have, in that process, an effective safety-valve for the release of stress and tensions associated with even increasing inequality, which could otherwise accumulate and become potent sources for social disorganization. In other words, low levels of conflict may be associated both with very low, and with very high, levels of mobility; it is when the ideology of unlimited mobility has taken hold, but the reality of social institutions, and of social experience, does not accord with the ideology, that a high density of conflict may come to mark a society.

A high rate of mobility cannot be taken for granted even when the society is, in principle, 'open'; for informal closures may nevertheless restrict mobility severely. Intense conflicts can still emerge in 'open' societies when the prized opportunities are effectively available only through informal social networks and the like. On the other hand, closed societies may dissipate the potentials for conflict, inherent in inequality, through ideology. But when an ideology of inequality, or hierarchy, breaks down, closed societies encounter intense conflicts pertaining to the structure of existing relations.

Another reaction to the earlier sociological thinking on conflict in the Marxian vein, came from Dahrendorf (1959). He argued that structurally significant conflict arises in relations of dominance. Drawing insights from Weber, he argued that even moderately complex societies require that the activity of many persons and groups be coordinated; therefore, it is structurally imperative that their distribution of power and authority is unequal (see Epilogue).

While every relation of dominance may be seen as carrying the germs of conflict, the relations flowing from the overarching authority of the state are especially significant. At various levels of polity, the process of decision-making implies authority—and is inherently prone to conflict. The basis of legitimacy of authority, the manipulation of consent for its exercise, the spheres and processes of decision-making, the effectiveness of the machineries to oversee its use/abuse, etc.: all these are crucial to understanding political conflicts.

Since the extent of concentration of power, and the basis of its legitimacy, vary between societies, we may broadly posit a continuum—with democracy and totalitarianism constituting its two ends, and real regimes lying in between. In theory, power is vested in the people in a modern democracy who elect representatives to exercise authority on their behalf. The legitimacy of authority is derived from the institution of elections, and its exercise is governed by what Weber (1964: 328) termed legal-rational considerations. There are institutional mechanisms, such as an election commission and a judiciary, to oversee the process of endowing individuals with authority—and to ensure that they exercise it legitimately.

In a totalitarian regime, power is concentrated in the hands of a single individual ('leader' or 'dictator') or a small group of individuals ('junta' or 'coterie') who claim to exercise authority in the interest of the larger populace. The legitimacy of authority here rests on the charisma, of the leader or of a ruling dynasty, or on the hold he or the group has over the armed forces and the party machinery. The exercise of authority responds to the will of the leader or the group— and is beyond all scrutiny.

The contrast between democracy and totalitarianism is generally applied to the political sphere, within the boundaries of a nation state. However, we may also consider various limited spheres of authority, such as a family, a work organization, a church, or a political party in terms of this contrast. We may, for instance, distinguish between an authoritarian, patriarchal family and an egalitarian nuclear family, or between an autocratic business concern and a participatory democratic enterprise.

Democratic societies and groups accept free expressions of difference and dissent. These are more likely to institutionalize conflict (see Epilogue), evolving mechanisms suitable for handling it. Since it is relatively easy in this setting to enter conflicts openly, there is a great er chance that these would be resolved periodically, and not allowed to accumulate and intensify. Hence, conflicts in democratic societies offer only limited scope for abrupt structural changes, such as can attend a revolution, especially in the short run.

On the contrary, difference and dissent are not allowed free

expression in totalitarian regimes. Such regimes cannot institutionalize conflict; and the machineries for handling conflict, if these
exist at all, by and large function to endorse the authority of the
leader or a coterie. There is a possibility that issues which cause
conflict may accumulate if they are left unattended. Therefore,
when conflict does break out, it could do so with a force which
could sweep away the established order.

The everyday life of human beings is significantly influenced
by values and norms, which take the form of symbols and codes.
In a small scale, homogeneous society, where activities like hunt-
ing and gathering provide the principal resource base, such
symbols and codes are more or less shared by its members; but,
in a complex, heterogeneous society, different groups of people
adhere to different sets of symbols and codes. This situation is
fraught with potential for conflict between ethnic groups, religious
and linguistic communities, caste groups, and the like. It must be
ob served, however, that the symbolic element may not always
be a source of conflict on its own, suigeneris; rather, it may be
drawn in to buttress economic and/or political interest. Selections
in Section II of this Reader make the point well.

Heterogeneous societies evolve various devices for minimizing
conflicts resulting from the plurality of symbolic systems: adoption
of an overarching neutral set of codes for general use (e.g. a
secular Constitution), or granting overarching status to the code
of the predominant ethnic group or religious community (e.g. a
theocratic Constitution). Yet the overarching code may on occasion break down, or segmental codes reassert themselves, resulting in conflict.

The composition and distribution of population in a heterogeneous society, the historical experiences of the different groups
within it, the relative levels of their socioeconomic development,
the sociopsychological predispositions of the different groups, their
relative sense of unity and strength, the interest evinced by outside
groups or forces, the effectiveness of the overarching codes: such
variables are significant in understanding conflict emanating from
or involving the symbolic sphere. Several selections in this volume
illustrate conflicts of this kind (see Epilogue: Appendix).

There are important psychosocial implications for the parties
in a conflict irrespective of the sphere in which a conflict originates
and is shaped. What did one's needs, conscious and unconscious,

contribute to one's stance in the conflict, and how did its course and consequences affect one's psyche? The biopsychological, unconscious basis of conflict, and its conscious, historical experience, will engage us in Parts 5 and 6 below.

A potential for conflict marks all inter-personal relationships. Likes and dislikes, preferences and avoidances, attitudes and opinions, hopes and expectations—such elements are basic, though not confined, to such relationships. These elements have an important bearing on personality adjustment. The strength and vitality of a relationship depend upon the compatibility or otherwise of the personalities involved.

Several factors appear to be important in understanding sociopsychological conflicts: the historically shaped codes which govern inter-personal relationships, the basis for their legitimacy, the process of socialization of the person and internalization of those codes by him or her, the extent of autonomy—social, economic, psychological— attained by the person, the stakes involved in the relationship, the influence of a third party, and so forth.

We have been considering a range of sources of conflict, one at a time; yet even when a conflict begins with a single definite cause, secondary issues may soon transform the scene. In actual situations of conflict, one can see an overlapping of causes. For instance, in a case of insider-outsider conflict, the basic cause may be economic (some of the limited job opportunities going to outsiders) but it may take on an ethnic form, as linguistic or regional conflict, (see Leonard 1978). Similarly, in intra-caste conflict between the 'left' and the 'right' groups among the ex-untouchable castes in south India, the crux of contention may be political (inadequate representation in the state cabinet) but it may be joined in a cultural field (rights of worship in a temple).

A multiplicity of issues may lead to an accumulation of tension. Hardgrave (1977) has shown how the peasant revolt in Malabar in the early 1920s, the Mapilla Rebellion, was exacerbated by a convergence of a variety of issues: agrarian discontent, a perceived threat to Islam, the Khilafat agitation, inflammatory newspaper reports, and provocation by government officials, and police. The superimposition of different causes may serve to crystallize conflict, as seen succinctly in the hardening of the communal divide between Hindus and Muslims in India, the tenacity of the conflict between them, and the associated violence.

### INTENSITY OF CONFLICT

Conflicts vary in their causes and content—and in their intensity too. The intensity of conflict is a function of the combatants' socio-psychological commitment to the issues at stake; we distinguish it from the extent of destructiveness of conflict, defined in terms of the magnitude of violence accompanying it. Intensity and destructiveness of conflict vary independently, however, and each may range from high to low. Gandhian non-cooperation, for instance, may be intense, yet non-violent; *dharna* and *satyagraha* are forms of protest associated with it. Strike, *bandh, rasta roko,* and *gherao* may be violent forms of protest, whose intensity may vary. The underlying conflict can be both intense and violent, as in armed rebel lion and various forms of terrorism.

One measure of the intensity of conflict is its duration. Conflicts could be chronic and pervasive (having a long history) or transient and episodic (of short duration). Hindu-Muslim communal conflict, in some localities, illustrates the former; a fight between two student factions on a college campus the latter. It is important to note that the mode of characterizing a conflict—whether as 'chronic and pervasive' or as 'transient and episodic'—reflects how the memory of the conflict is constructed in the society, or by particular persons and scholars. For example, for the authors of *Communalism and the Writing of Indian History* (Thapar, Mukhia and Chandra 1969), and for Pandey (1990) more recently, communal conflict was essentially a phenomenon of the colonial period, and reflected the pernicious influence of the colonialists. Others may regard communal conflict as reflecting antipathies which have endured for many more centuries—and which draw on well-entrenched ideas in myth, history, and religious symbol ism, selectively, for their continuing sustenance.

### OBJECTIVES OF CONFLICT

Simmel's seminal work noted that engaging in conflict, in struggle, giving expression to our hostile, aggressive feelings, gives us satisfaction. It may help clear the air; it is cathartic (Simmel 1955: 19; Coser 1956: Ch. 3). More recently Fanon (1967: 73) enlarged on the 'cleansing power of conflict and, indeed, of violence, especially for those who have lived through the humiliation of being colonized—or otherwise subjugated.

Coser sees greater ambiguity in the release of aggressive feelings in situations of conflict; its implications need analysis. We could begin by separating hostile feelings from actual conflict. Hostile feelings may be discharged in substitute ways—say in competitive sports, or by watching sports like boxing on television; or these may be discharged towards substitute objects—as in the familiar series of a boss rebuking his manager, who does it to his foreman, who takes it out on a shop-floor worker, who goes home and yells at his wife, who spanks her child, who goes out and kicks the dog. . . . Such activities may give one temporary relief from the tensions of hostility; and this may be partially functional for some of those who are involved. Enabling the release of, perhaps, paralysing antagonisms, it may permit them to return for a while to more or less normal activity.

Yet such emotional release does not tackle the root causes of the hostile feelings which, therefore, may keep getting renewed, becoming part of a recurring cycle. That cycle is weakened or broken only when the conflict is joined with the real source of one's sense of hostility. Hence Coser's distinction between two types of conflicts (1956: 48–55): realistic and non-realistic. Realistic conflict is 'a means toward a specific end.' It arises from 'frustration of specific demands within the relationship and from estimates of gains of the participants.' It is 'directed at the presumed frustrating object' '(F)unctional alternatives as to means' are possible in this category.

Non-realistic conflict, on the other hand, is an end in itself. Though it involves interaction between two or more persons, it is 'not occasioned by the rival ends of the antagonists, but by the need for tension release of at least one of them'. In this case there exist only 'functional alternatives as to objects'.[12]

[12] van der Dennen (1987: 26ff) makes the distinction somewhat differently. *How* aggression is released has wider consequences. For hostilities, and for drives which are ordinarily *suppressed* in the group, a society may carry institutional-ized—socially sanctioned—outlets, eg in duel. Release of aggressive drives in such forms is accommodated well; it would not ordinarily disrupt relationships within the groups. Elsewhere, there may be no channels available for releasing hostility safely *against the source that earned the hostility* originally. Here, aggression may be *displaced*, then, on to substitute objects, as in witchcraft accusations. This second case corresponds to Coser's non-realistic conflict.

The contrast between realistic and non-realistic conflict may be drawn in terms of a particular kind of social situation. A worker may engage in strike activity to press for a rise in his wages, his status, or the power of his union. Alternatively, he may enter into a dispute with his supervisor in order to release his pent up hostilities: he releases them against his supervisor, for he sees in him a father figure—upon whom the antagonisms against his own father, embedded deep in the worker's unconscious, are thus discharged. Clearly, these are dissimilar types of conflict: for the first situation, it may be possible to devise reasonable solutions; for the second, it would not be as easy.

A realistic conflict may have some non-realistic elements within it. While realistic conflicts can be seen as flowing from conflicting claims to scarce status, power and resources, and from adherence to contending values and codes, non-realistic conflicts can be seen as rooted in the rigidity of social and/or personality structure. The claims, the values, and the codes can scarcely be pressed, however, except in contexts of society and personality; and therefore non-realistic elements can cast their shadow on realistic conflicts all too easily.

What Coser leaves unsaid is that the patterns of social conflict—that is, just how people pursue their interests, cope with their frustrations, and the like—are only partly a matter of individual psychology. How one acts in a particular situation is not only a function of one's own personality but also of the historical tradition in which one's personality came to acquire its form—and in which one's social milieu came to acquire its form.

We may then re-state Coser's distinction between realistic and non-realistic conflict in Weberian terms. Social conflict may take a course in which the adversaries attend to a discriminating selection of ends and means, to realistic, purposive deliberation over them; or it may follow a course shaped largely by inherited, or unconsciously set, patterns of action, without either ends or means getting fresh thought. That is to say: social conflict too may take a course dictated by various rational considerations; or it may be dictated by non-rational considerations, one's hostilities finding targets, say, on unconscious grounds.

## CONFLICT: THE UNCONSCIOUS
## AND THE BIOLOGICAL BASIS

The ubiquity and inevitability of conflict, and the attempts to institutionalize it, have often led scholars to wonder if there are some innate, endemic qualities in societies—and human beings—which predispose them, more or less unconsciously, to engage in conflict. Presuming that 'nothing can move us to act in particular ways more strongly than those elements of our psyche that we are completely unaware of' (Reynolds, Falger and Vine 1987: xvi), sociobiologists have been investigating whether some aspects of the proclivity for conflict may be ingrained in 'the genetic code' (Macdonald 1975: 210).

A major focus of interest here is the universal cultural phenomenon of in-group/out-group relations, and the tendency to look upon out-groups with hostility, a phenomenon labelled 'ethnocentrism' by Sumner (1911). In terms of evolutionary continuity, the sociobiologists explore the link between ethnocentrism and the comparable element in the behaviour of animals, namely, their preference for relatives over strangers; for the latter, they claim to have found solid genetic basis. Insights from such explorations have been synthesized by van der Dennen (1987); we summarize his argument here.

The evidence from evolutionary studies and the study of apes, 'man's nearest relatives,' suggests that 'development of a higher level of intelligence . . . would mean an increased vulnerability to emotional disturbance,' specifically, susceptibilities to fear (ibid.: 45). Human fears are legion: 'of the stranger and . . . the strange, the unknown, the out-of-control, the potential chaos, the potential evil, the potential impurity, contamination and pollution, the potential threat and danger' (ibid.: 43f). There is much evidence, from observation of animals as well as infants and children, for a possibly biologically grounded fear of strangers—and for a tendency for aggression towards them (ibid.: 18–22). Similarly, 'natural selection' among humans may well have favoured, in Lorenz's words, a 'programmed love for traditional custom'. Such biological predisposition would favour intolerance towards challenges—and towards the challengers—to a society's beliefs (ibid.: 19). This would be a kind of ground level: the biological base on which varied social arrangements and cultural resources build.

There are other, uniquely human elements which enter our consciousness, and therefore our propensity for conflict: especially the possible consequences for us of our extraordinary abilities with languages, symbols, and ideologies—and our associated ability to create religions, institutions, technologies, and much else. Van der Dennen's implication is that these man-made resources may cut either way. Depending on the tenor and the content of our cultural resources, these may serve to give us a sense of security, so as to neutralize the play of the biologically given base of suspiciousness, fear and the like; or these may serve to activate those potentials further, driving us into frenzies. Whether these man-made resources act one way or the other would depend on the precise patterns of belief, symbol, myth, ideology and practice which stand for the society's historic experiences (ibid.: 38–57).

Apropos these latter, van der Dennen notes the contributions made, to human conflict and violence, by:

> highly complex and elaborate, abstract and rule-governed, cognitive conceptual and symbolic processes, meanings and constructs of reality, attitudes, norms, values, codes of conduct, anticipations, strategies, etc. This, in turn, has its negative side: the ability of man to create psychological 'distancing devices', to dehumanize, diabolize, to exterminate his enemies like vermin in fantasy and in reality; and to generate Weltanschauungen (worldviews) in which only a small portion of humanity fits, and social paradises from which the misfits have to be expelled. Furthermore, the human being has a very vulnerable sense of self-esteem and group identity (ibid.: 42).

The prevailing myths and folklore may offer, to their carriers and audiences, models for acting aggressively towards certain others, and expectations of similar conduct from the latter too. Beck (1982) has analysed what may be a sixteenth century folk epic from a part of Tamil Nadu. This account projects close kin—agnates and affines—as being among the most likely adversaries, whose mutual relationships are heavily loaded with tension, envy, hostility, and the like. We may have a paradoxical situation here: the values may be shared, but these may serve to promote not mutual trust but conflict.

At work, here, is the mechanism of stereotyping. Certain categories of thought, more or less entrenched in one's preconscious, predispose one to expect a category of others—say Bengalis or capitalists or cricketers—to act in one or another set manner, disregarding contrary evidence about their actual behaviour. The category of others at issue may have come to be de fined in various ways: one's siblings (Beck 1982); out-groups, say Hindus (Gaborieau 1972: 92ff) or Muslims (Kakar 1982: 60, 63, 87); or, indeed, one self: one may have grown up, in a particular social ambience, imbibing the self-image of a warrior, which may predispose one to everyday social combativeness, even without wielding sticks or bombs![13] Carried into the unconscious, the same mechanism leads to entrenched categories of social opposition (see Kakar).

It should be remembered that the act of recognizing shared interests is largely a matter of perception. The situation comes to be defined in one way or another; and this moment of defining may allow the actor a measure of option. To consider a special case, a group of persons may have made considerable emotional, and other, investment in their membership in a certain religious sect or a close knit political party. One's own sense of security may depend crucially on one's fellow members in the sect or party. That is to say, one's own confidence in oneself may depend on one's fellow members accepting, and continually reconfirming, the worldview received from one's sect or party. In such a situation, anyone who shows signs of deviation may be seen as a greater threat than another who has never been associated with the worldview. Hence the intensity of conflicts within such social entities (Coser 1956: 67–72).

## CONFLICT: THE CONSCIOUS, HISTORICAL EXPERIENCE

Irrespective of how much of a biological base we concede for social conflict, the operative aspects of conflicts and their immediate consequences are essentially cultural and sociohistorical. Among the most frequent 'resources' in a conflict are issues which arise from earlier skirmishes, and which concern related combatants. Dumont (1986: 310) heard echoes of 'old quarrels suddenly revived' in the early morning brawls in his Tamil village;

---

13 We refrain from citing a particular case because we do not wish to contribute to the process of stereotyping.

and every successive Hindu-Muslim skirmish is fraught with rhetoric of earlier perfidies. Time and circumstance may give the conflict new contours—somewhat different issues, somewhat altered adversaries' ranks—but the old spirit, if one may say so, pervades the new scene.

Contributing to this continuity, amidst changes and transformations in issues and personnel, is a reciprocally acting relationship between 'conflicts' on one hand and 'identities' and social boundaries on the other. Conflicts may strengthen the combatants' own social identities and bound aries (Coser 1956: 33–48, 72–81, 87–95). One's identity, in turn, may be constituted in good measure out of the memories, recent or ancient, of earlier conflicts: the 'other's' intentions, then, are inherently suspect.

The course of social conflicts, as of other human enterprises, hinges crucially on how the actors in them define, or interpret, the (changing) situation, on what meanings they attribute to events, actions and reactions, and to the others' intentions. Between what your intentions are and how I interpret them, there can be a large margin of difference, especially if I assume, and do not try to verify, what your intentions really are. You may well be surprised at my reaction to your action, for I may have reacted not to your actual intention but to my (mistaken) conception of your intention (see Epilogue on the role of mediators). This is one reason why conflicts, as well as other social processes, are suffused with all manner of unintended and unforeseeable consequences of our actions.

Once conflict takes off, the combatants may engage in mobilizing their resources consciously. These may cover manpower, symbols, status, wealth, skills, weaponry, and much else; their ultimate limits may be set only by the combatants' ingenuity. How wide a range of resources gets assembled for a particular encounter depends on the combatants' standing, their skills, their past experience, the general quality of their judgement, and their judgement about the stakes in a particular episode.

We have to remember, however, that actors in a particular situation may draw upon, or be buoyed up by, ideas and images which carry heavy emotional charges and are deeply embedded in their culture and worldview: what Turner called 'root paradigms' (1974; Barnes 1969). Such images and ideals as that of the martyr, rooted in hallowed memory of events past, may drive one to endeavours of extraordinary fortitude and sacrifice. Other hallowed cultural resources may be amenable to, and effective in, novel situations. Several observers have commented on the manner in which the old Indian practice of *dharna*, a form of forcing one's grievances on public attention, has been deployed in recent times. Nineteenth century Benares (Dharampal 1971; Freitag 1990), Garhwal (Guha 1991), and Gujarat (Spodek 1971) provide examples close to the old practice; Gandhi's *satyagraha* transformed that practice into a mode that enabled him to face an empire.

## TOWARD A SOCIOLOGY OF CONFLICT IN INDIA

India displays an unparalleled variety of conflicts, owing partly to the complexity of her cultural traditions and social structure. In seeking a perspective on this milieu, we proceed eclectically, being receptive to different theoretical approaches, modes of enquiry, and data bases. What follows will outline the scope for a sociology of conflict in India.

### BACKGROUND AND CONTEXT

Conflicts in India today arise against a historical backdrop which has seen much mixing of cultural codes (see Epilogue), the inevitable clashes of these diverse codes, and the countless dislocations attending industrialization, urban growth, and the like. We continue to repeat slogans like 'unity in diversity' as if these emanated from some inexorable law in our social existence, despite the daily experience of conflicts arising from that diversity.

In course of the colonial encounter, numerous European ways of doing things—general laws, bureaucracy (as against the commoner officialdom), governmental monopoly over exercise of power, and much else—entered proc esses which have become crucial to the functioning of our societies. The implication of this has varied from affecting the indigenous modes of conflict resolution to generating grounds where the Western and the Indian ways of doing things—Western and Indian 'codes'—come into collision. What follows pays particular attention to the implications of this encounter with Europe; it could be just as instructive to explore the implications, for patterns of conflict, of other political and cultural encounters in earlier centuries (see, for example, Pollock 1993).[14]

The logic of colonialism served to recast our subcontinental economy in a fundamental way. At the time of independence, India and a basic economic and institutional infrastructure which enabled it to embark on planned economic development. Its economic successes since that time are often recounted in phrases like the 'green revolution' and the 'white revolution', even though the fruits of these 'revolutions' and, more generally, of economic development have gone very unevenly to different regions, and to various social groups and strata in any given region. All this has stimulated aspirations of a magnitude which sometimes defy the limits of the feasible, at least in the foreseeable future.

Much legislation was also enacted, and welfare measures begun, which have stirred Indian society to its core. Ideologies of protest and revolt have made much headway. Egalitarian ideologies, embodied for example in universal adult franchise, have shattering blows brought to bear on the received, hierarchical order. The skills for raising issues combatively, and for mobilizing for struggles, appear to have grown substantially. In contrast, there has been a marked lag over the skills, and the institutions, needed for (1) stimulating wider, collective purposes, (2) negotiating differences, and resolving conflicts, in ways that would advance such shared purposes, and (3) sustaining collective effort directed at long-term societal achievements. To legitimize all manner of challenge and struggle, while neglecting the skills and habits for resolving them in orderly ways, makes the milieu cacophonous, dense with conflicts.

MANIFESTATION AND CONTENT

The profusion of conflicts in India may be analysed in terms of the dimensions outlined above. Instead, as a backdrop for the substantive selections to follow, we shall move here along two

---

[14] We thank Dr Bhagwan Josh for calling our attention to Pollock's important paper.

overlapping continua: (1) the nature and scale of the aggregates involved in the conflict: it may involve two persons at one end, and large aggregates such as two religious communities or states at the other; and (2) the magnitude of consequences of conflict for the society and the country: its significance may be structural, having wide ramifications, at one end, or, at the other, the significance and implications may be confined to the persons or groups immediately involved.

To open the scale, there are innumerable inter-personal conflicts in everyday life. Their content varies greatly, depending partly on their institutional context (family, work site, market place, etc.). Commonly, these turn on claims over property, status, or power, disagreement over role assignment or division of labour, or simply problems of personality adjustment. This last is crucial. It tends to inject non-realistic elements into a dispute—which would persist even after the realistic elements have been resolved. Violence[15] may sharpen and intensify such conflict—and indeed terminate the relationship itself.

The structural significance of inter-personal conflicts depends on how close the relationship is, and on whether the very basis of the relationship is in dispute. The ideology governing the particular relationship (e.g. male-female, elder-younger, superior-inferior) may help resolve, or aggravate, the conflict. Where ideological support is weak or missing, such conflicts may be resolved only through external intervention, whether informally by a common friend, or by a court of law. Given the growing frequency of inter-personal conflicts in particular areas, special institutions may serve to help cope with them e.g. family courts (Parashar 1992).

Higher up the scale we have limited intra-group conflict: who gets cast into the 'opposing parties,' would depend on the nature of groups active in the milieu. Conflict within a joint family is common enough, turning on claims over ancestral property or titles, temple honours, ritual rights, and marital alliances. In extreme cases, such conflicts can be violent. Traditionally these have been resolved through: the mediation of a third party, usually a village elder; arbitration by the caste panchayat; the intervention of a religious authority—or through a consensual decision to

---

15 Violence, may it be noted, can enter *any* conflict.

separate (see Madan and Rizvi). Such mechanisms still work, especially in rural areas, while recourse to courts of law is growing in urban areas.

Further up the scale lie a variety of inter-group conflicts involving primordial aggregates. Given the entrenched place, and continuing strength, of such entities as castes, subcastes, tribes, and sects in Indian society, conflicts between them are frequent. Opposition between any two entities tends to be confined to a geographical area, e.g.the conflicts between the Sunnis and Shias in Lucknow, the Syrian Christians and Roman Catholics in central Kerala, the Reddis and Kammas in Andhra Pradesh, and the Vadagalai Iyengars and Tengalai Iyengars in Kancheepuram. Yet, some of them, drawing in larger categories, may come to have much wider spreads: between the caste Hindus and the scheduled castes (see Alm), between the 'left' and the 'right' groups among ex-untouchable castes in some south Indian states, the non-Brahmin attack on Brahmins in Tamil Nadu and Karnataka, and so forth. The anti-Mandal agitation in 1990 was the acutest expression of a pan-Indian caste conflict, pitching the 'backward against the 'forward' castes.

Group conflicts often originate in interpersonal conflicts: an incident of ragging may trigger off a communal riot. Conversely, group conflict may sour interpersonal relations between two persons. The move from interpersonal to group conflict involves collective mobilization—a crucial variable in the sociology of conflict.

The issues in inter-group conflicts involving primordial aggregates are mixed. The echo our earlier distinction between the realistic and the non-realistic elements in conflict, it may be difficult to tell where resolvable, public issues end, and intractable personality difficulties begin. Claims over symbols, use of public space/amenities, temple honours, social status, privileges, concessions and the like are the staple for such conflicts. If an economic issue, say job opportunities, or a political one, say representation in cabinet, gives the dispute a focus, a tense situation may come to a boil (Alm).

A special case of conflict involving primordial aggregates concerns tribal peoples vis-a-vis other tribes or the mainstream society. The 'we'–'they' feeling is more pronounced in the latter case, reinforced by the tribes' geographical isolation; it may add up to secessionist urges. Cultural identity is primary, though economic issues are also significant. Phadnis illustrates the situation of armed insurgency in the Northeast.

The other end of the overlapping continua carries communal conflicts, Hindu-Muslim conflict has become almost pan-Indian. It has long antecedents, and it often takes violent forms. Conflicts involving other religious categories, Hindu-Christian or Muslim-Christian are confined to limited pockets (e.g.Kerala). These do not have a long history, are sporadic, and are relatively easily contained. Though communal conflict appears to turn on questions of religious symbols and practices, often these come to stand for rivalries over land or other economic sources or in the market (see fn. 10). The invoking of religious symbols, and of memories of past 'perfidies' and conflicts, gives communal conflict its emotional edge.

Located somewhere in the middle of the continua, a number of perennial conflicts relate to the economic sphere, both industrial and agrarian. By the criterion of organizational scale, the 'industrial' encompasses a vast range of organization, from a small factory to vast bureaucracies; and it subsumes different sets of conflict relations: between employer and employees or, on their behalf, between an employers' association and trade union(s), between the unions themselves, etc. Industrial conflict is more or less institutionalized now. These relations are governed by various laws, and their conflicts regulated by particular institutions, e.g.joint management councils, or legislatively established procedures for conciliation, mediation, and arbitration. Nevertheless, such machinery may cease to be effective, allowing a conflict to grow and spread (see Ramaswamy, van Wersch).

The agrarian sector carries its own load of conflictual relations: in class terms, between landlords and peasants or between either of them and landless labourers; or in factional terms, among landlords or peasants themselves. Yet other conflicts may pit peasants against the government, say as the supplier of key agricultural inputs and regulator of the farmer's costs and earnings through subsidies (Lindberg 1992). Agricultural work has tended to be organized in units of small scale, and therefore its conflicts have remained uninstitutionalized, though the scene appears to be shifting. Kerala has long been a notable exception, reflecting the work of the Communist Parties there (see Oommen). Since a significant majority of the population lives in rural areas, agrarian conflicts are an existential reality for them. Consequently, in many a state, a good deal of political mobilization follows cleavages in the agrarian relations; and peasant movements and farmers' agitations are social realities of great import (Shah 1990: 32–84).

Similarly located on the scale are political conflicts. These may engage different political parties or factions within a party. Inter-party conflict, essentially a struggle for power, may be institutionalized. Its main arenas are the periodical elections, followed by debates in representative bodies; but it may go to the courts of law—and even to the streets. Political conflict necessitates mobilization of people around some symbols, slogans, ideology, or programme, which are incorporated in the party's manifesto. The sharpness of the conflict obviously depends upon the capacity of each party to rally people round it, which in turn is determined by the appeal of its ideology, its capacity to organize cadres and convince people, its leaders' stature, its past role in the polity, and its material resources. Political scandal and assassination, breakdown of law and order, perceived assault on religion: under certain conditions of public opinion, any happening may help to galvanize such mobilization—and define the battlelines. The course and consequence of the conflict will depend on how far the parties abide by the polity's established rules of the game.

Intra-party or factional conflict, on the other hand, is more likely to be centred on personality rather than ideology. It has to do with the past position and experience of the leaders within the party, and their command over substantial support within it. Such conflict may follow from differences over policies or programmes of the party and their implementation. In its extreme form factional conflict is schismatic, leading to a split in the party (see Rastogi). The course and consequences of such a conflict depend on the changing configurations of political parties, of the factional leaders' clout, and their party's high command's capacity to handle the pressures.

Even territorial units like the states may become parties to a conflict. Inter-state borders (e.g.between Karnataka and Maharashtra) or *river waters* (e.g.between Karnataka and Tamil Nadu or Andhra Pradesh and Maharashtra) illustrate such contention (Jain 1971; Hussain 1972). Generally confined to institutional fora

like Parliament, courts, and tribunals, yet they get easily politicized; and an inter-state conflict may precipitate violence between people from the different states. Unresolved, for whatever
political or factional reasons, such conflicts may affect not only
the relationships between the states and their people, but also
the nation's federal fabric. If the linguistic reorganization of states
gave a fillip to linguistic chauvinism, the disparities in development between them have nurtured thoughts of 'the sons of the
soil' (Weiner 1978). Behind the apparently cultural conflicts
between linguistic groups, commonly there are significant economic elements, like scarce job opportunities, or business rivalries. Within the Roman Catholic Church in Bangalore, the
Kannada-and the Tamil-speaking laity are at odds with each
other; and there are the various insider-outsider, or the local-
migrants, conflicts, e.g.the Mulki-non-Mulki in Hyderabad, the
Maharashtrian-Madrasi in Bombay, Assamese-Bengali in Assam
(Leonard 1978; Weiner 1978; Oommen 1982). Primarily economic in nature, these also have cultural overtones.

When such conflicts get articulated explicitly, and people
rallied around them, these acquire a drive for separate tribal,
linguistic, or religious identities. What starts as a not-so-violent
protest movement, demanding say a separate Jharkhand or
Gorkhaland, may well turn into terrorism and secessionism,
making a bid for a separate Khalistan, Kashmir, or Bodoland.

## THE STRATEGY

The selections in this volume, and the editorial discussions surrounding them, rest on some assumptions concerning the process
of mastering a complex task. We see two phases to this process.

In the first phase the learner imbibes a set of interconnected
concepts bearing on the task. While acquiring these concepts
need not necessarily be through explicit instruction in words and
sentences, still, whether one is knitting a sweater or analyzing a
society, it takes a good deal of skill—and this always has underlying
concepts, even if one is not aware of them. Building up one's set
of interconnected concepts, concerning any task or subject, is
slow work; and it would help to have the concepts presented
explicitly. The editors' texts, as well as several of the selections,

seek to display the use of various concepts, or analytic styles, with some clarity.

Once the learner has mastered this set of interconnected concepts, this cognitive frame, he should be able to grasp the essentials of complex real-life situations, in a corresponding domain, relatively speedily. Anyone who has learned the elements of riding a bicycle or driving a car can make split second judgements in very complex traffic conditions. Correspondingly, our selections include several accounts of the involuted intricacies of real-life conflicts. Given the set of concepts being offered, the reader should be able to construct his basic cognitive frameworks for appraising situations of conflict. The accounts of complex, real-life conflict situations would then give him the opportunity to test the cognitive frameworks for their effectiveness in comprehending that complexity in its fullness. This distinction appears to correspond to two clearly distinct, yet both crucial, kinds of learning processes (Bloch 1990).

Academics commonly imagine that the level of concepts, or 'theory', is properly the level where good academics should function; this lays us open to the charge of 'bookish' learning. Testing our concepts and theories against good, detailed published accounts would be a step towards learning how to appraise situations of real-life conflict adequately, both as observers and as participants.

# I

# Family Sphere

Of the innumerable inter-personal conflicts which we encounter in everyday life, those which take place in the family sphere are perhaps sociologically the most significant. This is because the family is the basic unit of society, and still the most important primary group known to humankind. Since the structure of family is itself a variable, the sources, the nature and the consequences of conflict within it are obviously varied. However, it can hardly be gainsaid that conflict within the family has far reaching consequences for the wider social fabric.

The five papers in this section deal with conflicts in the family sphere in a variety of settings ranging from rural Kashmir (Madan) to Bangalore city (Ramu). They delineate the nuances of conflict among communities observing different kinship norms—patrilineal Kashmiri Pandits (Madan), matrilineal Nayars of Kerala (Jeffrey), and patrilineal Multani Lohars (Rizvi). They cover different periods of history—from the colonial era (Chandra and Jeffrey) to contemporary times (Ramu).

These papers highlight how conflict originates from within the structural arrangement of a family and the cultural norms and values governing it. Since the family is linked to other institutional orders of society, changes taking place elsewhere in society can exacerbate conflict within the family and bring about changes in it. In a traditional joint family, one major consequence of conflict between members is partition, leading to the division of family property among co-owners, so that they hold it in severalty, as well as the breakup of the household as a residential unit into two or more such units. In a modern nuclear family, the consequences can lead to the breakup of the marital bond.

The papers in this section try to capture the dynamics of the family in the context of stronger social forces impinging on it and the conflict situations which crop up within it and with which it has to cope. They deploy a variety of research techniques— observation and case study (Madan and Rizvi), historical analysis (Jeffrey), and several kinds of interview (Ramu). They work in different disciplinary perspectives—anthropological (Madan and Rizvi), historical (Jeffrey and Chandra) and sociological (Ramu)— and emphasize the importance of multi-disciplinary approach to the study of social phenomena.

In the opening paper the social anthropologist T.N. Madan analyses the partition of the *chulah*[1] (household) among the Pandits of rural Kashmir. His data was gathered in 1957–8 in the course of a larger study of family and kinship. While the data is a generation old, the insights which Madan derives from them are relevant even today, and are useful in understanding and interpreting the breakup of patrilineal-extended joint families elsewhere in the country.

According to Madan, partition is a crucial reality in the development cycle of the Pandit household though the 'joint *chulah*' is considered to be the ideal. The ideal is maintained through the fair behaviour of the patriarch as long as he is alive. The death of the patriarch alters the situation, with each brother seeking to protect the interests of his own wife and children. Thus, the two 'structural conditions' for partition are the death of the father and the marriage of two or more brothers. These conditions, Madan cautions, should not be confused with the immediate causes or real reasons for conflict between brothers leading to partition. Madan delineates the jural, moral and economic conditions

---

[1] *Chulah* (*choolah*), literally oven or the cooking place, is used to refer to the 'hearth group,' the co-resident and commensal domestic group, or the household.

which preclude any revolt by sons against fathers. Conflict between brothers, which is generally seen as the culprit, most often
arises because of the status differentiation within the family and
the differences over running the household. These differences are
likely to occur in spheres of mutual competition and in situations
where rights and duties are not clearly defined. While the mother
is passive, the daughters-in-law are shown to hatch such conflict.
Madan clarifies that partition need not necessarily be related
to conflict. Partition is viewed as a normal occurrence by the
Pandits, and they even have 'a traditional expectation' about it;
but it is not culturally approved. Though very rare, there are
instances of reunion of households.

That the breakup of the household is a contingent aspect of the
development cycle of patrilineal system among the Muslims is also
confirmed by the second selection. Sociologist S.M. Akram Rizvi
explores here the impact of the growth of industrial enterprise
among the Multani Lohars, known popularly as *Karkhanedars*
(*karkhana*, workshop; *-dar*, owner), on the structure and composition of their households. His data come from his fieldwork in an
old Delhi locality during 1971–2. While his substantive focus is on
a Muslim community, the general insights he provides on the
impact of entrepreneurship on family structure have a far wider
relevance.

Following A.M. Shah, Rizvi classifies *Karkhanedar* households
as simple (comprising either a nuclear family or an incomplete
one) and complex (consisting of extra-nuclear family kin). An
independent *choolah* (hearth) determines separateness of a household, so that within the same large building there may be many
households. Often the *karkhanedars* exhibit apparent solidarity
for purposes of business, but behind that facade they are divided.
The separateness of *choolah* is the symbol of the separateness of
income.

Contrary to the observations, such as those of Milton Singer,
that industrialization has not resulted in the breakdown of the
joint family, Rizvi's data suggest that improved material conditions
do lead to it. He analyses the new sources of tensions as well as
the old sources in the new setting in *karkhanedar* households. He
shows how the traditional tension management mechanisms are
hardly effective in dealing with the tensions confronted by those
households at this point in time.

Interestingly, though the settings and communities are different, there seem to be noticeable parallels between Madan's Pandit households and Rizvi's *karkhanedar* households, especially as regards the process of partition and breakup of joint households following conflict between brothers. In both the cases, the structural conditions mentioned earlier with reference to Pandits, as well as the role of women (daughters-in-law) as originators of conflict, are the same. However, Rizvi highlights also the impact of the changing environment, especially the growing individualism among the members of the joint household.

While partition is a crucial phase in the development cycle of the joint household in the patrilineal system, the development cycle is itself prone to collapse when the material and moral environment changes drastically. Moving to the other end of the country, historian Robin Jeffrey documents such a collapse by elucidating the disintegration of the institution of the matrilineal joint family, the *taravad*, among the Nayars of Kerala. His analysis is part of a larger study of the decline of Nayar dominance over half a century (1847–1908). While Jeffrey's main interest is in the interplay between society and politics in the princely state of Travancore, he offers instructive sociological insights on how exogenous forces brought about the decline of a system which had been the mainstay of society in Kerala for centuries.

According to Jeffrey, the spread of cash economy, the increased value of land, and the land becoming a commodity are primary forces which set in motion a whole series of changes. The spread of education affected the attitudes and values of the Nayars about their family system, which was the butt of ridicule by the educated castes and classes. Education and, through it, employment in the government introduced new conflicts of interest within *taravads*. The incidence of litigation rose, which in turn ruined many a *taravad*.

For centuries the Nayar *taravad* was impartible. Jeffrey traces how various forces set in motion a process which culminated in accelerating partitions among the Nayars. He analyses the intense debate within the community and in the governmental fora over the issue, and examines the consequences of litigation and partition on the community. The conflict arising within the households in their transition from matrilineal joint households to nuclear households awaits sociological investigation.

Another historian Sudhir Chandra's paper takes us to the 1880s. In it he analyses an important and controversial case of restitution of conjugal rights that came up before the Bombay High Court in 1884. Chandra's primary objective is to expose the myth of the emancipatory role of the British Indian legal system. Ignoring his iconoclastic fervour, here we find him concentrating on the juxtaposition between indigenous reality and the implanted legal norms revolving round an inter-spouse conflict. That is, like Jeffrey, Chandra also examines the consequences for the domestic domain of the encounter of two traditions, a theme which is considered at length in Section V and in the Epilogue.

Central to the case analysed by Chandra are marital and domestic relations among Hindus belonging to Suthar or Pachkalshi caste. The conflict between the spouses in this case highlights the traditional subordination of women. The crux of the case is the maintainability of a restitution suit among Hindus. Chandra shows how the colonial state tended to subvert traditional communities as centres of socio-cultural authority in resolving conflicts.

In the last selection, sociologist G.N. Ramu brings us back to contemporary times. He focuses on marital interaction and adjustment in urban nuclear families. His data comes from interviews with a random sample of 245 single- and 245 dual-earner couples (980 respondents in all) in Bangalore city. These were collected in two phases, in 1979 and 1984.

Ramu underscores the importance of day-to-day relations for marital solidarity and adjustment. According to him, the absence of strong bonds in nuclear families cannot be explained by reference to structural restraints as in the case of rural joint families, but by the inability of the spouses to cultivate such bonds. Examining the impact of the wife's economic status on various dimensions of marital interaction, he finds that a much higher percentage of wives in families where both the spouses earn reports marital happiness in comparison to families where only the husband earns (i.e. 'single-earner wives').

According to Ramu, marital relations become meaningful only in their specific cultural context. Traditional religious values, ineffective laws, and insecure economic conditions perpetuate the wife's dependence on her husband. As a consequence she shuns marital conflict, let alone think of divorce as a means of resolving it. Women continue to take it upon themselves to compromise, accommodate and make sacrifices to preserve marital stability; and this explains why Ramu's data does not categorically show that the wife's work status has a bearing on interpersonal differences among couples.

# Partition of the Household*

## T.N. MADAN

So long as adult men are living together, with their wives and children, under the tutelage of their father, the Pandit ideal of the joint *chulah* is easy to maintain. Not only is the moral and jural authority of a man over his sons responsible for this, but the general expectation that a man will not discriminate between his sons is also conducive to it. If he does favour one son against another, dissension is bound to arise, and the chances of cleavage in the household become real though they may not be realized in his lifetime. The father may remedy the situation before it becomes too explosive for the survival of the household. More often the aggrieved son bides his time, unwilling to come into open conflict with his father and thereby risk general disapproval of his behaviour. His mother also may act as a sobering influence.

But the situation in the household changes drastically when the father dies. Each brother seeks to protect the interests of his own wife and children, and in doing so comes into conflict with the others. The mother, if alive, still tries to keep her sons together, but generally without much success as she lacks the jural authority over them which her husband had enjoyed as the head of the household. Moreover, her own conflicts with her daughters-in-law may dispose her to take sides between them, and thereby accentuate domestic strife.

Joint living is still the ideal, but the divergence of interests

* Excerpted from T.N. Madan, 'Partition of the Household', *Family and Kinship: A Study of the Pandits of Rural Kashmir*, Bombay: Asia Publishing House, 1965, pp. 144–58.

between the brothers usually becomes so large as to be beyond compromise. Partition[1] is, therefore, a normal occurrence in Pandit society though it lacks cultural approval. However, should economic and other interests so dictate, a man composes his differences with one or more of his brothers, and a reunion of households takes place.

## PARTITION IN RELATION TO HOUSEHOLD STRUCTURE

. . . [T]he eighty-seven households of Utrassu-Umanagri are in different phases of development, and . . . no household contains more than three generations, or kin more distantly related than first cousins (if we exclude the solitary instance of second cousins living in a single household owing to its exceptional nature). Enquiries in several other villages reveal some instances of four-generation *chulahs*, but none of second cousins living in the same household. In fact, the number of households which attain the maximum extension of three or four generations and first degree cousinship is generally small; there are only four such cases in Utrassu-Umanagri. The question which arises here is: What prevents further expansion of the household? As the following analysis will show, death and partition are the crucial events which are responsible for arresting the extension of the composition of the household.

During 1957 no partition took place in the village, although several were incipient. Nevertheless, I was able to obtain fairly full details of fifty partitions from Utrassu-Umanagri and the nearby villages of Kreri and Naogam. Thirty-six of these partitions had occurred in the previous twenty-five years. In forty or four-fifths of these cases, partition occurred between brothers; in two cases between a widow and her deceased husband's brothers; and in one case between first cousins. The remaining seven were inter-generation partitions.

In thirty-eight of the forty partitions between brothers, the

---

[1] Throughout the following discussion, 'partition' is used to mean both the division of the estate between co-owners, so that they may hold it in severalty, as also the breakup of the household as a residential unit into two or more such units.

seceding brother, or at least one of the group of seceding brothers, was married and had children. Similarly, of the brothers of whom partition was demanded, at least one was married and had children. Only in three cases did a childless couple secede from the joint household consisting of two or more couples.

In all cases of partition which involved, among others, unmarried brothers, each single man sided with one, or a group of his married brothers. No case of an unmarried man separating from his natal household to set up his own independent *chulah* was reported to me.

In six of the forty partitions under consideration, the mother was alive when her sons separated. Two of these widows are still alive, each living with one of her sons. When a woman's sons finally decide to separate in spite of her exhortations to stay together, she has no option but to choose to live with one of them, though this does not mean that she has strained relations with the other(s).

It is of interest to note that in thirty-three of these forty households, the maximum degree of extension that may be encountered in a Pandit household—represented by three or four generations and first degree cousins—had not been reached by the time of partition.

The two cases of partition between a widow and her deceased husband's brothers also are, in fact, instances of partition in fraternal-extended and joint households. One of these widows had a young son and married daughters, and the other had only married daughters. The daughters were living patrivirilocally in both cases.

Of the seven inter-generation partitions, one occurred between a man and his deceased brother's son, and another between a man and his son on the one hand, and his deceased son's son on the other. In both these cases, a man whose father had died young obtained his share of the joint estate after he had been married.

The remaining five inter-generation partitions took place between a man and his son(s) in four cases, and between a man and his patriuxorilocally married daughter in one case. The earliest of these five partitions occurred in 1910 (and the latest in 1955), disproving the assertion of many villagers that partitions between fathers and sons are a recent phenomenon.

In two of these cases, including the earliest, a relatively older man's remarriage after his wife's death provoked his married son(s) by the earlier marriage to press for partition. Strained relations between the newly-arrived step-mother and her married step-son(s) and his (their) wife (wives) were the immediate cause of partition in both the cases. But it seems that the real reason was the desire of each seceding son to safeguard his interest in the joint estate in the face of a possible reduction in the size of the shares following the likely birth of sons to his step-mother.

The third case of partition between father and son is recent, and illustrates the importance which the cash income of individual members of the household has come to acquire nowadays. Nilakanth has five adult sons, but only the eldest of these, Tarachand, was earning a cash income, being a government employee. Three of the brothers, including Tarachand, were married and had children. In fact, Tarachand's eldest son also was a government employee. Desirous of getting the full benefit of his own and his son's cash incomes, Tarachand obtained his share from his old father and set up an independent household, consisting of himself, his wife, three sons and the eldest son's wife.

The fourth case of partition between a man and his sons was an unusual one involving charges of adultery by the sons, one of them married, against their widowed father.

The only instance of partition between a man and his daughter is remarkable for the complete lack of acrimony and conflict. It seems that Maheshwarnath agreed to live patriuxorilocally* because his parents-in-law had only one young son, Dayaram. When the latter grew up to be a young man, Maheshwarnath approached his father-in-law to be allowed to set up a household of his own. He had no jural right to make such a request except as his wife's guardian and spokesman. But his relations with his parents-in-law were cordial, and he had for several years made a contribution to the income of his wife's natal household. He was, therefore, allowed to secede and his wife received a one-third share in her father's estate as by then her mother had given birth to a second son.

---

* *Patriuxorilocal residence is an arrangement in which a man takes up residence with his wife's natal household. This, however, is not the norm among the Pandits. It is resorted to only to overcome the hardships which the elderly people are likely to undergo in a patrilineal system if they do not have male progeny to look after them. [Eds]*

On the basis of the foregoing analysis, we may conclude that whereas the average age expectancy and the average age at marriage usually prevent a household from extending into a fourth or fifth generation, it is partition which breaks up a fraternal-extended joint household. It is also obvious that whereas partition between a man and his son(s) is rare, joint living between married brothers is, in the long run, even more rare because of the conflict between the fraternal bond on the one hand and the conjugal and the parental bonds on the other.

## PARTITION: STRUCTURAL CONDITIONS

The right to demand partition is acquired in Pandit society by a man at his birth, but in most cases a son does not enforce his rights as a coparcener against his father. Instead he behaves as if his father were the sole owner of the estate, and his own rights in it contingent upon his father's death. Besides his father's moral and jural authority and the demands of filial piety already referred to above, self interest also may preclude a man from demanding his share from his father. The latter is entitled to retain a share for himself in his individual capacity as a coparcener, thus reducing the size of the share which a seceding son of his can get. Moreover, his sons have no claim to his self-acquired property during his lifetime. In view of these jural, moral and economic considerations, it is not surprising that a man rarely revolts against his father, but generally does so against his brother. Therefore, . . . the first structural condition for the occurrence of partition between brothers is that their father should be dead.

A Pandit is unable to take advantage of his right to secede from his joint household unless he is able to set up a household of his own, and this he can do only if he is married. In rare cases a man may depend upon his mother or sister (unmarried, or married but widowed) to run his home for him, but it is usually the wife who does this. His mother, if too old, would not be expected to live long. If his unmarried sister is grown up enough to keep house for him, then she is also of marriageable age and will have to be married off before long. . . . Further, an unmarried man is not subject to the same contrary pulls which a married man is. Marriage creates new bonds for a man—between him and his wife and children—which do not harmonize with his old bonds—between him and his brothers—and also places him in a situation which enables him to set up an independent household when doing so seems to be to his best advantage. It is, however, only rarely that marriage immediately results in partition. In only one of the forty-two cases of partition in fraternal-extended joint households, discussed above, did a man separate from his elder brother immediately after his own marriage.

Whenever a Pandit couple have two or more sons, the basic precondition for a future partition (between the brothers) may be said to obtain. But it is not till their father is dead, and at least two of the brothers are married, that a partition is likely to take place.

## PARTITION: CAUSES

The structural conditions within which partition is usually achieved are in no way the causative conditions which actually bring it about. . . . Conflicts arise out of the fundamental situation that prevails in the fraternal-extended household. It consists of several nuclear families which are related through the sibling bond. Between these brothers there is a feeling of uneasiness. As sons of the same parents, and as coparceners, they are equals. But according to the Pandit norms, age differences give rise to differential status: the older men, by virtue of their being older, have authority over their younger brothers, who are expected to be deferential and respectful towards them. Moreover, the eldest brother customarily succeeds to his father's position as head of the household when the father dies. As paterfamilias the eldest brother is elevated to the position of the father himself—a fact which his younger brothers, particularly those close to him in age, do not always like. The eldest brother himself is under strain due to his personal loyalty towards his own wife and children, and his moral obligation to treat all members of the household equally without discrimination.

Conflicts between the brothers usually arise over the running of the household, the distribution of food, clothes and other rewards to *chulah* members, and the rearing of children. Underlying these disagreements is a deeper feeling of antagonism and heartburning. Estrangement between adult siblings is a salient feature of the Pandit family system. As children, siblings who are close to each other in age grow up together and there is much friendliness and devotion between them. When on attaining adulthood a man is married, new 'interests enter his life, and he even starts thinking of the day when he will have a household of his own. He develops an attachment to his wife and children and indicates his interest in their welfare. Such interest often brings him into conflict with his siblings. The aggrieved siblings retaliate. On other occasions he is similarly hurt by the devotion which his brothers show to their wives and children in preference to him. Their relations thus become strained.

So far as sisters are concerned, they are not deeply involved in these conflicts. Before relations between a man and his sister become very strained, she is married out of the household. Not only is she removed physically from her natal home, her rights as an agnate are also limited. She is not a coparcener, unless married patriuxorilocally, and does not pose any threat to the interests of her brothers. But no such resolution of conflict is possible between brothers, and their dissensions proceed invariably towards partition.

The Pandits greatly emphasize the part which the wives of brothers play in these dissensions. Sisters-in-law are in almost all cases unrelated before their marriage. After their marriage and during the lifetime of their mother-in-law, they are all under her supervision and control. But when she dies they come under the control of the wife of the eldest brother; though it is unusual, she may not be also the eldest of them all in age. The other sisters-in-law do not like the elevation of one of them to the status of the mistress of the house, and always try to assert their equality with her in status, and even their personal superiority over her as housewives.

When there are more than two sisters-in-law in a household they have disagreements with each other, though they do also form temporary alliances. They quarrel over their own relative importance in terms of the contribution their husbands make to the upkeep of the household and the management of the estate. They disagree over whose natal household is of higher standing and more prosperous, and who among them receives more and better gifts from her parents. They also quarrel over their children, each accusing the other of discrimination in favour of her own children, and telling her that her children are misbehaved and spoilt. There are also conflicts over the distribution of work. In short, sisters-in-law seem to be always disagreeing with each other, so much so that if two particular sisters-in-law do not have any disputes, the Pandits regard it as rather unusual.

The main reason for these bickerings between sisters-in-law is that they constantly find themselves in situations within the household in which their rights and duties are not clearly defined, and in which each appears as a competitor of the others. Moreover, sisters-in-law are not inhibited in their relations with each other to the same extent by considerations of morality and kinship sentiment as are their husbands. Whereas a man may be willing to work under his brother, and partially subordinate his personal interests for the sake of his brothers, nephews and nieces, his wife generally does not like to do this. Her husband's agnates are no kin of hers. She wants independence and seeks the fulfilment which a woman finds only when she is the mistress of her own household. Again, the attitude of a woman towards her sisters-in-law in sometimes influenced by her parents who exhort her to exercise her rights and not to be submissive.

The quarrels between sisters-in-law would neither be so frequent nor so important as to lead to partition, were not the brothers indirect participants in them and interested in their development. Such quarrels are contributory factors towards the partition of the household, but they become of decisive importance only after the solidarity of brothers has been greatly weakened. The brothers in a fraternal-extended household are in a dilemma. There is a conflict in their minds between the ideal of fraternal amity and co-operation on the one hand, and immediate and long-term personal advantage on the other. According to Pandit kinship morality, quarrels between brothers are of much greater significance, than are the bickerings between their wives, as they lead directly to partition. When two brothers desire to partition the household and the estate, they also desire to avoid social disapproval, and try to blame each other for intransigence. They also invariably blame their wives for alienating brother from brother but connive at their bickerings and even encourage them. . . . Pandit men thus measure out moral sentiment against personal feelings and advantage, and avoid facing the problem

of conflict between these two frontally. Instead they try to resolve
it indirectly by quarrelling through their wives, as it were. And
when the end has been achieved—the household and the estate
partitioned—they tend to put the blame on their wives. It is likely
that this rationalization is partly unconscious, but it is a rationalization nonetheless.

In some cases, a man is less circumspect than others, and
readily comes to blows with his brothers. But the Pandits most
emphatically disapprove of such conduct, particularly if it is the
elder brother who is induced into physically fighting his younger
brothers. Partition, though a normal feature of Pandit kinship, is
deprecated, particularly if prior to its achievement (to quote one
of my informants) 'brothers fought as if they were strangers,
forgetting their common origin'. In the nature of things the
achievement of partition is in most cases accompanied by tensions
and conflict; hence the Pandit brothers' dilemma. That they
usually decide to partition the household and the estate is due to
both their personal interest and the attitude of their wives.

Sometimes a fraternal-extended household of two brothers may
weather these early storms and not break up till their sons grow
up into adults. Even a third (junior) generation may be added to
the household. When tensions arise in this phase of development,
the forces working for partition are very strong. . . . [F]raternal
conflicts are strongly reflected in the relations between paternal
uncles and nephews, and find almost unmitigated expression in
hostility between cousins. The feelings of kinship sentiment and
the considerations of morality and social disapproval, which
suppress open expression of hostility between brothers, are less
compulsive in inter-cousin relations. Paternal cousins usually quarrel without the qualms which inhibit their fathers, and tend to
support their mothers in their desire for partition.

Howsoever the Pandits may deprecate it, the fraternal bond
always breaks down in the face of conflict with the conjugal and
parental bonds and self-interest. There are no households in
Utrassu-Umanagri in which the senior generation includes first
paternal cousins, nor have any such *chulahs* been there in the last
[few decades]. The Pandits maintain that disputes between
brothers were less common in the past. It may be conjectured
that they were not less common, but did not in all cases inevitably
lead to partition. This is quite likely considering the economic

and social advantages that accrued to households with bigger land holdings, although the partition of bigger estates must also have been economically less disadvantageous than the partition of smaller land holdings. Moreover, very few Pandits earned personal incomes in past days. Nevertheless, cases of large joint and extended households, including cousins in the senior generation, must have been rare. I was not able to record any such instance, although. . . . I was able to get details of two cases of partition between a man and his deceased brother's adult son. . . . Nowadays, with more Pandits earning personal incomes than ever before, and at unequal rates, the ideal of the individual estate is gaining ground. It seems that in future, partition between brothers will occur as often as it does now, but considerations of economic advantage will play a greater and more decisive part in bringing them about than at present.

## A CASE HISTORY

As an illustration of the kind of data on which the foregoing analysis is based we may now present a brief description of two cases of partition. Kailas was the only son of his parents, and inherited from his father a three-storeyed house (built in 1899), a walnut tree, several cows and calves, and occupancy rights in

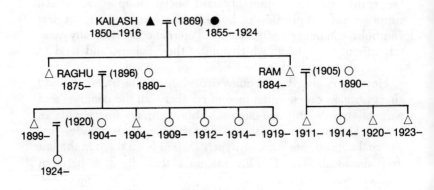

Figure 1

about 26 acres of land. He died in 1916, and was survived by his widow, two sons, and their wives and children. (For the sake of convenience no mention will be made of dead children and married daughters in this case history.) Kailas's widow died in 1924.

A year later Raghu celebrated the marriages of his second son and eldest daughter with considerable pomp and show. It seems that Ram wanted the initiation rites of his five-year-old son to be performed on the same occasion, but Raghu suggested that the same could take place a couple of years later. Ram was much annoyed by what he regarded his elder brother's selfishness, highhandedness and extravagance. He started grumbling about the manner in which Raghu was spending cash savings of the household which had been accumulated from the sale of surplus grain. A few months after the marriage Ram's wife quarrelled with Raghu's wife, telling the latter that the household would become impoverished by the time all her daughters were married. It may be noted here that Ram had only two daughters, the elder of whom had been married in 1920, whereas Raghu had four daughters. Raghu's wife reported this to her husband who felt that his honesty was being doubted and his children had been counted. The Pandits believe that counting children brings illness and even death to them; therefore, if a person mentions the large number of another's children, the latter takes it ill. Accordingly Raghu asked Ram to reprimand his wife, but the latter asserted that his wife had done no wrong. He also told several villagers that he was making a sacrifice in not demanding partition, pointing out that he had only four children as against Raghu's six children, one daughter-in-law, and one grandchild. Raghu, on hearing of this, complained that his children had been counted again; therefore, he suggested that they divide the household and their joint estate, and Ram readily agreed to this.

The partition was achieved fairly smoothly. Raghu took possession of the left half of their house, and Ram of the right half. All other property (occupancy rights in land, grain, domestic utensils, bedding, etc.) were also divided without much difficulty. There was some disagreement over cattle, but Ram finally agreed to accept only one milch cow and two calves, leaving two cows and three calves to his elder brother. The cowshed, the granary, and two walnut trees (of unequal age) were not divided. It was decided that the total number of walnuts would be divided equally each year. The use of the courtyard also was unaffected by the partition, but the kitchen garden was divided into two equal parts.

By 1954, when Ram died, his household had grown into a three generation fifteen member paternal-extended family. Besides thirteen acres of land which the household owned, Ram had been also running a grocery shop since 1929, and had constructed a new house in 1944 after selling his share in the ancestral house to Raghu's sons. His youngest son Janki was employed as a school teacher and his grandson Gopi as a land revenue record-keeper.

The relations between Ram's sons had been somewhat strained since Janki's marriage; his wife came of a rich household from a neighbouring town, and her behaviour annoyed her mother-in-law and sisters-in-law who regarded her as an upstart. The fact of Janki's being posted in another village, however, kept the conflict under check. But Dina's differences with his elder brother Sri, who was now the head of the household, kept widening. He did not like to be subservient to Sri who, he thought, was concealing the full extent of his son Gopi's income. The amount of Gopi's meagre salary was, of course, known to everybody, but he is a clever young man believed to earn a sizeable additional income by the distribution of favours.

In 1956 Dina persuaded Janki to join him in demanding partition from Sri. The former was keen on enlisting the latter's support, probably because if the two stayed together the blame would in all likelihood fall upon Sri. It is, moreover, probable that Janki's salary also entered into Dina's calculations. Janki did not need much persuasion as he was already under pressure from his wife to seek a division. But he felt that he had to join one of

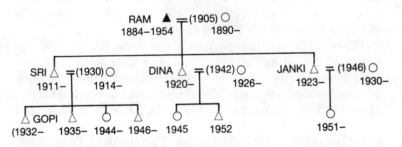

Figure 2

his elder brothers' households as his wife and child would be otherwise left alone; if he were to take them away with him his interests, above all in land, would suffer by default.

Ram's old widow was much distressed by the happenings, and chose to live with her eldest son. Her dislike of her youngest daughter-in-law was the major factor in her choice. She also probably realized that Dina was the main force behind the move to partition the household and the estate.

The division of assets turned out to be a very complicated and protracted process. The shop proved to be the main problem, and Sri ultimately succeeded in getting sole possession of it by buying out his brother's interest in it. However, he had to be content with only four rooms out of a total of 13 in their house. The division of assets took several months to settle, but nobody seemed to be satisfied with what had been agreed upon even a year after the partition had taken place.

## THE PROCESS OF PARTITION

Among the members of a household only co-arceners can demand partition. Legally only 'majors' may do so, but it seems that in practice any adult (in the physical sense of the term) is able to bring it about. While I was in Utrassu-Umanagri, a partition occurred in the nearby village of Naogam when a boy, aged 17, and legally a 'minor', obtained shares on behalf of himself and his 12-year-old sister from his father, alleging maltreatment by their step-mother and step-brothers. A patriuxorilocally married female agnate also can demand partition, but an unmarried or a patrivirilocally married female agnate (even if the latter may have returned to her natal home after her widowhood), does not have the jural right to ask for division. The position of a wife is intermediate. She may ask for partition, in the name of her deceased husband, on her own behalf, or on behalf of her children. But she does not acquire a vested right in her share of the estate, and cannot alienate it. If she is childless, the estate reverts to her husband's collateral heirs after her death. If she has children, they hold vested rights in it. The Pandit wife can ask for maintenance but has no rights of inheritance in her conjugal household.

When demanding partition, a coparcener need not advance any reason for his action, as it is his 'birth-right' to make such a claim. Therefore, partition is a traditional expectation of the Pandit family system. The timing of partition is, however, based, not on the caprice of individuals, but on predictable crucial events and structural and economic strains. When a man asks for partition, his coparceners may try to avoid it, but cannot refuse him if he insists on it. A man loses the right to demand partition only if he is insane; he loses the right of inheritance also if he becomes a convert to Islam, or deserts the village of his birth. But if a man becomes a Muslim, or deserts his village, after obtaining partition, he retains his individually owned estate. . . . If a coparcener is temporarily absent, his rights are not affected in any way, although if he is unable to be present at the time of the apportionment of shares, he may receive less than is his due.

In most cases it is one of the younger brothers who asks for partition. This, as may be expected, is because of the privileged position of the eldest brother and his wife, as also his moral obligation towards his younger siblings. Older people are expected to have patience and forgive the young for their misbehaviour. For an elder brother to force partition on his younger brother amounts to the abandonment of the former's kinship and moral responsibilities, and this is sure to provoke criticism from their common kin and other villagers.

After partition has been agreed upon, the coparceners take a decision regarding the extent and form of partition. In some cases the disputing brothers decide that the source of conflict lies in the working out of domestic relations and the distribution of consumer's goods at home and, therefore, only the partition of the *chulah* as a residential and consumption unit is called for. The *chulah* is a multifunctional group, and can be broken up with reference to only some of its functions. Thus, a *partial* partition takes place; the *chulah* as a residential and consumption unit is broken up, but its members continue to hold immovable property in common. . . . Even when the parties to a dispute decide on a complete severance of residential and economic ties, this may not be possible because of the impartability of some kinds of property, like the dwelling house, cattle and fruit trees as also sacred household pottery and icons. Therefore, partition between brothers is usually partial, and they continue to hold some property in common. Partition of the household is not a single act, but a continuing process which may go on for two, or even three, generations. When impartable property becomes relatively valueless by intrinsic loss of value (like dead cattle, or old fruit trees which bear little or no fruit), or by the diminished value of potential shares, some coparceners may abandon their claims to such property, or transfer it to others, either with or without some consideration in return. It is only then that complete partition is achieved.

## REUNION OF HOUSEHOLDS

Once a partition has been agreed upon, and its details worked out, it is usually final although the working out of these details may take several years. The reunion of households, or the amalgamation of separate estates, is very rare; it has happened only thrice in Utrassu-Umanagri in the past [few decades]. In two of these cases two brothers joined their separate households after having earlier broken away from a bigger fraternal-extended household. . . . There is reason to anticipate that when these smaller fraternal-extended households develop further, the union will be again dissolved.

The third case was rather unusual. Jialal obtained his share of the joint estate from his father's brother's sons, Mahtabram and Makundram, who were much older than him. Later he died and was survived by his mother, wife and daughter. Subsequently his wife married one of Mahtabram's sons and the two households reunited. This is incidentally the only household in the village in which second cousins are living together.

In Pandit society partition is the solution of the conflict between the fraternal bond on the one hand, and the conjugal and the parental bonds on the other. This conflict is regarded as regrettable but inevitable; in the general manner of its resolution—partition—may be seen the dominance of personal considerations, such as economic gain and the happiness of one's wife, over the kinship morality which should bind brothers together. In recognition of this tragic inevitability, brothers sometimes decide upon a partition before their relations become very strained. Three of the forty-two cases of partition in fraternal-extended households, and one of the seven inter-generation partitions described above, were amicable settlements of this kind. Partition partly removes the sources of exacerbation between brothers and usually restores to some extent peaceful relations between them, their wives and adult children. But it also usually separates them for ever into groups, and the bitterness generated during and just before the partition never completely disappears. 'Human relations are like a jar of pickles', said Sarwanand; 'once the rot sets in, it can never be eradicated, no matter how much you are willing to throw out of the jar.' Partition is thus a crucial event in the developmental cycle of the Pandit household. . . .

Partition enables emerging sub-groups within a household to realize ambitions incompatible with the continued membership of a single household. After partition the members of the emergent household deal with one another far more on a group-to-group basis than on a person-to-person basis. The bonds that bind together the households of brothers and patrilineally related cousins is that of agnatic kinship and territorial proximity. In the absence of the latter agnation stands out as the surviving link. The emphasis upon agnation, already prominent in intra-household relations, becomes very pronounced in inter-household relations. . . .

# Muslim Karkhanedars in Delhi[*]

## S.M. AKRAM RIZVI

The present study . . . deals with a Muslim *biradari* (community) called the Multani Lohars. The name indicates the place of origin (Multan) and the ancestral occupation of the group. Living deep inside the narrow lanes of the old city of Delhi, the Multani Lohars are popularly known as the karkhanedars. . . . Karkhanedar[1] is a vernacular term used for a person engaged in the business of manufacturing of which he is generally the owner. . . . The karkhanas under study operate in domestic conditions and, there-fore, have certain pervasive effects on the life of the karkhanedars who work in them. Particularly when such industries initiate changes in the day-to-day life, the institutional behaviour of the people tends to be adaptive. But this does not mean that such industries are themselves not affected by the social forces operat-ing in a society. . . . This paper explores th[e] interrelationship and interdependence between social structure and industry by focusing upon how the economic forces generated by the growth of karkhanas have affected the kinship structure of the karkhanedars. More specifically, it examines the changes that have come about in the structure and composition of households, the range of kin ties and the marriage preferences of the karkhanedars as a result of their improved economic conditions.

[*] Excerpted from S.M. Akram Rizvi, 'Kinship and Industry among the Muslim Karkhanedars in Delhi', *in* Imtiaz Ahmad, ed., *Family, Kinship and Marriage among Muslims in India*, New Delhi: Manohar, 1976, pp. 27–48.

[1] This paper is based on field work carried out among Muslim Karkhanedars in the locality called Pandit Kuchan in Old Delhi between September 1971 and July 1972.

There are no authentic accounts covering the period before
the arrival of the karkhanedars in Multan, nor for the period
during which they stayed there. . . . Many of them came to Delhi
towards the end of the nineteenth century. Around this time
various factories and engineering workshops were being established in Delhi. The karkhanedars got employment in these as
foremen, mechanics, turners and fitters. . . .

[ . . . ]

The knowledge and the experience that the karkhanedars thus
acquired prompted some of them to set up their own karkhanas.
In 1918, one Haji Abdul Shakoor, a foreman in Ganesh Flour
Mills, established his own karkhana. He kept his job in the Flour
Mills and devoted his spare time to his karkhana. He steadily
expanded his establishment, and by 1925 he was in a position to
employ over a hundred of his *biradari*-fellows in his karkhana.
Shakoor also helped some members of the *biradari* to open their
own karkhanas by providing them financial assistance and technical guidance. By 1947 there were three karkhanas owned by
the karkhanedars.

[ . . . ]

The expansion of entrepreneurial opportunities arising out of
the rapid industrialization of Delhi in the post-Independence
period and a ban on the import of certain machines created a
congenial climate for indigenous production. The karkhanedars
exploited this opportunity by starting their own karkhanas and
manufacturing the items which were banned. There was a rapid
growth of karkhanas[2] so much so that a large majority of the
karkhanedars started their own karkhanas. Thus, of the eighty-
eight karkhanedar households covered, seventy (79.5 per cent)
own their own karkhanas, while the members of sixteen households (18.2 per cent) depend on employment in karkhanas. The
remaining two households (2.3 per cent) have mixed sources of
income; some members of a household are employed in karkhanas as *karigars*, while some own their own karkhanas. . . .

---

[2] Karkhanas fall into two main types according to the place of work—house-
based and shop-based karkhanas. A house-based karkhana is installed in the
house where the karkhanedar lives. A shop-based karkhana is installed in a shop
outside the owner's residence. When a karkhanedar wishes to set up a karkhana,
he usually begins by establishing one in his own house because it requires less
investment than a shop-based karkhana.

# HOUSEHOLD COMPOSITION

The Karkhanedars are a patrilineal community, and the mode of residence at marriage is patrilocal. For analytical purposes I have divided their households into two broad categories: simple and complex. . . . A simple household is one which comprises either a nuclear family (a married couple with unmarried children) or an incomplete one, such as, husband and wife. A complex household, on the other hand, includes kinsmen other than those forming a nuclear family, such as, married brothers with their wives and children. _ . . [o]f the eighty-eight Karkhanedar households covered, thirty-nine are simple and forty-nine are complex.

The living space in a house (building) is shared by a number of households. Every household has its own separate *choolah* (hearth). In other words, a *choolah* determines the separateness of a household. To an external observer, however, all the members of a house may appear to form one large household. The Karkhanedars themselves try to convey this impression as a way of displaying a high degree of solidarity among the different persons living in the building. This is because joint living, especially among married brothers, has long been valued in the Karkhanedar community. Among the Karkhanedars married brothers normally pool their income from a karkhana, which they may have started jointly, and household expenses are met from a common fund. They generally try to be as frugal as possible in meeting their domestic requirements in order to invest as much as possible in their karkhana. When a man no longer pools his income in a common purse, it signifies his desire to separate himself and his immediate family members from the larger unit.

There are studies which suggest that the joint family has not broken down in the wake of industrialization. . . . Our data, however, tend to suggest that changes in the composition of households are indeed taking place as a result of the improved material conditions of the Karkhanedars though there are factors which also tend to keep complex households together. Let us first examine the factors tending to keep complex households intact despite changes in material conditions.

## SOCIAL INSURANCE AGAINST THE COLLAPSE OF INFANT KARKHANAS

The main sources of capital available to the Karkhanedar who wishes to set up a karkhana are usually: savings from wages; earlier savings; borrowed money (*qarz*) from friends or agnatic relations; loans (*qarza*) from a bank or a government agency; and help from affines. Savings from wages has been the most preponderant source of capital among the Karkhanedars. For instance, 46 (65.8 per cent) of the karkhanas studied had been set up with savings from wages, 12 (17.1 per cent) with previous savings and the remaining 12 (16.9 per cent) with other sources. Savings from wages are slow to accumulate. If several brothers live jointly they can also save enough for starting a venture. The following case illustrates this observation.

Sultan, aged forty years, owns a shop-based karkhana with his three younger brothers. It was started in 1959 in the house where all the brothers now live. Sultan was employed in a factory as a foreman and was proficient in his craft. At that time two of his younger brothers were also employed in different factories. They were together earning between 900 and 1,000 rupees a month. They were living in a complex household of which Sultan was the head. He was the only married brother. One day he suggested that if all of them made a joint effort, they could have their own karkhana. One of the brothers asked, 'How can we when we do not have money for investment.' Sultan replied, 'We shall not give up our present jobs. Instead, we shall try to save as much as possible from our wages and thereby manufacture our own machines as we accumulate money.'

It took two years for the brothers to manufacture one lathe, one drill, and one grinding machine. They made a total investment of Rs 2,600. Throughout this period they remained employed, and they continued to be so for another two years after the establishment of a karkhana in their house. Initially, they manufactured pistons, which fetched a good price. Five years after the installation of the karkhana in the house they shifted it to a shop which they rented after paying Rs 10,000 as *pagri*.[3]

Infant karkhanas also need constant attention in the early stages of development. If a karkhana is jointly started by several brothers

---

[3] *Pagri* is a lump sum which one is often required to pay at the time of renting accommodation and is in addition to the monthly rent.

living together, they can also give their collective attention to the karkhana as well as plough back their meagre profits into their business.

## DOMINANT ROLE OF FATHER OR ELDER BROTHER

The father, or, in his absence, an elder brother, is the head of a complex household. The head of the household is held in great esteem by his sons or brothers, and, therefore, enjoys a dominant position. At the same time, an elder brother as the head of a household does not enjoy the same dominance as a father does. The head of the household shoulders the responsibility of running the house. The successful carrying out of his functions depends on the degree of respect accorded to him by other members of the house. As head of the household, he is also supposed to resolve the conflicts between the wives of his brothers and his sons. If his own wife is involved in a conflict with his brother or brother's wife, the situation tends to become complex and may ultimately lead to a great deal of tension in the household. An elder brother as the head of a household has a more difficult task, therefore, than a father. Among the Karkhanedars the members of a complex household abide by the wishes of the head. This conforms to the traditional means of tension management through which disputes among members are resolved. The following case illustrates this.

Qamar, aged sixty-five years, lives with his five sons, two of them married, in a complex household. He owns a shop-based karkhana in which his sons are partners, and they work with him in the karkhana. One of the married sons has three children, while the other has four. Conflicts between the wives of Qamar's sons is a daily feature. Sometimes they quarrel over minor things, such as the use of utensils and the playing of their children in the house. These conflicts are usually quickly resolved and the tension lasts only for a short time. But there are occasions when these minor disputes take a serious turn. One day Qamar came back from the karkhana for lunch and found his sons' wives quarrelling among themselves. The point of dispute was that a child had been beaten by his aunt on the ground that he had snatched food from his cousin. The mother of the beaten child took a very serious stand and threatened to live separately. Qamar realized the gravity of the situation and told the lady who had beaten the child that it was bad on her part to beat the child so severely, though she had every right to beat him. He then said that he would not take his lunch unless the incident was forgotten and the concerned women promised not to convey it to their husbands.

However, the improved material conditions of the Karkhanedars have resulted in new sources of tension in their households which cannot be resolved through the traditional means of tension management. Let us now examine the sources of these tensions which have tended to influence the composition of complex households.

## NEW SOURCES OF TENSIONS IN KARKHANEDAR HOUSEHOLDS

An important source of tension in Karkhanedar households has been generated by the new entrepreneurial opportunities arising from the growth of industries in Delhi. Their tradition of craftsmanship made it possible for the Karkhanedars to exploit the new economic opportunities. As shown earlier, from a community of craftsmen who depended on others for employment, they had emerged as a community of self-employed, small manufacturers owning their own means of production. The ownership of the means of production became a means of enhancing one's prestige in the eyes of the community. Being an employee in a factory, on the other hand, began to be looked down upon by its members.

The improved material conditions of the Karkhanedars, resulting from the establishment of their own karkhanas, influenced the composition of their households. The desire to set up independent karkhanas was the driving force which affected the ties in complex households. The members of several complex households decided to have separate *choolahs* in the same house. Let me illustrate this point by a case.

Yousuf, aged fifty-five years, an employee in a karkhana, was the head of a complex household of five brothers, three of whom were married. . . . Of the five brothers, four were employed in various karkhanas. Yousuf, as the eldest brother, had the responsibility of running the house and meeting the expenses from the common purse in which all his brothers pooled their monthly wages. In 1955, they decided to start a karkhana from their savings. They hired a shop and jointly launched a karkhana. They manufactured motor parts till July 1959. During this period the fourth brother also got married and the fifth, who was till then working in another karkhana, joined the family enterprise. In July 1959, they successfully fabricated a replica of a type of compressor valve which had been imported from Germany till 1956. Owing to the ban on its import the indigenous production of this item fetched a good price. By 1962 they were manufacturing compressor valves and three kinds of motor parts in three different shops. At this stage, the three youngest brothers were tempted to separately own the means of production in order to reap the profits individually. This move was initially opposed by Yousuf and his immediate younger brother. The conflict went on for some time, and finally it was decided that the two brothers who were opposed to separation would own their karkhana jointly, while the others might have separate karkhanas. The three shops were then divided among four brothers, and the fifth was given finance for hiring a shop to start another karkhana. This had an immediate effect on their household. All the brothers, except the two who jointly shared a karkhana decided to have separate *choolahs* in the same house because, they argued, they had separate sources of income.

The establishment of a karkhana within a house also influences the composition of the household. This happens because a portion of the house is used for housing the karkhana. If there is already a shortage of living space, some of the members may be required to vacate the house in order to provide space for the proposed karkhana. The solution, therefore, is to allow some of the members of the household to set up independent households. But the process of moving out is not simple and is liable to create friction among the members. For instance, there is the problem of who should move out. However, those who agree to move out get financial assistance for hiring another place. Sometimes it turns out to be of benefit to both parties as both establish separate karkhanas. The following case illustrates this.

Mahmood, aged forty years, was living with his two younger brothers, one of whom was married. He had three children and was the head of the complex household. All the three brothers were employed in various karkhanas and factories as skilled workers. Mahmood successfully fabricated a replica of a motor part the import of which had

been banned. This greatly encouraged him to start his own karkhana. . . . Later it was decided that two karkhanas should be set
up to manufacture the motor part. One was to be owned by the two
elder brothers, and the other by the youngest, provided he set up a
separate household. In this way the youngest brother, Rasheed, set
up an independent household, consisting of his wife and unmarried
children. Therefore, one complex household, comprising three married brothers, gave birth to a simple household as a result of new
entrepreneurial opportunities.

Another development leading to change is when married sons
seek permission from their parents to set up separate households.
In such cases permission is sometimes accorded by the parents
themselves because they want to avoid the conflicts which may
arise from living jointly. In their financial condition permits, they
give some money to the married couple for meeting the expenses
of getting a place for residential purposes and setting up a
karkhana. There were also cases where the parents themselves
encouraged their sons to move out. . . . The following two cases
illustrate this.

Saghir, aged twenty-six years, was a partner in his father's karkhana.
He had three brothers, two of whom were working in the same
karkhana and shared the partnership equally. He was married to the
daughter of another Karkhanedar. Saghir's father, Rifaqat, who had
a well-established business, was manufacturing compressor valves, a
profitable item. Rifaqat, in consultation with his wife, suggested to
Saghir that he should acquire a place for himself in order to set up
an independent household. The latter did not like the idea and
requested his mother to plead his case with his father. His mother
politely told him that Rifaqat did not have any ill-will towards him.
She pointed out that, 'That is being done for your own good; you
will be able to work harder, and the love and; affection between us
would grow; if we live together, this may possibly divide our hearts,
and that would be very bad.' In this way Saghir's parents tried to
persuade him to live separately and set up an independent karkhana,
the initial expenses of which were to be borne by them.

Sajid, aged twenty-four years, was granted permission to set up an
independent household and a karkhana. Majid, his father, owned a
shop-based karkhana. Sajid had two brothers and two sisters. When
Sajid got married, he made a personal to his mother that, if his father
permitted him, he would set up a separate household for his family.
He told her that he was scared of his father because he might take

it ill. He added, however, that if he had his own karkhana he would work diligently and in two years his karkhana would be a flourishing enterprise. He tried to persuade his mother to influence his father to endorse his plans. When Majid was approached for advice he said that he was quite doubtful about the success of his son's plans. However, he obtained the full details of the latter's plans and gave him some suggestions. Subsequently, Sajid set up a simple household and established a new karkhana.

It is important to note that in all the four cases of branching off the fathers owned their own karkhanas and were in a financially sound condition. Because of this their sons were able to set up separate households and karkhanas.

Differences in the degree of proficiency among a group of brothers may sometimes generate friction among them. Thus, a proficient member of a complex household may find that his efforts to succeed in business are frustrated by the other members. He, then, thinks of having a separate karkhana so that he can display his talents as he has full control over the management of the karkhana.

## OLD SOURCES OF TENSION IN THE NEW SETTING

The traditional means of tension management cannot resolve the conflicts arising from the growth of karkhanas and the changed material conditions of households. Conflicts over the share of income drived from the karkhana, for example, have influenced the composition of complex households. It is true that conflicts over the use of money have always been a source of tension and existed even before the emergence of the Karkhanedars as owners of karkhanas. But it has become disruptive under the changed material conditions of complex households.

The responsibility of running a household, though primarily that of the father or elder brother, is shared by all the adult members who are required to behave in a manner conducive to the solidarity of the household. Here women, in their role as wives, become important in determining whether a complex household will continue as one unit. We find that more often than not trouble starts from quarrels among the women over the use of money. . . . This is illustrated by two cases.

Seven brothers, five of whom were married, lived in a complex household along with their wives and children. They had an equal share in the karkhana, which was under the supervision of the eldest brother who was also the head of the household. The karkhana was prospering, but there was a conflict over the use of the income derived from it. This was mainly because two of the five married brothers each had five children, while two had four and two children respectively, and the fifth had one child. The wives of those who had fewer children complained that more money was being spent on the children of the other brothers.

The climax came on the occasion of *Id* in 1967 when purchases were being made for the festival. The two wives who had the least number of children complained that they wanted better clothes and other things for their families. The two unmarried brothers unsuccessfully tried to pacify them. The conciliatory efforts of their menfolk, including those of the head of the household, were also in vain. It was finally decided that each nuclear family should have its own *choolah*, and for this purpose a fixed amount would be divided equally among them from the income of the karkhana. In this way five *choolahs* came into being. The two unmarried brothers joined their eldest brother's household. Three years later, on the occasion of the sixth brother's marriage, the assets of the karkhana were also divided among the brothers. . . .

Shaboo, aged forty years, had three brothers. All of them were married and they were living together in a complex household of which he was the head. All the brothers together owned a shop-based karkhana. One day Shaboo was having his lunch at home when his younger brother Zahoor told him that he would like to have a household of his own. Shaboo became disturbed on hearing this, and asked his brother to explain why he wanted to do so. Zahoor told him that he had overheard the wife of another brother . . . complaining to a visitor that he was extravagant, and that the other members of the household had to tighten their belts for his sake. Shaboo called the lady concerned and asked her what was the matter. She denied Zahoor's charges, and a big quarrel ensued among the members of the household. . . . Finally, it was decided that it was high time for all the brothers to set up independent households in order to avoid friction in future. The assets were calculated and the money was divided among them. . . .

Another source of tension has been the shortage of living space. In pre-Independence India, when the Karkhanedars were not well-to-do, it was very difficult for them to set up independent households even if there was a conflict in the house. The members of a complex household had to live jointly and pool their resources for their economic survival. But with the Karkhanedars emerging as owners of the means of production, they can afford to set up independent households in the event of quarrels among members of a household. The natural growth of a household by marriage or birth brings about changes in its composition and creates shortage of living space.

The death of either parent also influences the composition of complex households. The parents are generally a great source of unity and solidarity in a complex household. They regulate and govern the behaviour of their married children and their wives. They always try to maintain the unity of the house by emphasizing certain norms and values. Since the Karkhanedars are experiencing an economic transition, the death of either parent normally leads to a loosening of unity and the household is often subjected to daily tensions, especially in matters pertaining to financial management. If a household breaks up, the next step is the setting up of separate *choolahs* by each nuclear unit. This ultimately leads to the division of the karkhana.

[ . . . ]

## CONCLUSION

This paper has been concerned with a discussion of the impact of the economic forces generated by the growth of karkhanas on the domestic life of the Karkhanedars. It has been argued that the improved material conditions of the Karkhanedars has been accompanied by the growth of economic individualism among them. This has resulted in new sources of tension in their households which cannot be resolved through the traditional means of tension management. Certain factors, such as the death of either parent or conflicts over the share of income in a complex household, which operated even in the past, have become disruptive in the changed economic conditions of the Karkhanedars. We tend to find that large households, comprising several brothers and their children, are getting partitioned into smaller units. The economic advancement of the community has thus influenced the composition of households.

This conclusion is in contrast to that of Singer (1968), for instance, who maintains that the joint family continues to be the norm of entrepreneurs in Madras. The point to be noted in his study is that the industrialists come from well-to-do families and go in for joint ventures. This they do in order to maintain possession of, and control over, a large establishment. Further, an enterprise owned by a joint family can secure certain concessions, such as a rebate on income tax. Among the Karkhanedars, however, joint ownership may not be of much benefit since they own small karkhanas. Moreover, since the establishment of a karkhana does not involve much capital investment, the members of a complex household are tempted to start karkhanas independently of each other. This is both a sign of economic individualism and a factor that contributes to its growth. Consequently, complex households are tending to diminish in size. This has its own implications on the stability of wider kin ties, which are becoming weaker.

[ . . . ]

# The Decline of Nayar *Taravads*[*]

ROBIN JEFFREY

[The Nayars of Kerala] followed the matrilineal *marumakkattayam* system of inheritance, based on the matrilocal joint-family called the *taravad*. All members of a *taravad* were descended from a common female ancestor, but the management of *taravad* affairs was vested in the eldest male member, the *karanavan*; the system was matrilineal, not matriarchal. The property and assets of the *taravad* were held in common by all members, and no individual could claim his share of the joint property.

. . . A single [*taravad*] house might sometimes contain a hundred people, spanning three or four generations. Each woman had her own room where her young children slept and where at night she was visited by her husbands, who might be Nambudiris, Kshatriyas, Nayars of the same or a higher subcaste, or even non-Malayali Brahmins. The male members of her own *taravad* similarly went out at night to visit their wives.

Marriages were contracted and ended with considerable ease. A man negotiated with a woman's *karanavan*, obtained the woman's agreement and presented her with a cloth. This was called *sambandham*, and a woman might have *sambandham* with a number of men at the same time. They had no rights over her or her children, but were expected to provide her with small presents of luxury items like bath oil and to pay her expenses

* Adapted from Robin Jeffrey, *The Decline of Nayar Dominance: Society and Politics in Travancore, 1847–1908*, New Delhi: Vikas Publishing House, 1976, pp. 15–16, 107–8, 148–54, 180–90, and 243–51.

when she had a child. Either the man or woman could end the *sambandham* union with little formality. Pre-pubescent Nayar girls also underwent an expensive 'mock-marriage' called *talikettu-kalyanam*.

[ . . . ]

On the surface, Nayars also appeared to benefit from the changing circumstances of the 1870s and 1880s. They flocked to the government schools, and their male literacy rate rose from 21 per cent in 1875 to 37 per cent in 1891. . . . At the same time, Nayars captured more than a quarter of the choicest posts in the *sirkar* service. . . . Yet Nayars' share of such jobs was slightly less than that of non-Malayali Brahmins, though their population was 17 times greater. Here lay the makings of a grievance.

Nayars, however, had another, greater problem. The impartable matrilineal joint-family, the *taravad*, increasingly proved an embarrassment and a handicap. Educated Nayars winced at the taunts that 'no Nayar knows his father', while *taravads* were torn by feuds over money and land. The idyllic 'communality' of interest which should have characterized the *taravad* began to crumble. Finding it difficult to raise capital, and having fixed ideas about what constituted respectable employment, Nayars took little part in the commercial activities which allowed some Syrians, Iravas and Christian converts to improve themselves materially.

In 1891 educated Nayars, worried by the state of the *taravad* and the declining prosperity of Nayars, gathered as many allies as possible from other castes and religions and led an assault on the heavy non-Malayali Brahmin representation in the *sirkar* service. If Nayars could re-establish their political supremacy of pre-British days, the argument seemed to run, all could be made right with the *taravad*. But that supremacy could never be recaptured, and by 1905 Nayars were to find themselves divided within, resisted by non-Malayali Brahmins, and under pressure from Syrians and even Iravas.

It was the spread of a cash economy and the increased value of land which were perhaps most important, though least noticeable, to men living in the 1870s and 1880s. What was readily apparent was the burgeoning government school system and the advantages of sending one's dependants to school. Yet this education helped to undermine many of the traditional Malayali values and led to intense competition for the best jobs in the government service. For the matrilineal joint-family of Nayars, the sum of these changes added up to tension, dispute and decay.

[ . . . ]

When Madhava Rao [the then Diwan of Travancore State] left Travancore in 1872, Nayars held a place of dominance which appeared both comfortable and secure. Amounting to 20 per cent of the population, they held much of the land and 60 per cent of the 14,700 jobs in the government service. More than 20 per cent of their men were literate, and they were responding enthusiastically to the *sirkar's* educational programme. Yet Madhava Rao noted two areas of inadequacy and potential dissatisfaction. He pointed . . . to the 'great paucity of Nairs on the benches of the higher Courts', and on another occasion, though warning of the dangers of over-legislation, concluded that

> . . . it has to be declared lawful for any member of a Malayali (native) family to insist upon a division of common property so far as he or she is individually concerned, if he or she wishes to separate. Not that such a law would be generally acted upon at once. The feeling in favour of relatives living together in an undivided state of property is too strong to yield to reason in the present generation. But it is obviously the province of Government to see that a general feeling of the kind does not operate as an instrument of tyranny over individuals.

Questions of the *taravad* and of patronage in the higher echelons of the government service were to preoccupy Nayars for the next 60 years.

In the costly sphere of college education, Nayars led all other Malayalis, but could not compete with non-Malayali Brahmins. . . . Nayars were to argue that the dominance of non-Malayali Brahmins in the government kept Nayars from their just share of patronage and discouraged them from taking degrees. Among themselves, they dwelt on the cost of higher education and the question of who was to pay: the father of the child or the child's *taravad*.

Madhava Rao . . . intended to give a spur to his education system by making academic qualifications necessary for *sirkar* employment, even in the lower grades. Nayars quickly read his message and sent their dependents to school. . . . The question of education concerned virtually every *taravad*, and usually meant increased costs and changed attitudes.

What did students learn in these government-supervised vernacular schools? At the lowest level was the unaided vernacular primary school, the traditional village school, but now occasionally visited by the local school inspector. From such institutions, though they accounted for a third of the total enrolment, 'the regeneration of the masses' was not to be expected. . . .

In aided schools, however, a certain set of books was prescribed and in theory at least, a rough syllabus was followed. . . . At the level of the district English schools and the Maharaja's High School and College, leading figures like Vishakham Tirunal urged students to read Ruskin, Kinglake, Carlyle and Samuel Smiles. It is reasonable to suggest that such studies helped to propagate an individualism which was incompatible with the 'community' of the old *taravad*. . . .

The new education system also promoted mobility and independence. If a boy was to obtain the required qualifications for a job in the *sirkar* service, he often had to leave his village school and travel to the nearest town. . . . In travelling to and from school, in living in a town and in eating meals away from the *taravad* house, Nayar youths experienced new influences. In the upper schools there were team sports, debating clubs and dramatic societies, sometimes with officers elected from among the boys. Students were exposed to teachers of different castes, to European missionaries, and even to 'a clever Cambridge atheist', H.N. Read, the Scottish science professor and later principal of the Maharaja's College.

Students could not avoid hearing open attacks on Nayar marriage and morals. Augusta M. Blandford, who spent 40 years evangelizing among Nayars around Trivandrum and whose Fort Girls' School produced the first Nayar woman matriculate, described 'the customs of their caste with regard to marriage' as 'very revolting'. Rev. A.F. Painter, who moved freely among Nayars in north Travancore for more than 20 years, wrote of 'a system so horrible that even its defenders are ashamed of it as it stands'. What was worse for Nayars, however, were the jibes of other Hindus. Nagam Aiya in his 1875 census report felt obliged to make a brief apology for 'the looseness of the prevailing morals and the unbinding nature of the marriage tie which possesses such fascinations for the majority of our population'.

Growing numbers of Nayars were coming to agree with the

Tamil Brahmin. In pre-British days . . . polyandry was practised among Nayars, and either the man or woman could end a liaison virtually at will. Nambudiris, Pottis, Kshatriyas and non-Malayali Brahmins were also permitted to enjoy Nayar women. Yet by 1875 the Rev. Henry Baker, Jr. suggested that 'in many respectable families' there was not 'that state of profligacy the want of a *legal* marriage tie would imply'. Baker knew of Nayar couples who had been faithful to each other for 17 years. Perhaps in imitation of Smarta Brahmins, *sambandham* between first cousins was said to be the ideal among many Nayar families. However, even if such examples of lasting marriages were the rule, there were enough examples of the old laxity to embarrass educated Nayars. . . .

Education affected Nayar attitudes, but it also affected the *taravad* economically. Few *taravads* were so wealthy that they could afford school fees for half a dozen or more boys. The question of which boys were to be educated created dissension in the *taravad* and forced fathers to make alternative arrangements for their sons. 'It is a well-known fact', a leading Nayar wrote, 'that most Malayalis, whose *karanavans* are distant kinsmen, owe their education to their fathers'. But such fathers obviously had *taravads* and nephews of their own who should have had first call on their affections and resources. . . . [T]he *taravad* was often unable or unwilling to provide the cost. And if it did pay, it was generally after arguments and intrigues over which boys were to benefit.

The *taravad* was increasingly unable to bear financial strains. The largest of the joint families might profit from the rise in the value of their surplus rice, but this could also mean more spoils to fight over, more dissensions within. For the smaller landholding *taravads* . . . the abolition of slavery, and the rising cost of labour and rice were calculated to strain resources. Moreover, members of the *taravad* showed a growing concern for their own, rather than the joint-family's, interests.

Madhava Rao's Pattam Proclamation of 1865, which gave ownership rights to tenants on 200,000 acres of *sirkar pattam* land,*

---

* *The sirkar pattam was the new land tenure system which was brought into force by Maharaja Marthanda Varma in the 18th century. Under this system, the sirkar (the Maharaja) was the de jure owner of the land, and the tenant cultivated it under*

helped to accelerate the decay of the *taravad*.  In the year after the Pattam Proclamation, litigation in *munsiff's* courts rose from 9,804 cases to 18,441, as people attempted to realise the new value of land. Still more striking, and directly concerning Nayars, were the suits for the partition of *taravad* property. In the 5 years after the proclamation, these totalled 284. For dissatisfied members of *taravads*, the proclamation made partition more desirable. The joint-family could not sell its holdings of *sirkar pattam* land, and the share of each member would be enhanced thereby. However, after repeated court decisions refusing to grant partition—in accordance with the 'well established rule that division cannot take place unless all those who would be entitled to a share agree to it'—suits in the second quinquennium following the proclamation fell to only 28. . . . [I]n the 1880s, as the stresses within the joint-family grew and were accompanied by economic pressures, suits for partition again increased. Between 1881 and 1891, they numbered 660. The cases which reached the courts—especially since the courts were widely known to be unreceptive to the partition plea—represented only a tiny fraction of the discontent within the *taravad*.

This tension and economic pressure, however, were mitigated in the 1880s by Nayars' continued numerical dominance of the *sirkar* service. By 1881 their share of jobs in the expanding government service had increased to more than 65 per cent and a large proportion of *taravads* had at least one member working for the *sirkar*. To be sure, most Nayars were in jobs worth less than Rs 10 a month, but with the average cost of living at about Rs 30 a year, such positions were a vital asset to *taravads* increasingly unable to live solely from their land. Moreover, control of the lower levels of the government service allowed Nayars to enforce their caste privileges. . . .

By the mid-1880s two problems troubled educated Nayars in Travancore. The first was the decay of the *taravad*: the dissension within it, the ridicule it provoked, the mismanagement to which it was prone. The second problem was the hold of non-Malayali

---

*a pattam (tenure). Prior to 1865 the pattam holder could only enjoy the produce of the land, and the pattam land could not be sold or mortgaged, nor would a tenant get compensation for his improvement if he surrendered the land or was evicted. By discouraging transfers of land, this system supported the status quo. [Eds]*

Brahmins on the most powerful positions in the *sirkar* service. Having eschewed trade and the plantation business, Nayars more than ever needed to find extensive employment in the government. Yet they saw their way to the top being blocked. College-educated Nayars came to view reform of the matrilineal system as something which could be effected only after Nayars had regained supremacy in the highest positions under government. In the 1880s they formed the Malayali Sabha. Its original purpose was to promote education and work for modest social reform.

[ . . . ]

[T]he decay of Nayar social institutions became increasingly clear during the 1890s. This decay affected the vast majority of Nayars, not merely the educated elite who felt embarrassment at the absence of a marriage law. Leading officials like Thanu Pillai saw that Nayars' position in society was threatened by the basic inadequacy of their social institutions; but their attempts at remedy were mild and unsuccessful. . . . It was difficult—indeed almost impossible—for most of them to advocate radical social reform and thereby disavow those customs which had contributed to the traditional greatness of Nayars.

The major problem for Nayar society was its impartable matrilineal joint-family. . . . In the ideal *taravad* of pre-British times, the *karanavan* [the eldest male member and manager of a *taravad*] was selfless. A seasoned old soldier, devoted to the interests of his house and locality, he was charged with the supervision of the women, land and slaves, thus leaving the young men free to follow their raja and to fight. In the ideal *taravad*, there was a perfect 'communality' of spirit. Although the number of relatives in a single house might exceed 100, all were seldom at home together, for each *taravad* has responsibilities in war and government.

This was the ideal type, and whether it had actually existed was not so important by the 1890s as the fact that some Nayars believed that it had. It was part of a golden age when Nayars moved through the country as prosperous soldiers and gentry, respected and feared. With such a picture, the situation in the 1890s compared unfavourably. 'Incessant disputes, heart-burnings and litigation spring up; many families are sinking into ruin', wrote one well-informed, though not disinterested, observer, 'and the Nairs are, on the whole, diminishing in wealth and position'. The *karanavan* had become a greedy villain, and the *taravad* the scene of endless dissension among aggressive mothers, layabout youths and scheming elders.

The large ideal *taravad* had probably begun to dissolve in Travancore before other parts of Kerala as a result of Maharaja Marthanda Varma's subordination of the Nayars in the 18th century. Certainly by the 1870s, . . . monogamous marriages—though they were not backed by the courts—were becoming common. At the same time, *taravads* were increasingly agreeing to divide themselves into a number of branches, each with its

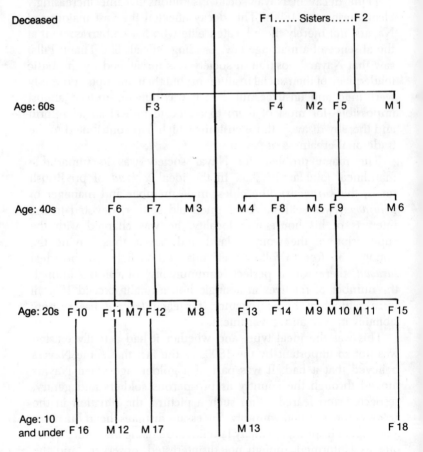

Figure showing descent and possibilities
for partition in a hypothetical *taravad*

own house and lands; but these divisions were similarly without the force of law and could be overturned in the courts. It is difficult not to burlesque the potential legal troubles of a *taravad*, but let us examine a hypothetical case for illustration. The diagram [may] help to make the situation clearer:

F1 and F2 are sisters, both dead. They have 29 descendants, and the *taravad* has extensive, scattered holdings of land. The *karanavan* is M1, the eldest male descendant* of the two sisters. M3, dissatisfied with M1's management, persuades his mother, F3, and his sisters, F6 and F7, and their families, to establish themselves on family lands a few miles distant from the old *taravad* house; there, M3 acts as the manager. Legally, however, M1 is solely responsible for the administration of the whole *taravad*. He can claim the revenue from the lands on which M3 is living, and, indeed, can alienate them if he can convince the purchaser or mortgagee (and, by extension, a court) that the alienation is for *taravad* necessities. M3, on the other hand, can challenge such alienations on the grounds that the *karanavan* did not have the consent of all the adult members of the *taravad*.

The permutations of even such a simplified example, and the scope for mismanagement and litigation, are extensive. For example, the *karanavan*, M1, may have been supporting his wife and children with *taravad* resources and neglecting even his own nephew, much less the nephews of his cousin, M2. M6, unlikely ever to be *karanavan* though he holds a well-paying government job, leaves the *taravad* to set up his own household with his wife in Trivandrum; his resources are lost to the *taravad*, and his nephews, M10 and M11, are neglected and unproductive. On his death, however, his nephews and *taravad* are his legal heirs and can claim all his self-acquired property, thus leaving his wife destitute, or at least with only her own *taravad* to fall back on. F13 is permitted to have *sambandham* with a penniless non-Malayali Brahmin who is unable to pay her confinement expenses and eventually disappears. . . .

Litigation . . . increased steadily. In the decade 1879–80/1888–9, there was an average of 60 suits a year for *taravad* partition,

---

\* *Within the taravad 'lateral succession' was the norm. The order of succession to the position of karanavan (manager) was from the eldest male member to his successive younger brothers, and when that generation was exhausted, to the sisters' sons, again in order of age. [Eds]*

in spite of the known policy of the courts to grant such decrees only when all the adult members of a *taravad* agreed. From 1889–90 to 1898–9, the average increased to 80 suits annually; from 1899–1900 to 1903–4, when figures stopped being published, the average was 96 a year. Thus in 25 years, nearly 1,800 *taravads* of the perhaps 30,000 in Travancore had taken the extreme step of going to law; as an indication of the malaise affecting the *taravad*, these cases were the tip of the iceberg.

By 1890 appalling stories were circulating about the state of poverty to which some families had been reduced by foolish litigation and haphazard management. It was said that some *taravads* were forcing their young girls into *sambandhams* with old Brahmins who could afford to pay a price. Nayars had always permitted *sambandhams* with non-Malayali Brahmins, but the latter were less attractive husbands than Nambudiris, Kshatriyas or even some subcastes of Nayars. As educated Nayars came to know more of Hinduism in the rest of India, their embarrassment at a custom which other Hindus regarded as both comical and disgraceful grew. . . .

The remedies suggested for the decaying *taravad* were various. Some men, embarrassed by the jibes at the laxity of Nayar morals, advocated a more binding marriage tie, recognised by law. Others asked how a mere marriage law could ameliorate the condition of the *taravad*, while a few radicals called for partition on demand: the right of any member to ask for and receive his share of the *taravad*'s assets. . . .

One of the aims of the Malayali Sabha had of course been reform of Nayar marriage customs; but by 1890 the Sabha's leading figures were deeply involved in the [Malayali] Memorial[*] and the *sirkar*-service issue. In that year, however, C. Sankaran Nair, a member of the Madras Legislative Council and the leading Nayar in the Madras Presidency, introduced a bill to permit Nayars in British India to register their *sambandhams*. This would make the *sambandham* legally binding and enable Nayars to dispose part of their self-acquired property on their wives and children. The proposed bill met with immediate opposition—from Nayars who defended the old system in its entirety, from Nayars

---

[*] *Malayali Memorial was a petition which claimed to express the grievances of all Malayalis irrespective of religion and caste. [Eds]*

who urged cautions slow changes, and from Nambudiris, Kshatriyas and non-Malayali Brahmins who saw their traditional domestic arrangements threatened.

The Madras Government created the Malabar Marriage Commission,* headed by Sir T. Muthuswami Aiyar, the most distinguished Brahmin in the Presidency, to examine the whole subject. . . . The commission examined witnesses in Malabar in mid-1891, and requested written opinions from Travancoreans. . . . The Commission's report was published towards the end of 1891 and suggested a modest, voluntary bill. But the report was forwarded to the Government of India, where it rotated with other files for two years, and it was not until 1896 that the Malabar Marriage Bill became law. Under its provisions people of any caste in Malabar following the *marumakkattayam* system could register their *sambandham* with government. This made the *sambandham* a legal marriage, entitled a man to make over his self-acquired property to his wife and children, and conferred on *marumakkattayis* such benefits of English law as bigamy, adultery and divorce. Yet the act was purely permissive: to those who did not register it did not apply. During its first 10 years on the statute books, fewer than 100 people registered their marriages; by 1906 it was pronounced 'a dead letter'.

The terms and passage of the act were watched closely in Travancore, especially after the Memorial and the virtual dissolution of the Malayali Sabha. Thanu Pillai pointed out that the error of [the] bill was in not recognising a public *sambandham* ceremony as a legal marriage. . . . Only by granting such recognition could the large majority of *marumakkattayis* be brought within the scope of the law and minimal rights given to wives and children.

As early as 1882, the Special Commission on Malabar Land Tenures, headed by William Logan, drew attention to the need to give Nayars the right to make a will and to leave their self-acquired property to their wives and children. . . . In 1887 the Malayali Sabha circulated a draft of a marriage bill among its members, but the Travancore *sirkar* showed no inclination to accept legislative proposals from an organization which it regarded as suspect.

* *Before independence, Travancore was a Princely State and Malabar was a part of the Madras Presidency. Both became part of the post-independence State of Kerala. [Eds]*

It was a measure of the good relations existing between leading Nayar officials and the new Dewan when early in 1896 Shungarasoobyer 'advised, encouraged and prompted' Thanu Pillai to introduce a bill in the Travancore Legislative Council. The bill . . . provided legal recognition for all marriages solemnized by 'the presentation of a cloth or some other recognised ceremony'. It did not undertake to change the system of inheritance; on a man's death, his *taravad* and his nephews remained his rightful heirs. But it removed any doubt about a man's right to provide for his wife and children from his self-acquired property during his lifetime, and it aimed to end the ridicule directed at the laxity of Nayar morals.

[ . . . ]

In the course of the next six months the bill became 'the chief subject of discussion' in the state; opinions were 'greatly divided'. The select committee presented a majority report, signed by Krishnaswami Rao, Thanu Pillai and Kuruvila, in January 1897. It recommended only one change in the proposed bill: the provision of optional registration for those who wished to make recognition of their *sambandham* unquestionable.

[ . . . ]

In the long term, Thanu Pillai's bill could be seen as a step towards ending the hypergamy of Nayar women and their deference to the high castes. Its immediate effect would be to make high-caste men, who had performed *sambandham* with a pretty Nayar girl and later changed their affections, liable to a criminal prosecution for adultery and bigamy. . . .

The marriage bill continued to excite interest throughout 1897, but it was virtually pushed off the Legislative Council agenda and never appeared likely to become law. During the next 5 days, though never formally killed, it languished and died. . . . The sudden death of Thanu Pillai at the age of 48 in May 1902 removed the most influential Nayar in the *sirkar* service and the bill's sponsor.

Educated Nayars, however, had achieved a small reform in 1899 with the passage of the Travancore Will Act. Again their apparently satisfactory relations with Shungarasoobyer, and, initially, with his successor, Krishnaswami Rao, who had been in Travancore service from 1884, first as chief justice and then as Dewan, facilitated action in the Legislative Council. The bill conferred on *marumakkattayis* the right to bequeath up to one-half of their self-acquired property to their wives and children. In the absence of a will, their *taravads* and nephews remained their sole legal heirs. Because the bill made no alteration to the law affecting marriage, it aroused less enthusiasm among educated Nayars; the stigma, the taunts and the exploitation of their women remained. Yet opposition was also lessened, and the bill passed without difficulty. . . .

[ . . . ]

## THE MARUMAKKATTAYAM COMMITTEE OF 1908

The Keraliya Nair Samaj's second annual conference held in Trivandrum in October 1907, shortly before the Assembly session, attracted the largest gathering of Nayars hitherto seen in Kerala. One of British Malabar leading Nayars, M. Krishnan Nair, a lawyer and member of the Madras Legislative Council, accepted the chairmanship, and delegates attended from British Malabar and Cochin. For the first time a Nayar meeting passed resolutions making specific recommendations for the reform of Nayar customs. In his opening speech Krishnan Nair stressed the urgent need for such reform, the key to which was a change in the law governing *taravad* partition. . . . He realized, he said, that his outspoken advocacy of radical reforms would cause 'violent disturbances', but the time for such reform was ripe.

The resolutions were not as radical as his speech called for. . . . The first and most important resolution . . . prescribed cautions moves towards a patrilineal family. . . . Stopping short of individual partition, it advocated: i) giving children a legal claim for maintenance from their fathers; ii) making a man's self-acquired property heritable only by descendants of that branch of his *taravad* originating from his mother; iii) allotting half of a man's self-acquired property to his wife and children on his death. Put into practice, such measures would not have ended the *taravad*, but they would have encouraged remotely related branches to sever all connections and partition family property voluntarily. . . .

The second resolution was mild enough: it called for recognition of the ceremony of *sambandham* as a legal marriage. Other resolutions, advocating dissemination of education among Nayars and the organization of village branches or *karayogams*, recalled Nayar meetings of earlier years. The two resolutions requiring changes in the law were forwarded to the governments of Travancore, Cochin and Madras.

Within a month, the Assembly met in Trivandrum under the presidency of the new Dewan, P. Rajagopalachari. . . . [H]e announced the creation of a committee . . . to investigate . . . proposed reforms of the joint-family, marriage, and inheritance customs of Nayars.

[ . . . ]

The committee toured the state throughout 1908, heard 1,021 witnesses and published its report at the end of the year. It recommended: the recognition of the ceremony of *sambandham* as a legal marriage; the outlawing of polyandry and polygamy; divorce by mutual consent certified by a registered document; compelling *karanavans* to keep careful accounts of their use of *taravad* assets; the grant to wives and children of a half share of the self-acquired property of a man dying intestate; and the right of any branch of a *taravad* descended from the same woman to demand partition. The last recommendation fell short of the right of individual partition . . . but it would have been enough to destroy the big *taravad*. In a *taravad* of 20 members, for example, a mother, her brother, her 3 children and their 2 children, would have been empowered to demand 7/20ths of the *taravad* assets and separate themselves completely.

[ . . . ]

Like the opponents of partition, the committee's first concern was the land. It collected figures on all sales and mortgages in the state for 18 months prior to the beginning of the Malayalam month of Makaram (January-February) 1908. . . . Under a system which in theory made property inalienable without proof of necessity or the consent of all adult members of the *taravad*, Nayars had alienated by sale or mortgage property worth Rs 18.77 lakhs more than they had acquired. Samantas, a matrilineal caste [ranking between Nayars and Kshatriyas] numbering no more than a thousand or so in north Travancore, had a similar net loss of Rs 35,651. Among patrilineal groups, on the other hand, Christians of all kinds had a net gain of Rs 11,71,007 worth of property; Iravas, Rs 2,94,386; and Shanars, Rs 83,009.

Christians and Iravas were acquiring land. Where was it coming from? The answer was obvious: from Nayars. And what was happening to the money which Nayars gained from hypothecating their land? That question led the Marumakkattayam Committee to its second concern: litigation.

Table 1

Suits Involving *Karanavans*, Brought by *Taravad* Members, 1073–1082 M.E. (1897–8/1906–7)

| | Type of Suit | Number |
|---|---|---|
| 1. | Suits to cancel a *karanavan*'s alienations | 4,365 |
| 2. | Suits to remove a *karanavan* | 295 |
| 3. | Suits to set aside decrees made against a *karanavan*'s alienations | 142 |
| 4. | Suits to set aside attachment of *taravad* property for a *karanavan*'s debts | 67 |
| | | 4,869 |

*Source*: Report of the Marumakkattayam Committee, Travancore, 1908, Appendix I, p. 73.

As Table 1 shows, disputes over the *karanavan*'s management provoked an average of 487 suits a year over the preceding 10 years. [It was] estimated the annual expenses incurred by Nayars in legal disputes arising from the *marumakkattayam* system at Rs 2 lakhs. If a Nayar won such a suit, another Nayar lost, and the fruits of victory were eaten up in litigation. The only Nayars to gain were vakils.

Finally, the Committee produced statistics to show a growing movement against the *taravad* way of life. . . . Agreed partitions had risen from 301 in 1896–7 to 516 in 1906–7. From such figures it would appear that over the 10-year period more than 3,000 *taravads* had unanimously agreed to partitions of one kind or another, and had executed the partition in the courts. At the same time, more members wishing to live apart from their *taravad* negotiated agreements for maintenance. In 1896–7, 205 such agreements were executed; in 1906–7, 385. In the same period, gifts to children, legally carried out, doubled. These figures, moreover, were undoubtedly only a tiny fraction of the *de facto* gifts, partitions and maintenance grants which were arranged without reference to the courts.

To these statistics the Committee added its opinion that 'residence [of the mother and children] with the father should be encouraged by the law on the ground of public policy'. It also endorsed the view of one of its witnesses that in 'the great majority' of *taravads*,

> instead of unanimity and mutual co-operation what one really finds is disunion and ill-will. . . . The credit of the average existing *Tarwads* will likewise be found to be very low, and it cannot be otherwise, for the credit of a country where civil war is being waged with determination on both sides, cannot ordinarily be high. And lastly, if prestige has any place, it is surely not in a *Tarwad*, one of the common pastimes of whose members is the institution of criminal proceedings against each other for assault, theft, forgery and even attempts to commit murder.

Having endorsed such views, the Committee not surprisingly advocated a modified form of partition. Yet in doing so it was acknowledging that the condition of Nayars was so serious that the very basis of their traditional organization had to be abolished if they were to retain the power which had been theirs in the past.

[ . . . ]

# Restitution of Conjugal Rights
## A Controversial Case in
## Colonial Bombay[*]

### SUDHIR CHANDRA

. . . I propose to indicate in this paper the need to rethink some of the notions that continue to be entertained about the emancipatory role of the British Indian legal system. Focusing on an important and controversial case of restitution of conjugal rights that came up before the Bombay High Court in 1884, I shall discuss if, in terms of legal procedure as well as substantive legal provisions, the colonial mediation necessarily brought in a whiff of fresh and invigorating air in an ossified inegalitarian society.

[ . . . ]

### I

Here is a brief description of the case. Known as Dadaji Bhikaji vs. Rukhmabai case, it began unnoticed around March 1884 with Dadaji moving the Bombay High Court to direct his wife, Rukhmabai, to live with him. A Suthar or Pachkalshi by caste, Rukhmabai was married, around 1873, when she was either eleven or thirteen to nineteen-year old Dadaji. Rukhmabai lived

* Excerpted from Sudhir Chandra, 'Whose Laws?: Notes on a Legitimizing Myth of the Colonial Indian State', *Studies in History*, 8 (2), 1992, pp. 187–211.

at the house of her step-father, Dr Sakharam Arjun, a noted physician and public figure of Bombay. Dadaji, a distant relative of Dr Sakharam, visited the family from time to time. The marriage, however, was not consummated. Eleven years after the marriage, Dadaji called upon Rukhmabai to go to his house and live with him. She refused. He thereupon filed a case for restitution of conjugal rights.

The case came up for hearing before Mr Justice Pinhey who gave his judgement on 21 September 1885. Awarding costs to the defendant, Pinhey held that the suit was not maintainable. . . . Dadaji was advised to appeal against Pinhey's judgement, which he quickly did. After listening to arguments from both the sides on 12 March, Chief Justice Sir Charles Sargent and Mr Justice Bayley held, on 18 March 1886, that the suit was maintainable, and that the case should be remanded for a decision on the merits.

Meanwhile Pinhey had retired and the case came up before Mr Justice Farran. Perhaps sensing the inevitable from the tenor of the appellate bench's judgement, Inverarity thought it prudent to tell the court that his client, Rukhmabai, had determined not to live with the plaintiff as husband and wife; which meant that in the event of an adverse decree she would, as judgement debtor, rather court imprisonment for six months. 'She certainly would not make any attempt to obviate', Inverarity clarified, 'but, on the contrary, was ready to bear the consequences'. The inevitable did happen. On 4 March 1887 Farran ordered Rukhmabai to go and live with Dadaji within one month, or else face the prospect of six months in prison.

While this resolution of the case produced a wide range of reactions, there seemed near unanimity about the impropriety of Rukhmabai being forced into prison for recusancy. Even the sections of the Hindu society that had solidly stood behind Dadaji expressed revulsion at such a prospect. . . .

A visibly worried Bombay government wrote to the Government of India on 30 March 1887. Stressing that the young lady seemed determined to accept the extreme penalty rather than the court's decree, the Bombay government suggested a short legislation as a possible way out of the almost certain impasse. Little did the Bombay authorities realise that the Viceroy himself was following the case with some concern. For, the same day—30

March—from his Camp he sent the following telegram to A.R. Scoble, the Law Member: 'I hope you are keeping your eye on the Rukhmabai case. It would never do to allow her to be put into prison'. Thus began a flurry of deliberations within the supreme government, which also sought the opinions of local governments and sections of the public, in order that the immediate crisis created by the case as well as its embarrassing legal implications could be coped with.

About the same time, an influential committee was formed to take up Rukhmabai case. Consisting of men and women who constituted the very elite of Bombay's society, and having Principal Wordsworth as its chairman, the Rukhmabai Defence Committee was intended to raise funds and take necessary action on her behalf.

More to gain time, it is clear in retrospect, than with any hope of success, an appeal was filed against Farran's judgement before a division bench of the Bombay High Court. Moreover, efforts were simultaneously initiated to bring about a compromise. These bore fruit in the first week of July 1888, and Dadaji agreed to relinquish his claims on Rukhmabai for a payment of two thousand rupees. Soon thereafter Rukhmabai sailed for England to train as a doctor.

## II

A crucial issue on which hung the fate of Rukhmabai's case was whether a suit for restitution of conjugal rights was maintainable among Hindus. While her illustrious counsel—Advocate-General Latham, Inverarity and Telang—advanced more than one reason why Rukhmabai should not be forced to live with Dadaji, they carried conviction with Pinhey only on the ground that such a suit did not lie among Hindus. . . .

It was 'a misnomer', Pinhey ruled, 'to call this a suit for the restitution of conjugal rights', because no such rights had ever been instituted between Dadaji and Rukhmabai. He observed that it was according to the practice in England, and according to the later practice of the courts in India that a suit for restitution of conjugal rights could be brought by one who was party to a traditional Indian marriage. But for such a suit to be maintainable, the essential requirement of English legal practice needed to be fulfilled: i.e., the married couple must have cohabited before separating and living apart. . . .

Pinhey regretted that suits for restitution of conjugal rights were permitted in the wake of post-1857 legal changes. He felt particularly anguished that this had happened at a time when in England the practice had 'become much discredited' and been 'rendered almost inoperative by the legislation of the past year'. Since, however, the practice had been introduced into this country, Pinhey admitted that he was 'bound to follow it so far as it has received the sanction of this Court or of the Privy Council.' But he was 'certainly not disposed to make a precedent, or to extend the practice of the Court in respect of suits of this nature. . . .'

[ . . . ]

When the case came up before Sargent and Bayley, the counsel for the appellant—Macpherson, Vicaji and Mankar—cited a number of judicial decisions to argue along the following lines:

> The rights of the parties are complete when the marriage ceremony is performed. The wife becomes a member of her husband's family, and ought to reside with him. . . . Consummation is not necessary to effectuate marriage. The husband has a right to the society of his wife, and the Court is bound to enforce that right. . . . If the right and its incidents be the same among Christians, Mahomedans, Parsis and Hindus, why should the remedy be denied to Hindus? The Court has no discretion.

Pinhey, we may notice, had not ruled that the marriage between Dadaji and Rukhmabai was void or incomplete. His ruling rested on a distinction between *restitution* and *institution* of conjugal rights. Finding no precedent to so construct restitution as to subsume institution, he was loath to create one himself. In arguing before the appellate bench, that Dadaji's rights as a husband were complete in spite of the absence of consummation, the counsel for the appellant were not demolishing Pinhey's point about suits for restitution of conjugal rights not being maintainable among Hindus. They were rather seeking from the appellate court the kind of extension of English legal practice to India that Pinhey had opposed on juristic as well as moral grounds. . . .

They need not have done that, though. Sargent and Bayley

took pains, in their judgement, to demonstrate that the distinction made by Pinhey between restitution and institution of conjugal rights appeared 'to be based on a misapprehension as to the principles on which the Ecclesiastical Courts in England exercised this jurisdiction'. This certainly gave them a reasonable ground to reverse Pinhey's verdict in the Rukhmabai case. But it also underscored Pinhey's point that suits for restitution of conjugal rights in British Indian law courts owed their existence to English practice.

[ . . . ]

If Pinhey's point about the nature of the suits in question remained unscathed by the arguments for the appellant, it was natural that it should receive support from Latham and Telang, the counsel for Rukhmabai. Opening the argument for the respondent, Latham supported Pinhey's judgement on two grounds: (*a*) 'that a suit for restitution of conjugal rights does not lie between Hindus'; and (*b*) 'that the present case is one without precedent, being a suit for rights not yet enjoyed. There is no English authority for enforcing the commencement of cohabitation'.

As to the first point, Latham admitted that he was 'asking the Court to decide contrary to a series of cases between Hindus' which had come up recently; the earliest of these being only ten years old. Besides the moral—and not negligible—consideration that suits of this kind were repulsive to civilized notions, the cases involving Hindu spouses seemed to have been admitted on the authority of two cases decided by the Privy Council. One of these cases—Ardaseer Cursetjee v. Perozebye—was between Parsis, and the other—Moonshee Buzloor Ruheem v. Shumsoonissa Begum—was between Muslims. 'In none of them', Latham emphasized, 'do the Courts appear to have considered what the Hindu law is upon the subject.' He, moreover, drew the court's attention to the Privy Council's declaration in Ardaseer Cursetjee v. Perozebye 'that ecclesiastical law has no application in India, that we are to have regard only to the law and usages of the people of this country.' So, unless shown to be known to Hindu law, suits for restitution of conjugal rights should not be extended to Hindus.

But the courts never cared to show this. Rather, since the 1867 Privy Council decision in Moonshee Buzloor Ruheem v. Shumsoonissa Begum, they began assuming that 'a suit for restitution of conjugal rights lies between Hindus'; and in doing this they ignored the fact that 'the observations made in the judgement were not intended to apply to cases between Hindus'. That, Latham submitted, 'was a mistake.' . . .

Carrying on the argument for the respondent, Telang [said that]. . . . '[w]hile the Hindu law books . . . prescribe the duties of husband and wife', they 'say little as to the mode of enforcing their performance.' These duties being religious, they are enforced by religious institutions. . . . The texts do not discuss the question of restitution. The law contemplates a husband's desertion of his wife, 'and that only results in a fine to the king.' In the absence of any 'provision at all for the case of a wife separating from her husband', Telang was prepared to assume that the same remedy or punishment would be applied to an erring wife as well.

Moving from Hindu law books to customary law or usage, Telang admitted that the caste could always have ordered a deserting wife to go back to her husband. The caste, he further admitted, could still do that. But not the civil courts. For, what had devolved upon the civil courts was 'the authority which belonged to the king when the Hindu law books were written', and not the functions exercised by the caste. Telang maintained that even where a wife's desertion of her husband was contemplated, Hindu law did not provide that 'the king shall order her to go back'. . . .

Pinhey and the counsel for Rukhmabai had thus shown that a suit for restitution of conjugal rights did not lie between Hindus. This impressive demonstration was sought to be destroyed by Macpherson with a clever technical twist. Knowing that he could not produce any sanction for such suits in Hindu law, he said: 'There may be no direct authority for the suit in Hindu law', but 'that law contains nothing forbidding it'.

With this bit of negative logic—turning the absence of evidence into a decisive argument—Macpherson carried the day. Indeed, he ensured for posterity that suits for restitution of conjugal rights would lie between Hindus. Of course, this became possible because Sargent and Bayley were more than inclined to go along with him. They almost echoed Macpherson in their judgement and made short work of Telang's contention that the civil courts had inherited the authority of the king and not the functions of the caste:

We may, however, remark that although no text may be found in the Hindu law books which provides for the king ordering a husband or wife to return, no text was cited forbidding or deprecating compulsion, and that it was admitted that the duties appertaining to the relationship of husband and wife have always been the subject of caste discipline, and, therefore, that *with the establishment of a systematic administration of justice* the Civil Courts would properly and almost necessarily assume to themselves the jurisdiction over conjugal rights as determined by Hindu law, and enforce them according to their own modes of procedure. (Italics added)

In the apparently casual, almost passing, reference to 'the establishment of a systematic administration of justice'—with the unstated assumption of a host of other benefits ensuing therefrom—we can sense the belief in the civilisational transformation initiated by the colonisers among the colonised. The depth of the collective superciliousness that sustained this belief among the colonisers is indicated by the fact that it remained unruffled even by the realisation that the legal provision of compulsion would profoundly violate human feelings.

So far as the provision of compulsion in the event of recusancy was concerned, even Sargent and Bayley admitted that 'the law should not adopt stringent measures to compel the performance of conjugal duties'. Still, with regard to actual administration of the much wonted systematic justice, they felt incompetent to entertain any objection which goes to the root of the jurisdiction, such as that urged by Mr Telang, viz., that the Hindu law books do not recognize a compulsory discharge of marital duties, but treat them as duties of imperfect obligation to be enforced by religious sanction'. All they could do was to administer the law as it was. Similarly, while claiming as a matter of right the disciplinary function discharged by the caste, they did not care to ensure that the justice thus imparted was not vitiated by the axiomatic acceptance of a procedural fetish called 'consistency and uniformity of practice'. Hence their claim that the jurisdiction exercised by civil courts over the conjugal rights of Hindus would be 'determined by Hindu law', but the courts would enforce those rights 'according to their own modes of procedure'.

[ . . . ]

The preference shown by Pinhey . . . for a critical and comparative understanding of jurisprudence across cultural frontiers was exceptional. It enabled [him] to look beyond the universal claims of [his] own culture and appreciate the underlying values and assumptions of socio-legal systems that were different from the one to which [he himself] belonged. Without forsaking faith in the soundness of [his] own system, [he] could see the distortions that characterised the British Indian legal network. Significantly, [he] could do this not only in terms of its deviation from the current English legal practice and principles: [he] could see also how its break from the erstwhile indigenous systems was in itself a retrogressive measure.

[ . . . ]

### III

. . . It can be argued that at least in the context of the Rukhmabai case the British Indian legal system was far from sustaining the hold of any myth, juristic or other, that may be supposed to have brought the subject people under its sway. If anything, the case was used by the latter to assail not only the new legal system but also the culture that had brought it to India. Whatever their differences, virtually all Hindu/Indian reactions to the case converged on one point: what was being administered was British and not Hindu law.

But there was no agreement as to what the Hindu law on the subject was. Indeed, . . . the same people could look upon something simultaneously as an assertion and also a violation of Hindu law. And this happened primarily as a result of the anxiety to preserve their cultural dignity vis-à-vis the rulers; an anxiety that could, at least at times, lead them into contrary positions. In the case of the 'reformist' response the internal contrariety was not so marked. Consequently, while maintaining in all soberness that restitution of conjugal rights was a notion alien to Hindu law, [a 'reformist'] could enthusiastically support legislation in India long the lines of legal changes in England that had done away with imprisonment for recusancy in 'restitution' cases. Also, people with a reformist orientation were willing to admit that social changes along desirable lines had been ushered into their society under the colonial dispensation.

[ . . . ]

Thus it happened that, following the fundamental change the British had brought about in the very conception of Hindu or/and Indian law, whereby traditional plurality gave way to a body of unified codes, even the pundits in the field tended to uphold the idea of a Hindu law as against the multiplicity of local and customary laws and usages. . . .

. . . The judicial practice conformed to the newly awakening Hindu conception of Hindu law. Almost overnight, as it were, the British had revolutionised not only the Hindu/Indian laws but also the conception that the Hindus/Indians would have of their own laws and society. The State would now legitimately, and inexorably, ease out traditional communities as parallel centres of socio-cultural authority.

# Marital Interaction and Adjustment[*]

## G.N. RAMU

The day-to-day relations between spouses are quite important for marital solidarity and adjustment. From a sociological point of view, they serve as crucial indicators of the level of affection, companionship, and communication between husband and wife. Moreover, life in a nuclear family encourages activities that centre around the couple, and this provides scope for a spouse to demonstrate his/her likes and dislikes towards the other easily and frequently. Therefore, if strong bonds do not exist in nuclear families, it is not due to structural restraints such as those found in rural joint families, but due to the inability of the spouses to cultivate such bonds. In this study,[**] we explore the marital interaction among single- and dual-earner households in relation to the patterns of recreation, day-to-day relations, marital discord, and marital-satisfaction. Our main purpose [is] to assess the impact, if any, of the wife's economic status on various dimensions of marital interaction.

---

[*] Excerpted from G.N. Ramu, 'Women, Work and Marital Patterns', *Women, Work and Marriage in Urban India: A Study of Dual- and Single-earner Couples*, New Delhi: Sage Publications, 1989, pp. 170–86.

[**] *This study involves a comparison between single- and dual-earner households. Its data, gathered in Bangalore, come from four samples, each comprising 245 respondents: husbands in single-earner households (SEH), wives in single-earner households (SEW), husbands in dual-earner households (DEH), and wives in dual-earner households (DEW). In the single-earner households the husband alone is the earner. (Eds)*

## PATTERNS OF RECREATION

[ . . . ]
While a spouse in an urban setting can go out for a walk in a park, see a movie, visit a restaurant, or attend a concert alone, to do so is increasingly perceived as improper, especially for the wife. This is because it is a negative reflection of conjugal solidarity, and a source of marital conflict. Furthermore, attending such events as a couple is not only a reaffirmation of togetherness in public, but also gives the couple an opportunity to be closer to each other without intrusions from children and others. With these considerations, the respondents were asked 'how frequently do you go out together', and 'usually where do you go when you get out of your homes'. The responses are summarized in Tables 1 and 2.

Table 1
The Percentage Distribution of Respondents by the Frequency of Going Out Together

| Frequency | DEW N(%) | DEH N(%) | SEW N(%) | SEH N(%) |
|---|---|---|---|---|
| Rare/never | 43(17.6) | 10(4.1) | 140(57.1) | 113(46.1) |
| Several times a week | 98(40.0) | 52(21.3) | 9(3.7) | 20(6.1) |
| About once a week | 94(38.4) | 147(60.0) | 35(14.3) | 43(17.6) |
| Only on special occasions | 10(4.0) | 36(14.6) | 61(24.9) | 69(28.2) |

N = 245 for each sample.

The data in Table 1 suggest that a significantly higher percentage of dual-earner spouses went out, either several times or once a week, than did single-earner spouses. About half of the single-earner spouses reported either never or only rarely going out together. Analysis of data controlling for SES variables did not yield any significant differences for dual-earner spouses, but for single-earner couples the husband's occupation had an effect on the frequency of going out: those in assembly-line and other occupational categories tended to report 'never' or 'rarely'. The data in Table 2 indicate that movies and shopping attracted more spouses from both samples (dual- and single-earner) than any other activity, although for dual-earners, centres of worship was the second frequently visited spot which partially accounts for their traditional disposition.

Table 2
The Percentage Distribution of Respondents by the Places they Visit When they Go Out

| Place | DEW N(%) | DEH N(%) | SEW N(%) | SEH N(%) |
|---|---|---|---|---|
| Never visit | 43(17.6) | 10(4.1) | 140(57.1) | 113(46.1) |
| Shopping/movies | 107(43.7) | 112(45.7) | 80(32.7) | 89(36.4) |
| Church/temple/mosque | 53(21.6) | 60(24.5) | 20(8.2) | 26(10.6) |
| Other | 42(17.1) | 63(25.7) | 5(2.0) | 17(6.9) |

N = 245 for each sample.

The data in Tables 1 and 2 permit the conclusion that living in urban nuclear families and the availability of various public forms of entertainment alone do not necessarily lead spouses to frequent 'outings'. The wife's work status has a critical influence not only on whether a couple goes out but also on the frequency of the outings. It has many facilitating conditions which might have contributed to the high frequency of their 'outings'. First, most dual-earner spouses worked in the same industry, and this made it possible for many of them, especially for those who had scooters, to commute together. The fact that they commuted together, either by themselves or via public transport, gave them the freedom to periodically shop or eat in a restaurant. By contrast, for many single-earner spouses, going out had to be planned ahead of time, as if it were an expedition. When planning is involved, given the authoritarian disposition of the SEHs . . . , men often have the dissenting voice. Second, the dual-earner couples had more economic resources for such ventures than did most of the single-earner spouses. Third, a DEW could legitimately demand of her husband that he take her out, whereas SEWs had to depend on the husband's moods and inclinations. Finally, a higher proportion of dual-earner couples had the benefit of maid-servants who could be relied on for child care than did the single-earners.

For many single-earner spouses, going out without children was impractical for at least three reasons. First, such practices as baby-sitting, common in Western societies, is virtually absent here. Parents have to frequently rely on neighbours or kind to look after children during their absence. Although it is legitimate to call on the assistance of neighbours and kin in emergencies, it is perceived as improper to do so regularly, and particularly during a couple's outing. Second, even if they have understanding kin or neighbours to look after children while they are away, the meaning and purpose of an 'outing' is not seen by many single-earner spouses in terms of conjugal solidarity; this is because the emphasis in marital relations has shifted from the couple to the family. Finally, middle-class dual-earner families are a novel phenomenon and thus their conduct is evaluated rather more leniently than that of single-earner couples. Single-earner households are still expected to adhere to customary patterns of behaviour. Consequently, husbands in such households tend to go on 'outings' with other men rather than with their wives. If husbands in dual-earner families engage in such behaviour routinely, it would initiate marital discord.

In our interviews, we noted that the issue of 'outings' was more contentious between single-earner spouses than among their counterparts. Many of the SEWs felt confined, and children were just an excuse for their husbands to go out by themselves or with other men. One SEW (Adi Laksmi Narasimmappa) reported:

> My husband, like all other men, used to take me out to cinemas and hotels when we were first married. He took me to Mysore. He took me to KRS several times [Mysore and KRS are places of tourist attraction]. We used to go to Cubbon Park almost every week. It was so nice going out together. It all stopped after the birth of our second child. He found going to a cinema or even to a park with children bothersome. Once in six months or a year he takes us all out and that too after all of us beg him. I agree that we have a lot of children, but they are an excuse for my husband not to take us out. He now likes going out with his friends. He goes out with them to cinemas, to Cubbon Park, to MTR [a popular restaurant in Bangalore] or wherever they want. I am stuck here when he is eating nice things in MTR with his friends. [Q. Do you or can you go out

to see a cinema in Majestic with other women?] Yes . . . some times. But it is not like going with your husband . . . (SEW-11).

Such views were not confined to wives of assembly-line workers because on certain aspects of marital interaction, gender (apart from wife's economic status) and not social class, tends to influence the behaviour of husbands. Take the case of Tirtha Ram (age 33), a quality control engineer. While he publicly maintained liberal attitudes on marital and family issues, in practise he was conservative as reported by his wife, Kala. Tirtha Ram said that demands made on him by his children and wife were too excessive and he could not relax when they went out with him. In his words,

> Imagine taking my three small children and my wife on a scooter to Majestic to see a film or to a hotel on a Sunday afternoon. For me that is worse than going to work on a Monday morning. It is nothing but misery. Children want everything they see in Kempegowda circle. They want to eat everything that is sold on the footpath. . . . They are restless in the theatre. My wife does not care because she is more interested in watching the movie. There are days I have spent more time taking these children to the toilet than watching the film. You take them to a hotel, they make a mess. It looks bad . . . sometimes I wished I was not there because of their behaviour. By the time I come home, I am so uptight I go out alone for a walk and smoke a cigarette or two. [Q. What do you usually do for relaxation? Do you go out alone with friends?] Yes . . . once in a while . . . sometimes they come here for a game of cards on Sundays. Otherwise, I stay home and play with the children (SEH-12).

It is likely that Tirtha Ram is more sensitive than most Indian fathers/husbands about the conduct of their young children. But he is one among the Indian husbands who have not yet come to terms with the changing demands of the urban family.

In sum, our findings suggest that the recreational activities among single-earner spouses were not as couple-centred as they were among the dual-earners. The opportunities for spouses in single-earner households to go out together or do things together were not as regularly or frequently available as they were to dual-earner couples. Also, leisure and relaxation were more likely to become a prerogative of the husband in single-earner than among dual-earner households.

# SELECTED PATTERNS OF MARITAL INTERACTION

. . . [W]e attempted to inquire about certain specific activities which would shed light on the nature of interaction between the spouses. To this end, a query was set as follows: Couples often do like to do some things together. Please tell us which of the following you and your spouse did together in the last two weeks. All the items referred to activities that were coupled-centred and based on a sense of intimacy, and demanded close interaction as well as joint planning. By asking them to report the occurrence of these activities within a two-week span, we wanted to exclude those interactional events which were special and somewhat mandatory (e.g., birthday parties and religious feasts). The findings are summarized in Table 3.

Table 3

The Percentage Distribution of Respondents by Selected Items on Marital Interaction

| Items | DEW N(%) | DEH N(%) | SEW N(%) | SEH N(%) |
|---|---|---|---|---|
| Spent an evening just chatting | | | | |
| Yes | 192(78.8) | 179(73.1) | 123(50.2) | 139(56.3) |
| No | 52(21.2) | 66(26.9) | 122(49.8) | 106(43.7) |
| Did something special which the spouse appreciated | | | | |
| Yes | 178(72.6) | 185(75.5) | 136(55.5) | 101(41.2) |
| No | 67(27.4) | 60(24.5) | 109(44.5) | 144(58.8) |
| Entertained kin/friends at home | | | | |
| Yes | 115(46.9) | 125(51.0) | 154(62.9) | 109(44.5) |
| No | 78(31.8) | 98(40.0) | 115(46.9) | 126(51.4) |
| Visited kin/friends together | | | | |
| Yes | 167(68.2) | 147(60.0) | 130(53.1) | 119(48.6) |
| No | 78(31.8) | 98(40.0) | 115(46.9) | 126(51.4) |
| Went out for a movie | | | | |
| Yes | 203(82.9) | 217(88.6) | 103(42.0) | 112(45.7) |
| No | 42(17.1) | 28(11.4) | 142(58.0) | 133(54.3) |

| Items | DEW<br>N(%) | DEH<br>N(%) | SEW<br>N(%) | SEH<br>N(%) |
|---|---|---|---|---|
| Went to a restaurant | | | | |
| Yes | 181(73.9) | 167(68.2) | 83(33.9) | 92(37.5) |
| No | 64(26.1) | 78(31.8) | 162(66.1) | 153(62.5) |

N = 245 for each sample.

The data in Table 3 suggest that husbands and wives differed within about a 5 to 10 per cent margin while reporting on most items. Nevertheless, the percentage of dual-earner couples who reported involvement in activities that enhanced and reinforced marital harmony was significantly higher than single-earner spouses. The most common form of shared activity among the dual-earners was 'going out to see a movie', while 'chatting with each other' was for single-earner spouses. The general pattern of interaction based on six items . . . allows us to conclude that a wife's employment enhances the primacy of the conjugal unit by providing numerous opportunities for shared activities that sustain and reinforce companionship and communication.

More important, most of the dual-earner spouses not only did things together but also enjoyed doing certain things together. It is true, as many spouses reported during interviews, that things have become fairly routine, and this takes away the element of surprise in their lives. For example, going out to see a movie or shopping was part of the weekly or biweekly schedule of most dual-earner couples. Buying things for each other or for the children on pay-day was part of the routine as well. And yet most of the couples preferred maintaining such standardized practices to not having them at all, because these permitted them to be physically together as also to be mutually dependent.

## MARITAL ADJUSTMENT

The cultural context in which relations between husband and wife are defined should be kept in mind when evaluating the notion of marital adjustment in the Indian context. . . . [R]eligious values, ineffective laws, and economic conditions perpetuate the dependency of a wife upon her husband. Such dependency entails several things. First, it is incumbent upon a wife to adjust to the needs of her husband. . . . Second, part of the adjustment process is making compromises, even if such compromises lead to sacrificing one's own needs. Third, women, more than men, are expected to contribute to domestic harmony. Fourth, marital conflict is feared by wives, and they often refrain from those acts that lead to dissension. This is due to the fact that in situations of marital conflict, husbands and their kin can, and often do, exercise coercive power. The use of such power is too frequent among urban middle-class families, as is suggested by journalistic evidence (e.g., daily reports on suicide by wives who could not cope with marital problems, or dowry-related homicides). Finally, although divorce is legally permitted, few ever seek it as an ultimate means of resolving marital conflict. Consequently, it is imperative that all forms of marital dissension be resolved by spouses themselves, thus placing immense onus on women to compromise, adjust, and make sacrifices in favour of marital stability.

Although the cultural context moderates, if not defines, the process of marital adjustment among couples, contemporary marital relations are more complex than the female-male dependency theory posits. While domestic violence against, and the exploitation of, women continues unabated among certain sections of society, the structure of marital relations is simultaneously undergoing a subtle change, as is evident from our findings on patterns of decision-making, recreation, and interaction among the respondents. Men are less patriarchal and more pliable in the area of interpersonal relations than they are in matters of housework. Nonetheless, husbands zealously guard their public image as masters of the household, just as wives are careful about preserving such an image. Such an implicit arrangement between spouses provides flexibility in matters pertaining to marital adjustment.

[ . . . ]

## MARITAL DISSENSIONS AMONG THE RESPONDENTS

In order to assess whether the wife's employment had any influence on selected aspects of marital dissension among the respondents, the following was posed: Here is a list of things on which couples sometimes agree or disagree; please check which ones caused disagreements, leading to problems between you and your spouse during the last two weeks. The findings are presented in Table 4. The proportion of those who reported arguments and discord due to spouse's physical fatigue was high for the DEWs and SEHs. . . . Fatigue due to role overload among employed wives and its impact on domestic relations have been noted by previous researchers. The husbands and children of these women make too many demands . . . which naturally leads to friction. However, a high proportion of the SEWs and a still higher proportion of their husbands reported fatigue as a source of marital conflict as well. It is likely that for a good many of the spouses who are dependent on industrial work, tension and physical stress are common, and that these do leave a negative impact on marital harmony.

Table 4
Respondents' Opinions on Selected Items
on Marital Dissension

| Items | DEW N(%) | DEH N(%) | SEW N(%) | SEH N(%) |
|-------|----------|----------|----------|----------|
| About your being tired all the time | | | | |
| Yes | 188(76.7) | 106(43.3) | 143(58.4) | 172(70.2) |
| No | 57(23.3) | 139(56.7) | 102(41.6) | 73(29.8) |
| About spouse spending time with friends | | | | |
| Yes | 187(76.3) | 65(26.5) | 204(83.3) | 36(14.7) |
| No | 58(23.7) | 180(73.5) | 41(16.7) | 209(85.3) |
| About household expenses | | | | |
| Yes | 113(46.1) | 129(52.6) | 153(62.4) | 178(72.6) |
| No | 132(53.9) | 116(47.4) | 92(37.6) | 67(27.4) |
| Spouse's irritating personal habits | | | | |
| Yes | 129(52.6) | 103(42.0) | 142(58.0) | 83(33.9) |
| No | 116(47.4) | 142(58.0) | 103(42.0) | 162(66.1) |

| Items | DEW N(%) | DEH N(%) | SEW N(%) | SEH N(%) |
|---|---|---|---|---|
| Spouse not sharing enough love and affection | | | | |
| Yes | 102(41.6) | 121(49.4) | 113(46.1) | 127(51.8) |
| No | 143(58.4) | 124(50.6) | 132(53.9) | 118(48.2) |
| In-laws' or other kin's interference | | | | |
| Yes | 93(38.0) | 108(44.1) | 119(48.6) | 90(36.7) |
| No | 152(62.0) | 137(55.9) | 126(51.4) | 155(63.3) |
| Your spouse being away from home all the time | | | | |
| Yes | 92(37.6) | 95(38.9) | 189(77.1) | 105(42.9) |
| No | 153(62.4) | 150(61.1) | 56(22.9) | 140(57.1) |
| Spouse's preoccupation with job | | | | |
| Yes | 42(17.1) | 35(14.3) | 22(9.0) | – |
| No | 203(82.9) | 210(85.7) | 223(91.0) | 245(100) |

N = 245 for each sample.

From the point of view of most wives in this study, the time their husbands spent with their friends was a source of marital stress, whereas most husbands did not consider this an issue. . . . [I]t is quite common for men to cultivate and retain friendship with other men, regardless of their marital status, whereas women are less likely to do so. It was not just their husbands' friendship with other men that disturbed most wives in this study, but the disproportionate amount of time and attention (which should be legitimately given to one's family) that such a friendship extracts. The dual-earner couples spent more time interacting with each other than did single-earner spouses, but even then the proportion of wives in both groups that reported husbands' time with friends as an irritant to marital solidarity was comparable.

Even when the husband spent just as much time with his wife as he did with his friends, this was deemed as sufficient basis for complaint and quarrel by the wife according to Kesavan (age 32), a production supervisor, who maintained extremely traditional views on practically every issue that concerned women. He sarcastically noted,

Women think when we marry them we should turn into bonded peons hanging around their sarees all the time. They can't make friends, and when they make friends they can't keep them for long. It is not our problem if we can have good friends and have a good time with them. If I go home an hour or two late, she starts moping and making noises. Women turn mean when they cannot adjust to their husbands' men friends. They don't realize men do what women have failed to do in their lives. [Q. And that is?] To make friends and keep them . . . and then there is the usual . . . [expletive deleted] statement, which all wives use to insult their husbands, 'if you like so much being with them [friends] all the time, you should have married them, why did you marry me then?' (DEH-15).

Dissensions due to household expenses and spouse's personal habits were also reported by a significant proportion of respondents. . . . Matters relating to money among wage earners are usually contentious, since expenses have to be tailored to monthly income. Furthermore, because there is always daily spending on one item or the other that is essential to the management of the household, there is potential for frequent argument about expenses. The disagreements were slightly higher among single-earner than among dual-earner spouses; this may be due to their relatively low family income. Irritating personal habits of the spouse is also a cause for domestic dispute, although this may not be as severe as, for example, disputes on account of monetary issues. The findings suggest that a higher proportion of wives were worried about their husbands' personal habits than were the husbands. Many wives reported disliking their husbands smoking and drinking, or their sheer untidiness when at home. As one wife put it, 'To pick up after a grown up man is disgusting . . . all those stinky ash trays and beer glasses. It is worse when they meet for a game of cards on Sundays' (SEW-12).

Of the remaining five items . . . 'spouse being away from home all the time' was more contentious among single-earner than among dual-earner spouses. For example, about 77 per cent of the SEWs reported disagreements on this item, whereas only a little over a third of the dual-earner spouses complained of this problem. The vast majority did not believe that in-laws encouraged marital discord, while inadequate demonstration of affection and love towards one's spouse in a higher proportion of husbands than wives indicated disagreements with their spouses. Finally, the spouse's preoccupation with his/her work was the least contentious issue. This may be due to the nature of the work that most respondents did. Unlike professionals, whose work schedule is flexible and encourages committed individuals to be workaholics, industrial jobs are arranged according to specific shifts. Consequently, most employed respondents in this study were precluded from carrying work home.

In sum, the differences among single- and dual-earner spouses, although significant on certain items, showed no clear pattern that would permit the conclusion that the wife's work status has a bearing on interpersonal differences among couples in both samples. The nature and level of marital discord among the respondents could be expected in most urban middle-class families. If differences between samples existed, they were due more to interpersonal differences among spouses than to the wife's work status.

Another dimension of marital discord was the respondents' evaluation of their marital problems relative to those families with which they interacted. If, in their perception, there were more disagreements in their marriage than in those of their relatives, friends, and neighbours, this led to distress and other psychological consequences for individual spouses. If, on the other hand, they perceived their marital problems as being neither more nor less than those of others, they were likely to treat their own problems as normal. This, in turn, facilitated a relatively smooth domestic life. In this regard, the respondents were asked the following question: Would you say that disagreements between you and your spouse come up more often, about the same, or less often than among other couples you know? In Table 5, their responses are reported.

There was considerable variation in perception among respondents about the frequency of disagreements in their own and other people's marriages. . . . Clearly, most dual-earner spouses tended to perceive that their marital differences were about the same as, or less than, those among their acquaintances. However, the disparities in this regard were somewhat striking among the single-earner spouses. About 30 per cent of the SEWs reported more frequent conflicts in their marriages than in those of their friends or neighbours, whereas a similar proportion of the SEHs perceived less frequent disagreements. This datum is consistent

Table 5
Distribution of Respondents by their Perception of the
Frequency of Marital Disagreements Among their
Friends/Kin/Neighbours

| Frequency | DEW N(%) | DEH N(%) | SEW N(%) | SEH N(%) |
|---|---|---|---|---|
| More often | 40(16.3) | 45(18.4) | 73(29.8) | 36(14.7) |
| About the same | 108(44.0) | 91(37.1) | 139(56.7) | 127(51.8) |
| Less often | 97(39.7) | 109(44.5) | 33(14.5) | 82(33.5) |

N = 245 for each sample.

with the pattern of responses by single-earner spouses: that is, husbands and wives tended to define their marital realities slightly differently. The SEWs tended to perceive certain aspects of their domestic and marital lives as more problematic than did their husbands. In turn, those husbands who were the most modern in orientation tended not to grasp the gap in attitudes and perceptions between themselves and their wives.

### CONFLICT RESOLUTION

For most urban couples, a resolution of marital conflicts depends essentially on their own interpersonal skills and talents, mainly because there are few institutionalized means for settling inter-spousal disputes. For example, in rural areas serious differences between husband and wife are discussed and settled by elderly kin or by the village council. With the weakening of the extended kin ties in urban areas, intervention by kin is impractical and often produces no positive results. Unlike in Western societies, marriage counselling is neither well institutionalized nor popular even among the urban middle class. . . .

Furthermore, although separation and divorce are legally per-mitted, few couples with troubled marriages consider them as a viable means of resolution. Social and economic conditions are not conducive, especially for women, to seek divorce, and those women who do so find it extremely difficult to reconstruct their lives. . . . For example, in this study we asked four questions on separation and divorce, and the responses were almost uniformly against such measures. Only 4 per cent of all respondents reported that they had occasionally thought of separation but decided against it because this was, in their view, an impractical solution to a troubled marriage. To our question, 'Have you ever considered divorcing your spouse for reasons of irresolvable differences?' even fewer (2.5 per cent) reported in the affirmative. Divorce was not seen as a resolution to marital problems by spouses in this study.

In some marriages, coercion is used as an instrument of resolution of differences. Domestic violence, either psychological or physical, remains a method of resolving husband-wife differences. Barring a few exceptional cases, domestic violence is directed against women, and often aimed at bringing them to behave according to the wishes of their husbands. However, among most urban middle-class families, frequent use of violent means to settle marital disputes is not only perceived as illegitimate but would also lead to legal action; this could result in separation and/or divorce, besides punishment to the offending party. Therefore, for most ordinary couples, the resolution of marital conflict lies in strategies that demand accommodation, adjustment, compromise, and tolerance. . . .

In order to understand how respondents in this study settled their marital differences, the following question was posed: When you and your spouse differ about something and quarrel, do you usually give in and do it your spouse's way, or does he/she usually came around to your point of view? The responses are presented in Table 6 and indicate that there was a greater consensus between dual-earner spouses on the methods of conflict resolution than

Table 6

Distribution of Respondents on the Method of
Conflict Resolution

| *Madras* | *DEW* N(%) | *DEH* N(%) | *SEW* N(%) | *SEH* N(%) |
|---|---|---|---|---|
| Do it husband's way | 89(36.3) | 96(39.2) | 98(40.0) | 72(29.4) |
| Do it wife's way | 76(31.0) | 52(21.2) | 37(15.1) | 87(35.5) |
| We make compromises | 80(32.7) | 97(39.6) | 110(44.9) | 86(35.1) |

N = 245 for each sample.

among single-earner couples. The SEHs tended to maintain a perception of how differences were resolved which was significantly different from their wives. However, the responses did not yield a clear pattern in that there was neither husband nor wife dominance in resolving marital conflicts. Adjustment and compromise appeared to be common to both groups of spouses.

## MARITAL SATISFACTION

There is considerable debate about using terms such as 'marital satisfaction' and 'marital happiness', because these are not only extremely subjective but also methodologically difficult to measure. . . . [These notions are] further complicated because of customary assumptions and practices about marriage and family life. Although happiness, contentment, prosperity, and success are considered worthwhile goals of marital life, these are tempered by the overall nature and purpose of marriage.

For example, unlike in Western societies, in India most individuals do not enter into a marital contract, but their families and/or kinship groups do. Also, most marriages are not initially contracted for reasons of romantic love and personal well-being. While romance and sensuality are expected to follow within marriage, the failure to cultivate these or their absence does not necessarily constitute legitimate grounds to withdraw from the contract. Furthermore, there is a belief that a marital alliance is predestined, and its purpose higher than person-centred sensuality and pleasure-oriented romance. This is not to imply that individual couples do not strive to attain personal pleasures within their union. But self-gratification is not a major consideration in the subjective definition of a successful marriage.

In short, most couples define satisfaction within marriage in the context of customary assumptions about marriage, the nature of the marital contract (which seldom permits easy dissolution) and material and physical comforts that their marital union provides. It is in this light that the data (Table 7) on the respondents' perception of the level of satisfaction in their marriage should be seen. The responses reported were to the question: Taking all things together, how happy would you say your marriage has been?

Table 7
The Distribution of Respondents by the Degree of
Reported Marital Happiness

| Level of Happiness | DEW N(%) | DEH N(%) | SEW N(%) | SEH N(%) |
|---|---|---|---|---|
| Very happy | 72(29.4) | 127(51.8) | 24(9.8) | 73(29.8) |
| Quite happy | 91(37.2) | 61(24.9) | 71(29.0) | 99(40.4) |
| Somewhat happy | 49(20.0) | 29(11.8) | 76(31.0) | 45(18.4) |
| Not too happy | 16(6.5) | 15(6.1) | 53(21.6) | 10(4.1) |
| Very unhappy | 17(6.9) | 13(5.3) | 21(8.6) | 18(7.4) |

N = 245 for each sample.

The husbands, especially the DEHs, in this study reported higher levels of marital satisfaction. The proportion of those who reported various levels of unhappiness was very small for dual-earner spouses. A comparison of responses of the wives in both samples suggested that the SEWs were generally less satisfied in their marriages than the DEWs: over 30 per cent of SEWs reported unhappiness, while only about 13 per cent of the DEWs did the same. In general, although the vast majority of the couples were satisfied in their marriages, there was greater consensus among dual-earner spouses than among single-earner spouses on the issue of marital satisfaction. . . .

[ . . . ]

## FURTHER READINGS

Shalini Bharat and Murli Desai, eds, *Research on Families with Problems in India: Issues and Implications* (2 vols). Bombay: Tata Institute of Social Sciences, 1991.

A source book covering the most recent research on families with problems in India. Among other topics the papers here deal with family crisis, marital problems, and abuse and violence in families. They are critical of the indiscriminate application of Western theoretical models to the understanding of the family in India. Primarily written by and for social workers, these papers offer an interface between the perspectives of sociology and social work.

Patricia Uberoi, ed., *Family, Kinship and Marriage in India*. Delhi: Oxford University Press, 1993.

Papers in this anthology capture the great variety of family types and marriage practices in India, and the theoretical formulations which try to explain it. The selections in Section III: marriage, alliance, and affinal transactions, and Section IV: family, household and social change provide an insightful background to an understanding of conflict and change in the family sphere. They also try to integrate a concern for gender issues into the study of Indian family.

Promilla Kapur, *Marriage and the Working Woman in India*. Delhi: Vikas Publications, 1970.

A pioneering exploratory study which analyses factors contributing to adjustment and maladjustment in marriage of the educated working women in India. Primarily sociological in orientation it highlights the importance of combining quantitative (social survey) and qualitative (case study) techniques in family research.

C.J. Fuller, *The Nayars Today.* Cambridge: Cambridge University Press, 1976.

An update of the kinship and marriage practices of Kerala's matrilineal Nayar community in the light of the traditional system. It assesses the changes that have taken place in recent times and the factors that have contributed to the total disintegration of the matrilineal joint-family system (*taravad*).

John S. Augustine, ed., *The Indian Family in Transition.* New Delhi: Vikas Publishing House, 1982.

Papers in this volume locate and interpret the changes taking place in the Indian family. They emphasize the 'transitionality' of the family, and portray the various factors of family change in different social and cultural milieux.

Archana Parashar, *Women and Family Law Reform in India.* New Delhi: Sage, 1992.

A critical study of the role of law in perpetuating discrimination against women, and the role of the state in improving the status of women by reforming religious personal laws. The focus is mainly on family law, and the arguments are built around historical records, parliamentary proceedings, legislative enactments, court cases, and pulpit and platform orations.

M.P. Sharma and K.D. Gangrade, eds, *Inter-Generational Conflict in India.* Bombay: Nachiketa Publications, 1971.

The first part of the book presents the findings of a socio-psychological study on inter-generational conflict which emphasize the disjunction between the values of two generations as the crux of the issue. The essays in the second part analyse the various facets of inter-generational conflict from an inter-disciplinary perspective.

# II

# Cultural Sphere

It is conflicts over identities and over 'symbols', more than over material interests, that pervade the studies in this section. Identities concern our sense of the self. How one's sense of the self is constituted depends on one's experiences while growing up, on the 'process of socialization', in one's particular social milieu. The early psychoanalytic insight into the importance of childhood experiences in shaping the adult personality is now a widely shared principle in the social sciences. (Kakar and Chowdhry in Section III explore its importance in the making of a student leader.)

One's salient identity may be that of being a mountaineer, a jailbird, a tycoon, or whatever. We are concerned here, rather, with *group* identities. These too may be variously defined: farmers, slum-dwellers, Brahmins, and so forth. Where the identities have come to be derived from the moment of one's birth, that is, ascriptive identities, these are often defined as mutually exclusive: you cannot be both a Brahmin and a Rajput—though you can be a jailbird and a tycoon, a farmer and a Brahmin, or even a Shia and a Muslim at the same time.

Exclusive identities may be rooted in religious difference (Chakrabarty, Kakar, Das), caste difference (Alm, Dirks), the tribal past (Phadnis), and so on. Such exclusive identities are particularly prone to conflict. Their conflicts may become recurrent, and the recurrent pattern may include varied measures of violence. Feelings that our identity is threatened can serve to arouse us to a high emotional pitch, which may be directed against people believed to be one's enemies. It is common enough for emotionally excited groups to get into orgies of violence.

Violence apart, conflicts display, and feed on, varied levels of communication too. Such communication may seek to stir memories, animosities, and latent identities; summon one's 'own group' to activity and assertion; insult those thought to be adversaries; and do much else. Ordinary language is always available; yet protagonists work with special resources too. They may employ complex rhetorical strategies (Das); goad adversaries through extravagant public challenges, say by killing a pig or a cow or by attacking the other group's women's honour (Chakrabarty, Alm); or register defiance in silent, telling gestures of resistance (Dirks). Indeed the contenders may know but dimly how their messages get across to, or are interpreted by, others. On both sides, the underlying memories, beliefs, and representations, which go into making or interpreting particular gestures or messages, may long since have settled into their respective *un*conscious (Kakar).

The opening paper in this set, by a young Swedish anthropologist, Bjorn Alm, begins with a local 'caste riot' which caught him in the course of his anthropological fieldwork near Dindigul in Tamil Nadu. He shows us that the riot had two faces: on one side, the local struggle for status, following economic (and other) changes; on the other, a larger argument, for a bigger slice of the cake, addressed to a 'national' audience.

Tension had been building up in the area between the Kallar, a relatively well-established middle level caste, and the Pallar, a scheduled caste, whom the Kallar saw as being provocatively aggressive. The spark igniting the tinder came in a speech by a Pallar leader, visiting from another district. The distinctive quality of Alm's paper, however, lies elsewhere. It lies in his attempt to track how the wider national and state-level policies of protective discrimination link up with local conflicts of this kind.

The adversaries' perceptions of, and interpretations of, everyday experiences are shaped crucially in terms of issues and impulses arising in these policies of wide application; and this facilitates the spreading of the contagion of local conflicts into wide-ranging riots. To demonstrate the wider play of such inter-level linkages, and therefore the more general applicability of analysis in this mould, Alm also examines an earlier conflict.

The battlelines are not drawn along the boundaries of the classic *jati* but, around the 'mega-categories' of caste which have been stirring into activity since the late 1800s. A riot is intended, in some cases, to push the State into conceding the demands of the category which precipitates the riot. A conflict's immediate history may be local, yet its motivations follow from wider, national policies and politics. Alm's analysis echoes, in some measure, the peeling of the layers of conflicts, over somewhat related issues, in two villages in southern Orissa by F.G. Bailey in the early 1950s (Gupta 1991: 387–98).

This linkage between the locality and the wider world is pivotal to the next selection also: Chakrabarty's rich study of Hooghlyside jute-mill workers near Calcutta, and their connexions with the metropolis, in the 1890s. The immigrants among them had come from areas of present day Bihar and Uttar Pradesh. They had brought with them social bonds, ideas and symbols, which they employed to recreate a sense of community which was defined along religious boundaries. This sense of community, and its social bonds, were useful as social buffers, cushioning them against the bumps of life in the jute mills' unfriendly universe. For example, potential seekers of employment far exceeded the available openings; and rivalries at the workplace found expression outside also.

However, the traditions which the immigrant workers had brought with them included (1) a sense of separation from 'the others', defined most clearly in religious terms, and (2) a range of activities, familiar from previous experience in their home areas, which could be trusted to produce a sense of outrage among persons of the 'other' category.

On the one hand, these older identities, as Hindu and Muslim, drew these workers into communal conflict. On the other hand, the Muslim workers occasionally saw themselves as part of a pan-Islamic world due to the efforts of a big merchant and the local Maulvis. The big men of the metropolis may have had their own reasons for responding to, and spreading, the expansive pan-Islamic message.

The Muslims of Calcutta functioned in a world of limited opportunities; many of them were under sustained pressure from Marwari merchants who had come from Rajasthan. The latter were mounting pressure on a broad front: subjecting Muslim merchants to stiff commercial competition, buying up precious land in central Calcutta, and displacing poor Muslims who had lived on it earlier. Secular public leadership was scarce in those times. For want of anything more responsive, succor for all too many everyday anxieties was sought along channels which were available: these happened to be religious or, seen differently, communal.

The psychoanalyst Sudhir Kakar's search for the roots of ethnic violence in India takes him into the unconscious, and his essay draws upon varied sorts of data: his earlier study at a temple near Bharatpur in Rajasthan, where mentally disturbed patients are brought in the hope of being healed through the temple's healing rites, his own clinical patients, and his observations at Amritsar's Golden Temple and at other large religious congregations.

Within the general psychoanalytic perspective (see the first para in this sectional introduction), Kakar argues in his paper here that our images of our 'own' group and of 'other' groups are formed in early childhood. Furthermore, we tend to 'project' what we see as our own undesirable qualities on to these 'other' groups—whose images already carry negative 'charges' in our conscious and preconscious. (Veena Das's paper below reiterates this theme.) That large religious congregations may have psycho-physical effects similar to those of a riotous mob is a novel, immensely disturbing, and undoubtedly debatable suggestion.

The reading on Mizoram comes from the work of the late Professor Urmila Phadnis. The conflict considered was between sections of Mizo society which took to insurgency in 1966 and proclaimed independence, and the State of the Republic of India. Given their geographical location, the Mizos—like other 'tribal' societies of the northeast—had not interacted with the larger Indian society very closely in past time. (The physical and social distances here were much greater than those considered by Romila Thapar and Majid Hayat Siddiqi in their study of Chota Nagpur, excerpted in Gupta 1991: 419–28.)

The manner in which the Mizo sense of alienation from Indian society grew to the point of armed insurgency is sensitively traced by Professor Phadnis. The uprising was sustained for nearly two decades, with some encouragement from across the borders. The resolution of the conflict depended on complex strategies on both sides: it depended partly on the course of the armed struggle, with much stronger forces controlled by the government; and partly on the willingness of the leaders of insurgency to respond to the government's offer to accommodate them in the structure of power in Mizoram. In some historical settings, the application of armed force can be the key to power.

In her 'Time, Self, and Community' Veena Das examines not the course of a particular conflict but, rather, a set of documents, written and oral, produced by Sikh militants between the years 1981 and 1984. These texts used a variety of rhetorical strategies in arousing their audiences' sense of outrage at the Sikhs' situation in Indian society and polity. These strategies included the propagation of suitably doctored versions of historical, as well as contemporary, events.

These versions had been doctored so as to excite a virile, masculine 'Sikh' identity—and complementary identities for 'Muslim' and 'Hindu'. The Indian State was seen to partake of the effeminate qualities of the 'Hindus' since they constitute a majority and have provided the bulk of political leadership. Given the protagonists' intense commitment to the 'Sikh' cause, they identify their principal social category of the 'other', namely the 'Hindus', with the Indian State virtually completely. The consequences of these beliefs, accurate or otherwise, for Punjab, are too well known to need reiteration.

Conflict takes much subtler forms in Nicholas Dirks' 'Ritual and resistance', which brings us back full circle to inter-caste conflict. His central assault is on the anthropological orthodoxy which used to see ritual as bulwark for established social arrangements. Not so, says Dirks, arguing with accounts from his Pudukkottai corpus. His combatants do battle, often silently, in village-sized encounters, over such issues as whether or not to mount a festival in honour of Aiyanar, the great Tamil deity. Ritual is a kind of folk theatre. Behind the scenes of its public enactments, there may be a good deal of negotiation, and jockeying for advantage. Refusing to co-operate, holding break-away festivals of one's own, and mocking the pretentions of the powerful even as one dances to their commands: these are some of the forms of quiet resistance—amidst ritual which the participants may proclaim to be age-old routines!

# The State and Caste Conflicts
# Two Cases from Tamil Nadu

## BJÖRN ALM

In this essay I will discuss some aspects of caste riots in Tamil Nadu. As examples I will use the riots in Cumbum Valley in 1989 and the Vanniyar riots in 1987–8. I will also briefly refer to some less well-known riots in the Dindigul area.

I will argue that to understand why the riots occurred, who was rioting, and how the riots spread, two levels of analysis are necessary: a national/regional (Tamil Nadu) level and a local level. The local level involves looking at local caste ranking, changing economic conditions, and antagonism and competition between groups. The national/regional level is concerned with state policies with regard to caste, like the system of positive discrimination, and the caste associations emerging in the beginning of the century. The two levels can be viewed separately, but in reality they are intertwined and determine each other. So, for example, the policy of an unequal distribution of state resources, in the system of positive discrimination, is one cause for resentment, and hostility, between local groups. The hostility may erupt in riots, aimed at reaffirming or questioning the local order, as well as influencing state policies. An outcome of my argument is that the system of positive discrimination is closely linked with competition and antagonism between castes. And inter-caste violence is possibly a sign of the effectiveness of that system.

There are several aspects of the riots which I will not discuss in this essay. I will not say much about the role of politicians, local and national, in the riots, nor about the role of the Cumbum Valley riots in national Indian and Tamil politics. Neither will I discuss the problem of violence as such in rural Tamil society, nor the common conflicts between local village groups.


## SOURCES OF INFORMATION

The Cumbum Valley riots occurred over a large area and in many different places. Most of the Cumbum Valley was affected, and so were many places outside the Valley. I was living in a village northeast of Cumbum Valley when the riots broke out. The village remained calm, while brief riots took place in neighbouring villages. I did not observe any riots personally, neither did I travel in the Valley during the worst days. Travelling at that time was dangerous. Some people, like politicians, did travel in the Valley with strong police escorts, but some of them were nevertheless attacked.

My sources of information about the Cumbum Valley riots were mainly of four kinds. One source was the mass media; newspapers in Tamil and English, in particular. Newspapers were also an important source of information for the villagers. Generally, the newspapers, as well as other media, attempted to tone down the conflict. They sided with the established order and gave large space to the government's attempts to quell the riots. Tamil newspapers were, however, less reluctant than English ones to name involved people and groups. As the riots became a national political issue the Tamil Newspapers showed their party sympathies more openly than the English newspapers did.

A second source of information was people who had been rioters or victims. Several villagers were trapped in Cumbum Valley when the riots broke out, others went there to participate in the riots. Their information was a mixture of what they had actually seen and of hearsay. The information had a piecemeal nature, dealing with local events and lacking a wider view of the riots. Naturally, most informants tried to avoid the riots because of concern for their own safety.

Rumours, a third source, were an important local source of information. Rumours spread quickly over wide areas, and strongly influenced the development of the riots. As information about the riots, they may be used only with great caution, but they cannot be altogether discarded.

A fourth source of information was villagers' discussions about the riots. The discussions were a running commentary on information from other sources, and gave the popular views. Their nature was, of course, very subjective.

All my sources of information on the riots have shortcomings. But, bearing those shortcomings in mind, the sources taken together may give a fairly good picture of the riots. A caution is, however, that this picture may tell more about how the riots were locally perceived, than about what actually happened.

## RIOTS IN CUMBUM VALLEY

By the afternoon on the 16th of September 1989, the village where I lived was tense and quiet. The main road was deserted; buses, lorries, ox-carts had all vanished. The square in front of the village temple, usually the hub of afternoon activity, was quiet but not deserted. On an ordinary afternoon it would have been full of noisy people; coming back from work, waiting for a bus, taking snacks and tea in a stall, shopping in the bazaar, or just strolling chatting with friends. This afternoon, however, there were only men in the square, and they were having urgent discussions in tight, small groups. There was little of the usual moving back and forth between groups, and most notably of all, there were no people belonging to the Scheduled Castes present. Only rumours moved freely in the village that afternoon and evening.

The following morning the newspapers confirmed the previous day's rumours. The *Indian Express* headline read:

'5 killed in group clash in Thevaram'

This was the beginning of a week of extensive rioting in Cumbum Valley. The riots quickly spread over the whole Valley and beyond it, over a distance of more than sixty kilometres. During the week's rioting twenty-eight people were killed, about a hundred were injured and hospitalized, and hundreds of houses and shops were looted and burned down.

The mass media followed the conventional rules of reporting about communal violence and toned down their reports from the

Valley. But obviously, the events in Cumbum Valley were of a different order than the occasional eruptions of violence in rural society. This was no local clash of the stab-and-run type, but full scale caste riots akin to minor warfare. Within hours the riots had spread over the Valley, villages were burned and people killed in places widely apart, and police patrols and roaming armed mobs made the valley dangerous.

Riots did not break out in the village where I lived. People of one hamlet decided to march on another hamlet, but were deterred by a strong police force placed at a nearby cross-road. Though calm, the village was tense. The castes rioting in Cumbum Valley were also numerous in the village. People were excited and scared, and tried to keep to their homes and streets as much as possible. A drunken brawl in a food-stall and a dispute in the bazaar, which ordinarily would have attracted limited attention, were discussed as caste antagonism and with dark forebodings meant to be the first incidents of a local clash.

After three days the buses started running again, which meant that the government had regained some control of the riot area. The government had reacted quickly and forcefully. As early as the third day, the newspapers said, there were more than 1,900 armed policemen in Cumbum Valley. They controlled the towns and the larger villages, but their control of the countryside was less secure. The police had isolated the Valley by putting strong forces at all cross-roads. The last major incident occurred on the eighth day when forty huts were burned down just outside the valley, but by then the police forces had pacified Cumbum Valley. The police admitted having killed eleven of the twenty-eight people killed in the riots. After the Valley had been pacified the newspapers named the rioters as belonging to the Kallar and the Pallar castes, which, of course, had been common local knowledge all along.

According to popular opinion a speech by Mr John Pandian, a visiting Pallar leader from Tirunelveli, was the cause of the riots. According to one widely believed story a Pallar girl had been seduced by a Kallar youth. He had promised to marry her, but had broken his promise after pressure from his family. To get rid of the girl some of his relatives kidnapped, raped and killed her. The girl's family took the body to a police station, but the police refused to investigate the murder claiming that it had happened outside their territory. Believing that the police were protecting the murderers the girl's family turned to Pallar leaders for help. A meeting was called at which Mr Pandian made a fiery speech. He was said to have demanded that Kallar girls should be given as brides to Pallar men. If Kallar girls were not given voluntarily, they should be kidnapped and forcefully married to Pallar men. That speech provoked the Kallars to attack the Pallars in Thevaram, and so that rioting began.

Mr Pandian's call to kidnap and marry Kallar girls was obviously not meant to be taken literally. A Pallar informant interpreted the call as a revenge against Kallars in general. Few Pallars were particularly interested in marrying Kallar girls, but the call was an insult to Kallar pride. Its implicit meaning was that the Pallars, a formerly untouchable caste, considered themselves to be the Kallars' equals. The speech was a public challenge of the superior status of the Kallars.

The villagers explained the Cumbum Valley riots in several different ways. Some thought that a speech like Mr John Pandian's was all that was needed to cause riots. Another explanation, which grew in popularity after the riots, was that the riots were engineered by local politicians to harm political opponents.

The most common explanation was, however, that the riots were bound to start, sooner or later, because of the tension in the area. The tension was the result of the growing prosperity of the Pallars and their demands for higher social status. There was a 'Pallar' version of this explanation, and a 'Kallar' version.

According to the Pallar version, the Pallars were doing quite well in Cumbum Valley. Many had become as prosperous as, or more so than, the Kallars. The prosperity had been achieved thanks to their own diligence, thanks to new economic opportunities and relative freedom from restraints, and thanks to benefits from the state. Economically, and in education, many Pallars had become others' equals, but socially they were still treated as inferiors, as untouchables. Kallars, in particular, would neither accept the rising fortune of the Pallars, nor treat them as equals, because of the Kallars' pride and arrogance. And the Kallars were looking for pretexts to suppress the Pallars to uphold their own superiority. Without protection by the state, the Pallars would be at the mercy of the Kallars and others.

The Kallar version built on the same premise: that the Pallars' prosperity was rising. Their prosperity was, however, entirely due to the preferential treatment they got from the state, according to this version. The Pallars, as well as other Scheduled Castes, were pampered by the state and by politicians, at the expense of others. And even though the Pallars' prosperity was growing, there was no sign of abolishing their preferential treatment.

A main resentment against the Pallars was their attitude toward others. The Pallars, it was said, were lazy, troublesome, arrogant and trying to lord it over others. They were not content with being equals but wanted to be masters. And, however prosperous they would become at the expense of others, they would complain of discrimination, and would claim protection and preferential treatment from the state.

A Kallar informant, a youth political leader, said to me that he did not envy the Pallars their benefits, but he resented their use of their protected status.

> If I quarrel with a Pallar, he said, he may shout any abuse he likes against me or my caste, and there is nothing I can do about it. But if I shout something against his caste he will report me at the police station and get me arrested for discrimination against a Scheduled Caste.

There is some truth in all of the villagers' explanations. The first explanation fails, however, to explain why the riots spread so quickly and widely. It does not explain why people in places so widely apart were ready to fight each other. Mr Pandian's speech undoubtedly acted as a trigger, but it is unlikely that it caused more than the first riot in Thevaram. An attack on women's honour is a sensitive subject, but is unlikely to cause riots in places sixty kilometres apart. The subsequent riots in Thevaram and other places must have had other local causes as well.

Politicians did undoubtedly have a hand in the riots, but it is unlikely that there existed a politicians' conspiracy to engineer the riots. On the other hand, once started the riots quickly became political propaganda material. The riots were finally used as an argument for dismissing the government of Tamil Nadu and to introduce president's rule.

The third explanation seems to be the most pertinent. When stripped of their partiality the Kallar and the Pallar versions tell the same story of economic change, resentment over preferential treatment by the state, and demands for recognition of higher social status.

At least some of the Pallars in Cumbum Valley seem to have been doing well—economically, educationally and in getting white–collar jobs—and to be catching up with socially higher castes. And that may go together with demands for the recognition of higher social status. Such demands are also partly supported by the laws of the state, like the ban against untouchability. And the Kallars, maybe the caste most threatened by the demands, reacted with violence to put the 'up-starts' back in their place. The crux of the matter is, however, that while demanding social equality on the basis of rising prosperity, the Pallars also wish to keep their relatively privileged position as a Scheduled Caste with the preferential treatment by the state which it entails.

To see the Kallars as the defenders of an old order would, however, be an over-simplification. The Kallars are part of a new order just as much as the Pallars, and there is little left of an old order to defend. Pallars receive benefits from the state, and so do Kallars. Kallars are classified as a Backward Caste and are given preferential treatment too, even if less preferential than the Pallars'. If Kallars question the system of preferential treatment as such, they also question their own benefits.

## POSITIVE DISCRIMINATION

In Tamil Nadu today, a person is classified as belonging to one of the categories of the system of positive discrimination: Scheduled Tribe, Scheduled Caste, Most Backward Caste, Backward Caste, or Forward Caste. Each of those categories are made up of a number of castes. Positive discrimination, in short, means a preferential treatment of lower categories by the state: Scheduled Tribe and Caste are the most benefited, Most Backward and Backward Castes somewhat less, while Forward Castes receive no special benefits at all.

The reasoning behind the system is that the higher castes have systematically oppressed and exploited the lower castes. In modern society everyone should have the same opportunities, and to ensure that, the depressed have to be given, temporarily, better opportunities than the higher castes. They need help to 'catch up'. Caste as such should disappear, according to the official ideology, but until this happens it is the duty of the state to protect and help the depressed castes.

The system of positive discrimination was started during the British time when some castes were classified as scheduled or backwards. Today the system is stronger than ever in Tamil Nadu, and the majority of the population is classified as either Scheduled, Most Backward or Backward.

Parts of the state's resources are distributed through the system of positive discrimination. These resources are popularly referred to as benefits. There is a broad variety of such benefits, ranging from reserved government jobs and political posts, to free slates, books and uniforms for children in elementary school. Many development schemes are also planned on the principles of positive discrimination.

The benefits of positive discrimination are important to many people. They might well survive without them, but the benefits may make their lives somewhat easier. Most importantly, the system of positive discrimination offers the possibility of education and white-collar jobs to people of low castes, and thus gives them a possibility to realise what they see as a better life. Consequently, the classification of one's caste is an important issue.

Resentment over the sharing of state resources in the form of benefits played an important role in the local explanations of the riots. The unequal sharing of benefits was seen as one of the main causes of the tension between castes. Leila Dushkin, who discusses a similar system of positive discrimination in Karnataka (1985: 389–413), comes to a different conclusion. She writes that there seems to be a relative legitimacy of caste politics in Karnataka, which makes it possible to handle such demands politically. Otherwise, these demands might result in inter-caste violence. The Cumbum Valley riots, however, seem to be a case when the division of benefits is closely connected with inter-caste violence. That connection was explicit in a series of riots between Vanniyars and Paraiyars in the central districts of Tamil Nadu in 1987–8.

## THE VANNIYAR RIOTS

The Paraiyars are a formerly untouchable caste classified as

Scheduled Caste, like the Pallars. Like the Kallars, the Vanniyars were then classified as Backward Caste, but Vanniyar political organizations tried to influence the state to change their classification in order to get a greater share of benefits.

The Vanniyars have been a political force since the end of the nineteenth century. At that time they tried to raise their caste's status by being classified as Kshatriyas in the censuses. By the 1930's they had created efficient and powerful caste associations. In the election in 1952 Vanniyar parties won thirty-one seats in the legislature assembly of Madras, and got two cabinet seats in the state government (Rudolph & Rudolph 1987: 49–61, 88–91). The Vanniyars are still a strong political force, but since the elections in 1967 their influence has diminished because of internal divisions. In 1986 the Vanniyar Sangam, a militant caste organization under the leadership of Mr Ramdos, grew strong among the Vanniyars, and soon riots between Vanniyars and Paraiyars became common. When the riots came to a climax in 1987–8, the issue was not to get the Vanniyars recognized as Kshatriyas, but to press the Sangam's demand for increased state benefits through a lower classification.

Political life was turbulent after the death of the Tamil Nadu Chief Minister M.G. Ramachandran, and the Vanniyar Sangam, claiming to represent the Vanniyar vote, played off the political parties against each other. The Sangam threatened to boycott or stop the imminent election, unless their demands were accepted. The main demands were a 20 per cent reservation in educational institutions and government jobs at state level and a 2 per cent reservation at central level, to the Vanniyars alone (*Aside* 1989 1–15 April).

To substantiate the Sangam's threats, Mr Ramdos claimed that the Sangam had an army of two and a half million youths trained as 'liberation tigers'. They were said to be organized in five wings: the security guards, the suicide squad, the yellow cat squad, the black leopards and the black cobras. And they were said to be trained in guerilla warfare by a former police officer, and by Sikh and Sri Lankan terrorists (*Aside* 1988 16–30 November).

The election was held and the new DMK-government partly fulfilled the Sangam's demands. A new category was established, Most Backward Caste, in which the Vanniyars were included among other castes. This category got a 20 per cent reservation in educational institutions and government jobs. The final list of reservations in 1989 was: 18 per cent to Scheduled Castes and Tribes, 20 per cent to Most Backward Castes, 30 per cent to Backward Castes, and 32 per cent to remain in open competition (*Aside* 1989 1–15 April).

Mr Ramdos was not satisfied with the allotment. He wanted a 20 per cent reservation to the Vanniyars alone (*Aside* 1989 1–15 April). The government refused to concede more, and with strong police forces in the field, and the election over, rioting ceased.

The Sangam's leaders repeatedly stated that they were not the enemies of Scheduled Caste, but that they simply wanted justice from the state for the Vanniyars. They wanted the preferential treatment they thought was due to the Vanniyars as poor people.

The Sangam's rhetoric focussed on the system of positive discrimination. The Vanniyars and the Paraiyars belonged to two different categories of that system, Backward and Scheduled Caste. The same was the case in Cumbum Valley where Kallars, Backward Caste, stood against Pallars, Scheduled Caste. In neither the Cumbum Valley riots nor the Vanniyar riots, however, did these categories act as united communities. The categories were not mobilized in the riots. The rioters belonged to much smaller groups within the categories. That the categories were not acting as united communities is, incidentally, shown by the fact that Mr Pandian of Cumbum Valley fame later turned up as a political ally of Mr Ramdos.

CASTE ASSOCIATIONS AND MEGA-CATEGORIES

To explain the mobilization of rioters it is useful to look at an essay by Washbrook on the emergence of caste politics in Madras Presidency (1975: 150–203). He notes that many caste associations were created at the end of the nineteenth century and in the first decades of the twentieth century. Appeals to caste solidarity were then already established in the political language. Caste associations in the provincial politics were, according to Washbrook, a new phenomenon, which had little to do with earlier caste institutions. Caste had earlier been of little importance in both local and provincial politics, Washbrook argues. Political power was earlier in the hands of locally powerful men and the local administration, and the government at Madras had little influence in local; rural society.

Washbrook traces the emergence of caste associations to political change in the Presidency: the expanding activities of the government of Madras and the increasing involvement of Indians in provincial political life and administration. The tasks of the provincial administration grew and its influence in rural society was increasing at the beginning of the twentieth century. With increased activity of the provincial government and the involvement of Indians in provincial politics, senior British administrators' ideas of the nature of the province became crucial. To interpret the province's peoples as belonging to different, distinct castes was an obvious way for the British to get some order out of the vast, diverse collection of peoples and lands which made up the province they were ruling. Castes were thought to be natural political groups and interest groups. Moreover, caste was assumed to be the traditional order of the Indian society. The provincial government's activities became increasingly directed by caste concerns, and the idea of exclusion and inclusion by caste steadily gained acceptance in the administration. Once the administrators had formed their view of how the people of the Presidency were ordered, or ought to be ordered, caste associations answering to this view started to emerge, Washbrook writes. (Irschick 1986 argues in a similar way about how the dichotomy between Brahmans and non-Brahmans was developed by British administrators and given political and legal sanction.)

The caste associations were based on a concept of caste which was different from earlier caste institutions. That concept Washbrook calls mega-category. Mega-categories were indirectly created by the provincial government and administration by the political role they were given.

The mega-category can be described as a broad status category composed of local castes which are unconnected spatially as well as by kinship. The unifying factors may be approximately similar positions in different local caste hierarchies, a common caste-name, and putative historical identity. The mega-categories are often vaguely defined, and controversies about which mega-category a caste properly belongs to occur. A mega-category can be made up of hundreds of castes, divided from each other by locality and by other reasons. Mega-categories make up much of the categories in the system of positive discrimination. The rioters discussed in this essay—Kallar, Pallar, Vanniyar and Paraiyar—are all examples of mega-categories.

Rather than being riots between people of different categories of the system of positive discrimination, the Cumbum Valley and the Vanniyar riots were riots between people of different mega-categories. The categories of positive discrimination are creations of the modern state, while mega-categories were created during the colonial time. Both are today inseparable parts of the political system. Antagonism and competition grows between mega-categories within the framework of positive discrimination. Rioting can then be seen as an intense form of competition over state resources, a way of influencing the state and of questioning what is seen as an unfair division, and as competition over political influence. Positive discrimination strengthens mega-category identity and solidarity, which expresses itself in riots over large areas. Local riots trigger off new riots in other places, between antagonists of the same mega-categories. Rioters were mobilized not so much along the lines of the categories of positive discrimination, as along the lines of mega-categories. But the causes of rioting are to be found partly in the system of positive discrimination.

## LOCAL CAUSES OF RIOTS

The analysis above tells us something about the patterns of the riots, but it does not really say very much about why local riots start. To understand that, it is also necessary to look at local causes. I will discuss a few of such causes which are relevant to the Cumbum Valley riots, the Vanniyar riots and to some other riots in the Dindigul area.

In Cumbum Valley the first riot in Thevaram was triggered off by an attack on women's honour. Such attacks are quite common causes of local conflicts. In the 1890's there was a large-scale agitation against Kallar village watchmen around Dindigul. The aim of the agitation was to drive the Kallars from the area, and it became quite violent. The anti-Kallar agitation started by what was seen as a Kallar affront to the honour of women of the Idaiyar caste (Francis 1906: 91–2). Another example of a riot started by a similar reason was told to me by a Vanniyar informant. In his village violence started after some Vanniyar youths had 'taken photographs' of Paraiyar girls.

The same informant also said that the 'uppishness' of the Paraiyars was a cause for tension in his village. The Paraiyars had stopped giving proper respect to their 'betters', the Vanniyar landlords.

The small village where the informant lived is dominated by Vanniyars, while the Paraiyars live in a hamlet outside the village. The Vanniyars own most of the land, while most of the Paraiyars are landless agricultural labourers. The relationship between the two castes had become strained and one night the Vanniyars decided to attack the Paraiyars because of their 'uppishness', to put them back in their 'right' place. One night Vanniyars stormed the Paraiyar hamlet and burned it down. The Paraiyars managed to flee into the surrounding fields where one old Paraiyar woman died from the night chill. The next day there were rumours saying that 'ten thousand' armed Paraiyars from the surrounding countryside were marching on the Vanniyar village to take revenge. The Vanniyars barricaded their village and spent an uneasy day and night waiting for the Paraiyars' attack. Instead of Paraiyar avengers an armed police force came to the village. The police officer read the law to the villagers and told them that if they caused any more trouble the police would come back and shoot every one of them. That ended the riot, but the Vanniyars decided that they would boycott the Paraiyars. No landowner or householder should employ a Paraiyar in the future. The Pallars of Cumbum Valley were similarly accused of being 'uppish'. They were also said to be arrogant and wanting to be the others' masters.

The wish to settle old scores and grievances is a common cause of violence. Grievances may stem from conflict unconnected with earlier riots, like disputes between landlords and labourers, disputes over land, and disputes over temple honours. But obviously, a riot also breeds new riots, when past injuries are to be revenged. In Dindigul in 1990 there was a brief two-day riot between Hindus and Muslims in which two people were killed, one Muslim and one Hindu. The Hindu came from a village outside Dindigul, and on the day of his funeral a mob gathered in his village, planning to go to Dindigul to take revenge on the Muslims. A police force stopped them from leaving the village.

The Hindu-Muslim riot in Dindigul also provides an example of the role of agitators in causing riots. Weeks before the riot broke out, street-corner agitators from a militant Hindu organization were preparing the ground by making fiery anti-Muslim speeches. Timed to coincide with a local Hindu festival, the agitators finally provoked the Muslims by shouting anti-Muslim slogans outside the main mosque. Needless to say, that ensured their purpose of creating a riot. I do not know if such professional agitators, apart from Mr Pandian, were present in Cumbum Valley. But after the Valley had been pacified, the newspapers reported that several visitors of that type were arriving, fishing in troubled waters.

A public challenge of social superiors was a cause of the first riot in Thevaram. Such challenges are a way of questioning ranking in local hierarchies. And they are, I believe, closely connected with changes in the relative prosperity of local groups. In Cumbum Valley the main cause of the tension seems to be the relative prosperity of the Pallars. Until the end of the nine-teenth century Cumbum Valley was a marginal area to the political and economic centres of South India. Politically Cumbum Valley had been ruled by local chieftains, *poligars*. After the suppression of the poligars in the early nineteenth century the Valley seems to have been stagnating. Although several rivers flow through the Valley, little of the land was irrigated. Roads were in a bad condition and transport costly. At the beginning of the nineteenth century surplus of grain was left to rot in the granaries because of the high transport costs as Nelson wrote in 1868 (1868: vol. V: 118–19).

The agrarian economy of the Valley received a boost when the Periyar irrigation project was started at the end of the nine-teenth century. The river Periyar was diverted into Tamil Nadu where its water was to be utilised for irrigation around Madurai. The water flows through Cumbum Valley, and much of the water was utilized there (Baker 1984: 474). Water and improved means of communication made the cultivation of cash-crops possible. It also meant immigration of people from neighbouring areas where conditions were less advantageous.

Today, Cumbum Valley is considered to be a prosperous

Valley by the local people. Agriculture supports half a dozen bustling market towns, and the products of the Valley find a ready market there and in the markets of Madurai. The land is fertile and intensively cultivated, and there are jobs to be found in agriculture and in the towns (cf Ramachandran 1990). The Valley is also considered to have less of a rigid social hierarchy than surrounding areas. In Cumbum Valley, it is said, caste is less of a barrier to prosperity than elsewhere. There Scheduled Caste people are also land-owners, and may become as prosperous as others. Not surprisingly, the Valley still attracts immigrants.

The prosperity of the Pallars has to be seen in the perspective of the prosperity of the Valley in general. But if the Pallars' prosperity rises relative to other castes, it will cause tension. This is because their prosperity is explained by their antagonists as a result of benefits from the state and therefore at others' expense. If former untouchables, the labourers and servants of the others, become landlords, doctors and administrators, they take on a new role in relation to their old masters. Only a small fraction of the Pallars in Cumbum Valley are, of course, prosperous, or have become landlords or white-collar workers, but the few who have succeeded are probably enough to intensify resentment and antagonism between castes.

## CONCLUSION

'There are conflicts in every village. If there are no conflicts, it is not a true Indian village', my research assistant used to tell me. His opinion is certainly realistic. Conflicts are common in Tamil villages: within families and between families, between factions and between local caste groups, between landlords, and between landlords and labourers. The conflicts I have been discussing in this essay are, however, of a different scale. They involved thousands of people, they spread over large areas, and they turned far more bloody and ferocious than village conflicts.

Caste conflicts of this type are not a new phenomenon in the Tamil countryside. Ludden (1989), Hardgrave (1969) and others describe similar conflicts in earlier days. What is new in the Cumbum Valley riots and the Vanniyar riots is, however, the role of the state. Through the policy of positive discrimination the state sanctions a division of the population in caste mega-categories. To the British that division was a way of 'divide and rule', on which the modern Tamil state has continued to build. The system of positive discrimination, the state's grand scheme for social and economical change, is planned on caste-lines and cast in the language of caste. Castes, or rather mega-categories, are made into interest groups as well as political groups. The riots cannot, then, be seen as conflicts between local groups only. Riots may well be about settling local scores and grievances, but they are also about the relation to the state. The state not only acts as an arbitrator and pacifier in the conflicts, but also as the distributor of benefits and protection. And it is possible to influence the state through rioting. The Vanniyar riots are a rather successful example of that.

A kind of mega-category identity and solidarity seems to be the best explanation for the spread of the riots. Washbrook stressed the role of the colonial government in the emergence of mega-categories in provincial politics. There is, however, no reason to think that the British invented the concept of mega-categories by themselves. The concept as such, albeit vaguely defined, probably existed earlier. But, with the importance attached to caste mega-categories in politics, and with the development of the system of positive discrimination by the modern state, caste mega-categories have taken on a reality and identity they did not have earlier. Today, it may safely be said that caste identity, in the form of mega-category identity, has its supreme importance in relation to the state. As discussed in the latter part of the essay, mega-categories and positive discrimination do not, however, tell us much about why local riots start. To understand that, the local contexts have to be included in the analysis.

Contrary to Leila Dushkin's conclusion that a system of positive discrimination may restrain inter-caste violence, I think that the system of positive discrimination creates some of the causes of the riots. When state resources are to be shared, the 'slicing of the pie' can turn quite violent. It has to be remembered, however, that caste politics and positive discrimination are nowadays so well entrenched in state politics, that a change to something else would be very difficult.

Inter-caste violence can also be seen as an indication of social and economic change, towards the equality visualized by the state.

Fighting over the 'slicing of the pie' implies that there is some sharing already. If former untouchables, like the Pallars and the Paraiyars, were unable to aspire to a better life, and to succeed, there would be no need for the Kallars and the Vanniyars to try to put them back in their 'right' place.

# Communal Riots and Labour
# Bengal's Jute Mill-hands in the 1890s*

## DIPESH CHAKRABARTY

A series of riots and disturbances . . . broke out unexpectedly among the jute mill operatives of Bengal between the years 1894 and 1897. Interestingly, most of these riots turned around religious and community sentiments and not around purely economic issues. The riots show strong communal (Hindu-Muslim) divisions existing among the workers. Some of the riots, those of 1896, were in fact caused by disturbances between Hindus and Muslims. A prominent example of the issues involved in such communal riots is seen in the Muslim worker's desire to kill cows on the occasion of festivals such as Bakr-Id, and in the active opposition to this sacrifice by Hindu workers. But there were also instances—some in 1894–5 and in the Talla riot of 1897–when only Muslims or Hindus rioted against the authorities over essentially communal demands. The period, it seems, saw the growth of 'community consciousness' among significant sections of the mill workers.

The official finger pointed to 'the masses of ignorant up-country mill hands [who] . . . evince now-a-days a greater tendency to combine readily than was formerly the case' as the main source of trouble.[1] The up-country men referred to were the Hindi- or

---

* Excerpted from Dipesh Chakrabarty, Communal Riots and Labour: Bengal's Jute Mill-hands in the 1890s, in Veena Das, ed., *Mirrors of Violence: Communities, Riots, and Survivors in South Asia*, Delhi: Oxford University Press, 1990, pp. 146–84. Also consulted original version in *Past and Present*, May 1981, 91: 140–69.
[1] West Bengal State Archives (hereafter W.B.S.A.) Jdl. (Pol.), Sept. 1897,

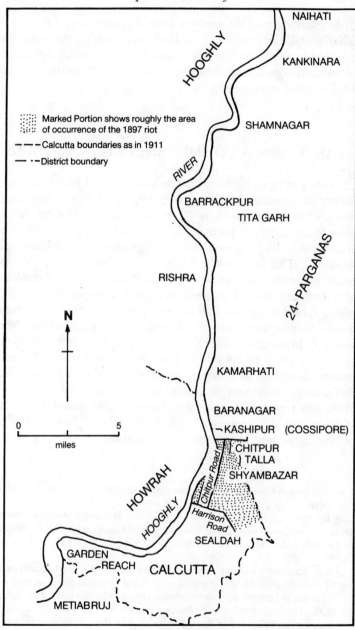

Communal Map
Areas Affected by Mill Disturbances 1894–7

Urdu-speaking migrant workers from the areas now covered by
Bihar and Uttar Pradesh. . . . They were indeed the main participants in the riots; from all available evidence this appears to
be true, though official thinking about them obviously involved
a lot of racist stereotyping.[2] . . .

[ . . . ]

## EARLY 1890s–A COMMUNAL CULTURE EMERGES

Calcutta and its surburbs appear to have enjoyed a fairly peaceful
history of communal relations over large parts of the nineteenth
century.[3] But from the early 1890s onwards a communal culture
grew in the northern parts of Calcutta and its northern suburbs,
areas which had concentrations of immigrant merchants and
labourers. The first recorded Muslim riot broke out at Shyambazar in north Calcutta in 1891. The issue was the demolition
of a building alleged to be a mosque.[4] Interestingly, the 5000
strong crowd in the riot had a very large up-country component,
mostly Jolahas, members of a Muslim weaving caste from Bihar
and U.P. Immediately after the Shyambazar riot several incidents
of conflict between Hindus and Muslims took place in the area
loosely described as Chitpur, especially at Machuabazar which
had a large settlement of immigrant Muslims.[5] The Urdu press
of the city reported in detail the Hindu-Muslim 'kine-killing riots'
of Bihar and U.P. of the early 1890s. In 1894 the Muslim leaders
of the city—most of them Urdu-speaking—memorialized the

A no. 92; Bengal Chamber of Commerce (hereafter B.C.C.), *Report, Feb. 1895–
Jan. 1896*, 2 vols (Calcutta, 1896), II, pp. 695–6.

  [2] By 1898, up-country men were described as having 'unknown antecedents . . . extremely excitable at times and . . . likely to act together.' National
Archives of India, New Delhi (hereafter N.A.I.), Home Pol., June 1898, A nos.
133–47.

  [3] S.N. Mukherjee's current research on the social history of Calcutta in the
period 1806–66 confirms this impression: personal communication to me.

  [4] This was to become a frequent issue for rioting in north Calcutta throughout
the 1890s. The Talla riots of 1897 discussed below fall into this pattern.

  [5] See, for example, *Amrita Bazar Patrika*, 21 July 1893, 'Editorial'; Report on
Native Press (Bengal) (hereafter R.N.P.B.), 29 Apr. 1893, 6 July 1895. By 'Chitpur'
I refer to the area through which the Chitpur Road ran.

government on the subject of its circular restricting cow-killing in the Bengal municipalities.[6]

[ . . . ]

A significant rumbling of communal demands was also heard in the years 1894–5 in the jute mills. Sections of the mill workers became extremely assertive about observing their religious festivals, including those of Id, Bakr-Id, Muharram and Rath Jatra. Disturbances occurred over demands for paid leave during these festivals. There was a Bakr-Id riot, for instance, at Baranagar Jute Mills in 1894, and 'a little disturbance' at Kamarhati Jute Mills where the Muslim workers were refused leave. In 1895 similar riots took place at the mills in Titagarh, Baranagar and Kamarhati. At the Gourepore Jute and Oil Mills, Muslims demanded holidays for the Id, Bakr-Id and Muharram festivals, while Hindus asked for leave on the day of Rath Jatra.[7] The Empress of India Cotton Mills granted such leave, and so did the Victoria Jute Mills in Hooghly, where the Hindus also 'were given half a day for Rath Jatra'. At the cotton mills at Shamnagar no holidays were given for Rath Jatra or Muharram. The mill-hands therefore took them 'forcibly' by 'threatening' the mill with a strike.

[ . . . ]

The most interesting point about these demands is of course their novelty—'Last year [1894] and in the former years they were never demanded'. This new accent on religious and community festivals revealed to the authorities 'quite a new attitude on the part of the mill coolies'. Thus the Baranagar Jute Mill workers in 1895 were reportedly 'more exacting than they had been hitherto. . . . Last year they had no Muharram holidays at all, but this year they took them'.

The demands also reveal a new community consciousness on the part of the workers. The Muslim worker was emphasizing the Muslim part of his identity, while the Hindu emphasized the Hindu part. In 1894–5 this did not yet lead to communal (that is Hindu-Muslim) conflicts, but the 1896 Bakr-Id riots in the jute mills were indeed communal. As our discussion of these and the 1897 riot will show, such community consciousness on the part

---

[6] *Muhammadan Observer*, 11 Jan. 1894, p. 13.

[7] . . . The Hindus were probably too divided by caste to have the same festivals for all. This may explain the Muslim preponderance in the area.

of the mill worker, especially the migrant, was only to grow over time both in its depth and spread.

## THE MILL RIOTS OF 1896

The Bakr-Id riot at Titagarh in 1896 started when Mahomed Hossain, an up-country bricklayer working at the construction site of the Standard Jute Mills, brought in a heifer to be sacrificed. The heifer was stolen by a group of four men—Ganesh Lalla, Ganesh Misr (both *durwans* or watchmen at the construction site), Chowki (a Hindu bricklayer), and Ghamundi (a caterer employed by a firm of contractors, Anderson Wallace and Company).[8] These men (Lalla and Misr suggesting up-country origin) were opposed to the sacrifice of cows on Bakr-Id. In the ensuing riots, however, workers of the neighbouring Titagarh Paper Mills and the Titagarh Jute Mills joined in, taking sides according to communal allegiance. Word had spread from the 'Titaghur mosque', where about 300 Muslims from neighbouring areas congregated on the morning of Bakr-Id and where Mahomed Hossain and other Muslim bricklayers had gone to say their prayers. About '300 or more Hindus and 180 Mahomedans' took part in the riot where slogans like 'Mar Hindu sala log (Beat up the blasted Hindus!)' were frequently shouted in frenzied outbursts.[9] A newspaper account of some of the principal Muslims accused (and later convicted) in the case gives in idea of the kind of people involved in the riot: 'Dhanuk [Sheik] is a boiler maker ['the second boiler sirdar' in the Titagarh Paper Mills], Shamad Ali a labourer but [who] now sells vegetables; Roja [Sheikh] is a coolie in the old Jute Mills; Ramjan [Sheikh] used to work in the paper mills, but now works in the Jute Mills—where Sukur, another of the accused, was also employed.[10] These men fought for their right to sacrifice cows on Bakr-Id. Obviously a feeling of community embraced them all—the relatively skilled, the unskilled and the former factory worker.

[ . . . ]

8 W.B.S.A., Jdl. (Pol.), Aug. 1896, A nos 4–5.
9 Ibid., nos 13–14; *Englishman*, 2 June 1896, p. 3.
10 *Englishman*, 2 June 1896, p. 3; Ibid., 26 June 1896, p. 6.

Communal passions were similarly aroused to a high pitch in the Bakr-Id riot at Rishra (in Serampore, Hooghly district), where Hindu and Muslim employees of the Hastings Jute Mill were involved.[11] The Muslims had made it known in the locality that they would be sacrificing a cow that year, and a petition in protest of the sacrifice was made to Mr Lister, the sub-divisional officer by Hindu mill-hands as well as shopkeepers, 'mainly . . . telis'[12] of the 'Rishra Bustee', headed by a 'rich Marwari shopkeeper'. One of the petitioners said: 'Eight days ago I heard Buna Mian, a worker in Hasting Mill, say that they would kill cows. He also heard Khuda Mian, a weaver, say [that] three days ago'. This was on 18 May, six days before Bakr-Id. On 21 May Lister received a petition from Muslim workers, headed by one Multan Mian, asking for permission to kill cows, whereupon a counter-petition was submitted by fifty Hindus saying that '*Korbani* [animal sacrifice] at Rishra should be forbidden'.

. . . Only measures which included a strong police detachment near the mosque forced stoppage of 'Ingress of Mahomedans into the town' and bands of constables patrolling all over the town succeeded in preventing a riot.

## COW KILLING: AN IMPORTED ISSUE

What is the import of this sudden emphasis placed by mill-hands on communal issues such as cow-killing?

The very fact that cow-killing became such an important issue in the 1894–6 riots strongly suggests the up-country social origins of the rioters. For cow-killing riots had never been seen in Bengal to any significant extent,[13] whereas they raged in districts of Bihar and U.P. such as Ballia, Benares, Azamgarh, Arrah, Saran, Gaya

---

[11] This account is based on W.B.S.A., Jdl. (Pol.), July 1898, A nos 52–7; *Englishman*, 29 May 1896, p. 6; R.N.P.B., 13 June 1896.

[12] *Teli*, literally 'oil pressers', traditional money-lenders in Bengal.

[13] Compare the reaction of a Bengali newspaper to the mill riots of 1896: 'This is the first year in which cow-killing quarrels have taken place in Bengal, and that in the vicinity of the metropolis': R.N.P.B., 27 June 1896. But there were a few minor and individual cases of Hindu zamindar oppression of Muslim peasants over this question, especially in the eastern districts of Bengal (now Bangladesh): R.N.P.B., for the years 1893–6.

and Patna throughout the years 1888–93, i.e. the period just
preceding the troubled years at the Calcutta jute mills.[14] The
districts affected were also typically the supply areas for immigrant
labourers in Bengal's jute mills and other industries. 'Cow-killing'
thus seems to have been an 'imported' issue. Some observations
of contemporary officials confirm this. For instance, during the
Rishra riot (1896), Mr J. Laing, the magistrate of Hooghly who
had his 'own personal experience in the kine-killing [riots at]
. . . Gaya, Arrah and Saran', observed that 'the disturbing element at Rishra was composed of the very same low-class, ignorant,
religious fanatics whom I had to deal with in those districts . . . '.[15]

[ . . . ]

## COMMUNITY CONSCIOUSNESS AND
## THE LABOUR MARKET

What was happening, however, was not just a mere transfer of
past attitudes into a new situation of industrial work. Life in
industry had elements which helped such attitudes to persist and
grow. To explain that phenomenon, we now turn to a discussion
of the jute mill labour market. In the absence of any significant
growth of other industries in the narrow industrial belt around
Calcutta, especially in the absence of any significant engineering
industry, the jute mills were the most important employers of
industrial labour in a market where supply of labour always
outstripped demand. In 1911, for example, jute mills employed
more than 73 per cent of the factory labour force in the industrial
areas of Hooghly, Howrah, 24-Parganas and Calcutta.

[ . . . ]

Work in the jute mills required a low degree of skill and little
rigorous training. Workers therefore were highly replaceable, and
since the mills had a pull on the entire labour market of Bihar,
U.P. and Orissa, the industry could easily afford to change the
social composition of its work-force whenever this was to its
advantage. . . .

What concerned the industry most, then, was a steady supply
and control of labour. Also, being a labour-intensive industry

14 See N.A.I., Home (Public), Jan. 1894, B nos 309–414.
15 W.B.S.A., Jdl. (Pol.), July 1896, A nos 55–6.

where labour alone accounted for more than 50 per cent of the 'cost of conversion',[16] the jute had to find a relatively less expensive means of recruiting and controlling its labour force. For instance housing, which involved capital expenditure, was never thought of as a means of control: in 1897 only 13.5 per cent of the work-force lived in company-built coolie lines.[17] The industry's answer to its problem of supply and control was the *sardari* system.

*Sardari* . . . is probably an example of a pre-colonial, pre-capitalist institution being made an essential feature of the process of industrialization in a colony. Simply put, the *sardar* was both a recruiter and supervisor of labour. He was of the same social origin as the ordinary worker. He had the power also to effect dismissal. He indulged in all kinds of financial extortions, which included taking a dastoory (commission) from each of his recruits. In the jute mills he was also the workers' money-lender and landlord, and his major economic instrument of control was debt-bondage.

The *sardar's* mode of operation had some crucial pre-capitalist elements. For one thing, he always recruited on the basis of the often overlapping networks of community, village and kin, making such links extremely valuable to the worker. The basis of the *sardar's* social control of the work-force lay in manoeuvring these relationships, and the ideologies and social norms associated with them. *Sardars* would thus have dominated the caste panchayats of up-country Hindu workers which were already in existence in 1890 and which the contemporary Factory Commission reported on.[18] Muslim *ulama* (priests), whose influence over up-country Muslim workers was so visible during the riot at Rishra in 1896,[19] must have had the *sardars* as their patrons and cohorts. For the *ulama* were attached to mosques, and mosques in working-class localities situated in jute mill districts are still named after important *sardars*.[20]

[16] Buchanan (1934), p. 250.

[17] W.B.S.A., Jdl. (Pol.), Sept. 1897, A nos 95–9. Calculated from a list submitted by the inspector-general of police, Bengal.

[18] *Report of the Indian Factory Commission of 1890* (Calcutta, 1890), p. 85.

[19] An *alim* (Muslim priest), for example, declared Rishra during the 1896 riot to be a '*dur-ul-harb*' i.e. 'a country of kafirs [unbelievers] against whom it is lawful to make war of jihad': R.N.P.B., 13 June 1896.

[20] This information is based on my own fieldwork, including an interview (on 5 Aug. 1976) with a ninety-year-old up-country *sardar* in the Bhatpara area, called Ishaque Sardar, who has a mosque in his own name in that area. Note

Thus the *sardari* mode of recruitment and control went hand in hand with the retention of community consciousness and other forms of pre-capitalist ideology in the working-class milieu. In the mid-1890s, as demand for jobs grew, the *sardar's* powers increased, and with that the worker's community consciousness became more manifest.

. . . The scramble for jobs (especially when the mills were expanding in the mid-1890s) and the consequent weakening of the workers' bargaining power is reflected in the wage data. The index of the average real wage (taking the average for 1890–4 as the base) for the jute mill workers fell first from 108 in 1895 to 105 in 1896, and then to 91 in 1897.[21]

In such a scramble for work, the *sardar* in his capacity of recruiter would undoubtedly have been crucial to the worker's life.[22] Communal connections through which the *sardar* found his recruits, and therefore community consciousness (which *sardari* control fostered anyway), would have become extremely important to the worker, especially to the migrant in search of work. . . .

Community consciousness was then, in a sense, the migrant worker's substitute for closed-shop trade-unionism.[23] Yet surely it was much more than just that. In a life characterized by the preponderance of men, unstable marriages, precarious living conditions, and desperate gambling in years of rising prices, socialization usually took place along communal lines. Hindus and Muslims often lived in separate *bustis* (slum dwellings). The caste panchayats of the Hindu migrants, or the Muslim *ulama* acting as communal figureheads for the Jolaha weavers from U.P.,[24] would all serve the same function: to fulfil the immigrant's need to hold on to certain constants in a hostile and changing

---

also how mosques figure in all the riots of 1896.

[21] K.L. Datta, *Report on Enquiry into the Rise in Prices in India*, 8 vols (Calcutta, 1914), ii, pp. 194–5.

[22] Indeed from 1893 onwards we hear increasingly of powerful and oppressive *sardars* in the jute mills: W.B.S.A., Jdl. (Pol.), Jan. 1896, A nos 6–11; *Bengal Administration Report, 1895–6*.

[23] We can now see why the first organization of mill workers, formed at Kankinara in 1895, would call itself the Mahomedan Association and have as its principal objectives the recruiting of more Muslims to jute mill work and the renovating of mosques: *Indian Factory Labour Commission*, II, pp. 263–4.

[24] On the traditionally strong *ulama* influence on Jolahas from UP, see Robinson 1974 and Crooke 1896: 70.

environment. Community consciousness thus also gave to these socially marginal people psychological comfort and security.

This is what made Muslim workers receptive to the politics they received at the hands of the city's Muslim leaders who controlled the Muslim (especially Urdu) press, and from the itinerant 'maulavis and oolamas' who naturally spoke a religious language. This is not to suggest that the Hindu migrant was any less (or more) communal. It was just that for the Hindus, as the following discussion will show, such organized leadership was not available.

## WORKERS AND COMMUNAL LEADERSHIP: A DOCUMENT

The character of the social leadership that these community-conscious working men often sought in this period is remarkably brought out in a letter written by the imam of Rishra, Nazir Mian, to Haji (*Hadji*) Nur Muhammad Zakaria, an important Muslim trader living in north Calcutta, asking for help during the *Bakr-Id* riot of 1896:

> It is informed that in village Rishra, police station Serampore, district Hooghly, the Hindus are going to create a row during the *Bakr-Id* (cow) slaughter; they say they do not sacrifice here, if you do so, we [Hindus] will create row. Therefore, I request that you assist us. We are poor people and work in mills. You better give this information to Muhammadans in the Friday prayers that it is religious act and everybody should assist as possible.[25]

The letter is significant. Part of it merely shows the poor man's sense of his position ('We are poor people and work in mills'), but the invocation of a 'religious act' and the whole purpose of writing the letter clearly bring out my point about the growth of community consciousness.

The letter, further, suggests a situation. We have here at the end of the nineteenth century a group of up-country workers, acutely conscious of being Muslims, approaching a wealthy Muslim of the city for his support of their communal demands. The haji must have appeared in their eyes as a community leader.

[25] W.B.S.A., Jdl. (Pol.), July 1896, A nos 55–6.

## THE TALLA RIOT OF 1897

Evidence is lacking on the question of how, or what sort of, connections were formed between the haji and the Muslim mill-hands. But we may use the Talla riot of 1897 in Calcutta and the events connected with it to prove indirectly a basic point: a person like Haji Zakaria was accepted by the poor Muslims in and around the city as their protector and guide. It is to men of this sort that they repeatedly turned for leadership in trying to solve their problems.

The Talla riot was the first ever large-scale riot to break out in Calcutta. It started on 29 June over the issue of the eviction by court order of a Muslim mason named Himmat Khan from a piece of land at Talla in north Calcutta. . . . Himmat Khan, faced with the court order, declared his hut to be 'a Masjid of long standing'. The 'mosque' was subsequently demolished by the police, and this sparked off the riot.[26] It blazed in the northern parts of the city until 2 July. . . . Eighty-seven people were ultimately sent up for trial on charges of rioting, and eighty-one were convicted.[27]

Throughout the history of the riot Haji Zakaria and other leading Muslims of Calcutta figure as the people involved in the events leading up to the outbreak of the riot, as in those which finally culminated in its quelling. In fact as soon as the police had pulled down Himmat Khan's 'mosque', Himmat with two of his Muslim neighbours . . . 'came to the Nakhoda's mosque in Chitpore Road, and failing to find Haji Nur Mohamed [Zakaria], went over to his house at Amratolla Street, where they informed him of what had happened'. The haji contacted Golam Ariff, a wealthy silk merchant in the city from Gujarat, and the next morning they both went with the 'Talla men' to the house of Maulvi Shams-ul-Huda, where they were joined by Khan Bahadur Seraj-ul-Islam, Maulvi Jowad, Abdur Rehim and Jowad-ul-Rahim, all of them practising advocates except Abdur Rahim who was a barrister. . . . 'The Talla Mahomedans were . . . advised to rebuild their mosque [and] to resist any attempt to dispossess them; acting

---

[26] Ibid., Nov. 1897, A nos 12–13, 39–43; *Amrita Bazar Patrika*, 2 July 1897; R.N.P.B., 17 July 1897.

[27] N.A.I., Home (Public), Jan. 1898, A nos 55–7; Oct. 1897, A no. 150.

upon this advice the ignorant Mahomedans of Talla, Chitpur, Baranagar and Nikaripara assembled at the spot on the night of Tuesday, the 29th June'—the fateful night when the riot started.[28]

The haji and Shams-ul-Huda were the only two gentlemen ever to appear at the actual scene of the riot, where they addressed a large assembly of the rioters at a Muslim *busti* 'on the west of the demolished mosque'.[29] . . . . The haji's importance to the rioters is finally illustrated in the manner in which the riot ended. It was necessary for the haji to issue a religious *fatwa* (decree) before the rioters would calm down. The *fatwa* was to the effect that 'no one could build a mosque on another's land, and that no mosque could be built on a land which is not wakf (Charitable Trust) and if a landlord did not give his permission, then it was not lawful to offer Friday prayers on his land'.[30]

[ . . . ]

## ZAKARIA, HIS AUDIENCE AND COMMUNITY CONSCIOUSNESS

Haji Zakaria was an important member of the Kutchi Memon community living in the Chitpur quarters of the city. . . . The Memons were a trading community from Gujarat who had started to migrate to Calcutta in 1770 following the decline of Surat.[31] . . . It is this community which later gave its name to the biggest mosque in the city—the Nakhoda Mosque, which evolved out of an earlier mosque the haji had founded, named the Zakaria Mosque.[32] In the 1870s we see the haji running his own firm called Haji Jackariah Mahomed and Company[33] when he was secretary of the Indian Trades Association in Calcutta. In this latter capacity he was considered important enough to

[28] This paragraph is based on a confidential note by Mr James, Calcutta police commissioner, appended to C.W. Bolton's letter, 1 Aug. 1897: N.A.I., Home (Public), Oct. 1897, A nos 124–57.

[29] *Amrita Bazar Patrika*, 2 July 1897, p. 4.

[30] See Ahmed 1974: 201–2.

[31] See *Statesman*, 5 May 1929, p. 10; *Gazetteer of the Bombay Presidency*, 23 vols (Bombay, 1876–1901), IV, pt. 2, p. 51.

[32] Interview on 15 Aug. 1976 with Abdur Razzak, a descendant of Zakaria. . . .

[33] N.A.I., Home (Public), Feb. 1878, B no. 215.

be consulted by the government for his views on the first Factories Act proposed for India,[34] which was passed in 1881.

What might otherwise have only been conjectured from the letter of Nazir Mian, the imam of Rishra, can now be seen as reality. In 1897 we have a wealthy Muslim trader who is at the same time a 'religious' man (as evidenced by his founding a mosque) and who enjoys a great deal of social importance, commanding a following from among the more indigent Muslims in the city. The haji's followers were a motley crowd, men of different labouring occupations. . . . But looking through some newspaper reports on rioting at Talla near the site of the mosque, we do indeed catch glimpses of the mob, and can identify some faces—few in number, but they may be indicative of the social composition of the men who fought to save the demolished mosque. There was for example Sheikh Chadi, a fifty-year-old rioter killed by the police, who was a 'thatcher by profession'.[35] So was Gajadhar Kurmi, a fifteen-year-old boy, also killed by police firing. Natra Abdul, another of the rioters, was a 'coolie' who declared in court that 'he and several others kept away from work' during the riot on 30 June. Another accused, Nanku Khan, 'worked in Jetty and lived in Subedarpara, an area of rioting'.[36] One Nabijan was identified as having been among a group of labourers accused of assaulting a certain Mr Slotter, engineer in the Ashcroft Jute Press at Chitpur[37]—Chitpur and Kashipur (Cossipore) being two places where many of the local jute presses were located. Himmat Khan, the man at the centre of events in the Talla riot, was himself a mason; the newspapers[38] carried reports on the 'hundreds of masons and coolies' who fought a see-saw battle with the police throughout the two days of rioting'.[39] The commissioner of police later reported that the rioters were composed mostly of 'low class' Muslim weavers, perhaps Jolahas, and 'bricklayers, who were joined by bad characters of the

---

[34] W.B.S.A., General Misc., May 1879, A no. 1.

[35] *Amrita Bazar Patrika*, 16 July 1897, p. 4.

[36] Ibid., 25 July 1897, p. 5.

[37] Ibid., 22 July 1897, p. 5.

[38] *Amrita Bazar Patrika*, 2 July 1897, p. 4.

[39] The police 'demolished the mosque as often as the Musalmans built and rebuilt it': R.N.P.B., 17 July 1897.

disturbed area,[40] while another newspaper identified the bulk of the rioters as 'up-countrymen'.

These, then, were the poor up-country Muslims of the city who made up the Talla rioters and accepted the social leadership of Haji Zakaria—the mason, the thatcher, the bricklayer, the coolie, the jetty worker and the labourer from a jute press in north Calcutta. These and many other up-country Muslims working in mills north of the city shared certain communal bonds and were, in other words, community conscious. . . . This is why Nazir Mian of Rishra had earlier thought that his appeal for help from Muslims in fighting Hindus during the Rishra riots would find a receptive ear in the city.

## PAN-ISLAMISM, THE PLAGUE AND THE POOR IN 1897

Haji Zakaria was one of the earliest and most confirmed pan-Is-lamists in Calcutta. His allegiance dated from the time when the first wave of pan-Islamism reached the city during the Russo-Turkish war of 1876–8.[41] In the pro-Turkish agitation he was regarded as one of the 'most active of Muhammadans at present' in Calcutta, another one being 'Hajee Ahmad of Burra Bazar'. . . . 'They are in constant communication with Bombay and the North-West Provinces. They have been appointed as treasurers to transmit to Bombay the money raised in Calcutta.'[42] The haji's dedication to the pan-Islamist cause is also shown by frequent meetings held at his house[43] or at his mosque. . . .

Apparently many of the earlier enthusiasts dropped out of the pan-Islamist group when the second wave of the movements reached the city during the Greco-Turkish war of 1896. . . . 'A small fund was collected for the relief of Mahomedans who had suffered in Crete, but it has not been remitted, and is not now likely to be'.[44] The lack of response is perhaps explained by the

[40] W.B.S.A., Jdl. (Pol.), Nov. 1897, A nos 39–43.
[41] See Bamford 1925: 110, Shukla 1973: 96, 100, 176, and Hardy 1972: 118.
[42] N.A.I., Home (Public), Feb. 1878, B no. 217.
[43] Ibid.
[44] Bolton's letter, 1 Aug. 1897: N.A.I., Home (Public), Oct. 1897, A nos 124–57.

fact that, unlike the years 1876–8 when Great Britain supported
Turkey, pan-Islamism in 1896–7 had an anti-British corollary. Most
Muslim leaders in the city played a fairly safe and compromising
politics, avoiding mass contacts and concentrating their efforts on
demands for more jobs and education for Muslims.

Even in these lean years of pan-Islamism in the city, Haji
Zakaria remained a consistent follower of the creed. People who
stood by him in this were also the men who had signed his
religious *fatwa* during the Talla riot, the men who were described
officially as enjoying the confidence of the rioters: Shams-ul-Huda,
'Haji Mahomed Abdur Rezak, Sheikh Buksh Elahi, Syed
Mahomed Tahir and others'. Of course they were not anti-British
as such, and showed 'every disposition to please the authorities'.[45]
But in their pan-Islamism they did form a 'party', which was
described as having been

> active in holding up the Sultan as the head of Islam, in representing
> him as being unjustly harassed by Great Britain and the European
> powers, and in magnifying his might as manifested by victories over
> the Greeks.[46] . . .

Thus if the men who gave social leadership to the Talla rioters
were pan-Islamist, it is interesting to observe that pan-Islamism
also formed an important part of the feelings that circulated during
the riot. The Talla incident, wrote a correspondent to the *Amrita
Bazar Patrika*, 'has its origin in a current of feeling which was
inspired by the manner in which the news of the victory of the
Sultan over the Greeks were so freely circulated among the
Mahomedan population in the country'. 'The educated Mahomedans were the agents in circulating the news', so much so that
the Talla rioters often thought that they were fighting 'the cause
of the Sultan and the [Afghan] Amir'.[47] . . .

[ . . . ]

Rumours current during the Talla riots also point to the
pan-Islamist content of the riot. The *Amrita Bazar Patrika*, in an
editorial after the Talla events, wrote of the 'very many' stories

---

[45] Bolton's confidential letter, 7 Sept. 1897: N.A.I., Home (Public), Oct. 1897,
A nos 124–57.

[46] Bolton's letter, 1 Aug. 1897: N.A.I., Home (Public), Oct. 1897, A nos
124–57. It should be noted that the 'party' consisted mainly of traders and
professionals (pleaders), who may have enjoyed a patron–client relationship.

[47] *Amrita Bazar Patrika*, 11 July 1897, p. 5, letter from 'K'.

circulating on the subject of the rioters. One such story held 'that they sent telegrams to the Sultan and the Amir asking for help, and received favourable replies'. 'Of course, there is no truth in the above', the *Patrika* commented, 'but it is certain that the rioters were led to believe that telegrams were actually sent and that their appeals have extorted favourable replies'.[48] . . .

It was not only the distant reality of the Sultan that came to be looked upon with pan-Islamist eyes by the poor Muslim; the ideology of pan-Islamism seems to have gone deeper. Even things nearer to the daily lives of the city poor often received a pan-Islamist interpretation. The mid-1890s were problem years as much for the city poor as they were for the jute mill workers. . . .

. . . Early in the year, Calcutta was 'restive with rumours about plague regulations', and the 'wildest possible notions' were being 'freely supported'. The Muslims especially disliked the restrictions the government had put on haj pilgrimage; in April 1897 the pilgrimage had been temporarily stopped by the government under the Epidemic Diseases Act.[49] This was interpreted by the Muslim labourers as an action which ran counter to pan-Islamism. The *Amrita Bazar Patrika* wrote:

> To say that the dispute about a cotta of land is the cause of the Talla riot . . . is to show ignorance of human character. The feelings had been simmering long before the present riot occurred; and the reason which offended the Musalman community, or rather the lower class of the community, was openly proclaimed by the rioters during the hottest part of their work at Talah. This was heard by our reporters and hundreds of others. They said that the plague regulations were a myth, and the Government had an ulterior object in view in preventing them from going to Mecca. The Government, they said, feared that if the Musalmans of India went to Mecca, they would come in contact with the soldiers of the Sultan; and the result would be that the Indian Musalman would come to this country, re-enforced by the Sultan's men, and thus the British-raj would come to end![50]

[ . . . ]

---

[48] *Amrita Bazar Patrika*, 7 July 1897, p. 4.
[49] See Elgin to Hamilton, 17 Feb., 10, 24 Mar., 21 Apr. 1897: I.O.L., Elgin Papers, MSS. Eur. F 84/15.
[50] *Amrita Bazar Patrika*, 2 July 1897, p. 4.

## THE COMMUNAL QUESTION AND PROBLEMS OF SOCIAL LEADERSHIP IN THE 1890s

Why were the immigrant Muslim traders of the Chitpur area so interested in linking up with the Muslim poor? After the Shyambazar riots of 1891 over the issue of the Nikaripara mosque, Kasim Ariff (father of the wealthy Gujarati silk merchant Golam Ariff) purchased the disputed piece of land for Rs 4500 and made it over to the rioters so that they could have their *masjid*.[51] These Muslim merchants did the same when two other decrees were issued by the civil court in 1893, 'for possession of plots of land held by Mahomedans on which there were huts alleged to be mosques.[52] Additionally, 'the Haji had subscribed largely for the defence, in court, of the Shambazar rioters', whom the *vakil* (pleader) Shamsul-Huda defended.[53] . . . Abdur Rahim and Muhammad Yusuf had . . . tried to help the Muslim mill workers of Rishra during the 1896 riot.[54]

Muslim charity or factional politics may have been important factors in these developments, but a police document of 1910 suggests an interesting alternative explanation. Such an explanation can again only be speculative in the absence of hard data.

The document in question relates to the anti-cow-killing agitation in Chitpur in 1910.[55] The agitation was led by immigrant Marwari traders from Rajasthan, Hindu or Jain by religion, who were to dominate much of Calcutta's business history in the twentieth century. The document shows that by 1910 Marwaris were pushing into the residential areas of Muslim traders and labourers, and were prepared to use communalism to displace them. The marwaris, who were deeply entrenched in the trade of rice and jute, the two principal twentieth century crops in Bengal, brought with them new chains of retail and wholesale

[51] Bolton's letter, 1 Aug. 1897, in 'Notes': N.A.I., Home (Public), Oct. 1897, A nos 124–57, and James's report appended thereto. . . .

[52] Bolton's letter, 1 Aug. 1897: N.A.I. Home (Public), Oct. 1897, A nos 124–57.

[53] *Amrita Bazar Patrika*, 2 July 1897, p. 4. This was also promised by the merchants to the Talla rioters if they would calm down.

[54] See *Englishman*, 27 May 1896, p. 5; W.B.S.A., Jdl. (Pol.), July 1896, A nos 52–3.

[55] W.B.S.A., Home Pol., Special Branch, confidential file no. 290/1910, nos 1–3.

trade connections. Their entry into the Chitpur area, the central business district of the city, may have been of importance to their interests.

[ . . . ]

Such Marwari incursions into the Muslim residential areas of Chitpur and Burrabazar did not start in 1910. Indirect evidence points to an earlier beginning. The formation of a Marwari-inspired Cow Protection Society in Burrabazar in 1894, or Marwari gambling that was particularly rife in 1896 in Chitpur,[56] suggest a growing Marwari presence in these areas in the 1890s. If this is true, then it would partly explain why in the decade the poor migrant Muslims were often fighting the demolition of 'alleged mosques'. Their settlements were under pressure from developments in the local land market. The residential areas of the old Muslim traders were being invaded by the Marwaris. They may have faced business competition, too, from the Marwaris. The Zakarias and Ariffs were probably on the defensive and therefore keen to link up with the poorer migrant Muslims so as to be able to use their own 'communalism' against that of the Marwaris. In this, a pan-Islamist ideology could be a very good bond to cement the Muslim rich and poor.

The leadership of the up-country mill-hand, by contrast, went by default. His communalism may have received occasional support from Hindus important in the locality. . . . But the chain of patronage would hardly go beyond the locality.[57]

The Bengali *bhadralok* ('respectable person' of the middle class) in the nineteenth century, with his 'education, clean clothes, and hands unsoiled with manual labour',[58] perhaps felt distant from the world of men who worked in the mills. In the 1890s, with a large number of immigrant mill-hands, the gulf between the *bhadralok* and working men was only to grow wider. The Bengali *bhadralok* were not sufficiently equipped culturally to communicate with such groups. Their premier political organization, the Indian Association, reacted to the Talla riot by petitioning the viceroy to 'open a volunteer corps and train the Bengalis in the

[56] See 'Proceedings of the General Committee of the Calcutta Corporation for 21 Aug. 1896', pp. 243–6 (copy at Calcutta Corporation Archives).

[57] Organized Marwari (and up-country Hindu) patronage for communal riots was to become really important in the twentieth century.

[58] The description is from Sarkar 1973: 509.

use of arms . . . [which] would . . . help them to resist the rowdy rioters.[59]

[ . . . ]

It was in this context of a social and cultural hiatus between the *bhadralok* and the migrant workers that the community consciousness of Hindu mill-workers found foster-parents in the idiosyncratic communalism of an Annapurna Devi or a Hindu mill babu, while Muslim migrants found similar support in the broader community politics of someone like Haji Zakaria. Bengal did not provide them with any alternative social leadership.

[59] See Bengal 1953: 129.

# Some Unconscious Aspects of Ethnic Violence in India[*]

## SUDHIR KAKAR

The need to integrate social and psychological theory in the analysis of cultural conflicts, i.e. conflicts between ethnic and religious groups, has long been felt while its absence has been equally long deplored. Though everyone agrees on the theoretical questions involved—how do these conflicts originate, develop, and get resolved; how do they result in violent aggression—a general agreement on the answers or even on how to get these answers moves further and further away.

A large part of the problem in the study of these questions lies with the nature of and the crisis within the social sciences. The declining fortunes of logical positivism, hastened in the last twenty years by the widespread circulation and absorption of the views of such thinkers as Gadamer, Habermas, Derrida, Ricouer and Foucault, has led to a plethora of new models in the sciences of man and society. The dominant model of yesteryears—social science as social physics—is now only one among several clamouring for allegiance and adherents. It incorporates only one view among many on the nature of social reality and of social science knowledge. Anthropology, sociology, political science, psychology and even economics are all becoming more pluralistic and scattering into frameworks. In such a

* Excerpted from Sudhir Kakar, Some Unconscious Aspects of Ethnic Violence in India, in Veena Das, ed., *Mirrors of Violence: Communities, Riots, and Survivors in South Asia*, Delhi: Oxford University Press, 1990, pp. 135–45.

situation, the calls for a general theory of ethnic violence or indeed (as Clifford Geertz has remarked) of anything *social*, sound increasingly hollow, and the claims to have one science seem megalomaniacal.[1] Thus, without taking recourse to other disciplines and even ignoring the grand theories of human aggression in psychology itself—those of animal ethology, sociology, Freudian Thanatos and so on—I would like to present some limited 'local knowledge' observations on ethnic violence in India from a psychoanalytic perspective.

In the manner of a clinician, let me begin with the concrete data on which I base my observations on the first question, namely the origins of ethnic conflict. The data for these observations, and those which follow, come from diverse sources: spirit possession in north India, dreams of psychotherapy patients, eavesdropping on group discussions at the Golden Temple complex in July 1984, and finally, personal participation in large religious assemblies.

## THE OTHER IN ETHNIC CONFLICT

Some years ago, while studying the phenomenon of possession by spirits in rural north India, I was struck by a curious fact.[2] In a very large number of cases, 15 out of 28, the *bhuta* or malignant spirit possessing Hindu men and women turned out to be a Muslim. When, during the healing ritual, the patient went into a trance and the spirit started expressing its wishes, these wishes invariably turned out to be those which would have been horrifying to the patient's conscious self. In one case, the Muslim spirit possessing an elderly Brahmin priest vigorously insisted on eating kababs. The five women surrounding the man who had engaged the *bhuta* in conversation were distinctly disheartened that he had turned out to be a *Sayyad* and one of them lamented: 'These Mussulmans! They have ruined our *dharma* but they are so strong they can withstand our gods.' In another case, the *bhuta* inhabiting a young married woman not only expressed derogatory sentiments towards her 'lord and master' but also openly stated

---

[1] See Geertz (1983).
[2] See Kakar (1982).

its intentions of bringing the mother-in-law to a violent and preferably bloody end.

Possession by a Muslim *bhuta*, then, seemed to reflect the afflicted person's desperate efforts to convince himself and others that his hunger for forbidden foods and uncontrolled rage towards those who should be loved and respected, as well as all other imagined transgressions and sins of the heart, belonged to the Muslim destroyer of taboos and were furthest away from his 'good' Hindu self. In that Muslim *bhutas* were universally considered to be the strongest, vilest, the most malignant and the most stubborn of the evil spirits, the Muslim seemed to symbolize the alien and the demonic in the unconscious part of the Hindu mind.

The division of humans into mutually exclusive group identities of tribe, nation, caste, religion and class thus seems to serve two important psychological functions. The first is to increase the feeling of well being in the narcissistic realm by locating one's own group at the centre of the universe, superior to others. The shared grandiose self, maintained by legends, myths and rituals, seems to demand a concomitant conviction that other groups are inferior.

India has not been exempt from this universal rule. Whatever idealizing tendencies we might have in viewing our past history, it is difficult to deny that every social group in its tales, ritual and other literature, has sought to portray itself nearer to a purer, divine state while denigrating and banishing others to the periphery. It is also undeniable that sharing a common ego-ideal and giving one's own group a super-individual significance can inspire valued human attributes of loyalty and heroic self-sacrifice. All this is familiar to students of culture and need not detain us further here.

For the psychoanalyst it is the second function of division into ethnic groups, namely the need to have other groups as containers for one's disavowed aspects, which is of greater significance. These disavowed aspects, or the demonic spirits, take birth during that period of our childhood when the child, made conscious of good and bad, right and wrong, begins to divide himself into two parts, one that is the judge and the other that is being judged. The unacceptable, condemned parts of the self are projected outside, the projective processes being primitive attempts to relieve pain by externalizing it. The expelled parts of the self are then attached to various beings—animal and human—as well as to whole castes, ethnic and religious communities. This early split within our nature, which gives us a future license to view and treat others as if they were no better than the worst in ourselves, is normally completed by the time the child is six to seven years old. The earliest defenses for dealing with the unacceptable aspects of the self—namely their denial, the splitting from awareness and projection onto another group—require the active participation of the members of the child's group-parents and other adults who must support such a denial and projection. They are shared group defenses. The family and extended group of a Hindu upper-caste child, for instance, not only provides him with its myths and rituals which increase his sense of group cohesion and of narcissism in belonging to such an exalted entity, but also help him in elaborating and fleshing out his demonology of other ethnic and religious groups. The *purana* of the Muslim demon, for instance, as elaborated by many Hindu groups, has nothing to do with Sufi saints, the prophet's sayings or the more profound sentiments of Islam. Instead, its stories are of rape and pillage by the legions of Ghazni and Timur as well as other more local accounts of Muslim mayhem.

The Muslim demon is, so to say, the traditional container of Hindu conflicts over aggressive impulses. It is the transgressor of deeply-held taboos, especially over the expression of physical violence. Recent events in Punjab, I am afraid, are creating yet another demon in the Hindu psyche of north India. Over the last few years, tales of Bhindranwale's dark malevolence and the lore of murderous terrorists has led to a number of reported dreams from patients where Sikhs have appeared as symbols of the patient's own aggressive and sadistic superego. A group of Sikhs with raised swords chasing a patient who has broken into an old woman's shop, a Nihang stabbing a man repeatedly with a spear on the street while another patient as a frightened child looks down upon the scene from an upstairs window—these are two of many such dream images. Leaving aside the role played by these images in the patients' individual dramas, the projection of the feared aggressive parts of the self on the figure of the Sikh is an unhappy portent for the future relationship between the two communities. The fantasy of being overwhelmed by the frightening aggressive strength of the Sikhs can, in periods of upheaval and danger—when widespread regression in ego takes place and the touch with reality is weakened—lead to psychotic delusions about Sikh intentions.

## SIKH MILITANCY

Until this point I have used some psychoanalytic, especially Kleinian, concepts of splitting and projective identification to understand data that bears on the question of ethnic conflict. More specifically, I have outlined the origins of certain pre-conscious attitudes of Hindus towards Muslims and Sikhs. These attitudes reflect the psychological needs of the child, and the adult, to split off his bad impulses, especially those relating to violence, and to attach them to other communities, a process supported and reinforced by other members of the group. Let me now use another set of analytical concepts of group identity and narcissism, narcissistic hurt and rage, to understand the phenomenon of Sikh militancy. To avoid any misunderstanding let me state at the outset that I am primarily talking about the militant Sikh youth of Punjab, not of all Sikh youths, and certainly not of the Sikh community as a whole. Also, the word narcissism in psycho-analysis is not used in a pejorative sense but, together with sexuality and aggression, as the third major and fundamental motivational factor in human beings which is concerned with the maintenance of self-esteem. The data for these observations comes from being an observer of heated and anguished discussions among randomly formed groups which were being spontaneously held all over the Golden Temple complex in Amritsar, five weeks after Operation Blue Star. As I have said elsewhere,[3] the aftermath of Blue Star, which heightened the awareness of their cultural identity among many Sikhs, also brought out in relief one of its less conscious aspects. I have called it the Khalsa warrior element of Sikh identity which, at least since the tenth guru and at least among the Jats, has expressed itself in images of 'lifting up the

---

[3] See Kakar (1985). Operation 'Blue Star' was the code name for the army action to clear the Golden Temple of Sikh militants in June 1984, in which the militant leader Bhindranwale died. The operation resulted in extensive damage to the sacred site.

sword' against the 'oppression of a tyrannical ruler', and whose associated legends only countenance two possible outcomes—complete victory (*fateh*) or martyrdom (*shaheedi*) of those engaged in the battle. The surrounding society has of course reinforced this identity element over the years by its constant talk of Sikh martial prowess and valour. The Sikh youth's acceptance of these projections of heroic militancy made by the Hindu can lead to his overestimation of this aspect of his identity as he comes to feel that it is his very essence. All other qualities which may compromise heroic militancy, such as yearnings for passivity, softness and patience, will tend to be denied, split off and projected onto other, despised groups. The damage done to the Akal Takht—as much a symbol of corporate militancy as of religious piety—reinforced the two M's—militance and martyrdom—the inner counterparts of the well-known five K's which constitute the outer markers of the Khalsa warrior identity. The exaggerated value placed on martyrdom is hard to understand for Hindus since oppressors in *their* mythology—the Hindu equivalent of Sikh legendary history—tended to be destroyed by divine intervention rather than by the sacrifice of martyrs.

The army action was then a hurt to Sikh religious sentiments in a very different way from the sense in which a Hindu understands the term. It was an affront to group narcissism, to a shared grandiose self. The consequent feelings were of narcissistic hurt and rage. This was brought home to me again and again as I listened to groups of anguished men and women in front of the ruins of the Akal Takht. Most men stood in attitudes of sullen defeat, scorned and derided by the women with such sentences as 'Where is the starch in your moustache now?'

Given the collective need for the preservation of this core of the group identity, the Golden Temple action automatically completed a circle of associations. The army action to clear Akal Takht from desperadoes became an attack on the Sikh nation by a tyrannical 'Delhi durbar'. It was seen as an assault designed to wipe out all its traces, its *nishan*—since this is how it was in the past. The Sikhs killed in the attack were now defenders of the faith and martyrs—since this too is a pattern from the past. The encounter was viewed as a momentous battle, an oppressive empire's defeat of the forces of the Khalsa. The relatively heavy army losses are not a consequence of its restraint but a testimony to the fighting qualities of the Khalsa warrior. Paradoxically, the terrorist losses were exaggerated to simultaneously show the overwhelming strength of the army and the Khalsa readiness to die in martyrdom when victory is not possible.

Bhindranwale, in dramatically exemplifying the two M's of militancy and martyrdom, has touched deep chords. His status with much of the Sikh youth today is very near that of an eleventh guru. Initially, Bhindranwale may have been one of many *sants*, though more militant than most, who dot the countryside in Punjab. What began the process of his elevation was his successful defiance of the government—echoes, again of Sikh history, of defiant gurus contesting state authority. In setting the date and terms of his arrest ('*Santji* gave arrest', and not 'He was arrested', is how the people at the Temple complex put it),[4] and predicting the day of his release, Bhindranwale began to be transformed from a mortal preacher to a 'realized' saint with miraculous powers. (And the reputation of being able to work miracles is, we know, essential for those aspiring to enter the portals of gurudom in all religious traditions.) His 'martyrdom' has now cemented the transformation and made his elevation into the Sikh militant pantheon irreversible. The tortures and murders in the Temple complex or outside are no longer his responsibility, being seen as the doings of deluded associates, acts of which Santji was, of course, unaware.

It is obvious that after the army action there was a threat to the cultural identity of at least a section of the Jat Sikh youth. This led to regressive transformations in the narcisstic realm, where reality is interpreted only as a balm to narcissistic hurt and as a coolant for narcissistic rage. It needs to be asked what precisely constituted this threat. I would tend to see the threat to the Jat Sikh group identity as part of a universal modernizing process to which many groups all over the world have been and continue to be exposed. This group though has preferred to change a social-psychological issue into a political one. The cultural decay and spiritual disintegration talked of in the Anand-pur resolution are then viewed as an aspect of majority-minority relations rather than as an existential condition brought on by

---

[4] This referred to the arrest of Bhindranwale in 1981, after the murder of Lala Jagat Narayan in Punjab.

the workings of a historical fate. A feeling of inner threat is projected outside as oppression, a conflict around tradition and modernity as a conflict around power.

Narcissistic rage, then, is the core of the militancy of Sikh youth and Sikh terrorism. As Kohut (1972) says about this rage: 'The need for revenge, for righting a wrong, for undoing a hurt by whatever means, and a deeply anchored, unrelenting compulsion in the pursuit of all these aims, gives no rest to those who have suffered a narcissistic injury.' For the analyst, this becomes paramount in the understanding of youthful militancy, the foreground, while political, social and other issues recede into the background.

Let me now make a few observations on the question of ethnic conflict resulting in violent aggression, i.e. on mob violence. My data for these remarks is, paradoxically, personal participation in largely peaceful and loving groups engaged in religious and spiritual endeavours. Yet many of the psychological processes are common to the two kinds of groups. Both emotionally charged religious assemblies and mobs on the rampage bring out in relief the vulnerability of human individual ego functions confronted with the power of group processes. In the face of these, the 'integrity', 'autonomy', and 'independence' of the ego seem to be wishful illusions and hypothetical constructs. Mobs, more than religious congregations, provide striking examples of the massive inducement, by group processes, of individuals towards a new identity and behaviour of the sort that would ordinarily be repudiated by a great majority of the individuals so induced. They illustrate, more clearly than in any other comparable social situation, the evanescence of rational thought, the fragility of internalized behavioural controls, values, and moral and ethical standards.

The most immediate experience in being part of a crowd is the sensual pounding received in the press of other bodies. At first there may be a sense of unease as the body, the container of our individuality and the demarcator of our boundaries in space, is sharply wrenched away from its habitual way of experiencing others. For, as we grow up, the touch of others, once so deliberately courted and responded to with delight, increasingly becomes a problem. Coming from a loved one, touch is deliciously welcomed; with strangers, on the other hand, there is an involuntary shrinking of the body, their touch taking on the menacing air of invasion by the other.

But once the fear of touch disappears in the fierce press of other bodies and the individual lets himself become a part of the crowd's density, the original apprehension is transformed into an expansiveness that stretches to include others. Distances and differences—of class, status, age, caste hierarchy—disappear in an exhilarating feeling that individual boundaries can indeed be transcended and were perhaps illusory in the first place. Of course, touch is only one of the sensual stimuli that hammers at the gate of individual identity. Other excitations, channelled through vision, hearing and smell, are also very much involved. In addition, there are exchanges of body heat, muscle tension and body rhythms which take place in a crowd. In short, the crowd's assault on the sense of individuality, its invitation to transcend one's individual boundaries and its offer of a freedom from personal doubts and anxieties is well nigh irresistible.

The need and search for 'self-transcending' experience, to lose one's self in the group, suspend judgement and reality-testing, is, I believe, the primary motivational factor in both religious assembly and violent mob, even though the stated purpose is spiritual uplift in one and mayhem and murder in the other. Self-transcendence, rooted in the blurring of our body image, not only opens us to the influx of the divine but also heightens our receptivity to the demonic. The surge of love also washes away the defences against the emergence of archaic hates. In psychoanalytic terms, regression in the body image is simultaneous with regression in the superego system. Whether the ego reacts to this regression in a disintegrated fashion with panic that manifests itself (in a mob) in senseless rage and destructive acts—or in a release of love encompassing the group and the world outside—depends on the structure provided to the group. Without the rituals which make tradition palpable and thus extend the group in time by giving assurances of continuity to the beleaguered ego, and without the permanent visibility of leaders whose presence is marked by conspicuous external insignia and who replace the benign and loving functions of the superego, religious crowds can easily turn into marauding mobs. Transcending individuality by merging into a group can generate heroic self-sacrifice but also unimaginable brutality. To get out of one's skin in a devotional assembly is also at the same time to have less regard for saving it in a mob.

## SOME IMPLICATIONS

The implications of my remarks, I know, are not too comforting. The need for communities, our own to take care of our narcissistic needs and of others to serve as recipients for our hostility and destructiveness, are perhaps built into our very ground-plan as human beings. Well meaning educative efforts in classrooms or in national integration seminars are for the most part too late and too little in that they are misdirected. They are too late since most of the evidence indicates that the communal imagination is well entrenched by the time a child enters school. They are misdirected in that they never frankly address the collective—and mostly preconscious—fears and wishes of the various communities. Demons do not much care for 'correct' interpretations of religious texts by scholars, nor are they amenable to humanist pleas of reason to change into good and loving beings. All we can do is accept their existence but reduce their potential for causing actual physical violence and destruction.

[ . . . ]

# Mizoram: Ethnic Dynamics of Autonomy and Secession[*]

## URMILA PHADNIS

[U]nlike the Presidencies of Madras, Bombay and Bengal in which the British had entrenched themselves during the eighteenth century, their annexation of the hilly tracts of Eastern India including Mizoram (designated by them as Lushai Hills) took place by the end of the nineteenth century. However, the British found it politically expedient and economically beneficial to maintain the indigenous patriarchical system of tribal/clan chieftainship under their overarching dominance and control. Under the 1935 Act, for instance, the Mizo Hills were designated as 'excluded areas' under the direct control of the chief executive of the area, i.e., the governor of Assam.

The British pattern of dominance facilitated the political insularity of the area *vis-à-vis* the rest of the country. Besides, in their recognition of the chieftainship, the socio-political *status quo* was maintained within the area. Although the practice of shifting 'jhum' cultivation was not disturbed, the recognition of the chief as the owner of all land in his domain required extraction of land revenue or tribute to the British. The colonial government classified the tribal groups into relatively wider tribal conglomerates and designated them in the census reports as Lushai, Hmar, Chakma, Pawi, Lakher, Kuki, etc.

* Excerpted from Urmila Phadnis, Mizoram: Ethnic Dynamics of Autonomy and Secession, *Ethnicity and Nation-building in South Asia*, New Delhi: Sage, 1990, pp. 148–60, 288–90.

Among these groups, the Lushais formed the majority in the area. Notwithstanding the intra-tribal differences, the acceptance of a general name provided them an identity with a wide space and meaning. Almost simultaneously, the induction of Christianity was a significant factor during the period. Thus, according to the 1951 Census, Christians accounted for 90 per cent of the total population in Mizoram. Among the Lushais, the conversion was almost 100 per cent. The situation hardly changed in the later decades.[1]

Christianity provided linguistic and territorial integrity and a 'sense of cultural homogeneity, specially in the central part of the territory'.[2] In the process, it also gave rise to a new educated elite which developed a sense of relative deprivation *vis-à-vis* the tribal chiefs and sought change. However, it was not easy to challenge the dominance of the chiefs as they were virtually the protégés of the colonial government. Nonetheless, the processes of transfer of power during 1946–7 did provide them an opportunity to ventilate their protest against the then prevailing system.

In April 1946 the Mizo Common People's Union (MCPU) was formed. It demanded equal voting rights for the 'common man' and the chiefs in the elections for the District Conference which was the locus of political power in the district. Led by young educated Christians belonging to various tribes, the MCPU re-christened itself as Mizo Union (MU). During 1946–7, the spurt of political activity in the area reflected an emphasis on 'Mizoness' by the contending factions of the emerging elite, claiming to represent the commoners (vantlang) versus the established elite— the chiefs (Lal). It seems that the emphasis on the term 'Mizo' was ingenious as well as innovative. An indigenous term, translated as 'highlander' or 'hillman', it cut across tribal boundaries and had wider territorial connotations. In effect however, the leadership as well as the rank and file of these groups were mainly from the numerically preponderant tribe of Lushais who were rechristened as Mizos in the post-independence censuses. Despite the different courses of action propounded by these groups, they underscored the distinctiveness of the Mizo people as a 'nation'. . . .

[1] For details see Roy Burman, 1970: 31; Census of India 1971: 88.
[2] Goswami 1979: 24.

Thus, the left wingers in the Mizo Union wanted the abolition of chieftainship, representation of the Mizos in the Assam Legislature and their socio-economic amelioration 'as a "backward" nation'.[3] On the other hand, a move for the possible independent status of the Lushai Hills was also being canvassed. It comprised a segment of the Mizo Union and the chiefs. It was supported financially by rich businessmen and politically by the British administration. Organising itself as the United Mizo Freedom Organisation (UMFO), the party came into being on 4 July 1947 with the avowed object of the Lushai Hills joining Burma. An alternative scheme was also floated by Professor R. Coupland at this juncture, which suggested the creation of the 'Crown Colony of Eastern Agency', consisting of the hill areas of Assam and Burma which would in due course be an independent state.[4]

Of these alternatives (*a*) the option to join India; (*b*) that of becoming a separate state; (*c*) union with Burma; and (*d*) continuance as a Crown colony, the last three options did not seem to be politically feasible, partly because of the Burmese Prime Minister U Nu's attitude on the issue and partly due to the firm and open proclamation of the Indian leaders, perceiving such moves as hostile actions *vis-à-vis* the new government. Also, as regards the secessionist demand, it was obvious that it could not fructify unless and until it had an external/colonial prop. Nonetheless, the secessionist group (encouraged by the British officers in the area) was highly antagonistic to the option of joining India.

With feelings running high among the MU and the UMFO, a meeting was held on 14 August 1947 under the chairmanship of the British Superintendent of the Lushai Hills which was attended by representatives of both the groups. The conference first inquired as to whether the Lushai Hills district's option of joining any other dominion, i.e., Pakistan or Burma, apart from the Indian Union, was open. In the event of such an option being closed, the group's main demands were:

1.  The continuance of the existing safeguards of the customary laws and land tenure, etc.
2.  Retention of the Chin Hills Regulation of 1896 and Bengal

[3] Extracts of draft constitution of the MU in *ibid.*: 133.
[4] Roy Burman 1970: 133–37.

Eastern Frontier Regulations of 1873 until the Lushais, through their District Council or other parallel district authority declared that these could be abrogated.

3.    After a period of ten years, the Lushais, if so intended, would be allowed to opt out of the Indian Union.[5]

The last clause was similar to the one put forward by the Naga National Council (NNC) headed by A.Z. Phizo in its memorandum to the Nehru government. In fact, there is enough evidence to show that during 1946-7, the NNC leaders were in touch with the leadership of the Mizo Union. In fact, as late as April 1947, Phizo had invited the Mizo leaders to join hands with the Nagas and fight for political independence. He even suggested that the Mizo language could become the *lingua franca* of the independent state of Naga and Mizo Hills. The Mizo Union leaders however declined the offer.[6]

This was understandable. As mentioned earlier, the young leadership of the Mizo Union perceived in the Indian National Congress an ally which would abolish the system of chieftainship which was perceived as a prop of the British. Alongside, in such a changed scenario, they would become the legatees of the power resources. And the greater was their autonomy, the more was their power accretion. The emphasis on Mizo identity and personality, though for different reasons, was however, as important to the autonomists as to the secessionist stream which starting as the UMFO, decided to merge with the Eastern Indian Tribal Union (EITU) in 1957, having as its object the formation of a Hill state comprising the hill districts of Assam, Manipur, Tripura, Nagaland and the North East Frontier Agency (now Arunachal Pradesh). As regards the MU leadership, almost since its inception, while on the one hand it was prepared to link its political destiny with Assam, on the other, it was equally keen to maintain the autonomy of Lushai Hills which it wished to rechristen as Mizoram.[7] In this respect, the Sixth Schedule of the Constitution

[5] For the text of the resolution, see Goswami 1979: 135.

[6] Sarin 1980: 146-8.

[7] This is evident from the statements of the MU leaders as early as April 1947 when they gave their evidence to the sub-committee of the Constituent Assembly under the Chairmanship of Gopinath Bardoloi. India, Constituent Assembly 1947: 27.

provided the solution by endowing a fair degree of self-government to the district as an Autonomous District Council within Assam.

During the first decade, the MU dominated the district politics. In the District Council elections held in 1952, it won twenty-three out of twenty-four seats. It succeeded in persuading the Congress-led Assam government to abolish the system of hereditary chieftainship in 1954, changed the name of the District from 'Lushai Hills' to 'Mizo Hills' and introduced certain socio-economic reforms. Though the Congress was hardly a force in this area during the 1950s, it worked in close co-operation with it till 1957.

However, the MU leadership was unable to give substance to its socio-economic reforms. To a great extent, this was due to the politics of patronage. Besides, the opposition charged that the failure of the MU was due to its acquiescence to the Assamese government which discriminated against the hillmen in favour of the plains people. The decline in the popularity of the MU was evident in the 1957 elections which ended in a plurality with the MU winning eleven and the UMFO eight out of twenty-four seats.

The district level competition of these two groups however, found a co-existential frame at the state level. This was an indication of the efforts of the Centre to maintain a certain degree of administrative autonomy at the local level as well as incorporate them in the power structure of the state. Such an inclusionary strategy of the Centre was manifested in the inclusion of tribal leaders of both the groups in the Cabinet, following Nehru's visit to Shillong in 1957.

However, such an equilibrium was given a rude jolt by a state level issue—that of language—and, a local crisis, i.e., famine. As regards the former, the enactment of the Assam Official Language Bill in 1961, making Assamese the official language in the state, evoked a violent reaction from the hill districts. In 1960, various parties in the hill areas including the Mizo Union, decided to merge in the All Party Hill Leaders Conference (APHLC). It resolved that all the Hill Districts should be separated from Assam to form an Eastern Hill State. Thus, the earlier rapport between the Mizo Union and the Congress was somewhat strained. Although the MU, under the Congress umbrella, did very well at the 1962 polls, it found in the rise of the Mizo National Front (MNF), a militant political adversary.

## THE FAMINE OF 1959 AND
## THE EVOLUTION OF THE MNF

The immediate impetus to the founding of the MNF could be traced to the famine of 1959, an acute natural disaster called Mautam.[8] During the famine, the relief measures provided by the Assam government were perceived as inadequate by all the political forces in the district. Thus, the members of the MU, as a symbolic gesture of protest, left the Congress Legislature Party and joined the APHLC. On the other hand, members of the EITU as well as others, formed the Mizo National Famine Front (MNFF) which combined its welfare activities with political activism. It also launched a newspaper called the *Voice of the Mizos*. After the relief work subsided, the organisation was rechristened as the Mizo National Front (MNF) with Laldenga as its President.[9]

. . . [It] is not without significance that in its initial phase, the MNF, despite its secessionist goal, participated in electoral politics. . . . In the 1962 elections, at the District Council level as well as in the Assam Legislative Assembly (where the district was allotted three seats), it did badly. But within a year it had wrested from the MU two seats in the interior of the district. Thus, in the Village Council elections held in 1963, as against the Mizo Union's 228 seats, the MNF had won 145. The Congress got 16, the EITU 12, and the Independents 10.[10]

However, the MNF, alongside its electoral participation was also strengthening its military wing—the Mizo National Army (MNA). It seems that its rank and file who had already been given training in arms (in adjacent areas of East Pakistan) could not be kept inactive for long, particularly after the breakaway of Vanlawama, a veteran secessionist, who prescribed violent means to achieve independence. Besides, with the unemployed youth providing the rank and file of the MNF, the nature of its support

---

[8] According to the Mizos, the *Mautam* has a fifty year cycle. A particular type of bamboo which grows in the area abundantly starts flowering after every 50 years. And when rats eat the seeds, their fertility increases tremendously. Consequently, the rodents attack the crops and eat them up. This happened in the first decade of the present century and recurred in 1959.

[9] Animesh Roy 1982: 132–4; Goswami 1979: 143–4.

[10] Roy 1982: 135.

structure coupled with the ideology as adumbrated by the MNF leadership had a logic of its own: action.

The MNF ideology had positive as well as negative aspects. To begin with, it emphasised the distinct identity of the Mizos as a nation incorporating the various tribal identities therein. According to Laldenga,

> *The Mizos from time immemorial lived in complete independence. . . . The Mizo country was subsequently brought under the British political control in December 1895, when a little more than half the country was arbitrarily carved out and named Lushai Hills and the rest of their land was parcelled out of their hands . . . the Mizo people are inseparably knitted together by their strong bond of tradition, custom, language, social life and religion wherever they are. The Mizo stood [sic] a separate nation, even before the advent of the British Government having a nationality distinct and separate from that of India.*[11]

Some of the veteran tribal heroes of the region were eulogised and battalions were named after them. . . . [T]he fact that these heroes belonged to the major Mizo ethnic groups, provided a certain degree of multi-ethnic symbol congruence to emphasise the politico-cultural identity of the Mizo people.

Alongside such selective tribal symbolism which were roused to facilitate tribal fervour and solidarity, Christianity and its values were also harnessed. As a powerful speaker and a devout Christian, Laldenga was perceived by many as a messiah. What he was projecting in his speeches was the vision of a millennium. A promise of the land of the Mizos also implied a land of Christians. Thus, tribal symbolism and Christianity were blended into a new political religion of the MNF which attracted the youth as well as others.

Implicit in such a vision of the Mizo Nation or Homeland of Mizos, the other ethnic groups, such as Hmar, Lakher, and Chakma, who asserted their identity as distinct from the Mizos, were played down in the discussion of the political identity of Mizoram. Nor were the territorial boundaries of the envisaged state spelt out clearly except through such appellations as the areas comprising the Mizo inhabitants in adjacent states, with Mizoram being the core area. However, the MNF assault in February 1966 was restricted to the Mizo District only.

---

[11] Cited in Nibedon 1980: 40.

The tribal-Christian component of the MNF ideology had, as its broad reference groups, the non-tribal/non-Christian plains people. These were projected and perceived as intruders and exploiters. The Centre and the state government of Assam were viewed as symbolic of such reference groups *vis-à-vis* whom a sense of discrimination and relative deprivation was evoked. Broadly speaking, the MNF maintained that the administration had failed to bring about economic development in the area. Secondly, in view of the lack of economic development, there were few jobs to absorb the increasing number of educated Mizos. As and when there were jobs, most of them were appropriated by non-Mizos. It is not without significance that the ideological stances of the MNF had a highly localistic as well as nativistic content. The 'freedom' slogan also implied the concern for the 'sons of the soil'.

Finally, using the word 'vai' (outsiders) in a somewhat derogatory sense, Laldenga maintained that the Mizos and other tribes of Assam did not consider themselves Indians in view of their socio-cultural distinctiveness and in any case, even when they joined India, it was with a clear understanding that the issue would be reopened after ten years. In a memorandum submitted to the Prime Minister of India in October 1965, the MNF stated that despite close contact and association with India since independence, the

> *Mizo people had not been able to feel at home with Indian [sic] or in India, nor have they been able to feel that their joys and sorrows have really ever been shared by India. They do not, therefore, feel Indian. They refused [sic] to occupy a place within India as they consider it to be unworthy of their national dignity and harmful to the interest of their posterity. Nationalism and patriotism inspired by the political consciousness has now reached its maturity and the cry for political self-determination is the only wish and aspiration of the people. It is, the only final and perfect embodiment of the social living for them. The only aspiration and political cry is the creation of Mizoram, a free and sovereign state to govern herself to work out her own destiny and to formulate her own foreign policy.*[12]

Alongside this subjective basis, the objective basis of the MNF had found expression in such phrases as the 'increase of Indian

---

[12] Goswami 1979: 149–51.

officers', 'economic frustration'. There is no doubt that coming as it did in the wake of the famine, the claims of the MNF evoked considerable support. In the process, they laid bare the economic stagnation of the area on the one hand and the poor development work of the government on the other.

With a solitary road linking Aizawl (the capital) to Silchar and with very few jeepable roads within the districts, the communication lines had remained unsatisfactory. Nor were there adequate water or electricity facilities. The traditional mode of shifting cultivation had hardly changed and even when people tried to grow cash crops, the market facilities were meagre. Besides, in industrial terms, Mizoram had remained one of the most backward districts of Assam.

There is no doubt that the consequences of an agelong insularity of the area could not be corrected easily. Nonetheless, the fact remained that the benefits of developmental grants from the state had not percolated down. Thus, as late as 1959, it was reported that more than half the families in the rural areas were indebted, with the main source of loan being the trader who in many cases was a non-Mizo.[13] With its high rate of literacy and equally high rate of unemployment, the nature and tenor of underdevelopment in the area became an effective source of political mobilisation. This was particularly so with the educated youth. Many of them were in their teens and they felt that they had highly limited opportunity structures for employment. And it was the youth who provided the cadre to the MNF, initially as volunteers and later as the rank and file of the new party. It is not without significance that out of the 40-odd legislators in the MNF's organisational structure in 1966, over half were graduates. Underemployed or unemployed as the youth was, it perceived in the MNF ideology and goal an explanation as well as an alternative to remedy its frustrations.

While the youth provided the major segment of the MNF, Laldenga had also succeeded in winning the support of the UMFO and MU factions which had nurtured secessionist ideas earlier. He also had the support of the local contractors who were unhappy with the Public Works Department being dominated by outsiders. Added to these were the chiefs who had lost their

[13] Roy Burman 1970: 223, 279.

privileges and rights under the new dispensation. Finally, there were the ex-servicemen who were enrolled during World War II and had been fairly exposed to the outside world. After independence, many of them were in the Assam regiment which was disbanded due to a number of reasons and these ex-servicemen had to come back to Mizoram. They had thus a grudge against the government. Those who joined the MNF trained the villagers in guerrilla activities.

An able organiser, Laldenga used traditional as well as modern devices to build up the MNF. Thus, the traditional tribal mode of dormitories (Zawlbuk), which had provided training and discipline to the tribal youth in the past and operated as a centre for conferring status and honour on the brave and worthy, was revived. The youth were given lectures on Mizo nationalism recalling the bravery of Mizos in the past, trained to use firearms and promised a place in the 'New Mizoram'. Besides, Laldenga showed an ingenuity in using the signal corps for dissemination of information as well as giving commands. As early as 1947, some young Mizos had formed an unofficial signal corps which transmitted messages in the Mizo language by Morse Code and through torch battery signals. This was developed to the extent that any news in the Mizo District could be transmitted from one corner to another in a couple of hours. This mode of communication was used so effectively by the MNF that after the MNF uprising, the government decided to ban the sale of torch cells as well as torches, for some time.

Alongside the mode of communication within the district, the MNF also had regular contacts in erstwhile East Pakistan and China where training was given to members of the MNF. Arms as well as ammunition were also procured. By 1965, the MNF had formed a shadow government called Mizoram Sarkar (Mizoram government) with Laldenga as its President. A detailed blueprint for the executive, bicameral legislature (senate and house of representatives) and judiciary was also worked out. Last but not the least, an important part of the underground network was the Mizo National Army in which the MNF ex-servicemen played an important role. They were assigned ranks by the MNF leaders which were much higher than the ones they had held earlier. Promises of a bright future were made to them. The MNA formed battalions which were named after the well-known Mizo legendary heroes. Many girls also joined the MNA. As MNF volunteers, they acted as intelligence personnel.[14]

On 1 March 1966 the MNF declared its independence. The MNA launched attacks on the key centres of defence and administration. For nearly a week, the civilian installations, Assam Rifles, and the Border Security Forces were the special targets of the insurgents. The Aizawl-Silchar road which linked the district with the rest of the country was unusable as the bridge was blown up. It took the army a week to make its presence felt and almost a month before it could re-establish its effective control. The MNF was declared illegal and its hard core escaped to East Pakistan. However, it continued its hit and run activities.[15]

The MNF revolt indicated that while the proclamation of independence was easy, its sustenance was not. Nor was it possible for the government to exterminate insurgency altogether. The insurgency was a manifestation of the weakening of the earlier Mizo insularity, its increasing exposure to the world beyond it, and the mobilisation of a certain section of the Mizo society by insurgent leadership in ethnic terms. . . . In the wake of the secessionist move of the MNF, the immediate response of the government was that of a counter-insurgency operation. However, the long-term perspective of a political-economic solution of the insurgency was not obviated either. . . .

In addition to banning the MNF, the Mizo District was declared a Disturbed Area under the Assam Disturbed Area Act of 1955, extending the powers of the civil and military administration. Alongside, the Armed Forces Special Powers Act, 1958 was also invoked. These acts gave wide-ranging powers to the military to cope with the insurgency. . . .

However, the most significant strategy of the counter-insurgency was the regrouping of villages, leading to the shifting of remote villages to a vantage point, especially along the main road. These were called Protected and Progressive Villages (PPV). The regrouping was also done along secondary roads. It was only in 1970 that the army handed over the control of these areas to the civilians. In the process, about 80 per cent of the rural population

---

[14] Goswami 1979: 161. For details on the military strength of the MNF see Johri, 1970: 206–8.

[15] For details of the MNF's activities during 1966–79, see Nibedon 1980.

was shifted. Such a move certainly disturbed the traditional style of living of the Mizos and while it was officially justified partly as a counter-insurgency measure but more so, as a measure which could facilitate the development of the area through the clustering of villages, there is no doubt that the removal of the Mizos from their habitat coupled with the military supervision and control in the area did provide more recruits to the MNF, at least initially.[16] However, though the political and administrative machinery was disrupted for a while, it was gradually restored.

While no elections could be held in 1967, the government decided to hold them in 1970 to bring about political normalcy and also routinise electoral politics. By this time, the MU disassociated itself from the All Party Hill Leaders Conference and instead of seeking the old APHLC demand of a hill state of all the hill districts, it sought a separate status of a state for Mizoram within the Indian Union. The MU won the elections decisively with the Congress trailing behind. Interestingly, three ex-MNF members (who had surrendered or were released after serving their jail terms) who contested as the Congress candidates lost the election.

In 1972, after the formation of Mizoram as a Union Territory, the MU held on its own once again. However, in 1974 it decided to join the Congress, a step which seemed to be its own undoing. On the one hand, such a move provided an impetus to the Mizo militants and, on the other, gave a push to Brigadier Sailo's newly formed party—the People's Conference—with its emphasis on the protection of human rights. There is no doubt that as regards the common man, caught as he was between the crossfire of the military and the militants, the People's Conference was perceived as an alternative worth trying.

In the April 1984 elections, however, the PC lost to the Congress. With the 'returnees' seeking refuge in the Congress since the late 1960s, the Congress could be viewed as comprising a significant component of the ex-MNF who had abjured violence and had resorted to electoral politics. The Congress Chief Minister Lalthanhawala, for example, was imprisoned during 1966–67 and again in 1968. In 1973 he became the President of the party.

---

[16] For an incisive account of the implications of village groupings see Rangaswami 1978: 653–62.

Though the peace parleys between Laldenga and the government proved abortive in 1976 and also in 1980, it was evident that, within the Congress, there were persons in close touch with Laldenga.[17]

## 'RETURNEES' AND NEW RECRUITS

At this point, the nature and character of the insurgency as it had evolved over the last two decades requires a perusal. With the creation of Bangladesh, the Mizo base in the Chittagong Hill Tracts had to be shifted. Subsequently, though with the Chittagong Hill Tract tribals rising in arms against Dacca, the Mizo rebels did find in them an ally, yet the earlier extent of underground manoeuvrability was lost to them in the area. Besides, the fairly liberal terms of amnesty seemed to provide adequate impetus to a number of insurgents to surrender. Though personal experiences, a sense of adventurism and kinship networks did prompt a number of young men and women to go underground, the proportion of 'returnees' seemed to be much larger than the new recruits. And though there were a few cases of vendetta, yet their absorption by the state Congress itself was telling.

More so, by 1978, factionalism within the MNF[18] had come into the open, with Laldenga resigning from the Presidentship, and Biakchunga, the Army Chief, elected the new President. As the emissary of the MNF in his parleys with the representatives of the Centre, Laldenga perhaps had already fallen foul with some of his underground comrades. Nonetheless, he had retrieved his position as the President of the MNF in no time. During 1980–82 his negotiations with the Centre clearly indicated that he was prepared to settle for statehood for Mizoram provided he was made the Chief Minister. Needless to add, the then Chief Minister, Brigadier Sailo, was not in a mood to oblige the insurgent leader.

There is no doubt that nothing could have been more propitious for Laldenga in this respect than the victory of the Congress in 1984 for which he could also take some credit by supporting

---

[17] For the linkages of the Congress with the MNF as well as the ups and downs in the peace parleys, see Hemendra Narayan 1984a, 1984b.

[18] For details on factionalism within the MNF see Nibedon 1980: 204–62.

it through a tape-recorded message.[19] His unilateral command to cease-fire from his self-imposed exile in England, and his abnegation of the demand for secession to the late Mrs Gandhi in his correspondence, indicated that politics in Mizoram had turned a full circle.

It may be mentioned that in 1976 Laldenga had made a similar promise but it broke down in no time. However, 1984 was not 1976. Unlike the earlier time, the Church leaders threw their weight in the peace parleys. More so, the willingness of the Congress Chief Minister to step down in favour of his one-time chief, provided other terms and conditions could be mutually settled, was a significant factor at this juncture.

These were spelt out in a Memorandum of Settlement signed on 30 June 1986 between Laldenga, the Union Home Secretary, R.D. Pradhan and the Chief Secretary of Mizoram, Lalkhama. On its part, the MNF promised to take steps to end underground activities, ensure the surrender of insurgents with their arms and ensure their return to civilian life. The Centre agreed to accord statehood to Mizoram and the requisite assistance to help the Mizoram government rehabilitate the insurgents. It also promised certain constitutional guarantees (as provided to certain states and regions under Article 371) for the religious or social practices of the Mizos, Mizo customary laws and procedures, administration of civil and customary justice according to Mizo customary laws and, finally, regulation of ownership as well as transfer of land to the Mizos.[20]

As an unwritten part of the accord, the ruling Congress-I Ministry resigned and an interim coalition government with Laldenga as the Chief Minister and Lalthanhawala as the Deputy Chief Minister took over in August 1986. This was an interim government for six months after which elections were held. The MNF won 25 seats with the Congress getting 12 and the PC trailing behind with 3 seats. The movement party had an impressive victory in Aizawl—the capital—as also in the district as a whole (23 out of 28 seats). In Lunglei district, it had modest success capturing 3 out of 7 seats. In the southern district of Chimptui

---

[19] Sumanta Sen 1984: 30–31.
[20] For the full text of the accord see India, Ministry of Information and Broadcasting, *Mizoram Accord* 1986.

pui, mostly inhabited by non-Mizo ethnic groups (Pawi, Lakher, Chakma, etc.), it drew a blank.[21] Even earlier, these groups had not supported the activities of the MNF, presumably because they perceived, in the collective appellation of Mizo identity, a majoritarian thrust.

Herein lay the ambivalence in the use of the term 'Mizo' which was manipulated by the leadership of various political groups as it suited them. Thus, at one level, the census category of Mizo referred to the differentiation between 'Mizo tribes' and others. At the state level however, the term 'Mizoram' could be interpreted as the land of all the hillmen or the land of Mizo tribes. Finally, the concept of greater Mizoram referred to the amalgamation of tribal constellations in the adjacent states. In his statements Laldenga used the term 'Mizo' as a people, as a 'nation'. His emphasis was not merely on the dominant-subordinate relationship between the 'outsiders' and 'insiders', the plainsmen and the hillsmen but also between the frontier area as the periphery and the Centre. Though projected in ethnic terms, the Mizo demand for self-determination had strong political and economic implications for the tribal people.

As mentioned earlier, the village regrouping scheme had virtually disrupted the tribal habitat. In the late 1970s, the tribal people were allowed to return to their respective villages. However, as they were placed under their respective parent group centres, the issues pertaining to an integrated programme of development in various areas were skewed. More so, in the three vital areas of food, water and roads, the performances of successive governments appeared to be tardy. What is more, the development grant from the Centre increased appreciably over the decades without much development. 'It seems,' commented an observer 'that those concerned with development have given greater priority to such schemes as construction of warehouses, though there is little to store, and to the development of industries, for which neither the raw materials nor skilled hands are available.'[22] In view of the insurgency, coupled with the strategic importance of the state, its leadership made strong claims on the Centre for greater assistance. In the wake of the

[21] Vipin Pubby 1987.
[22] C. Narayana Rao 1984: 242.

one-time insurgents turning into the governing elite, the issue of development remained equally pertinent in another way. A state ravaged by conflict required rehabilitation. In the absence of private entrepreneurs and landed interests, the resources in the hands of the governing elite continued to be considerable. However, going by the past record, its distributive nexus seemed to be corroded. Belonging to a small group, the wielders of political power, circulating among various political groups, while raising the issues of economic exploitation and social injustice tended to be in effect partners in perpetuating the unequal hierarchical system. The Mizo movement did provide an aggregation of the Mizo identity in the socio-political realm, but Mizo ethnicity hardly reckoned with the issues of exploitation and social justice, in effect.

# Time, Self, and Community: Features of the Sikh Militant Discourse[*]

## VEENA DAS

In this paper I shall examine the construction of the Sikh militant discourse in the Punjab in recent years. This discourse is part of the political language being evolved by the militant movement to create a politically active group and to forge an effective unity among the Sikhs. Thus, a 'we' group is sought to be created out of a heterogeneous community that can function as an effective political agency in the context of the structures of the modern state in India. It is interesting, therefore, to see that this discourse functions through a series of rigorous dualisms in which masculine and feminine, Hindu and Sikh, and state and community, function as counter concepts. However, it is important to remember that not all these concepts have the same status. Some oppositions such as that of masculine and feminine are seen as belonging to nature; others are seen as products of history. The rigorous dualisms as part of an unstable, evolving, political language are new; they bear the stamp of contemporaneity, and some may well become neutralised in course of time. Hence it is important to see that the militant discourse sees the sacred and the eternal as breaking into modern political events. This is characteristic of the language through which linguistic and political self-recognition is sought to be created among the Sikhs, but this language is part

* Excerpted from Veena Das, Time, Self, and Community: Features of the Sikh Militant Discourse, *Contributions to Indian Sociology* 1992, n.s. 26: 245–59.

of the contemporary political culture in India rather than being a trace or remnant of the past.

The emergence of a militant movement among the Sikhs, both in India and among emigrant Sikhs, is an important phenomenon of the last decade. It is not my intention to provide a comprehensive account of this complex process here, for which the reader may refer to the excellent 'Introduction' in Kapur (1987). What concerns me in this paper is the period between 1981 and 1984, when Sikh leaders led a series of mass civil disobedience campaigns against the Indian government for the fulfilment of several demands. It was also the period when the use of terror and violence for the fulfilment of Sikh demands began to be defended. These demands had been most clearly articulated in a document known as the Anandpur Sahib Resolution, which had been adopted by the Working Committee of a major regional party of the Sikhs—the Akali Dal—in 1973. Depending upon the context in which this document is being articulated, it can be read as either asking for greater autonomy for the Punjab within a federal structure of the state in India or for an independent state of Khalistan. For example, in defending the Resolution in forums of all opposition parties, Sikh leaders have argued that it asks for greater autonomy for the different states in India, but at meetings addressed by militant leaders in many *gurudwaras* it has been explicitly articulated as providing the charter for the Sikh struggle for a separate homeland. . . .

I shall analyse a selection of the written and oral discourses which were produced in the period under discussion (1981–1984) by the Sikh militants. My analysis of the written discourse is taken from the monthly magazine *Shamsher Dast*, which was the organ of the All India Sikh Students Federation till it was banned in 1982; some of the published reports of the Shiromani Gurudwara Prabandhak Committee, and two prominent publications, the *Khalsa Times* and the *Akal Times*. For the analysis of the oral discourse I have depended upon the lectures given by Bhindranwale and some other militant leaders in the *gurudwaras*, especially at Mehta Chowk and in Amritsar. These recordings of meetings at which lectures were delivered are not easily available at present, but they enjoyed a wide circulation as recorded lectures during the period under discussion.

It is the characteristic of the written discourse that it strives towards a rational organisation of ideas. Further, the tone of the written discourse often varies according to the assumed addressee. At one level the 'you' of the oral discourse is directly present to the speaker which gives it the character of a performance, and allows the use of many kinds of rhetorical strategies by the use of voice and body. At another level the oral discourse also addresses certain absent others in which the people present become an audience to an imaginary conversation between the speaker and the presumed addressee. This is especially true when the state is sought to be addressed. Both the cases we are discussing belong to political rhetoric and there are certain imperatives which are embedded in both kinds of discourse, making them closer to performative forms of speech acts. The emotional role of several tropes such as synecdoche, irony and metonymy in the organisation of such discourse has been noted by several authors (cf. Friedrich 1989) and is amply demonstrated in the militant literature. Let us turn to the main features of this discourse.

## TIME, SELF, AND OTHER

In the most direct forms of speech, the aim of the militant movement is expressed in terms of an anxiety over the preservation of a separate Sikh identity. The greatest threat to this identity is seen to be the Hindu character and the state in India. Through a series of interesting slippages these come to stand for each other.

The movement for the preservation of Sikh identity is framed in a language that immediately places it in the context of modern nation-states since it is replete with references to rights of minorities, the international covenants and the centrality of territory as a means of preserving identity. Yet, as mentioned earlier, this struggle is also represented as a continuation of a series of struggles that Sikhs have had to wage in history in order to preserve their identity. By imputing an identity of events and return of certain key constellations in the history of the Sikhs, a contemporaneity is established between non-contemporaneous events. The function of language here is to create an optical illusion of the contemporaneity of the non-contemporaneous which comes to be encapsulated in the use of words. Language then functions more to *produce* a particular reality rather than to *represent* it. In this sense neither Sikh identity nor Hindu identity can be treated as having an unchanging essence—rather, these are identities that are produced anew in every period and narratives of the past are part of the process of producing these identities.

In this narrative, the Sikh community is defined in the contemporary period with reference to certain key events of the past, which emphasise the building up of the community on the basis of its heroic deeds. Thus, the construction of memory in this case is strongly tied up with the construction of a concrete identity, and, as Assmann (1988) has noted, this has a positive aspect (that is how we are) and a negative aspect (that is our opposite). In other words, the self is given shape and form by opposing it to its 'others'. There are two communities that are posited as the counterpoints of the Sikh community, the relevant others, in the building of this narrative. The first are the Muslims, as holders of power in the medieval period, whose unjust practices the Sikh gurus had consistently defied. However, the position of the Muslims in the modern period as a 'minority' resembles the position of the Sikhs. This is an interesting example of the manner in which political exigencies have led to a redistribution of attributes among the three terms in the triad of Hindu/Sikh/Muslim. For a long period of their history, the Sikhs represented historical events in terms of the antinomies between the Sikhs and Muslims in which Hindus were the weak partners of the Sikhs. These antinomies played an important role in the construction of popular imagination until the partition of India. It is therefore significant that the strong opposition between Sikh and Muslim is neutralised in contemporary militant discourse.

The second opposing community is that of the Hindus who are represented as weak, effeminate and cunning—people towards whom the Sikhs are shown to have had contempt but whom they consistently protected. The emergence of this particular dualism reflects the reverse process to that of the neutralisation of the Sikh/Muslim dualism mentioned earlier. The self of the Sikh as it emerges from this particular organisation of images is that of the martyr whose sacrifices have fed the community with its energy in the past, while the Hindu is weak and effeminate or cunning and sly. In both cases the Hindu 'character' is envisaged in terms of the dangers that it poses to the masculinity of the Sikh.

Even when there are differences of emphasis an important image in all these texts is that of *charkhi chadhna* and *khopdi utarvana*—i.e., being slowly ground to death over a churning wheel, or offering one's head at the stake—punishments that the defiant Sikhs are said to have received from the Mughal emperors.

Consider the following example in which the construction of the past and the construction of the self appear as conjoint themes.

> History has always been repeating itself. Sikh people passed through such a critical phase after the death of Banda Bahadur Baba Gurbaksh Singh in 1716, that some historians called it the darkest period of Sikh history. . . . Time again took a new turn with the martyrdom of Bhai Mani Singh in 1734 AD. . . . In this way began once again the era of struggle for the Sikhs which subsequently was converted into the golden age of the Sikhs. Which sacrifice is there in the history of the world that Sikhs had not to pay for this conversion? A terribly dark route from the teeth of *'charkhi'* to the edge of the sword was traversed. Every inch of the land where we today have assembled was covered with the precious blood of the Khalsa. Then and then only could we harness the days when Kashmir, Jamraud and Ladakh bowed before the Kesri Nisan Sahib and Nanak-Shahi coins could replace the Muslim one's [sic].[1]

Just as the heroic character of the Sikh is sought to be established through a particular reading of Sikh history in terms of their defiance of the powerful Muslim rulers, so the character of the Hindu, the negative 'other' of the Sikh, is established through the historical narrative of the modern period pertaining to the nationalist movement. It is the consistent complaint of the writers of these journals that the contributions of the Sikhs in the creation of modern India have been undermined by the Hindu chroniclers of the nationalist movement. By a careful choice of episodes which happened primarily in the Punjab, they are able to argue that the sacrifices of the Sikhs were far weightier than the sacrifices of the other communities, and yet Sikh symbols such as the *nishan sahib*—the flag—which used to fly over Lahore in the times of Raja Ranjit Singh were given no recognition in modern India. The people responsible for this denial to the Sikhs of their rightful

[1] 'Message to the Delegates of the First Annual Dal Khalsa Conference', held at Gurdaspur, 8 to 9 December 1979, by S. Gajinder Singh, Panch Dal Khalsa.

place in history are the Hindus who have bestowed modern India with their own 'effeminate' and 'cunning' character through their dominance of the state apparatus as well as the ideology of the nation.

Let me take as example a poster circulated by the All India Sikh Students' Federation entitled, '*Lala Lajpat Rai di maut kiven hoi?*' (How did Lala Lajpat Rai die?). Addressed to the Sikhs, the first paragraph reads as follows:

> The politicians of India have always tried to keep the minorities suppressed. We have a well-known saying that a Hindu does not kill a snake. He asks the Muslim to kill the snake. The meaning of this is that if the snake dies, an enemy dies. But if the snake bites the Muslim then its meaning will also be that an enemy will die. This saying makes the character of the Hindu crystal clear—of what temperament are they the masters.

The poster then goes on to exemplify the character of the Hindus through the discussion of a historical event. It mentions the visit of the Simon Commission in 1928 and the decision taken by several prominent politicians in the Punjab to boycott it. A procession was organised, according to this poster, by the Akali Dal with the help of several Muslims and Congressmen to greet the members of the Commission with black flags. Thirty thousand people came to protest against the visit of the Simon Commission, of whom 19,000 to 20,000 were Sikhs.

According to the poster, the story of Lala Lajpat Rai's so-called heroism is as follows:

The procession was being led by Master Tara Singh, Lala Lajpat Rai, Dr Satpal Dang and Abdul Kadar, when a *lathi* charge against it was ordered. According to the poster, Gopi Chand, Satpal Dang and Abdul Kadar were wounded. Lala Lajpat Rai received one *lathi* blow on the head but was protected by his umbrella. This is why he could continue to lead the procession to its final destination. The procession was organised on 30 October 1928. Lala Lajpat Rai died of heart failure on 17 November. Yet, his death was linked with the *lathi* charge and it was circulated that as he lay wounded, he had uttered the famous words that every *lathi* falling on his body would become a nail in the coffin of the British Raj.

Even as the misrepresentation of events in this and several

other such posters would be easy to show, the truth that history books linked the event with Lala Lajpat Rai and the protest organised by the Congress, understating or ignoring the contribution of the others, can hardly be denied. Indeed, as many historians (especially those writing under the genre of Subaltern Studies) have pointed out, there has been a tendency in nationalist history writing to assimilate local histories into the master narrative of nationalist history, with agency being vested in the nationalist leadership alone.[2] What is interesting from my point of view, however, is that the author of this poster is not content to challenge the national narrative and expand the consciousness of the reader by giving voice to the silences in this narrative. There is a further move to establish that the history of the Sikhs which is inscribed on the body of the martyr is a reflection of Sikh character while the history of the Indian nation, in that it takes the character of the Hindu as paradigmatic of national character, becomes nothing more and nothing less than a writing of Hindu history. This point becomes clearer if we turn our attention to the construction of masculinity as the defining feature of the Sikh community.

## COMMUNITY, KIN, AND MASCULINITY

Anderson (1983: 131) has drawn attention to the fact that the style of thought in which large collectivities such as the nation are invested with the status of a 'natural' entity often involves the use of kinship terms as metaphors for defining the relationship between individual and collectivity. Such metaphors are used extensively in the oral discourse of the militants to create a sense of community. What is specific to the Sikh militant discourse, however, is the emphasis on ties between *men* as the defining ties of community. In one of his speeches Bhindranwale stated, '*khalsa ji* (you, who are the pure ones), the Sikhs are the sons of the true king Guru Gobind Singh *ji*. Now you know that a son must resemble his father. If the son does not resemble his father, then you know the term used for him. If he does not behave like his father, then people begin to view him with suspicion. They say

---

[2] See the five volumes of *Subaltern Studies* edited by Ranajit Guha (1982–1987).

the Sikhs are the descendants of Hindus. Are they pointing a finger at our pure ancestry—how can a Sikh bear to be called any one else's son?'

In the written discourse, the position of Mahatma Gandhi as the Father of the Nation is contested on the grounds that it was the sacrifices of the Sikhs that are said to have brought independence to the country. In the oral discourse there is a palpable anxiety about the non-violence and passivity implied in a movement based upon principles of non-violence, because of its feminine character. In one of his speeches, Bhindranwale propounded the idea that it was an insult for the Sikhs to be included in a nation that considered Mahatma Gandhi to be its father, for his techniques of fighting were quintessentially feminine. He was symbolised by the *charkha*, the spinning wheel, which was a symbol of women. 'Can those', asked the Sikh leader, 'who are the sons of the valiant guru, whose symbol is the sword, ever accept a woman like Mahatma as their *father*? Those are the techniques of the weak, not of a race that has never bowed its head before any injustice—a race whose history is written in the blood of martyrs.'

Thus, the construction of the past in terms of a genealogy of father/son relations is also a construction of the self and the other. Through the particular narrative web of Sikh history as a history of martyrs, a Sikh character is sought to be simultaneously created of which the negative counterpart is the Hindu character. The dangers of a 'Hindu' history are not just that Sikhs are denied their rightful place in history but also, as many of the authors state, it is a conspiracy to make the martial Sikhs into a weak race.

> . . . the Sikhs have been softened and conditioned during the last fifty years to bear and put up with insults to their religion and all forms of other oppression, patiently and without demur, under the sinister preaching and spell of the narcotic cult of non-violence, much against the clear directive of their Gurus, their Prophets, not to turn the other cheek before a tyrant, not to take lying down any insult to their religion, their self-respect, and their human dignity.[3]

The danger is not of a heroic confrontation with a masculine

---

[3] See *They massacre Sikhs*. A White Paper by the Sikh Religious Parliament (Shiromani Gurudwara Prabandhak Committee), Amritsar. Date not given.

other, but that the feminine other will completely dissolve the masculine self of the Sikh. 'With such an enemy', says one warning, 'even your story will be wiped out from the face of the earth'.

In view of this particular articulation of community as the community of men, it is not surprising that there are direct exhortations in the oral discourse to the Sikhs to shed their femininity. The most visible sign of the masculinity of the Sikh in this discourse is his sword. In many speeches there is the simple exhortation, '*shastrdhari howo*', become the bearer of weapons. In one of his speeches Bhindranwale cites an example from the mythology surrounding the saint-poet Tulasidas. Pleased with the poet, Lord Rama appeared in person before him to give him *darshan* (a privileged viewing). Tulasidas, however, saw that Rama did not have his bow and arrow with him, and he refused to bow before him saying, 'Tulasi's head will only bow before you when you have the bow and arrow in your hand'. The question as to how the militant leader took an example from what is considered a sacred Hindu text will be taken up later. Here I want to juxtapose it with stories of a different genre, that derived from the experiences of modernity. In one of his speeches Bhindranwale referred to the fact that Indian Airlines and Air India do not allow Sikhs to carry their swords into the aircraft. He then stated, 'If a Hindu can wear his sacred thread (*janeu*) which is his sign, why can't a Sikh carry his sword?' . . .

The sword is the sign of the masculinity of the Sikh that is external and a product of history. The other visible sign of Sikh masculinity is his beard. Bhindranwale exhorts the Sikhs to let their beards grow. 'If you do not want beards then you should ask the women to become men and you become women. Or else ask nature that it should stop this growth on your faces. Then there will be no need to exhort you to wear long beards. Then there will be no need for me to preach (*prachar karna*), no need to break my head on this (lit., *matha khapai karna*).' Another leader, a functionary of the Akali Dal, stated that the flowing beard of the Sikh man is a direct challenge to the authority of the state. When the threat to the Sikh community is articulated, it is often stated that 'they' have their eyes on 'your' sword, on 'your' beard (*ona di nazar twadi kirpan te hai—ona di nazar twadi dadi te hai*). Thus, we see the same theme of the feminine other destroying the community by robbing it of its masculinity and bestowing on it a feminine character.

## TIME, REPETITION, AND WILFUL FORGETTING

The construction of the past and the present in the mode of repetition becomes the major cognitive tool through which a single and rigid character is sought to be bestowed upon the Sikh community on the one hand, and the Hindu community on the other. There is no willingness to subject the character of the community to chances of transformation. This is directly tied up with the obsession to mechanically analogise new events to a limited stock of past events. Such a view of the past does not allow for freedom from the arrested preconceptions about the Sikh character, hence from the *idée fixe* that every future event repeats the past, and can only be understood within the framework of repetition. Thus the assassins of Mrs Gandhi are seen to be reincarnations of two characters, Sukha Singh and Mehtab Singh, who had avenged the desecration of Harmandar Sahib (the Golden Temple in Amritsar) by a small Muslim chieftain, Massarangara, in 1752 by assassinating him. Similarly, even the sacrificial death of young Sikh children is eulogised as evidence of the heroic character of the Sikhs, a repetition of the past sacrifices of the two young sons of Guru Gobind Singh. It is not that there is no outrage at such events, but it becomes a muted link in the master narratives of Sikh history and Sikh character.

As may be expected, such a unified master narrative that absorbs in itself all voices within the community cannot be built without a systematic 'forgetting'. In the master narrative of Sikh history, this forgetting is essentially of the close links between Hindus and Sikhs—the bonds of language, common mythology, shared worship, and the community created through exchanges in everyday life (just as the bonds with Persian, with Urdu poetry, with important elements of Islamic ideology, and the everyday relations with Muslims were forgotten in the traumatic period of communal violence in the late 1940s in the Punjab). In fact, the participation of the Sikhs in the communal riots against the Muslims, testimony of which is not only present in textbooks of history but in the personal lives of the people, is not acknowledged at all. All the darker aspects of the past are purged by being projected on the Hindus.[4]

As one example of this kind of 'forgetting', incidents of communal tensions from the 1920s are discussed primarily in terms of Hindu-Muslim conflicts as if the Sikhs did not figure in these at all. Under the subheading, 'It happened before', the White Paper prepared by the SGPC, *They massacre Sikhs* (see fn. 3), states the following:

> This phenomenon in which Sikh religious sensibility is calculatedly outraged and their human dignity cruelly injured, has its historical antecedents in this part of the world. It was in the late twenties of this century that a cultural ancestor of the present anti-Sikh Hindu urban crust [*sic*] wrote and published a small book, purporting to be a research-paper in history under the title of *Rangila Rasul*: 'Mohammad, the pleasure loving Prophet'. . . . The entire Muslim world of India writhed in anguish at this gross insult to and attack on the Muslim community but they were laughed at and chided by the citified Hindu press of Lahore. . . . But the process of events that led to bloody communal riots in various parts of India till the creation of India and Pakistan and the partition of the country itself, with tragic losses in men, money and property, is directly and rightly traceable to a section of the majority community exemplified in the matter of *Rangila Rasul*. . . ' *(pp. 29–30).*

The first act of wilful forgetting, then, is related to the purging of the community of any evil, now projected on to 'the citified Hindu majority'. The second act of forgetting is to construe all acts of violence, both those directed within the Sikh community in such institutional practices as feud, and those directed outward in communal violence, as the violence of martyrdom. Finally is

---

[4] The relation between memory and forgetting in constituting the community has been noted in many contexts in recent years. In a very interesting paper, Gross (1986) shows the importance of memory in the resistance to totalitarianism, and of simultaneous forgetting for the construction of community as purged of its past evil in the case of Polish-Jewish relations during the Second World War. He comments powerfully on the Polish conviction that 'a halfway victory over totalitarianism's attempts to destroy social solidarity would still be won if the community's history were rescued from the regime's ambition to determine not only the country's future but also its past.' Yet the same Polish people developed elaborate myths to conceal from themselves the nature of Polish-Jewish relations and the anti-Semitism in Polish society which led to both covert and overt support being given to the fascist ideology of scapegoating the Jew.

the assumption that the state is an *external institution*, in fact a Hindu institution that has been imposed upon the Sikh community rather than created through the practices prevalent in the region itself. In the next section I discuss in greater detail the last two processes which allow the Sikh community to absolve itself from all blame in relation to the corrupt practices of the institution of the state which are projected on to the Hindu character.

## INDIVIDUAL BIOGRAPHY, SOCIAL TEXT, AND VIOLENCE

What are the processes by which the community manages to suppress from collective memory the individual memories of some events such as the participation of Sikhs in the riots and abduction of women at the time of the partition of India, and sanctify other memories such as the oppression and illegalities of the police against the Sikhs in the present context? To my mind, this question is intimately related to the issue of how individual biography becomes social text.

One of the most important characteristics of the oral discourse under discussion is its use of detailed local knowledge through which people are recognised and named and their individual misery transformed into the misfortunes of the community. In every meeting addressed by Bhindranwale, there is detailed use of local examples. For instance, he would say, 'Ajaib Singh[5] from village Todda, who is present here—the police came one night and dragged his son away and the whole night they tortured him with hot iron rods. Is this not a sign of the *gulami* (slavery) of the Sikhs in India?'

Sometimes expression is given to the most tabooed subjects if they relate to police excesses. For example, at one meeting Bhindranwale pointed to an old man who was present in the congregation and stated that the man had been dragged to the police station in Ferozepur along with his daughter and that they forced him to have sexual relations with her (*onane pyo dhi vich sambandh karaya*, lit., they made the father and daughter have a relation). It would seem from these examples that local knowledge

---

[5] Names of persons and villages have been altered here.

of police atrocities and its reiteration in the context of the narratives of the community is very important in our understanding
of how the state comes to be experienced in everyday life and
how this experience is transformed in the making of a violent
community.

Once the community becomes the conduit through which the
individual experience of having been violated can be seen as
the experience of the whole community, the next step is to
explain the violence committed by the community against others
as a response to injustice. References to violence abound in the
speeches of Bhindranwale and other militant leaders and they
are framed by the creation of active and passive solidarities
around victims of violence belonging to the Sikh community.
For example, in one of the speeches Bhindranwale refers to
some villagers who came to Guru Teg Bahadur and exhorted
him as the true king to protect them from the raids of Muslim
soldiers. After they had represented their case repeatedly for
three days, the Guru replied that he did not wish to hear that
they had been raided; he wished to hear what reply they had
given to the raiders. This is followed by the exhortation that
those who had insulted the Sikh faith, burnt the sacred book,
and made the women of the Sikhs naked could only be made
to 'board the train'—a favourite colloquial expression used by
Bhindranwale to refer to the act of killing/assassination.

It is important to appreciate the juxtaposition of the stories of
how Sikhs had been insulted and oppressed, the allusions to
mythology and folklore about the past heroic deeds of the Sikhs,
and the exhortations to violence. Where active agency is vested
in the Sikh as killer, it is framed there by the context of the fight
for justice. Corresponding to this is the imperative that an armed
Sikh should not kill someone who is unarmed.

It is well-known that many killings by the militants have been
done not in heroic confrontation with an armed adversary, but
by ambushing unarmed people and shooting them unawares.
There is considerable ambiguity in references made to these kinds
of killings, which are represented as acts by people who were out
of control. For instance, in the context of the murder of Lala Jagat
Narain by armed militants, it is stated that he was publishing
insulting remarks about the President of the SGPC (Sri Gurudwara
Prabandhak Committee); that he had written an article saying

that the latter's passport should be impounded and that even after being warned he continued to write ignoble things about the Sikhs in his newspaper. As Bhindranwale said in his speech, 'Finally some lover (of the Sikhs) could not restrain himself and he made him mount the train'. In the written discourse, the more formal language—'finally his murder happened'—replaces the colloquial usage. The common point, however, is that in both cases agency is deleted.

The effort to justify the use of violence is further supported by reflections about the nature of the present. It is repeatedly stated that this particular moment in history is pregnant with new possibilities. It only requires conviction and the capacity to sacrifice in order to ensure that the brief period of Sikh glory during the Sikh rule can be revived again. Precisely because the nature of time is seen as extraordinary, it is also assumed that ordinary morality does not apply. In various warnings that were issued both in written and oral forms to individuals seen to be opposing the Sikhs, the threats were framed by references to the particularity of the historical moment. 'We would regret if something were to happen to you—but the time is such that every action has to be geared towards the recovery of the lost Sikh glory.'

By what process does the state, which is seen as the major aggressor, come to stand for the citified Hindu? First of all this is done by creating a genealogy and an ancestry for the holders of office. The then Prime Minister, Indira Gandhi, is always referred to as '*Pandatan de ghar jammi*'—she who was born in the house of the Pandits. Others are either referred to as born of Brahmins, if they belong to high castes, or as belonging to groups which had earlier suffered all kinds of humiliation (those who did not have the permission to wear the sacred thread, those who were not permitted to ride a horse, those who had to perform weddings at night because they were not allowed to take bridal parties through the streets in the morning). In either case, their rule is declared illegitimate because of their ancestry. The Brahmin's task was not to rule but to provide ritual service, while the lower castes were subservient in both ritual and power hierarchies. But typical of this discourse is the juxtaposition of this kind of reasoning with a logic derived from contemporary, democratic societies. Thus, Indira Gandhi's rule was illegitimate because she was born in a family of Pandits, because she was a woman, because she was a widow, but also because in a speech she had said that if the Sikhs demanded a homeland then Sikhs living outside the Punjab would be subjected to civil violence, thereby admitting that the state was unable to protect its citizens.

There is a great distrust of alternate definitions of the Sikh community. This comes to the fore in the relation of the Sikh militants with communities on the peripheries of Sikhism itself. One such case is that of the Nirankaris, who may be considered a sectarian development within Sikhism itself. However, since the followers of this sect worship a living guru, contrary to orthodox Sikh teaching, they were declared to be enemies of the *panth* in 1973 by priests of the Golden Temple. In April 1978, some of Bhindranwale followers clashed violently with the Nirankaris on the holy day of Vaisakhi in Amritsar. There were deaths and injuries on both sides. Some Nirankaris were arrested but were later found to have acted in self-defence. In April 1980 the Nirankari guru was assassinated and several murders of Nirankaris followed. In the reporting of these episodes in the militant litera-ture, the very use of Sikh symbols by the Nirankaris is considered an insult. Although it is acknowledged that the Nirankaris were a historical sect with close connections with the Sikhs, their present forms of worship are considered unacceptable and they are declared to be 'counterfeit Nirankaris'. By a mental exchange of images it is not the Nirankaris who are seen to be the victims of the violence by the militants but rather the Sikh community which is the victim. Further, they are declared to be agents of the Hindu government whose only mission is to destroy the Sikhs. Yet, a certain ambivalence towards the violence directed against them by the militants is discernible in the phrase with which the killing of the Nirankari Baba is described: *'akhir ona da katal ho gaya'*, lit., 'finally, his murder happened'. The use of the impersonal voice signals a distance from the act of violence as if in dim recognition of the violence this would do to the notion of the community itself.

## CONCLUDING COMMENTS

We can now pull together the main strands of the argument regarding the features of the militant discourse. These features are:

(*i*) the use of rigorous dualisms to define self and other; (*ii*) the creation of contemporaneity between non-contemporaneous events; (*iii*) the weaving of individual biography into social text through the use of local knowledge; and (*iv*) the justification of violence with reference to both mythological motifs and contemporary political practices.

It may be best to bring these features together by focusing on the quality of time in the militant discourse. The present, in this discourse, is the site of the militant movement. It is the pregnant moment which may give birth to a resplendent future. However, this very characteristic of the present makes it subject to manipulation, since rules of normal morality do not apply. The ambivalence of such a position is reflected in the deletion of agency when abhorrent events, such as murders, are described and justified.

In its construction of the past, the Hindu and the Muslim may be described as the feminine other and the masculine other in relation to the Sikh. As the feminine other, the Hindu was seen as part of the self. Weak and effeminate, he needed the protection of the Sikh who could experience himself as the protective masculine half of the Hindu. This is why stories of the past are replete with incidents in which the insults to the Hindu faith, or injustice to Brahmins meted out by the Mughal court are avenged through the martyrdom of the Sikh gurus. In contrast to the Hindu, the presence of the Muslim in the past is as the masculine other. Heroic confrontation with the powerful Muslim kings or chiefs, even when it leads to defeat, confirms the heroic self of the Sikh.

The danger to Sikh identity in the contemporary period is the danger that the masculine self faces from a feminine other. In confrontation with a masculine other, the militant discourse seems to postulate, the travails one faces may lead to physical extinction of the person but the self is affirmed. The danger of the feminine other, on the other hand, is the seductive danger of becoming totally merged in the other and being gifted with a false self. Hence the palpable anxiety about the 'narcotic' cult of non-violence and about being merged in a nation that takes the feminine leader Mahatma Gandhi as the 'father' of the nation.

In relation to this past, the present is a spectral present. It has memories of the Muslim as the oppressor, but these are now transformed by the notions of minority communities in danger from a 'Hindu state'. The Sikhs and Muslims are both said to face this danger, in which a modern discourse of state, minorities and cultural rights is permeated with a second discourse of Sikh history, in which there is the intervention of Sikh gurus in present political events, and reincarnation of historical Sikh personalities to guide and alter the course of history. The emergence of novelty is thus subsumed within repetition and the coevalness of events that are chronologically distant is established through the magical properties of language. Thus Hindu and Sikh, as concepts, come to possess a socio-political plenitude which leaves the traces of contemporaneity even in discussions that are framed by events located in a distant past.

Does the construction of Hindu identity in the militant discourse of the Sikhs reflect back on the Hindus' own conception of the self? We would have to make a similar analysis of present political discourse in the militant movements of the Hindus in order to answer this question in any depth. Meanwhile, it may only be noted that at least on two issues—that of the 'feminine' identity of the Hindu and the relation between Hinduism and the culture of the state—the militant discourse of the Sikhs is refracted, if not reflected, in the modern political movements for a recrafted Hindu identity.

# Ritual and Resistance
## Subversion as a Social Fact*

## NICHOLAS B. DIRKS

*There is subversion, no end of subversion, only not for us.*[1]

[ . . . ]

As we increasingly, and from differing perspectives, examine ordinary life, the fixtures of ordinariness give way to fractures and we see that struggle is everywhere, even where it is least dramatic, and least visible.[2] Struggle becomes visible where previously we could not see it, a trope for a critical vision of the world. Consensus is no longer assumed unless proven otherwise, but even more unsettling for our social science, rebellion and resistance can no longer be identified through traditional indices of the extraordinary. The ordinary and the extraordinary trade places.

In the study of rural India, anthropology has provided most of our social scientific terms of reference. And in anthropology 'order' has always been the chief ordering principle of discourse. When anthropology puts particular emphasis on order, it sanctifies it with the adjective 'ritual'. Ritual is not only principally about order, it

---

* Excerpted from Nicholas B. Dirks, Ritual and Resistance: Subversion as a Social Fact, *in* D. Haynes and G. Prakash, eds, *Contesting Power: Resistance and Everyday Social Relations in South Asia*, Delhi: Oxford University Press, 1991, pp. 213–38. [*The study is located in central Tamilnadu. – Ed.*]

[1] Greenblatt's transformation of Kafka. See S. Greenblatt 1988..

[2] See M. de Certeau 1984.

is often the domain in which our sociological conception of society is properly realized. . . . Anthropologists have often viewed rituals in terms of religious or cultural meanings. They have interpreted the social significance rituals have either directly in terms of these meanings, or—in what is just a slight transformation of this view—as productive of social solidarity. In this view, social relations are displayed and renewed and the hierarchical forms underlying social relations confirmed and strengthened by ritual.

[ . . . ] .

However, Jean Comaroff among others has argued that ritual need not be about order and domination alone. She has found, at least in her work on southern Africa, that

> ritual provides an appropriate medium through which the values and structures of a contradictory world may be addressed and manipulated. . . . The widespread syncretistic movements that have accompanied capitalist penetration into the Third World are frequently also subversive bricolages; that is, they are motivated by an opposition to the dominant system. While they have generally lacked the degree of self-consciousness of some religious or aesthetic movements, or of the marginal youth cultures of the modern West, they are nevertheless a purposive attempt to defy the authority of the hegemonic order. . . . Such exercises do more than just express revolt, they are also more than mere acts of self-representation. Rather, they are at once both expressive and pragmatic, for they aim to change the real world by inducing transformations in the world of symbol and rite.[3]

It is this mode of situating ritual practice and ideology in a world of hegemony and struggle in which representation itself is one of the most contested resources which I follow in this paper.

But I also seek to go further, as also to start with a more basic premise. I will not evaluate ritual practice on the basis of whether or not it aims to change the real world, however much it may lack self-consciousness. Rather, I will look at traditional village rituals in India which at face value have the effect of restoring social relations and upholding relations of authority both within the village and between it and the larger political unit of the kingdom or later state. And I will seek to determine if the way in which order and disorder have been narrativized as basic components of ritual practice, is in fact adequate to the multiple

[3] J. Comaroff 1985.

foci and forms of disorder as I encountered them. For anthropologists have viewed ritual not only as merely a sociological mechanism for the production of order, but also as a cosmological and symbolic site for the containment of chaos and the regeneration of the world (as we, or they, know it).

Elsewhere I have argued that current anthropological writing on ritual underplays, both at the level of kingdoms or large political units and at the level of village rituals and festivals, the social fact that ritual constitutes a tremendously important arena for the cultural construction of authority and the dramatic display of the social lineaments of power.[4] However, although I presented examples of conflict, I saw them largely as products of the breakdown of authority under colonialism. Here I shall argue that precisely because of the centrality of authority to the ritual process, ritual has always been a crucial site of struggle, involving both claims about authority and struggles against (and within) it. By historicizing the study of ritual, we can see that while rituals provide critical moments for the definition of collectivities and the articulation of rank and power, they often occasion more conflict than consensus, and that each consensus is provisional, as much a social moment of liminality in which all relations of power (and powerlessness) are up for grabs as it is a time for the reconstitution and celebration of a highly political (and thus disorderly) ritual order. Resistance to authority can be seen to occur precisely when and where it is least expected.

The ritual I will focus on is crucial here because although it is only one of several village rituals it is the one that inaugurates all other village rituals, often setting the calendrical and cosmological agenda for the yearly ritual cycle. The Aiyanar festival, called the *kutirai etuppu*, was critical also in that it vividly reflected and displayed the hierarchical relations within the village, with the village headman, or *ampalam*, as the ostensive centre of these relations. The priests for this ritual, who also acted as the potters who made the clay horses that were consecrated in the central ritual action, had to obtain permission from the village headman in order to begin making the horses for the festival. The *ampalam* was the host for the festival which began and ended at his house and his emblems were as importantly involved in the procession

4 N. Dirks 1987.

as were the clay horses themselves; the *ampalam* received the first honours, which he then distributed to the other members of the village at the conclusion of the ritual. In short, the *ampalam* represented the totality of the village in a rite which was seen and said by some to celebrate and regenerate the village itself.

When I was in the field—for me the little kingdom of Puduk-kottai, one of the largest of the little kingdoms in the early modern period of the Tamil-speaking region of southern India and later under the British Raj the only Princely State in the Tamil country—it took little time to realize that Aiyanar was a critical deity, and the yearly festival in his honour a crucial festival, in the ritual life of the social formations constituting the focus of my general ethno-historical research. Village elders and headmen would regularly take me to their own Aiyanar shrine as the most important stop on the village tour. They would tell me all about their village festival, how it was famous for miles around, how I would be able to observe and recognize the political centrality of the headman, that I should definitely plan to return to their village on the occasion of the festival. Clearly ritual was important, and clearly this was the social ritual par excellence, at least in the post-independence days of a post-royal kingdom. During the course of my fieldwork, I attended and took extensive notes on about twelve of these festivals in different villages throughout the state. Because of my interest in local social relations and structures of authority, I was drawn into this festival, which became, quite by surprise, a chief focus of my ethnographic research.

There was one festival in particular that I looked forward to attending. The village headman had been an especially rewarding informant, or guide, and spent many hours telling me about the complex details of social organization in his village and his *natu*, the territorial unit that was coterminous with the settlement zone of his subcaste group (also called *natu*) of Kallars, the royal caste in Pudukkottai. He was a patriarch of classic proportions. He told me about the Aiyanar festival with the care and comprehension of a radio cricket commentator, and as the festival neared he even visited my house in town on two occasions to submit to further questions and my tape recorder. I was told exactly when the festival would begin, and we agreed that I would arrive soon after dusk, to participate in the final preparations which would culminate in the commencement of the festival around midnight

(like many of these rituals, it was to take place through the night).
When the festival was still a week away, I expected a formal visit
from the headman to invite me as an honoured outside guest,
but when he failed to turn up I assumed he was unable to come
because he was enmeshed in the myriad preparations for the
festival. So on the appointed evening I drove my motorcycle the
requisite thirty-five miles across potholed tarmac and dusty bullock
cart tracks, only to arrive in a village that was virtually dark, with
no visible evidence of any approaching festivities. The village
headman looked dismayed and surprised as I rolled up on my
Enfield, though less dismayed than me since I heard, as I switched
off my engine, the unmistakable hiss of a rapidly deflating tyre,
the devastating effect of a large acacia thorn's union with my
non-radial Dunlop. The headman told me that the festival had
been called off, and that he had hoped I would have guessed
this since he had not come with the formal invitation. In any case,
he said, he could not have come to tell me that there would be
no festival, since this would have been inauspicious, and would
have made it even more unlikely than it already was that the
festival could take place. But, of course, this admirable foresight
had not turned things around; the festival could not be organized,
a long-standing factional dispute in the village was not in the end
resolved, and the festival became yet another casualty of this
dispute. My immediate concern, apart from the fact that my tyre
was flat and I was not carrying a spare, was that I had lost a
brilliant opportunity to match theory, narrative, and practice, to
follow up the story of a festival that I had been tracking industrious-
ly over the preceding weeks and months. But as my host instructed
his son and assorted relatives to hitch the bullock cart to arrange
for my long and bumpy transport back to town, my disappointment yielded to bewilderment. For I learned that the festival on
which I had such exquisite detail had not taken place for seven
years, and that no one in the village had any genuine expectation
that it would take place this year.

Most fieldwork stories are similarly allegorized. We begin with
calm self-confidence, our initial assumptions and convictions yet
unchecked by the chaotic realities and serendipities of the field.
We then find ourselves in some disastrous predicament which,
in unsettling us (and sometimes them), enables us to cross the
fault line of cultural difference, to familiarize ourselves with the

concerns and logics of new social terrains, to achieve new forms of communion with our anthropological subjects, to achieve wisdom. In fact, at the time I was simply seriously annoyed. Yet, I should also note that although I had been aware of the extent to which Aiyanar festivals gave rise to conflict and dispute at the time, it was only then, and increasingly over the years since, that I have realized the extent to which this story illustrates the flip side of my concern with how village rituals reflected and displayed political authority and political relations. I had begun thinking about Aiyanar by using the Aiyanar festival to attack Dumont's notion (which he developed in a number of places but not insignificantly in an important article on the Aiyanar festival in Tamil Nadu) that religion/ritual always encompasses politics/power.[5] Having established this, it was still difficult to come to terms with the fact that Aiyanar festivals were always sites for struggle and contestation; that speech about the festivals reflected concerns about ritual order and auspiciousness that were part of a different ritual order than the ritual event itself; that even when the ritual event did not happen it was as significant as when it did. The non-event of the called-off ritual was not, in fact, a non-event, after all.

During the rest of my fieldwork I learned that many of the other great events of ritual calendars were similar non-events, that Aiyanar festivals did not happen almost as often as they did, and that when they happened they did not always include everyone in the village, or result in the village communal harmony that I had previously assumed, and indeed that this communal harmony was disturbed not only along the so-called traditional lines of caste or faction but along developing class lines as well. I also learned that while at one level the festival was about the re-establishment of control over the disorder of a threatening nature, it was also about the range of possibilities that existed precisely at the moment of maximal contact between order and disorder. But it is now time to backtrack to the festival itself, before we allow it, as it did that night for me, to deconstruct itself.

In Pudukkottai, Aiyanar was often the principal village deity, though there are villages which include Aiyanar temples in which the village deity was said to be a goddess. According to most of

---

[5] L. Dumont 1959: 75–87.

my informants, the most significant feature of Aiyanar was his role as the protector. He was more specifically called the protection diety, the protector of boundaries, and the one who protected those who took refuge with him. The *kutirai etuppu* festival—or the installation of the horses—began a month before the main festival day. The head of the potters (Velars), the community that made the terracotta offerings and often acted as principal priests for Aiyanar, would take a handful of clay (*pitiman*) from the village tank. The *pitiman* was placed in a brass plate and handed to the village *ampalam*, who then returned it to the Velars, along with the ritual dues. The *ampalam* had to make this gift, signifying his permission for the festival to begin, to entitle the Velars to proceed with the preparation of the offerings. The gift was made in part in the form of puja, as the blessed return of a gift that was first offered to the superior being. The central position of the *ampalam* was thus enunciated and displayed at the moment of the festival's inauguration.

Throughout the festival itself, though each one varied in details, the role of the *ampalam* was particularly conspicuous, as important as the deity. The festival began and ended at his house, the central locus of all village gatherings. There the first ritual action of the festival had taken place a month earlier, when the *ampalam* returned the *pitiman* to the head of the Velars. Similarly, the first ritual action of the festival day was often the puja performed to the *ampalam*'s family deity, adorned with the emblems which represented and encapsulated the family's heritage. Granted by the Raja, and passed from generation to generation within the family, these emblems now symbolized that this festival was sponsored by the village *ampalam*, a festival at once personal and public, the private puja of the *ampalam*'s family and the public performance of the entire village.

In Dumont's well-known analysis of this festival he places too much importance both on the opposition between purity and impurity (deducing from diet that Aiyanar is principally modelled on the Brahman, even though in behaviour and legend Aiyanar is far more like the king) and on his contention that Aiyanar's relation to other village deities reflects the subordination of the political to the religious. The kingly aspects of the deity and the critical role of the *ampalam* are either ignored or accorded only secondary importance. Dumont's failure to provide a fully satisfactory analysis of Aiyanar and his festival is part of his larger refusal to grant that a king can, in certain contexts, encompass and incorporate the divine, the brahmanic, as well as the social and political constituents of caste solidarity and warrior strength. In the village, where the king was represented by the *ampalam*, the festival at once elevated the *ampalam* and his political authority, displayed the *ampalam*'s relation to the king, effected an identity between the latter and the village, and produced, through the celebration of a festival on behalf of a god who so dramatically exemplified the royal function, the conditions under which the village could be victorious against the forces of evil.

But this is not the whole story. For it is precisely the political permeability of ritual that makes possible a succession of contested performances, readings, and tellings. In India kingship had been the dominant trope for the political, but far from the only one. As I stated at the beginning, the Aiyanar festival frequently did not happen, or occasioned everything from violent dispute to multiple celebration, as in one village where three separate village festivals took place under the leadership of three rival castes and their factional affiliates.

[ . . . ]

I found many other instances in which ritual turned out to be a core arena for resistance, particularly for groups such as artisans and untouchables who could resist by simply withholding their services. The closest thing to a municipal strike in the history of Pudukkottai town took place in the early 1930s when the untouchables protested the establishment of a municipal crematorium by withholding their ritual funeral services for all their patron groups. The municipality backed down in short order because of the consternation of one high-caste family after another who felt they were dishonouring their dead. Kathleen Gough has vividly documented the breakdown of village ritual in rural Tanjavur where untouchable groups, fired in part by the growth of a local communist movement, increasingly withheld their ritual services from village festivals.[6] Nonetheless, Gough's assertion that village rituals would not recover from the effects of recent change and growing class consciousness has not been sustained by the experience of the last thirty years. In fact, village

[6] K. Gough 1955.

rituals continue to be important precisely because of their association with conflict.

Although village rituals were clearly sites for struggle between
elite groups and their factions over who was in charge,[7] this was
only part of the story. Rituals were sites for struggle of all kinds,
including—as my earlier story suggests—the struggle between discourse and event. Ritual was a discursive and practical field in
which a great deal was at stake and a great deal was up for grabs.
But when conflict developed in ritual it always made the ritual a
site for appropriation as well as for struggle. The headman of the
darkened quiet village appropriated the interpretive function of
a ritual that he always knew would not take place, and was
embarrassed only when I pressed my curiosity and showed up
without the proper invitation. . . . Anthropologists have appropriated ritual to advocate the religious dimensions, character, and
force of the social, which in the case of Dumont's transformation
of Durkheim is located in a world of religiously validated hierarchy. Appadurai and Breckenridge found struggle at the top level
of ritual and argued that temples provided political arenas of
dispute.[8] These appropriations—like my own—are all examples of
the way ritual has become central to the field of power relations
in southern India. Further, these appropriations have never fully
succeeded in containing the power of ritual, and they are all
checked by the profoundly subversive character of traditional
ritual practice (at least as I observed, and did not observe, it in
southern India). Not only did ritual discourse and ritual practice
operate at angles to each other, both discourse and practice were
open to a multiplicity of contesting and resisting agencies, even
when these agencies were themselves constituted by (or in relation
to) the concealed agencies of colonial hegemony.

But I have so far completely ignored one of the most important
but also complex sources of agency and action in the Aiyanar
festival. I do not mean the lord Aiyanar himself, but rather his
incarnation in the form of the *camiyatis*, the people in the village
who during the course of the festival were routinely possessed by
the lord Aiyanar. Possession was an absolutely critical part of this
and other village festivals in the south. Apart from the goat

---

[7] See N. Dirks 1987.

[8] A. Appadurai and C. Breckenridge 1976.

sacrifice and the feast it was the most charged event in village ritual practice. Once again I must retell the festival, which I will do with reference to the Aiyanar festival celebrated in the predominantly Kallar village of Puvaracakuti, in Vallanatu, about eight miles southeast of Pudukkottai town in early July 1982.

The festival began at the house of the *ampalam*. When I arrived the *ampalam* was bathing and a number of village folk and members of the *ampalam*'s family were busy decorating the *ampalam*'s house, festooning it with mango and coconut leaves. The Paraiyars who had assembled some distance from the house built small fires to tune their drums. Flowers, coconuts, and other items for the puja were brought to the front porch of the house. There were five red ribbons to tie on the horns of the horses and bulls, five towels for the possessed *camiyatis* and towels for the service castes such as the dhobi, barber, and Paraiyars. The *ampalam* came to the front porch after his bath, and worshipped the images of gods and goddesses hung on the interior walls of the porch.

The emblems of the *ampalam* were brought out from the vacant house next door, called the big house, which was unoccupied because of a quarrel within the *ampalam*'s family between collateral contestants for the position of *ampalam*. These emblems consisted of a spear, a sword, a cane, and a club. The emblems symbolized the office and authority of the *ampalam*, and were said to have been presented many generations before by the Raja. Under a small tiled roof *mandapam* (pavilion) about twenty yards to the west of the *ampalam*'s house, they were placed next to the *pattavan*, a sword representing an ancestor of the *ampalam*'s family who was worshipped as the family deity. The emblems and the *pattavan* were shown the flame, camphor was burnt, and coconuts were broken, the three most common elements of any performance of puja. After this, the emblems were carried by other Kallars in the village, and the *ampalam* was summoned. The first procession of the day was ready to begin.

The emblems were carried by Kallars. The entire procession was led by Paraiyars beating their drums. Though the *ampalam* was the central character, attention was increasingly focused on the *camiyatis*, here five Kallars who were to be possessed by the god. Initially chosen for possessing special spiritual powers, they were the hereditary *camiyatis* who participated in the festival each year. They walked immediately behind the drum-beating Paraiyars. Not yet in full trance, the *camiyatis* began to show signs of possession as they walked on to the beat of the drums, their bodies sporadically quivering at the touch of Aiyanar, who was shortly to enter into them. The procession walked straight to the small structural temple to Aiyanar. A puja was performed for Aiyanar, and sacred ash was distributed to all those present. The *camiyatis* then picked up bags of ash and began walking back to the village, accompanied by the Paraiyars. As they walked through the village, the women of each house came towards them and poured water over their feet to cool them. The *camiyatis* blessed the women with the ash they carried. We walked through the Kallar section of town, via the *ampalam*'s house, to the Velar settlement on the eastern side of the village. There the procession was welcomed by the playing of the *mela telam* (drum) by the Melakkarars (the pipers) of a nearby temple and by exploding fire crackers. Six terracotta figures, each about four feet high, were lined up on the Velar street—one elephant, three horses, and two bulls—in the final stages of decoration. They had been whitewashed, painted with coloured stripes, and crowned with stalks of flowering paddy and the ribbons from the *ampalam*'s house. The five Kallar *camiyatis* stood in front of the terracotta figures. A Paraiyar from a nearby village came forward, and carefully dressed the *camiyatis* in special clothes. The Paraiyar wore a garland made of silver balls, his head was wrapped with a red cloth, his chest was draped with multicoloured strands of cloth, a new towel was tied around his waist, and garlands of bells were wrapped around him. His face was painted with vermilion and sandal paste. This Paraiyar was called the *munnoti*, the leader or the one who went first. In a few minutes he became possessed on his own, to the music of the drums and *nadaswaram* played by the Melakkarars. He began to jump wildly when the incense and camphor smoke were shown to him and he stared fixedly at the sky. He suddenly leapt into the crowd, snatched the *ampalam*'s spear, and began to beat the ground with it. He was jumping and running around and through the crowd, all the while circumambulating the six figures. The *ampalam* then came up to him, garlanded him and smeared sacred ash on his forehead. After this, the *munnoti* led the other *camiyatis* into states of possession. Someone whispered in my ear that the *munnoti* was the burning lamp which lights other lamps. Full possession was achieved when the *munnoti* held the camphor up to the *camiyatis*, one by one.

Now that the *camiyatis* were fully possessed, the procession was ready to commence. The Paraiyars went first, followed at some distance by the Melakkarars, then by the *munnoti* and the five *camiyatis*, then the terracotta offerings, with the elephant in the lead, followed by the smaller offerings of individual villagers. Behind them walked the *ampalam*, surrounded by many of his kinsmen. As the procession moved around the village, on its way back to the Aiyanar temple, villagers came up to the *camiyatis* to be blessed, often asking questions about the future which the *camiyatis* answered. When we reached the temple, the eyes of the terracotta figures were opened with the blood of a cock, sacrificed by the *munnoti* (who was then given the cock). The terracotta animals were then installed in front of the temple. A grand puja was held to Aiyanar. The Velar priests offered tamarind rice, broke coconuts, and then showed the light, after which they offered ash to the worshippers. Then the priests left the Aiyanar shrine, shutting its doors. Aiyanar was said to be vegetarian, and ought not to see the sacrifice to Karuppar, the fierce black god whose shrine is always next to Aiyanar.

Moving to Karuppar, the priests performed puja again. The villagers surged forward en masse to obtain some ash. One of the priests laid a stone a few yards in front of the Karuppar temple. The villagers assembled in a circle; finally a goat was brought forward, and judged proper. The fifth *camiyati* came forward bearing a large sword taken from the Karuppar shrine. With one swift slice he cut off the goat's head. As they intently watched the spilling of blood and the final convulsions of the goat's body, the crowd became increasingly excited and jubilant. The carcass of the goat, which had been donated by the *ampalam*'s family, was now handed over to the Velar priests.

A cloth was laid on the ground for the *ampalam* to sit on. The Velars brought him the huge bowl of tamarind rice and all the *pracatam* from the puja: flowers, coconuts, and plantains. Sitting there the *ampalam* distributed the honours, first to the Kallar lineage heads, then to the Valaiyars, and the artisans. Finally, the village elders took up the *ampalam*'s emblems once again, and beckoned to him to lead the procession back to the village. All returned to his house, where the emblems were returned to their accustomed place. This concluded, the village Kallars and Paraiyars were given their *pracatam* in the village square in front of the *ampalam*'s house, along with sufficient rice and a chicken for a feast of their own.

The final distribution of honours both confirmed the authority of the *ampalam* and displayed the hierarchical relations of all the caste groups in the village. Or so it seemed. This harmonious village festival began to deconstruct itself when I came to realize shortly after I attended the festival that a rival group of Konars, traditionally herders but now an increasingly powerful agricultural caste, had seceded from the ritual performance and instead held their own *kutirai etuppu* some weeks later. Thus the appearance of harmony that presented itself so forcefully began to unravel as soon as I began to poke into the affairs of the village. After what I have already argued in this paper, this is hardly surprising. But here I will comment on one important aspect of the festival that I completely ignored in my earlier analysis. From the account it is clearly seen that possession was a central part of the ritual drama. However, what was possession all about, what did it signify?

Most of the literature on possession deals with the nasty kind, when it is the devil rather than the lord who has taken up residence within our mortal coil. And so rather than the exorcist we have its opposite—a man whose skill and power is precisely to induce possession rather than rid us of it. But this too is an extraordinary form of power, and one that has many dangers. It is significant that for this role an untouchable is chosen; while all the regular *camiyatis* are of the dominant Kallar caste, the one person who makes their possession possible could never be invited into their houses nor be allowed to dine with them. And his power was not completely contained by hierarchy, for there were moments of real fear when he seized the *ampalam*'s spear and began dancing wildly about. The fear of Aiyanar was clearly enhanced by his choice of this unruly Paraiyar as his principal vehicle and agent. When I went to visit him he was completely drunk, and he combined in his person an exaggerated deference and a smouldering bitterness. On the one hand he acted as if he was deeply honoured that I should visit him; his failure to recognize me for a moment or two seemed due more to drink than any difficulty in remembering my presence in the festival through the daze of his own possession. On the other hand, he was the one who told me that there was a rival festival in the village hosted by Konars or shepherds, and as he told me this he almost laughed at the hollow claims of the Kallar headmen who could no longer control an inferior caste group.

Indeed, this was not the only moment of danger, not the only reason why containment was a live issue throughout the festival. Aiyanar was clearly hard to handle, and his agents in possession had to negotiate a delicate balance between play-acting and overacting. I was repeatedly told that the possession was real, that it took many years to learn how to accept the visitation of the lord, that it required the supervision of a man of special powers both to learn and to do, and that after a spell of possession it would take days and sometimes weeks for the possessed person, exhausted and shaken by the experience, to return fully to normal. And I was told that if a *camiyati* turned out not to be really possessed, simply play-acting, they would ridicule him and exclude him completely from the festival and its proceedings.

After all, the festival was critical for the well-being of the village, and if Aiyanar was misrepresented by an impostor, then the festival might fail, and certainly the advice handed down by the lord to the anxious and enquiring villagers would be spurious. But there were also times when possession could prove too much; the *camiyati* was called the vessel, and when this vessel could not contain the concentrated power of the lord, it might crack. In such instances the *camiyati* would not recover from possession, would stay deranged and disturbed, and then there would be need of an exorcist.

It is possible to account for all of this with a traditional view of ritual. Van Gennep was keenly aware of the danger and disorder that was part of ritual, and built this into his explanation of liminality and ritual transformation.[9] But his theory has a tendency to contain danger too readily, too automatically, and to assume that disorder is epiphenomenal. I would propose here that possession was yet another aspect in which ritual practice was genuinely dangerous and always already subversive. Part of

[9] A. Van Gennep 1960.

the subversiveness had to do with what we have already considered, the constant possibility of conflict, fission, paralysis, and
hermeneutic if not agonistic explosion. But the subversiveness
had also to do with the politics of representation and misrepresentation inherent in both the role of the headman and that of the
*camiyatis*.

First, the festival was a powerful spectacle precisely because of
the role of the possessed *camiyatis*. The festival seemed to me at
times, particularly since I attended many different festivals in
different villages, like theatre. Victor Turner has already commented on this correlation, using the term 'ritual drama', by which
he meant that ritual could be analysed as if it was an unfolding
drama with the participants as actors who engaged in the unseen
forces of life through the vicarious agencies of ritualistic enactment.[10] But if what I witnessed was theatre to the participants, it
was very different from what has come to be accepted as theatre
in the West. Stephen Greenblatt has noted that 'the theatre elicits
from us complicity rather than belief.[11] But in rural southern India
there were elements of both complicity and belief; there were
roles and masquerades that depended on far more than skilful
artifice and conceit. This was 'theatre lived' not 'theatre played'
as Greenblatt observed when citing an ethnographic example.[12]
But even this opposition does not capture the power of this ritual
experience. For there was the possibility that something could go
wrong, and this provided an urgency and unpredictability to the
drama that renders a theatrical metaphor too dramatic and possibly sacrilegious. One of the inescapable implications of the
*camiyati*'s predicament—the risk that possession could be in-
authentic—was that all agency and all representation in the ritual
was at risk as well. Identity was most fragile at the moment of its
transformation and multiple reference. And the risk that the
possessed might be faking it no doubt raised the possibility that
the headman, whose authority and connections with the king were
both celebrated and renewed in the festival, might also be faking
it. After all, everyone knew (though at the time I did not) that
the headman claimed a sovereignty over the entire village that
was not granted by the rival shepherds. Thus, participation in the

[10] V. Turner 1969.
[11] See Greenblatt 1988.
[12] Ibid.

festival was highly politicized. Indeed, even the role of the lord was thus politicized: on whose side was which god? But it was the compelling, contestable, and dangerous components of the ritual drama that also raised the stakes. The spectators did not simply gaze, they vied with each other to participate more actively and more centrally in the festival, to interlocute the *camiyatis*, to see the cutting of the goat, and to collect and consume the prasada—the transubstantiated return—of the lord. They also vied with one another to celebrate, to control, and to interpret the ritual.

I have given just a few illustrations to suggest what I might mean by the subversive nature of ritual practice and discourse. I will close with one last observation. Each ritual event is patterned activity to be sure, but it is also invented anew as it happens. When I witnessed one festival, there was frequent confusion about what was to be done. At one point a participant in the festival leaned over to me, realizing that I had seen many similar festivals, and asked me what I thought they should do next. At the time I thought that I was already intruding too much on the authenticity of the ritual event and that to offer an opinion would be to go across the fragile threshold of legitimate participation implied in the oxymoronic motto of anthropology: participant observation. But I was wrong, for the authenticity of the event was inscribed in its performance, not in some time and custom sanctioned version of the ritual. And the authenticity of the Aiyanar festival was in particular inscribed in its uncertainty and its contestability, even when it didn't actually take place.

## FURTHER READINGS

Sandria Freitag, *Collective Action and Community: Public Arenas and the Emergence of Communalism in North India.* Berkeley: University of California Press, 1989.

Investigates 19th century happenings in cities of latter-day Uttar Pradesh: social, economic, and political equations were becoming fluid with the passage to the colonial regime. Competing for public space—as in religious processions—was an aspect of re-negotiating the equations in status and power. Ways of acting, later marking aggressive communalism, were taking form.

D. Haynes and G. Prakash, eds, *Contesting Power: Resistance and Everyday Social Relations in South Asia.* Delhi: Oxford University Press, 1991.

Interesting studies on the general theme that neither the use of power nor the practice of resistance, overt or covert, can be understood by itself; rather, each helps shape and condition the other. The focus is on the colonial period, with earlier and later periods on the margins.

Ratna Naidu, *The Communal Edge to Plural Societies: India and Malaysia.* New Delhi: Vikas, 1980.

Examines 'communalism' on the national canvases of Malaysia and India, from a comparative perspective: historical origins of communal interfaces, the colonial experiences, the nationalist articulations against colonialism, the politico-economic struggles both long-term and recent, the social logic of communal riots and the unconscious, pathological underpinnings of much associated activity.

Veena Das, ed., *Mirrors of Violence: Communities, Riots, and Survivors in South Asia.* Delhi: Oxford University Press, 1990.

An imaginative collection on riots in Sri Lanka, Pakistan, and India—concerned especially with the 'meaning' of the experience for those who survive the trauma. Papers by historians, political scientists, sociologists, psychologists, and others.

Rabindra Ray, *The Naxalites and their Ideology*. Delhi: Oxford University Press, 1988.

Draws on both sociology and philosophy for an explanation for Calcutta's late 60s/early 70s student terrorists—the Naxalites. Sees them as profoundly nihilistic, driven to demolish, but short on positive vision: qualities judged to have risen in the prevailing Bengali values and social and economic experiences.

# III

# Political Sphere

The unequal distribution of power and authority is ubiquitous and pervasive. It is often regarded as a structural imperative of complex social organization. While societies and groups have evolved ideologies legitimizing this inequality, none of them has ever experienced unquestioned acceptance of its legitimacy. Conflicts over the distribution and exercise of power, and challenges to authority, are ever present. Such conflicts and challenges are fraught with far reaching consequences for the societies and groups concerned.

This section brings together four papers on conflicts/challenges in the political sphere. They focus on a variety of themes: student unrest (Kakar and Chowdhry), rebellion as custom (Guha), factional conflict (Rastogi), and interaction between local and regional politics (Attwood). They cover different time periods: from the pre-independence era (Guha) through the sixties (Rastogi, Kakar and Chowdhry) to more recent times (Attwood); from diverse disciplinary backgrounds: anthropology (Attwood), psychoanalysis (Kakar and Chowdhry), and sociology (Guha, Rastogi); with divergent intellectual objectives: model building

(Rastogi, Attwood) socio-historical reconstruction (Guha) and psychoanalysis (Kakar and Chowdhry).

The opening selection from Ramachandra Guha's work on peasant response to ecological—and governmental policy—changes takes us through the history of Tehri Garhwal from the second half of the nineteenth century to the era of the freedom struggle. Guha focuses on the customary nature of protest in this region of Uttar Pradesh in the institution of *dhandak*. He documents the early *dhandaks* resisting forest management, provides a case study of the *dhandak* at Raiwan in 1930, and contrasts them with the Kisan *andolan* of 1944–8.

An inherent feature of the *dhandaks*, Guha emphasizes, is that they were never directed at the monarch. Their targets of protest and revolt were the functionaries of the state who were perceived as 'the true exploiters'. Refusal to cooperate with rules and the officials who enforced them, and in extreme cases fleeing to jungles or across political frontiers, were classic features of this form of protest. Barring isolated attacks on officials, they were generally free from physical violence. This form of protest was predicated on the traditional relationship between the *raja* and his *praja*, as also on the democratic nature of the peasant communities.

Guha shows how the traditional methods of conflict resolution broke down and customary relations between *raja* and *praja* underwent change because of certain exogenous forces such as the revision of forest settlement, the spread of freedom movement, the incorporation of the peasants into the market economy, etc. Guha's work is proof *par excellence* of the immense utility of archival records and vernacular newspapers in reconstructing social history in general and analysis of customary and long-term conflicts in particular.

Of the various categories of population the one which is regarded as most rebellious, and often as being inherently so, is youth. Psychoanalyst Sudhir Kakar and management specialist Kamla Chowdhry have tried to locate Indian youth in its changing society. The selection included here dwells on unrest among a section of the youth, namely, the students. Following Alexander Mitscherlich, they distinguish between protest and revolution, and observe that, in the rebellion of the youth, elements of both these are mixed in varying proportions. They stress the need to delve deeper, underneath the superficial stereotypes of the student leader and student unrest.

Substantively, Kakar and Chowdhry present the case history of a student agitation in a south Indian state in 1965 protesting against increase in tuition fee and analyze the life history of one of its student leaders. They are not interested as much in the *internal dynamics* of the agitation as in its *meaning* in the present state of the student community (i.e., the social context) and in the life-history of the leader (i.e., the personal context).

Kakar and Chowdhry, and Guha, are aware that their analyses of single cases do not permit them to make generalizations. Yet their insights from these case studies help deepen our understanding of a host of similar cases, illustrating the significance of the case study as a strategy for sociological research.

Nowhere is conflict in the political sphere more apparent and pervasive than in the relations between political parties on the one hand, and among individuals and groups within a party on the other. Inter-party conflict over claims to power is institutionalized as a competition, partly carried on according to the rules of the electoral game. Intra-party, or factional conflict, however, is not institutionalized; yet it determines the dynamics of the party as a political organization as well as its strength and stature as a competitor for political power.

The next selection from sociologist P.N. Rastogi's work examines the nature and dynamics of factional conflict. It begins with a theoretical framework for the analysis of factional conflict in which Rastogi tries to show how the changing character of factionalism in a group is related to the dynamics of its faction situation. This is illustrated by a detailed case study of factionalism in the Indian National Congress in the sixties which culminated in its breakup in 1969.

Rastogi employs three modes of analysis—structure of a faction situation, analysis of factions, and dynamics of factionalism—which supplement each other to provide a comprehensive picture of factionalism. His effort reveals how a sociologist can bring to bear his analytical tools on a subject which is primarily of interest to political scientists. It also highlights the importance of newspaper reports and secondary data in sociological analysis of conflicts.

Akin to the analysis of the development cycle of patrilineal joint households by Madan and Rizvi, in the last paper D.W. Attwood outlines a cyclical model for the analysis of political conflict, distinguishing between stable, cyclical, and evolutionary elements, which in reality are often combined in situations of conflicts. Drawing from his rich fieldwork experience in Maharashtra, he illustrates the working of this model. He then contrasts the cyclical model with four competing models, namely, the encapsulation model (F.G. Bailey), the competitive patronage model (Paul Brass), the class conflict model (Mary Carras), and the patronal elite model (Anthony Carter).

The specific case which Attwood elaborates relates to the Olegao cooperative sugar factory in Pune district. He traces the evolution of local conflict through cyclical phases, and shows how political changes come about through access to new resources and to contacts with regional networks. Drawing upon similar observations from the works of Scarlet Epstein and Alan Beals in rural Karnataka, he is able to suggest that his model may have wider applicability.

# Rebellion as Custom[*]

## RAMACHANDRA GUHA

[ . . . ]

A recurring feature of peasant and tribal revolts has been attacks on functionaries of the state. The state, or the monarch, appears as an abstract entity far removed from the scene of exploitation, while its functionaries become the targets of popular uprisings. The situation of the actual exploiter—the state and the interests which the state represents—is obscured in the minds of rural communities, and surrogate officials are perceived as the true exploiters. The notion of a 'just' government, integral to the Hindu tradition, is another factor which influences popular perceptions; thus, tyrannical officials are seen as breaching the ethical code of justice governing relations between ruler and ruled.

The king's concern for the welfare of his subjects is, therefore, contingent on the degree of competence of his officials. Without competent officials (*yogya karamchari*) the king was helpless. The lofty ideals of Raja Narendra Shah [of Tehri Garhwal] were circumscribed, according to his subjects, by the highhandedness and unconcern of the high officials of the durbar, notably the new dewan (chief minister) Chakradhar Juyal [c. 1928]. Juyal, it was alleged, had achieved high office not by virtue of competence but through flattery and other devious machinations. The king was constantly enjoined to be aware of the troubles of his

* Excerpted from Ramachandra Guha, 'Rebellion as Custom,' *The Unquiet Woods: Ecological Change and Peasant Resistance*, Delhi: Oxford University Press, 1989, pp. 62–98.

subjects and not place sole faith on officials like the present dewan. . . .

The tension to which this relationship was subject was particularly manifest in periods of the king's minority, when administrative responsibility vested exclusively in a council of regency and no direct channel of communication existed between raja [king] and praja [citizens]. During the minority of Kirti Shah, who took over the gaddi [throne] in 1892, the desire was persistently expressed that the councillors should be removed and the young prince left to rule entirely on his own. . . .

## THE DHANDAK

In the ruling ideology of kingship, the harmonious relationship between raja and praja was complicated in this manner by officials to whom the king had delegated administrative powers and the day-to-day functioning of the state. These powers were always liable to be misused. While this was not an infrequent occurrence, there existed in the moral order of society mechanisms whereby the peasantry could draw the attention of the monarch to the wrongdoings of officials. Traditionally, peasant protest in Uttarakhand took the form of individual and collective resistance to tyranny by officials with a simultaneous call to the monarch to restore justice. This form of protest was known as the dhandak, derived from 'dand kiye gi', the admonition used by Garhwali mothers to hush troublesome children. Dhandaks were never directed at the king or at the institution of kingship; rather, they emerged in response to what was perceived as oppression by subordinate officials and/or the introduction of new taxes and regulations. On punishments being inflicted upon the erring officials, the dhandak invariably died down, only to flare up again when fresh cases of tyranny occurred.

The dhandak typically encompassed two major forms of protest. First, peasants refused to co-operate with new rules and the officials who enforced them. Alternatively, when the demands grew excessive and were backed by force, villagers fled to the jungles or across political frontiers into British territory—a classic form of protest. Occasionally, peasants caught hold of the offending official, shaved off his hair and moustaches, blackened his face, put him on a donkey with his face towards the tail, and turned him out of the state. Such non-co-operation at a local level was often accompanied by a march to the capital. A mass gathering would be proclaimed by the beating of drums, and peasants from surrounding villages would gather at an appointed spot, often a shrine. Here they would decide not to cultivate their fields or pay revenue and march to the capital demanding an audience with the king. On the king appearing in person and promising redress, the crowd would disperse.

In the dhandak the absence of physical violence, barring isolated attacks on officials, was marked. The moral and cultural idiom of the dhandak was predicated firstly on the traditional relationship between raja and praja, and secondly on the democratic character of these peasant communities. The rebels did not mean any harm to the king, whom they regarded as the embodiment of Badrinath. In fact they actually believed they were helping the king restore justice.

Interestingly, the officials, particularly those deputed from British India, who were often the targets of such revolts were unable to comprehend the social context of the dhandak. They invariably took any large demonstration to be an act of hostile rebellion. . . . [I]n 1925 C.D. Juyal described the people of the pargana of Rawain as being able to 'reap the pleasures of Heaven on this earth merely for their extreme religious devotion and unequalled loyalty towards your highness'. But a mere five years later, following the 1930 dhandak in which he figured prominently, Juyal thought the rebels 'a formidable and strongly armed gang of outlaws'. . . . Actually Juyal himself, who was later to epitomize the callous and wicked official, had at one time been praised by his fellow hillmen for his administrative abilities in British India. This hiatus between the self-perceptions of dhandakis and the views of targeted functionaries may be traced to the theme of the wicked official as one who disturbs the traditional relationship between raja and praja.

The dhandak essentially represents a right to revolt traditionally sanctioned by custom. Hindu scriptures urged obedience to the sovereign, subject to the right to revolt when the king failed to protect his people. In the trans-Yamuna Simla states a form of protest called the *dum* or *dujam*, not dissimilar to the dhandak, was widely prevalent. Such revolts were not directed at the monarch, the peasantry being convinced of his divine origins. In order to draw the king's attention to some specific grievance the cultivators would abandon work in the fields and march to the capital or to other prominent places. As the suspension of farm work affected revenue collection, the king would usually concede the demands of the striking farmers.

## EARLY RESISTANCE TO FOREST MANAGEMENT

. . . [F]orest management, whether under the British or the aegis of the raja himself, produces uniform results with regard to peasant access to forest produce and pasture. Rationalized timber production can only be ensured . . . by the regulation of traditionally exercised rights. As over time the greater part of the revenue of the Tehri durbar came to be realized from its rich forests, the raja steadily introduced a policy of stricter forest conservancy modelled on the system prevailing in British territory. This met with stiff resistance from villagers. . . . In response to the difficulties created by the reservation of forests, 2500 people of Rawain—a pargana in the north-western part of the state—marched to Tehri to demand an audience with their sovereign. Meanwhile, Pratap Shah [the monarch] died and, according to one chronicler, the peasants took pity on the widowed maharani. Deeming it unjust to put pressure on her, they returned to their homes. Soon afterwards, during the minority of Kirti Shah, the peasants of Patti Ramoli submitted a long list of grievances to the political agent. These included complaints at the extend of begar [forced labour] taken by officials, restrictions on the collection of grass and leaves, and various other taxes levied on land and buffaloes. . . .

The next recorded dhandak concerning forests occurred around 1904 in the patti of Khujni, lying to the south of the capital, Tehri. This was a consequence of the repeated demands for bardaish* made by the conservator of forests, Keshavanand Mamgain, and his staff, and the new taxes levied on cattle for which the forests were the main source of fodder. When villagers refused to meet what they regarded as excessive and unjustified levies, the forest staff entered their homes, broke vessels, and

---

* *Free supply of milk and other materials for touring officials. [Eds]*

attempted to arrest the strikers. Peasants resisted and beat up Mamgain's men; meanwhile some men fled to Tehri. In an affirmation of solidarity and their democratic spirit, the village councils of Khujni resolved that whosoever did not join the rebels would be expelled from the community. Kirti Shah sent a high minister, Hari Singh, to pacify the rebels, who put him under arrest. . . . [T]hey were not satisfied with the king's emissary—they needed an assurance from the monarch himself. Ultimately, the new taxes had to be lifted and Mamgain's men were withdrawn from forest work in Khujni.

The man who succeeded Mamgain as conservator, Pandit Sadanand Gairola, was to suffer a worse fate at the hands of enraged villagers. Gairola was directing forest settlement operations in the patti of Khas. Subsequent developments have been described by the official report on the dhandak:

On December 27th, 1906, the forests surrounding the Chandrabadni temple about 14 miles from Tehri town were being inspected, preparatory to their being demarcated and brought under reservation. It is reported that the villagers both then and previously had taken exception to the reservation of these forests, but it was not supposed that their objections would extend beyond the refusal of supplies and petty obstructions. On the morning of the 28th December, however, about 200 villagers armed with sticks assembled at the camping ground where the officials' tents were pitched and objected to *any* state interference with forests over which they claimed *full* and *exclusive* rights. They attacked the Conservator against whom they are alleged to have had a special grudge as a *foreigner* to the state, introducing *unaccustomed* forest customs and regulations. It is reported that they beat him, branded him with a hot iron, tore down his tents, pillaged his baggage and took away and broke his guns. He is represented as having escaped with much difficulty into Tehri.

Unnerved by the strength of the opposition to forest conservancy, the raja resorted to a show of force and, when that failed, asked the British for assistance. Clearly, the recurring dhandaks had forced the sovereign to consider new methods—apart from those socially sanctioned—to contain discontent.

Two aspects of the repeated protests against state forestry need mention: (*i*) their localized nature, and (*ii*) the total isolation from political developments elsewhere in India. . . .

## THE DHANDAK AT RAWAIN, 1930

The decisive breakdown of traditional methods of conflict resolution was yet to come. This followed a dhandak in Rawain in opposition to the revision of the forest settlement based on the recommendations of the German expert Franz Heske. . . . Under the new settlement forest concessions were said to have been considerably reduced. It was rumoured that the prescriptions of the settlement could disallow each family from keeping more than ten heads of sheep, one cow and one buffalo—this in an economy largely dependent on sheep and cattle rearing. Villagers were to be levied taxes on herds exceeding the prescribed limit. Peasants complained, too, that very little waste land had been left outside the reserved forests. They were also no longer allowed to cut or lop *kokat* (hollow) trees without a permit. Villagers sent several representations to the durbar; when these elicited no response they resorted to the time-honoured means of obtaining redress—the dhandak.

The dhandak soon spread from Rawain to the neighbouring pargana of Jaunpur. . . . The resisters sent a telegram demanding the king's personal intervention. As the monarch had gone to Europe, the durbar sent Harikrishna Raturi, the former dewan, . . . an old official of the state who first codified its law, [and] was well acquainted with dhandaks. Apprising the peasants of the king's absence, he asked them to stay quiet till his return. They agreed on condition that the durbar stayed the new forest restrictions in the mean time.

Raturi's agreement was, however, not ratified by the dewan. Instead, Juyal conveyed orders to the local magistrate, Surendra Dutt Nautiyal, to arrest the leaders. . . . [This] episode provided an additional impetus to the dhandak. It began to spread rapidly. In a manner characteristic of peasant upsurges, rumours circulated to the effect that the raja had not gone to Europe but had been held in internment by the present dewan, a foreigner to the state. The dhandakis appointed Hira Singh, pradhan [head] of Nagangaon, as their head. He, along with the shopkeeper Ramprasad and Baijram of Khamundi village, assumed leadership of the movement. Villagers were asked to endorse blank papers called *dharmpattas* affirming their support. Village headmen received notices that unless they joined the dhandak within a specified time they would be robbed and beaten up. . . . Hira Singh designated himself prime minister of the 'Shri 108 Sarkar'. The appellation clearly indicates the king's continuing legitimacy in the eyes of his subjects, who believed that through their actions they were helping him regain his lost powers. Meetings of this independent authority or Azad panchayat were convened at Tiladi, a vast expanse of level ground overlooking the Yamuna.

Alarmed at the rapid turn of events, Juyal moved to Nainital to confer with N.C. Stiffe, commissioner of Kumaun division and political agent to Tehri Garhwal state. Undoubtedly influenced by the civil disobedience movement then at its height in British India, Stiffe advised Juyal to take punitive action. . . . When the troop commander, Colonel Sunder Singh, refused to march on his kinsmen, the dewan removed him from the post and . . . personally assumed charge of the troops. . . . The dewan sent two villagers to the dhandakis, asking them to surrender. Their response was that when their president (presumably Hira Singh) returned, he would send a reply if he so wished.

Instead, . . . the troops marched to Tiladi, where the villagers had gathered. Juyal's men fired several rounds and an indeterminate number of peasants was killed (estimates vary from four to two hundred). Others frantically jumped into the Yamuna and were drowned. Many villagers fled to the jungles or into British-ruled Jaunsar Bawar. The army also indulged in looting; 164 people were later arrested and confined in Narendranagar jail. Of these, 80 were freed and the remaining awarded sentences ranging from one day to twelve years in jail. . . .

In his report the dewan portrayed the striking peasants as a gang of outlaws engaged in dacoities and murders throughout the state. He did not explain how a band of outlaws chose as their rendezvous a virtually defenceless field enclosed on three sides by hills. If the villagers had been as well equipped as Juyal made believe, it is difficult to comprehend how the army did not suffer any casualties. Clearly, the dewan was hoping to gain the support of the higher authorities for his attack on unarmed villagers. But his distortion of events was only in part a wilful one; it was also informed by his lack of acquaintance with the cultural idiom of the dhandak. As a police officer from British India, his training equipped him to view any sign of popular unrest with suspicion. In a fashion typical of functionaries of the raj, Juyal blamed urban politicians for fomenting trouble to undermine his authority. . . .

On the king's return from Europe the dewan was able to convince him that the gravity of the situation called for a punitive expedition. Despite several representations, the people of Rawain were unable to acquaint the king with their version of events. Shortly afterwards, Narendra Shah deplored the outbreak, criticizing the Rawain folk for deviating from their peaceful ways. Pinning the blame on 'unworthy' headmen, the sovereign asserted that as villagers were ignorant of forest conservancy, he had called in a foreign expert to advise him. In a conciliatory gesture the king promised to end utar* by building better roads. In response, the *Garhwali* agreed that while forest management was necessary the present commercial orientation left the wants of peasants unfulfilled. The continuing burden of utar and the ban on private distillation also came in for criticism.

Narendra Shah's failure to dismiss Juyal and make amends epitomized the changing relations between the peasantry and the monarch. . . . Constrained by the imperatives of scientific forestry, and wary of the political movements in British India, the administration of Tehri Garhwal began to exhibit a visible strain: inevitable because an increasingly bureaucratic system impinged on the highly personalized structure of traditional authority. Simultaneously, the continuing protests forced the king to adopt a more autocratic style of rule, one reinforced by his closer contacts with British colonialism. . . .

It was, however, the dewan and his rapacious behaviour which figured prominently in the popular consciousness. Wild rumours began to circulate that the all-powerful Juyal had proposed new taxes on women and drinking water and an enhanced tax on potato cultivation. His attack on the Rawain peasant lives on in peasant folksongs which recount the awesome terror of the dewan's rule. . . .

## THE KISAN ANDOLAN, 1944–8

These intermittent and localized protests were to crystallize into a widespread movement, engulfing large areas of the state, that

---

* *Services rendered without payment, as for repairing roads. [Eds]*

culminated in the merger of Tehri Garhwal with the Indian Union. Resembling the archetypal peasant movement far more than the dhandak, the Tehri kisan andolan was nevertheless composed of different strands. On the one hand the spread of the nationalist movement into princely India led to the formation of the Tehri Rajya Praja Mandal at Dehradun in 1939. On the other the growing incorporation of the Tehri peasants into the market economy rendered them more vulnerable to its fluctuations, notably during the depression and World War II. The situation engendered by the loss of control over forests, by now almost complete, was further aggravated by the new taxes the durbar imposed on an unwilling peasantry. The intervention of the Tehri Praja Mandal (itself no replication of the Congress, with its activists rooted in the cultural milieu of the state) was, therefore, mediated through a peasant uprising whose idiom was determined rather more directly by a distinctive social history of protest.

The oppressive forest rules continued to be met with suspicion. The rates at which villagers could buy timber in excess of their allotment far exceeded those at which the durbar sold wood to outside agents. In 1939 the forests between the Bhilagna and Bhageerathi rivers caught fire. Many heads of cattle perished, as did nine peasants who attempted to extinguish the blaze. The durbar refused to award any compensation. Outside the forest restrictions, Juyal had introduced a new tax called *pauntoti*, a form of customs duty levied on the belongings of subjects as and when they entered the state. As a greater number of Garhwalis were now dependent on outside employment, this levy was the cause of much resentment. So was the cess on potatoes, one of the state's chief crops.

The Praja Mandal (Citizens' Forum), established on 3 January 1939, took up the issues of begar and pauntoti. Its outstanding leader, Sridev Suman, was . . . (a) member of the Congress since his youth. . . . Determined to set up an organizational forum to mediate between raja and praja, Suman wrote articles and delivered speeches on both local and national struggles. . . . In and out of the state Suman had a strong influence on the students of the college in Tehri. . . . Postal employees in Tehri, who sympathized with Suman, were able to sabotage the censorship enforced by the authorities. On 21 July 1941 Suman embarked on a hunger strike outside the Tehri police station; this continued for several days, and attracted much attention and support.

Externed from the state, Suman continued his work in British India. On his release from a spell of imprisonment in Agra jail, he re-entered Tehri state and began to tour villages and organize meetings. He was arrested and lodged in Tehri jail. Here he embarked on an indefinite hunger strike, appealing that: (*i*) the Praja Mandal should be recognized and allowed to work in the state; (*ii*) the cases against him should be personally heard by the maharaja; (*iii*) he should be allowed contact with the outside world. When these demands went unheeded, Suman succumbed to pneumonia and heart failure after a fast that lasted eighty-four days.

[ . . . ]

Suman's supreme sacrifice (*balidan*) was to be of immense propaganda value in the years to come. In the year of his death the durbar embarked on a fresh land survey and settlement, in revision of the settlement operations of 1917–26. . . . The extensive operations, carried out under the supervision of the settlement officer, Ramprasad Dobhal, involved the measurement of land and fixation of the new (enhanced) rates of revenue. Immediately, surveying officials had to contend with non-co-operation by peasants who refused to submit to the survey.

Sustained opposition to the settlement followed the submission of interim reports by the *amins* and patwaris, when the settlement officer himself held court to ratify the survey. Dobhal's large entourage, which included his guests and dancing parties, claimed *bara* (services) and begar as a matter of course. Despite rules prescribing payment for rations and transport, officials were taking services at nominal rates and claiming receipts for the full amount. Complaints were made about the arbitrary manner in which *nazrana* (revenue) rates were fixed and impediments put on the breaking of fresh ground for cultivation. Peasants also demanded the right to alienate land enjoyed by their counterparts in British Garhwal. Simultaneously, the forest department's highhandedness came in for sharp criticism. . . .

The first meeting to oppose the settlement, attended by about a thousand peasants, was held on 21 April 1946. The movement, one largely autonomous of the Praja Mandal, was led by a retired employee of the postal department, Dada Daulatram. It spread rapidly to Barjula, Kadakhot, Dangchaura and Akhri pattis. Refusing to supply bara and begar, peasants forced Dobhal's entourage to cook and clean utensils themselves. Nor could they move camp without hiring costly coolies. Refusing to submit to intimidation, villagers desisted from attending *muqabala* (settlements) in Dobhal's court. Instead, the relevant cases were decided in the village panchayat. In some localities peasants tore up the settlement papers which attempted to codify the state's demands. . . . Under Daulatram's leadership a *jatha* (group) of peasants marched to Narendranagar, the new capital, raising slogans against begar and nazrana. Daulatram and his associates were arrested and jailed on 21 July 1946.

On hearing of their leader's arrest another jatha proceeded to Tehri. Led by Lachman Singh Bist, an ex-soldier of the Indian National Army, this party had the object of releasing the prisoners from jail and proceeding to Narendranagar to celebrate '1942 day' on 9 August. In the ensuing scuffle several peasants were arrested but the rest, including Lachman Singh, evaded arrest. Meanwhile, Daulatram and several colleagues, including the young communist Nagendra Saklani, went on a hunger strike in protest against the durbar's actions.

At this juncture the Congress stepped in to mediate between the peasantry and the durbar. The party's traditional suspicion of peasant movements over which it did not exercise control was perhaps reinforced in this case by the immediacy of the interim government in which it was to hold power. Accordingly, a delegation led by Jainarayan Vyas and Khuslanand Gairola visited Tehri Garhwal between 10 and 20 August. An agreement was reached with the durbar whereby the Praja Mandal was registered and allowed to hold processions and meetings. The pact also envisaged the release of those activists in jail. Under its new constitution the 'ultimate object' of the Praja Mandal was the 'achievement of responsible government under the aegis of His Highness . . . by constitutional, legitimate and peaceful means'. Triumphantly, the resident proclaimed that this article constituted 'a very considerable success for the Darbar'.

The terms of the pact were, however, not adhered to by the durbar. While several prisoners were released on furnishing personal bonds, others including Daulatram and the Praja Mandal president, Paripurnanand Painuli, were still in jail and being tried.

Daulatram had also been refused defence counsel. On 13 September Painuli, labelled a 'communist' by the authorities, and several other prisoners commenced an indefinite hunger strike, demanding a repeal of the Registration of Associations act under which the Praja Mandal had been derecognized.

. . . Strongly protesting the durbar's actions . . . Chandra Singh Garhwali accused Jainarayan Vyas of deliberately allowing the durbar to sabotage the pact. . . .

The Praja Mandal had its first open meeting in Tehri on 26 and 27 May 1947, and Daulatram was chosen its head for the next year. On 14 August Painuli sent a wire to the maharaja, warning him of his intention to enter the state on Independence Day. He was promptly arrested on arrival. Gathering momentum, the movement had spread to Saklana. . . . In Saklana, a major potato producing area, peasants had been protesting extortion by the potato 'syndicate' to whom the durbar had accorded sole rights of collection and sale. Muleteers were also desisting from paying the tax levied on transport. When the police arrested striking peasants, the refusal to pay taxes became more widespread. Some villagers fled to Dehradun district. The police also raided houses and beat up the inhabitants. Angered, the kisans encircled durbar officials and forced them to leave Saklana. The *muafidars* [revenue collectors] voluntarily abdicated and left for Dehradun. In the last week of December victorious peasants formed an *azad* panchayat which abolished taxes and declared that each cultivator had ownership rights.

As news of the development at Saklana spread, azad panchayats were formed in several other pattis. In Badyargarh events took a dramatic turn at the Dhadi Ghandiyal *jath*. At this fair, held every twelve years, peasants paid homage to the local deity of Ghandiyal. Shrewdly utilizing this opportunity, Daulatram and his colleagues arranged to address the crowd on the Saklana and Kadakhot dhandaks. The gathering was informed of the impending march on Kirtinagar, where peasants from different parts of the state were expected to congregate.

Following the Dhadi jath, activists fanned out into the villages. In several places *chowkis* (offices) were captured and their patwaris replaced by men chosen from among the peasantry. Survey officials were made to return bribes extorted from villagers.

Occasionally, liquor contractors were beaten up and their stills smashed.

Jathas of around fifty peasants each were rapidly sent onwards to Kirtinagar. On 30 December policemen came searching for Daulatram. The constables were arrested by the villagers and asked by Daulatram to report at the court at Kirtinagar. The next day, when the police fired on a crowd at Jakhni village, angry peasants captured the court and police station at Kirtinagar. The police inspector's house, where the deputy collector was also taking refuge, was surrounded. When the officials refused to surrender, the crowd collected kerosene preparatory to burning the house. The deputy collector was caught while trying to escape and taken across the Alakananda river to Srinagar. The police party who had fired at Jakhni on the 31st were found tied up on the road. They were taken to the office of the District Congress Committee at Pauri and made to sign letters of resignation. In Devprayag, too, the court had been captured by the dhandakis. The same night Daulatram and Painuli were spirited away to Narendranagar for negotiations with the durbar.

Meanwhile, thousands of peasants had collected at Kirtinagar. Daulatram himself returned on 9 January. The town had initially been cleared of all officials and an azad panchayat had been proclaimed. In response, the durbar sent an armed force led by Baldev Singh Panwar, a close kinsman of the raja. This force arranged a meeting with Daulatram in the local court. However, as soon as Daulatram returned, soldiers fired teargas shells and bullets at the waiting crowd. When fire was set to the building, senior officials tried to flee. The crowd chased them, whereupon one officer fired several bullets, killing the young communist Saklani.

The next day the crowd took the bodies of Saklani and Moluram (a peasant killed in the firing outside the court) and proceeded to Tehri via Devprayag. En route the jatha exhibited the corpses in different hamlets. A second jatha, led by Daulatram and including the captured officials, proceeded directly to Tehri. On 14 January the two jathas met and immersed the martyrs in the confluence of the Bhageerathi and Bhilagna rivers. The army having fled, an azad panchayat took over Tehri under its pradhan, Virendra Dutt Saklani.

Hoping to win over the people through his presence, the raja rushed to Tehri from Narendranagar. His attempt to enter Tehri was foiled when the bridge across the Bhageerathi was shut. The physical gulf that separated him from his people became invested with a deeper meaning: as one peasant recounted, on one bank were the massed subjects, on the other their ruler (*Us taraf raja, is taraf praja*).

The raja had now lost control. Thousands of peasants from Jaunpur and Rawain gathered at Bhavan and handcuffed police inspector Baijram, the man responsible for Suman's arrest. Functionaries of the police, revenue and forest departments were forced out of the locality and an azad panchayat established. In defeat, the raja called in the Praja Mandal leaders for negotiations. A ministry headed by Dr Gairola was established, which held office till the state's merger with Uttar Pradesh the following year.

## PEASANTS AND PARTIES

The kisan andolan differed from the preceding dhandaks in two major respects, one of which was in its spread. The initial confluence of several local movements gained an additional impetus with the Kirtinagar khand (firing) and came to cover much of the state. Secondly, this movement had an organizational forum in the shape of the Praja Mandal. The dyadic relationship between raja and praja was therefore complicated by the presence of Congress-inspired nationalists. The specific linkages between the Praja Mandal and the praja it claimed to represent thus need to be examined.

The relationship between the Praja Mandal and the peasantry can be viewed at several levels, each invested with different layers of meaning. The Praja Mandal's aims initially encompassed the reformation of an administration viewed through the prism of modern nationalism as *samantshahi* (feudal). In fact, in the early part of the movement there were reports that the peasant leader Daulatram had 'been disowned by the Praja Mandal'. . . .

On assuming power on 15 August 1947 the Congress attitude towards the Tehri movements underwent a major shift. The desire to integrate princely states with the Indian Union, coupled with the growing pressure of the peasant movement itself, led the Congress to view Daulatram and his associates in a more favourable light. Now the Praja Mandal agitation imperfectly merged with the kisan andolan in a movement that generated its own dynamic: the outcome perhaps exceeding what either the Praja Mandal or the peasantry had envisaged.

The hiatus between the Praja Mandal and those it professed to represent remained, at the level of perception, a considerable one. As a young activist later recounted, the attempt to popularize the slogan 'Inquilab Zindabad' . . . at village meetings met with a miserable failure. As the slogan was raised along with the national tricolour, peasants interpreted it in a manner more representative of their feelings. They responded by shouting 'Yanno Khala Jandabad' (this is the way we will bring about the rule of the flag). Although the Praja Mandal attempted to explain the original slogan and its significance, the same misperception repeated itself at the next village.

Interestingly, whereas Praja Mandal activists explained the origins of the Kirtinagar 'satyagraha' in terms of India having won freedom while Tehri was in bondage, peasants were emphatic that their struggle was against the oppressive taxes and the settlement operations that came in their wake. But it was not merely at the level of perception that this duality persisted; it was imbricated in the significance attached to different actions. Thus, peasant participants recounted, with evident satisfaction, how patwaris had been overthrown and symbolically replaced by their own men, adding that their nominees continued to hold office for some time. . . . On the other hand, Praja Mandal activists emphasized the formation of the interim ministry as a major fulfilment of their goals.

Peasants were also insistent that the king did not himself know of the injustice (*anniyayi*) being perpetrated in his name. . . . The fear of retribution from the police was adduced as an important factor which dissuaded peasants from approaching the king. For its part, the Praja Mandal had a far more ambivalent attitude. Its eagerness to share power with the durbar was nevertheless accompanied by an ideology which was implicitly anti-monarchical.

## ELEMENTARY ASPECTS OF
## CUSTOMARY REBELLION

. . . [I]n Tehri Garhwal the mechanisms of social protest drew heavily on the indigenous tradition of resistance known as dhandak. Yet, for all its distinctiveness, the dhandak is representative of a type of rebellion widely prevalent in pre-industrial and pre-capitalist monarchies. Variations on the dhandak theme have been reported from other parts of Asia, and Africa and Europe as well. The dhandak is a sub-type of what one might call 'customary' rebellion: a form of rebellion that draws its legitimacy from custom and does not seek to overthrow the social order. . . .

Typically, the origins of rebellion in traditional chiefdoms and monarchies stem from a perceived breach of the covenant between ruler and ruled. This covenant between high and low, or patron and client, is normally couched in the idiom of father and son. Being by definition the ruler *par excellence*, the monarch patronizes his subjects not only in the economic sphere but in the socio-political and judicial spheres as well. According to the dominant ideology, the peasantry looks to the king for impartial arbitration and social justice. . . . The symbolism of father and son well epitomized the essentially patriarchal style of domination, where 'protection' of the peasantry harmonized with the kingly ideal of benevolent rule. . . .

This covenant, while indicating the limits of arbitrary action by both rulers and subjects, is continually under threat. For, intermediate between the king and the peasantry are myriad laws relating to the land, the forests, and the waters of the kingdom, and myriad officials to enforce these laws. And in the eyes of the peasantry officials are invariably tyrannical and high-handed; moreover, they tend to pervert the king's commands and interpret laws in their favour and against the interests of the peasants. . . . Often ethnically and economically distinct from the peasant masses, these officials are both despised and feared. In times of revolutionary change . . . peasants seize the opportunity to appoint their own men in place of officials deputed from outside. . . . [They] take matters into their own hands, physically attacking officials even as they break the new laws. In this act of trespass peasants could cry . . . 'long live the king, down with the Forest

Administration'. . . . Alternatively, . . . they could march to the capital demanding an audience with the king. . . .

Such appeals to the king were made in the name of 'custom'—namely the argument that the new laws were contravening time-honoured social (and natural) arrangements. . . . Yet such invocations are not merely tactical; the opposition to new laws and their enforcing officials has often been strengthened . . . by the profound conviction that the king was on their side. In general, appeals to the monarch rested on two core assumptions: that the king symbolized the spirit of the collectivity and that, as the temporal and spiritual head, he was the very fount of justice. . . . [H]is persona is avowedly sacred, not secular. . . . As the mediating link between the sacred and the profane, the king takes on some of the attributes of the gods: he is quasi-divine. . . . The divinity of kingship is further heightened in isolated and protected tracts, such as Garhwal, where the tranquillity of the cosmic order and its integration with society remain relatively undisturbed by cataclysmic social or natural events.

In his mediating role the king must faithfully observe the rituals of investiture, symbolically undertake the first annual ploughing, and enact the other societally varying magico-religious ceremonies which are believed to constitute royal power and assure social harmony. Failure to do so may bring the wrath of his subjects upon him or his office. . . . Apart from the correct observance of traditional rituals, the physical presence of the king is required—especially at crucial times like the harvest. . . .

As the embodiment of the spirit of the collectivity, the protector of his subjects and the fountain of justice, the monarch is the ultimate court of appeal for rebels claiming the sanction of custom. Here lies one major difference between the idiom of customary rebellion in small, relatively homogeneous and well integrated states like Tehri Garhwal, and in states organized according to different political and economic principles. In large monarchies, for example, one important variant on the theme of customary rebellion is the appearance of a 'pretender'. This phenomenon normally occurs in the far-flung corners of a huge kingdom, where peasants are far removed from the centre of authority and are unlikely to have ever seen a member of the royal family. A pretender comes among the villagers, claiming to be the true monarch . . . he asks, and frequently gets, their support in a social movement directed against corrupt officials. The dhandak can also be distinguished from the phenomenon of regicide found in the segmentary states of Africa, where disaffected subjects can call upon a chief to replace the incumbent to whose inadequacies are attributed current economic and political tensions. In Tehri Garhwal, loyalty was owed to the person occupying the throne, not simply to the institution of kingship; there was no question of the rebels calling upon another person to replace the one in power.

# Protest, Revolution and the Student Leader[*]

## SUDHIR KAKAR AND KAMLA CHOWDHRY

'Unrest', 'protest', 'indiscipline', 'rebellion', 'revolution', are a few of the many terms which are being used today to describe the explosive situation prevailing among young Indian students. The proliferation of terms is perhaps also an indication of the confusion as to the dynamics of this 'student unrest'. The explanations offered have ranged all the way from the individual to the epidemiological. The student unrest has been seen by some as a part of the normative maturation crisis which every young person goes through, while others have seen in it the echoes of a worldwide phenomenon. . . .

To consider the Indian situation in a worldwide perspective and to compare it with similar manifestations in other countries, especially in the West, it is perhaps necessary to distinguish between the categories—*protest* and *revolution*, a distinction first made by Mitscherlich.[1]

The roots of protest are firmly anchored in the experience of early childhood and are thus greatly influenced by the child's relationship with its parents. Protest is the cry of the child whose wishes have been frustrated, a cry which is much louder and much more uninhibited than the protest of an adult who is faced

---

[*] Excerpted from Sudhir Kakar and Kamla Chowdhry, *Conflict and Choice: Indian Youth in a Changing Society*, Somaiya Publications, Bombay, 1970, pp. 11–32.

[1] See Mitscherlich 1969.

with similar frustrations in later life. During the course of development, protest becomes muted, its intensity modified by the individual's increasing awareness of the reality in which he lives and his increasing ability to empathise with others who come in the way of his uninhibited realisation of pleasure. Youth, however, is a period in which the feelings and conflicts of early childhood once again become active. The protest of early childhood against the restrictive authority of the parents, or against early deprivations, once again rises to the surface, to be channelled (under certain conditions) into protest against the whole of the older generation.

In contrast, in *revolution* the focus of protest is shifted from significant individuals of the past to the social conditions prevailing in the present. It calls for a greater awareness and perception of reality, an emancipation from the conflicts and deprivations of childhood. Its genesis does not lie in the unconscious individual past but rather in the conscious social present. It is not directed against parental oppression but against a perceived social oppression. Most of the terms which are used at present to describe unrest can thus be subsumed under one or other of the two categories. Once again it should be emphasised that 'protest' and 'revolution' are abstract entities . . . they are rarely, if ever, to be found in their pure states in actual behaviour. In the life history of any young rebel, the elements of both *protest* and *revolution* are found to be mixed in varying proportions. There is little doubt that both these elements, the personal and the social, influence each other and we can separate them for the purposes of analysis only. Interestingly enough, this combination of personal and the social factors in rebellion is brought to its sharpest focus in case of the much-maligned student leader.

The stereotype of an Indian student leader usually consists of an academically poor student, much older than his fellow students who, with the active or covert support of a political party, spends most of his time in organising agitations, mostly violent, on the most trivial of issues. He is often regarded as one of the main villains in what has come to be called 'student indiscipline' or 'student unrest'. The opinion that, given the moribund state [of] and the widespread dissatisfaction with our institutions in general and our universities in particular, student indiscipline might be a positive factor, the only way that change can take place, has been rarely expressed. This does not mean that we intend to play the devil's advocate here, to argue for violence as a desirable means for social change or even enter into a discussion on the ethics of ends and means. The point is that at the present moment social scientists do not really know enough about the way change takes place in social institutions to condemn student 'indiscipline', even in its violent form, completely out of hand. . . .

In any case we need to delve deeper into the superficial stereotypes of the student leader and student 'unrest'. We need to know whether most of the issues are really as trivial as they appear on the surface or whether they also contain more fundamental differences, the 'hidden agenda', in the confrontations with social institutions. The following case history of a student strike and the life history of a student leader attempt to clarify some of the questions posed by 'rebellious youth'.

In April 1965, the Government of a south Indian state ordered an increase of more than 100 per cent in the tuition fees of the pre-university courses in the faculties of Arts, Science and Commerce, thus setting the stage for a confrontation with the students. Since the announcement did not make the headliness in the local newspapers and the University was closed for the summer vacation, there were no immediate reactions to the increase. A month later, Rajan, a student of the engineering college in the capital city of the State, and his friend, Seshan, a practising lawyer also studying for his master's degree in law, were accosted by a journalist friend and informed about the fee increase. Their reaction to the news was strong and swift. Rajan writes as follows:

> Any fee increase in education could touch a responsive chord in me. I was born in a lower-middle-class family whose sustenance was on a month-to-month basis. My entire education, till then, had been on merit scholarships and freeships. I had gone through an agonising period of doubt as to whether I could study further into university after I passed my matric with 80 per cent [marks]. I had seen my friends who were less lucky dropping out to become clerks or factory workers. If one was poor, one must be academically brilliant—or else, one stands no chance of studying even if one is moderately good. I felt it was our duty, as articulate ones amongst students, to represent to the Government to reconsider its order. Seshan agreed readily.

He hailed from a similar background and we thought on the same wavelength.

Both Rajan and Seshan were well placed to take the initiative on behalf of the students. They were well known amongst the student community for their leading part in many extra-curricular activities. Rajan held office in a number of scientific, literary and other cultural forums around the city and had often represented the university in debating competitions. Rajan and Seshan, though not personally affected by the fee increase, decided to pick representatives from the various courses and to ask for an appointment with the Education Minister. The meeting with the Minister took place the next day and proved to be abortive. . . .
[ . . . ]
During the course of years, the university had acquired a notoriety for the predictable violence of its student agitations. Every year the students would go on violent strike on issues ranging from postponement of examinations to travel concessions. . . . Remembering the past agitations, Rajan says that he was determined that this time there be no violence. . . . Thus when Rajan heard of rumblings in this direction in the second city $X$, he and Seshan hurried to confer with the student leaders there.

The meeting was a heated one as the student leaders of $X$ wanted to repeat the earlier violent pattern. One of them, referring to the authorities, stated his viewpoint bluntly, 'These sons-of-thieves will wake up only if we break the [street] lamps.' However, in the past agitations, a pattern had been set in which the students of $X$ and the other towns always followed the leadership of the capital city. Rajan and Seshan persuaded their colleagues from $X$ to hold back till a delegation had again met the Education Minister and tried to persuade him to reconsider his decision. The student leaders of $X$ were pessimistic about the outcome of the second meeting, but agreed to Rajan's proposals.

We then stated that if it failed and the Minister refused to budge, then we would call for a general strike and abstention from classes—but never with old tactics. We also extracted a promise that in case of a strike, they would religiously adhere to these methods in conducting the agitation and that if any violence broke out in any part of the State, we would withdraw publicly our participation in the strike and condemn the violence. These decisions were agreed to by all.

[ . . . ]

The second meeting with the Minister was formal and businesslike. The Secretary of the State's Education Department, who was also present, read out a list of figures showing that with the recent increase in fees the State was only trying to catch up with the fee levels prevailing in other States. The student delegation replied with statistics as to the low per capita income of the State and the greater size of the average family and pointed out that the first casualty of the measure would be the higher education of girls, as parents, faced with a choice, would inevitably choose to pay for a son's education. The Minister 'listened with no change in his attitude. . . . There would not be even a reconsideration, let alone revision, of the fee increase.' The students decided to call for a strike.

In the capital city, Rajan and Seshan, now joined by another old friend, Krishnan, shared the burden for the preparation of the strike which was scheduled to take place three days later. . . .

We worked like devils to make it true. We had very little money and no vehicles to move about, except a cycle between us. All we had were friends and acquaintances in great strength and contacts around colleges. All through the night, we went around the city's streets with makeshift brushes made out of brooms tied with rags—dipping them into borrowed buckets of lime and painting the city with calls for strike and abstention from classes. We rushed through the press of a friend, leaflets explaining the pros and cons of the issue involved and that we had been compelled to take recourse to strike. We collected a band of workers and volunteers from students of all colleges and divided the vast city's colleges, spread out in different parts, into responsibility areas under each one of us. . . .

. . . This was the first and most important test of Rajan's efforts. His success was complete. The students of Law College abstained from classes in sympathy with the agitation. A nucleus of marchers was built up from amongst the Law students and the procession went around the different colleges in the city to persuade them to strike. Here is Rajan's description:

At each place, we followed a regular pattern. The procession would be stopped at a distance outside the gates; we would request the principal to permit us to address the students. Some of them [the principals] out of sympathy for the genuineness of the cause, some out of admiration for the new look of agitation and some out of a mistaken fear that the crowd would surge in, permitted us. Students seldom needed a lot of persuasion. It was fun to miss classes. . . .

The only difficulty Rajan encountered was at a girls' college whose principal was reputed to be 'tough'. Seeing him standing at the gate, the girls were afraid to come out. Rajan notes that it was extremely important for the strike to have the girls join them.

Also the build up to the boys, seeing the girls come out would be great. Above all, I thought, any temptation for unruly behaviour would be curbed in the presence of girls, as the boys' attention would be riveted on them. The police would be reassured too. The popularity with the public for the cause would go up a lot, if girls joined in. . . . I said, 'I want to tell you something the Chief Minister told us. We told him that girls' education would suffer if the fees went up. He replied, "Oh. What does it matter if they don't study? After all they have to get married and stay at home." Now you decide for yourself whether you want to come or not.' They trooped out in a body and a roar went up from the crowd. I could not help smirking a little, even though—by God!—that was one of the few straight pure white lies I have said in my life.

By the afternoon, it was known that the strike had been an unqualified success throughout the State. In the capital city alone, twenty thousand students had marched to the State Assembly. In the evening, in one of the hostel rooms serving as an 'office', the active volunteers, almost thirty now, gathered to give the agitation a formal organisation. Rajan, Seshan and Krishnan were all brahmins. Because of the strength of the communal and anti-brahmin feeling in the State, they decided that a Students' Action Committee be formed with the majority of its positions including that of the Chairman to be held by non-brahmins. The three friends were named as spokesmen for the Committee. This was an act of political prudence which avoided any hint of communal bias in the student agitation. The strike continued successfully for four days without any violent incidents to mar its 'new look'. Citizens' Committees, some by well-meaning citizens and some by political parties 'who wanted to be on the popularity bandwagon', were formed to support the students' demands. . . .

After four days of the strike, from a district headquarter there came the news of a stone-throwing incident. Students or, some maintained, the youth wing of a political party, threw stones at a police van and some students were arrested. Rajan felt that their control over the agitation was slipping. They could be sure of their control only in the two principal cities. They had trusted that the distant towns would follow the model set by the two cities. They had no money to travel and lacked the resources of a formal organisation. They were now haunted by the possibility that the strike could turn violent and completely slip from their grasp, allowing the various political parties to do their 'dirty work'. However, on the fifth day, to Rajan's great relief, the Chief Minister of the State announced a review of the fee increase issue and the strike could now be gracefully called off.

The history of this particular student agitation can be analysed at two different levels. First we could narrow our attention to its *internal* dynamics—the way an agitation starts, the leaders and the coalitions they build, the different stages of an agitation, the role of the political parties—in short, the anatomy of a student agitation and the points where this specific case differs from the conventional views on the nature of student agitations. For example, are the student leaders academically and intellectually below average? Of the three student leaders in this particular case, one went on to the Harvard Law School on a fellowship obtaining his Master's degree with distinction, the second became a trade union leader and was elected as the youngest member to the State Assembly while the third graduated from an all-India professional institution at the top of his class and was awarded a doctoral fellowship in the University of California to prepare for a teaching career in a university. Their past academic records were checkered, brilliance in part alternating with failure. Our purpose here is however different, the analysis is on a second level. We are interested in finding the *meaning* of the agitation in two different though related contexts, namely, what does the agitation really mean in the present state of the student *community*—the social context, and what does it mean in the life-history of the *leader*—the personal context.

The older generation has often expressed the view, sorrowfully, ruefully or in anger, that the present generation of students have no 'higher' cause like that of the earlier Independence movement in which they could channel their youthful energies. This energy, for the lack of such a worthwhile outlet, now erupts in heedless violent rampages and aimless riots. Sensitive representatives of the younger generation agree with this evaluation and Rajan himself, talking of the students taking part in the agitation, eloquently gives expression to this:

> They [students] belong to the generation of the 40's. By the time they could perceive the world beyond their homes, war was over and the struggle for Independence too. They grew up without having undergone the rigours and pleasures of rebellion; they never knew the luxury of idealism and pride of patriotism. . . . An influx of superficial western values washed off old values—values like faith in religion, acceptance of one's lot with equanimity or resignation and such others. Nothing new was substituted. A spiritual vacuum, if one may use a loose term, was created. The surplus energy of youth, hardly catered to by the outdated educational system, cried out for an outlet. . . . The annual strikes in my university were, I believe, acts of spiritual masturbation.

What Rajan is here expressing is the role of a period of historical transition in exacerbating the normal conflict of adolescence. In this conflict youth's need for an *ideology*, and we use the term in Erikson's sense of an unconscious striving for a world-view (*Weltanschauung*), convincing enough to support the collective and individual sense of identity, is well known and well documented.[2] This need for ideology is however much greater in periods of historical transition such as the present, than in the relatively quiet periods of history. It does not matter if the ideology or the cause offered is a simplification or inconsistent with existing knowledge. What matters is that in youth there is a developmental, almost existential need for the offering of devotion to a ' . . . utopian outlook, a cosmic mood, or a doctrinal logic, all shared as self-evident beyond any need for demonstration.'[3] This need to give *devotion* is one aspect in the identity formation of youth. It is this need which is not being fulfilled when the older generation talks of the lack of a worthwhile cause and which leads Rajan to

[2] Erikson, 1958: 22.
[3] Ibid.: 41.

aptly describe the violent strikes as 'spiritual masturbation' since these strikes, having no ideology as a loved partner, thus become masturbatory.

But gaining a sense of identity, the step towards maturity, demands not only *devotion* but also *repudiation,* which often means the rejection of life styles intrinsic to the parents' generation. The violence and the intensity of this rejection is influenced not only by the vacuum created by periods of historical transition but also the manner in which youth perceives the probity or the integrity of the older generation. The greater the perceived 'betrayal' or the 'hypocrisy' of the older generation the more violent the youthful repudiation is likely to be and likely to go to much greater lengths than the 'normal' developmental rejection of the parents' generation. Thus the common thread tying up the various student agitations on a variety of issues appears to be a *repudiation* which is more than a 'generational conflict'. In the absence of a positive cause (devotion) the negative one (repudiation) becomes predominant.

Earlier we mentioned the violence and intensity of this repudiation being partly dependent upon the image that the students hold of the older generation. It is in the intensity of its expression that we see the repudiation as more than a conflict between generations. Conflict at least assumes a semblance of mutual respect but here we find amongst the students a thinly disguised contempt for the older generation, for their 'great betrayal' which somehow serves as a justification for the student violence. 'They are sons-of-thieves who only wake up when the lamps are broken,' and 'This is *goonda* regime—and it is goondaism that pays here,' are some of the remarks made about the political authorities by the student leaders of the strike. . . .

With a feeling of horrified outrage the student leaders tell of a State Cabinet Minister who advised them to continue their agitation, the hidden agenda being that the Education Minister was on the point of resigning on this issue, making the political promotion of this minister possible. 'Hence he was prepared to encourage (all in hush-hush of course) the protest against his own government and disrupt the educational machinery further.' But the older generation does not only comprise of the political authorities.

[ . . . ]

Thus in the absence of a 'cause', it is this sense (conscious and unconscious) of angry contempt and betrayal by the older generation which turns a normal generational repudiation into a cause in itself. The periodic violent and destructive agitations by the students are thus not only rejections of a 'dirty' authority but also serve as communal 'purification' rituals for the young.

In the foregoing observations we have very briefly tried to find the meaning of the agitation for the students both in terms of history (the nature of the transitional period leading to a technological society) as well as in terms of present student beliefs and attitudes toward the older generation. The agitation has however also a meaning in the life history of the leader. First of all we suspect, and the evidence in Rajan's autobiography demonstrates the suspicion to be well founded, that the abdication of responsibility by the parents is a complaint also directed against Rajan's own father. The contempt towards the older generation, shared by Rajan's contemporaries, has in his particular case, its origins in his life history which also contains other themes related to Rajan's leadership of the agitation.

Rajan was the ninth and the last child of his parents. Of the other eight children only two elder brothers had survived their infancy. Rajan's father was a minor government official earning about Rs 150 per month and Rajan thinks of his social origins as low middle class. It was a close knit family with many relatives with whom the children were in close contact. From his early childhood, Rajan had developed a sense of being a chosen one, of having a superior destiny in store for him. . . . This sense of superior destiny was heightened by Rajan's early precociousness. He went to school at the age of four and stood first in the class from the very beginning, winning prizes in literary activities, music, recitation and mimicry. He appeared in a stage play at the age of four and 'loved the limelight from then onwards'. His parents, pleased at Rajan's early successes, looked toward Rajan as one who would rise above them and have great success. . . . 'There was parental pressure for success on me, especially since my brothers had been failures. But this pressure was not exerted at the cost of freedom to me.' In his frank and lucid autobiography, Rajan however shows an uncertainty as to the strength of his parents' love for him. At one place he writes, 'They did not discriminate between their three children and loved us equally well.'

However, at another place, writing of his relationship with his eldest brother, eight years his senior, a plaintive doubt creeps in:

> He [the brother] was the first child to live after the death of six children. Hence obviously he was coddled and was the life and soul to my parents. My father was quite lavish in spending on his clothes [an obsession my brother still has!] and welfare. Even after the birth of my elder brother, who was a very quiet baby, my eldest brother continued to dominate the family scene.

Thus Rajan as a child, though the exclusive centre of his parents', especially his father's *ambition*, is unsure whether he is also the centre of their exclusive *love*. Superiority is not enough for a child; he also wants to be loved by significant others for this superiority. Looking for an almost exclusive love as his natural reward for being the chosen one, the child starts doubting his own worth if this love is not forthcoming in a constant reassuring stream. He becomes intensely self conscious in relation to others. . . .

This sense of superiority given by the parents is then a vulnerable one, for it depends upon the love and affection given to the child as its manifest proof. It is made more vulnerable by an isolation from one's peers by a perceived sense of inferiority, extenuated by the child's hypersensitivity, in Rajan's case, we suspect, the smallness of stature—'My physique was very slight. . . . Lack of nutrition, being born late in my parents' life, my mother's slight physique and continuing delicate health—all these made me small in body.' The leader as a child, and let us here admit our own methodological predilections, and the leader as a young man, conscious of a superior destiny but hypersensitive and beset by doubts, constantly seeks situations where leadership can be exercised and reassurances of the early superiority sought—a theme common in the life history of many other historical leaders. In another context Rajan gives evidence of this:

> I was on the whole the most successful debater in the university and created records for individual and institutional prize winning. Still, an occasional second prize instead of first prize would make me feel as if I had failed miserably and I would be satisfied with nothing but the best . . . a rather feverish attempt to prove to myself and the world at large my supremacy on every occasion and, in the process, try to forget anxieties about my supposed diffidence, inferiority complexes and uncertainties about the future.

A second theme in Rajan's personality, that is related to his leadership, is his contempt of authority, of the older generation who seemed to have abdicated their responsibility for the younger one.

In his autobiography, Rajan depicts his father as an exemplary one—affectionate, kind, encouraging—and one who had a great influence in moulding his sons' values. He talks of his father as the most honest man he knows, uncorrupt in a naive, god-fearing, society-fearing way. The father was proud of his son's various successes though leaving all decisions regarding career, choice of place to study, etc. to his son *but*—he still failed as a father. To understand this better it is necessary to consider the role of a father, of *being* a father, in some detail.

Talcott Parsons has pointed out that the father-image can be analytically broken down into its two main components, the *authority* which breaks up the boy's earlier dependency on his mother and the *model* for the boy's assumption of masculine roles.[4] Both these components are interdependent and a breakdown is only *analytically* possible. The provision of guidance and authority by the father is essential to a child's growing up and this is what the boy looks for. It does not matter whether, in the judgment of others, the father is strict or harsh; what he must be for the boy is to *be there*, be 'tangible', a bedrock of guidance on which the boy can always depend upon. 'Good' but weak fathers can be the worst. If the father does not fulfil this role, or if he abdicates it altogether, he has *failed*. In Rajan's family, ' . . . mother was the disciplinarian of the family naturally, as my father was away for days at a time.' Much more revealing (in connection with an incident to be discussed later), Rajan tells of his feelings toward his father:

> My ambivalent feelings towards my father—protective feelings towards him, image of him as vulnerable and naive. . . . It is a fact that I have always, paradoxically, taken a patronising attitude toward my father, explaining things to him, advising him and believing that he needs guidance.

Here we see a reversal of the traditional father-son relationship and we would contend, on the basis of clinical reports of several such relationships, that Rajan's indubitable love for his father is

[4] See Talcott Parsons 1964.

also combined with a contempt and hostility against him. Rajan's later 'search for a father' who would provide the authority and the guidance that Rajan lacked while growing up, a search that failed because of his great emotional investment in it, is amply documented in his autobiography. The father who fails is not an uncommon one and normally the son comes to some sort of *modus vivendi* by aggression and rebellion in his adolescence so that the *individual* reaction to the father as a person can be replaced by more or less objective *evaluation*. In Rajan's case, the father however made this necessary aggression against himself impossible, not only by his kindness and love for his son but by the son's feeling of guilt, connected (we strongly suspect) with a childhood incident. . . .

. . . Here we must emphasise that we are neither postulating nor advocating a simple displacement of private emotions into public affairs, nor are we choosing between the personal and social aspects of Rajan's leadership. Our attempt is to see both the themes—the personal and the social—in the leadership of a student agitation. However, our account would be incomplete without introducing another dimension on the personal level, the stage of life Rajan was in when the agitation took place.

Upto his intermediate examination, Rajan had had a brilliant academic career. But now, as he expresses it, 'came a major young man's crossroads problem in choice of a career'. He thought that his aptitude lay in the field of humanities, and English literature was his preferred field of study. 'But then most people around thought that it was silly of me to renounce lucrative opportunities in engineering or medicine and take up literature.' Rajan was young, at the beginning of his adolescence period, and bowing to this pressure he enrolled for his Bachelor's degree in Science. Finding himself in a field which did not interest him at all, he became listless, his attendance at classes irregular and sporadic. He passed his Bachelor's degree with a second class, the first 'failure' of his career. He then drifted into the engineering college, which he hated, and the adolescence crisis, reactivating the old doubts of his childhood, approached a climax, culminating in what can only be called a neurotic episode, later perceived by Rajan as such.

Rajan spent a year at home, recovering. Here amidst the warm acceptance of his parents, regressing to the scene of the childhood triumphs when his superior destiny seemed so manifest, he was able to put himself together again and regain a sense of wholeness. Recovering from the crisis, he returned to the engineering college to finish his studies. It is at this point that the student agitation took place in which Rajan played such a leading role. The agitation was thus in a sense a continuation of his self-therapy. For by combining a purposeful activity toward clear goals with his leadership role which served as a reassurance of the old sense of superiority, the agitation helped in restoring Rajan's fragmented personality.

Here we have briefly considered the leadership of a student agitation from different aspects of the student community and the life histories of a student leader in an attempt to find a configuration which gave a 'meaning' to this leadership. Limitations of data more than the limitations of space (though these are also present) have prevented us from considering each of these aspects as exhaustively as we would have liked to. However, it is our belief that the key to understanding student agitations and student leadership in India, as anywhere else, lies in more case studies of this type. For though a single case of this type does not permit valid generalizations, it often happens that, by providing new insights, a single case deepens the understanding of a host of similar cases.

# Dynamics of Factional Conflict
# The Break-up of the Indian
# National Congress in 1969[*]

## P.N. RASTOGI

The changing character of factionalism in a social group is related to the dynamics of its faction situation. The dynamics refer to the nature of relationships and interactions between structural elements that yield as their output the fluctuating character of factional phenomenon. . . .

## I

## STRUCTURE AND DYNAMICS

The structuring elements of a faction situation are basic to its dynamics. They represent the nodal points around which the system dynamics are apt to revolve. For this purpose it may be useful to trace the course of a faction situation in terms of the sequential appearance of its structuring elements. A faction situation emerges and begins at a particular period and takes some time to develop all the elements of its structure.

[*] Adapted from P.N. Rastogi, 'Dynamics of the Conflict Process,' and 'The Analysis of a Conflict Situation: The Break-up of the Indian National Congress,' *The Nature and Dynamics of Factional Conflict*, Delhi: Macmillan India, 1975, pp. 57–93.

The starting point in this context is the appearance of major changes in the group's environment. The changes may be social, economic, political and cultural. They generate schisms in the group which are subsumed under the general term 'clash of interests' between leading members of the group. The latter come to represent alignments of group members along antithetical positions regarding the group's policies and activities. As the schisms persist, competitors begin to develop a closed system outlook, i.e., 'perceptual setting of interest closure'. This aspect, after a varying delay period, leads to an adverse impact on interpersonal relationships, and a tendency towards the cessation of cooperative activities in the transactions of the group is initiated. The development of such a state of affairs seriously violates the reciprocity of expectations in the social interaction of group members. At this stage the conflict comes into an overt phase. The factions blame one another and see the opposite side as responsible for the loss of group solidarity and the noneffective realisation of group goals. This stage tends to generate psychological tensions which amplify as the conditions of mutual recrimination, loss of cooperation and damage to group interests continue. Activation of conflict-resolution elements is apt to occur at this juncture and their effectiveness may reduce the tension and restore cooperation. Alternatively, the tensions may lead to provocative activities in terms of a factional strategy to harm and humiliate the rival side. Activities on the one side generate corresponding responses from the other and a vicious circle of action, reaction and 'evening up the score' is apt to arise. This would provide the psychological tensions with a momentum and in the process enlarge the area of clash of interest. The initial issues may be supplanted by larger ones. The cycle of interaction and the formation of a faction situation is complete at this point.

## REACTIVE PATTERN OF POSITIVE FEEDBACK

The continuation of the situation then follows the repetitions of the above interaction cycle. The circular reactive structure outlined above reveals the pattern of a positive feedback loop. The time cycles of the loop can manifest both the growth and decline phases of the phenomenon. The phases would depend upon the initial values of the structuring elements and the varying periods of delays, i.e., time constants between the sequential stages of loop interaction. The dynamics of the process may then be represented in the form of a positive feedback loop as in Figure 1.

## THE DYNAMIC STRUCTURE OF FACTIONALISM

The positive feedback loop in Figure 1 presents the essential outline of the dynamic pattern of factional conflict. The process starts from an unresolved clash of interests which reflects the impact of major changes in the group's environment. It proceeds through the sequential stages with a period of delay at each stage and cycles back to the starting point. The periods of delay depend upon the empirical situation and its changing nature. A growing situation may be characterised by progressively shorter delays in the loop cycles while the reverse would be the case in a declining situation.

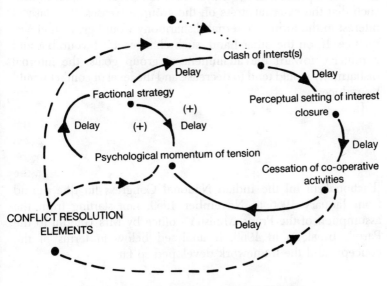

Figure 1

The conflict resolution elements may be external, i.e., persons, groups and social agencies connected with the group's activities and/or internal, i.e., some non-aligned group members. They seek to dampen and insulate the conflict process. Their activation is, however, more likely after the cessation of cooperation makes the conflict overt. The decline, growth and accommodation of factions would depend upon the relative effectiveness of these elements. If the conflict resolution elements are successful in their efforts, the loop would enter a decline phase, i.e., the conflict would progressively lessen. If they are only partially successful, the situation would persist at a given level of opprobrium. If, on the other hand, they are unsuccessful or absent from the scene, the situation would progressively worsen, leading to either the elimination of one faction or the break-up of the group into two separate groups. The growth phase of the loop, if unchecked in its course, would eventuate in the collapse or disintegration of the existing system.

Major changes in the group's environment may similarly affect the conflict process in two ways. If certain adverse changes occur such that the external stress on the group increases, the clash of interest in the form of internal disharmony would grow in consequence. If, on the other hand, such changes are favourable and conducive toward the attainment of group goals, the internal disharmony would tend to decrease and the level of conflict would be reduced.

[ . . . ]

## II

[Factionalism in] the Indian National Congress [in t]he period from January 1966 to November 1969, i.e., starting from the assumption of the Prime Minister's office by Mrs Gandhi to the Party's break-up in 1969, is analysed below in terms of the concepts and the framework developed so far.

## THE STRUCTURE OF THE FACTION SITUATION

The analysis here begins with the changes occurring in the party's environment followed by an outline of the structuring elements of the faction situation.

## CHANGES IN THE PARTY'S ENVIRONMENT

[ . . . ]

The Congress Party during the period under review functioned without the advantage of a leader of Nehru's stature. The Party could no longer capitalise on its role in the freedom movement after two decades of rule and the death of its most illustrious leaders. Politico-military pressure from China and Pakistan was continuing. Failure of two successive monsoons had created near famine conditions in some parts of the country and adversely affected economic growth. Problems of unemployment, labour militancy in West Bengal, Naxalite violence in Andhra, Bihar and West Bengal, regionalism in Punjab and Madras [now, Tamil Nadu], tribal insurrections in Assam and general economic recession in the country, were producing severe stresses on the political system. The public dissatisfaction with the government resulted in the Party's poorest ever electoral performance in 1967. The currency had to be devalued in the same year. All these factors induced strains within the Party's internal relationships. The Party's pre-eminence in national affairs was declining.

## THE STRUCTURAL ELEMENTS OF THE FACTION SITUATION

### CLASH OF INTERESTS

This is the first structuring element of a faction situation. It is concerned with the lines of internal divisiveness within a group. The clash of interests here involved status, power and authority. The formulation of the discord was however over the relationship between the Party and the Government wings. The Party leaders wanted a major role in governmental policies and the exercise of power as they felt [that they] had had to justify and defend Government policies before the electorate. The Government wing's consistent view was that Government policies and decisions depended on many factors, some of which may be confidential, and the Party's role in administration would create confusion in the lines of authority. The Party's role according to them was restricted to the selection of candidates for elections, ideological matters and general policy lines for the guidance of the Government. During the Nehru era, the issue came to the surface many times but did not become a crisis owing to Nehru's hold over the Party and the fact that the Party President was often a man of his choice. He himself combined both the functions for some time. With a decline in the Party's importance in national affairs, the antagonism between both the wings sharpened.

Factional schisms in the present situation were accordingly observable along two major lines: the Party organisation wing *v.* the Government Parliamentary wing, and the rightists *v.* the centrists and a small section of leftists. Senior Party leaders, most of whom were rightists, allied with the sections of rightists in the Government wing to depose Mrs Gandhi and her followers. This produced a bipolar situation.

The Party President Nijalingappa and other Party leaders like Sanjiva Reddy, Atulya Ghosh and Morarji Desai (Deputy Prime Minister) were rightists. K. Kamraj, a former Party President, was a leftist but joined the rightist faction owing to his strained relations with Mrs Gandhi. On the opposite side in the Government wing were Mrs Gandhi, F.A. Ahmad and J. Ram, all left of the centre centrists. Y.B. Chavan (government wing centrist) first aligned with the rightist faction but later supported Mrs Gandhi in the pre-split situation.

The issue that upset the Party leaders was the Government's failure to consult them on the devaluation issue. The Party leaders at this juncture were anxious to remove Mrs Gandhi if need be and supplant her by someone more pliable. Morarji Desai was both able and willing to play this role. In the immediate contest provided by [President] Zakir Hussain's death, election of their faction candidate would have enabled them to remove Mrs Gandhi by a Presidential ordinance in the then fluid conditions of Parliamentary majority. Mrs Gandhi perceived the situation in much the same way and wanted J. Ram, a trusted colleague, or the then Vice-President, V.V. Giri, to be accepted as the Party's nominee. The clash of power and authority was supplemented by the status rivalry between the Prime Minister and the Deputy Prime Minister. The rightist faction came to be known by the term 'Syndicate'. Mrs Gandhi's group was termed 'Indicate' but its use did not catch on.

## PERCEPTUAL SETTING OF INTEREST CLOSURE

This developed gradually as the opposite sections realised that they would not be able to shape the Party and the Government in their image without the removal of the other. Syndicate members perceived the Government wing as insensitive and unresponsive to their views and advice for the improvement of the administration and the Party's future. It was, according to them, therefore necessary to make Mrs Gandhi compliant to the Party leadership or alternatively seek her removal. Mrs Gandhi and her followers saw the Syndicate moves as undue interference in the Government's functioning and an effort to erode her position as leader of the Parliamentary Party. Such a mutually exclusive way of perception suddenly sharpened in focus in the context of the Presidential election in August 1969. As the situation unfolded, the persons, the issues and the happenings came to be increasingly adjudged by the labels 'pro-Indira' and 'anti-Indira'.

## CESSATION OF COOPERATIVE ACTIVITY

This aspect makes the conflict visible. Rival factions blamed each other for their respective failure to extend proper cooperation in the elections. The electoral defeat of some prominent rightist leaders in the February 1967 elections was attributed to the active negative role of the leftist Party members. Cooperation faded further after the 1967 elections. In January 1968, Mrs Gandhi failed to get Dinesh Singh, a member of her cabinet, elected to the Party's Working Committee. In July 1969, both the factions failed to agree on a list of economic programmes and could not cooperate in the unanimous selection of a candidate for the Presidential election. Mrs Gandhi refused to support the candidature of Sanjiva Reddy, the nominee of the Syndicate faction. Her faction mobilised to get him defeated in August 1969.

Cooperation at the Working Committee level ended next. The Party President removed three pro-Indira members from the Party's Working Committee. Her faction withdrew its participation from the Committee meetings in consequence and was 'expelled from the party' soon after. Cooperation at the governmental level ended with the removals and resignations of Syndicate supporters from the Central Ministry.

## PERIPHERAL NATURE OF DISJUNCTIONS

This element, as discussed previously, refers to a basic defining characteristic of factionalism as a species of conflict. Factions do not differ with each other over the fundamental goals and objectives of the group of which they are a part. The discords concern the policies and the activities pursued by the group to achieve those goals and objectives. In the situation under review, both the factions agreed with one another over the goal of ensuring the dominance of the Congress Party in the national government and political affairs; both of them realised that it was only their party that could tackle the important tasks of economic reconstruction and political stability. They however differed over their approach toward realising these goals. They saw one another as pursuing and advocating erroneous policies and to that extent being responsible for the Party's declining prestige and hold over the masses. With the passage of time, these differences grew. They came to be characterised by an increasing degree of emotional estrangement between the Party's prominent leaders. This aspect of emotionalism, termed here as the psychological momentum of tension, provides the next structuring focus of the faction situation.

## PSYCHOLOGICAL MOMENTUM OF TENSION

This structuring element seeks to stabilise a faction situation. Psychological tensions here were evidenced by the frequent polemical exchanges between supporters of the rival faction leaders. After the [nomination of Sanjiva Reddy], informal contacts and communication between the rival leaders nearly ceased. Formal and sharply worded exchange of letters and notes became the rule. Public statements became more vituperative. Derogatory references and stereotypes, and slanderous leaflets and pamphlets circulated amongst the Members of Parliament and State Legislatures who constituted the electorate for the Presidential election. The Party meetings became platforms for mud-slinging.

## Factional Strategy

The structuring element reinforces and widens the clash of interest. Factional strategy in this situation was going on covertly for a long time. It primarily took the form of preventing the nomination and election of candidates perceived as belonging to the opposite faction. Occasionally it took the form of embarrassing the Government by putting forth awkward questions directly and indirectly. Critical references to the Government in public speeches and writings also came under this category.

The intensification of conflict at the central level followed when the Syndicate, as part of its strategy to weaken Mrs Gandhi, refused to have Dinesh Singh in the Working Committee and later turned down Mrs Gandhi's choice for Presidential candidate. Mrs Gandhi responded immediately by relieving Morarji Desai, the Deputy Prime Minister, of his finance portfolio and thus forcing him to resign. She further enacted leftist economic measures like bank nationalisation and moved to abolish the privy purses of former princely rulers.

These moves were meant to damage the image of the rightist faction. As part of her counter strategy she refused to endorse the candidature of Sanjiva Reddy and her faction mobilised the support of other opposition parties like the Muslim League, Communists, DMK and Akali Dal for V.V. Giri. The Syndicate was already soliciting the support of the rightist parties like Jan Sangh and Swatantra. After Sanjiva Reddy's defeat, the Syndicate sought to humiliate Mrs Gandhi by demanding a public apology and threatening her with expulsion. Mrs Gandhi responded by dismissing four junior ministers and the railway minister known to be Syndicate supporters and initiated a signature campaign to call a general meeting of the Party to impeach Nijalingappa and elect a new President. The Syndicate responded by expelling the supporters of Mrs Gandhi from the Working Committee. Finally, after issuing a notice to Mrs Gandhi, the Party Working Committee dominated by the Syndicate expelled Mrs Gandhi, J. Ram, and F.A. Ahmad from the party on 12th November 1969. Indira Gandhi's faction then called an A.I.C.C. meeting and elected a new Party President. At this stage, the Party split was complete. Two Congress parties came into existence.

The objective of factional strategy for both the factions was to weaken and damage the public image of the rival side in order to achieve the dominance of their own faction.

## UNRESOLVED NATURE OF THE CONFLICT

This is another basic defining attribute of factional conflict. The nature and course of conflict was lacking in the commonly agreed and socially established modalities for a lasting resolution of the discords. The majority decisions of the Party's Working Committee and the Central Parliamentary Board, which were dominated by the Syndicate faction, were unacceptable to Mrs Gandhi's faction and led to retaliatory moves on her part. Similarly, her policies and decisions were unacceptable to the Syndicate who were insensitive to her problems and wanted to direct the functioning of the Government over her head. Regulatory devices like mediation and arbitration had been rendered ineffective by the middle of 1969. There was no prestigious figure in the Party who commanded the trust and confidence of both the rival factions. In the absence of such regulatory mechanisms, the conflict could not be insulated and continued to grow leading to the eventual split of the Party.

In 1966 and 1967, the conflict resolution elements were active and effective. They succeeded in preserving party unity by avoiding a disruptive contest for Prime Ministership. They managed to have Mrs Gandhi elected leader of the Parliamentary Party without contest. The role of Kamraj, a former Party President and a veteran Congress leader from Madras, was notable in this context.

The prestige of Kamraj, however, slumped after his defeat in the 1967 general elections and the poor performance of the Congress Party in the Madras (now, Tamil Nadu) State where the DMK party formed the state government. He gradually moved closer to the Syndicate owing to his differences with Mrs Gandhi. By 1969, there was no effective Party leader of stature who could insulate the conflict. Mediation efforts by Y.B. Chavan and the last minute efforts by some State Chief Ministers, represented the ineffective operation of the internal conflict resolution elements.

This structuring element is basically concerned with the fact that in factional conflict there is no lasting settlement of the conflict. Specific disputes and discords may apparently be resolved for the time being only to be reactivated again and intermittently, whenever new occasions for the clash of interest arise. This is what has happened time and again since 1966 and earlier. . . .

## PARADIGM FOR FACTION ANALYSIS

The preceding discussion of the structure of the Congress Party faction situation has provided an analytic overview of the situation as a whole. This analysis has essentially been in terms of descriptive and static categories. A paradigm for the analysis of factions on the other hand focusses on the group aspects of the situation. It provides a picture of a conflict situation during a given period. A series of such pictures would then provide one with a dynamic picture of an evolving situation. The analytic categories are descriptive and static here too. But a comparison of the information over an extended period of time enables the analysis to reflect the dynamic aspects of the situation as well. The paradigm hence provides a mode of analysis that is both static and dynamic at the same time.

The factionalism in the Congress Party (1966–69) is analysed through this paradigm. The analysis is given in a tabular form (see Table 1) for ease of comparison and conciseness. The Table juxtaposes three successive pictures of the conflict situation. They refer to the situation as it existed at the beginning (January 1966), at a midway turning point (March 1967) and at the end (November 1969). The remarks column amplifies the information where necessary but omits the details given earlier. . . . The Table illustrates some dimensions and categories only with reference to Mrs Gandhi's faction. This, however, does not unnecessarily limit the analysis. The situation with reference to the Syndicate faction may be inferred by the obvious implications.

Table 1

Paradigm for Faction Analysis in the Congress Party (1966–69)

| Dimensions | Analytic Category I-Beginning (Jan. 1966) | Analytic Category II-Midway (March 1967) | Analytic Category III-End (Nov. 1969) | Remarks |
|---|---|---|---|---|
| 1. Number of factions | Two | Two | Two | Factions in the early stages were generally known as rightists and left of the centre centrists. Towards the end, they came to be known as Indira faction and anti-Indira faction. The latter was also known as 'the Syndicate'. |
| 2. Proportion of group membership. | Majority of the members at every level of the Party and Government wings. | More than half of the Party members in Parliament; about half of the membership in the Party's Working Committee and Central | In the Parliamentary Party 432 members out of a total of 543; ten members out of twenty-one in the Working Committee; even numbers in the | Factional alignments operated at the level of Party's Parliamentary group, Central Parliamentary Board, Party's Working Committee and the State Chief Ministers. |

| Dimensions | Analytic Category I-Beginning (Jan. 1966) | Analytic Category II-Midway (March 1967) | Analytic Category III-End (Nov. 1969) | Remarks |
|---|---|---|---|---|
| | | Parliamentary Board; more than half of the Chief Ministers in the States with Congress Governments. | Central Parliamentary Board; eight out of eleven Chief Ministers; 407 delegates of AICC out of a total of 703. | |
| 3. Stability of membership over a given period. | Fairly stable. | Infrequent changes. | Fairly stable in the sense that there were few if any defections *from Mrs Gandhi's faction.* | Changes became frequent during the period between late 1967 and early 1969. The hard core of both the factions however did not change sides. |
| 4. Relative magnitude of change in membership. | Little or no change. | Proportional decrease in faction size. | Marked proportional increase in faction size. | K. Kamraj went over to the Syndicate side in 1969. Y.B. Chavan changed over to Mrs Gandhi's side after August 1969. Mrs Gandhi's faction grew in size after |

| Dimensions | Analytic Category I-Beginning (Jan. 1966) | Analytic Category II-Midway (March 1967) | Analytic Category III-End (Nov. 1969) | Remarks |
| --- | --- | --- | --- | --- |
| | | | | July 1969 following her leftist policy measures like bank nationalisation. Her faction withdrew its participation from the Party's Working Committee on the eve of the Party's split, i.e., November 1969. |
| 5. Beginning of dissension. | Particular event and period, i.e., Desai's second failure to secure Prime Ministership; recent. | Poor performance of the Party in 1967 elections and Desai's third failure to secure Prime Ministership; recurrent. | The impending election of a new President following Zakir Hussain's death in May 1969; recurrent. | Dissensions during each of the three periods received a fresh impetus from a particular event during the period concerned. The dissensions acquired a recurrent character following the successive bids for power by the rightist faction. Desai's first failure was against Shastri in 1964 following Nehru's death. |

| Dimensions | Analytic Category I-Beginning (Jan. 1966) | Analytic Category II-Midway (March 1967) | Analytic Category III-End (Nov. 1969) | Remarks |
|---|---|---|---|---|
| 6. Nature of dissension during a given period. | Quiescent | Intermittent | Ongoing and intensified. | Factional activities were coextensive at the Party, Parliament and state levels. |
| 7. Issues of discord. | Specific, simple, few and narrow. | Diffuse, complex, many and narrow. | Specific, simple, few and wide. | In 1966, the issues of discord were relatively specific and simple, i.e., those relating to the sharing of power. By 1967, they had become diffuse, complex and numerous. In addition to the issues related to the sharing of power, others relating to election affairs, ideological considerations, the Party's role and importance and the Government's policies, emerged and magnified. Toward the second half of |

| Dimensions | Analytic Category I-Beginning (Jan. 1966) | Analytic Category II-Midway (March 1967) | Analytic Category III-End (Nov. 1969) | Remarks |
|---|---|---|---|---|
| | | | | 1969, they were simplified into 'remove Indira' and 'dislodge the Syndicate' goals of the rival factions. |
| 8. Nature of interests and values involved. | Power, status and authority. | Power, status and authority. | Power, status, authority and ego considerations. | Ideological formulation of the discords was the supremacy of the party wing v. the government wing, and the radical economic measures v. a conservative approach. |
| 9. Intensity of conflict. | Social distance. | Social distance and avoidance. | Overt provocative activities. | Polemics and non-cooperation represented the situation during the period mid-1967 to mid-1969. From July 1969, the conflict went beyond this level although polemics and non-co-operation increased further. |

| Dimensions | Analytic Category I-Beginning (Jan. 1966) | Analytic Category II-Midway (March 1967) | Analytic Category III-End (Nov. 1969) | Remarks |
|---|---|---|---|---|
| 10. Scope of conflict. | Limited primarily to the parliamentary group, i.e., one sub-system level. | Limited primarily to two sub-system levels, i.e., Party's Working Committee and the Party's Parliamentary group. | Extension to the system as a whole, i.e., all the sub-system levels: Parliamentary group, Working Committee, Central Parliamentary Board, AICC delegates, state legislatures and party organisations. | During the 1969 presidential election, both the factions sought to develop links with other political parties. The Indira group sought the help of Akali Dal, Communists and DMK parties while the Syndicate aligned with Jan Sangh and Swatantra parties. Communists extended support to Mrs Gandhi's government during the post-split period also. |
| 11. Social bonds among faction members. | Common interests. | Common interests and shared opprobrium. | Common interests, shared opprobrium and reciprocity of obligations. | Progressive widening of the conflict amongst the Party's top leadership increasingly involved their associates and followers in an expanding |

| Dimensions | Analytic Category I-Beginning (Jan. 1966) | Analytic Category II-Midway (March 1967) | Analytic Category III-End (Nov. 1969) | Remarks |
|---|---|---|---|---|
| | | | | orbit reaching down to the Party's grass-root levels. |
| 12. Status of conflict resolution elements. | Active and influential. | Active and moderately influential. | Active and non-influential. | During periods I and II, and even earlier, Kamraj played a notable role in resolving the problem of succession to the Prime Ministership. Later he joined the Syndicate faction. Y.B. Chavan tried to play a conciliatory role in July 1969 but failed. Last minute efforts by some Congress Chief Ministers in November 1969, to avert the party split, also failed. |
| 13. Location of conflict resolution elements. | Internal to system. | Internal to system. | Internal to system. | |

These three successive pictures of the conflict situation give us an idea of the changes occurring in a dynamic situation. These changes are reflected in the changing entries in the rows of the paradigm. Each successive entry depicts the qualitative and/or quantitative changes occurring in the situation as it developed in time. The situation is seen to be moving in a particular direction, i.e., toward increasing tension and instability.

The paradigm supplements our knowledge of the situation by highlighting its group aspects at changing points in time. The number, nature and strength of the factions, the beginning and ongoing character of the dissensions, the nature, number and objects of discord, the scope and extension of conflict and the status of conflict resolution elements, give us the relevant and necessary information to understand the functioning of factions. This understanding is gained both with reference to the situation at a given time and across that point in time.

Both the paradigm and the structure of a faction situation enable us to understand the 'what' and 'how' of the situation in their respective terms. They organise the available data and information in such a manner that orderly patterns may be discerned in the mass of apparently unrelated data and information. They are however unable to represent the 'why' of the phenomenon as it changes or could have changed in its time path. The 'why' aspect of a phenomenon requires its formulation in dynamic terms and the introduction of causal relationships in its representation. This purpose is served by the third mode of analysis, i.e., the dynamics of the process.

## THE DYNAMICS OF THE PROCESS

Factionalism as a process of conflict was seen to be representable in the form of a circular reactive structure of a positive feedback loop (Figure 1). Five of the seven structural elements of a faction situation, i.e., clash of interest, perceptual setting of interest closure, cessation of cooperative activity, psychological momentum of tension, and factional strategy, constitute the process variables of the positive feedback loop.

The loop pattern then signifies that a clash of interests gives rise to a perceptual setting of interest closure; this closure leads toward a cessation of cooperative activity; the cessation generates a psychological momentum of tension which in its turn gives rise to a factional strategy. This factional strategy then reinforces the psychological tensions on the one hand and augments the clash of interests on the other. The loop is complete at this point and cycles again from the clash of interests onward.

Each variable in the loop is linked to the next one through a non-linear relationship and an intervening random period of delay. These non-linear relationships may be interpreted here as causal links, and the loop as a whole then represents a circular chain of causation. A non-linear relationship is one in which regular variations in the antecedent variable produce irregular and non-proportional variations in the consequent variable. A non- linear relationship between the two variables attended by a random delay period, signifies that one variable affects the other in a delayed manner such that the initial response is slow, followed by a more rapid response. In the context of the present situation, the pattern of the loop relationships means that the conflict increases very gradually at first, followed by a relatively rapid escalation. As the loop continues to cycle along its path in time, the situation develops gradually over three years and reaches a critical stage in the fourth year when the system breaks up.

[ . . . ]

The external variables—conflict resolution elements and changes in the group's environment—affect the loop variables from the outside. Conflict resolution elements, if effective, would reduce the values of the concerned loop variables and check the growth of the conflict. Such was the case up to 1967. Thereafter, the conflict resolution elements became ineffective and could not avert the growth of dissensions. Changes in the environment that produce stress on the group, serve to aggravate the internal conflict. Such stressful environmental change occurred in May 1969, when Dr Zakir Hussain, the then President of India, died. This external event induced a sudden increase (step input) in the value of the clash of interest variable, thereby affecting other variables and hastening the system toward its disintegration. The period from May 1969 to November 1969 is covered by the last seven cycles of the loop. During these cycles, the external factor of Hussain's death seriously and suddenly enlarged the clash of interests in the context of electing a new President for the nation.

Both the factions perceived that the wide powers vested in the Presidency would be decisive in determining their own political survival in the then prevailing conditions of political uncertainty. This sudden and significant increase in the first loop variable, then rapidly amplified the values of the other variables in a nonlinear manner. The loop could not then proceed beyond a few cycles as its variables were approaching their critical limits. The system disintegrated explosively in its forty-seventh cycle in early November 1969. This aspect is highlighted by the rapid escalation of factional strategy and psychological tensions during the last four cycles from July to November 1969. The moves and the countermoves of the two sides during this period are given in Table 2.

Table 2
Tension and Strategy in the Congress Party Factionalism
During July to November 1969

| Syndicate Faction | Mrs Gandhi's Faction |
|---|---|
| *July:* | |
| 1 (a) Sanjiva Reddy selected as the Party nominee for Presidential election against Mrs Gandhi's efforts. | 1 (a) Mrs Gandhi relieves Desai of the finance portfolio, who then resigns to save his 'self-respect'. She also announces the nationalisation of fourteen major commercial banks as a part of her efforts to damage the public image of the Syndicate. |
| (b) Indications that Reddy would try to use the wide but as yet untested powers of Presidency against the Prime Minister. | (b) Mrs Gandhi refuses to endorse Reddy's candidature to Congress members of the Parliament. Her supporters call for a 'free vote' of conscience in the election. |

| Syndicate Faction | | Mrs Gandhi's Faction | |
|---|---|---|---|

*August:*

| 2. | Syndicate seeks electoral support for Reddy from the Jan Sangh and Swatantra, the two rightist parties. | 2. | Her supporters mobilise support for V.V. Giri from the Akali Dal, Communists, DMK and Muslim League parties. Reddy was defeated in the election on August 16. |
|---|---|---|---|

*September-October:*

| 3. | In heated discussions, Mrs Gandhi is accused of indiscipline, intrigue, disruption, corruption and anti-party activities by the Party President Nijalingappa and his friends. | 3 (a) | Mrs Gandhi removes four junior ministers who were Syndicate supporters from her cabinet. |
|---|---|---|---|
| | | (b) | In abrasive exchanges, the Syndicate is accused of being reactionary, representing vested interests, anti-socialist and an enemy of the masses. |

*November:*

| 4. | Nijalingappa drops three of Mrs Gandhi's supporters from the Working Committee during its meeting on November 1. | 4. | Mrs Gandhi and her supporters boycott the Working Committee meeting and organise a parallel meeting at her residence. They resolve to hold a meeting of AICC at Delhi on Nov. 22, to elect a new Congress President. |
|---|---|---|---|

| *Syndicate Faction* | *Mrs Gandhi's Faction* |
|---|---|
| 5 (a) Congress President and his supporters reject a compromise formula worked out by Congress Chief Ministers. They refuse to withdraw charges against Mrs Gandhi. | 5 (a) Mrs Gandhi's faction launches a signature campaign among the members of AICC to impeach Nijalingappa and elect a new Congress President by the end of the year. |
| (b) With eleven members out of twenty-one who attended the regular Working Committee meeting, Syndicate declares the requisition move to call the AICC meeting 'illegal' and serves a 'show-cause' notice on Mrs Gandhi for her 'anti-party' activities. | (b) She cancels an afternoon meeting with Nijalingappa on Nov. 7 arranged by Congress Chief Ministers. Mrs Gandhi removes the Railway Minister, Dr Ram Subhag Singh, a Syndicate supporter. |
| (c) Three supporters of Mrs Gandhi suspended from Party's primary membership for rowdy demonstrations. | (c) Two other ministers leave her cabinet. |
| (d) On Nov. 12, Syndicate's Working Committee expels Mrs Gandhi from the Congress and instructs the Congress Parliamentary Party to elect a new leader. | |

The dynamics of the process also elucidate the alternative possibilities regarding what could have happened. The two external variables play a crucial role in this context. Had the death of Dr Hussain not occurred when it did, the conflict would not have escalated so rapidly. This would have resulted in delaying the party's split, if not preventing it altogether. Similarly, if the conflict resolution elements could have remained effective, the dissensions would have been manageable. The earlier problems of Shastri's succession in 1964 and the unanimous election of a Prime Minister after the fourth general election in 1967 were much more serious, yet they were effectively tackled. The decline of conflict resolution elements, as discussed earlier, can be traced to Kamraj's loss of standing by his and the Party's defeat in his home state in the 1967 elections and his subsequent alignment with the Syndicate. The Party at this stage functioned without the benefit of the moderating influence of a reputed leader and its capacity to handle the internal discords was accordingly reduced.

The positive feedback character of the process dynamics implies that factionalism in a social system would occur owing to a persisting clash of interests and grow because of the self-sustaining circular causation of a closed loop. Conflict resolution elements as an external variable serve to dampen the process and reverse or check its growth. Environmental changes may increase or depress the process depending on their impact on the clash of interests. The actual and fluctuating character of the phenomenon is then accounted for by the varying combination of the two external variables and their resultant impact on the cycling of the loop.

# Conflict Cycles: The Interaction of Local and Regional Politics in India*

## D.W. ATTWOOD

[ . . . ]
The purpose of this article is to argue that, in our studies of local politics and their connexions with regional power systems, we must be alert to the problem of distinguishing between processes which are (1) homeostatic or repetitive; (2) evolutionary or revolutionary; and (3) cyclical over the medium term (and which may easily appear, in some phases, under the guise of the other two). Most real-world processes probably involve some combination of stable, cyclical and evolutionary elements, and it is no doubt artificial to attempt to draw too fine a line between them. Nevertheless, some important theoretical problems hinge on the perception that situations which appear to be either stable or linearly progressive may in fact be merely quiescent or active phases of a medium-term cycle. . . .

[ . . . ]
. . . The model I propose to discuss here is not intended to be general but merely illustrative. It is presented in order to support the general point that taking note of [political] cycles may lead to more rigorous testing of the two polar (and often unstated) assumptions that local political power is either distributed in a static pattern based on 'tradition' or else is being steadily redistributed into a configuration which is more 'modern' or revolutionary.

* Excerpted from D.W. Attwood, 'Conflict Cycles: The Interaction of Local and Regional Politics in India,' *Man* (NS), 14, 1979, pp. 145–60.

. . . I suggest the following propositions regarding cyclical processes in political conflict:

(1) Observations of political conflict at different times and places within a given society may generate what appear to be meaningless variations unless one looks for regular phases of a cyclical process (or processes).

(2) Observation of a single arena in a short time period may lead to erroneous conclusions either that
  (a) there is a fixed pattern of power differentiation and conflict; or that
  (b) the observed dynamics will intensify into the indefinite future.

I am not suggesting that permanent differentiation or linear evolution are nonexistent in political (or economic) affairs; my position is exactly the opposite, in fact. However, we cannot properly distinguish what is stable nor what is changing over the long run, unless we are also careful to sort out variations which are primarily cyclical in nature.

This article is based on a particular example of a conflict cycle, derived from observations in rural western India. This particular cycle occurred not once but several times, during the last thirty years or so, in a number of overlapping arenas which were crucial for the transfer of political demands and resources between local and regional institutions. The same cycle has probably occurred in a number of empirically similar situations, but it would be premature to attempt to specify the conditions under which it is or is not likely to occur. Even within a single society, conflicts can vary along a wide range of dimensions, and no doubt conflict cycles come in many forms besides the one discussed here. . . . Consequently, a good deal of comparative investigation is necessary before we can begin to specify what conflict cycles, if any, are likely to occur under a given set of conditions.

[ . . . ]

After presenting the conflict cycle model, and the case study data which support it, I propose to compare it with four other models of local-regional political interaction which have appeared in the literature on Indian politics. Like the conflict cycle, these four competing models are based on case study material. They all have features which are important for an understanding of local politics in India and probably in other agrarian states as well. However, in one way or another, these four models appear to be unnecessarily static or linear in their assumptions. I hope to demonstrate that much of the behaviour which is accounted for by these competing models could be subsumed under the different phases of the conflict cycle model.

## THE CONFLICT CYCLE MODEL

The conflict cycle begins with:

*Phase One*: When an arena is controlled by a stable ruling group, it takes on the pattern of an *elite council*, in which the ruling group is able to conceal its internal competitions, from outsiders and subordinates alike, behind a facade of 'consensus' (Bailey 1965). The power of a local ruling group of this type usually depends heavily on access to a regional elite network. Using this access, local leaders can offer patronage favours (or sometimes threats) to their clients or subordinates. Subordinates are kept in their place by lack of access to the regional network.

*Phase Two*: Consists of a challenge by subordinates against the ruling elite, through a process of *group mobilisation*. If subordinates find they are unable to satisfy their ambitions and demands through individual connexions with the elite (that is, through patron-client alliances), they may develop a sense of common interests and mobilise against the ruling group. In reality, the usual situation is not quite so simple, for those who lead the rebellion are often those who have at least limited access to power already but who expect to gain greater control through group mobilisation, that is, through widening the scope of their competition with other power-holders. . . .

Just as the local elite council is embedded in a regional elite network, so the local group mobilisation is related to processes at the regional level. The local rebels may be stimulated by changes or expected changes in the control of regional systems; and more directly, they may also be stimulated by power shifts in overlapping local and intermediary institutions.

*Phase Three*: Follows the group mobilisation effort, if it is successful. Members of the former out-group have forced their way into the regular decision-making process in the arena. They bring with them new bases of support and corresponding new demands. As a result, it becomes uncertain just what kinds of leadership, alliances, strategies, demands, and so forth, will determine the decisions to be made. There follows a period of experimentation, in which alliances shift very rapidly, with no regard to previous group interests and loyalties. This is the phase of *anarchic* or 'pervasive' *factionalism* (Siegel & Beals 1960), in which individual opportunism predominates.

Given the lack of consistent group loyalties, it is difficult to perceive any pattern in this phase, particularly if it lasts for a long time. However, there is a pattern at work, one of selective pressure on the political survival of individual competitors. This selective pressure derives from the new bases of support and their corresponding demands. The old leaders must learn to manipulate (and satisfy) these new groups of supporters, or else, in the scramble of new alliances and shifting attacks, they will be driven out of power, one by one, as *individual* losers. (Of course, it is likely that some were already driven out in Phase Two.) The old guard are no longer being challenged, or trying to defend themselves, as a group: the selective pressure acts on individuals and their mutable alliances. On the other hand, some members of the old guard may become highly successful at the new techniques of wielding power.

*Phase Four.* Begins when the problems of experimentation are resolved and some leader or clique is able to fit the new and old sources of power together in a stable fashion. The new stability is less like that of an elite council and more like an *arena council* (Bailey 1965), in which the constituents are capable of exerting more organised pressure on the official decision-makers. Phase Four resembles Phase One, but it may also represent a small, linear step towards greater overall participation by the constituents, a step which was made possible by the success of the group mobilisation in Phase Two and by the intense competition (for support from below as well as for patronage from above) of Phase Three.

In order to achieve this new stability, two conditions must be satisfied. First, the new sources of local demands and support must be balanced into a workable coalition; and second, the local leaders must gain efficient access to a regional elite network. Put another way, the conflict cycle has two sources of energy. One source is the local discontent of subordinates, who are willing to follow new leaders in the hope of a larger collective share of the pie and new opportunities for individual ambition. An equally important source of change derives from the external connexions which rising local leaders make with politicians, administrators, and businessmen in other arenas. When power relations are changing in the outside world, they provide opportunities for new kinds of connexions to be made. Such connexions tie the local conflict cycle to the political process of the surrounding region, and they may have a determining effect on the timing, intensity, and outcome of the different phases.

## *Examples of the Conflict Cycle in Action*

At this point it will help to illustrate the workings of the conflict cycle with an actual case from Western India. The outline below is a very brief summary of the findings presented in a previous paper (Attwood 1977); it also emphasises a number of new points concerning the connexions between local conflicts and regional politics. The focal arena in this case is the Olegao co-operative sugar factory, located in Poona district, Maharashtra state.[1] Like other co-operative sugar factories in the region, this one is a crucial arena for the working out of local ambitions and conflicts, because of the value of the resources which it controls. . . .

The factory is owned and controlled by some 2,700 shareholders, each having one vote. The vast majority of the shareholders are medium- and small-scale cultivators living in thirteen villages near the factory and belonging to one of the peasant castes of Maharashtra: either the Maratha caste (which accounts for about 50 per cent of the shareholders), or the minority peasant castes (of which there are four, accounting for a total of about 35 per cent of the shareholders).

---

[1] The research in Poona District began in October 1969 and ended in September 1971. (Statements made in the present tense in this article refer to conditions in 1970–1.) All names of persons and localities within the district are fictitious.

*Phase One*: The Olegao co-operative sugar factory was founded in 1955, largely through the organising efforts of one large-scale cane grower who did not belong to the peasant castes. This man, the first chairman of the factory, was a Brahman who had built up a large farm operation by the use of his education, business skills, and connexions in the regional networks of business and public administration. These qualities were also the ones necessary successfully to establish the Olegao factory.

The initial Board of Management was appointed by the state government, for a period of five years. The chairman was supported on the Board by a few other Brahmans and merchant-caste cultivators, plus some wealthy peasant-caste representatives. With great care, this Board managed to build the factory into an efficient business enterprise.

*Phase Two*: After the initial five years of getting the business established, a new Board was to be elected by the shareholders. The first election, in 1960, provided the occasion for certain conflicts to come out into the open. Local leaders belonging to the Maratha and other peasant castes wanted to gain control of the Board, since they represented the majority castes.[2] These challengers naturally sought support first from their numerous kin. The latter, for their part, saw in this turn of events an opportunity to press their leaders for employment in the factory or other favours. The result was a form of political bargaining, patronage politics, in which votes were exchanged for potential favours. One could hope for more favours from a kinsman or fellow villager than from a comparative stranger; therefore, the advantage in this game lay with leaders from the larger peasant lineages.

In seeking to gain control of the factory, the peasant-caste leaders were following a regional trend: anti-Brahman feelings had been simmering in the region for decades, due to the disproportionate influence of the highly-educated Brahman minority in the realms of public administration, politics, and the professions. The universal franchise, instituted in 1952, coupled with an expanded system of local councils and agricultural

---

[2] This was not just a phase of caste conflict. There were issues involving economic class interests which cut across caste loyalties; and alliances were also affected by specifically political interests, by kinship connexions, etc. These cross-cutting interests are analysed in more detail in the earlier paper (Attwood 1977).

co-operatives, gave the rural majority (dominated by the landowning peasant lineages) the leverage needed to take control of various political arenas. The ambitions of the peasant-caste leaders within the Olegao factory were not merely stimulated by awareness of this trend at the regional level. Several of them had acquired political experience and leverage in overlapping arenas, such as the District Central Co-operative Bank. Gains made in some arenas could produce a domino effect in others, particularly in the case of the co-operatives, which had interlocking directorates built into their formal structure.

The old high-caste elite, supported by some of the wealthier peasant-caste leaders, managed to cope with the new challengers by splitting the opposition. It was not only the Brahman and merchant-caste leaders who feared the voting power of the Marathas, the largest peasant caste; so did the leaders of the minority peasant castes. The old elite assembled a carefully balanced election slate, in which they were joined by representatives of all the minority peasant castes, plus two Marathas. This coalition won nine out of eleven seats on the new Board of Management.

*Phase Three*:  Once the Maratha threat was temporarily subdued, the minority coalition lost most of its cohesion when it came to selecting a new chairman of the Board. Eventually, the only compromise candidate they could agree on was, of all things, a Maratha: a choice which pleased no one. As the minority coalition fell apart, the old elite finally lost any semblance of control as a group: the scope of political competition had been irrevocably widened, leading to fluid competition among a host of peasant-caste leaders and factions. From 1961 to 1967, in this phase of competitive patronage, no coalition endured from one election to the next, and the chairmanship changed hands repeatedly. The peasant castes were in control, but their leaders derived from five different castes, thirteen villages, a score of major lineages, and innumerable factions. It was extremely difficult to assemble a coalition which would satisfy all these blocs of constituents. In retrospect, it is also evident that this anarchic phase lasted as long as it did because there happened to be no local leaders with really powerful connexions to regional institutions such as the Congress party and the state assembly.

*Phase Four:* Such a connexion was provided finally in 1967. A young Congress party worker (who had his own personal connexion with a powerful leader in the national cabinet) was elected as local Member of the Legislative Assembly (MLA). He assembled a ruling coalition out of three small factions on the Olegao factory Board; and subsequently, in 1970, he supervised the selection of candidates for the re-election of this coalition. Since he was in a position to grant or withhold important favours, he could maintain a certain amount of discipline among his personal supporters and weld them into some semblance of a cohesive unit.

As a consequence of its new internal stability and efficient connexions with regional political networks, the factory was now in a better position to bargain for its interests with institutions at higher levels. In 1967 the factory sent a deputation with the MLA to the Prime Minister to ask for changes in the government's sugar price policies. In the two years immediately following, prices were much more beneficial to the co-operative sugar factories and their shareholders.

Does a similar cycle help explain other cases? There seems to be some evidence that it does, in places where anthropologists have restudied local politics after an absence of a decade or more. For example, Epstein (1962) has described Wangala, a recently irrigated village, where in 1955 a group of newly-rich peasants were attempting to acquire some of the political and ritual authority held by the heads of less-wealthy but longer-established lineages. Epstein's first fieldwork was done when this conflict was just beginning to intensify; as she discovered later (1973: 179–83) this situation soon led to open competition for community support in a recurrent ritual context (comparable to Phase Two group mobilisation). Epstein admits that, when she returned to the field in 1970, she expected to find the same conflicts had continued or intensified. Instead, she discovered a situation of peaceful coexistence: the newly-rich peasants had made it too expensive for the traditional elders to continue the competition, and the former were now in charge (a situation comparable to Phase Four). In this case, Phase One existed, by implication, before the rebels commenced their struggle; but there is no mention of anarchic factionalism comparable to Phase Three. Even if Phase Three did not occur in this case, the general point still stands:

local politics was neither set in a fixed mould nor moving in a simple linear direction (towards ever-increasing factionalism, for example).

Similar conclusions can be drawn from observations by Beals (1974: 167–70), who also restudied a local political situation seen earlier in quite a different light. In 1953, Namhalli village was in a condition of pervasive factionalism (Phase Three), which appeared to be the result of increasing contacts with the outside world, and which the authors apparently expected to continue as these contacts inevitably intensified (Siegel & Beals 1960). However, in 1966 Namhalli had settled down into a quiet Phase Four, in which a group of educated young men with factory jobs and urban ties had assumed control of village affairs. It can be inferred from this that perhaps at some point a Phase Two situation had developed, in which these young men first attempted to share power with the elders who had previously dominated the village; though it is possible in this case that Phase Two grew out of Phase Three, instead of vice versa. In any case, the general point still stands: the dynamics of one political trend may lead eventually to a reversal instead of a linear intensification.

We may conclude from these two cases that local conflicts in India (and possibly in other agrarian states) are indeed likely to move through cyclical phases; that political changes are likely to come about through the introduction of new resources and connexions with regional networks; and that, in a short period of observation, it is possible to mistake the dynamics of a particular phase for a long-term trend.

## COMPETING MODELS OF LOCAL-REGIONAL INTERACTION

We turn now to the discussion of four competing models, based on case studies of local-regional political interaction in India. Each of these models has a valuable dynamic aspect, corresponding, it is claimed, to similar features in the conflict cycle. At the same time, however, each of the four competing models has its particular static aspect, which the conflict cycle attempts to avoid. For the sake of convenience, the four competing models may be labelled: (1) the encapsulation model (Bailey 1969); (2) the competitive patronage model (Brass 1965); (3) the class conflict model

(Carras 1972); and (4) the patronal elite model (Carter 1974). Discussion is confined to the idiosyncratic ways in which these four models are used by these particular authors; but it is possible that the following comparative analysis will provide, if not insights, then at least relevant questions which could be applied to other models bearing similar labels.

Let us begin with a discussion of *encapsulation* (Bailey 1969: 144–85). Bailey has designed the encapsulation model in order to show how villages which are for geographical or other reasons on the margins of state systems, become incorporated as the state expands the scope and functions of its administration. Once these villages are affected by more than a small number of external contacts, then 'the situation of encapsulation has given way to integration' (1969: 175–6). This suggests that encapsulation is the preliminary stage in the general incorporation of autonomous or semi-autonomous localities into the state. The region in India which provides the data for Bailey's model is highland Orissa, where 'the frequency of interaction between the villagers and the world outside is still low compared to that found in other areas of India' (1969: 175). In fact, one could easily argue that most of India's rural population, living in the nuclear zones of Indian civilisation, passed through the stage of encapsulation centuries ago, since most Indian villages have long had regular contacts with state administrations and regional market networks. Be that as it may, there can be no doubt that the frequency and intensity of local-regional interactions have been increasing rapidly in all parts of India. Consequently, Bailey's model, in drawing attention to changes in local politics caused by increasing external contacts, is helpful even where a locality has passed beyond encapsulation to integration. The conflict cycle model suggests, however, that increasing integration may have cyclical as well as linear effects on local politics. In Wangala and Namhalli villages, for example, factionalism did not increase indefinitely, as had been expected.

A second valuable feature of the encapsulation model is the emphasis on political middlemen, who influence the terms of interaction between the village and the state. The only problem with Bailey's approach to this aspect is that he sees the local middleman as one who interprets, screens, guides, or distorts the impact of the regional on the local system. Middlemen certainly do these things, but that is not all they do. In another paper

(Attwood 1974) I have argued that there are at least two complementary role types for political middlemen: the patron and the group mobiliser. The patron is one who manipulates resources or sanctions originating from outside the local area. The group mobiliser, on the other hand, activates local supporters in order to demand changes in the regional distributive system. (The same person may play both roles, of course.) In contexts such as the non-Brahman movement, the nationalist movement, and many caste uplift movements, for example, local group mobilisers have been active for decades in many regions of India. . . . [I]t is possible for group mobilisers to have an effect on the regional system, even when they are acting on purely local demands. For our present purposes, one relevant example would be the delegation from the Olegao sugar factory to the Prime Minister in 1967.

The problem with Bailey's model, then, is that it is one-sided. As he himself observes, 'The arrows of causation between a political structure and its environment point both ways. But, as far as is possible, the encapsulated political structure will be treated as the dependent variable and the environment will be the independent variable' (1969: 146–7). This would seem a dubious short-cut in situations where local demands and initiatives have had an influence on state policy and administration.

The conflict cycle and encapsulation models, consequently, share a concern with the actions of political middlemen and with the effects on local politics of changes in regional institutions. The conflict cycle model differs, however, in two additional points of emphasis: (1) it assumes that increased encapsulation or integration may cause cyclical as well as linear changes in local politics; and (2) it also assumes that local demands and initiatives may have reciprocal effects on the regional system, particularly through the process of group mobilisation.

The *competitive patronage model* is simple, plausible and widely used. A good expression of this model is given by Brass, in his discussion of the connexions between local and regional factions: 'Factions are vertical structures of power oriented towards influence, that is, towards the establishment of links which will provide for the transmission of favours and services' (1965: 244). In other words, factional cleavages are a result of competition for patronage resources. State and district-level politicians, who can influence the allocation of state resources (for development projects, etc.), need voters to support them. Local-level faction leaders become attached to the higher-level leaders so that blocs of votes can be exchanged for patronage. There is competition among these leaders at every level, meaning that factional splits at the state level tend to be replicated among subordinate leaders at the local level. Given the high degree of competition and individual mobility, there are also frequent opportunities for leaders to shift their alliances according to expediency. This contributes to the growth of a 'patternless politics' in which group loyalties (whether based on caste, class, religion, or something else) are frequently overridden by cross-cutting alliances (Brass 1965: 32). Brass is aware that interest-group conflicts may also enter the political process; but he suggests that group mobilisation and class conflict are inhibited by factionalism (1965: 244), over-looking the possibility that these different types of conflict may alternate in a causal-feedback relationship, as they are assumed to do in the conflict cycle model.

The competitive patronage model shares with the conflict cycle an emphasis on individual competition and mobility of political middlemen. These are undoubtedly important sources of change in the interaction between local and regional political processes, because competition tends to generate a search for new resources and bases of support. (For example, it was the high-caste leaders, under pressure from the Marathas, who brought the minority peasant castes into a position of unusual power on the Olegao factory Board in 1960.) However, in de-emphasising the possibility of group mobilisation as an outcome of such competition, the competitive patronage model acquires a static aspect: schemati-cally, the approach suggests that vertical patronage alliances combined with vertical factional cleavages inhibit the formation of horizontal class cleavages.

An explicitly antagonistic model, emphasising *class conflict*, is put forth by Carras (1972) in her study of district council factions in Maharashtra state. These district council factions are seen as representing, on one side, the class interests of rising rural polit-icians, who are based in the agricultural cooperatives and repre-sent the great mass of the voters, in opposition to more urbanised politicians on the other side, who are based in the upper echelons of the Congress party, and are said to represent the big industrial and mercantile interests in the state (1972: 14–15). Thus district factions stem from the problems of a 'mixed economy', the conflicts of interest between the co-operative and private sectors.

In some districts, at least, Carras's data on the 1962 district council elections point to a phase of relatively coherent confrontation between two interest groups (a rising rural elite and an established urban elite). However, Carras does not conceive of these data (which are purely synchronic survey data) as reflecting a passing phase of a larger process. Her analysis posits a fixed association between economic classes and functional, systemic 'needs': a blending of Marx and Parsons. She conceives of a fixed, horizontal division of class interests between the 'political constituency' (the rural masses) and the 'economic constituency' (the urban businessmen). These constituencies serve, respectively, the 'integrative' and 'adaptive' needs or 'imperative functions' of the political system (1972: 18–22). Carras sees evidence of this cleavage at both the state and district levels of the system; but she does not explore the actual transactions between political actors at different levels, as Brass did, which tends to make her rejection of his model less convincing. She seems to assume that political alliances must form between actors with equivalent, but not complementary, interests. Later study of some of the same district councils suggests that the interest groups which may have formed in 1962 were quickly dissolved in the course of factional competition (Rosenthal 1972).

Carras expresses concern that the rural based 'political constituency' might overwhelm the district councils and somehow destabilise the 'system' (1972: 188–9). Thus her model of the connexion between local and regional politics appears to be one of a permanent, horizontal division, which must be maintained to keep the system in balance: the alternative is a 'convulsive crisis' (1972: 188). As Dahrendorf (1959: 131) noted, discussing Marx and Parsons, this sort of model actually tells us very little about a society in which change is pervasive, which is neither in a state of functional balance nor of revolutionary upheaval. Carras's model, which might appear dynamic at first glance, is actually one of fragile homeostasis.

The conflict cycle model, on the other hand, recognises that class (or caste) interests may be divided during a phase of group mobilisation, but views this as a normal outgrowth of increased political participation and the growth of institutional networks between the rural populace and urban centres. The 'system' is constantly destabilised, by such events as the nationalist and non-Brahman movements, among others; but group mobilisation seldom leads to the outright disruption of a regional system. It may, in fact, cause only a change in actors (e.g., non-Brahmans replacing Brahmans); or it may also lead to incremental changes in the overall level of political participation.

The fourth model, which I call the *patronal elite model*, combines elements of the two preceding ones. This model is also based on a study of local politics in Maharashtra state (Carter 1974). Carter argues that there is a strong horizontal cleavage between the dominant 'political class' and the remainder of the rural populace (1974: 5, 151–61). He thus agrees with Carras on the existence (though not the nature) of a permanent and all-important division of class interests in local politics. Within the dominant class, which stretches across the region in what I have called an elite network, political alliances are the typical, fluid coalitions between faction leaders, based on opportunistic competition for control of patronage resources. This aspect of Carter's model corresponds to the competitive patronage model used by Brass. On the other hand, local alliances between leaders and their followers (between members and nonmembers of the dominant 'political class') are said to be more stable than the coalitions between faction leaders, for the simple reason that the clients have no bargaining power: they are forced to depend on the will of their patrons. In spite of this assumption, however, Carter notes that a leader could lose his followers if he does not provide them with enough patronage (1974: 159). This implies that, as patrons compete strenuously for control of resources (1974: 128–38), they may also be competing for the loyalty of their clients.

In effect, this is an expansion and elaboration of the 'dominant caste' model of Indian village politics. As articulated by Bailey (1963: 118), the original model assumes that, in the village, patronage alliances:

> 'run up and down between families in the dominant caste and families in the service castes. Only the dominant caste has an autonomous political existence, not as a corporate political group, but as a field for political competition.'

These few words on village politics contain all the major assumptions which guide Carter's study on a somewhat larger scale.

The patronal elite model is more complex than the others, yet it is also static. Even though Carter refers, in passing, to the local history of elite circulation (1974: 3, 177–8), he does not incorporate this process into his basic model. The model emphasises rigid stratification at the expense of group mobilisation and individual mobility. It is interesting that, in defining the political class, Carter relies heavily on the category of people known as 'vatandar Marathas'–that is, the dominant, landholding patrilineages from which the village headmen were formerly appointed (1974: 5, 46–8). Carter's work offers insights into the social, political and economic sources of power of these lineages; but his model tends to suggest that this status category is rigid over time. Some of his data suggest otherwise. In one village, there are several 'attached' lineages which even now are being absorbed into the vatandar Maratha category (1974: 81–4). Presumably, this process of absorption is stimulated by economic mobility, as with the case recorded by Epstein, in which immigrant lineages rose, within a few decades, to become equivalent in ritual status to the 'founders' of the village (Epstein 1973: 179–82).

The vatandar category is not closed to new recruits, nor is it the tiny minority which Carter implies. The numerical data marshalled to demonstrate that Girvi village is dominated by a small minority can actually be reinterpreted to show that political control is won by the *largest* descent groups, working through multicaste coalitions. In this village, the vatandar Marathas consist of two main lineages totalling 25 per cent of the population. The rest of the village is divided among thirty-two other Maratha lineages (comprising 32 per cent of the population) and nineteen other castes (43 per cent of the population) (Carter 1974: 16, 96). If the vatandars are able to operate as a cohesive unit, it is small wonder they can outweigh these other fragmentary groupings. However, even the vatandar lineages do not attempt to operate alone: elections are decided by multicaste coalitions (1974: 117–18).

Throughout the book runs the assumption that status groups form irreducible, cohesive units in political and economic affairs. Thus we learn how much land, labour and credit is controlled by the vatandars as a whole (1974: chs 5, 7), but there is no statistical comparison between *individual* class membership and *vatandar* status. (How many *vatandars* are poor? How many non-*vatandars* are rich? And how do these anomalous individuals behave politically?) Since they are ignored as analytic units, the model provides no insight into the mobility of individuals—still less of the groups which they mobilise to acquire political power.

The patronal elite model portrays a situation of fluidity at the upper levels (within the dominant 'political class') coupled with rigidity, due to lower ascriptive status and economic dependence, at the bottom. Although Carter mentions the circulation of elites in passing (1974: 3, 177–8), his model does not really account for the competitive circulation of individuals into and out of the political class, a process which could be a potential source of change in the recruitment of political support and the utilisation of regional connexions. Even less does the patronal elite model allow for the possibility of group mobilisation and change in the balance of power between various groups.

## CONCLUSIONS

An observer who makes a short-term study of political conflict in what happens to be a Phase Three situation will probably conclude that the arena studied contains a great deal of fluid competition, but no trace of class conflict or change in the class basis of local power. A real shift in the basis of power is only evident if we have comparative data from Phases One and Two. We may speculate that the competitive patronage model is based primarily on observations made in Phase Three situations, with some admixture of Phases One or Four (which involve more discreet competition for patronage resources). The advantage of the competitive patronage model is that it explains the rapid shifting of alliances and the mobility of individual careers. It has a corresponding static aspect, however, which is the assumption that competitive patronage simply generates resistance to group mobilisation and class conflict. The conflict-cycle model, on the other hand, assumes a possible causal-feedback relation over time between factionalism and class conflict, between patronage and group mobilisation.

By the same token, if the observer happens to make a short-term study of conflict in Phase Two, he is likely to conclude that the real basis of conflict lies in the divergence of class interests. This probably explains the origin of the class conflict model propounded by Carras. The class conflict model is potentially valuable for understanding the processes of group mobilisation and change in the bases of political support. However, the use which Carras makes of this model is quite static: hers is a model, not of ongoing restratification, but of an absolute dichotomy between balance and upheaval. And even if this class conflict model were more dynamic in itself, it would not give a very good account of other phases in which alliances are fluid and individual opportunism is rampant.

Lastly, if the observer should make his study in a Phase One or Phase Four situation (with possibly some admixture from Phase Three), he might be inclined to advocate a patronal elite model. This model of a restricted elite, which does not allow its internal competitions even to be observed by subordinates, is equivalent to the 'elite council' situation in Phase One (cf. Carter 1974: 153–8; Bailey 1965). The patronal elite model accounts for individual mobility within the political class, but it does not account for individual mobility from below, nor for group mobilisation and change in the balance of power between groups.

Thus we conclude this comparative discussion with the speculations that: (1) many of the empirical variations in local politics reported in the literature might be subsumed under a small set of dynamic processes, of which the present conflict cycle is but one example; and (2) some conclusions concerning the permanent distribution of political power, or linear trends in that distribution, may need modification in the light of longer-term studies of cyclical changes.

As a final note, we might observe that to focus on the conflict cycle in the Olegao factory does not preclude awareness of the important secular trend towards increased political participation and power within the landowning peasant lineages; nor need it occlude our perception of certain elements of stability, such as the continuing importance of personal wealth, education, and regional elite connexions as normal prerequisites for the acquisition of local political power.

# FURTHER READINGS

Paul R. Brass, *The Politics of India since Independence* (The New Cambridge History of India, IV–1). Cambridge: Cambridge University Press, 1990.

An useful introduction to the political history of post-independence India. It outlines the systemic crisis confronted by the Indian state, society and economy and analyzes how the political system and political practices have been altered in the post-Nehruvian era in ways which have intensified tensions, exacerbated a variety of group struggles and increased the stakes of political conflict.

Zoya Hasan, S.N. Jha, and Rasheeduddin Khan, eds, *The State, Political Processes and Identity: Reflections on Modern India*. New Delhi: Sage, 1989.

The essays in this volume focus attention on state power and on the ways in which state intervention has affected the relationship between modern institutions and caste-community identities. Though rooted in political science and couched in a Marxian perspective, they provide valuable insights into the political sociology of conflict in India.

Francine R. Frankel and M.S.A. Rao, eds, *Dominance and State Power in Modern India: Decline of a Social Order* (2 vols). Delhi: Oxford University Press, 1989.

An ambitious exercise in an integrated approach to the understanding of social change in India. Cutting across the boundaries of history, political science, and sociology, contributors adopt here a common set of concepts to analyze the changing relations between dominance and state power embracing diverse cultural regions and in an elongated time horizon.

F. Tomasson Jannuzi, *India in Transition: Issues of Political Economy in a Plural Society*. Hyderabad: Orient Longman, 1990.

This slim book takes on issues of political economy

that are likely to be persistent in India for many years to come. Its thesis is that India is a peculiar type of plural society within which consensus-reaching among its disparate elements will remain difficult, whatever the system of governance.

Satish Saberwal, *India: The Roots of Crisis*. Delhi: Oxford University Press, 1986.

This short work tackles the social crisis in contemporary India, whose roots are searched by comparing the specific forms of historical evolution of institutions and norms in India with those in Europe. Advancing from ordinary descriptive procedures, it attempts to construct a socio-historical model of explanation.

Rabindra Ray, *The Naxalites and their Ideology*. Delhi: Oxford University Press, 1988.

An intimate and comprehensive study of the Naxalite movement and its distinct ideology. It draws on both sociology and philosophy to explain the rise of communist revolutionary terrorism in Bengali society in the late sixties and early seventies.

Ghanshyam Shah, *Social Movements in India: A Review of the Literature*. New Delhi: Sage, 1990.

A critical review of the burgeoning body of literature covering social movements in India from 1857 to the present. The studies are divided into eight groups based on the participants and the issues involved: peasant, tribal, *dalit*, backward caste, women, student, middle class, and industrial working class.

# IV

# Work Sphere

Human beings are distinguished from other animals by their capacity to produce their material means of subsistence. Production more than many other social activities requires patterned relations between workers. Such activity, though premised upon cooperation, carries an in-built proclivity for conflict. This is because of the conflict of interests implicit in the generally inequitable relations between categories of persons involved in a particular productive activity.

The four papers in this section deal with conflict in two major kinds of work, namely, agrarian and industrial. The first two analyze the nature of agrarian relations and tensions, the other two dwell on industrial relations and strikes. A distinctive feature of both the agrarian and industrial conflicts is that they are inter-group conflicts, or they tend to become so even if they begin with only two persons. It is the group dimension of these conflicts which makes them structurally significant.

In the agrarian sector the conflict is typically between the landlords and tenants/landless labourers, and in the industrial sector between the employers and workers/trade unions. In both these categories generally the state machinery—legislature, executive and judiciary—is drawn in as a third party. The group orientation of the conflict necessarily implies mobilization by the respective groups in order to strengthen their relative positions. At this stage political parties enter, and the conflict acquires a political dimension.

The mobilization may take place on many bases, including primordial social categories, such as caste, religion, or region. This potential for crystallization of conflict may however be neutralized by the alliances and coalitions due to exigencies of the changing situation. Nevertheless, to the extent that conflict in the work sphere draws on social sources which are not directly related to work *per se*, their mobilization has far reaching consequences for the economy, polity and society in which they take place.

In the opening paper André Béteille describes agrarian relations in Tanjore District of Tamil Nadu, where he did extensive fieldwork during the sixties. This district has been characterized by extremes of inequality and a sharp division between the landowners and the landless, and it has witnessed major economic and political changes since independence.

Béteille sheds light on how traditional patterns of stratification respond to changes in the economic and political spheres. He argues that rural society cannot be fully explained exclusively in terms of the caste system. Emphasizing the importance of ownership, control and use of land he delineates the subtle and complex relationship between caste and class. Thus, his analysis of agrarian relations is pitched on the plane of social stratification.

Béteille urges caution against easy and hasty generalizations about agrarian relations at the macro level. He painstakingly establishes the importance of ecological factors (especially the distinction between the old and the new delta, and the eastern and the western taluks in the old delta), the different modes of production (the *waram*, the *kuttahai*, and the *pannaiyal*), and the various programmes of development in understanding the nature and manifestations of agrarian relations.

According to Béteille, the popular presumption that extremes of inequality in the material conditions of existence inevitably lead to conflict, and that cooperation can be based only on equality, is not supported by sociological evidence. The relation between inequality and conflict is a complex one, and only under certain conditions does inequality lead to conflict. He delineates these conditions.

The paper by T.K. Oommen surveys the internecine agrarian tension in Kerala. Based on a case study of Alleppey district Oommen argues that the presumed relationship between the Green Revolution and agrarian conflict is naive and simplistic, and tries to show how politics plays a crucial role in the origin and spread of agrarian unrest.

Oommen examines how such economic factors as the high density of population and the extremely low land-man ratio, the decline of the coir industry and its impact on trade and commerce, and the resulting growth of unemployment have accentuated the agrarian crisis in several ways. This crisis is placed in the social context of the traditional division between castes and communities, and the erosion of the traditional social bonds which were essentially non-contractual in nature.

Oommen then explains how the tension-prone situation was transformed into a patterned agrarian conflict because of the intervention of such forces as the rural wings of political parties, acting as agrarian pressure groups, and the organizational innovations by the state government. For managing the tension-prone situation in Alleppey, the Marxist government appointed the Kuttanad Industrial Relations Committee (IRC), and Oommen reviews the working of IRC as an instrument of tension-management.

Turning from the rural agrarian to the urban industrial scene we have two papers exploring conflict in work relations in Bombay. The selection from E.A. Ramaswamy provides a general survey of the nature of industrial conflict in the premier industrial metropolis of the country. And, excerpts from H. van Wersch examine the strategies employed by the contending parties in a historic strike.

In his book Ramaswamy surveys the industrial relations scene in Bombay, Madras, Bangalore and Calcutta, and highlights its unique features and general trends. The focus in our selection is on Bombay, where there is an organic linkage between the vitality of the labour movement and the eclecticism and adaptability of private, and in particular multinational, enterprise.

According to Ramaswamy, the unique feature of the labour movement in Bombay is the sway of independent trade unionists who disclaim allegiance to political parties and their trade union federations. Equally important is the self-conscious and assertive shop-floor leadership, which too is non-ideological. He examines the dynamics of leadership within the unions and how the managements get embroiled in it on the one hand, and the implications of such leadership for industrial relations on the other.

Ramaswamy contrasts the leadership styles of Datta Samant and R.J. Mehta in the course of industrial conflicts. He reviews collective bargaining as a machinery for settling industrial disputes and highlights the cost at which the leaders 'achieve' benefits for their followers. The loss of confidence in leadership among Bombay workers and their seemingly endless quest for more appropriate leadership are explained against this background.

The Bombay textile strike of 1982–3, directly involving a quarter of a million workers and lasting nearly a year and a half, is perhaps the greatest industrial cataclysm of its kind anywhere in the world. The last selection in this section, drawn from the first full-scale study of this unprecedented strike by van Wersch, describes the strategies adopted by the textile workers and their leaders, most notably the consummate militant Datta Samant, on the one hand, and the millowners and the state government on the other.

Beginning with an outline of the position of various unions *vis-à-vis* the strike, van Wersch notes the ambivalence of the Communist unions. He examines the misconceptions about the role of workers' committees in the strike. And he highlights the importance of rural connections in the course of the agitation, especially in providing sanctuary to the workers leaving Bombay, in the food collection drives, and in the jail *bharo* campaigns.

An important aspect of the textile strike which has drawn critical attention is the use of violence by Samant and his followers. H. van Wersch examines the evidence available on this and reflects on the image of the strikers which was sought to be created by the millowners in collaboration with the police and the media. He is particularly critical of the role of the state and its police in the suppression of the strikers. He concludes with a review of the strategies adopted by the millowners.

# Agrarian Relations in Tanjore District*

## ANDRÉ BÉTEILLE

### I

Tanjore district in South India offers certain advantages for the
investigation of agrarian relations as an aspect of the broader
problem of social stratification. It displays extremes of inequality
in regard to both caste and class and a close, though changing,
relationship between the two. There is first the threefold division
of the population into Brahmins, Non-Brahmins and Adi-Dravidas.
This division is visible in the physical structure of the village
where even today the three groups inhabit different residential
areas. Each group retains a degree of cultural unity and there are
areas of social and ceremonial life in which Brahmins, Non-Brahmins and Adi-Dravidas constitute relatively autonomous systems.
Even in the past the outlines of the agrarian structure were not
as sharp and clear as the divisions separating the three groups of
castes. To use broad and general categories, landowners, tenants
and agricultural labourers did not constitute mutually exclusive
groups or have the kind of cultural identity characteristic of the
broad groupings among castes. It is true none the less that the
division between landowners and the landless was sharper in
Tanjore district than in most other parts of the country.

Even though the district is a relatively small and compact unit,
it is not a homogeneous unit. Tanjore district offers the special

* Excerpted from André Béteille, 'Agrarian Relations in Tanjore District,'
in *Studies in Agrarian Social Structure*, Oxford University Press, Delhi, 1974,
pp. 142–70.

advantage of having within a relatively restricted area more than one clear pattern of social organization. The district may be divided into the Old Delta and the New Delta,[1] each with its characteristic pattern of agrarian relations corresponding on the one hand to differences in ecological conditions and on the other to differences in the structure of caste. Within the Old Delta itself there are differences of a lesser magnitude between the Western and the Eastern *taluks*. The sharpest difference from the viewpoint of agrarian relations is between the Eastern *taluks* of the Old Delta and the *taluks* of the New Delta.

[ . . . ]

[T]he contrast between the Old and the New Delta is not merely an economic contrast but also a cultural one. On the one hand, there are differences in ecology (including water supply), crop pattern (including intensity of cultivation) and density of population (including settlement pattern). On the other hand, there are differences in antiquity of settlement, concentration of temples and places of pilgrimage, and the development and cultivation of the arts of life. These two sets of differences are interconnected. On the whole, one notices the greatest cultural elaborateness in those areas where ecological conditions have in the past been most favourable to the development of intensive cultivation.

In Tanjore district cultural elaborateness is closely associated with elaborateness of social structure. In the Old Delta, and particularly in the Western parts, the settlements are not only older and larger, they have also a more complex pattern of social organization. This complexity has many aspects but we are interested in it mainly from the viewpoint of social stratification. The system of stratification is less rigid and elaborate in the New Delta than in the Old. This is true in regard to both the structure of caste and the organization of classes.

The proportion of both Brahmins and Adi-Dravidas is much higher in the Old Delta than in the New. These represent the

---

[1] The area which has been irrigated for centuries [by channels of river Kaveri—ed.] is actually the one we refer to as the Old Delta. It covers the entire northern and eastern portions of the district. The New Delta is that portion of the 'non-deltaic' part of the district which is now irrigated by the Grand Anicut Canal and the Vadavar Canal, both completed in 1934.

extremes of the hierarchy of caste. The New Delta has a high concentration of castes belonging to the middle levels of the hierarchy. The Old Delta has also a higher proportion of both large landowners and landless labourers. In the New Delta there are very few large landowners and the proportion of agricultural labourers is also quite small. The close relationship between caste and class is nowhere more evident than in Tanjore district; one can see the two vary in the same manner as one moves from one *taluk* to another.

## II

[ . . . ]

Traditionally at least three modes of productive organization were known in the area. They have been characterized as the *waram*, the *kuttahai* and the *pannaiyal* systems. *Waram* and *kuttahai* are both forms of tenancy. According to *waram* the tenant gives a stipulated share of the produce to the landlord; according to *kuttahai* he gives a particular amount earlier agreed upon. The *waram* system seems to have become obsolete several decades ago but the *kuttahai* system is still widely prevalent. In the *pannaiyal* system, also widely prevalent, the landowner has his land cultivated by labourers to whom he pays wages. In addition to tenancy (*kuttahai*) and wage labour (*pannaiyal*), production is also organized by many on the basis of family labour.

[ . . . ]

Tenancy is a blanket term which represents a complex pattern of rights and obligations having a number of variants. The terms and conditions of tenancy differ greatly from one crop to another. We shall discuss here only those arrangements which prevail in the cultivation of paddy which is by far the most important crop grown in the district. The legislative and political problems centering around tenancy in Tanjore almost all relate to the practice of tenancy in paddy cultivation.

Tenancy as a mode of productive organization is far more common in the Old Delta than in the New. In the past it was probably equally common in all parts of the Old Delta but in recent years it seems to have been replaced to some extent by wage labour in the eastern *taluks*. From what I could gather in the course of a brief stay in 1968 very little change seems to have occurred in the extent of tenancy in the western *taluks*. This would be consistent with the limited change in productive arrangements in general in this area as compared with the other parts of Tanjore district.

. . . In . . . villages . . . located in the western part of the Old Delta, the typical landowner is the Brahmin *mirasdar*. The Brahmin *mirasdar* is debarred by ritual sanctions from the use of the plough, and cultivation is inconsistent with his traditional style of life. Since wet paddy cultivation is both arduous and onerous, Non-Brahmin landowners also try to get the rough and heavy work done by others whenever they can afford to. In order to understand why tenancy is so widespread here we have to recognize that it has been established in the area for a long time on the basis not only of the economic calculation of costs and benefits but also of the social evaluation of work and leisure.

[ . . . ]

In Tanjore district tenancy is an unequal relationship since land is scarce and labour plentiful. In the past when a man had enough land he did not need to till it himself; and the demand for land was such that tenants could always be secured to work on terms which by today's standards would appear very unfavourable. In the past the landlord often extracted as much as 70 or 75 per cent of the produce. The traditional relationship between landlord and tenant was however an enduring one and the tenant, in spite of his low economic and political position, enjoyed a measure of security. With changes in economic and political conditions in the present century, tenants began to demand a higher share of the produce and this the landlords frequently countered by threats of eviction.

This is the setting in which a series of legislative enactments was initiated soon after Independence with a view to improving the economic and political position of tenants in relation to their landlords. The first in the series was the Tanjore Tenants and Pannaiyal Protection Act of 1952. Then came the Madras Cultivating Tenants Protection Act, 1955 which reduced the landlord's share to 60 per cent of the produce; and after that the Madras Cultivating Tenants (Payment of Fair Rent) Act, 1956 which reduced it further to 40 per cent. The most recent legislative moves seek to reduce it still further to 25 per cent of the produce.

In addition to increasing the share of the tenant, these enactments have also attempted to give him security of tenure.

Tenancy legislation seems to have had two kinds of effects which are somewhat opposite in nature. Powerful and enterprising landowners have in some cases succeeded in evicting their tenants and then re-engaging them as wage labourers; this seems to have happened more extensively in the eastern parts of the Old Delta than in the western. But where tenants have resisted eviction they have on the whole improved their economic and political position, although this does not mean that they are able to secure all the advantages which the laws guarantee.

Organizing production by the use of wage labour is not new in Tanjore district, and it is to be found everywhere although one encounters it in its most characteristic forms in the eastern *taluks* of the Old Delta. While it is easy to see that the *kuttahai* and the *pannaiyal* systems have coexisted for a long time, it is difficult to determine the factors in terms of which the individual landowner might choose the one rather than the other mode of productive organization. Today there seems to be a preference among land-owners for wage labour over tenancy, but we must never forget that the conditions which determined these choices in the past were different from those of today.

[T]he largest farms in Tanjore are to be found in the eastern *taluks* of the Old Delta. Many of these are run on a commercial basis including some which have changed from paddy to sugar-cane production. Here economic calculations of costs and benefits are very much in the forefront. Agriculture is viewed as a field for the investment of capital and the application of the most modern techniques available. A few of the really wealthy and enterprising landowners in this area engage managers selected for their knowledge of scientific agriculture and experience in farm management.

It hardly needs to be said that on farms of this kind production is organized through wage labour. In some cases tenants have been converted into wage labourers but how extensively this has happened it is impossible to determine. If tenancy is an unequal relationship, the element of inequality is even more marked in the relationship between landowners and wage labourers. The wage labourer has less economic security and lower social prestige than even the tenant. . . .

The third mode of productive organization is that based on family labour. When one talks of a peasant society, this is the kind of productive organization that one regards as its basis. This can be the predominant mode of organization in an area only when certain conditions are met. The distribution of land should be such that holdings are not too large in relation to the available technology and not too many of those who have to live by agriculture are landless. These conditions are both met in the New Delta and it is in the New Delta that we find production based on family labour to be the predominant mode, although it is found in other parts of the district as well.

[ . . . ]

It is particularly important to remember that the different modes of productive organization are not in reality separated into water-tight compartments. They not only coexist within the same district and the same village but are frequently combined on the same farm. This means that if we are to discriminate between the different parts of Tanjore district we can do so only in terms of broad differences of mix, saying, for instance, that production on the basis of family labour is the predominant mode in the New Delta while wage labour forms the main basis of productive organization in the eastern *taluks* of the Old Delta, although all the three modes of productive organization are and have been for long present in each of the three parts of the district.

The modalities of combination may be best illustrated by describing the kinds of cases which I investigated in Sripuram in 1961–2 and observed again in 1968. A man owning twenty-two acres of land leases out a total of thirteen acres to three different persons. The rest of the land he has under 'personal cultivation' which means that he pays wage labourers to cultivate them and engages a supervisor to see that the work is being properly done. Or, one can take a slightly more complex case. A man with six acres of land leases it out for cultivation on the *kuttahai* system. The *kuttahaidar*, who himself owns three acres, leases in two more acres from another landowner, thus giving himself an operational holding of eleven acres. Out of these he sub-leases five acres to someone who is distantly related to him, and has the rest cultivated by a combination of wage labour and family labour, the propor-tions of which vary from year to year.

[ . . . ]

## III

As we have seen, the examination of the different modes of productive organization leads to a consideration of a number of social categories such as landlords, owner-cultivators, tenants, sharecroppers and agricultural labourers. These categories may be viewed either in terms of relations of equality and inequality or in terms of relations of co-operation and conflict. One can easily see that these two perspectives are not unrelated.

Let us consider first the hierarchical aspects of the categories I have identified. One can see in them at least three forms of inequality: (i) between landlord and tenant; (ii) between landowner and wage labourer; and (iii) between large, medium and small proprietors. The first two constitute dichotomous divisions while the third constitutes a set of graded distinctions. In their pure forms they have very different implications for social conflict.

The nature of stratification varies from one village to another although certain broad patterns are discernible. One important difference is in regard to the elaborateness of the system of stratification. The simplest marker of this is the number of layers or strata present in the community. A village which has large, medium and small landlords, owner-cultivators, sharecroppers and landless labourers may be said to have a more elaborate pattern of stratification than one which is composed predominantly of owner-cultivators and wage labourers. From this point of view it can definitely be said that the Old Delta shows more elaborate patterns of stratification than the New.

Another way of comparing systems of stratification is in terms of the social distance between the top and the bottom of the pyramid. This we may call the extremity as opposed to the elaborateness of stratification. There is a close relationship between the two but they are not identical. A system of stratification may be quite elaborate within a relatively narrow spectrum, while another may be made up of only two terms representing the two extremes of the scale.

Here again the difference between the Old and the New Delta is clear. In the Old Delta villages with large landowners at one end and landless people without employment at the other are quite common; in the New Delta the distinction between landowners and the landless though present is less sharp. Beyond this there are certain other differences which are however a little more difficult to describe. In the eastern *taluks* of the Old Delta one often encounters villages which show a greater extremity of stratification than in the west, but less elaborateness; this is particularly true of those villages where tenants have been converted by eviction into wage labourers.

The nature of these categories and their mutual relations can never be fully understood unless we view them in relation to caste, but in doing so we have to proceed with great caution. . . . [T]here are two kinds of relationship between caste and the agrarian class structure. The first is what I call a surface relationship which is revealed by the fact that landowners belong predominantly to the upper castes and the landless to the lower castes. The second is a deeper relationship in which the hierarchical values of caste sustained and legitimized the unequal relations among landowners, tenants and agricultural labourers.

[ . . . ]

At the surface level one notices certain differences between the categories of caste and the categories of class. . . . The boundaries separating the different strata are much less clear in regard to class than in regard to caste. Castes are exclusive categories whereas classes are not; this means that the same individual cannot be a Brahmin and a Non-Brahmin, but he can be at the same time a landowner as well as a tenant. We have to examine the implications of this phenomenon because when it occurs on a large scale it may become difficult to talk meaningfully about classes as opposed categories.

It is easy enough to discriminate between the top and the bottom of the agrarian hierarchy. There are clear and numerous differences between big landlords and landless labourers both in life chances and in life styles. They differ firstly in their relationship to work. Big landlords do not engage in manual work, invariably among Brahmins and very generally among Non-Brahmins. This difference between them and the landless, which is present among men, is particularly conspicuous among women; when one sees women working in the paddy fields in Tanjore one can be certain that they occupy a low position not only in the caste structure but also in the agrarian hierarchy.

There are clear differences between the landlords and the landless not only in what they do but also in how much they earn. With the application of the new technology incomes have risen on both sides, but it is not entirely clear whether the income gap has been reduced or widened. Economic position has to be viewed not only in terms of more tangible factors like income but also in terms of less tangible ones like security. The economic security of landless labourers has declined in Tanjore district even where their incomes have risen. Finally, one has to consider the very considerable differences in levels of living between the landlords and the landless.

When on the other hand we consider large, medium and small landowners, we find the differences between them to be fewer and less clear. For one thing, the lines that we draw between them are bound to be subjective and to that extent arbitrary. A man owning five acres of land may be a small landowner in the dry parts of the New Delta but not necessarily in the western parts of the Old Delta. Further, minor differences in the size of holdings may be mitigated by a variety of other factors such as family size, efficiency of cultivation, adoption of new techniques, availability of credit and so on. Finally, the same individual may pass from one category to another in the course of a few years. When we are dealing with economic distinctions at this level we can easily see how different they are from the distinctions of caste.

Even the distinction between landlord and tenant need not always be sharp although in Tanjore district it has generally been so. Perhaps as a class the tenants have undergone the greatest change since about 1950. There were those who were evicted and transformed into landless labourers. But there were others who improved both their earnings and their economic security first as a consequence of the land reforms and then by taking advantage of the Package Programme. Thus in the days to come it is conceivable that a tenant having a lease on ten acres of land might enjoy an economic position not much inferior to that of someone who owns a similar amount of land.

The contrast between the wealth and affluence of the landlords and the poverty and squalor of the landless is much sharper in the Old Delta than in the New. These differences are visible in dress, deportment and habitation and, clearly, they are associated not only with distinctions of class but also with distinctions of caste. Here again one notices the close association between caste and class although this association is now changing. Wealthy landowners in the eastern *taluks*—and particularly those of the younger generation—are now adopting common patterns of dress and habitation whether they are Brahmins, Naidus or Vellalas.

In Tanjore the ownership of land is not only a source of wealth, it is also a source of prestige and power. It would hardly be an exaggeration to say that every cultivator in Tanjore aspires to be a *mirasdar* for the status that such a position confers. When I did fieldwork in Sripuram I knew two persons—one a Brahmin and the other a Christian Vellala—who had made large sums of money by running a fleet of buses from Tanjore. They had both bought land in the village not so much to enhance their wealth and power as to set a seal on their status as *mirasdars*.

In an area where land is scarce and labour plentiful, the ownership of land gives one control not only over material resources but also over persons. In spite of the protection given to tenants by the law, landowners continue to enjoy great power over them. The lease is usually an oral lease. Sometimes the landowner uses lease deeds printed by him in a local press. Although they do not seem to be legally binding, such lease deeds emphasize the obligations of the tenant rather than of the landlord. Contrary to what is usually set forth in such private lease deeds, the Fair Rents Act of 1956 emphasizes the rights rather than the obligations of the tenants. The two documents, the legal Act and the lease deed actually in use, sum up nicely the ambiguity in the relationship between landlord and tenant in contemporary Tanjore.

The landlord might use his power to engage a landless person as either a tenant or a wage labourer. . . . Since the wage labourer has often to seek employment from day to day (unlike the tenant whose position is secure for at least a season), he is in a sense much more beholden to the landowner than is the tenant.

From what has been said above it will be evident that patterns of agrarian hierarchy in Tanjore are extremely complex and it will be difficult if not misleading to say anything general about the changes taking place in them as a whole. We may perhaps say that the agrarian hierarchy is becoming less elaborate than it was in the past although, to repeat once again, this does not mean that the distance between the top and the bottom is being necessarily reduced. The extent of tenancy is on the decline and the tenants who remain will probably acquire greater economic security in the future. But the basic problem in the agrarian system continues to centre around the relationship between the landowners and the landless. This problem is acquiring certain new forms. In order to understand them we shall now consider certain political forces in the district.

## IV

[ . . . ]

It has been widely believed that conflict is generated directly by extremes of inequality in the material conditions of existence. The view that inequality leads necessarily to conflict and that co-operation can be based only on equality, though widely held among idealists, does not find much support in sociological research. If there is a relationship between inequality and conflict, it is a complex one, and we shall now examine some of the conditions under which inequality does become a source of conflict.

*Mirasdars, kuttahaidars, pannaiyals* and others have had relations of inter-dependence in this area for many generations. Even if we admit, for the sake of argument, that inequalities between landowners and the landless have increased in recent years, there is no question whatever but that there were severe inequalities in the past and that the landless have for long lived a life of poverty and squalor. In spite of this there was a measure of co-operation among the classes in the process of production. This does not mean, of course, that there were no tensions or conflicts between individual landowners and their individual tenants or labourers in their day-to-day relations. It only means that these tensions and conflicts did not generally lead to the kind of organized antagonism between groups which has become an important feature of social and political life in certain parts of Tanjore district.

It is impossible to give a general sociological answer to the question as to why human beings who live under conditions of extreme inequality at a certain time begin to find these conditions intolerable at another time. A number of different things have happened in Tanjore district—as in other parts of the country—which might have combined to make inequality appear less tolerable than it was in the past. Of these, two seem to be of particular importance. The hierarchical values on which the caste system was based, and which gave legitimacy to the unequal relations between the landowners and the landless, have been gradually eroded. With this has declined a whole range of obligations which the upper strata had towards the lower, so that the moral components in the relations between them are now liable to be superseded by political components.

In considering the conflict of classes we find once again certain differences between the Old and the New Delta which become more marked when the New Delta is contrasted with the eastern *taluks* of the Old Delta. Obviously this contrast is related to the contrasts . . . in terms of modes of productive organization and of agrarian hierarchy between the different parts of the district. But caution is advisable against any hasty generalization about the inevitability of conflict, for similar modes of productive organization and of agrarian hierarchy have existed in the past without necessarily generating conflict in east Tanjore.

Agrarian unrest is not altogether new to Tanjore district but the issues have changed and also the forms of conflict. Kathleen Gough, who did her fieldwork in 1951-2, was greatly struck by the clash of interests between landowners and the landless and she had concluded that 'economic and class conflicts, whatever their outcome, will in the future increasingly weaken the identities of caste' (1960: 59). These conflicts do not appear to have developed along a linear path as Gough probably anticipated they would, but the purpose in drawing attention to her statement is to indicate that the structural conditions for these conflicts were present long before the inception of the Package Programme.

Agrarian unrest can be transformed into a conflict of classes only through the action of political associations or parties. The Communist Party has been active in the district since the early forties. . . . When Kathleen Gough did her fieldwork the Communist Party was active in the district and the conflict of classes was close to the surface. Between 1957 and 1967 the Communist Party underwent a decline and the conflict was also subdued. In 1967 the Communists made a comeback in the district and this was followed by intense and sometimes violent conflict between landowners and the landless.

It is obvious that political factors alone cannot explain these conflicts between the landowners and the landless. Some of the structural cleavages in the agrarian system have already been described. I would now argue that these cleavages not only foster the development of certain political forces but are in turn deepened by them.

In the first decade after Independence the problem of the relationship between the landowners and the landless had two forms. There was the relationship between landlords and tenants which centered around the issue of tenancy; and there was also the relationship between landowners and agricultural labourers which centered around the issue of wages. Although tenants and wage labourers were both landless, their interests were by no means always identical, and where tenants themselves employed wage labourers they could even become contradictory.

In the fifties the attention of left-wing political parties was focussed on the issue of tenancy. The agitations of the peasant associations also centered around this issue. (Since tenancy was of small importance in the New Delta, the main arena of conflict was the Old Delta.) The land reform legislation of the fifties was directed mainly towards the problem of tenancy. This problem is politically far less significant today. Firstly, the eviction of tenants, particularly in the eastern *taluks*, has reduced the magnitude of the problem. Secondly, the tenants who remain are probably on the way towards arriving at some kind of stable arrangement with their landlords on the basis of the new legislation. This leaves the relationship between landowners and wage labourers as the principal political problem in the agrarian system of Tanjore district.

The decline of tenancy led to a simplification of the relations between landowners and the landless in the eastern *taluks* of the Old Delta. Tenants no longer stand as a kind of buffer between landowners and wage labourers as they do in many areas in the country including some parts of Tanjore district. Further, there seems to be very little combination of roles in these areas as even small landowners do not usually hire themselves out, and wage labourers have no other sources of livelihood besides agricultural labour. Elsewhere there is a mixed category of dwarf cultivators and sharecroppers who at certain times hire themselves out and at other times hire others to work for them; this leads to a mitigation of conflict between wage labourers and the employers of wage labour. In the eastern *taluks* of the Old Delta landowners and landless labourers come much closer than elsewhere in Tanjore district to being mutually exclusive groups.

It has been argued that the Green Revolution has contributed to an increase in the antagonism between classes although the nature of its contribution is not easy to assess. It has certainly led agriculture to be organized on a commercial basis. Mention has been made of farms in the eastern *taluks* which have changed from paddy to sugarcane and where production is organized with the help of professional managers on a clear calculation of costs and benefits. When this happens on a large scale it is natural for both landowners and wage labourers to become increasingly conscious of their respective economic interests and to perceive such contradictions as there are between them.

The series of disputes between landowners and wage labourers which led to the death of forty-two persons in Kizhavenmani—and which continue to this day—have a clear and evident connexion with the shift from single to double cropping in the eastern *taluks* which began to take place around 1967. This change led to an increase in the demand for labour. The labourers, having already achieved some measure of political organization, . . . adopt a bargaining strategy. . . . Some of the landowners (more often the smaller ones) concede the demands of the *kisans* or arrive at a settlement. Others . . . might try to bring in labour from outside and at the same time seek police protection. In the latter case violence is a likely outcome.

We now have to ask what it is that gives wage labourers their bargaining strength. It appears that they derive this strength in east Tanjore from an unusual combination of factors which are not generally combined in the same way in other parts of the country. How unusual this combination is we can easily see by contrasting the eastern *taluks* of the Old Delta with the New Delta of Tanjore district.

The economic homogeneity of the landless in the eastern *taluks* has already been noted; economically they constitute a pure category of wage labourers to a much greater extent than elsewhere. We have to add to this the quite extraordinary numerical strength of agricultural labourers in east Tanjore. . . .

Tanjore district has a higher proportion of agricultural labourers in the agricultural work force (comprising cultivators and agricultural labourers) than Tamil Nadu as a whole which in turn has a higher proportion than the country as a whole. Within the district the proportion is over 60 per cent in the three eastern *taluks* of Nagapattinam, Nannilam and Sirkali and below 35 per cent in the three *taluks* of Arantangi, Orathanad and Pattukottai which comprise the New Delta. The proportion of agricultural labourers in Nagapattinam is about six times as high as the proportion in Arantangi. In the western *taluks* and in *taluks* like Mannargudi, which are partly in the Old Delta and partly in the New, proportions come close to the average for the district.

We saw a little while ago that the massive concentration of agricultural labourers in the eastern *taluks* is unusually homogeneous economically. We will now see that it is unusually homogeneous in its caste composition. Agricultural labourers have everywhere in the country a high proportion of Harijans and this characteristic is especially marked in areas of wet paddy cultivation. In Tanjore district it is much more marked in the eastern *taluks* than in the New Delta, the western *taluks* showing, once again, figures which correspond to those for the district as a whole.

Even where the landless are homogeneous economically, they are often divided socially and culturally. In rural India caste often acts as a divisive force, driving a wedge between people who might share the same general economic condition, but live separately, eat separately and marry separately. Even where the barriers of caste are being otherwise broken, the line which separates caste Hindus from Harijans continues to be sharply drawn. In other parts of rural India it has proved difficult to persuade caste Hindu agricultural labourers to make common cause with their Harijan counterparts. In east Tanjore the position is different because here the overwhelming majority of agricultural labourers are not divided by caste, but united by the fact that they are Harijans.

The unity of Harijan agricultural labourers is reinforced by a feature which is characteristic of the layout of settlements in rural Tanjore. Harijans are residentially segregated everywhere in rural India but to a much greater extent in rural Tanjore than in most parts of the country. They live in separate streets called *cheris* which are often at a distance of several furlongs from the main settlement where the caste Hindus live. The social life of the Pallacheri or the Paracheri has a measure of autonomy, and not infrequently the different *cheris* are grouped together in a way which cuts across the grouping of the caste Hindu settlements into revenue units.

The economic and cultural unity of the Harijan agricultural workers in the eastern *taluks* and their physical isolation in the *cheris* has made it particularly easy for them to be organized into a class for the purpose of political action. I would like to insist once again that these conditions are unusual rather than general for rural India as a whole. They do not prevail even in the New Delta where agricultural workers are fewer in number, economically and culturally heterogeneous and residentially scattered among the different sectors of the villages.

In these circumstances it is not surprising that the Kisan Sabha has built up a powerful organization among agricultural workers in east Tanjore whereas in the west its organization has been weak and sporadic. As far as the New Delta is concerned, it has hardly any presence there. . . . I have tried to present arguments which will help us to understand how this organization has come to be strengthened in this area and also why it has not spread very much in the other parts of Tanjore district.

The success of the Kisan Sabha itself depends on the operation of wider political forces and in particular on the relations among the different political parties in the state. In the 1967 elections the Communist Party (Marxist) gained a position of strength in the area which it had never had before. The key constituencies of Nagapattinam, Thiruvarur and Kuttalam were all won by the Communists who at once became the most powerful political party in the area. It is true that the success of the CPI(M) was itself in no small measure due to the polarization described earlier, but one must not forget that the Communists were singularly unsuccessful in both 1957 and 1962.

It is interesting—and perhaps expected—that the organization of the landowners should grow apace with the organization of the workers. Tanjore has not only a powerful Kisan Sabha, it has also a powerful Paddy Producers' Association. Further, the Paddy Producers' Association has a strong organization in precisely those areas where the Kisan Sabha is strong. Where the Kisan Sabha is absent or very weak, as in the New Delta, the Paddy Producers' Association is also absent or weak.

In east Tanjore the relations between landowners and agricultural workers have during the last few years acquired the textbook characteristics of the relations between classes. They confront each other politically. The two modes of political action adopted are widespread agitation by workers at the farm and village levels, and organized collective bargaining at the district level. In both cases the main issues are of the right to work and of wages. Collective bargaining is organized through Tripartite Agreements involving the Collector and representatives of the Kisan Sabha and of the Paddy Producers' Association. Such agreements have become a well known feature of agrarian relations in Tanjore district but it is doubtful that they can ever provide a full guarantee against what may be described as direct action.

## V

[ . . . ]
Since 1967 developments in Tanjore have attracted the attention of a large number of people. Many of them have understandably sought to view these developments in the light of the Green Revolution which is itself a subject of considerable interest. Not everyone is equally convinced that a Green Revolution is in fact taking place in Tanjore. Those who are convinced about this are again divided on its implications for the relations among classes.

Some would argue that the Green Revolution heightens the polarization between the landowners and the landless and thus leads inevitably to a conflict of classes. Others would maintain that by rapidly raising production, it leads to an overall improvement in levels of living and a consequent reduction in inequality and tension between classes. Both arguments are somewhat misleading. Those who argue that the Green Revolution leads to class conflict would point to east Tanjore, but their opponents might with equal justification point to the New Delta.

The Tanjore experience makes it clear that something like the Green Revolution may lead to one set of consequences in one area and to a very different set of consequences in another. One may of course argue against this and say that we ought to make a distinction between the short term and the long term consequences of these phenomena. Here also the same facts may lead to opposite conclusions. Those who believe that the conflict of classes is inevitable will maintain that what has happened in the eastern *taluks* is bound to happen in the other *taluks* as soon as some of the fortuitous obstacles to the growth of class consciousness present there are removed. From the other side the argument would be that it is the New Delta and not the Old which foreshadows the shape of things to come.

When we examine the New Delta we see that there can be a rapid rise in production without any serious tensions developing among the classes. When we examine the eastern *taluks* of the Old Delta a little closely we see that tensions between classes can take a fairly acute form without the agency of a Green Revolution. . . .

What seems to be evident from a consideration of the Tanjore case is that a social fact like agrarian unrest has many causes, and that the same cause produces different results at different places because it never acts in combination with the same factors everywhere. I think that it would be futile to look for a single factor in regard to which we will be able to say that that alone is the cause of the conflict of classes, or that wherever it occurs there will also be a conflict of classes. There are in my belief very important structural reasons which make it impossible to predict phenomena of this nature.

The conflict of classes presupposes at least two sets of factors: (i) a given set of existential conditions and (ii) a given state of consciousness. All the historical evidence tends to show that the relationship between the two is indeterminate. The statement that a given state of consciousness is always associated with a given set of existential conditions is demonstrably false; the statement that the former will come to be aligned with the latter in the long run is meaningless.

There is another way in which we may view the development of class conflict in a specified area. It may be generated by endogenous factors or brought into being by exogenous factors. Those who speak of the inevitability of class conflict assign a crucial role to endogenous factors and are generally inclined to argue that exogenous factors are of little or no significance. Clearly class conflict cannot be sustained from outside if the internal conditions are unsuitable for its generation. But the converse of this is not true. Even when the internal conditions for class conflict are appropriate in a specific area, it can be crushed by forces operating from outside.

If we carefully study the relations between the landowners and the landless in east Tanjore from 1944 onwards, we will find that they have not developed along a linear path. It would be a gross distortion of facts to say that the landless have sought confrontation with the landowners with steadily increasing vigour during the course of this period. The confrontation has had its ups and downs and it seems much more fruitful to try to relate these to the political fortunes of the Communist parties in the state as a whole. It would be naive to believe that the landless can sustain a confrontation with the landowners without the support of the Kisan Sabha or that this support will be equally strong whatever may be the fate of the political party of which it is a limb.

These considerations lead me to conclude that we may seek to interpret broad social facts like the relations among the classes, but we cannot offer explanations of them of the kind which are common in the natural sciences. There are so many factors involved and the relations among them are so often indeterminate that it would be futile to look for ineluctable laws of growth, development or change. The sociologist can never predict the emergence of agrarian unrest in the way in which the astronomer can predict the appearance of a comet. But he can interpret meaningfully what has happened in the past, and this gives us some indication of future possibilities within a given constellation of factors.

# The Politics of Agrarian Tension
# in Kerala[*]

## T.K. OOMMEN

I have argued [elsewhere] that the presumed relationship between Green Revolution and agrarian conflict is naive and simplistic and indicated that politics plays a crucial role in the origin and spread of agrarian unrest. This [paper] attempts an empirical explication of the argument through a case study of Alleppey district from Kerala. Alleppey . . . is Kerala's Intensive Agricultural Development Programme (IADP) district where Green Revolution has occurred, and it is well-known for agrarian unrest.

[. . .]

While paddy is the major food crop of Alleppey, coconut is its chief commercial crop for products such as oil and coir. Alleppey town, presently the district headquarters, was a thriving centre of coir trade and industry, providing employment to thousands of rural migrants. . . . Being the centre of the . . . highly unionized coir industry, Alleppey town was in the forefront of trade union activities. Since a large number of coir workers commuted from the neighbouring villages, Alleppey town functioned as a disseminating centre of trade union ideas, a recruitment base for political leaders, and a testing ground for political ideology. This has contributed in a large measure to the politicization of agricultural labourers in the district.

* Adapted from T.K. Oommen, 'The Politics of Agrarian Tension in India: A Case Study', *Social Structure and Politics: Studies in Independent India*, New Delhi: Hindustan Publishing Corporation, 1984, pp. 148–80.

[. . .]

## AGRICULTURAL PRODUCTION, WAGES, AND PRICES

The data relating to production of rice in Kerala and Alleppey from 1957–58 to 1967–68 . . . indicate an erratic . . . pattern. Of the eleven years for which data are available, the production figures of Alleppey are lower in five years and higher only in six years, as compared with the State as a whole. Apart from this, in terms of both the area under new varieties of rice and the productivity of rice, the situation in Alleppey district compares unfavourably with Kerala as a whole. . . . [But] the increase in daily real wages rate has been the highest in Alleppey between 1962–63 and 1967–68.

[From the facts] that agricultural production in Alleppey has not registered any marked increase and that agricultural wages have increased substantially, it can be argued that the disparity between the cultivators and the agricultural workers has narrowed. However, before accepting this conclusion let us relate the rise in the wages of agricultural labourers to the increase in price. We will pursue our analysis with special reference to paddy since it is the principal crop of the district.

[T]here has been a steady increase in the wages of agricultural labourers in Alleppey during the period 1957–58 to 1967–68, with minor downward trends occasionally. Over this period the increase in money wages was a little over 2.5 times, and that of the price of paddy four times. This means, by and large, the increase in agricultural wages kept pace with the increase in the price of paddy. At any rate, it appears that the 'prosperity' of the cultivators cannot be traced to the increase in agricultural productivity as such but due to the increased price of agricultural commodities. Then, it is not the Green Revolution which accentuated the disparity between the cultivators and the agricultural labourers, . . . but the increase in the price of paddy.

Apart from this, the question of increased or increasing disparity between the rich and the poor in the context of Green Revolution cannot be adequately understood unless the issue is discussed in relation to the number of days worked by the agricultural labourers. While the surplus labour days available per worker per year on an all-India basis was only 66.62 in 1956–57, it was as high as 121.26 for Kerala. . . . [T]here is hardly any improvement in the employment situation in Alleppey due to IADP. That is to say, increase in the wage rate of agricultural labourers in itself is hardly any guide to understand the decrease in disparity between the rural rich and the poor. In those areas where unemployment of farm labour is acute and widespread, as in Alleppey, the probability is that agrarian tension will accentuate even after an appreciable increase in agricultural wages.

## ECONOMIC FACTORS CONTRIBUTING TO AGRARIAN UNREST

The density of population in Alleppey district is estimated to be 1,091 per sq km in 1965. Of the twenty lakh people in Alleppey, 18 per cent are cultivators and 19 per cent are agricultural labourers. The [land-man] ratio is extremely low, the per capita land available in the district being only 0.25 acres, as compared with 0.56 acres in Kerala. The land-man ration of cultivable land in the district is still lower (0.23 acres) and 96 per cent of the land is already cultivated. This means, the scope for bringing new land under plough is extremely limited.

[. . .]

[A sample survey by the state government's Bureau of Economics and Statistics (1968)] found that only 2.1 per cent of the households belong to the category of landlords (non-cultivating land owners) in Alleppey district. Over 56.0 per cent households are owner-cultivators, and tenants are only 14.6 per cent of the population which is the lowest proportion in the State. However, the percentage of hutment-dwellers in Alleppey district, locally known as *kudikidappukars*, is the highest (27.7) in the State. Traditionally, hutment-dwellers were attached labourers who were permitted by landlords to erect huts for residence on the farm. However, they were not entitled to cultivate the land (surroundings of the hut) or to take any yield therein, although the restriction was imposed strictly only in regard to coconut. Being landless, the hutment-dwellers are entirely dependent upon seasonal agricultural work for their income. . . .

Seventy-one per cent of hutment-dwellers in Kerala have an

annual income of less than Rs 1,000 while only 3.5 per cent of
them have an annual income of Rs 2,000 or above. It is equally
important to note that only 18.9 per cent of the landlords, 3.0 per
cent of the owner-cultivators, and 1.2 per cent of the tenants have
an annual income of more than Rs 6,000. Although rural poverty
in Alleppey is appalling, the disparity between the rich and the
poor in the district is low.

Given the [land-man] ratio and the extent of land already
brought under cultivation, industrialization seems to be the only
way to better the economic conditions of the rural poor in
Alleppey. Paradoxically enough, Alleppey district in general, and
Alleppey town in particular, have been steadily on the decline as
far as industry, commerce and trade are concerned.

[. . .]

The coir industry started declining by the early fifties after
having enjoyed a period of boom during and after the Second
World War. From 1952 onwards, several coir manufacturing units
had started retrenching workers, and by 1960 mass retrenchment
became the order of the day. Nearly 15 major factories were
closed down resulting in the unemployment of a large number
of workers. However, a substantial number of them found employment in 'feeder factories' subsequently started by the erstwhile
factory employees: some as co-operative ventures, and others as
individual enterprises. Most of the new small entrepreneurs were
those who held supervisory positions in the closed-down factories.
A typical 'feeder factory' employs five to seven persons and
manufactures coir products to be sold to merchant exporters.
Most of the merchant exporters are the erstwhile manufacturing
exporters.

There are two reasons for keeping the size of feeder factories
small: first, to escape the provisions of the Factories Act, and,
second, to keep the labourers under control. At present there
are nearly 2,000 small 'factories' in and around Alleppey town
manufacturing coir and products. Usually, a person or a family
owns several factories registered under different names. Not only
has the wage rate of coir workers declined due to the fragmentation of the industry, but also fringe benefits such as bonus,
Employees' State Insurance, provident fund, etc., are not given
to the workers. In the early fifties, the average daily wage rate
was Rs 5 for a coir worker, and work was available for about 250

days in a year, but in the mid-sixties the daily wage rate came down to Rs 1.25.

It is necessary to recall here that this was not only a period of economic depression for the coir workers but also one of political inactivity. Notwithstanding the long history of the struggle of the Travancore Coir Factory Workers' Union, the political climate rendered impossible any unified effort on the part of coir workers. Several of our informants commented that there was a steep decline in the membership of trade unions after the fifties. . . . With the formal split of the Communist Party of India in 1964, the two Communist parties—C.P.I. and C.P.(M)—organized separate unions. . . .

The decline of organized large-scale coir industry accentuated agrarian crisis in several ways. Although we could not estimate the extent of unemployment caused by the closing down of big coir manufacturing units in Alleppey town, several informants reported that at least a few thousands of these workers returned to their villages, to join the agricultural labour force. Also, since wages in the feeder factories were low, coir workers, especially women, sought jobs in agriculture in the busy seasons. However, there is no deterioration in the availability of employment to agricultural workers. This has been possible due to the increased employment opportunities due to intensive cultivation, especially the increase in the number of crops raised in a year.

Transport and communications are well-developed in Alleppey district and this immensely facilitates the movement of men. It is a common sight during harvest seasons that men and women commute in buses to agricultural fields. Hundreds of men and women often flock to paddy fields and forcibly join the harvesters. While the local agricultural labourers consider it their right to harvest the fields of their village they do not resist the intruders. Big landlords prefer to have a large labour force because it shortens the period of harvesting. But sometimes this leads to agrarian tension.

## THE SOCIAL CONTEXT OF AGRARIAN TENSION

. . . Traditionally, landlords in Alleppey were *devaswams* (temple tenants), Brahmins, and a few rich Nair chieftains. The land was

cultivated mainly by Syrian Christians or Nairs on very unfavourable terms. Until the early forties most cultivators were
eking out a hand-to-mouth existence. Paddy fields were cultivated,
especially in the water-logged areas of the district, only once in
two or three years. However, the cultivator experienced a sudden
prosperity due to the immense rise in the price of agricultural
commodities during the Second World War. One of our informants estimated that the rise in the price of paddy was to the tune
of 120 times. . . . Although the tenant-cultivators bettered their
economic condition, their subservient relationship continued in
the social contexts since they did not own the land.

Although the Kerala Agrarian Relations Bill of 1957 was not
passed, with its introduction the landlords started experiencing a
sense of insecurity as the Bill sought to confer upon the tenants
the right of possession of land they cultivated.[1] The landlords,
particularly the rich ones, started selling their land. Since the
tenant-cultivators could not be evicted, landlords had to sell their
land to the tenants at low prices. Thus, gradually the land came
to be owned by the former tenants and in the place of a few
non-cultivating land-owning rich families there emerged a middle
class of owner-cultivators, mostly Syrian Christian. The erstwhile
landlords shifted their investment from agriculture to new business
ventures. Due to the subsidies given by the government, agriculture
became a business proposition and the newly emerged owner-cultivators soon became members of a prosperous middle class. Some
of the disgruntled ex-landlords, particularly from among the Nairs,
turned to radical movements and revolutionary ideologies.

. . . A close look at the rural situation in Alleppey (as indeed
in Kerala) unfolds that the agrarian classes are differentiated by

---

[1] The Kerala Agrarian Relations Bill, 1957, introduced by the first ministry
led by the Communist Party was a comprehensive piece of agrarian legislation.
The two most important provisions of the Bill relevant for our purpose are: (1)
the Bill granted fixity of tenure to landless occupants of homesteads known as
*Kudikidappukars*, and (2) tenants were given the right to purchase the land already
in their possession. The tenant had to pay only 16 times the fair rent fixed under
the Bill, or 12 times the contract rent. He could pay the price in 16 equal annual
instalments. The Bill could not be passed due to the political turmoil in Kerala
leading to the dismissal of the ministry by the President of India. However, the
Kerala Agrarian Relations Act of 1960, passed by the coalition ministry which
came into power in 1960, contained most of the essential provisions of the 1957
Bill.

the local population based on property relations and occupational differences. This categorization can be viewed as a dichotomy on the one hand and a continuum on the other.

The dichotomous categorization of the rural population in the district falls into two categories: *melans* (masters) and *adiyans* (attached labourers). The *melan-adiyan* relationship may be viewed as a patron-client or employer-employee relationship. If we view agrarian classes as falling into a continuum, we note the *jenmie* (land-owner non-cultivator) at the apex and the *adiyan* at the bottom. Since a *jenmie* does not cultivate the land he owns, he has no direct contact with agricultural labourers. The *karshakan* (owner-cultivator) comes next to *jenmie* in status. The persons who cultivate the land not owned by them, the *pattakkar* or *veethakkar* (rentiers or share-croppers), come next to owner-cultivators in status. It is difficult to draw clear boundaries between each of these categories, as a person may be a *jenmie* and a *karshakan* at the same time. For instance, if a *jenmie* owns land in several villages it is usual that he cultivates some of the land which he can directly supervise and lets out the remaining land for rent or for share-cropping. Similarly, a *karshakan* with a small patch of land may also be a sharecropper.

The agricultural workers, too, can be grouped into several categories. Those at the bottom of the hierarchy are *adiyans*, who are paid the lowest daily wages, although they are compensated through other customary payments. Above the *adiyans* come *koolikkar* (casual labourers) who are unattached and earn a higher wage compared to the former. Until recently wage rates reflected one's caste or community status since labourers from higher castes were paid more for the same work. Generally speaking, agricultural labourers from higher castes (e.g. Nairs) are not involved in patron-client relationship. As for a lower caste agricultural labourer, he may be an *adiyan* to one *melan*, but a *koolikkaran* to another, thus having a dual status in the context of employer-employee relationship.

Traditionally, Pulayas were *adiyans* [of] *melans* drawn from Brahmins, Nairs, and Syrian Christians. The poor Ezhavas were also invariably involved with the higher castes in a patron-client relationship. While the patron-client relationship continues to exist, it is undergoing fast and radical changes. *Adiyans* were given small patches of land free of rent to put up huts. Usually these huts were near paddy fields owned by the landlords. Payments to agricultural labourers were made in kind for harvesting and threshing, and in cash for such operations as weeding, bunding, transplantation, etc. The wages for the latter varied for the attached and non-attached labourers, the former being paid less. However, they were compensated by the landlords in other ways, such as a house-site, continuous employment, financial assistance at the time of life-cycle rites, etc.

Even when the traditional patron-client relationship was intact, it was not possible for a cultivator to manage his work exclusively through his *adiyans* especially at the time of harvesting. An overwhelming majority of harvesters in the *padasekharams* of Kuttanad are migrant labourers from other parts of the districts. The usual practice is to finish harvesting in a given block . . . before threshing starts. Obviously, the migrant harvesters are put to hardships since they are not likely to carry enough food and money with them. In order to keep them going during the days between harvesting and threshing, they were given a bundle of paddy, *katta*, locally referred to as *theerpu*, every second or third day. Before 1950, *theerpu* was given only to the migrant labourers, but by the early fifties the labourers from the same village, including *adiyans*, started demanding it. The farmers resisted this demand, and this led to several confrontations between them and their attached labourers. However, by 1955 the practice of giving *theerpu* became widespread, especially in lower Kuttanad.

In April 1957, the first Communist ministry led by E.M.S. Namboodripad came into power. The Communist-led agricultural workers' organizations were hitherto not very effective in getting concessions from the cultivators. However, with the Communist ministry in power, the cultivators were compelled to accept the demands of local party leaders. Most of the agrarian tensions in the mid-fifties were caused by the demand by agricultural labourers for increased wages. For instance, hitherto the labourers' share of paddy was one-tenth for harvesting and threshing. The new demand was for one-eighth of the total paddy. While these demands were by and large conceded by the bigger landlords, partly because they were helpless in that they could not harvest their fields themselves, the small land-owners often refused to meet the new demands. Some of them tried to harvest their fields by themselves or with the cooperation of relatives and neighbours.

Since most of the agricultural labourers were Pulayas and Ezhavas and the farmers were Syrian Christians and Nairs, class interests converged with caste loyalties. The situation become explosive when a group of Pulaya agricultural workers attacked a Christian farmer and his family while they were harvesting the small patch of land they cultivated, in Niranam village in the Tiruvella *taluk* of Alleppey district, in May 1957. The Christians felt humiliated at the recalcitrance of their traditional *adiyans*. Suddenly, a volcano of communal tension exploded in the form of Christian-Pulaya conflict. Hundreds of armed Christians attacked the Pulayas in the area. A large number of Pulayas were disabled and a few killed. It appears that the Niranam incident marked the end of the traditional coercive and subservient relationship between farmers and their *adiyans* in Alleppey.

## THE POLITICS OF AGRARIAN TENSION

Our discussion on the economic and social situation in Alleppey unfolds the tension-prone character of the district. However, the submerged discontent can manifest in overt conflicts only if there exists certain context to express it. It is our contention that agrarian pressure groups which are the rural wings of political parties and organizational innovation by the government provide the context for tension. . . .

Agrarian pressure groups can be broadly divided into two types: those catering to the needs of agricultural labourers, and those meant to look after the welfare of farmers and landlords. We found four agricultural labour unions and two farmers' associations fairly active in Alleppey district. These associations frequently create confusion in the minds of agricultural workers and farmers in the process of making claims and counter-claims. Apart from this, in their eagerness to establish their authenticity that they are really working for the welfare of their clients, these associations not only accentuate inter-class but also provide occasions for intra-class confrontations.

The first agricultural labour union in Kuttanad was formed in 1939, as a branch of the Travancore Karshaka Thozhilali (Agricultural Labour) Union (TKTU). The activities of the union, in its early phase, were confined to Alleppey town and the surrounding rural areas. . . . One of the outstanding labour union leaders of Alleppey became the Labour Minister in 1957, when the Communists first came into power in Kerala. Two of the important measures introduced by the Labour Minister for the uplift of agricultural workers were the appointment of a committee to fix minimum wages for agricultural labourers and the formation of the Industrial Relations Committee (IRC), a tripartite body consisting of the representatives of the government, farmers and agricultural labourers. This made it possible for the agricultural labour unions to represent their cases in a formal way. . . .

The TKTU was by and large an organization of the Communists. In order to make its presence felt on the agricultural labour front, the Indian National Congress organized the Travancore Cochin Karshaka Thozhilali Sangham (TCKTS) in 1953. At present, the membership of the TCKTS consists mainly of lower middle class workers such as engine drivers, poultry farmers or those who carry headloads. It is important to note that while its membership is equally drawn from Christians, Nairs, and Ezhavas, the number of Harijans is very small. In 1970, this union claimed a membership of 6,000 in Alleppey district, although other unions contest this figure.

Consequent upon the split of Communist Party of India in 1964, the TKTU too was split into two: The Kerala Karshaka Thozhilali Federation (KKTF) organized by C.P.I. and the Kerala State Karshaka Thozhilali Union (KSKTU) led by C.P.(M). Both these unions draw most of their members from the Pulayas and the Ezhavas, the traditional agricultural labourers of the district. However, in terms of their size, the two vary considerably. The KKTF claims a membership of 5,000, while the KSKTU claims 15,000 members in Alleppey district.

Another active agrarian association is the Kuttanad Karshaka Thozhilali Union (KKTU), although its influence is confined to a few pockets. The KKTU came into existence only in 1968 and is led by the Revolutionary Socialist Party (R.S.P.). It claims a membership of 1,200.

In our discussions with the agricultural labour union officials in Alleppey, we found that there existed considerable political rivalry between these unions. While the Marxist-led labour union was eulogising the achievements of the Marxist ministry which came into power in 1967, it was keen to criticize the C.P.I-led ministry and its 'anti-labour' policies. On the other hand, the officials of the unions owing allegiance to C.P.I. and R.S.P. described in glowing terms the achievements of the mini-front ministry of which they were partners. In contrast, the officials of Congress-led union (TCKTS) were emphasizing the unlawful and disorderly activities unleashed by leftists in general and Marxists in particular.

The officials of all the unions we contacted agreed that these unions worked at cross-purposes. For instance, one of the officials of the KKTU (the R.S.P.-led union) confessed that the union was started mainly to sabotage the Marxist attempts to 'use' poor and innocent agricultural workers for their party ends. (The Marxists were in power from 1967 to 1969.) In their attempt to project themselves as 'progressive,' each union is trying to put forward more and more demands on behalf of agricultural labourers. It appears that some of these unions are endlessly in search of 'causes' for agitations.

Frequently, the acceptance or rejection of a demand or benefit by an association is based on its political affiliation. Even when a given demand sponsored by a union is beneficial to all the labourers, the other unions try to underplay the demand. We have been told that agricultural labourers, said to be Marxists, are willing to work for lower wages in certain areas where non-Marxist unions are strong in order to discredit the rival unions. The non-Marxist labourers indulge in precisely the same kind of activity elsewhere. The net result of this inter-union rivalry is often to undermine the bargaining power of the unions.

Agricultural labour unions of Alleppey are widely believed to be corrupt bodies. Several of our informants reported that labour union leaders were bribed by rich farmers to avoid troubles in their fields. The fact that the farmers resort to bribing the leaders of the labour unions is partially indicative of the lack of co-operation among the former. However, wherever the farmers' associations are strong, they do not resort to corruption.

The Kuttanad Karshaka Sangham (KKS), one of the two important farmers' associations in Alleppey district, came into existence in 1939. In the beginning, its membership was confined to the top land-owners in the area and it was merely an association to secure economic benefits such as debt relief, loan, bunding, subsidy, irrigation facilities, etc., from the government. Although small land-owners of the area felt aggrieved against this association, the KKS remained indifferent to their discontent till 1957 when, with the installation of the first Communist ministry in power, agrarian unrest started spreading fast. Realizing their numerical weakness to resist the labour unions of leftist orientation, the big land-owners found it expedient to join hands with small and medium cultivators.

The KKS is much less organized as compared to the labour unions in Alleppey district. Family feuds and personal rivalries, not to speak of political animosities, hamper the cooperation of farmers as a united front against labour unions. In lower Kuttanad, the KKS is particularly weak due to the fact that the size of middle class population is very small and the few rich families are rarely mutually cooperative. In contrast, the upper Kuttanad area, with very few big land-owners and with a large middle class population, has a well-organized Karshaka Sangham.

At present, the Upper Kuttanad Karshaka Sangham has 17 branches, established on the basis of *panchayat*, with a membership of 8,200. The Sangham has associate members, too, and the majority of them are (nearly 2,000) agricultural labourers attached to the farmer-members. The KKS claims 12,000 sympathizers apart from its registered membership. The Sangham is dominated by Christian farmers (with a membership of 75%) , and about 18 per cent of its membership is drawn from Nairs and the rest from Brahmins and Ezhavas. Among the associate members, about 95 per cent are Christians and the rest are Pulayas and Ezhavas. Although the KKS disclaims any official association with political parties, most of its active workers are also active Kerala Congress workers. Most of the persons associated with the KKS openly admit that they are opposed to Marxists. The hotbed of the activities of Upper Kuttanad Karshaka Sangham are a few villages in Tiruvella and Chengannur *talukas*, a traditional bulwark of Christian aristocracy, under the leadership of John Jacob, a Kerala Congress M.L.A.

The other known farmers' association is organized by C.P.(M). Faced with the dilemma of losing small farmers from their fold, the Marxists found it necessary to organize small farmers under the banner of Kerala Karshaka Sangham, which is affiliated to the All India Kisan Sabha. The Kerala Karshaka Sangham came into existence only in 1967 and its activities are limited and achievements modest as the Marxists concentrate on agricultural labourers.

## THE KUTTANAD I.R.C. AS AN INSTRUMENT OF TENSION-MANAGEMENT

Under the traditional system, when the patron-client relationship was strong, there were no fixed hours of work for agricultural labourers. Agricultural labourers, particularly *adiyans*, went to fields for work early in the morning and left only by sun-set. The hours of work ranged from 10 to 12. As the traditional agrarian relations started showing signs of disintegration, the labourers protested against the unstipulated working hours. They came 'late' for work and left the fields 'early'. This was objected to by the employers which frequently led to altercations or violence. This situation called for the specification of working hours for agricultural labourers.

There was no uniformity of wages paid to agricultural workers in different *taluks* and villages. Again, no differentiation between the various farming operations was made for the purpose of wage payment. There were three different rates of payment for the same work, depending upon the status of the worker. The Harijans who were *adiyans* were paid the lowest wage, the non-Harijans were paid the highest wage, and the wage-rate of Harijans who were not *adiyans* came in between.

With the gradual weakening of the patron-client relationship, the problem of hiring agricultural workers frequently created tensions. While the employers wanted full rights to determine who they should employ, the local workers asserted their right to be employed in preference to others. This situation necessitated the intervention of a statutory body.

The worsening of the labour situation prompted some big land-owners to go in for mechanized farming. This move was promptly resisted by the labourers as they feared the accentuation of the existing unemployment situation.

The importance of the appointment of the Kuttanad Industrial Relations Committee (IRC) and its decisions are to be understood against the backdrop of this tension-prone situation in Alleppey. A tripartite committee consisting of the representatives of the government, farmers, and agricultural labourers, was established by the Government of Kerala on 17 July 1957. The disputes between the agricultural workers and their employees were less frequent till 1957, and there was no need felt for a statutory organization to prescribe norms to farmers and agricultural labourers. The IRC was instituted with a view to examining all the problems relating to the agricultural labour in Kuttanad area.

The IRC consists of 6 government nominees, 15 representatives of employer farmers, and 13 representatives of agricultural labourers. The six government nominees are: the District Collectors of Alleppey and Kottayam, the Labour Commissioner who acts as the convener of the Committee and three political workers from Alleppey or Kottayam, usually members of the Kerala Legislative Assembly. The representatives of farmers and agricultural workers are drawn from the various agrarian associations and/or those who are said to be politically neutral. Although the persons included in the Committee change from the time to time, the basic composition of the Committee remains undisturbed.

[ . . . ]

One of the first decisions of the IRC related to fixing of wages for agricultural labourers. In 1958, the Committee recommended Rs 1.25 for men and Rs 0.87 for women for an eight-hour working day. This wage rate was recommended for 'ordinary operations' such as transplanting, weeding, bunding etc. For other types of operations such as ploughing with bullocks Rs 1.37 was fixed for a five-hour working day. Usually the wage payment for these operations was in cash and for harvesting and related operations it was in kind. The rate of payment recommended for harvesting and threshing was two-nineteenths of the produce, in addition to *theerpu*, wherever it was in vogue. (The specific proportion to be paid as *theerpu* was left to the discretion of the farmer.) The Committee also recommended additional remuneration to the workers if they carried harvested but unthreshed paddy (*katta*) for a distance over one furlong from the paddy field. Earlier no payment was made for such operations.

Although the Committee recommended payment for certain types of operations for which no payment was made hitherto, the wage rate was unspecified. This created problems in the transactions between cultivators and agricultural labourers, particularly during harvesting seasons as these operations were related to harvesting. Most cultivators were unprepared to accept the recommendation. Even when payments were made reluctantly by the cultivators, the workers were dissatisfied. The dissatisfaction on both sides called for the specification of wage rate for these types of operations by 1959.

Payment of *theerpu*, which was a customary practice for temporary relief to migrant workers, became a statutory right for all agricultural labourers. Although a separate payment was recommended by the IRC for carrying hay from the field to farmer's house, it was not obligatory on the part of workers to undertake these operations. Since harvesting and threshing is much more paying, they leave these operations unfinished to take up harvesting in other fields, which leads to loss and inconvenience to farmers.

The migrant labourers who go to Kuttanad area during the harvesting season usually move with their families as the season spreads over six to eight weeks. These labourers were permitted to construct temporary huts in the land of their employers and the construction charges were met by the workers. Similarly, the responsibility of securing drinking water was that of the workers and they had to walk two to three miles for this purpose.[2] The IRC at its meeting held in December 1962 recommended that the employers should provide temporary sheds for migrant labourers and drinking water to all labourers in those areas where it was not easily available.

Usually, the labourers move from one village to another at the instance of employers. However, the latter are not in a position to provide work continuously and this creates hardships for the migrant workers. In order to remedy this, the IRC recommended (in December 1962) that those employers who brought agricultural workers from far-off places should either find work for them or pay them a subsistence allowance for the days they were not engaged. This subsistence allowance was fixed at 1.5 kg of paddy per day.

The wage rate of agricultural labourers was revised periodically by the IRC. In October 1967, the Committee recommended a daily wage of Rs 4.85 for men and Rs 2.88 for women which was further raised to Rs 3.40 in September 1969. Thus, from Rs 1.25

---

[2] The sub-soil water in certain parts of Alleppey district becomes salty during the months of February, March and April which is the major harvesting season.

in 1957 the daily wage recommended for a male agricultural worker rose to Rs 4.85 in 1969 and that of the female worker from Rs 0.87 to Rs 3.40. However, it is wrong to assume that the workers are always paid at the rate recommended by the Committee. The wage rates recommended by the IRC are only indicative of the general rise in agricultural wages.

Another issue on which the IRC arbitrated relates to the employment of agricultural workers. From 1964 onwards the big cultivators in Alleppey district were trying to introduce tractors for ploughing paddy fields, partly to grapple with the troubled labour situation and partly to bring down the cost of cultivation. Although the number of tractors used is very small, agricultural labourers consider the introduction of tractors a threat to their interests. The IRC at its meeting on 19 March 1969 recommended that the cultivators should compulsorily employ agricultural workers for the second and third round of the ploughing, if tractor was used for ploughing in the first round. Thus, the displacement of ploughmen by tractors was rendered impossible.

The problems relating to the day-to-day hiring of labourers, too, called for the intervention of the IRC. Due to acute agrarian unrest in 1967, when the C.P.(M) came into power, it was impossible for employers to discipline workers. Agricultural workers who belonged to the C.P.(M) (and their number was substantial) secured physical and moral support from the party to challenge the employers. This situation compelled the employers to hire those workers who they thought were disciplined and/or those who were known to be sympathizers of parties other than the C.P.(M). This resulted in protests by the Marxist workers. Frequently, they entered the fields forcibly and 'worked.' The 'employers' were reduced to the position of dumb observers of such actions and were forced to pay for the labour of men whom they did not employ. As such incidents increased, the Kuttanad Karshaka Sangham made a representation to the IRC. The Committee recommended that the primary qualification for employment of agricultural labourers in *padasekharams* should be the proximity of their residence to the fields. Thus, cultivators were required to employ *parisarathozhilalikal* (labourers from the vicinity) in their fields. This recommendation provided the grist for countless conflicts, as a clear interpretation of the recommendation was difficult.

On the whole, the data presented in this section strongly suggest that the IRC has been able to resolve issues bringing a balanced relationship between farmers and agricultural labourers. On the other hand, in a highly politicized, well-organized and articulate agrarian society, new issues keep coming up as old ones are resolved.

## THE EXTENT OF AGRARIAN TENSION

Kerala is notorious for political instability. The present State of Kerala came into being on 1 November 1957, combining three areas: Travancore, Cochin, and Malabar. The Congress was the ruling party from 1948 to 1956, prior to the emergence of united Kerala, except for the small interlude from 16 March 1953 to 14 February 1955 when the Praja Socialist Party was in power with Congress support. The first Communist ministry came into power in 1957. The major open agrarian conflicts took place in 1954–55 and the number of these clashes varied with the changing political situation in the State.

A number of measures were introduced by the Communist government (1957–59) for the welfare of the agricultural labourers. These measures led not only to an improvement in the material conditions of the rural poor but also instilled a new faith in them that it was possible to better their conditions through collective bargaining. Their aspirations soared, and they started making more demands. The landlords, on the other hand, were not prepared to recognize the growing strength of their *adiyans*.

The second leftist ministry led by the C.P.(M) came into power in 1967. The increased confrontation between agricultural labourers and cultivators had increased in number and had diversified considerably by this time. The earlier agitations were mainly directed for securing benefits to the agricultural labourers. The political content of agrarian unrest increased considerably during the C.P.(M) rule from 1967 to 1969. The Marxist-led coalition government fell in October 1969, and the owner *versus* labour conflict took a new turn. The agricultural labour agitations had been receiving explicit support so far from the well-organized party organs of the C.P.(M) and implicit support from the Marxist-led government. The farmer's interests were being protected by some parties within the coalition, thus maintaining a balance of conflicting interests. With the fall of the C.P.(M)-led coalition, agrarian tensions became violent and widespread as manifested in the land grab agitation. While it is difficult to establish a direct relationship between the growth of political parties which endorse and pursue conflict as a means of change and the increase in agrarian tension, the available evidence suggests this possibility.

Table 1

Cases Relating to Agrarian Agitations in Alleppey District From 1.1.1965 to 31.12.1969[3]

*(Annual averages are shown within bracket)*

| Party in Power and Period of Rule | Total Number of Cases Registered by Police and Charged to Courts | No. of Persons Arrested | Total Number Hurt | Violence of Other Types |
|---|---|---|---|---|
| President's Rule 1.1.1965 to 31.12.1966 (2 years) | 6(3) | 132(66) | 0 | 6(3) |
| United Front with C.P.(M) as the major partner 1.1.1967 to 31.12.1969 (3 years) | 96(32) | 477(159) | 51(17) | 44(15) |

The extent of agrarian tension from 1965 to 1969, presented in Table 1 makes it amply clear that agrarian agitations were far more widespread during the United Front regime. We are handicapped in this comparison between the two time periods in that President's rule preceded the United Front regime. However, it is our overall assessment that the functioning of law and order

[3] The exact period during which the C.P.(M)-led ministry was in power was from 7 March 1967 to 31 October 1969, and the exact period of President's rule was from 10 September 1964 to 6 March 1967.

institutions during the period of Presidential rule was not markedly different as compared with the period earlier to that. It appears, then, if a political party which endorses violence as a means to effect change is in power it is probable that the number of conflicts in that State will increase considerably. It is also likely that violent agitations will spread and become intense if such a party is the chief and a substantial political opposition.

Let us now look at the situation in 1970, when the agrarian scene in Alleppey was particularly turbulent due to the land grab agitation led by the C.P.(M) as an opposition party.

On 1 November 1969, the mini-front led by Achuta Menon (C.P.I.) assumed power and the new government declared that the Kerala Land Reforms (Amendment) Act, 1969, would be implemented with effect from 1 January 1970. The Act visualized a vigorous programme of distribution of excess land under the ownership of the government, public endowments, and private individuals to the landless. Apart from this, ownership rights were to be conferred upon all hutment-dwellers (*kudikidappukar*) in 7.5 cents (100 cents make an acre) of land around the huts they dwell. However, they were required to submit an application to the revenue authorities requesting the transfer of title deeds. Moreover, the hutment-dwellers were expected to pay 12.5 per cent of the market value of the land in twelve instalments.

Although a party to the Act, the Marxists created obstacles in its implementation, now that they were out of power. In a joint State convention of the Marxist-controlled Kerala Karshaka Sangham (Farmers' Association) and the Kerala State Karshaka Thozhilali Union (Labourers' Union) held at Alleppey on 13 and 14 December 1969, the following decisions were taken: (1) No rent should be paid by hutment-dwellers to landlords and land-owners; (2) all excess land should be forcibly occupied; (3) ten cents of land around their huts should be fenced by hutment-dwellers and they should start taking yield from such plots; and (4) all steps by the government, courts, police, and landlords against these attempts should be resisted.

The Land Reforms (Amendment) Act came into force on 1 January 1970. Marxist volunteers commenced encroachment of government and private lands and constructed huts in many places in the State. In several areas hutment-dwellers took forcible possession of ten cents of land each around their huts and erected fences. They plucked coconuts and took other yields from the occupied lands. Although not very satisfactory, the only method of measuring the extent of tension is to take note of the number of cases registered in civil and criminal courts, and the number of persons arrested by the police in connection with the agitation.

According to our estimate, over 20,000 hutment-dwellers stood by the 'Alleppey decision' of the C.P.(M) and nearly 2,000 cases relating to the land grab agitation were registered in the eleven civil and criminal courts in Alleppey district from 1 January 1970 to 31 May 1970; the total number of accused in these cases was estimated to be over 25,000. According to police records, the total number of encroachments were 931 and the number of houses or huts built were 338. The total number of persons arrested in the 734 cases registered by the police was 4,881. Of these, excepting two who belonged to S.S.P. all were either members or sympathizers of the C.P.(M). Only 32 of the arrested persons were land-owners, the rest being agricultural labourers. The fact that almost all the land grabbers belonged to C.P.(M), supports our contention that the agrarian tension is unleashed mainly by political parties.

As the tempo of the agitation was whittling down, the C.P.(M)-led Kerala Karshaka Sangham held a three-day State convention at Kottayam in the last week of May 1970 to revive the agitation. The convention gave a call to commence the second phase of the struggle for land. The hutment-dwellers were asked to negotiate with all landlords who had filed suits for arrears of rent against the tenants and to organize agitation in front of the houses of such landlords who refused to compromise.

Usually, the encroachments when directed against privately-owned lands were confined to those families which did not have much numerical strength and/or those which were unable to field a group of able-bodied men to resist such attempts. Apart from this, those landlords who were said to be Marxist or Marxist sympathizers were rarely the target of attack. In most cases of encroachment the land-owners were Congress sympathizers. Finally, most land grabbers were physically strong men from locally significant communities. Thus, the land grab agitation as it was conducted in Alleppey district was not a confrontation between the haves and the have-nots but a systematic attempt by those who belonged to a political party to usurp [the land of] those who identified themselves with other political parties. It was also an attack on the physically weak individuals and groups by the physically strong.

According to the estimates of the District Collector, the total number of hutment-dwellers in Alleppey is about 65,000. They are required to submit their applications in the prescribed form in order that necessary steps may be taken to confer ownership rights on them. Till 3 May 1970, four months after the Act came into force, only 5,710 cases came in for legal formalities, and of these, 5,371 cases were disposed of. Of these, as many as 4,800 hutment-dwellers secured the certificate of purchase after paying the first instalment. About 20,000 settled the transfer through mutual consent. The rest did not submit the required application. It is widely held by land-owners, bureaucrats, and non-Marxists that these hutment-dwellers refused to undergo the prescribed legal requirement due to Marxist pressures. The hutment-dwellers are impressed easily by two arguments put forward by Marxist workers: (1) the legal procedure takes a long time and there is no need to wait, and (2) if a hutment-dweller takes to the legal procedure it is incumbent upon him to pay 12.5 per cent of the market value of land as compensation; by forcible occupation both these requirements can be overlooked.

That the hutment-dwellers are easily convinced by these arguments is not surprising. They have been victims of bureaucratic red-tape and upper class oppression all along; quick results attract them easily. The District Collector of Alleppey, while claiming that his district is in the vanguard in implementing the provisions of the new Land Reforms Act, confessed that the progress relating to transfer of ownership rights to hutment-dwellers was very slow for want of staff. His estimate is that it will take at least three years for all the legal formalities to be completed in all the cases in his district.

[ . . . ]

## CONSEQUENCE OF TENSION

[ . . . ]

The present tendency among the big land-owners is to sell their land, although it is extremely difficult to arrive at a clear picture of the amount of land sold. One of the landlords at the conclusion of my interview with him said: 'I am going to the field and I am not sure whether I will return home alive.' Another land-owner lamented: 'We no longer expect any police or legal protection. The State apparatus is always in favour of the poor.' Some landlords of lower Kuttanad have already left their ancestral villages to settle in nearby towns, where they feel more secure. Most of them plan to divert their investments to safer sectors such as plantations, industries, etc., as these areas are not only more profitable but safer. Those who plan to continue with cultivation of land seem to be disinclined to make heavy investments, and occasionally even let their land lie fallow. The natural conditions in Alleppey district, particularly in the Kuttanad *taluk*, are such that they call for huge investments. Operations such as bunding and dewatering cannot be done for small patches of land. The only viable alternative seems to be State farms or cooperative farming by small individual owners. However, this cannot be accomplished in the immediate future, and it appears that with the liquidation of big cultivators the productivity of land will be adversely affected. A senior Congress politician, who is also a prosperous farmer, remarked: 'The possibility is that Kuttanad will soon become a colony of the poor.'

An interesting indirect consequence of agrarian tension in Alleppey is the emergence of a new politico-rich class. The big landlords are eager to sell their land and to divert their investments to safer sectors. The new buyers are, generally, those who are identified with political parties of leftist orientations particularly C.P.(M). Several of the local party leaders (village, *panchayat*) had become traders, money-lenders, or land-owners. The source of income of these local politicians is, interestingly enough, politics itself. In order to avoid labour troubles during busy seasons of transplantations, harvesting, etc., the landlords are compelled to bribe local party officials. Usually, the cultivators bribe the village or *panchayat* level party workers who control partymen at the grass-root level. However, big cultivators occasionally bribe the State or district level leaders, too, to seek their help in·averting troubles in their fields. One of the factors which contributes to corruption in this context seems to be the lack of cooperation among cultivators. In those areas where the Kuttanad Karshaka Sangham is strong and well-organized, political bribes are much less common as compared with those areas where the cultivators are not united.

An immediate consequence of agrarian tension in Alleppey appears to be fall in food production in the district, notwithstanding the advantages accrued through the inputs such as improved seed, fertilizers, etc.

## TOWARDS AN EXPLANATION OF AGRARIAN TENSION

. . . Our point of departure is that disparity is a *necessary* but *not a sufficient* condition for conflicts to erupt. Alleppey's dense population, low [land-man] ratio, highly developed transport and communications, high literacy rate, and agriculture-based economy, together provide a structure that generates tension. We have shown that the impact of Green Revolution in Alleppey, despite the IADP, is weak and that the wages of agricultural labourers have gone up substantially. However, unemployment among the agricultural labourers is high and the increase in wage rate is offset by inflation. The agrarian situation in the district deteriorated due to the decline of coir industry, the principal extra-agricultural avenue for labour absorption. We have argued that while there is no evidence to suggest that the disparity in incomes between the rural rich and the poor widened in recent years, there are good reasons to believe that the *perception* of the disparity by the rural poor has crystallized due to their politicization.

An analysis of the labour union activities in the recent past in Alleppey shows that the agricultural labourers are politically organized. The political mobilization of agricultural labourers is easy, thanks to the support provided by a number of political parties, notably C.P.(M), C.P.I. and R.S.P., through their agricultural labour unions. On the other hand, farmers' associations supported by political parties accentuate polarizations of social classes. When the political parties of leftist persuasion gained power in the State the labour force received powerful support against the employers. Thus, sporadic conflicts between the farmers and agricultural labourers started in the mid-fifties, and they became a frequent occurrence by the mid-sixties.

The conflicts in recent years gradually eroded the traditional social bonds which were essentially non-contractual in character. In its place an employer-employee, contractual, market-oriented relationship emerged. Statutory bodies such as the IRC provided legal recognition to the representatives of labour organizations and enhanced their formal power and they, in turn, piloted the demands for higher wages, shorter and stipulated working hours, right to employment and other welfare measures.

The dislodging of agricultural labourers from the traditional patron-client relationship and the absence of new structures to replace the old increased the labourers' sense of insecurity. At the same time, legislative reforms gave a boost to the rising aspirations of the rural poor. Adult franchise has engendered a feeling among the poor that they are part of an egalitarian society, yet they suffer deprivation. This discrepancy between the avowed objectives of the society and the existing economic disparities goads the poor into violent action. Thus, a multiplicity of structural factors and a series of social changes contribute to agrarian conflicts.

# Worker Consciousness and Trade Union Response in Bombay[*]

## E.A. RAMASWAMY

Bombay is arguably the premier industrial metropolis of the country. The city compels attention with the sheer size and range of its industry and the colour and vitality of its labour movement. Bombay must undoubtedly be central to any study of contemporary trade unionism in India. The overwhelming aspect of industry here is the dominance of private, and in particular multinational, capital. . . . [T]here is an organic linkage between the buccaneering spirit of Bombay unions and the eclecticism and adaptability of private enterprise. It would be hard to visualize this kind of trade unionism in Bangalore or Hyderabad dominated by the public sector with its bureaucratic controls, centralized managerial practices and staid rigidities. . . .

The driving force of the Bombay labour movement are union leaders who disclaim allegiance to political parties and their trade union federations. . . . The communist AITUC which had the advantage of an early start had all but withered away by the mid-sixties. Hopes of a Marxist revival raised by the more radical CITU were soon nipped by the onslaughts of independents. George Fernandes and his socialist ideology which ascended to prominence in the sixties did not go far beyond the confines of the service sector. . . . The imagination of workers was captured

* Excerpted from E.A. Ramaswamy, 'Bombay', *Worker Consciousness and Trade Union Response*, Delhi: Oxford University Press, 1988, pp. 17–78.

for a while by the Shiv Sena with its militant regionalist ideology, but they are no longer a force to reckon with. The INTUC has support in petroleum refining and a few other pockets, although its claim to the loyalty of the large textile labour force stands completely exposed by the historic strike under the leadership of Datta Samant. Of all the national federations, it is probably the Bharatiya Mazdoor Sangh (BMS) with its Hindu ideology which has grown rather than declined in recent times. BMS support is however too modest to establish it as a major force.

The most important power in the labour movement after the independent trade unionists is in fact the home-grown, internal shop-floor leadership, which is of course just as businesslike and non-ideological. If Bombay has witnessed the meteoric rise of high-flying militants, it is also the home of a self-conscious and assertive internal leadership. . . .

## CONFLICT AND CHANGE

The common pattern of organization, especially in the newer industries, is for workers to form themselves into a single trade union at the level of the enterprise. Multiple unions competing for the loyalty of workers is not the norm, although it does exist. In spite of this favourable structural feature, the city has been rocked by bloody trade union rivalries. If elsewhere in the country rival trade unions are locked in combat for supremacy over the enterprise, conflict here is typically between segments of the same union extending support to rival leaders.

The process has its genesis in worker dissatisfaction with the existing leadership and desire for change, a situation fraught with conflict because the reigning leader does not readily abdicate when the challenger throws the gauntlet. The management also become embroiled in the conflict because of their anxiety to avert a change of leadership. . . .

Worker dissatisfaction with the union and the conflict attending efforts at changing the leader have mounted steadily over the years, the most powerful recent evidence of this being the bitterly fought textile strike. In the more extreme cases workers have gone so far as to seek a change of leader each time a settlement comes up for negotiation. They flit from one leader to another, often coming back to the same person after a while since the choice of leaders is not infinite. The employers are dismayed at the instability: many have signed long-term settlements with a leader whom they thought to be representative of the men only to find him jettisoned overnight in favour of another. The events have cast their shadow above all on the labour movement itself. The arduous task of organizing a trade union from scratch has suddenly lost its relevance: the easier path to ascendance as a leader is to take over existing organizations. Raiding and poaching rather than laborious organizing are the norm. And yet, the fact is also that, barring exceptions, the challenger enters not at his own initiative but at the behest of the workers.

The forces which have culminated in these developments are deeply rooted in the system of industrial relations. Apart from the absence of democratic procedures in trade unions and the resulting inability of workers to vent their grievances, two other factors surface prominently. The foremost among them is the gross inadequacy of the conventional processes of dispute resolution. Comments Radha Iyer, a frequent contributor to financial dailies on Bombay industrial relations:

> Nearly ten lakh cases are pending before industrial tribunals and labour courts. And there is no hope of the backlog being cleared in the near future. A number of these courts do not have a judge at all and therefore do not function. . . . In Calico Chemicals where a protracted struggle is going on under Dr Samant (in the year 1980), the charter of demands was presented sometime in 1964. At that time workers had high hopes in the legal machinery and agreed to go to court. The award of the industrial tribunal came only in 1971. The company went in appeal against this to the High Court. When it failed, it went before the division bench of the same High Court and then to the Supreme Court where the case is pending at present. . . . In the meanwhile, for the past 21 years since 1958 when the company first started production there has been no revision in pay scales and wage structure. . . . Now the workers have been on strike for over 10 months led by Dr Samant. If the strike goes on for another 10 months, Dr Samant at least would not give in. That is the kind of leader the workers want, that is the mood.[1]

There is wide agreement that established procedures are

---

[1] Radha Iyer 1980.

murderously slow. P.K. Kunte, a leader of the CITU, views the militancy as the product of the present chaotic system and goes on to cite an example: 'In 1972 the CITU had organised a 22-day strike in the woollen industry. The matter was referred to the industrial court and the award was announced just a few days ago, nine years after the strike. The award is in any case irrelevant in today's condition of high inflation.'[2] Comments Datta Samant: 'There is need for a lot of changes. The Industrial Disputes Act . . . has a number of loopholes. When the workers get something good from the lower courts, the employer goes to the Supreme Court and straightaway 10–15 years are lost. The worker naturally cannot afford to wait for so long to get things changed.'[3]

P.W. Khandekar, Personnel Director of Siemens, . . . observes in reply to the question whether the conciliation machinery has been effective: 'Not at all. First of all, the approach is too legalistic. In Bombay at any rate—and I think it is the same elsewhere in the country—the conciliation process does not take place at all. The two parties are asked what they have to say and the negotiating officer does not make any suggestions. He is a . . . paid employee who takes a very formal approach. He does not declare his opinion. . . . As far as the industrial tribunal machinery is concerned, it is far too dilatory. I would say that the workers and the trade union leaders are to a very great extent justified in not having too much trust in the tribunals and the conciliation machinery.' He goes on to comment that the system works in favour of the employer: 'I feel employers tend to use it. . . . Certain kinds of employers use the delaying nature of the industrial relations machinery to their own advantage, frustrating all attempts to settle disputes. . . . It is a fact that the employers misuse it; it is a fact that the government machinery is too dilatory.'[4]

The second major factor contributing to the present state is the inability of established unions to respond to the new challenges. The national federations have been essentially conservative and rule-bound in their approach to problems, and this includes the more radical ones as well. Pendse notes of the communist unions: 'Their most important [attribute] is the inability to change

[2] D.K. Varma 1981.
[3] *Transindia* 1978.
[4] Ibid.

with the times. The communist unions seem to be rooted in the milieu in which they were formed . . . . The inadequacy in grasping change is seen with regard to even the traditional demands. In 1977, for example, the norms regarding the quantum of wage rise underwent a drastic change. Most unions including the red flag ones were surprised at the workers 'adamance' and ultimate management capitulation. . . . An ironic situation perhaps is that red flag unions are considered by managements to be 'responsible', i.e., they accept the norms of capitalism in practice if not in theory. They are overall defensive organizations geared to the backward sections of society. The limitations of the red flag unions created a vacuum of leadership and representation among the Bombay working class. The Datta Samant wave could only be conceivable in such a vacuum.'[5]

[ . . . ]

The inertia of established trade unions, their touching faith in legal and constitutional procedures, their lack of empathy with shop-floor activists and their aspirations, the inability or unwillingness of even radical unions to mount militant campaigns, the gross inadequacy of established procedures to settle conflict equitably and expeditiously, and the abuse of the system by employers to put the lid on labour, cumulated to produce an enormous upheaval. None of the circumstances which have rocked Bombay are really unique to the city. The system of industrial relations with this reliance on conciliation and adjudication is the same all over the country. If anything, Bombay has more advanced statutory provisions for trade union recognition which are often held out as a model for others to emulate. . . . What sets Bombay apart are more the specifics than the generalities: the scale of the eruption which is partly a function of the scale of organized industry; the search for an alternative in non-political leadership; and the methods adopted by the leadership to gain redress.

## CONTRASTING LEADERSHIP STYLES

The militancy of workers which their own unions could neither perceive nor charmelize has found expression through Datta

[5] Sandip Pendse 1981.

Samant, the man who has symbolized labour protest for over a decade. Samant is not the only leader operating with unconventional methods outside the framework of political parties and their trade union federations, but he is by far the most popular among them. For this reason his style of leadership has to be considered in some detail.

A doctor by profession, Samant was attracted to trade unionism in the mid-sixties by the plight of stone quarry workers whom he ministered. He shot to fame in 1972 when he was invited by the workers of Godrej and Boyce, a firm manufacturing consumer durables, to dislodge their trade union. Samant met with stiff resistance not merely from the established union and the employer but also from the police and the government although he had by then joined the Congress party. Large scale violence erupted, leading to the death of several persons, and Samant was arrested and denied bail for inciting the violence. Samant's arrest provoked workers into a powerful display of solidarity to demand his release, firmly establishing him as a major force in the labour movement. The Godrej campaign had all the attributes that were to characterize the many struggles under his leadership: he was entering at the invitation of workers to dislodge an unpopular union, he used methods which were direct if also violent, and displayed scant regard for legal and procedural niceties.

The next major turning point was the Emergency and the years immediately following, which saw Samant bloom to his full potential. Although a Congressman working within the folds of the INTUC at the time of the Emergency, he opposed the government's policy of stifling labour protest, and spent much of the period in jail under the dreaded Maintenance of Internal Security Act. The outburst of labour protest all over the country upon the termination of the Emergency was spearheaded in Bombay by Samant. He led dozens of strikes all over Bombay at any given time. A mere charter of demands from him sent shivers down the spines of employers: it was the harbinger of conflict that would be liberally punctuated by assault, mob violence and murder and be prolonged for months if not years. Samant's empire expanded phenomenally—so much that many requests for intervention had to be declined.

By 1980 Samant was out of the Congress as well as of the INTUC. This made no difference to him since the affiliation was never more than nominal, and he needed the Congress and its union less than they needed him. The crowning event of his career came in 1982–3 when he took 200,000 textile workers out on strike for over 18 months. In the midst of the strike he floated a political party called the *Kamgar Aghadi* (Workers' Front), arguing that workers needed a party which would be under their control and push for legislation that was favourable to them. The textile strike which established the enormity of his following is also the biggest fiasco Samant has ever faced: the mills re-opened without a settlement. The defeat has not in any way affected his stature. It is impossible to give an accurate estimate of Samant's supporters. His own office does not have these figures because . . . it runs a campaign rather than a trade union. What is beyond doubt is that his is the overwhelming presence on the Bombay labour scene.

What are the methods which have made him so popular? 'The attraction that Samant held for workers can be fairly clearly understood. He represented direct, swift and uncompromising confrontations. . . . He would usually put forth a direct, simple lumpsum demand. . . . He did not seem to be unduly bothered by the intricacies of the modalities by which this was to be effected. Palpable, attractive quantums were the backbone of his demands . . . . Samant also effectively articulated the general distrust of capitalists which the workers were feeling. He echoed their disgust towards the legal system. It was not seen in any way as an aid to problem solving. . . . He has not only avoided legal procedures but has violated accepted legal norms. He has brushed aside injunctions, ignored questions of legality of his actions, trampled upon signed and concluded settlements. . . . The distrust which he displayed in the financial statements of the companies also echoed the workers' sentiments. He refused to accept these as the basis of any settlement, refused to even read them. He has repeatedly and openly called them fraudulent. The only basis for negotiations that he was accepted are his own demands. Intricate arguments about capacity to pay etc., he has treated as useless lies. He displayed in the same manner a contempt for negotia-tions . . . . They are only ways of delaying the proceedings and of trapping the workers. Trials of strength through immediate, direct confrontation was the foundation of his methodology.'[6]

A few remarks may be added to this lucid summary to

[6] Ibid.

complete the picture. Samant calculated profits and ability to pay in his own way with production figures obtained from workers, and based his demands on these calculations. Once the demand was formulated, he did no more than write a letter to the employer stating the demand. In particular, there was no attempt to start a dialogue. The employer had the option to either concede the demand or face a trial of strength.

While all this may convey the impression that Samant has got whatever he wanted, the facts are somewhat more complex. Along with remarkable successes, he has also suffered stunning reverses, the textile strike being only the most recent of them. His strategies, simple and effective in most cases, do not always succeed. In the words of a journalist, the chink in his armour is that, like a general who never plans for an ordered retreat if the need should arise, Samant does not know what to do with a campaign that runs into rough weather. . . .

[ . . . ]

Once the novelty wore off, employers learnt to cope with Samant. Numerous enterprises have institutionalized their relationship with him, and at least some have found a positive aspect to the relationship. The advantage in dealing with Samant is that he agrees to productivity deals and refrains from interfering in everyday industrial relations. . . . For those who are determined to resist Samant, his total lack of strategy to push the employer towards a settlement offers a major advantage. . . .

Another disturbing feature of Samant's campaigns is that the line between friend and foe has become blurred. The methods of early and late Samant have tended to vary. In the early phase he crusaded to free workers from collusive relationships between employers and obsequious trade union leaders. He himself has repeatedly said that he was a doctor and not a trade unionist by profession, and that if he entered a firm it was only because the workers wanted him. . . . With growing stature and ambition, these proprieties have tended to erode. While activists from obscure plants may still be sent back to collect signatures from the entire labour force, the request of a minority is often sufficient in the case of a prize target. The contrast between his early campaigns, such as the one at Godrej where he battled with a truly unpopular union, and the later ones where he took over unions which had a mass base, is indeed marked.

Once the quarry was identified, violence was the chief method of achieving the goal. When unpopular unions were attacked, violence was aimed at blacklegs and similar other elements to protect the mass of workers, and the vanguard of the attack was worker militants and activists. In the later campaigns, violence, ever more brutal, became a method of beating the majority into submission. The victims of the attack were worker militants battling to save their unions and the vanguard now consisted of the lumpen. This reversal of roles has tended to detract from the very purpose of Samant's entry into the labour movement.

A second independent trade unionist, way behind Samant in influence but nevertheless an important force, is R.J. Mehta whose major constituency is the engineering industry. An inveterate and implacable firebrand, Mehta has paled only because Samant is even more fearsome. His methods are however quite different from those of the latter. He takes to the courts as easily as Samant's squads take to the streets, and is skilled enough at turning a phrase to hold his own in the Supreme Court. With all this, adjudication is not the preferred method but only a necessary back-up. . . . Mehta is so sworn to collective bargaining that his agreements do not seek the legitimizing stamp of the government, as do many others even when they do not require the meditation of the labour department.[7]

Mehta is a business unionist par excellence who has little to do with political parties and their labour fronts. His union office is well equipped and efficiently managed by staff who enjoy the benefit of a regular salary including dearness allowance, provident fund, gratuity and pension. The members have to pay for the services and the money is collected straightaway through the employer by means of the settlement. All his settlements provide

---

[7] Mehta's settlements are signed invariably under Section 18(1) and not 12(3) of the Industrial Disputes Act. Since the latter provision encompasses the totality of the organization's labour force, majority support for the union has to be first ascertained by the labour department. In contrast, a settlement under the former provision extends only to members of the union signing the instrument and, therefore, does not require the intervention of the labour department. Another feature of Mehta's settlements is the provision containing management's recognition of his union. In normal circumstances recognition has to be obtained through the labour court under the Maharashtra Registration of Trade Unions and Prevention of Unfair Labour Practices Act. These methods are evidently aimed at keeping all third parties out of the industrial relationship.

for the deduction of 10 per cent of arrears as contribution to the general fund of the union, a further 2 per cent to the Free Trade Unions Multipurpose Project Trust for the welfare of rural and backward regions and Rs 24 as membership fee for the year. Given the substantial benefits offered by settlements and the mounting arrears because of the lag between the expiry of one settlement and the contracting of another, the union nets a neat pile in this manner. Since Mehta does not believe in servicing those who do not pay, an undertaking is appended to every settlement, and the benefits accrue only to those who sign the undertaking which provides, among other things, for the deduction. The only concession to ideology in his set-up is the social work the union undertakes in backward and rural areas and a mobile hospital it runs.

Mehta submits not a charter of demands, but the draft of the settlement which his union would like to sign with the employer, and pushes the management into agreement through bargaining. He will call a strike if necessary and keep up the fighting spirit with strike relief, but believes that violence does not pay. Being a generalized instrument for achieving a variety of objectives of the workers, the trade union and the management, Mehta's settlements make fascinating study. They have a strong element of quid pro quo, a trade-off between benefits to members and advantages to the employer. The members get many benefits, but are also tied to several obligations. All settlements carry an employment security clause whereby no worker can be laid off, retrenched or discharged without the consent of the union. They also offer significant benefits by way of increase in wages and allowances. The union, for its part, collects all the amounts due to it from the workers and gains recognition from the management through the settlement. However, it is the demands conceded to the employer which mark them off from run-of-the-mill settlements.

An important objective of the management is to curb absenteeism which has assumed serious proportions. A standard clause in all settlement is that workers who are absent for more than a certain number of days in a month . . . shall forfeit certain allowances for the entire month . . . , and that the amount shall be credited to the union. . . . Another clause, somewhat less common, reads: 'Any worker reporting late on more than three occasions in a month shall forfeit one day's casual leave. A worker who reports late further in a given month shall forfeit half a day's leave for every additional day he reports late, and may be further liable for disciplinary action as provided under the standing orders.'

Some other clauses which the management find advantageous are:

'During the course of this settlement there shall be no strike or go-slow and no stoppage of work . . . and there shall be no lockout or closure of the company.'

'There shall be no stoppage of work in any manner on account of the demise of a workman. However, all workmen of the company including managerial and technical staff shall observe two minutes silence at the place of work before the closing hours.'

'Workmen without uniforms or with unclean uniforms and shoes shall be sent home and shall not be paid wages for that day and washing allowance for that month.'

[ . . . ]

Another favourable aspect from the employer's point, especially common in the engineering industry, is the productivity clause in return for enhanced compensation. What is involved is not the usual affirmation of union support for efforts at increasing efficiency, but prescription of precise quantums to be turned out. Mehta is willing to have industrial engineers acceptable to the union study the work process and recommend production norms and manning levels.

Finally, the settlements display a strong touch of paternalistic union concern for the member and his family. Almost every settlement requires the company to preferentially employ children of workmen, and to maintain a list of heirs for this purpose. If a worker dies in harness, the firm is required to immediately employ a son or daughter. When a worker dies or is disabled, all workers are required to contribute half day's pay, and the employer a matching amount, to a benefit fund. Workers are required to have a compulsory medical check up, to be organized by the union's medical facility, every two years. A major objective of most settlements is to increase retirement benefits. Some also provide for long-term savings schemes to which employers contribute 50 per cent of the amount workers deposit. The most esoteric of all provisions—and one rooted in the social reality of industrial workers—concerns incorrigible alcoholics. One settlement provides that workers identified as 'habitual drunkards' shall forfeit several major allowances, and that the amount shall be handed over by the company at its expense to the wife if the worker is married, and to the parents if he is not. . . .

## COLLECTIVE BARGAINING: PAY, BENEFITS AND COUNTERVAILING DEMANDS

Independent trade unionists and internal leaders who together control the vast bulk of Bombay's industry have undoubtedly bargained wages and benefits which are better than possibly any other industrial centre in the country. Compensation is especially attractive in capital intensive and labour saving process industry. Petro-chemicals is currently the best paymaster, followed closely by pharmaceuticals. The older labour intensive industries such as engineering come way behind, and cotton textiles is close to the bottom.

[ . . . ]

[T]he handsome emoluments of Bombay workers come as part of a package which trims the size of the labour force and expects increased exertion from those left behind. This steps up the pressure on workers, making it especially difficult for the older ones to cope. They have the choice to either accept voluntary retirement and quit, or be constantly pressurized by the management and probably their own trade union to stretch themselves.

Getting increased benefits through the settlement is not a onetime effort. The major question is whether, and how often, the trade-off between benefits to workers and economies to the employer can be repeated, especially in the absence of significant investments in technology, as does frequently happen. Trade union leaders themselves doubt that such an exercise can continue. . . .

## DECISION MAKING IN TRADE UNIONS

All bargaining is an effort to balance the give and the take. Who decides the make-up of the package? Is the mix of what is given and what is got, of the workers' choosing or decided for them by the leader? Is there a broad-based consultation with workers before demands are finalized? Do the leaders get a draft settlement approved by the general body before committing to it? Answers to these questions have much to tell about the internal organization of the union which will inevitably have consequence for its external relations with the management.

The leaders who dominate the scene clearly do not stand out for their democratic practices. What Datta Samant leads is a movement, not an organization. Some do not even view it as a movement, but only as a struggle campaign, a perpetual charge. His organisations seem to be very loose structurally. The conduct of the day-to-day affairs is left to a local committee—self-appointed rather than elected in many cases. . . .

Mehta is not far different. Although his organizations are well structured and he himself is far more accessible, his decisions lack a popular base. . . . His settlements are indicative of the slender thread that links the member to the union. As already noted, Mehta collects through the settlement all that is due from the worker to the union . . . . What Mehta operates is in effect a closed shop which makes it hard for anyone to keep out of his union. . . .

[ . . . ]

Faced with the authoritarianism of the leader, the workers develop their own defenses. 'Reflecting on his own experiences of the history of the union in his plant, an activist from one of several plants controlled by a Dutch multinational told us he thought most reshuffles occurred after the signing of a settlement where the union had simply short-circuited the bargaining cycle, presenting workers with a *fait accompli* and promoting the settlement through propaganda rather than consultation and feedback. Changes in the union committee or the union as a whole are thus one form in which workers express their disapproval. . . . '[8]

Union leaders have not lagged behind workers in alacrity. In the continuing battle between workers and their own leaders to outsmart each other, the latest development is a restriction of the workers' right to choose their union. . . .

The overall picture that the Bombay labour movement conveys is one where workers' allegiance to their unions is tenuous and

[8] Jairus Banaji 1985.

the unions' own claim to speak for their members dubious. It is a situation where free-floating workers not only shift easily from one union to another but even choose different unions for different purposes. Indeed, loyalty itself appears outmoded and irrelevant in such an atmosphere. . . .

One can see why the free-wheeling independent unions have built no bridges between themselves and their members. They have neither an abiding ideology nor an organizational structure which draws in the worker. All that they have is a single point agenda appealing to his pecuniary instinct. What is more puzzling is that even Marxist trade unions have no ideological base, unlike their counterparts elsewhere in the country. Unable to match the militancy of Samant, and devoid of a base of dedicated support, the Marxists have in fact been the worst victims of rivalry and violence, first from the Shiv Sena and then from Datta Samant.

[ . . . ]

## CONCLUSION

Our analysis of the trade union scene in Bombay unmistakably indicates that workers are losing confidence in their own leaders, and consequently engaged in the quest, seemingly endless, for more appropriate leadership. The desire for better compensation is certainly an important source of dissatisfaction. Although Bombay workers are the best paid in the country, the fact is also that pay packets that sound attractive elsewhere look diminutive in this high cost city. However, it would be a grievous mistake to equate all the upheaval in the labour movement with the pecuniary instinct, for leaders who win the best packages have been uprooted as well. There clearly are other significant issues, and they are rooted in work rather than in money. Redundancy, loss of work identity, forced retirement euphemistically termed voluntary, shrinking job opportunities, increased work pace, rising work loads without matching inputs in technology, and lowered manning levels are important issues to ordinary workers. The workers . . . are concerned at the increased recourse to casual labour, decline in the permanent force, the contracting out of essential tasks such as security, transport operation and machinery maintenance, farming out of production reminiscent of the putting-out system to take advantage of cheap labour, threatened closure of entire sections, the consequent de-skilling and shuffling about of permanent employees and a host of similar problems.

Trade union leaders without a background of industrial employment rarely have much appreciation of non-monetary issues. They bring to every situation their conception of what workers require. The leader's stake to prominence is built on the size of his empire, which in turn is presumed to depend on how much money he can get for his followers. The leaders appraise themselves, and believe others to appraise them, merely along the monetary yardstick. The minimum that Datta Samant would accept through a settlement as additional monthly benefit runs into hundreds of rupees. This is a target set quite consciously at the highest levels of the MGKU [Samant's organization], and not the result of some informal processes of interest articulation by the members. The quantum finds expression in money with no reference to work issues. No leader decides on the workers' behalf that he would fight to finish the contract system or casual labour. . . .

The strategy adopted to win the demand is as standardized as the demand itself. Leaders have their convictions on how to go about, and the strategy is the same regardless of the situation.

There is a certain naiveté about pre-determining the quantum of desired benefit and the choice of strategy without regard for the specifics of the situation. An additional benefit of Rs 400 means one thing for a capital intensive process plant whose labour cost is some 5 to 7 per cent of manufacturing expense and quite another for a labour intensive textile mill or engineering factory whose labour cost hovers around 25 per cent. Even if a leader decides to ignore the management's protestations about ability to pay, he has to figure out the right strategy for applying pressure. A host of circumstances influence the staying power of labour and management. A petroleum refinery cannot parcel out the processing of crude among small scale refiners to beat down a strike whereas a firm in entertainment electronics can farm out jobs without much difficulty. On the other hand, a refinery can be manned by officers in an emergency, but not plants engaged in fabrication or assembly. There is not much evidence of strategy being tailored to the specifics of the situation.

The one corrective to this warped sense of priorities would be the generation of the charter of demands through the general body, or at least through a factory-based committee of activists. This rarely happens because most leaders see themselves as functioning on the workers' behalf, not at their behest. Strong, elected local committees are perceived as a threat to their authority. The *ad hoc*, self-appointed structures found in many places may be high on enthusiasm but have no perspective of the real issues nor the moral force to act as a corrective to the leader.

Having decided what demands to make and how to fight for them, the leader also decides which of the demands of the management to concede so as to clinch a deal. The critical element, once again, is the leader and not the requirements of the situation. What are given up, paradoxically, are the very issues which trouble workers. While workers are concerned about work and employment, it is precisely in these areas that they have conceded the most to the management.

It is not because of mere ignorance of workers' sentiments and aspirations that such deals are struck. The leaders are in the business of building their image, enhancing their following and becoming a force to reckon with. This is best achieved by concentrating on the most visible of all issues, which is money. A leader who settles for a modest package to prevent the closure of a section or stop the farming out of jobs, would scarcely hit newspaper headlines, gain fame or widen his sphere of influence.

By trading increased employer discretion over work and employment for higher benefits, the leaders are redistributing rather than creating income. What really happens is that ever increasing benefits are placed in the hands of ever shrinking numbers. Contract work, casual labour, redundancy and voluntary retirement create the surplus that is passed on to those left behind in permanent employment. The flow is from one segment of workers to another rather than from capital to labour. In a way, the heightened demand for further benefits has itself created the situation of Peter being robbed to pay Paul.

The final travesty is that some of the leaders have begun to discharge functions which are essentially managerial. The common response of managements when confronted with mounting union pressure has been to aggressively demand whether trade unions have only rights and no responsibilities. To managers it appears incontrovertible logic that those who ask for more from the system should also be responsible for enlarging the kitty. The managements themselves evidently take the responsibility for keeping their part of the bargain. Should not trade unions, which so freely promise co-operation while asking for more, be tied to action instead of being allowed to get away with words? How can any segment of the organization merely take without giving?

Under the weight of this logic, a new kind of 'responsible trade unionism' has grown. In earlier times, 'responsibility' meant that the union would be submissive, play the game within severe limits and accept management as the final arbiter of everyone's destiny. In the new style, unions are aggressive and demanding and refuse to accept that management have the final word, but team up with the management to ensure that workers perform as promised. In a bid to assuage employers that additional benefits to labour would come form the production of increased wealth, union leaders have begun to assume executive responsibility and thereby double as managers. They have become the honorary personnel and industrial relations managers of the organization. . . . In effect, the management have given out the man-management function on contract, and that to the trade union leader himself. . . . It is obvious that no one can offer the best to both labour and management, and the frequent change in union leadership is a manifestation of this simple truth.

It is in fact the leaders grown from the ranks who refuse to confine themselves to the package of benefits. Generalizing about internal leaders is hazardous because they range from the submissive to the militant, with the former being more numerous than the latter. . . . The assertive and independent worker leadership which is beginning to emerge is probably the hardest to deal with from the managerial point of view. Unlike outsiders who readily give in on the roundabout to gain on the swing, a trade-off with worker leaders is more difficult. . . . It is with this kind of leadership that the management feel the candle being burnt at both ends.

[ . . . ]

Whether employers would permit inside leadership of [the] highly vigilant and critical kind to function is the moot question. They would probably prefer to be dictated to by the most militant of outsiders than submit every managerial decision to searching scrutiny by worker leaders. It is relatively easier to part with even substantial quantities of money, especially in exchange for explicit or implicit legitimization of managerial control over areas other than worker compensation, than share power with inside leadership which is fully in the know of the happenings in the enterprise.

As for the workers themselves, the real choice open to most groups is between one outside leader and another. They cannot alter the basic character of this leadership. What they can do is to capitalize on the leader's strengths and try and mitigate his weaknesses. They capitalize on the leader's political influence, ability to mount sympathetic action by commandeering other worker groups and greater legitimacy in the view of the management, while keeping him on a leash through perpetual probation and application of pressure to pursue their interests rather than his own.

# Strategies in the Bombay Textile Strike, 1982–83*

## H. van WERSCH

## WORKERS' STRATEGIES

### Position of the Unions

The idea of a general strike in the textile industry emanated first from the left-oriented unions united in the Trade Unions' Joint Action Committee (TUJAC). Their sympathy for such action is clear from their contribution to the heating up of the atmosphere prior to the strike and their participation in warning strikes, such as those on 27 September 1981 and 6 January 1982. During the strike their support became visible in the collections of money and grain, organization of independent meetings as well as in their participation in rallies in which they shared the dais with Datta Samant and the Maharashtra Girni Kamgar Union, MGKU. However, their position was very ambivalent and their participation in strike-related activities remained moderate with the notable exception of the Sarva Shramik Sangh (SSS) which threw in its lot with Samant's MGKU. The hesitation of the other socialist and communist unions is understandable. Many leaders among them had right from the outset serious misgivings about the

* Excerpted from H. van Wersch, 'Strike Strategies', *The Bombay Textile Strike, 1982–83*, Bombay: Oxford University Press, 1992, pp. 155–233.

feasibility of an indefinite strike. On the other hand, they saw and sensed the mood of the workers and realized that if they wanted to avoid being swept away completely they were left with no other option than to jump onto the MGKU bandwagon.

Under the circumstances, moderate support promised the highest returns enabling them to sustain their (battered) position in the industry as some of the credit could be claimed in the event of success and most of the failure could be attributed to Samant in the event of failure. Datta Samant became increasingly aware of this and the realization in combination with insurmountable ideological differences largely explains why he was averse to negotiations with the Government and/or the millowners in the company of the red flag unions. However, his reluctance to involve them in negotiations, in attempts at conciliation or in the development of strike strategies would also militate against the success of the strike, apart from providing the left unions with a ready excuse to drop out. Not being tied to success as strongly as the MGKU/SSS combine, the red flag unions were in a better position to gauge much earlier and more accurately changes in the mood of the workers, but their motives being suspect, their warnings were too easily explained away as subtle attempts to undermine workers' morale.

[ . . . ]

## WORKER'S COMMITTEES

Possibly the most striking characteristic of the strike was its spontaneity, finding expression in the sudden shift of loyalty towards a complete outsider in the industry. This characteristic was also borne out by the formation of workers' committees, repeatedly declared to be the backbone of the strike, without which the strike would have collapsed much sooner. . . . These committees have also been credited with a leading role in the decision-making process during the strike. True, mill committees had already been formed before the strike began and they were instrumental in seeking Samant's leadership. Zone and area committees too operated at an early stage, a couple of months after the beginning of the struggle. But, unless one wishes to credit the various types of workers' committees with the bullying of strike-breakers and the beating up of Sangh-activists, there is little to support the contention that they were as crucial for the success of the strike as has been suggested.

In some cases it was only a matter of reviving committees which had been active in earlier struggles and had been lying dormant. In other cases young workers without former committee experience decided to establish a committee. As the police made the proper functioning of all these committees increasingly difficult (Section 144, arbitrary arrests), many active workers went underground and some resurfaced in zone and area committees. In every zone about six mill committees operated which were entrusted with the tasks of canvassing for the strike and providing a channel of communication between the workers and the strike leadership. The area committees were based in the suburbs and had to perform the same functions as the mill and zone committees in the city. About a year after the strike, zone and area committees were to be integrated in a Central Committee but at that stage disintegration, as a result of frictions with Samant, was already clearly visible.

What tasks were assigned to these workers' committees? They played a role in the organization of meetings and rallies, the collection and distribution of food and money, the organization of *morchas* [demonstrations or processions] and *gheraos* [encircling, making inaccessible, of person or building as a protest action] and, most importantly, in keeping in touch with the workers on strike. If the committees had been successful in performing all these tasks then one could rightly attribute a crucial role to them in the continuation of the struggle. But in spite of the unquestioned relevance of all these activities, only a small section of the workers in the sample appeared to be aware of even the existence of any workers' committees and a still smaller group attached much value to them. This came as a surprise because much had been made of these committees in many accounts of the strike. . . .

Great care was therefore taken that the workers in the sample understood the questions relating to the existence and the activities of mill, zone and area committees (various names and descriptions were tried) but it was all too obvious that apart from the food distribution, very few had come into contact with members of such committees. This was as much the case for workers in Bombay Dyeing (usually living in the heart of the textile area) as

for the Finlay workers (often staying far away and spread over the city). If these committees had been the link between the strike leadership and the rank and file of the workers, as various authors have claimed, then a great many more workers should at least have known about them. In some cases workers who themselves had been very active at the beginning of the strike and participated in the work of the committees appeared to have lost interest after a couple of months. . . . That committees did not fare well may also be deduced from repeated appeals to join such committees.
[ . . . ]
One is led to believe that workers who had returned to their villages during the strike had fewer opportunities of getting in touch with the workers' committees which would explain the general ignorance. But it was found that most of the workers who did not know about the activities of the committees appeared to have stayed in the city. In all, more than 62 per cent of the workers in the sample appeared to have no knowledge of the existence and activities of the workers' committees.

This raises the question of what created the impression that the various committees were vital for the prolongation of the strike. Part of the answer is provided by looking at the many tasks these committees were expected to perform and, undoubtedly, did perform in a number of cases. These tasks were vital and had the committees really been able to shoulder them it would certainly have had a great impact on the outcome of the strike. But assigning a task or attributing a function to a committee is not the same as living up to it. If we take into account the individuals by whom the committees were manned we find what usually the most active workers found a place in them as they were seeking ways of expressing their involvement in the strike and to influence its course. These workers would not have been satisfied with merely attending meetings and joining marches. It is to be expected that they, who one might term the vanguard of the rank and file of Samant's MGKU, would soon feel the need for greater action. Such workers would find each other at the mill gates or at the office of the MGKU and soon realize the need to get organized, first at mill level but later also at a higher (zone) level and would act accordingly. It appears, however, that there were far too few active workers to establish a force capable of reaching all levels of the textile labour field.

Other unions active in the textile industry too have and/or had a system of shop level presentation. Keeping such an elaborate system alive is, of course, much easier for the representative union than for contesting unions but even so mill committees, linked to opposing unions, existed in the past and were active in times of labour unrest. The formation of such committees in the present strike, therefore, was a continuation of a trend with a long history. But their rapid development may have been hampered by the exodus to the villages and what was beneficial for the survival of the strikers may well have been detrimental to the success of their organization. Apart from handling organizational tasks, the main purpose of these committees, whether attached to a union or not, has always been to convey the views of the workers to the strike leaders and to explain the strike strategy to the workers. In doing so the committees could exercise influence on both the leadership and the workers and in that way they could contribute to shaping events.

This strike was different in the sense that its leadership was tied down essentially to one man—Datta Samant. Unfortunately, Samant was not the type of person who cared much for consultation. The tremendous support he received was enough proof to him that he represented the workers' feelings, their hopes and anger. Every meeting convinced him that the workers were with him and he did not therefore feel the need for deliberations on the course of action which ran the risk of his strategy of militancy supported by endurance being watered down. Discussions with him were a one way traffic and those who entertained conflicting views hardly had an opportunity to air them and even less to influence his decisions.

As the strike progressed many active workers and many labour activists became increasingly dissatisfied with this and dropped out. Samant could afford such an attitude as he knew that there was no one else to whom the workers would turn and it was easy to create the impression that those who were not for him should be taken to be against him. The sheer presence of mill committees and a few zone and area committees cannot hide the fact that their influence on the decisions taken by Samant was by no means great. It would not be unjust to say, in fact, that Samant's very popularity blocked the way for massive and active participation of lakhs of workers in specific strike-related action. The mill and zone committees simply did not get a chance to work out different approaches to the strike even if they had wanted to. The leader was too powerful for that.

Things might have been different had Samant felt the need for a well thought out strategy for conducting the strike. For the development of such a plan and its execution he would have required detailed information and co-operation from the activists among the workers, from a network of committees. But no such strategy providing for massive, coercive and sustained action existed. The rural tour he made, a move displaying an awareness of the need to broaden the ambit of the struggle, was in idea suggested to him by the activists of the Lal Nishan Party (LNP) and one of the rare instances of the application of unconventional means. Typically, this campaign necessitated close co-operation from the LNP without which the whole operation might not have taken place.

On the whole Samant's tactics were simple, if not minimal. He did not go much beyond delivering speeches near mill gates and at mass rallies, and heading *morchas* and jail *bharos*.[1] For the initiation and organization of these activities he did not require an elaborate system of workers' committees although the success, particularly of the jail *bharo* campaigns, might have been far greater had such a network existed. With the assistance of a substantial cadre of worker–activists, together establishing an effective network, providing leadership at the lower level and sustaining the action in Samant's absence, the outcome of the strike might well have been different. The strike now seemed largely a one man show for the performance of which Samant relied on the endurance of the workers and the assistance of a handful of trusted lieutenants. . . . Datta Samant knew that the struggle would be long and fearing that the workers might be tempted to give in, he preferred not to have them around, which is why he sent them back to the villages.

---

[1] The term 'jail *bharo andolan*', a mixture of English and Hindi, signifies an agitation in the course of which the participants offer themselves for arrest. The reason for such a 'fill the jail campaign' is to call public attention to the need to redress a wrong experienced by a particular group. The method is derived from strategies propagated by Mahatma Gandhi in the course of India's struggle for freedom.

This is not to say that Samant was insincere in his efforts to find a solution or that he was basically motivated by personal aggrandizement but a proper infrastructure in his union empire was and still is painfully lacking. Such an infrastructure is indispensable in a struggle on the scale of the textile strike. Prior to the strike Samant had always dealt with labour struggles on a small scale and he was used to dealing with them single-handed. Now he adopted the same methods in the textile strike, but what had worked in single factories would not work for a whole industry. As long as only a few unions in his union empire conducted strikes, it was always possible to sustain a prolonged struggle with the assistance of the main body (solidarity strikes, collection of funds, food-grain and the like) but now that a whole industry was paralysed the policy of remaining on strike for better or for worse proved self-defeating.

A strong network of mill and zone committees would also have been able to detect changes in the mood of the workers at an early stage and might have been able to modify policies accordingly. This leads to another point illustrating that the mill and zone committees were ineffective. The fact that a majority of the workers in the sample [n=150] acknowledged that they had wanted to resume work after a period of about six months but refrained from doing so for fear of violence . . . , proves that the committees were either insufficiently aware of this change or chose to ignore it. In the first case they would clearly prove to have been out of touch with the workers and in the second they would rapidly become so.

Lastly, the question of how the impression prevailed that the workers' committees played such a dominant role in the strike should also be considered from the point of view of who reported on the strike. It must then be noted that the strike was followed closely by only a handful of labour correspondents, many of whom had little sympathy for Datta Samant's arbitrary behaviour. They attempted to discover the voice of the common worker and were inclined to believe that the mill and zonal committees were the platforms where the genuine feelings of the workers could be detected in their purest form. It is fairly certain that the misconception about the importance of the workers' committees originated here.

## The Rural Connection

*Exodus to the Villages:* [ . . . ]

It has been stated by advocates and adversaries of the strike alike that its incredibly long duration was essentially due to the rural connections of the workers who returned to their home villages. There is no denying that tens of thousands of textile workers boarded buses in the days following the commencement of the strike. In doing so they responded to appeals made by Datta Samant but they also acted in accordance with past behaviour and their realization that the village offered better chances of survival. In the history of the Bombay textile workers, the village always acted as a refuge for workers on strike. In the present exceptionally long strike, the importance of the rural hinterland could only be greater still. There is therefore no denying the significance of the rural connection for the strike at this general level but this changes as soon as one tries to be more specific.

. . . It was found that the estimates of the number of textile workers leaving the city during the strike vary greatly and are anywhere between 33 and 80 per cent of the entire labour force. It is tempting to fix the figure arbitrarily at 55 per cent but there would be no justification for this. It might very well be that some of the estimates are more realistic than others but, unfortunately, there is no way of finding out whose estimates deserve more credit.

[ . . . ]

No one seems to have paid attention to the fact that it would have been very difficult to arrive at a reliable estimate even if it had been possible to count the number of workers leaving the city. Thousands of workers returned after three, six or nine months to see what was going on. Many of them might even at that time have hoped or even tried to resume work but finding the atmosphere uncongenial or even downright hostile, may have decided to return to their villages once more. This is not as far-fetched as it may seem for a substantial majority of the workers in the sample who left for their villages mentioned having visited Bombay once, twice or more times during the strike. Some stayed just a couple of days, other lingered for weeks or months together. Many of those who returned to Bombay prior to finally resuming work (or finding that they had been dismissed), stated that they made an attempt to get their job back during their visit(s) to Bombay.

To add all these workers to the group who voluntarily stayed in the village throughout the strike would be incorrect. Neither would it be justifiable to add them to the group of Sangh supporters who remained in the city or to those that were opposed to the strike for different reasons—groups of unknown magnitude. There is also the problem of families who got separated during the strike (wife returning to the village, children remaining in Bombay for their schooling). It is pointless to fix a figure arbitrarily as the lack of evidence and the complexity of the situation does not allow for that. What may be said is that even if only 40 per cent of the workers returned to their villages, this group still comprised some 1,00,000 workers and that returning to the village, therefore, has to be considered an important avenue for survival.

While living in the village the workers were often without proper information about the situation in Bombay. They ran the risk of losing heart as a result and a visit by the strike leader to their places of origin would certainly do a lot to keep them united. If their active support could be enlisted to collect food and money this might even ease the problems of their fellow workers in the city. There was also the opportunity of pointing out the need for cooperation between industrial and agricultural labourers, which might create a bond between these different groups of workers. It was therefore decided that Datta Samant would undertake a rural tour in the second half of February and March. His visit to the rural areas, suggested and largely organized by LNP activists, did not go unnoticed. . . . This initiative deserves attention as it was an acknowledgement by the strike leadership of the importance of some of the less obvious aspects of the rural connection.

The presence of striking textile workers in the villages was bound to have an impact on village life, the scope of which naturally depended on the number of strikers in the village and their proportional share in the population but it also varied in accordance with the support from parties and groups that helped them to get organized. . . .

*Food Drives:* The support extended by the people living in the rural areas to the workers in Bombay in terms of food and money is indicative (though not the only indicator) of the significance of the rural connection. In assessing its scope it appears to be very difficult to arrive at a comprehensive view of the total support, be it in the form of food and monetary collections or any other strike-related activities. The situation for Bombay, where workers of many factories donated money for the success of the strike, is not much better. . . .

. . . In the heat of the struggle no-one bothered to carefully register donations in cash and kind. Whatever administration existed appears to have been haphazard. There was no central point in Bombay where all donations were first collected before being distributed to the needy workers. Apart from that, some donors organized their own distribution of money and food. . . . As a result the precise scope of the support given will remain unknown.

[ . . . ]

A different consideration is that even if the amounts of money and food that the strike leaders speak of were collected, this would still be a drop in the ocean. Rs 3 crores for at a minimum 1 lakh workers in the city would mean Rs 300 per person and 4,000 quintals of grain would come to 4 kgs per worker. It is true, certainly, that not all workers availed themselves of the support and with the passage of time ever more would resume work thereby leaving a greater share for those who continued the strike, but even so the donations could do little to relieve the distress.

. . . From all the workers in the sample some 40 per cent appeared to have received help in cash or in kind. These donations rarely exceeded 10 kg of wheat (portions of 5 kgs appeared to be the rule) or Rs 50 in cash, and in most cases the workers received help only once or twice. . . . If the sample results do provide an indication of the support received by workers from other mills then it must be concluded that in spite of statements to the contrary the total material support was very limited in scope.

The collection and distribution of food and money were not just limited in scope but also in time and took place mainly in the months following Datta Samant's rural tour in February 1982. After July nothing much is to be found in the papers on material support of any kind and it seems fair to assume that this support ebbed away. It could not be otherwise as there are tremendous problems involved in trying to sustain the attention and sympathy of the public in such long-drawn strikes.

This, of course, does not deny the possibility of the scale of support being unprecedented. In fact, this is likely to have been the case. To the best of my knowledge there have been no comparable food drives and money collections in earlier struggles. It tempts one to believe that this points to a growing awareness among agricultural labourers and small peasants in the rural hinterland that the struggles for better wages in the city and for higher income in the rural areas ought to be combined. This is questionable, however, and a matter of speculation. . . .

*Jail Bharo Campaigns:* The grain collections being over, another eruption of strike-related activities in the rural areas was to follow in August and September when jail *bharo* campaigns were launched (the first on 16 August) throughout Maharashtra, including Bombay. The news of the jail *bharo* campaigns was spread with the aid of pamphlets, posters and newspaper reports. . . . Samant claimed that some 50,000 workers courted arrest on 16 August but spokesmen of the police reduced that figure to 5,000 who were practically all released the same day. . . . The difference in figures is, apart from the customary overestimation and underrating, understandable as most workers who offered themselves for arrest were simply not arrested but dispersed. By refusing to arrest all those who offered themselves, the campaign was robbed of much of its glory and its badly needed martyrs. From the point of view of the state this was an effective answer to a campaign which might otherwise have unnerved the public and might have disrupted the entire jail system.

The second jail *bharo andolan* started on 17 September, a day on which 1,500 workers were arrested in Bombay but the zeal of the workers tapered off quickly. In the course of a week less than 5,000 workers courted arrest as against Samant's hope that this figure could be reached daily. . . . Even Datta Samant admitted that the participation was disappointing and ascribed this to the return of the textile workers to the villages . . . . But if this was really an explanation for the low response this time then it might rightly be asked why greater success was not achieved in the countryside.

A new vigorous attempt to draw public attention to the ongoing strike was made in October when yet another jail *bharo* campaign was planned in combination with a three days' strike in Samant-ruled industrial enterprises in Maharashtra starting on 11 October. Workers ignored the ban order regarding unlawful gatherings which resulted in violent clashes with the police on the first day of the strike and the arrest of 5,300 persons including Dada and Datta Samant. Datta Samant would be in jail for fourteen days. This campaign led to the unfortunate tussle with George Fernandes regarding the participation of the BEST [a major public utility, including the bus system] workers. . . . The success of the jail *bharo* campaign outside Bombay seems to have been moderate although a noteworthy aspect of it was the conspicuous participation of women in it. . . . With this last campaign the activities in the rural areas were practically over. In February and March 1983 there would follow a few long marches but these came too late to influence the outcome of the strike in any way.

[ . . . ]

Summarizing, it may be concluded that the rural connection had an important bearing on the chances for the survival of the workers. In this the present strike did not differ from similar struggles in the past. This connection (sometimes dubbed 'rural nexus') provided also the basis for collections of food and money as well as for participation in jail *bharo* campaigns, but the success of both these activities was limited even though it may have surpassed whatever was achieved in earlier struggles. Barring a few examples, there is no evidence that the strike had a significant impact on the unification of the struggles of agricultural and industrial labourers (the so-called worker–peasant alliance) and statements to that effect must be treated with caution. . . .

## THE USE OF VIOLENCE

*Impact of an Image*:  Millowners and Government have consistently attributed the unexpected success of the strike to the violent means supposedly adopted by Datta Samant and his MGKU. The Mill Owners' Association (MOA) used to speak of 'a fear psychosis' created in the minds of the workers as a result of beatings, stabbings and murders. Many newspapers uncritically aped this phrase without stopping to check the extent to which Samant's

MGKU could really be blamed for the use of means so easily attributed to it. The press reports about murders meanwhile did much to increase the tension and instilled fear in the hearts of countless textile workers. They also provided the millowners with an excuse to seek police protection for the workers who resumed duty and contributed considerably to a negative view of the strike by the public at large.

[ . . . ]

In order to establish the real proportion of violence the newspapers are of little use. . . . In order to obtain an overview of the situation during the strike, the office of the Commissioner of Police in Bombay collected information from the various police stations in the city in April/May 1987 and provided the statistics given [in Table 1]. . . .

Table 1
Cases of Violence Registered During Textile
Workers' Strike from 18.1.'82 to 1.8.'83

| Offences/ Criminal Acts | Total Cases | Total Accused Arrested | 'A' Cases* | Cases Pending Trial | No. Cases Convicted | No. Cases Acquitted |
|---|---|---|---|---|---|---|
| I | 178 | 237 | 49 | 29 | 3 | 97 |
| II | 59 | 72 | 18 | 9 | – | 32 |
| III | 3 | 3 | 2 | – | – | 1 |
| IV | 4 | 42 | – | 2 | – | 2 |
| V | 4 | 12 | 1 | 3 | – | – |
| Total | 248 | 366 | 70 | 43 | 3 | 132 |

\* 'A' Cases: true but undetected
I = Common assaults (beatings with or without weapons, stabbings)
II = Criminal intimidation (threats)
III = Violent acts (e.g. brickbatting, throwing soda water-bottles)
IV = Rioting
V = Murder cases
*Source:* Office Commissioner of Police, Bombay, May 1987

[ . . . ]

[A] word has to be said about the reliability of the information received from the police. The questions to be answered here are whether the police, as part of the law-enforcement machinery, could have a bias in reporting cases of violence and whether such a bias would lead to under-reporting incidences of violence or overrating them. The answer to these questions involves the role played by the police during the strike. This role went far beyond the maintenance of law and order. A bias may therefore not be excluded. From the involvement of the police in strike-breaking activities . . . it may be deduced that if any bias coloured the compilation of police statistics, it must have been a tendency to exaggerate the use of violence resorted to by Samant's MGKU and to minimize the use of violence by the Rashtriya Mill Mazdoor Sangh (RMMS)* (not to mention its own contribution).

[ . . . ]

The role of the police as an instrument for repression surfaced in its attempts to break the strike as reported by the press and attested to by workers during the interviews. . . .

The workers were questioned on their experience with or knowledge of violent incidents in order to ascertain the extent to which they were subjected to or influenced by violence of any kind during the strike. In tabling the results there was no alternative but to take the victims' surmises regarding the background of the assailants for granted. This implies that such tricky cases as a union assaulting its own members with the assistance of anonymous persons in order to discredit its opponent have gone undetected. It is impossible to say whether this techniques was resorted to by any of the unions. The results are presented in Table 2.

The answers confirm the impression that all the elements mentioned earlier, i.e. violence perpetrated by the MGKU, RMMS and the police, prevailed during the strike. Although the interviews were generally quite open it seems fair to assume that, if anything, the real incidence of violent encounters and threats was higher than appears from the Table. In any case, 27 workers out of a total of 150 (i.e. 18 per cent) were physically or verbally intimidated by any of the three agents, the MGKU, RMMS and

---

* *Rashtriya Mill Mazdoor Sangh (RMMS) is the representative union of textile workers founded in 1947. It is affiliated to the Indian National Trade Union Congress (INTUC), the trade union wing of the Congress Party. The union was preceded by the Rashtriya Girni Kamgar Sangh founded in 1939. (Eds)*

the police. It also appears that according to the findings in this sample the use of forceful means was more readily resorted to by adherents of the MGKU than by those of the RMMS. However, if we include the encounters with the police (and the pressure they put on workers to resume work) on the Sangh side, then there appears to be more of a balance. The justification for doing so would be that it matters little whether it was the Sangh or the police telling a worker to resume work if we want to map out the pressure to which workers were subjected. Roughly-speaking then we would find 16 acts of intimidation on the MGKU-side as against 11 on the part of the Sangh.

Table 2

Violent Encounters and Threats During Strike as Reported by Sample Workers

| Offence | Assailants | Mill A (n = 75) | Mill B (n = 75) |
|---------|-----------|-----------------|-----------------|
| Beating by | Samant-walas* | 3 | – |
| Stabbing by | Samant-walas | – | 1 |
| Threats by | Samant-walas | 8 | 4 |
| Beating by | Sangh-walas | 1 | – |
| Threats by | Sangh-walas | – | 3 |
| Beating by | Police | – | 1 |
| Threats by | Police | 2 | 4 |
| Total | | 14 | 13 |

* The Hindi and Marathi term 'wala' has a very flexible meaning and is used to denote persons employed with or concerned about something.

There are various problems connected with the evaluation of these data. One is that the seriousness of all these incidents is difficult to compare. A threat may seem to be more innocent than a beating but if the threat comes from a group of persons wielding knives and swords and visiting the victim at home (as happened to a RMMS-activist who thereupon left for his village), then it is certainly not less serious than the 'mild beating' reported by several workers who were stopped by 'MGKU-walas'. Again, a threat of dismissal (as given by 'Sangh-walas') may have a greater impact on a worker whose endurance has been tried far too long than would a mild beating.

[ . . . ]

Another problem is that a distortion of reality might have occurred in the sample as a result of contact with a worker who suffered from serious maltreatment by the police. This meeting was both shocking and revealing and would naturally lead me to ask the victim whether he knew of anybody else having undergone the same fate. In this fashion three more workers were contacted. As those who suffered from maltreatment by the police were known to each other, the result may well have been accumulation of relevant but possibly not very representative evidence. Even so, the accounts of the victims and the confirmation by other workers, in addition to the press reports, indicate such uniformity in the *modus operandi* of the police that there is no reason to believe that the extreme cases of harassment I chanced upon were restricted to the workers of the two mills under investigation.

*Contribution of the State*: The role of the police in Bombay city had far greater impact on the development of the strike than in the rural hinterland where the police usually did not go beyond telling a worker to resume duty and, if felt necessary, warning him if he did not do so. In Bombay the confrontations were much more grim and may as a result have contributed to an escalation of violence. In certain quarters police was stationed day and night, for the better part of the strike, to maintain law and order but also to bully activists. Warnings to resume duty were often given in threatening surroundings such as a police van or police station. If the worker appeared to be stubborn or an activist of the MGKU, policemen might go further and threaten his relatives as well. The display of force by the police would be such that workers preferred to stay at home rather than to go into the streets to avoid confrontations with them. In September 1982 Samant publicly complained that police and security guards of the mills obliged scores of workers to resume duty at the risk of being locked up in their rooms if they refused. . . . That this was no empty accusation is borne out by the account of Baluram, one of the sample workers, who was forbidden to contact his fellow workers and ordered to stay in his room. . . .

[ . . . ]

It has to be concluded that if the 248 registered cases refer to violence resorted to by adherents of the MGKU, as claimed by the police, then a few more cases are conspicuously absent in the statistics. It seems fair to assume that the registered criminal cases, apart from maintaining law and order, also served the purpose of undermining the morale of the striking workers. This impression is strengthened if we look at what happened to all these cases. Table 1 tells us that 53 per cent of all the cases were acquitted. These were compounded at the trial stage, a fate shared by more than 76 per cent of all the cases of assault in which assailants were apprehended. Of all cases of violence, 17 per cent are pending trial and a mere 1 per cent resulted in conviction.

It is true that the figure for convictions may become higher once the cases that are *sub judice* now are tried. Similarly, if the 28 per cent cases classified as 'true but undetected' had resulted in arrests the percentage of convictions might also have been higher. But, even if we allow for a tenfold increase in the number of convictions, there is no denying the fact that the percentage of convictions will be far below what might be expected if these cases had been supported by strong evidence. This calls into question the sincerity of the police in registering complaints about violence by MGKU adherents and lends credibility to the accusation that registration of criminal cases was intended not only for maintenance of the law but also harassment of the more determined workers.

## MILLOWNERS AND GOVERNMENT

### A COMMON FRONT

In order to cope with the strike millowners employed several different strategies. Naturally, their tactics changed as the strike progressed. If it is true that many millowners were initially not averse to the strike as demand for cloth was slack anyway and stocks were piling up, it is equally certain that these advantages gradually disappeared as by then new (and to many millowners, attractive) prospects surfaced. One has to bear in mind that the tactics used by individual millowners to survive the crisis differed and depended on the specific position of their mill in the textile industry. For the same reason their policy might not be in tune with policies followed by their representative bodies such as the MOA and Indian Cotton Mills' Federation (ICMF) where the voice of the owner of an affluent mill carries greater weight.

Some millowners attempted to remove the stocks from mill premises, others (or the same ones) explored the possibilities of maintaining production and sales by sub-contracting. In order to break the strike (and Samant along with it), workers were requested and in the end simply ordered to resume duty. In many mills workers were at first lured to return by offers of hospitality, free meals and lodging and with promises of police protection. At a later stage millowners would start recruiting labourers from elsewhere. As the strike did not collapse the millowners were offered the rare opportunity of carrying out rationalization and retrenchment and they liberally availed themselves of it. This policy was followed even as new recruits marched into the mills.

To be able to do all this the millowners needed harmonious relations with the powers that be, i.e. the Congress Government. The task to ensure this was entrusted to their representatives in the MOA and ICMF. It was also important to establish contact with the public in order to explain the millowners' views so that no aura of martyrdom would be attached to the striking workers. This task too fell to the MOA and the ICMF which sought to justify the millowners' stand with the aid of articles and advertisements in newspapers and by denouncing Datta Samant. But more important than image building were close relations with the Government at state as well as at national level. If required, the millowners would seek the help of the Centre to overrule decisions taken at state level and they were successful in this.

[ . . . ]

## THE EXECUTIVE AND THE LEGISLATURE

. . . [E]fforts by the Government to settle the strike issues were few. Apart from the half-hearted attempt at mediation in July 1982 (discussions from which Samant was excluded), there was another effort at the time when the strike had practically collapsed (March '83). There were also two offers: in July 1982 the Centre announced that, pending the results of the Deshpande Committee, an interim wage increase of Rs 30 was to be paid and an advance of Rs 650; in October 1982 when the State Government came with what was called 'a new formula' allowing for the same interim increase of Rs 30 but this time with an advance of Rs 1500. Both the advances were to be paid back by the workers. These were the only concrete offers by the Government. Apart from that, the Central Government might be credited with the appointment of the Tripartite Committee, but the composition of this Committee as well as its terms of reference were such that it could hardly contribute to the solution of the strike, and that may well have been the reason why the terms were not more specific.

The deliberate inertia displayed by the executive at the state and national levels is matched by the treatment the strike received in the legislature. Although it gradually dawned on everyone that India was witnessing its largest ever strike, no sustained efforts were made to come to terms with the problem and neither did the strike draw much attention in such parliamentary bodies as the Lok Sabha (House of the People), Rajya Sabha (Council of States), Vidhan Sabha (Legislative Assembly) and Vidhan Parishad (Legislative Council). To be sure, there is no dearth of casual references, brief skirmishes and questions about the textile strike in the course of the proceedings in 1982–3 but the number of debates devoted to the strike is very small and reflects a lack of serious concern about the plight of the workers. It is a rather unique phenomenon (one stressing the close links between trade unionism and politics in the Indian context) that several important actors in the strike drama, like A.T. (Bhai) Bhosale, Datta Samant, Haribhau Naik, Bhaurao Patil, were themselves members of one of the representative bodies. Yet this did not prevent the strike from being treated in a miserly way although it contributed to a lot of mud-slinging and strong abuses in the legislature which, of course, was not really helpful.

[ . . . ]

## FURTHER READINGS

A.R. Desai, ed., *Peasant Struggles in India*. Delhi: Oxford University Press, 1979.

This anthology examines various tribal and peasant uprisings and struggles against feudal overlords and colonialism, as also the response of various emerging social and political organizations to such struggles. By highlighting the innate strength of the peasants and tribals it explodes the myth of 'traditionally passive peasantry.' The papers are written by scholars as well as activists, and give a flavour of grass-root authenticity. Complementing this volume is the editor's *Agrarian struggles in India after independence* (Delhi: Oxford University Press, 1986). The mushrooming of agrarian struggles in this period is ascribed to the policies, such as land reforms, pursued by the government.

Venkatesh B. Athreya, Goran Djurfeldt, and Staffan Lindberg, *Barriers Broken: Production Relations and Agrarian Change in Tamil Nadu*. New Delhi: Sage, 1990.

Based on a survey of 367 households in rural Tamil Nadu, this book examines agrarian change and the factors which have the potential to control and direct the course of such change. It delineates the variations in agrarian relations in terms of two ecotypes, namely rainfed cultivation and irrigated agriculture. It offers a new quantitative methodology for studying agrarian class relations.

K.P. Kannan, *Of Rural Proletarian Struggles: Mobilization and Organization of Rural Workers in South-West India*. Delhi: Oxford University Press, 1988.

This study examines the nature of capitalist development and its impact on the position of propertyless labourers in rural Kerala. It outlines the historical process of proletarianization and the development of a proletarian consciousness leading to collective action. Case studies of toddy tappers, beedi workers and agricultural labourers are used to indicate the historical context and the dynamics of organization of rural proletarians.

E.A. Ramaswamy, *Power and Justice: The State in Industrial Relations*. Delhi: Oxford University Press, 1984.

Based on first-hand field data on major industrial disputes this book provides a sociological critique of the system of industrial relations in post-independence India and an assessment of the theories of the state. A good follow up to this is the author's *Worker consciousness and trade union response* (Delhi: Oxford University Press, 1988) which provides a comparative study of trade unionism in Bombay (excerpted in this volume), Calcutta, Madras and Bangalore.

Sujata Patel, *The Making of Industrial Relations: The Ahmedabad Textile Industry, 1918–1939*. Delhi: Oxford University Press, 1987.

Industrial relations in Ahmedabad offer a conspicuous model of peace that is distinguished by the rarity of strikes and lockouts. Combining sociological and historical methodologies, this study traces the evolution of this unique system of industrial relations to resolve disagreement between capital and labour.

Mark Holmstrom, *Industry and Inequality: The Social Anthropology of Indian Labour*. Cambridge: Cambridge University Press, 1985.

This pioneering study in industrial anthropology examines the uneasy relationship between 'organized sector' and 'unorganized sector' workers. The study attempts to understand the thoughts and actions of the workers and the wider economic and political aspects of their situation against the background of economic dualism.

# V

# Conflict Resolution

The following papers explore questions of conflict resolution, around three nodes. The first node concerns the *panchayat*, an indigenous social form for resolving disputes. The papers by the Freeds and by Madsen examine the functioning of the panchayats, and of other relatively informal procedures, in north Indian villages. Today, the panchayats function under the shadow of the urban court system—and of related kinds of bureaucratic interventions; and our *second* node reviews this counterposing, as witnessed by Cohn's paper.

During the 1700s, recourse to force had been a more normal aspect of societal functioning than it was to be later; and Cohn considers the key contrasts between the principles which underlay indigenous social arrangements, in villages around Banaras in eastern Uttar Pradesh, on one side and, on the other, the Western-inspired, initially colonially implanted, courts and other legal institutions. What happened when a *village* dispute ended up in a colonial *court* is examined closely by Saurabh Dube, working from court records for two such cases, out of the many in his files, in the 1930s. (Sudhir Chandra, pp. 79ff, also considers the working of colonial judicial institutions in their Indian setting—in

the very different context of a marital dispute in the courts in late
nineteenth century Bombay city.)

How does the Western-style court system function in Independent India?—this question sets our *third* node. Morrison reports
on the social milieu and social organization of lawyers, a key
professional group in the court system, in a district town in
Haryana. The two other papers focus explicitly on the alien origins
of these Western legal institutions in India and, from their different
angles, conclude that these Western ideas and institutions have
been domesticated far more than is often thought, or might have
been expected following Cohn's argument.

In a wide-angled review, Galanter is impressed with the tena-
cious survivability of the Western complex or, rather, with the
weakness of challenges to it on behalf of the indigenous traditions
of conflict resolution, such as the panchayat. Focussing on Bangalore and its vicinity, Kidder insists that the apparent 'flaws' in
its formal judicial apparatus arise not in its alien inspiration but
in the textures of its enveloping, multiplex social relationships and
expectations.

The chapter by Stanley and Ruth Freed draws on their meticu-
lous fieldwork in a village near Delhi during 1958–9. The cases
they report and analyse turned principally on ownership of
land—and on violence by upper caste on lower caste men. The
theme of conflict between the upper and the lower castes has
dominated several selections in this volume, especially Alm in
Section II; its muted echoes can be heard in some of the Freeds'
discussions.

In the resolution of these conflicts, we notice the working of
panchayats of several sorts, as we do again in the next paper by
Madsen. In the Freeds' village, recourse to panchayats was only
one of the ways of settling disputes. It alternated with beating, or
intimidating, the weak into compliance, using pressure and influence informally or through governmental agencies, and taking
issues to the courts.

A particular event may be perceived by different observers in
a variety of ways, and the Freeds are very sensitive to this diversity.
As becomes clear from their accounts of several cases, one's
perceptions concerning what 'really' happened in an event, and
why, depend largely on the narrator's interests, social location,
personal dispositions, and the like.

Madsen focuses on one case, but on a wider canvas. It does not concern the myriad disputes colouring everyday rural life but the ramifications of a single marriage: the marriage might have seemed innocuous enough, but difficulties arose. The principles of hierarchy and equality intermesh in north Indian society in complex ways. Within the *jati* 'By definition all Jat clans are considered equal.' Yet, in the prevailing ideology of marriage, the wife-giving family is ranked below the wife-taking one as a consequence of the particular marriage.

This relative ranking of the two families is held to make a difference to the other families in the two clans too, at least to families in the same village. Each marriage generates fresh affinal ranking of this kind; but this ranking is countered by other principles of Jat social organization. Thus, a Jat village commonly has only one major clan; and since a marriage *must* be outside the clan, the ranking makes no difference to its everyday relationships with its neighbours. Consequently, these differences in rank between families (and their clans) remain limited in range, and do not add up to generate a durable sense of hierarchy.

In the case Madsen examines, the bride happened to have clan-mates who lived in her bridegroom's village. Her clan-mates saw portents of a decline in rank for their clan vis-a-vis that of the bridegroom in her marriage. The gravity of the issues was widely recognized. During the next nine months, more than twenty panchayats were convened in villages far apart; and, pending a decision, over a hundred marriages were stalled!

Overshadowing the panchayats' functioning, in contemporary India, are the ideas of bureaucratic authority and the system of formal laws and courts and all their functionaries. Cohn surveys the scene from a Rajput-dominated area in eastern Uttar Pradesh. As an elderly Rajput told him, 'We took this land with the sword, these other people are our dependants.' The British colonial administration threw its weight behind institutions of a rather different kind. Cohn carefully traces the contrasts between the premises which informed the older modes of conflict resolution as against the legal style and apparatus fostered by the colonial regime. To these, Cohn might have added the point that Simmel made (1955:37) in his discussion of modern legal conflict in the West, namely, that there is an underlying assumption of:

a broad basis of unities and agreements between the enemies.
... The parties to a negotiation or a commercial affair ... recognize
norms binding and obligatory to both, irrespective of the opposition
of their interests.

These assumptions cannot be taken for granted in legal disputes
in India; the divergence between the two traditions has been
great. Insofar as older social arrangements and ideas remain alive
and influential too, the resources of this legal regime have tended
to be used less for resolving conflict than for harassing one's
enemies, as the studies by Dube and Kidder in our set will show.

While we have excellent anthropological reports on indigenous
modes of resolving conflicts, such as by the Freeds and by
Madsen, comparable accounts of how modern courts handle
disputes are hard to find. Hearings in a particular case may drag
for years and decades, even generations. It would not be easy to
match this rhythm with that of anthropological fieldwork, which
can rarely be stretched beyond a year or two. We can be grateful,
then, for Dube's reconstruction, and analysis, of two cases from
the 1920s and 1930s, drawing on rich court records.

In one case, a woman had left her husband to marry his
classificatory brother. The two branches of the family nursed their
hostility, which led up to a murder: an issue for trial in a court.
The other case turned on the contention between a large landlords' family and its many tenants. A land resettlement by government officials had redistributed rights to land use—and done so
ambiguously. To enforce what they insisted were *their* rights, the
tenants organized a social boycott, and harassment, of the landlords. What came to court was a case wherein the tenants were
accused of relieving two of the landlords' family of certain ornaments; the tenants denied this as a trumped up charge—and lost.
The premises underlying the villagers' conceptions of right and
wrong were sharply different from those reigning in the court;
and Dube emphasizes the difference.

Legal proceedings sought to establish the precise motives which
led to the singular act: the 'crime' in the court's lexicon. These
motives had taken shape, however, in a milieu whose exploration
leads us to the villagers' perception—or, at least, to many villagers'
perception—of the event's real meaning. That context gave evidence of complex plays of prevailing norms, of responses to social
transgressions, of the uses of force, will, and legal strategy, and

of ideologies—those of the Satnami tradition and of *swaraj*—which had come in from the wider world. Dube tests his interpretations against continuing, contemporary Chhatisgarhi ideas and practices, in the course of anthropological fieldwork—which he deftly combines with his historian's craft.

Our remaining selections on the Western-style court system focus not on the course of particular disputes, as Dube does, but (1) on analysing it as a *social space*, and (2) on how well this, essentially imported, social form fits in with the style and values of the host society. Morrison's paper embodies the first of these concerns. It evokes the sights and sounds (though, curiously, not the smells) pervading a north Indian district courts complex, as well as its operative social logics.

While one's caste background does affect one's life chances for entering the bar, it does not determine the professional conduct or relationships of those who manage to become practising lawyers. The social temper here is similar to that of other urban, educated, self-employed 'professionals'. The concluding account of an electoral contest in the local Bar Association, conveying something of the flavour of contestation in such urban, professional spaces generally, fits well into a Reader on *Conflict*.

The domestication of Western legal forms in Morrison's north Indian district court is forcefully seconded by Galanter and Kidder. Galanter addresses a 'dispute' in the wider public domain, over public policy, public institutions, and the like. The 'dispute' concerned a choice over the modes of settling disputes: Western modes of conflict resolution—that is the legal system—on one side and, on the other, the indigenous ones. Writing in the early 70s—and later trends confirm his analysis—Galanter noted that, during the decades since Independence, the Western legal system in India more than held its own amidst all the castigation of its foreignness.

It survives so well, Galanter notes because (1) it has generated influential structures of interests, and associated spokesmen—among lawyers, judges, and the like—much more powerful than those arising in the (unorganized) indigenous traditions of settling disputes, and (2) the latter's repertoire of forms has been limited: it has not been able to provide forms for resolving conflicts which could handle the great variety of issues arising in this society of growing complexity; the Western legal tradition was much more resourceful.

Kidder's stance is similar but his focus is local, not national. Like Morrison, Kidder too has worked with the local social organization: roles, attitudes, and practices among litigants in Bangalore, Mysore, and lesser centres in Karnataka. Yet Bangalore is a major state capital, its webs of legal relationships and activities more convoluted than in Morrison's district town.

The great bulk of this judicial effort does not yield clear adjudicative outcomes; rather, it appears to lead to a spell of court appearances during which the contestants may edge towards more realistic assessments of their own prospects, and thence to out-of-court settlements. Veteran litigants put 'a great variety of relationships, practices, transactions, and expectations' into advancing 'their own and other persons' litigation.' Kidder presents a challenging case for regarding the sometimes bizarre proceedings in Bangalore's courts as a function of these contemporary, multiplex social relationships and expectations—not of the system's erstwhile alien origins.

# Judicial Functions of Panchayats in Shanti Nagar*

## STANLEY A. FREED AND RUTH S. FREED

In addition to its administrative activities, the village panchayat had judicial functions. It did not deal with every dispute or infraction of law and custom that happened in the village. Some disputes were settled within the lineage, others resolved by informal counseling by respected elders, and still other disputes or transgressions were adjudicated by caste panchayats. A village panchayat usually was concerned with disputes between people of different castes, with cases that were too difficult for a caste panchayat, or with offenses against administrative decisions made by the panchayat in its executive role. In the case of disputes, the panchayat attempted to reconcile the two parties; for infractions, the village panchayat often fined a violator Rs 1.25.** Sometimes, however, he was forgiven if he promised not to repeat the offense.

Those cases regarded as most serious by the villagers, based on the small sample that came to our attention, developed from disputes over the ownership of land or involved a high-caste man's inflicting violence upon a low-caste man. These two causes could,

* Excerpted from Stanley A. Freed and Ruth S. Freed, 'Panchayat: Judicial Functions', *Shanti Nagar: The Effects of Urbanization in a Village in North India. I. Social Organization.* New York: Anthropological Papers of the American Museum of Natural History, 1976, v. 53, pt. 1, pp. 169–88.

** *This was in 1958–9. At 1993 prices, this would be equivalent to about Rs 10.* [Eds] of course, be elements of a single dispute. The village panchayat often lost control of such cases when the disputants invoked the police and/or resorted to the courts. In order to avoid police involvement, a multivillage panchayat might be convened to hear a case.

The police and courts were feared in cases involving violence because a villager might be sent to jail. For this reason, assaults of a high-caste man upon one of low-caste were viewed seriously. A low-caste man could obtain redress in the courts; if he had been seriously hurt, the temptation to go to the courts would have been great. Such a situation could easily be used by men of competing high-caste factions to try to injure their opponents. . . . The opposite situation, that of a low-caste man assaulting a high-caste man, was not as likely to occur and was not so serious. The more numerous and powerful high castes would simply beat a low-caste man in retaliation.

Although people often went to court in disputes over land, this was a serious step because of the expense involved and the fact that a decision imposed by a nonvillage authority could lead to lasting antagonisms. The two factions of Shanti Nagar stemmed from such a dispute. Sometimes, after a court had handed down a decision, a panchayat met to affirm it in an attempt to get the contesting parties to avoid costly appeals, and, hopefully, to cool tempers and to assuage hurt feelings. The proceedings of the judicial panchayat of Shanti Nagar mirrored a number of the major features of village life: the domination of the high over the low castes, the general distrust and fear of external intervention, the importance of landownership, the concern for prestige, and factionalism.

[ . . . ]

### LAND DISPUTE: LANDOWNERS VERSUS LANDLESS VILLAGERS

Disputes over land might go directly to the courts bypassing a hearing before the village panchayat because it might be an inappropriate body to adjudicate the dispute. Generally, panchayats were composed of Jat Farmers and Brahman Priests whose caste and lineage memberships might give them a vested interest in the decision. An illustrative dispute involved an attempt on the part of many, or most, of the large landowners to divide some village common land among themselves and the other land-owners. They were opposed by two leading villagers, a Jat and a Brahman. It would have been useless for the village panchayat to hear the dispute because all or most of the panchayat members were involved in the plan. This dispute took place before we lived in the village; consequently, our notes lack the detail that we might otherwise have obtained because we did not have the opportunity to interview the participants while the case was still fresh in their minds. We obtained a fairly full account from only one informant, who, however, was most reliable.

The land in question included approximately 8 acres of the habitation site and 9 acres of the common grazing land. When the landowners proposed to divide this area among themselves, the landless people approached a village Brahman skilled in dealing with the courts and asked him to prevent the division, which, if permitted, would deprive them of a place to live. The Brahman enlisted the aid of a Jat lumberdar,* the most powerful man in the village, and they both apparently opposed the rest of the larger landowners. The Brahman and his Jat friend won the case when they were able to show that one of their opponents had tried to include the 9 acres of village grazing land in the habitation site, but that the transfer had not been entered in the appropriate government records. The court before which the case was tried was not empowered to distribute pasture land; therefore, the 9 acres were safe. As for the other 8 acres in question, the area was considered too small to be divided among all the landowners who would have been entitled to a share. The Brahman claimed that he never recovered the five or six hundred rupees he spent on the case. His Jat supporter was said to have contributed no money.

The motives of neither the Brahman nor the Jat were clear to us in this dispute. For the Jat, it could have been a matter of prestige. He was the most important man in the village and he permitted no one to play the role of leader (*chaudhari*). He prevented people from becoming too important and powerful in

---

* *A lumberdar was a village official, often hereditary, responsible for collecting and transmitting land revenue to the government. Initially created by the colonial government, the office continued to be important in 1958–9. [Eds]*

the village. Prestige could have been a factor in the Brahman's participation or, perhaps, he believed that the low castes were being treated unjustly. However, there were probably other reasons for his actions of which we never learned. In the following case it will be observed that some of the facets of the relationship between a low-caste client and his patron and moneylender could influence the patron to support the low-caste client in a land dispute with another high-caste man.

## LAND DISPUTE: CHAMAR LEATHERWORKER VERSUS BRAHMAN PRIEST

A Chamar Leatherworker who had been cultivating the land of a Brahman Priest for a number of years attempted to claim it under the provisions of the Delhi Land Reforms Act of 1954. The intent of the act was to create a uniform body of peasant proprietors with no intermediaries. The act provided that tenants who had cultivated land since 1952 or before were to become its owners. In Shanti Nagar, the most common result of this legislation was that tenants voluntarily, or under varying degrees of pressure, furnished statements that they had not cultivated the land in question during the critical period. However, the Leatherworker was both combative and ambitious. In addition, he had a powerful ally, his patron, the Jat lumberdar whom we have frequently identified as the most powerful man in the village, who had lent him a substantial sum of money variously estimated by informants as from five to 15,000 rupees, the latter figure probably much exaggerated. The lumberdar was afraid that he might not be able to collect the debt if the Chamar lost the case. The other landlords of the village supported the Brahman. The Brahman eventually won.

We believe that the critical factor in the case was the lumberdar's lack of support from his Brahman friend who worked so skillfully in the courts. The Brahman told us that he had to support his caste fellow because they were related. He had a talk with his friend, the lumberdar, in which he urged him not to support the Leatherworker. The other landowners were also putting pressure on the lumberdar; finally, he capitulated. Nevertheless, the Chamar Leatherworker would have been in a strong legal position because he was listed in the land records for the village as the cultivator of the disputed land. However, the legally skilled Brahman was quite clever; he told us that he had had a lien placed on the Leatherworker's crops so that they could not be harvested. Thereupon the Leatherworker, in order to be allowed to harvest his crops, agreed to make a legal statement to the authorities that he had never farmed the disputed land.

This dispute is of interest because, although one of the disputants was a low-caste man, apparently it was settled by maneuvering among the high castes. Once his high-caste patron withdrew his support, the Leatherworker's position deteriorated. This case also illustrates the importance of the ability to use the courts skillfully. One informant said that a panchayat had been convened to consider the case, but its deliberations had apparently been ineffectual. Although the Chamar lost his dispute with the Brahman, he did win some land from a Jat Farmer on the basis of the new land reform legislation. For some reason, possibly because they were newcomers to the village, the Jats did not fight; the Leatherworker won about 2.5 acres and became the only Harijan in the village to own land. In commenting upon the behavior of the uncombative Jats, a Brahman said, 'You've got to have a big heart to hold the land.'

[ . . . ]

## ASSAULT: JAT FARMERS VERSUS ARTISANS

One of the largest Jat landowners of Shanti Nagar and the leader of one of the factions of the village became involved in a dispute with a man belonging to one of the middle-ranking, landless, artisan castes. Several differences between the two men had been festering for several years; finally, increasing tensions between the two families erupted in a fight in which the more numerous Jats severely beat the artisans.

A Bairagi Beggar woman, the wife of the village watchman, gave us a brief account of the happening the day after the fight. To simplify the various narratives of the episode and the account of its aftermath, we will use pseudonyms for some of the principals: Sher Singh for the Jat who had been involved in the fight; Hari Pal, for the artisan; Om Prakash, for the youthful Jat, a leading member of the faction opposed to Sher Singh; and Ram Krishna, for the senior man and head of the largest Jat lineage of which Om Prakash was a member. According to the watchman's wife, the artisan had been putting cattle dung in a place near his shop, an area claimed by Sher Singh and his brother. Sher Singh told Hari Pal to move the dung, but the artisan refused. The two families began to fight; Hari Pal's eldest son was beaten. Hari Pal sent the village watchman to summon the police.

Hari Pal's wife gave us a more complete but somewhat different account. She told us that, in the evening, her husband and eldest son were sitting in front of their shop when Sher Singh and his sons were returning from the fields. Sher Singh noticed that dung had been removed from the piece of land under dispute and he asked Hari Pal who had taken the dung and who had allowed it to be taken. Hari Pal answered that he had given the dung to another Jat Farmer who had asked for it because he had more than he needed. Sher Singh was outraged; he threatened the artisan because he regarded the land and the dung on it as his property. Hari Pal asked why Sher Singh was angry, since the dung belonged to him (Hari Pal). At this remark, Sher Singh ordered his sons to beat the artisans. The bus from Delhi arrived while the fight was in progress; the villagers who left the bus stopped it. Sher Singh threatened to renew the fight when the artisans went to their house. Their shop was situated on the outskirts of the village near the bus stop, but their house was in the heart of the village across a lane from Sher Singh's house and adjoining his cattle shed. To reach the artisans' house, one had to pass the house of Sher Singh. The artisans attempted to go to their house, but the Jats blocked the lane. A fight started. However, neighbors came quickly and separated the combatants before very much happened. Hari Pal and Om Prakash went to the police the same evening. Hari Pal's wife mentioned that her family used to work for Sher Singh, but as he had not paid them for two years, they had discontinued the relationship.

Sher Singh and various members of his family gave us versions of the actual fight that agreed reasonably well with that of the watchman's wife. They added, however, that the serious damage to the artisans had occurred after the fight and was part of a plot against them. Sher Singh's nephew, who was present at the fight, said that his uncle had asked Hari Pal to move the dung from the disputed land, but that he had refused. At this, his uncle leaped from his bullock cart in which he and another nephew were riding and seized Hari Pal's son by the neck. Our informant, who had been walking behind the cart, was afraid that his uncle would kill Hari Pal's son; so he stopped the fight. He said that when Hari Pal went to the police to report the incident, two of his teeth had been knocked out. He claimed, however, that the teeth had been knocked out, not by any member of his family, but by someone else in order to build a strong case against his uncle. He insisted that his uncle was a peaceable man, but so strong that he was dangerous when angered. Sher Singh's nephew pointed out that involvement in a fight can be costly, and added that some people liked to see this happen.

[ . . . ]

Sher Singh's brother essentially repeated his family's version of the quarrel. He characterized it as only a trivial argument, but charged that their factional opponent had taken the artisans outside the village where he had broken their teeth and bruised their faces and then had taken them to the police station to press charges. The two brothers had then gone to Hari Pal to ask why he had involved the police. They said it was only a minor dispute that could have been settled peaceably. The two brothers then went to the police station where they were told that the police would take no action if the dispute could be settled peacefully. Accordingly, the two brothers summoned three distinguished men from a neighboring town, all elected members of the Delhi Municipal Corporation, the governing body of the Union Territory of Delhi, and convened a large panchayat in an effort to resolve the quarrel.

Om Prakash justified his involvement, saying that he had accompanied Hari Pal to the police station because he was always on the side of the weak and the artisan was poor and politically weak. He said that when one person beat another, he could be tried under Law 325 and jailed for three years. Consequently, the sentiment of the villagers was to keep the case out of the courts, and he too was willing, provided Hari Pal agreed. One of Hari Pal's younger sons said that Om Prakash had always been a friend of his family and had accompanied Hari Pal to the police station in that capacity. He also observed that there were unfriendly feelings between the two Jat families. He said that Sher Singh habitually failed to pay for labor, and that Om Prakash used to tell him that this was not proper.

The panchayat meeting turned into a lengthy hearing that lasted from about 11:00 A.M. for more than three hours. A large crowd of men from Shanti Nagar and other villages was present. The three members of the Delhi Municipal Corporation who came to adjudicate the dispute were from a nearby town. One was a Brahman Priest, the second a Baniya Merchant, and the third a Jat Farmer. They arrived in a truck, went to the house of the late lumberdar for some refreshment, and waited while a crowd gathered at the Jat meeting house. Hari Pal sat on a cot with one of his sons, his grandson, and a relative from another village. Sher Singh and his brother arrived and sat on separate cots. There was preliminary conversation. Sher Singh remarked that he had never harmed Hari Pal. Hari Pal's eldest son set a conciliatory tone by saying, 'We work for you. We are yours and you are ours. Who will take care of us?' Sher Singh replied, 'I know that in anger people do many things.'

A corporation member initiated the proceedings by asking Hari Pal to relate the cause of the fight. The elderly artisan, who appeared to be under great physical and emotional strain, spoke in a weak voice. During his testimony, he offered to take an oath saying that if he lied his whole family would die. He began by relating one of his grievances. For two years he had not been paid for his labor and Sher Singh owed him [90 kg] of grain. Consequently, he had decided not to work for Sher Singh any longer. Once, he said, one of Sher Singh's sons had called him to come to work, but he gave an excuse and did not go. After that incident, Sher Singh's family had their work done in a neighboring village. Then Sher Singh himself had called Hari Pal to come to work; again he refused. A month before the panchayat meeting as he was passing Sher Singh's house, one of Sher Singh's sons called out telling him to move his house and that Sher Singh would fight him if he failed to comply. The young man said that in exchange his family was prepared to provide a house site for Hari Pal elsewhere. Sher Singh wanted Hari Pal's land, which adjoined his own, for his cattle. Hari Pal told the young Jat that he was like a son to him but that if Sher Singh wanted him to do something, he should tell him so himself. In other words, Hari Pal, an elderly man, the head of his family, believed that he should deal with the head of the Jat family and not with a junior member.

At this point, Sher Singh, disturbed by the gist of Hari Pal's testimony, interrupted to swear that if he (Sher Singh) lied, his whole family would be ruined. Many people then suggested, 'Let Hari Pal say what he has to say.' Hari Pal continued saying that Sher Singh's son had threatened him, telling him that if he did not change his house site he would have trouble. Then, one day, when all the Jats were returning from the fields, they charged the artisans with placing dung on their land. They said that because Hari Pal had been making so much trouble they would beat him. Hari Pal said that he had folded his hands to Sher Singh, saying that he was a poor man. At that point, Sher Singh's nephew descended from the cart and struck Hari Pal's son. Abruptly, Hari Pal interrupted his testimony and turned to Sher Singh to ask, 'Didn't I work for you?' Sher Singh said, 'Do you mean that I didn't pay you?' Hari Pal said, 'Yes, you didn't pay.' Sher Singh was astounded. 'This is impossible,' he said. 'Tell the panchayat that I have paid you everything. He's just like my son and he's telling lies. He ran away in the middle of my work and it suffered'. A corporation member tried to restore calm by saying, 'As you (Sher Singh) have said, people who are big should protect him. It's just like a family and you should forget. Hari Pal should also believe that we are just like a family and he should forget.'

[ . . . ]

Hari Pal, fearful that the panchayat was drifting toward a recommendation of reconciliation without resolving his grievances, said, 'I am a poor person.' One of the members of the corporation replied, 'Why are you a poor person? In the panchayat all are equal and no one person can ask another to remain silent. We can encourage you so much that you can work hard and become rich.' Ram Krishna, never varying from the theme of reconciliation, said, 'These things always happen and people are reconciled.'

Silent until this moment, Om Prakash arose to try to swing the panchayat from its emphasis on reconciliation to an attempt to learn who was at fault, so that justice could be done, and to a consideration of Hari Pal's grievances. 'I do not know who was at fault,' he said. 'I was not present at the time of the fight. Everyone else heard the noise and ran to the fight. Everyone must know what happened. Someone said that there is no justice in the village. If I'm telling lies, say so. It is good if a poor person is aided.' He then alluded to Sher Singh's contention that Om Prakash himself had beaten Hari Pal, remarking sarcastically that those who complain of having been beaten and can show their wounds are actually the people who administered the beating. He then said that Hari Pal wanted several concessions in order to settle the matter peacefully. Otherwise, he would fight in the courts.

A corporation member asked Hari Pal what he wanted. Hari Pal, a timid and not very bright man, missed the opening provided by the question and began to talk about the affection of the two families prior to the death of Sher Singh's wife and how recently, Sher Singh had not treated him properly. A corporation member, ignoring Hari Pal's remark about recent trouble, began to question him about the past good relations. Om Prakash became irritated and said, 'We have just agreed that Sher Singh has done something bad. Ask Hari Pal what he did that was wrong.' Everyone began to talk at once, demanding that Hari Pal be asked what he wanted. When quiet was restored, Hari Pal listed his three main problems: (1) he had not been paid for two years; (2) Sher Singh blocked the lane with his cart so that Hari Pal's family was unable to reach his house; and (3) for years he had put his cattle dung on a specific piece of land that was now being claimed by Sher Singh. He did not mention the dispute over his house site; however, that was tacitly included in the grievance about the blocking of the lane.

The investigation of Hari Pal's three grievances was begun by questioning him about the piece of land where he had put his cattle dung. The corporation members asked who owned the land. Hari Pal said that he owned it but that Sher Singh had occupied it. They asked Hari Pal if he had a place other than the disputed area to put his dung. He replied that he had such a place.

[ . . . ]

Then Hari Pal was asked if he would work for Sher Singh. Hari Pal said that he would if Sher Singh wished it. Sher Singh said that in the past he had given Hari Pal grain and would continue to in the future, implying that he had always paid for Hari Pal's work and that he would be willing to have Hari Pal work for him. At this point, Hari Pal's son interrupted, saying, 'You should bring water from the Ganges River for him to swear upon. It's been 10 years since the lumberdar told us to move our shop from the middle of the village.' For Hari Pal's son, whether or not they continued to work for Sher Singh was a minor issue; he was more concerned with being free from harassment to move their house. Sher Singh said, 'I will give them grain.' Angrily, Hari Pal's son replied, 'I don't care if he gives grain. If he is telling lies, we don't want it. When Sher Singh puts his cart in front of his house, he doesn't leave any space for us to pass. How can we bring our own cart to the house? He should empty his cart and take it away, not leave it overnight.' A corporation member agreed and said, 'All right, he won't leave his cart in the lane.' Sher Singh did not like the direction the inquiry was taking and said, 'There are 20 houses,' alluding to the approximate number of Jat households that would support him and to the fact that the artisan was the single representative of his caste in Shanti Nagar. A corporation member said, 'We are not worried about the number of houses. We are here to settle the dispute.'

The corporation members reverted to the problem concerning the disputed area. One of them said that Hari Pal should have some space for his dung, and suggested that either one landowner or the village donate such a space. Another member returned to the theme of reconciliation. He said that when all agreed that their hearts should be pure, there would be no trouble about the cattle dung, the grain payments, and the cart in the lane. He reminded Hari Pal that he used to have Sher Singh near to his heart and that he should reestablish the old relationship. He said that like children who sometimes talk nonsense, Hari Pal did too. Hari Pal's son, who had received the worst beating, commented that he was not sure that the two families could live amicably as they had formerly. Sher Singh's brother disagreed, saying that it was possible. Aware that the proceedings of the panchayat had developed very favorably for Hari Pal to this point, Om Prakash called for a written statement. 'Hari Pal has told us his grievances; if Sher Singh thinks they are inaccurate he should say so. If not, they should be written, and everyone will sign. That will be an agreement.' One corporation member increased the pressure on Sher Singh when he remarked, 'When the three of us came [from the nearby town], we assumed the responsibility for settling the dispute. If Sher Singh is not prepared to give the grain payment, I will give it, or the three of us will.' Hari Pal's son said, 'Bring Ganges water.' A corporation member reprimanded him, 'Anything said in the panchayat is just like swearing with Ganges water.'

A corporation member, who noticed Sher Singh sitting quietly, asked him to speak if he had anything to say. 'What can I say,' said Sher Singh, 'you believe him.' The corporation member protested that they were listening with open minds and that if Sher Singh had anything to say he should speak. An elderly village Brahman, alluding to the dispute over the ownership of the land where Hari Pal had kept his cattle dung, said, 'There are many old people here. Let them all speak.' Om Prakash, sensing that the favorable moment was slipping away, asked, 'On whose side should I speak?' The village Brahman reprimanded him, 'You should say what is right. You shouldn't talk for only one side.' A corporation member remarked, 'What is said in the panchayat is like Ganges water.' . . . Hari Pal's uncompromising son insisted, 'If one of the parties is telling lies, then people should say he's telling lies.' Ram Krishna, constantly pleading for reconciliation, suggested, 'You should come to an agreement. Tell Hari Pal where to put his dung.' Om Prakash, always aware of the feelings of Ram Krishna, the head of his lineage, carefully remarked, 'The person who doesn't want an agreement is the worst person. If two people want to agree and the third does not want them to do so, he is the worst person.' We interpreted this as a warning to Hari Pal's son that he was making a very bad impression with his intransigent hostility toward Sher Singh. . . . A corporation member said, 'If the space belongs to someone, then another person can't put his dung there. Now is the time to settle this point.' The panchayat therefore decided to inspect the land in question.

The point to be decided was a difficult one. Landless people did not own land in the habitation area, but they did have the right to use such land. Use of land, however, was subject to permission from the village landowners. If an area of land belonged to or was often used by landowners, then a landless artisan or worker could not use it, even if it was temporarily unused. The division of the habitation site among the landowners was not recorded in the land records of the village; only the agricultural land was so recorded.

At the site, the discussion dealt with whether the general area had been divided and among whom, and how it was being used. A division of the general area would indicate that the disputed space had been assigned to a landlord, possibly Sher Singh, although there was no clear evidence to substantiate this surmise. If it had not been divided, the panchayat then had to decide who had been using the area. If the general area had not been divided and Hari Pal was using the space, his plea would be strengthened. Of the several issues between Hari Pal and himself, Sher Singh regarded the ownership of the disputed land as most important. Of course, the other landowners were also concerned with any precedent that might be established on the basis of the decision in this case.

At the site of the disputed ground, Sher Singh declared, 'This case will not be settled here. It will go to the courts.' This served as a warning to the panchayat that with regard to the land Sher Singh would not accept an adverse decision. Hari Pal's son pointed to their dung cakes, saying that they had been moved from the disputed area. Sher Singh asked a Jat Farmer to tell who owned the space. Sher Singh, a canny politician, had addressed the question to a Jat who was a member of the same lineage as Om Prakash and yet had had disputes with him. The Jat avoided answering directly, but he identified two adjacent areas as belonging to Jats, thus strengthening Sher Singh's argument. However, a corporation member noted that there was no partition between the two areas specified by the Jat, thus weakening the contention that the space had been divided. Everyone noted that there were no written records, but Om Prakash declared that people should agree anyway. Another Jat, asked about the disputed area, said that he knew nothing. A respected Brahman elder concluded that the Jats themselves did not know who owned the piece of land. At this, Om Prakash's well-meaning but clumsy older brother, trying to help his younger brother, said, 'Everyone knows whose space this is. Those dung cakes belong to Hari Pal.' Sher Singh, ignoring the ineffectual older brother who only reflected his brother's opinions, angrily turned to Om Prakash and said, 'You are saying that this belongs to Hari Pal.' Om Prakash protested innocently, 'When did I say that ?' Sher Singh insisted that Om Prakash had said it and began to shout and talk rapidly. He was greatly disturbed. . . . For a moment, the patience of one of the corporation members wavered and he remarked, 'I have come to the conclusion that they are fighting only about dung.'

Everyone returned to the Jat meeting house to continue the discussion. The panchayat had been in session for a long time. Pressure began to build for a written agreement, even though no decision had yet been made as to the ownership of the land. Most of the pressure was directed toward Hari Pal. . . . The corporation members declared that the problem could be solved only by the villagers, who refused to take the responsibility. The corporation members suggested that Hari Pal and Sher Singh each nominate two trustworthy individuals and that these four should make the decision. Taking the position that he maintained to the end, that the problem of the land was separate from the fight and the other grievances, Sher Singh said, 'You can settle the fight, but you can't decide who owns the land.'

[ . . . ]

Ram Krishna became more forceful. Addressing Hari Pal, he said, 'The decision that is written by the panchayat must be followed by both of you. Sher Singh has always helped you and he will do so in the future. If you leave the village, you will be in trouble, and so will Sher Singh. If Sher Singh wants you to stay here, he won't put his cart in front of your door. You are pushing the matter too far. If you don't want to agree, you'll be sorry in the future.' However, no one changed his position. The Jats continued to maintain that they did not know who owned the land; each disputant repeated that he was the owner, and Ram Krishna continued to admonish them, saying that if they did not agree they would be sorry. Two elderly men expressed a growing sentiment of the group by asking the disputants, 'If you did not want to agree, why did you call everyone? People are busy and have to go.' . . .

The panchayat divided into small groups for final discussions. A corporation member put his arm around Hari Pal's shoulders and led him to one side where he talked to him earnestly. Then, one after another, all the older men talked to Hari Pal. Meanwhile, Sher Singh sat quietly on his cot, smoking the hookah. . . . Ram Krishna spoke to Hari Pal, 'All the people have come to help you. No one wants to harm you. There is a saying that people who are in the house are far away, but neighbors are near.' Hari Pal tried to leave, but people held him. A corporation member said, 'I have seen many people who disagreed with a panchayat's decision and were sorry.' One of the corporation members began to write. An elderly artisan from another village said, 'Let them make the decision. If we don't like it, we'll say so.' The written decision was circulated for thumb impressions and signatures. . . . A corporation member gave the written decision to Om Prakash to read. Om Prakash said, 'It is written that we agree.' Hari Pal's son said, 'We don't. If you haven't settled our problems, we don't agree.'

After the panchayat meeting, we traveled a few miles on the Delhi bus with the three corporation members who said that the dispute had been settled, that all the parties involved had signed the reconciliation agreement, and that it was decided that the land belonged to Sher Singh, but that Hari Pal would be permitted to put his dung there. Informants seemed to be in general agreement about the broad outlines of the settlement. . . . A Jat informant, saying that the fight had been foolish and that both sides had been foolish, summarized the agreement: first, the artisans were to work again for Sher Singh if he paid them the 90 [kg] seers of wheat he owed them for previous work; second, Sher Singh agreed not to put his bullock cart in front of Hari Pal's house and to refrain from harassing Hari Pal; and third, the villagers told Hari Pal to put his dung elsewhere, and he had agreed. The Jat informant also said that because the land had been undivided and Sher Singh had occupied it, he owned the land. The Jat informant explained the basic principle of land ownership: that those who did not own agricultural land did not own land in the habitation site. Landless people had usufruct rights in land in the habitation site based on the permission of the landowners. A nephew of Sher Singh said that the panchayat had ruled that the land belonged to Sher Singh and that Hari Pal had to move his dung. He said that since Hari Pal swore that Sher Singh owed him grain, Sher Singh would pay, but he indicated that Hari Pal had lied.

One of Hari Pal's younger sons, however, had the impression that Hari Pal had been awarded possession of the land. As for the grain payment, he noted that the panchayat had agreed that Sher Singh should pay what he owed. Hari Pal and his eldest son were bitter. Eleven days after the panchayat meeting, they told us that the panchayat had done nothing. They said that they had never agreed to the panchayat ruling. They complained that Sher Singh still blocked the lane with his cart and that they were afraid to go to his house for their grain because he might beat them or say that they were trying to steal something. When asked if Om Prakash should go with them, they replied emphatically in the negative, saying that the people who had rendered the decision should accompany them. Hari Pal's eldest son was very upset. He said he should kill Sher Singh and then die himself.

[ . . . ]

## DISPUTES, PANCHAYATS, AND CHARACTERISTICS OF VILLAGE LIFE

We have described at some length a number of legal cases, especially that of Sher Singh and Hari Pal, because they illustrated so well many characteristic features of village life and government. In Shanti Nagar, disputes over land were a basic cause of the most bitterly fought legal cases. Landless villagers could become involved in such disputes because of their usufruct rights in land in the habitation site as well as from the possibilities for claiming ownership in agricultural lands that were opened by land-reform legislation. Their traditional rights regarding agricultural land could also lead to other problems. . . . In the dispute between Hari Pal and Sher Singh, a side issue involved Hari Pal's right to give away surplus dung. Sher Singh was alleged to have told the artisan, 'For eight months your buffalo grazed in my fields and so the dung is mine.' Although Sher Singh was exaggerating the issue, it is of interest that he would indirectly protest the traditional right of landless people to graze their cattle in his fallow fields.

Part of the dispute between Sher Singh and Hari Pal was due to the changing statuses and roles between landowners and serving castes. The landowners were receiving somewhat less service from artisans and landless labourers than they had formerly. Some landowners seemed to believe that grazing and other rights in the use of land enjoyed by the serving castes depended on the service relationship between landowner and worker. If artisans and laborers did not provide the same services as formerly, they did not deserve the same privileges. Although most landowners did not openly express this attitude, they still made a strong effort to enforce what they considered to be the proper attitude and behavior among the dependent serving castes. For example, the landowners tried very hard to repress Hari Pal's son, who was only a few years younger than Om Prakash and whose behavior was not nearly so tempestuous, aggressive, or inappropriate. The difference as to what constituted acceptable behavior for these two young men depended on their status and rank. Nevertheless, during the dispute, both of them had to be taught their proper behavior and where their loyalties should lie, also that neither violence nor involving the police or the courts was an acceptable means of settling disputes. As the rulers of the village, the landowners preferred to handle disputes themselves. Thus, they were protecting their own interests, but, at the same time, preserving village unity, although on their own terms.

As a means of harassing each other, factional opponents could enter into disputes that did not directly concern them. Although high-caste people tended to stand together in disputes with the lower castes, high-caste patrons sometimes believed that it served their interests to support low-caste clients. Such support, however, was generally curtailed if the patron was not supported by his caste and lineage fellows as often happened. Villagers were suspicious of the courts and generally preferred to avoid them. However, the financial resources and the ability to use the courts skillfully gave a man a substantial advantage in village disputes. Violence usually failed to settle disputes but only served to complicate them. The possibility that violence could lead to a court case and a possible term of imprisonment for a villager was regarded most seriously.

The panchayat was a council rather than a court. . . . The members of the panchayat usually shared the functions of eliciting information, making decisions, and enforcement. Although the more powerful members exerted the most influence, this was seldom apparent in overt role playing in the panchayat. There were no formal roles, such as prosecutor, mediator, or judge, assigned to specific individuals. . . . Panchayat members generally have known the disputants (or the accused) all their lives, have discussed the circumstances in detail prior to the hearing, and often have definite opinions. . . . A panchayat was not so much interested in deciding who was right and who wrong as it was in reconciling the disputants so that village life would again be harmonious. The village population was very small; despite their

differences, its inhabitants had to continue to live in close proximity. When a panchayat considered an infraction of its own
administrative decisions, the accused was not presumed innocent.
A panchayat would not bother to convene unless the accused
was strongly suspected of being guilty. Often a fine was forgiven
if the offender apologized. No police officers enforced the decisions of the panchayat, but public opinion could not be safely
ignored. We observed many panchayats and were impressed with
their seriousness of purpose and the wisdom of their decisions.
The panchayat was well adapted to life in a small village; for the
solution of many problems, it seemed to us to be a more
appropriate forum than an impersonal city court. In all essential
respects, the multivillage panchayat resembled the village
panchayat; however, it gave added weight to the seriousness of
the proceedings because of the participation of distinguished men
from other villages.

As was true of many features of village life, the panchayat
system favored the landowners and was often used by them to
maintain their control over the serving castes. However, national
and state laws were causing changes in many aspects of village
life including the panchayat system. Panchayats under the new
legislation would be elected by all the eligible voters of the village
and would contain either representatives of the artisan and labor-
ing castes or members of other castes who owed their election
partly to the support of these castes. Such a situation could result
in more concern being given to the problems of the lower castes
while at the same time maintaining the virtues of the traditional
panchayat.

[ . . . ]

One evening after we had been living in Shanti Nagar for a
year, one of [the] factional leaders came to our house and charged
that of village politics we understood only about the worth of one
anna (about 6%; one rupee contains 16 annas). He then gave us
a lengthy account of political life in Shanti Nagar, replete with
examples of motives and strategies. The major points of his
analysis are worth noting here; most of them have been well
illustrated by the preceding disputes. In addition, our informant
certainly qualified as an expert on the affairs of the village. He
said three main motives were the basis of village politics, most
important of which was the ownership of agricultural land. Second

in importance was the control of land in the village habitation site and third was the desire to be a leader (*chaudhari*). He identified the principal tactic as the initiation of quarrels between people in order to weaken the position of one's opponents. He illustrated this kind of maneuver by recounting the successful effort of one of his factional opponents to cause or, at least, to aggravate a quarrel between him and one of his allies. Another tactic was a willingness to endure a loss in order to make one's enemies lose. Other villagers used to emphasize this point, saying that a man might consider it a victory to cause his opponent to lose one rupee even though he himself had had to lose two. In the mind of our informant, education was a tactic in village politics as was business acumen. He was much concerned with the prestige of leadership and spoke at length of the devious ways that men attained it. One must lie, he said, curry favor with important people in the village and in government, and keep the low castes in line by putting pressure on them. He said that such men go through the streets tensely. In his opinion, they would achieve nothing in this life. One could attain leadership, he said, only by following the path of truth, implying that he did so. Although the details of the disputers of which we learned and the strategies of various opponents were frequently complex, these could, without too much distortion, often be reduced to the principles suggested by our informant. We were pleased when, a few months later, he informed us that our understanding of village political life had reached the two-anna level.

# Clan, Kinship, and Panchayat Justice Among the Jats of Western Uttar Pradesh*

## STIG TOFT MADSEN

## WESTERN UTTAR PRADESH AND THE JATS

First I will introduce the caste with which this article is concerned and the area in which they live, i.e., the Hindu Jats living in the western parts of Uttar Pradesh in the districts of Muzaffarnagar and Meerut. . . .

Principal crops of the area are sugarcane and wheat. Since the big canals were constructed—the Eastern Yamuna canal in 1830 and sections of the Ganga canal in 1855 and 1860—the area has been relatively prosperous. The Jats in particular have been eulogized as hardworking by the British and others. To an extent the Jats have become a role-model for various castes in the area. . . .

Each village tends to be dominated politically and economically by one of the agricultural castes. Schwartzberg puts it this forcefully: 'in the villages in which the Jats live no other cultivating caste is represented, even by as much as a single household' (1965: 488f.). The same is often the case as regards other landowning cultivating castes such as Tyagis, Gujars, Ahirs, Yadavs,

* Excerpted from Stig Toft Madsen, 'Clan, Kinship and Panchayat Justice among the Jats of Western Uttar Pradesh', *Anthropos*, 1991, 86: 351–65.

and Sainis. As peasant proprietors generally working their field themselves, these castes sit very tightly on the land. Historically, they have to a large extent resisted de facto alienation of land to non-agricultural castes such as merchant castes (see Raheja 1988: 255 note 5). . . .

## CASTE CATEGORY AND CLAN

[ . . . ]
When Jats talk about themselves as a caste—as groups of male Jats tend to do—they often stress their 'democratic' values. . . .

Since the Jats generally only live in villages which they dominate politically, they see themselves as 'kings' in their own villages. The Jats consider themselves as well as Rajputs, Gujars, Ahirs, Sainis to compose a category of castes. They belong to the same *varna* or caste category: All are Kshatriyas or 'rulers' sharing hereditary martial proclivities or leadership qualities. . . .

The Jat notion of democracy leaves little room for the lower castes in their villages. As they have been subjugated by the Jats, they are not considered Kshatriyas. Jat 'democracy' is not for the weak: Only the strong can be equal.

The internal organization of the caste reveals other strong but less conspicuous egalitarian values. In particular, all the Jat clans or *gotras* are reckoned to be equal. A *gotra* is a patrilineal and exogamous descent group or clan. . . .

Marriages among the Jats are arranged between two families of different clans. While a family giving its daughter in marriage to another family thereby acquires a subordinate position *vis-à-vis* the wife-receiving family, the status of the clans to which the families belong are *not* supposed to be affected. By definition all Jat clans are considered equal. The dispute to be analysed arose precisely because one clan could claim that it had been reduced to an inferior status as a result of a particular marriage.

## CLAN TERRITORY AND BROTHERHOOD

According to the Jats' own version of their history, migrating clans or segments of clans settled the area by conquering existing villages or by creating new villages. The first village settled in the area is considered the head village of the clan. Gradually, the descendants of the original settlers would fan out and settle other nearby, but not necessarily adjacent, villages which remained affiliated to the head village. These affiliated villages form a *khap*, or clan territory. The ideal Jat landscape thus consists of clan territories each containing a large number of villages acknowledging a historical head village of the clan.

[ . . . ]

The Jats often say that the land of each village was initially divided equally among the Jat settlers. Later generations would divide the land equally among their sons—not their daughters—thereby gradually differentiating land holdings. In this way an egalitarian principle ('equality of the sons') accounts for the actual differences in the size of land holdings.

The living members of a *gotra* form a *biradari* or brotherhood among whom the norms of brotherhood, *bhaichara*, prevail. As Dumont has noted the concept of 'brother,' *bhai*, has a great encompassing capacity (Dumont 1988: 27, 166 f.). Generation-wise, the brotherhood members are classificatory 'brothers' and 'sisters' (*bhai-bahan*) to one another and as such cannot intermarry.

The head of a local descent group, typically a land-holding family, is called a *chaudhari*, i.e., headman, and may participate as such in the traditional political-juridical institution, the panchayat or caste council. Each higher segment of the clan is supposed to have a *chaudhari* representing that segment in panchayats. The *chaudhari* of the whole clan generally lives in the original head village. As clans are considered equal and of different origin, no *chaudhari* is *a priori* entitled to represent all the clans.

[ . . . ]

## MARRIAGE PROHIBITIONS

A marriage establishes an asymmetrical relationship between members of different clans and clan territories uniting two families or local descent groups of different *gotras* from different *khaps*. The marriage creates a relation of inferiority and superiority between the two descent groups: The wife-receiving family is ranked higher and is shown due respect by the wife-giving family in accordance with the general Hindu ethos. Yet, as we have seen, being Jat presupposes equality. The Jats, therefore, observe certain marriage prohibitions to ensure that clans and *khaps* remain of equal rank despite the inequality generated by a marriage.

[ . . . ]

Exchange of brides between two families in a reversible pattern is prohibited as it creates an alliance based on equality between two families. This could lead to the formation of closed groups exchanging brides among themselves weakening 'loyalty' to the clan (see Milner 1988: 150 f.).

[ . . . ]

As regards the prohibition of repetition Dumont said that it 'prohibits the *repetition* of intermarriage (in the same direction) between smaller units, i.e. households or families' by stating that 'a girl should not be married in the same house as her father's sister, or, in the jargon of the anthropologist, matrilateral cross-cousin marriage is barred' (1966: 105). The prohibition is wide-spread in North India among Hindus, and the contrast to South India is striking. In South India and parts of Sri Lanka marriage between cousins creates lasting alliances between local descent groups. . . .

To further ensure that marriages do not result in inequalities the Jats adhere to the so-called 'four *gotra* rule.' This rule prohibits marriage between a boy and a girl who share any of the *gotras* of their father, mother, father's mother or mother's mother. . . .

The Jat kinship system, thus, has a certain internal consistency. The marriage prohibitions are mechanisms to regulate marriages to ensure inter alia clan equality by putting a brake on both exchange marriages which may lead to the formation of closely related elite clans, and on repetitive unidirectional marriages which may create a hierarchical system of hypergamous clans. Yet, these marriage prohibitions alone cannot prevent conflicts in which opposing parties may both on the basis of sober interpreta-tion of Jat norms hold strong and conflicting views as to the proper course of action.

It would seem that the prohibitions on reversal and repetition and the 'four *gotra* rule' have to be seen in conjunction with the territorial rules, particularly the rules of village and *khap* exogamy. As Gould has noted 'the tendency to regard affinal and consanguineal kinship ties as mutually exclusive' goes hand in hand with the clan exogamy and village exogamy, and with territorial stabilization of kin groups in *khaps* or similar units (1961: 298; see also Gould 1960: 478; Dube 1974: 279, 292 f.).

[ . . . ]

## THE GOELA CASE

In 1981 a dispute arose in Goela village between Maliks and Balyans, two Jat clans. Together with the Tomar, . . . the Maliks and Balyans form the three biggest Jat *khaps* in western Uttar Pradesh (Bingley 1978: 47).

The Malik clan originally had 52 villages in the Muzaffarnagar, Meerut, and Ghaziabad districts. These villages formed the Gathwala . . . *khap*. At present only 34 of the 52 villages are wholly or partially Malik villages.

[ . . . ]

The Balyan *khap* is said to have comprised 84 villages, but only 47 villages are still in the hands of the Balyans. . . .

[ . . . ]

Goela village is a large village with 2,152 acres of land and a population of 6,299 of which 855 were classified as scheduled castes (Sinha 1971*b*). Jats are the dominant caste in the village, and the elected head of the village at the time of my fieldwork was a Jat. According to his estimate there were 4,000 voters 1,300 to 1,350 of which were Balyans, 450 Maliks, 700 scheduled caste, 500 Muslims, 300 Kahars, 150 Gosains, and the remaining 600 or so were Brahmins, Banias, and Nais, etc.

The Balyans live in five *pattis* in the western portion of the village. A *patti* is an old revenue unit originally based on major lineages or clan segments (Hershman 1981). The Maliks live in two *pattis* to the east. . . .

In June 1981 a Balyan boy from Goela was married to a Malik girl from Baral, a village approximately 35 kilometers from Goela. Baral has grown together with the village Kishanpur. The combined population of the twin village in 1971 was 5,614 (Sinha 1971*a*). Kishanpur-Baral is dominated by Tomar Jats, but between fifty and one hundred Maliks also lived there.

Weddings are always celebrated in the bride's village, and the

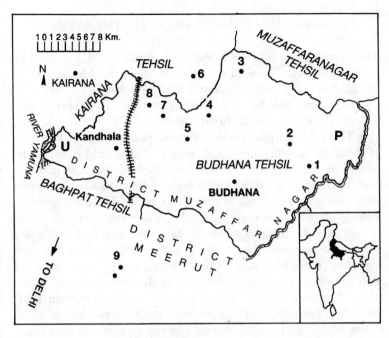

Map of Budhana Tehsil, Muzaffarnagar District, Uttar Pradesh, India.
Inset map shows the State of Uttar Pradesh. The numbers refer to
villages mentioned in text: 1. Goela; 2. Shoron; 3. Sisauli; 4. Kharar;
5. Phugana; 6. Chunsa; 7. Lisarh; 8. Salpha; 9. Kishanpur-Baral.

parents or relatives of the girl pay most of the expenditure. The
party of a bridegroom is often very big. In this instance the party
included a few Maliks from Goela. During the wedding ceremony . . . the Maliks from Goela realized that the bride was a
Malik. Knowing that Kishanpur-Baral was dominated by Tomars
they had assumed the bride to be a Tomar.

The Maliks from Goela were treated as superiors by the hosts
because they had come with the groom's party. They were given
small gifts as tokens of respect by the girl's real and classificatory
kinsmen at the ceremony of 'meeting' or 'mixing' (*milai*).

Receiving gifts intended for in-laws from a clansman made the
Maliks feel awkward. When they returned to Goela they narrated
their experience to other Maliks who, in the course of a few
weeks, mobilized an opinion on the incident.

## DIVERGING EXPLICATIONS OF THE CASE

The marriage was disputed because it 'destabilized' the ideal Jat social landscape. To deal with the situation, the Maliks framed two arguments employing different interpretations of brotherhood. One argument may be called the 'village-brotherhood argument,' the other the 'clan-brotherhood argument.'

1) The village-brotherhood argument posited that all Jats born in a village are 'brothers' and 'sisters' and should observe the norms of brotherhood or *bhaichara*. Nobody should marry a woman of any clan represented in the village as such a woman after taking up residence in the village would be simultaneously a bride (*dulhan*) or a younger brother's wife (*bahu*) of the village as well as a classificatory sister (*bahan*) to the men and unmarried women of her own clan residing in the village. As a *bahu* she would have to observe *parda* or *ghunghat*, i.e., to cover her head with her sari or shawl in the presence of all men considered senior to her husband . . . (see, e.g., Vatuk 1975: 182; Hershman 1981: 204). As a *bahan*, however, she would not have to observe *parda* in the village and would also be allowed to communicate more freely.

The Malik girl married into Goela would be both a bride and a sister: an impossible and almost incestuous combination, threatening to blur one of the most important roles in Jat society. The Maliks argued that all clans represented in the village ought to be spared the ordeal of having to see their own classificatory sisters acting as an in-law.

The marriage also reflected on the clan as a whole. If the marriage was accepted, the clan could be branded as inferior because it allowed a Malik girl to enter the village as a bride while being unable to reciprocate by bringing Balyan girls to the village as brides of Maliks. The possibility would arise that in the long run the Maliks would be turned into an inferior clan linked to Balyans in a hypergamous relationship. To preclude such an eventuality the Maliks of Goela emphasized the principle of village-brotherhood.

2) The clan-brotherhood argument also advanced by the Maliks posited that the clan which originally colonized the village was entitled to receive brides from all clans except, of course, their own and from any village not part of their *khap*. The same

argument was employed by the Balyans to legitimize the disputed marriage. The agreement on principles opened up a discussion as to who were the original settlers of Goela.

. . . Some of the information gathered by the Maliks came from their genealogist and was noted down by a Malik school-teacher. According to the Maliks, Goela was settled by one Nar Pal, a Malik from village Salpha in 928 AD. As surrounding villages were settled by aggressive Rajputs, Nar Pal, in 946 AD, asked for help from one Madan Pal from the nearby village Shoron which is an old Balyan village. Madan Pal stayed on in Goela. He had five sons from whom the five Balyan *pattis* of the village derive. Nar Pal had two sons from whom the Malik *pattis* derive. The Maliks were the original settlers and the Balyans were therefore not entitled to bring Malik brides into the village.

The Balyans claimed that this story could not be true as neither Shoron nor Goela had been settled at [the] time Maliks claimed. In accounting for the presence of the Maliks in Goela, the Balyans narrated several stories. In one, the Maliks were portrayed as descendants of one Chandra Pal, a Somval Rajput from village Faridpur who had one or two tribal or Jat wives. . . . The Maliks were not original settlers, much less conquerors, the Balyans [argued] and therefore had no right to determine whom the Balyans could marry.

[ . . . ]

As both clans claimed to be the original settlers, the debate turned to modern history. The Balyans said that the Maliks had, in fact, already accepted that Goela belonged to the Balyan *khap* by allowing several marriages between Balyans of Goela and Malik girls. . . . A few of these were of the type under dispute, i.e., of a Balyan boy of Goela to a Malik girl. The Maliks claimed that none of these marriages were representative. One was a love affair: Love being blind and anti-social, this marriage could have no bearing on social rules. Another involved a Malik girl who was brought up by her mother's brother and had adopted the clan of her mother. The Balyans did not accept this repudiation of the significance of precedence.

Thus, neither a clarification of rules nor a close reading of history allowed a decision on the point raised by the Maliks. Goela being an atypical village inhabited by two large clans, history did not have an unequivocal answer to the question raised by the marriage of a Balyan boy from Goela to a Malik girl from Baral.

## PANCHAYATS: THE VEHICLES
## OF DISPUTE PROCESSING

In such conflict situations a secondary institution is commonly called upon. This is the institution of a panchayat or caste council which, in one form or another, has been prevalent in the sub-continent. A panchayat is supposed to hear both or all sides of a case and to settle it according to accepted norms. The participants in a panchayat are *chaudharis* from the segments involved in the dispute and from the segment above, or indeed any headman or other knowledgeable person specifically invited or simply joining spontaneously. . . .

About two months after the marriage in Baral, on 8 August 1981, the Maliks of Goela contacted the headman of their *khap* segment. The segment comprised four villages, the head village of which was Phugana. Later, the headman of the Malik clan was contacted. He lived in Lisarh village. By October, the head of all Maliks in Uttar Pradesh and the neighbouring state Haryana had been contacted.

Collective action was directed against the family in Baral who had agreed to marry their daughter into a Malik village. Malik men staged several panchayats at the family's house and asked them to nullify the marriage by not sending the newly married woman to her husband. The panchayats guaranteed the family that money would be collected in all Malik villages in order to marry her off to some other party if the family complied with its wishes. The girl's family did not accept the 'offer' and ultimately contacted the District Magistrate who instructed the police to prevent further Malik panchayats in Baral.

Thus the Baral family openly went against the Malik panchayat. It is possible that they did this because Maliks in Baral had themselves been subjected to a humiliation comparable to the one the Maliks of Goela faced. The Maliks came to Baral from Lisarh as sons-in-law to cultivate the land of the fathers of their wives. In the last decade around seven marriages have been contracted between Malik girls from Lisarh and Tomars from

Kishanpur-Baral. The Maliks in Baral objected as these Maliks girls came from the very same village as they originally had come from, but their clansmen in Lisarh took no notice. Thus, the marriage to Goela provided the Baral Maliks an opportunity to foist a degradation on other Maliks, particularly on the Maliks from Lisarh.

The Maliks of Goela then contacted Mahendra Singh Tikait, the headman of the Balyans who lived in Sisauli, the head village of the Balyan *khap*. Through an emissary he initially replied that it was none of his concern to prevent a Malik from giving his daughter in marriage to Balyan. The Maliks also contacted the *chaudhari* of the Tomars, Sukbir Singh, residing in Baraut town. He avoided taking a stand on the issue. Then, on 27 December, at a panchayat in Lisarh attended by the Malik *chaudhari* from Haryana it was decided to impose a clan-wide ban on giving brides to Balyans.

This ban was already breached on 4 January 1982 when a Malik from village Chunsa, right in the center of the Gathwala *khap*, married his daughter to a Balyan from Sisauli. The marriage took place under police protection. The marriage party left Sisauli by tractor around 2 A.M. Upon reaching the bride's house, the groom was garlanded and sweets were distributed. No wedding ceremony proper took place and the sweets were consumed on the tractor during a hasty retreat to Sisauli. The girl's father was later excommunicated by a Malik panchayat.

No further breach of the ban occurred, but as the marriage season wore to an end, 52 marriages of Malik girls to Balyan boys were pending from the time before the ban. Seventy marriages of Malik boys to Balyan girls were also pending as the Balyans had decided to counter the Maliks by imposing a reciprocal boycott. In other words, many families who had honor and money at stake were suffering as a result of the conflict. Their interests lay in a compromise. On March 14 a panchayat was held in Phugana with representatives of both Maliks and Balyans. It was organized by Ilam Chand Arya, a Jat belonging to an altogether different clan. As a courtesy towards the suffering families waiting to get the arranged marriages solemnized, it was decided to cancel the ban on marriage and settle the Goela issue later. However, the issue was never settled.

[ . . . ]

## THE DILEMMA OF THE MALIKS

From the outset several alternatives were open to the Maliks of Goela. They could have concentrated exclusively on their own clan: Had all Maliks agreed that no-one should give a daughter in marriage to anyone in Goela, no 'sister' would ever appear in the village as a bride. Alternatively, Maliks could have concentrated on the Balyans of Goela, but the Balyans were in a clear majority and simply did not agree to a possible compromise based on the village-brotherhood argument. Instead, the Maliks imposed a marriage ban on the Balyan clan as a whole, but were unable to enforce it. Despite investing a considerable amount of effort and time, Maliks could not undo the injustice they perceived had been done.

[ . . . ]

## THE COMPROMISE

In the end the dispute was contained by the intervention of Ilam Chand Arya. His intervention was based on several factors. One of these was his connection to a confederation of all the eighteen *khaps* of the area called the Sarv Khap Panchayat (All Clan-territory Council).

The Sarv Khap Panchayat goes back several hundred years, but after the 1857 uprising in North India it ceased to function (Pradhan 1966). In the 1950s it was revived by men of Arya Samaj convictions. The Arya Samaj movement is a revivalist, antiritualist monotheistic movement founded by Swami Dayanand and very widespread among Hindu Jats. . . . For a time the Sarv Khap Panchayat was active in 'curbing social evils' such as dowry.

[ . . . ]

# Some Notes on Law and Change in North India[*]

## BERNARD C. COHN

### THE LITTLE KINGDOM

As the anthropologist has turned from the study of primitive, isolated, pre-literate societies to that of social units which are parts of great civilizations, a new range of problems calls for description and analysis. This essay is a description of the dispute settlement process in a local region in north India and the effects that the establishment of British rule had on indigenous dispute settlement procedures.

The complexity of the situation in an Indian village as regards law and the process of settling disputes can be only briefly catalogued here. To start, let me briefly summarize the social system of a particular region in India.

Senapur is a large, multicaste village in Jaunpur district of eastern Uttar Pradesh, and my remarks, unless otherwise specified, relate to Senapur and the immediately surrounding locality, which is called Dobhi taluka or tuppah. Dobhi taluka is an area of forty square miles with roughly one hundred villages. All the villages were 'owned' at one time by one lineage of Rajputs, locally termed 'Thakurs'. Thakurs are descendants of an agnatic ancestor who

* Excerpted from Bernard C. Cohn, 'Some Notes on Law and Change in North India', *An Anthropologist among the Historians and other Essays*, Delhi: Oxford University Press, 1987, pp. 554–74. Also consulted earlier publication in *Economic Development and Cultural Change*, 1959, 8: 79–90.

conquered the area in the seventeenth century. One of the underlying assumptions in this essay is that a local area of this kind, which I will style the 'little kingdom', was the basic jural unit of upper India in the eighteenth and nineteenth centuries.

The political organization of upper India in the latter part of the eighteenth century has to be viewed at two levels. At the top level were the successor states of the Mughal empire, most of them established by conquerors. Beneath this level were lineages which, as corporate groups, acted as the local rulers. A lineage, usually Rajput but occasionally Brahman, Bhumihar, Ahir, Jat or Gujar, controlled anything from a few villages up to several hundred. The British recognized a lineage or the headman of a lineage as the landlord of a village or a group of villages and made the lineage or headman responsible for the regular payment of land revenue and maintenance of law and order. In Mughal times, in addition to payment of land revenue, the lineage was also responsible for the provision of troops. These lineages governed the little kingdoms. In Mughal times there was little interference in the little kingdom on the part of the ruling state as long as the ruling lineage did not try to abrogate its tax or military obligation and as long as internecine warfare among the Rajput lineages did not break out into major battles.[1]

One of the lineage functions in the little kingdom was the settlement of disputes. Disputes regarding caste matters, such as marriage, rules of commensality and caste occupational regulations, were settled by the caste *panchayats* (councils) of the local region. As far as I could determine in the field [in] 1952–53, the jurisdiction of the various caste panchayats fell entirely within the boundary of the little kingdom. Caste matters that could not be settled by the caste panchayat could be, and often were, referred to the dominant caste, the Thakurs (Rajput landlords), whose lineage controlled the little kingdom. This referral of caste disputes to the Thakurs was usual in questions of property right, inheritance, inter-caste disputes or disputes which threatened the peace of the village or the region.

The Thakur's power to settle disputes arising in other castes resident in the little kingdom was based on their position as landlords, the fact that all castes were tied to them through social, economic, ceremonial and traditional ties, and the fact that the

[1] Jadunath Sarkar 1920: 16–17.

Thakurs were the rajas for the inhabitants. The Thakurs defined themselves and were defined by those below as the 'Lords'. The Thakurs attitude was summed up by one elderly Thakur who said, 'We took this land with the sword, these other people are our dependants'.

During the eighteenth and nineteenth centuries in a little kingdom, the dominant caste controlled all castes beneath it. The outside government did not ordinarily interfere with this relationship. Disputes among members of the dominant caste within the little kingdom, at least in eastern Uttar Pradesh, could ultimately be settled by a formally constituted council. Membership in this council was based on a regional division into twelve lineage segments, the basis of the judicial and governing body and landholding. The principal basis of dispute settlement in this council was probably arbitration and the balancing of power so well analysed by students of African political organizations.[2] The system of arbitration and power balance was reinforced by the expectation, in pre-British times, that internal strife in the dominant caste would be used by surrounding groups to destroy the suzerainty of the lineage over its little kingdom.

Thakurs also derived important status in their role, as settlers of disputes and judges, from their claims to be kings in a traditional social order. In Hindu political and legal doctrine part of the function of the king was the maintenance of the social order, which entailed prevention of what the law books terms 'the confusion castes'.[3] Every caste had its prescribed duties to perform, as well as the obligation of marrying within the caste. The king wielded the *danda* (literally, stick) to enforce the rules of the caste system. The Brahman was the advisor of the king and the interpreter of law, and he could prescribe punishment in the form of a ritual expiation, but it was the king's duty to see that the punishment was carried out. Theoretically, the castes were self-governing in terms of setting and enforcing their own standards of behaviour, but the king could always be resorted to by appeal from caste rulings. This aspect of the function of the king was preserved even into the twentieth century in those parts of the Indian subcontinent ruled by the Indian princes.[4]

[2] Gluckman 1955: 1–26.
[3] P.V. Kane 1946, vol. III, pp. 3, 57, 238, 281.
[4] A.M.T. Jackson 1907: 509–15; Census of India, 1911, vol. V, Part I, Report

The Thakurs in a particular village, backed ultimately by the local council of twelve, ruled and adjudicated for themselves and for the dependent castes in matters which the dependent castes could not settle themselves. The separate subcastes below the Thakurs lived, worked, and were the dependants (*praja*) of the Thakurs. These separate and independent subcastes usually settled intra-caste disputes.

[ . . . ]

## THE CHANGING POLITICAL, LEGAL, ECONOMIC AND SOCIAL SITUATION

Thus far I have been writing as if the village and little kingdom were unchanging isolated units, unaffected by outside events in north Indian society. Obviously this was not the case. I seriously doubt if the village of Senapur was at any time stable, since in the pre-British period warfare and famine must have had considerable effect on the social structure of the village and little kingdom. The description I have given is an abstraction and to some extent a caricature; however, since the establishment of British rule in the late eighteenth century, a number of developments have markedly changed the relationships within the village. The initial effect of the establishment of British rule was a stabilization of the society by guaranteeing the position of the Thakur as zamindar and by eliminating internal warfare. The British strengthened the position of the dominant caste by the extension of the cultivation of cash crops, notably indigo and sugarcane. The Thakurs as landlords derived the greatest benefit from the initial extension of the cash crop economy. In the nineteenth century the new sources of income were used by the Thakurs to strengthen their traditional way of life and their traditional position *vis-à-vis* low castes.

. . . [From] the beginning of the twentieth century to the present, [Senapur] has seen a large rise in population with the concomitant rise in pressure on land, which, coupled with a rise in agricultural prices, has made land a very valuable commodity.

---

by L.S.S. O'Malley, 1913: 452–8; also vol. XVI, Part I, Report by Govindbhai H. Desai, 1911: 255–6.

During this period Senapur, through the building of railroads and
the spread of 'Western style' manufactured goods, has increasingly
been drawn into an all-India market and ultimately a world
market. Higher standards of education and the rise of urban
occupations in commerce, industry and administration have increased opportunities for employment outside the village and
have exposed the villager to a wide range of urban contacts. The
establishment of British and, later, Indian administrations has
greatly weakened, if not destroyed, the importance of the little
kingdom as a political-judicial unit. Land reform has altered the
relationships among Thakurs and their dependants, and the nationalist struggle, democratic elections and movements for social
and economic uplift of the low castes have destroyed the moral
base of the relationships of superordination-subordination among
the Thakurs and their low-caste dependants. Even this brief listing
of some of the variables at work indicate the far-reaching changes
taking place in Senapur and the little kingdom.

## LEGAL CHANGES

In 1795, after twenty years of indirect rule, the full legal and
administrative structure of the East India Company was extended
to Banaras. The company's goal was the full and regular collection
of the land revenue, and as a step toward this goal courts were
established, the judges of whom were British employees of the
company. The principle disputes in these new courts were questions of ownership of land and rates of revenue and rent.

In the area of personal law (marriage, divorce, inheritance and
adoption) the district courts administered Hindu law for Hindus
and Muslim law for Muslims. The courts administered criminal
codes written in the middle of the nineteenth century which were
a mixture of British and Muslim criminal law, and acts and laws
passed by the various provincial legislatures and governors. This
latter group includes the very important topic of land law.

When the British established their courts in India they were
cognizant of substantive law, but did not think that the procedural
law and the courts, as they found them in the late eighteenth
century, were adequate. In fact, some of the early British administrators thought there was no court system other than that

which the Mughals had imposed in north India. They ignored
local indigenous adjudication procedures and modelled the process of adjudication in the courts on that of the British law courts
of the period.

Almost from the establishment of British courts in India, it was
apparent to the British that there were serious faults in these
courts. It took years for disputes to be resolved, and there were
too many appeals from lower courts. Use of forged documents
and perjury in the courts became endemic.[5] It was evident that
courts did not settle disputes but were used either as a form of
gambling on the part of legal speculators who were landlords or
merchants and who turned to the courts to wrest property from
the 'rightful' owners, or as a threat in a dispute. There is apparently
no quicker way of driving an opponent into bankruptcy than to
embroil him in a law suit. Most people would go to any length
to avoid going to court. It is likely that most of the cases that
went into courts were fabrications to cover the real disputes.[6] The
British were constantly concerned with reforming the courts. This
concern entailed, in Uttar Pradesh, the shifting of the language
of the court from Persian to Hindi, Urdu and English, imposing
severe penalties for bringing false cases, reform of the police and
establishment of local panchayats. But the flood of cases continues,
and, at least based on my experience in 1952–53 and on a brief
revisit in 1958, there is no apparent abatement in this cycle of
false cases and what an historian, Percival Spear, has termed the
Indian peasants' 'slot machine' attitude towards the courts.

It is my thesis that the present attitude of the Indian peasant
was an inevitable consequence of the British decision to establish
courts in India patterned on British procedural law. The way a
people settles disputes is part of its social structure and value
system. In attempting to introduce British procedural law into
their Indian courts the British confronted the Indians with a
situation in which there was a direct clash of the values of the
two societies; and the Indians in response thought only of manipulating the new situation and did not use the courts to settle
disputes but only to further them.

The British thought that, by providing an honest judge and

---

[5] Percival Spear, 1951.
[6] Robert Carstairs 1912; Cecil Walsh 1912; and Penderel Moon 1945.

establishing firm rules of evidence and court procedure, the judge could determine the facts in the case and, with his knowledge of the law, hand down a just decision. But from the brief description of the process of adjudication of intra- and inter-caste disputes which I have given above, several value conflicts are apparent.

## EQUALITY IN THE EYES OF THE LAW

Basic to British law is the idea of the equality of the individual before the law. North Indian society operates on the reverse value hypothesis: men are not born equal, and they have widely differing inherent worth. This theme or value is basic to the whole social structure and is expressed most clearly in the caste system. When Indians go into a court they are supposed by definition to lose their outside statuses. It is not Thakurs and Chamars who are having a dispute but a defendant and a complainant. The adversary system has developed to equalize the persons in court. To an Indian peasant this is an impossible situation to understand. The Chamar knows he is not equal to the Thakur. He may want to be equal but he knows he is not. The Thakur cannot be convinced in any way that the Chamar is his equal, but the court acts as if the parties to the dispute were equal.

## STATUS AND CONTRACT

As in the nineteenth century when Sir Henry Maine wrote about India, the Indian peasant society is one still largely dominated by values surrounding the concept of status. The landlord-tenant tie is not just a contractual relationship, as it is treated in law, but rather it is a hereditary relationship having important social and ceremonial concomitants which cannot be treated as contractual relations. Two Thakurs disputing over a piece of land are not only buyer and seller with a contractual tie but, in classificatory kinship terms, are brothers or uncle and nephew. In Max Gluckman's terms, the Indian village is a multiplex society in which people are tied by a network of relationships, and some of these ties cannot be summarily cut by a decision of a court. People must continue to live and work together in the multiplex society.

So decisions of the courts based in ideas of contract do not fit the value system and social structure of the Indian village.

## THE IMPORTANCE OF THE DECISION

Central to British law is the necessity of a decision, if a case comes to court. It appears that the indigenous adjudication procedure of India is geared to postponing a clear-cut decision as long as possible, the goal being to have the parties to the dispute compromise their differences in some way. If a compromise is not possible, the minimal requirement is to maintain at least the fiction of a compromise, especially in an intra-caste dispute. This fiction is not possible in the court, where the situation is defined in terms of winning or losing.

## SETTLING THE CASE AND ONLY THE CASE

The British legal system, as it has been adopted in India, rests on the idea that the courts will adjudicate the dispute that is presented to it. Very often, even in the caste meetings, the case which is ostensibly the crux of the dispute is only a minor expression of a long-standing antagonistic relationship between two families or groups. Often when I discussed a case with a villager, he would start out by discussing events and disputes of twenty years ago. A specific case does not stand alone but is usually part of a string of disputes. The caste meeting can and does deal with the string of disputes, and over a period of time will try to mediate the basis of the dispute. The British court, given the nature of the adjudication process, can deal only with the specific case presented by the contending parties.

## SUMMARY

I have detailed the areas of change and conflict which brought about the situation in which law is used not for settling disputes but for furthering them, and where the courts are looked upon as a place for harassment or a place in which to gain revenge.

The Rajputs, their way of life, values and power, were dominant in the little kingdom. Everyone else was subservient to them within the little kingdom, and although the dominant Rajputs were in a position of subordination to the Mughal government or, later, to the Raja of Banaras, these superordinate political powers did not in any way challenge the Rajputs' control in their own little kingdom. The Rajput landlords settled all disputes arising among the castes below them that were not of an intra-caste nature, and through the functioning of their own Council were able to settle disputes among themselves.

British legislation regarding land revenue was the first assault, albeit unintentional, on the solidarity of the Rajputs, by making engagement for revenue with individual members of the lineage and recognizing individual interests in the land of the little kingdom, rather than assessing the *taluka* as a unit and considering the land to be held by the entire lineage—both practices in effect before British rule. As a result of the British policies the Rajput saw that his economic position was not as tightly bound with that of the other members of the community as it had been. Although separate engagements were part of the land revenue settlements of 1789 and 1839–1942, they do not seem to have impinged strongly on the little kingdom until the settlement of 1880–1882, when, in conjunction with a rapidly expanding role network and increasing urban experience, the Rajputs began to look outward for prestige and power.

Before the end of the nineteenth century the little kingdom was an almost closed prestige system; prestige depended on the amount of land one inherited from his ancestors, the status of his family in relation to the founding ancestors, and the number of low-caste followers that he could muster. When the Rajputs began to turn government employment, education and business outside the little kingdom, a new source of wealth and prestige was introduced. A Thakur could now convert the money he had made as a police officer in the British administration to buying land, building a large house, marrying his daughter into a more prestigeful clan; and in a generation's time a family could move from a lowly position into one of great importance in the village and the local area. Election to a position on the district board enabled a Thakur to use his knowledge of the government and his acquaintanceship with government officials to better his position and to help his followers in the village. Education, in addition to opening up new opportunities which could be converted to higher status within the community, also resulted in a growing familiarity with law and the courts.

In addition to new sources of prestige and power which were in opposition to the principles on which the old prestige system was built, the expanded role network made the Thakur more aware of the possibilities of manipulation in the courts and what could be done through influence and the use of questionable practices.

The Rajputs have always had a highly developed sense of their own importance, honour and position. Their traditional occupation was warfare and they have a highly developed martial ethic. With the coming of the British, outside warfare stopped; the basis of the solidarity of the group was cut away; they no longer had to co-operate from fear of outside invasion or subjugation; and with the changes in land tenure it became advantageous for individuals to break their ties with the group. This change led to increased feuding, competition for position and attempts to ruin fellow Thakurs. In this new scramble for prestige the courts provided an excellent battleground in which to carry out a fight against both their caste fellows and the lower castes. A wealthy Thakur who went to court looked forward to not just one quick case, but to a series of cases, appeals, adjournments and counter appeals through which a poorer competitor could be ruined. Since British procedure and justice appeared capricious to the Indians, someone with a bad case was as prone to go to court as someone with a good case. The standard was not the justice of his case but his ability to outlast his opponents. It became a mark of pride among the Thakurs to outwit an opponent through the use of the courts and law, and the prestige of a family was tied to its success as a litigant and its ability to ruin its competitors in court.

# Village Disputes and Colonial Law
## Two Cases from Chhattisgarh, Central India[*]

### SAURABH DUBE

This paper focuses on two disputes of the 1920s and 1930s in different villages of Bilaspur District in Chhattisgarh, a large region bound through linguistic ties in Central India. The disputes were located in the domain of the familiar and the ordinary in village life and were seized, worked upon and fashioned into cases in the realm of colonial district judiciary. They traversed and brought together the two arenas. The paper opens with a dispute which was rooted in ties of kinship, neighbourhood and

[*] These excerpts from a larger study-in-progress have left out secondary theoretical references and contain the barest minimum of footnotes. The study brings together a close reading of archival material with field work. The Sessions Trial cases used in the text were consulted in the District and Sessions Record Room in the city of Raipur, which has been the main administrative and judicial centre of the Chhattisgarh region in south eastern Madhya Pradesh. The field work was carried out primarily in villages of Bilaspur District between November 1989 and April 1990. It consisted of extended discussions and interviews with groups and individuals of different castes to focus on the working of customary law and dispute settlement processes in villages, the local perceptions of colonial and modern law and law enforcement agencies, the working of law courts and the interpenetration between these domains. In addition I did focussed interviews with older judges and lawyers in Raipur and Bilaspur on these issues. I use the following abbreviations: DPW: Deposition of Prosecution Witness; EA: Examination of the Accused; J: Judgement; *LRS: Report on the Resettlement of the Khalsa of the Bilaspur District, 1927–32.*

conjugal relations among the Satnamis—a low caste and heretical group who combined the features of a caste and a sect—and involved a transgression of the norms of the community. In the other dispute tenants of different castes within a village came together to oppose a family of *malguzars* (village-proprietors) over the issue of rival claims to land and property. An account of these disputes allows us to trace the playing out of conflicts within varied relationships in village community life and to touch upon the local negotiation and uses of colonial law.

The disputes are contained in records of incrimination: the Bilaspur District Sessions Trial cases. The cases are made up of the charge under which the accused was/were sent up for trial to the Court of Sessions by the Committing Magistrate, the examination of the accused before the Committing Magistrate, a list and description of exhibits, the several documentary exhibits—including a copy of the first information report of the offence, and a map showing the scene of the offence drawn by the Patwari of the village—that were used in the proceedings, the depositions of witnesses for the prosecution and the defence, the examination of the accused, and, finally, the judgement in the Court of Session. It is from this evidence that I reconstruct the two stories of everyday life. The exercise is fraught with difficulties. The cases dealt with the events and the features of a dispute by designating it as a 'crime'. A dispute was fashioned into a case within the colonial judicial system through the privileging of a physical act (or a set of actions) that had a serious consequence. To take an example, a blow struck with an axe which led to a death. The act was constructed as the key event which defined the crime and occupied the centre of the stage; the other episodes and elements of the drama constituted the backdrop to this critical event.

The process was worked out through the discursive strategies of law. The depositions of witnesses for the prosecution were ordered in a fashion which diverged from the actual sequence of events: they were arranged in a sequence which highlighted the central event of the crime. The depositions of witnesses began with descriptions of acts of murder, injury, or dacoity and then retraced their steps to earlier events and to patterns of relationships to fill in the background. The questions posed during examinations of the accused were directed to explicate the major act of the crime. The master narrative of the judge drew upon the different accounts to construct a summary statement of the prehistory of the crime before seizing upon the final act—its immediate circumstances, the intention which underlay it, and the manner in which it was carried out—to determine, through the manifold requirements of judicial proof and evidence and 'a consolidation of his reason', the nature of the crime. There was a great deal at work in the constitution of guilt and innocence.

It is also possible, however, to prise open the cases and recover what the disputes tell us about the play of varied and differentially structured relationships within village life. Such a task necessitates a displacement: the final act of crime is no longer accorded a position of privilege; it is, instead, placed alongside other elements and events of the dispute as one part of a complex story. The sources allow us to effect such a displacement. The depositions of witnesses, we have noted, retraced their steps to fill in the background of the crime. What the witnesses constructed, particularly in the course of cross-examination, was a rich and vivid picture of the relationships, the patterns of solidarity and of enmity, and the occurrences within the village which went into the making of disputes.

It can be argued, in fact, that there was a gap, a lack of fit, between the limited range of facts required by the judgement and the plenitude offered by the depositions. It is by working within this gap, by picking up the fine detail and seizing upon the repetitions within the narratives of the witnesses, that we can trace the play between the concerns of ordered legalities and the processes of signification within village relationships. Moreover, by a curious logic, the examinations of the accused also come to our aid. The accused sought to establish enmity as the reason for their being framed by the prosecution and often admitted the history of the dispute as both cause and proof of this enmity. This once again makes possible a rehearsal of the narratives about the familiar and the everyday in village life. The gaps, the repetitions, the curious logic, the double binds are indeed a part of the larger story of the interface between colonial judicial and indigenous conceptions of criminality, legality and rival ways of constructing the person. I bracket for the moment a formal analysis of the exercise of power through colonial judicial discourse and practices and of the interface between colonial law and indigenous practices.

My main concern—even as I recognise the limits of the endeavour—is to tell one side of the larger story.

## KINSHIP, NEIGHBOURHOOD AND
## TRANSGRESSION: DISPUTE 1

An altercation and a fight between two Satnami families on the morning of 15 July 1927 in Karkhena village in the Janjgir Tahsil resulted in the death of a patriarch.[1] Itwari, Hagru, Dukhiram and Banda went to one of their fields, placed their sticks on its boundary, and began to plough. Soon afterwards Chandu, Sohgi, Sheodayal, and Nankai came to their field—which adjoined that of Itwari—and began to sow. They were joined by Samaru and Ramdayal. According to the prosecution, Chandu's group, the accused in the trial, began the fight. Sohgi went and picked up the sticks of the men of Itwari's family. Itwari noticed this and raised an alarm. The members of Chandu's group then said that since Itwari's family 'had got them fined so they would that day bathe in their blood.' Itwari and his group ran to a field close by, the other family in hot pursuit. The ploughmen in these fields interceded on behalf of Itwari. Chandu's family assured them that they were returning. When the ploughmen resumed their work Hagru and Itwari were attacked with sticks and an axe. Itwari was murdered. The case for the defence was that Itwari first rebuked Sohgi for enticing his daughter-in-law and then hit her. A fight broke out. Hagru was hurt and Itwari was killed in self-defence. We need to unravel the threads of this village family drama.

The families of Chandu and Itwari, Satnami cultivators, were neighbours who held adjoining fields and were related to each other. On one side, Chandu and Samaru were half-brothers, 'the sons of the same mother from different fathers': Chandu was the son of Sadhu, and Samaru was born from Dina. Chandu, who had a sister Nankai, was married to Sohgi and had two sons, Ramdayal and Sheodayal (see Figure 1). On the other side, Itwari and Dukhiram were brothers; Hagru was the son of Itwari and

---

[1] The reconstruction of this dispute is based on *King Emperor Vs. Samaru and others,* Sessions Trial No. 33 of 1927.

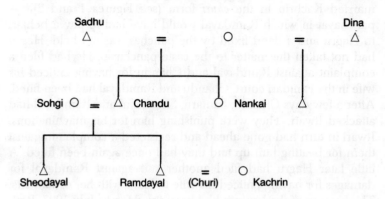

Figure 1: Chandu's Family

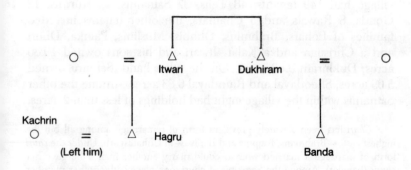

Figure 2: Itwari's Family

Banda was Dukhiram's son (see Figure 2). The two groups were related. Chandu and Dukhiram were cousins. Finally, the two families were linked through the break up of a marriage and the establishment of new conjugal ties.

Kachrin occupied a key role in the drama. She was married

to Hagru, left him, and started living with Ramdayal. Ramdayal married Kachrin in the *churi* form (see Figures 1 and 2).[2] A panchayat in which Ramdayal would have had to pay a behatri to Hagru and a dand fixed by the panchas was not held. Hagru had not taken the matter to the caste panchayat. He had filed a complaint against Ramdayal and Chandu for having enticed his wife in the Faujdari court. Chandu and Ramdayal had been fined. After a few days Chandu, Samaru, Sheodayal and Ramdayal had attacked Itwari. They were punishing him for his machinations. Itwari in turn had gone ahead and registered a complaint against them for beating him up and they had once again been fined. A little later Hagru had filed another suit against Ramdayal for damages for having enticed his wife to leave with her ornaments. The hearing of the law suit had been fixed for 14 July 1927. Both groups had been present for the hearing which had, however, been adjourned. The two groups had gone back in the evening. This was a day before the fight, the central event of the Sessions Trial case.

Karkhena was a primarily Teli and Satnami village which had a substantial Muslim malguzar with a landholding of 152.08 acres. Apart from two substantial plot-proprietors, both Kurmis, the village had 149 tenants: 48 Telis, 37 Satnamis, 12 Kurmis, 12 Gonds, 8 Rawats and 5 Chamars; the other tenants included families of Lohars, Brahmins, Dhobis, Muslims, Painka, Dhuri and a Christian and a Kalar. Itwari and his sons owned 19.80 acres, Dukhiram 9.63 acres. On the other hand, Samaru owned 5.09 acres, Sheodayal and Ramdayal 6.83 acres. Among the other Satnamis within the village eight had holdings of less than 2 acres,

---

[2] *Churi* has been a widely prevalent form of remarriage among all but the highest castes—Brahmans, Rajputs and Baniyas—in Chhattisgarh. Under the *churi* form of marriage a married woman could marry another man if he gave her *churis* (bangles). Among the Satnamis, if churi took place with another member of Satnampanth, the matter was deliberated by the *jat* (caste) panchayat: they fixed a certain *behatri* (compensation for bride price) which the new husband had to pay to the earlier husband and his family. The new husband also had to give a feast to the Satnamis—the number was decided by the Satnami elders in the village—which symbolised the incorporation of the woman into his home and the acceptance of the marriage by the community. The earlier husband, on the other hand, had to feed the Satnamis within the village in the form of a *marti jeeti bhat* which symbolised that the woman was dead to him. Finally, the new husband could be asked to pay a *dand* (punitive fine), a portion of which was kept for the guru and the rest used by the Satnamis in the village.

nine owned less than 5 acres and four each between 5 and 8 acres and 8 and 12 acres. Six Satnamis, apart from Itwari's family, had holdings of more than 12 acres. Itwari's family was among the most substantial Satnami cultivators and Chandu's group, although relatively better off than a number of Satnami tenants, was among the poorer cultivators in the village.[3]

Let me rehearse the prosecution story based upon the master narrative of the judgement and the evidence of the witnesses. On the morning of 15 July 1927, Itwari and Hagru along with Dukhiram and Banda went to their field. They carried three *nagars* (ploughs); Itwari, Banda and Hagru also carried a *tutari* (a stick with a sharp end to drive bullocks) and a *lathi* (stick). They kept the lathis on the *medh* (boundary) of their field and began to plough. In the meanwhile Chandu, Sheodayal, Sohgi and Nankai came with two ploughs to their fields. The two fields adjoined each other. Chandu and Sheodayal were carrying a lathi and a tutari. Sohgi brought a basket of seed grain and Nankai brought two pick axes and an axe. They began to sow their field. After some time Samaru and Ramdayal reached there. They were both carrying lathis. As soon as they came Sohgi went and picked up the lathis of Itwari and his group. Itwari noticed this and warned his 'party' that there was trouble ahead.

The men in Chandu's group declared that since Itwari's family 'had got them fined so they would on that day bathe in their blood' (DPW No. 5, Hagru). On hearing this Itwari's group ran with their ploughs to Dukhiram's field. They left the ploughs there and then ran to the field of Kasi. They asked Kasi to save them. When Chandu and his group reached there, Kasi remonstrated with them with folded hands. Chandu and his group, however, did not heed his request and repeated the statement about bathing in the blood of Itwari and his family (DPW No. 11, Dukhiram). Itwari and his men ran to Girdhari's field which offered greater safety: there were eleven ploughmen working there. When the ploughmen asked Chandu's family why they were chasing Itwari's group, they replied that they did not have any evil intentions. Kodu, a Gond labourer, stated that Chandu had said that they had taken away the lathis of Itwari's group because there was no

---

[3] Details culled from the land settlement records of Karkhena, Bandobast No. 124, Patwari Halka No. 57, Lakhatpur Group, 1928–29, Collectorate record room, Bilaspur.

reason for them to have brought them to the field (DPW No. 14). When Chandu's group was asked to return the lathis they said that they would do so in the village before the panchas and gave an assurance that they were going back. When they started moving away the ploughmen began working again. At that point Hagru was attacked and hit with a lathi till he fell down; Itwari was struck with an axe and a lathi and was killed.

The defence of the accused hinged on the argument of self defence. When Chandu, Sheodayal and Sohgi started working in the field they realised that they had not brought any seeds with them. Sohgi then started for home to get the seeds. On the way Itwari confronted, rebuked and abused her for enticing his daughter-in-law: '*Bhosda chodi hamar palodu la lae havas* [Cunt fucker you have taken away my daughter-in-law]' (EA, Chandu). Itwari then struck Sohgi twice with a stick. On hearing the noise Chandu and Samaru moved towards Sohgi and Itwari; Nankai, Sheodayal and Ramdayal, the defence argued, did not go in that direction. Chandu asked Itwari not to hit the old woman. Itwari turned to Chandu and attacked him with a stick. In his examination Chandu stated that he warded off Itwari's blows with a tutari and then, acting in self-defence, used it to hit him; Samaru joined him in hitting Itwari with a tutari; he could not be sure whether it was his or Samaru's blows which felled Itwari. Hagru, Dukhiram and Banda soon reached the spot. They attacked Chandu and Samaru with their sticks who defended themselves by wielding their tutaris. Samaru and Hagru fell down (EA, Chandu). Samaru in turn stated that he followed Chandu towards the scene of the fight between Itwari and Sohgi. 'I saw from a distance that . . . Sohgi fell down on the ground on account of two blows which Itwari dealt her on the head. Hot words were being exchanged between Chandu and Itwari.' At this point he was surrounded by Hagru, Dukhiram and Banda who had lathis in their hands and said, '*Bahen chod hamare bap ko mare bar jat ho* [You sister fucker, you are going to kill our father].' They started hitting Samaru with their sticks who defended himself with his tutari and struck a blow to Hagru, but then fell down because of successive blows from Dukhiram and Hagru. Hagru sat on Samaru's chest and dealt fist blows till he passed out. He did not know what had happened, 'I did not kill Itwari' (EA, Samaru). In brief, the defence argued that Itwari's family had attacked Sohgi, Chandu and

Samaru and, in the fight which ensued, Chandu and Samaru, acting in self-defence, had hurt Hagru and killed Itwari.

The dispute needs to be situated at an intersection of two axes: bonds of kinship and neighbourhood and Satnami notions of and engagement with forms of legality and justice. We know from the deposition of Dukhiram that Chandu was a cousin. The families of the 'accused' and the 'victim' were related through ties of blood. Moreover, the two families were neighbours: they held adjoining fields; and the pattern of settlement of castes in a Chhattisgarh village meant that the families of Chandu and Itwari would in all likelihood have lived in the Satnami/Chamar *para* (neighbourhood) with the thirty-five other Satnami families in Karkhena. We do not have evidence for the history of the relations between the two families before Kachrin left Hagru for Ramdayal. At the same time, what we know of the dispute was informed by the logic of the dynamics of relations of kinship and neighbourhood.

In village society in Chhattisgarh, relationships of affinity, friendship and kinship are double edged. The ties which bind are, on one hand, the basis of mutual support in everyday life; on the other hand, these bonds are the most fraught with risk and the possibility of a constant danger to a person, a family, a group, pregnant with the threat of rivalry, envy and disruption. In the course of discussing this dispute during field work Satnamis (and members of other castes) immediately recognised—through a quick affirmative 'ho' (yes) accompanied by a vigorous nod—the tension inherent in the relationship between the families of Itwari and Chandu: 'this is the way it always happens.' On two other occasions, in an effort to follow up the strained relations between Satnami families who were neighbours and related to each other, I enquired about the reasons behind the tension. My queries were met with good humoured laughter which signified that I was asking about the obvious: 'Don't you know, neighbours always fight.' I was enquiring about a norm and a pattern which governed everyday life.

The specific relationship between Ramdayal and Kachrin also carried a possible danger. Chandu and Dukhiram were cousins. Kachrin was Ramdayal's *bhauji* (brother's wife). Kachrin and Ramdayal, bhauji and *dewar* (husband's younger brother), were bound by a 'joking relationship'. The relationship between a bhauji and her dewar affords a high degree of freedom and licence and is replete with romantic and sexual overtones, which stands in contrast to the relationship of 'avoidance' between a woman and her father-in-law and her husband's elder brother. The *dadaria*, a genre of popular oral folk poetry of Chhattisgarh, for instance, repeatedly plays upon the longing of the bhauji and the dewar for each other.

> Sweet rings of sugar, the boys are eating
> Under every shade, Bhauji awaits me
>
> Mother-in-law's comments, sister-in-law's sarcasm
> Because of the young Dewar, my heart is not at rest.

There are, of course, well defined limits within which the jokes, the licence, the longing and attachment are meant to be played out. At the same time, it is only among close kin that an escape from these boundaries constitutes a transgression. Ramdayal and Kachrin were distant relatives: Kachrin's desertion of Hagru and her re-marriage with Ramdayal could not be considered a genuine violation of incest taboos. Ramdayal in marrying Kachrin worked upon a possibility that was inherent in the nature of the relationship between the members of the two families. Itwari's family seemed to underplay the element of Kachrin's volition and choice when they held Chandu's family responsible for enticing their daughter-in-law.

Matters internal to the Satnamis, particularly those relating to marriage, are settled by their panchayat. Indeed the twin inextricably bound characteristics of Satnampanth as a caste and a sect were premised upon affairs of the community being settled by the Satnami panchayat and, in case of serious transgressions, the organisational hierarchy set up by the gurus. Kachrin had not merely deserted Hagru; Kachrin and Ramdayal had been married in the churi form. The Satnami panchayat would have considered this within the bounds of fair play. None of the people—including some who sit as panchas in caste panchayats—with whom I discussed the dispute felt that Kachrin's marriage to Ramdayal constituted an outrage. It is not surprising then that Hagru, instead of taking the matter to the Satnami panchayat, had appealed to the Faujdari court. Itwari's family did not merely wish to recover a behatri. They wanted to go beyond the imposition of behatri and dand on Chandu's family and to avenge their loss of face in the village.

As substantial cultivators they were better suited than Chandu's family to take the matter to court: the move was, at the very least, bound to financially embarrass their opponents. The strategy paid off. Chandu's family was fined in the Faujdari court. According to Chandu's group the act of taking the matter to court and the subsequent imposition of a fine had crossed the well defined boundary of settling internal matters of the community in the Satnami panchayat. The action of Itwari's family, according to their opponents, was a transgression of norms of legality and justice of the community. Chandu when asked in his examination if he had been fined in the Faujdari said: '*Han nalish ki thi aur jurmana hua tha. Mor gavahi badal diye thhey* [Yes, there was a case and there was a fine imposed. My testimony/evidence had been changed]' (EA). The statement reveals the perception of Chandu's family of the legality and correctness of their position and their sharp feeling of having been tricked and wronged.

The four men of Chandu's family had consequently attacked Itwari; Itwari's family had taken them to court and they had been fined a second time for beating up the patriarch. The matter did not end there. Hagru once again dragged Chandu's family to the law court by filing a case against Ramdayal for damages for having enticed his wife to leave with her ornaments. The hearing of the case was to have been held the day before the fight occurred. The adjournment of the hearing would have left Chandu's family uncertain and worried about the outcome and angry about the expense and the trouble their relatively better off enemies were causing them. Itwari's family had stepped beyond the bounds of fair play; Chandu arguably reaffirmed the legality and norms of justice among Satnamis when he told the ploughmen that the sticks of Itwari's family would be returned before the caste panchayat. Chandu's family then redressed a loss, avenged a defeat, and punished a transgression.

In the universe of the familiar and the everyday, kinship and neighbourhood, colonial courts could simultaneously constitute an 'alien legality' and a strategy of settlement and revenge. 'You have got us fined so we shall on this day bathe in your blood.' Itwari's family in their desire for retribution sought to implicate their enemies by deploying this statement, possibly under the guidance of the counsel for the prosecution, to establish the common intention of all members of Chandu's family to kill Itwari and Hagru. Sheodayal, Sohgi and Nankai were acquitted; Ramdayal was imprisoned for only two years. Clearly the rules of colonial courts were difficult to master. At the same time, we are reminded of the distinction between 'traditional' processes of dispute settlement that are concerned with transgressions of norms and authority, and 'modern' legal systems which seek to establish the intention behind a crime as the central criterion of culpability. 'You have got us fined so we shall on this day bathe in your blood.' The statement of Chandu's family spoke of their construction of a transgression but was seized by judicial discourse to establish intention. Chandu's family had punished a transgression; Chandu and Samaru were convicted—and sentenced to transportation of life under section 302 and 305 of the Indian Penal Code—for intending the death of Itwari.

## PROPERTY, ENMITY AND CONFLICT: DISPUTE 2

The land revenue resettlement of the Bilaspur district between 1927 and 1932 led to the creation of two 'parties' in Murlidih village.[4] The 'tenant party' and the 'malguzar party'. The tenants belonged to different castes within the village; the malguzars, Chanahoo by caste, belonged to one family. The tension stemmed from conflicting claims over the *gochar* (village waste) and the *barcha* (land adjoining the village pond used for growing sugarcane), over the payment of rent and interest, and the issue of forced labour. There was, moreover, the intrusion of the notion of *swaraj* (freedom), reworked and reinterpreted by the tenants. What eventuated was a protracted battle of strategy and manoeuvre. In the course of this long drawn out conflict nine members of the 'tenant party'—eight Rawats and one Satnami— were accused of taking away a silver *chura* (an ornament worn above the wrist) and a gold *bali* (an ornament worn in the ear) from Govinda and Jagatram malguzars. When Govinda and Jagatram tried to get the ornaments back by making a payment, the money was kept but the ornaments were not returned. Finally, the tenants forced the malguzars to give them a receipt for *dhan*

---

[4] The reconstruction of this dispute is based upon King Emperor vs. Rendhia and six others, Sessions Trial No. 22 of 1932.

(unhusked paddy). This was the prosecution story. The defence of the accused was that they had not taken away the ornaments or the money. The trial in the court of the Additional Sessions Judge, Raipur, was concerned with the facts of the 'dacoity'; the tension between the malguzars and tenants constituted the antecedents of, the background to, this central event. We can, however, reverse the emphasis. The taking away of the *bali* and *chura*, the acts which helped fashion the dispute as a 'case', provides us a point of entry. We engage in an exercise to reconstruct the working out of a dispute between malguzars and tenants within village life in Murlidih.

What do we know about the village and the family of Chanahoo malguzars? Murlidih was populated in the main by Rawats; the other members of the village were Telis, Gandas, Bairagis and Satnamis. The overwhelming majority of the tenants of Murlidih had meagre landholdings: seven of the ten members of the 'tenant party', protagonists in the trial, had landholdings between 1.5 acres and 3.75 acres; Koli Rawat owned 6.74 acres and Baijnathdass 8.95 acres; Bidga Ganda owned no land.[5] The other details about the members of the 'tenant party' are contained in the table below.

Table: Details of the 'Tenant Party'

| Name | Caste | Approx. Age | Occupation | Status within the trial |
|------|-------|-------------|------------|------------------------|
| Rendhia | Rawat | 40 Years | Tobacco Seller | Accused |
| Orjhatia | Rawat | 30 Years | Cultivator | Accused |
| Sakharam | Satnami | 30 Years | Cultivator | Accused |
| Bhokna | Rawat | 45 Years | Cultivator | Accused |
| Buli | Rawat | 45 Years | Cultivator | Accused |
| Shivprasad | Rawat | 40 Years | Cultivator | Accused |
| Koli | Rawat | 60 Years | Cultivator | Accused |
| Mohan | Teli | 32 Years | Oil-presser | Approver |
| Baijnathdass | Bairagi | 50 Years | Cultivator | Approver |
| Bidga | Ganda | 42 Years | Cultivator | P.W. No. 10 |

[5] Murlidih, Bandobast No. 613, Patwari Halka No. 249, Jaijaipur Group, Janjgir Tahsil, 1929–30.

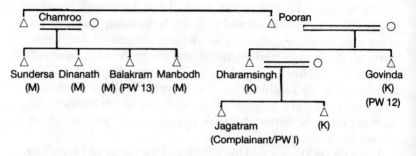

Figure 3: Family of Chanahoo Malguzars

The Chanahoo family, village proprietors of Murlidih, had two branches. One lived in Murlidih, the other in nearby Karbadih. The two villages were held jointly by the family: but the two branches cultivated their lands separately (see Figure 3).

The creation of the two 'parties' was rooted in the land revenue resettlement effected between 1927 and 1932. The malguzar Govinda stated, 'since last settlement the troubles between Malguzars and tenants have arisen.' (DPW No. 2.) The settlement was announced in the two villages in 1931. In August-September 1931 the malguzars and tenants had been divided into two parties. The two major points of tension, brought to the fore by settlement operations, were the gochar (village waste) lands for grazing, and the barcha for sugarcane cultivation in the village.

What did the settlement authority have to say about the two issues?

In the Khalsa of this district, definite areas of village waste have been exclusively reserved for the grazing of village cattle. The reservation of land for grazing purposes is an extremely controversial matter, but in view of the fact that much of the land reserved is practically unculturable and the consensus of opinion was in favour of such reservation, Government agreed to its continuance. But in order to preserve a certain degree of elasticity, it was ordered that power should be given to Deputy Commissioner to allow such changes during the currency of the settlement, as local circumstances might render desirable (*LRS*, Bilaspur, 1932: 32).

The story of the sugarcane fields was a little different.

The cane fields are either scattered plots situated in the holdings of individual agriculturists, or common lands locally known as barchas, which are appropriated permanently to the purpose and so situated as to facilitate irrigation from one of the village tanks. The barchas are either held by the Malguzar . . . and the tenants jointly, in which case each man has, each year, his plot from which he takes the rotation crop also in the following year, or it may entirely consist of the Malguzar[s] . . . home farm where the rights of the tenants are limited to its use for growing cane only in alternate years, the owner of the land taking whole of the rotation crop. *In those villages, where the barchas have been divided into strips and held permanently in severality the strips have been numbered and recorded separately according to possession.* (*LRS*, Bilaspur, 1932: 29; emphasis added.)

Murlidih had witnessed that 'certain degree of elasticity' left for government initiative in relation to gochar lands. 'The tenants of the village used to demand from us the Malguzars that they should be given the pakka gochar lands for cultivation. They said they would pay rent.' (DPW No. 1, Jagat.) Clearly the gochar land in Murlidih was not 'practically unculturable'. It was no doubt in keeping with these local circumstances that the government had allowed a change. The entire gochar of Murlidih was given over to and came to be in the sole possession of the malguzars (J). As we shall see, however, the measure went against the 'consensus of opinion' of the tenants.

Concerning barcha, Murlidih, it appears, was not one of the villages where it had been 'divided into strips and held in severality.' In the village, before the settlement, the malguzars alone used to occupy the barcha lands. It was their 'home farm.' The barcha of the village was 'surveyed, numbered and recorded separately'; the strips of this land were given to the tenants—along with the malguzars—of Murlidih to grow sugarcane (J). 'The tenants have been given rights for sugarcane and padti [gochar] land is allowed to the Malguzars by revenue officers' (DPW No. 6, Baijnathdass).

The decisions of the settlement authority about the gochar and the barcha in Murlidih effected a departure, then, from the earlier practice in the village. The gochar on which all the villagers had grazing rights became the property of malguzars. The barcha which had been held only by the malguzars was now distributed among the tenants and malguzars. Moreover, the changes were characterised by a certain ambiguity. There was a gap between what the settlement report said about gochar and barcha lands and what actually happened in Murlidih. It was, in fact, the break with past practices and this ambiguity which created the space for the contending and rival claims of the two parties within the village.

The conflicting claims of tenants and malguzar over gochar become clear from the statement of Jagatram malguzar: 'The tenants of the village used to demand from us the Malguzars that they should be given the Gochar . . . land for cultivation or else they would not allow us to cultivate the same. They said that they would pay rent and if the land was not given it may remain fallow. This year the idea became firm with the tenant' (DPW No. 1). The malguzars refused to budge. 'Applications were made to the Revenue Courts, but the tenants lost' (J). The loss would have been a disappointment, a blow. The claim of the tenants was backed by a certain legitimacy: if the gochar, the common property of the villagers in the recent past, was to be cultivated then the tenants should have a right in cultivation—they were willing to pay rent; at the same time, if they were not given this right they would not let the malguzars cultivate—the lands would remain fallow.

There was in addition the question of the barcha. The tenants had been given rights in the barcha after the settlement. The malguzars were, however, unwilling to part with what had been their land before the settlement: 'Malguzar was also not giving sugarcane lands to tenants for cultivation' (DPW No. 6, Baijnath-dass). There was a feeling among some of the tenants that the malguzar had lost their rights over both the gochar and the barcha, which bore testimony to the differential perceptions of the changes introduced by the settlement: 'Since last settlement it is decided that all the tenants have a right to grow cane on lands reserved for it and also on Gochar lands. The Malguzars sole possession is refused by the settlement' (DPW No. 5, Mohan).

The questions of the gochar and barcha got linked to two other contested issues within Murlidih: the payment of rent and interest to malguzars and *bhet begar* or unpaid labour rendered under custom—codified by the colonial regime—by tenants to their malguzars. The trouble over rent went back in time. Dharamsingh, the resident malguzar of Karbadih, had got together with Sundersa of Murlidih: the two had divided the tenants of Murlidih among themselves and had separately collected rent from them. This arrangement worked for a year. After that the tenants had refused to pay rent for three years. At the time when the tension over the barcha and gochar in the village became serious the malguzars were demanding rent with interest: but the tenant party, characteristically, was in no mood to pay. 'Sundersa and Dharamsingh divided the tenantry privately and in one year they recovered the rent privately from their respective tenants. For three years next none of them received rents and then after that arrears with interest were demanded. The tenants declined to pay interest and on this account also there are two parties—one for the tenant and one for the Malguzar.' (DPW, No. 5, Mohan.)

Equally, the settlement of 1927–32 had formally done away with the institution of bhet begar.

> Very little of the patriarchal idea now survives in the relations between landlords and tenants, and there is no reason why this relic of a medieval custom should be entered into the record of rights, particularly when there is so much cry against forced labour all over the world (*LRS*, Bilaspur, 1932: 32).

Govinda stated, 'In the last settlement Bhet Begar has been stopped and the tenants now refuse to give Bhet Begar and [the issue] has made them rise against their Malguzars' (DPW No. 2). The malguzar was, of course, lamenting the final demise of 'paternalist' ties. The tenants were freed of a burden and a critical marker of their subordination to the malguzar. 'This year we did not do Bhet Begar' (DPW No. 5, Mohan). The lines of battle stood clearly drawn.

The tenant initiative opened with the customary social boycott within village life, *nai dhobi bandh*, in which the critical services of the service castes, particularly the barber and the washerman, are stopped. 'The tenants stopped our servants and also barber and dhobis. This was in last Kuar [September-October]' (DPW No. 13, Balakram). The boycott was comprehensive. The malguzars were shunned. There was a ban, enforced by oaths in the name of relatives, on verbal interaction with the malguzar: 'The tenants had also asked the [other] tenants not to speak to the [malguzars] and had put oaths in the name of relatives' (DPW No. 13, Balakram). The social boycott was, of course, a form of censure, also expressed in other ways. The tenants would smear the doors of the malguzars' houses with shit and throw the polluting substance into their compounds. The malguzars' houses were pelted with stones, their chilli plants uprooted, their compound walls broken. The censure was aimed at preventing the malguzars from showing their face within the village. Balakram as the resident malguzar of Murlidih lamented, 'We had to keep our doors closed. We used to come from the backdoor side . . . . We kept inside the house all day long' (DPW, No. 13).

The tenants of Murlidih had initiated a major offensive. To effect a complete social boycott of the malguzars—who ordinarily called the shots in matters of censure and in relation to service castes in everyday village life—was to establish an alternative, oppositional centre of authority. The tenant enterprise was informed by the critical metaphor of *swaraj*. Budga Ganda made it clear: 'I was in the tenant party of Swaraj. The only persons excepted were Malguzars' (DPW No. 10). The repeated play with the metaphor within the depositions of witnesses underscores that the tenants believed that swaraj had indeed come to Murlidih. The dispute between tenants and malguzars in Murlidih was, in fact, a part of a larger pattern. Almost all over the Jaijaipur station area there was tension between Malguzars and tenants. Niaz Ahmad, the Circle Inspector of police, deposed: 'In many other villages in the said station house area there are disputes between tenants and Malguzars.' The police official had found out about the trouble in Murlidih when he was on tour 'making enquiries about the disputes' in the entire area (DPW No. 14).

In the first round of the Civil Disobedience movement in 1930–31 there were numerous forest satyagrahas in neighbouring Raipur district; the Congress organisation was active in the towns of Bilaspur district. It was the articulation of generalised notions of a challenge to (and displacement of) authority with tensions rooted in the processes of revenue settlement that defined the tenant opposition to malguzars in Jaijaipur station house area. The tenants of Murlidih seized upon the notion of swaraj within this matrix. In recent years we have had forceful reminders of the need to understand swaraj as a polysemic sign capable of generating and sustaining multiple perceptions. Swaraj was understood and worked upon in varied ways and came to be differentially implicated in the practices of varied social groups.

Mohan Teli explained, 'Swaraj in our village means that whoever can retain any article got should be allowed to retain that article as his own' (DPW No. 5). The obscure oil-presser's statement has possible links with Gramsci's observation about popular currents of natural law as 'the ensemble of opinions and beliefs concerning one's "own" rights which circulate uninterruptedly among the popular masses and are continuously renewed under the pressure of real living conditions' (Gramsci, 1985: 193). At the same time, Mohan Teli had come up with what was only one of the definitions of swaraj in Murlidih. Swaraj opened up several possibilities and was reworked in practice by the tenant 'party' of Murlidih: it informed an alternative centre of authority which effected a vigorous offensive of censure.

We get a glimpse of the shift in the nature of the tenant enterprise from the deposition of Jagatram malguzar. 'The disputes about Gochar land and other lands started from settlement time. The tenants used to damage our crops, since last Kartik [October–November] only. Before Kartik last i.e. before taking the ornaments the tenants used to damage the crops by cattle and after that they gathered the crops themselves' (DPW No. 1). Mohan Teli added: 'We were saying that Swaraj had come to our village and as Govinda and Jagat . . . were seeing the fields, we would call them and make them pay. This spirit has started since last Kartik' (DPW No. 5). The month of Kartik was the point which inaugurated the shift. There was a move from merely damaging the malguzars' property to staking an actual claim on it: the tenants did not allow the malguzars to gather their crops; they gathered the malguzar's crops.

The shift was also marked by an attack on bonds which inscribed debts to malguzars.

> The tenants then held a meeting which all the accused attended. We four brothers were called. . . . Sundersa asked why they were summoned. Accused Sukharam, Bhaluwa and Rendhia then said that we should tear out all the bonds for debts and an agreement would be made. We wanted four days time for consideration. On that Orzatia said that they should go away and Malguzars would not tear away

the bonds. The tenants went away one after the other and then we
brothers came back. They began to throw night soil in the compound
and we had to walk through it . . . the tenants began to trouble us
more and more (DPW No. 13, Balakram).

The four brothers referred to by Balaram were the four resident
malguzars of Murlidih. The tenants of Murlidih did not, in fact,
take loans from money-lenders outside the village. It was the
debt-bonds to the malguzars of the village which the tenants had
sought to destroy. This 'territoriality' of the tenants also brings us
to the central event of the trial.

I begin with the prosecution story. On 20 November 1931
Rendhia, Orjhatia, Bhukua, Balli, Shivprasad, Koli, Sakharam,
and Baijnathdass [see Table] were sitting near the house of Koli
Rawat. 'We were saying that Swaraj has come to our village and
we will make them pay' (DPW No.5, Mohan). Jagat and Govinda
were returning after seeing their field within the village. They had
reaped the crops of their fields the day before. When the two
malguzars passed the house of Koli Rawat they were called by
the tenants. 'We went there and were asked to sit down' (DPW
No. 2, Govinda). Rendhia and Bhulwa said that Govinda and
Jagatram should pay ten and fifteen Rupees respectively if they
wished to gather their crops. 'We stood up to go out saying why
should we pay' (DPW No. 1, Jagat). 'The accused then said we
should pay or else our fathers will pay and that would not do'
(DPW No. 2, Govinda). The two malguzars of Karbadih were
then surrounded with cries of 'pakdo, pakdo [catch them, catch
them]': 'I was caught hold of by Orjhatia and my uncle Govinda
was caught by hand. All of them said "chhino, chhino [grab,
grab]". Orjhatia then took out a silver Chura from my hands
. . . Rendhia took out a Bali from the ear of my uncle' (DPW
No. 1, Jagat). Jagat and Govinda were forbidden from entering
Murlidih; they went to the kotwar (watchman) of their village but
did not take the matter to the police. They had been threatened
that they would be killed if they talked about the incident. 'I
refused to make a report for fear of life' (DPW No. 1, Jagat).

A week later Jagat and Govinda went to Murlidih. They paid
eight Rupees to Sakharam Satnami and asked for the ornaments.
The money was kept but the chura and the bali were not returned.
About this time the tenants also forced the two malguzars to give
them a receipt. The receipt stated that malguzars had received

their share of the paddy from their lands which they had given the tenants to cultivate. These three acts of the tenants involved a play with territoriality. Jagat and Govinda were the non-resident malguzars of Murlidih: 'As Jagat and Govinda were non-resident Malguzars we decided to take the money from them. The others lived in my village' (DPW No. 5, Mohan). All these events came to light when the malguzars made a report to Circle Inspector Niaz Ahmad on 1 February 1932 when he went to the village for the second time within a month.

In their defence the accused denied that these three events had occurred. All of them claimed alibis and argued that the bali and the chura which had been seized by the police from Orjhatia and Rendhia belonged to the two Rawats. They were being framed by the malguzars on account of *adawat* (enmity), which had its roots in the quarrel over the barcha and gochar lands and the tenants' refusal to pay rent for three years. The endorsement of enmity, repeated by all the tenants in their examination, is significant for the reconstruction of the dispute.

In the judgement, delivered on 7 May 1932, the Additional Sessions Judge argued that the 'prosecution consists of the testimony of eye witnesses only and it is a case of believing or not believing the prosecution witness.' The Judge then went on to believe the prosecution witnesses in 'light of probabilities.' The defence of the accused was 'weak', the witnesses were 'interested', and the case of the prosecution stood 'unrebuked'. At the same time, the judgement qualified the central event: 'This is not a case of dacoity in the strict sense of the term, but is more or less technical dacoity. What the tenants really appeared to have desired was to coerce the Malguzars to subjugation.' The seven accused were each sentenced to rigourous imprisonment for seven months.

It we believe the prosecution story, the three central events of the dacoity were not freak occurrences. They were a part of a pattern. The tenants party in a new found spirit, charged with the possibilities opened up by swaraj, had begun making claims on village property. The 'accused' had taken away the chura and the bali, the money and the receipt, from the malguzars because of their perception of what was their legitimate due and entitlement. It is quite possible, however, as the tenants argued in their defence, that they were being implicated on trumped up charges and framed on account of their enmity with the malguzars. This enmity—the creation and existence of two 'parties'—was rooted in tensions and quarrels over the gochar and barcha lands, the refusal to pay rent and to render begar. A prime accused was asked a pointed question about the way the tenants used to trouble the malguzars. He admitted that they had thrown shit into the malguzar's house even as he made light of the event: '*Thoda sa maila dere mein ek din phenk diya tha* [One day a bit of shit was thrown into the compound]' (EA, Rendhia). The seven members of the 'tenant party', in fact, turned the admission of their quarrel with the malguzars into their defence. It is the nature and the working out of this quarrel that we were after. The events of the 'dacoity' provided us a point of entry to reconstruct a struggle launched by the tenants of an obscure village in Bilaspur district. The point of entry, provisionally, also has to be the moment of closure. My story of the dispute between the tenants and malguzars in Murlidih ends with the conviction of six Rawats and one Satnami to seven months rigorous imprisonment.

# Social Organization at the District Courts: Colleague Relationships Among Indian Lawyers*

## CHARLES MORRISON

In addition to containing religious centres of pilgrimage, regional and local markets, and educational establishments, a district headquarters town in India is, virtually by definition, the seat of a whole complex of law courts. The personnel whose activities contribute to the patterning of social life in such towns includes as an essential feature a small brotherhood of local legal practitioners. The present paper describes one such brotherhood: the advocates who practice in a district headquarters town in Haryana. The main problem with which I shall be concerned is that of isolating and describing the system of social relations, the interconnected set of behavioural patterns, that occurs in the daily interactions among a hundred or more professionals in the district courts.

[ . . . ]

The social organization of civilizational centres, whether of 'traditional' systems such as temples or 'nontraditional' systems such as modern law courts, can be considered as having two

* Excerpted from Charles Morrison, 'Social Organization at the District Courts: Colleague Relationships among Indian Lawyers', *Law and Society Review*, 1968–9, 3: 251–67.

aspects: first, relations between specialists and those they serve (in which the function of the center largely defines the content of the relationships); and second, relations among specialists (in which the content of the relationship may be tangential to the main function of the center). These two aspects overlap, of course, and there are many variations: an isolated specialist may have little interaction with others of his kind; or services usually reserved for nonspecialist clientele may be provided for fellow specialists; or specialists may have significant relations with allied specialists.

For the litigants of an Indian district, the courts are an important occasional social arena. For even the busiest of chronic litigants, however, they are only an *occasional* arena. The professional and administrative personnel of the legal system are necessarily somewhat marginal figures in the litigant's world, of not as much concern to him as the allies and opposite parties of his numerous lawsuits. For a vast majority of district legal practitioners in India, on the other hand, the courts are the arena, the physical and social setting, for a lifetime's work. . . .

In looking at the courts as the work context of the Indian district lawyer one can ask about some of the problems that occur in the description of any social system: How are relations distributed in space, what roles can be distinguished, what is the range of variation in role enactment, how does the purpose for which the system exists affect the formation of groups, how is authority distributed and so forth. Not all these problems are dealt with in this paper; and many important facets of lawyers' lives, activities that take place away from the courts, are left largely out of account.

## INTRODUCTION

First, I comment on caste and the composition of the bar. Then I examine the setting in which the lawyers' interactions with their colleagues occur. Next I discuss three kinds of informal grouping that differentiate the bar and give shape to its internal political structure. Finally, I examine the way in which these structural features were involved in a recent bar association election.

# THE CASTE COMPOSITION OF THÈ BAR

Table 1 shows the caste identity of the local lawyers discussed in this paper. All-India figures are not available, but knowledgeable metropolitan lawyers believe that Brahmins dominate the profession as a whole. The table reflects the marked lack of importance Brahmins have as a community in the public life of Punjab and Haryana. The castes that dominate the bar here (Aggarwal and Khatri) are those that also dominate the trading and business life of the town. The numerically dominant agricultural caste of the region is Jat, whose members comprise between 40–50% of the regional population.

### Table 1
#### Caste Composition of the Bar[*]

| Number | Caste | Traditional Occupation | Number of Lawyers |
|--------|-------|------------------------|-------------------|
| 1. | Aggarwal | Trade | 22 |
| 2. | Khatri | Trade | 21 |
| 3. | Arora | Trade | 12 |
| 4. | Jat | Agriculture | 12 |
| 5. | Brahmin | Priest | 11 |
| 6. | Jain | Trade | 7 |
| 7. | Ahluwalia | Distilling | 4 |
| 8. | Rajput | Agriculture | 2 |
| 9. | Chamar | Leather work | 1 |
| 10. | Gadariya | Shepherd | 1 |
| 11. | Kamboh | Agriculture | 1 |
| 12. | Kayasth | Clerk | 1 |
| 13. | Saini | Market gardening | 1 |
| | | Total | 96 |

[*] Assigning traditional occupations to castes is hazardous. Most of the castes listed here have, for generations, had members of several different occupations. On the other hand, Ahluwalias, for instance, have long since abandoned distilling and in this town, at any rate, appear to have mainly entered the professions and government service. . . .

In the day-to-day relations among members of the bar, caste is relatively unimportant as a determinant of social behavior. It is, of course, a factor in recruitment to the profession. An urban Aggarwal boy stands a better chance than does a rural Chamar boy of coming from a family in which literacy is high and other members are in government service or professions and where opportunities for law study are possible. But once both Chamar and Aggarwal become lawyers, their common professional identity tends to cancel the differences of caste identity. Of course, in the lives of lawyers outside the courts, caste is significant. For example, it is often a factor in regional political activity and in the management of various urban associations such as sectarian schools. In general, however, caste does not have the role-summation significance for city professionals that it has in village life.

## THE COURTS AS AN OCCUPATIONAL SETTING

The lawyers' localization in the courts gives them a position there akin to that of merchants in a marketplace, and in fact both lawyers and clients sometimes refer to the court compound as a bazaar. . . .

The district courts on which this paper is based are likely to give the casual visitor the impression of an improbable cross between a bustling, alfresco stock exchange at the peak of trading, a mainline platform before the express arrives, and a rural trade fair. Ramshackle kiosks, chairs, benches, tables and lean-tos are scattered seemingly at random in the dusty and apparently undifferentiated compound that stretches forlornly between verandaed office buildings of various PWD vintages. Through the compound wanders a curious mixture of urban and rural types. . . . Many just sit and stare. Others work furiously at antique typewriters or with the tattered files, battered dispatch boxes and the cloth bundles of Indian office life. From the rows of dilapidated tea stalls that fringe the compound, boys bring the inevitable refreshments. In season, a dust storm further enlivens the scene.

On entering one of the courtrooms, the visitor is likely to find the confusion only slightly abated. On a typical day, he will probably have difficulty even seeing the magistrate or judge, for the latter is usually obscured by a crush of advocates, witnesses and others crowded round the bench. A succession of unhushed conferences are likely to be in progress between various secondary officials and lawyers and it is not unusual for parts of two cases to appear to be in progress simultaneously. The occasional efforts of police and *chowkidars* to impose order only add to the hubbub.

In such a setting, the Indian district lawyer spends between a half and two-thirds of his working time. In the course of a day at the district courts described here, an advocate passes back and forth between several segments of this setting. For each of these segments there are appropriate modes of behavior and characteristic relationships. We will examine some of these distinctions in more detail.

First, however, a comment on the matter of confusion in juridical situations is relevant here. Anthropologists writing about law in the non-Western world have often noted the apparent disorder and informality of court proceedings. For instance, Epstein observes that the seeming casualness of African tribal courts is in marked contrast to the august atmosphere of their English counterparts but adds that such informality does not mean that the actual situation under inquiry is chaotic; rather it reflects how closely the work of the courts is bound up in the daily lives of the people. One of the admittedly minor differences between a 'traditional' or tribal legal system and a 'modern' (*i.e.*, Westernized) law court such as described here is that the latter is intended to cope, if not simultaneously, at least in relatively rapid and continuous succession with very many totally unconnected cases. Some of the seeming confusion in the district courts arises from the nature of the system. The rules of procedure in such a legal system necessitate the fragmentation of even the simplest case into perhaps as many as five or six different hearings. This in turn multiplies the frequency of interactions, if not the actual number of relationships, in which lawyers and litigants are involved with court officials and the judiciary. All this is relevant here not only because the fixing of dates for future hearings consumes much of a lawyer's time, but also because one of the skills of a successful lawyer is an ability to manipulate the court calendar to his own advantage. We might usefully make a distinction between 'complexity' (the multistranded nature of the system) and 'confusion' (the possibility of ambiguous situations and the sheer difficulty of stage management that results from the translation of this multiplicity into actual social relations).

In the town described here, the district lawyer's professional use of urban space has two clear divisions: home-office and courts. The latter has three subdivisions which will be discussed later. The home-office is easily accommodated by the domestic architectural conventions of north India. All homes in the economic class to which lawyers belong possess a multipurpose public room usually provided with direct access to the street and known here as a *baithak*. Depending on the size and stage of his career, a lawyer's *baithak*-office may be more or less exclusively reserved for law work. The ordering of behavior associated with the *baithak* in the minds of visitors and occupants provides, at least in this relatively prosperous area, an interesting continuity between the urban and the rural. The lawyer's office, the doctor's dispensary, and the politician's reception room are all recognizable urban variants of the rural 'men's house' or guest quarters of this region. The *baithaks* of many substantial villagers here are structurally and functionally identical with their urban variants. The storage of simple agricultural equipment, lawyer's files, compounder's medicines and the accommodation of guests, clients, patients, or political supporters are all well within the range of uses for such places.

[ . . . ]

In the court precincts, three distinct segments of social space can be recognized: the courts proper, the compound, and the bar association library. Each has a characteristic patterning of relationships. We are chiefly concerned with the last two. Activity in the courts proper is, as noted above, intense and bustling; but the behavior is also highly repetitive and focused. For almost everything that goes on in the courtroom, there exists somewhere a set of written rules—government manuals on court upkeep and organization, textbooks on advocacy, codes and case law. Colleague interactions here are highly legalistic in content and for the purposes of this paper of rather marginal relevance. Here my concern is with that area of the lawyer's identity that lies between this central, role-defining activity of court appearance and the broader field where professional identity merges with social class. In any case, it is *at* the courts rather than *in* court that the majority of district practitioners are to be found most of the time.

The second of the three segments is the compound; the third is the library. In both compound and library, lawyers interact with one another informally. The compound is, in addition, the chief area of lawyer-client interaction outside the courtroom. The compound also provides a place where potential clients can shop for lawyers, by observing their actions without entering into direct relations with them.

The special unit of identity in the compound is the *takht*, the platform table-bench that serves as an office and has some of the functions of a merchant's stall in a bazaar. *Takhts* themselves are not usually identified by name plates, although there is no actual rule against this. Many are ramshackle and there is no correspondence between the size or construction of a *takht* and the affluence or professional skill of its occupant. . . .

[ . . . ]

The bar association library at the courts described here is a collection of five or six rooms forming one of the buildings of the compound. The library also functions as a social club, general office, communications center, mess hall, and consulting room. The place has the usual *baithak*-office atmosphere, achieved in part by portrait photographs of late distinguished members. Sometimes clients come here but they are not encouraged to do so. In Goffman's terms, the library is a backstage area as far as lawyer-client relations are concerned.[1] Clients are likely to become suspicious if they see their own counsel joking with the opposite party's advocate in the library building. Typically, client visitors stay only long enough to locate their lawyer, usually to let him know their case has been called. . . .

## FRIENDSHIP SETS AND ETHNIC SECTIONS IN THE BAR

As already emphasized, members of the legal brotherhood spend much of their time in one another's company. Hours are consumed in informal conversation with colleagues while lawyers overtly wait for cases to be called or covertly wait for clients to materialize. In these sessions, as in the shorter courtroom confrontations, quick wit and verbal facility are valued. The peculiar

[1] E. Goffman (1959).

ethos of this gossipy, single purpose association is a somewhat paradoxical blend of egalitarianism status consciousness, camaraderie and mistrust.

In structural terms, three kinds of grouping can be discerned in the social relations of the lawyers described here. First, there are small, very informal, rather fluid, interconnected clusters or cliques of colleagues. Secondly, there is a more general grouping into two large sections on the basis of the ethnic distinction between 'refugees' and 'local.' The refugees are men who moved (or whose families moved) to this district at Partition in 1947. Thirdly, there is a rather transient form of grouping which cross-cuts the broader, dual division of refugees and locals. I will refer to these three kinds of grouping as sets or cliques, sections, and alliances. Sets are the small day-to-day colleague groups; sections are the broad, permanent, ethnic divisions; and alliances are the occasional transient ties of political expediency and interpersonal rivalry. Informal social control and socialization are achieved through sets for the most part; formal, internal political structure is chiefly expressed with reference to sections or alliances.

Although the section division of the bar here is explicitly recognized, it is felt to be 'wrong' and factionalistic. Not surprisingly in such a legalistic atmosphere, some informants contend that there is no jural basis for such a division. Others simply argue that the distinctions of twenty years ago should now be forgotten. It is often said that the division into sections has no real significance. But despite such pious disapproval, the division continues and is clearly marked in space. Local advocates have their *takhts* clustered at one end of the court compound, just outside the bar association library, near home as it were; refugees are clustered at the other side of the compound near the main entrance. A few isolated *takhts* dot the intervening space.

The basis on which sets or cliques are formed reflects the variety of associational ties available to educated urbanites. A common explanation for the origin of a bar friendship is the school tie. Involved here is a class or year identity rather than a differentiation based on competing institutions. Most lawyers received their legal training at the main state law college. Beginners who join the bar at about the same time often become friends, even if they were not college mates.

Caste is on the whole unimportant in the organization of the bar but it does sometimes provide the basis for a set. There is a Rajput set, for instance. Here the caste tie has been strengthened by a cooperative speculation in urban real estate. Common political interests (*e.g.*, support of a local party candidate in a constituency election) provide another kind of tie in the organization of some sets. Frequently members of sets say they came together originally because they shared a common approach to life. It is difficult to specify what this means and there are sets whose members seem to have contrasting personalities.

Kinship links are sometimes a factor in set formation; a number of lawyers are distantly related to one another. Links of this sort should be distinguished from the ties that unite fathers and sons, between whom the norms of deference and respect preclude the possibility of informal clique formation. In the district courts, every lawyer belongs to some set but the degree of importance that such clique activity assumes in day-to-day life differs among individuals.

Some cliques of young advocates span the division between refugees and locals. Some sets of older lawyers, on the other hand, are explicitly based on shared refugee status. In the socially heterogeneous milieu of the courts, the refugee-local distinction does not have the same significance that it possesses in the larger society of this region where it is possible to distinguish broad, general, and contrasting stereotypic refugee-local patterns of outlook and life style. In an anthropological account of commercial life in a small town of this area, the refugee businessman is depicted as an aggressive, extrovert, modernistic entrepreneur with a flair for manipulating the administration.[2] The local *bania*, in contrast, is depicted as conservative, miserly, tradition-ridden, and fearful or indifferent of the administration. The common activities and training of the legal profession, however, prevent or blur the development of distinctions of this order. The characteristics are recognizable among the lawyers, but they crosscut the section division. Thus, some who come close to the refugee stereotype sketched above are in fact locals; and there are some notoriously cautious and conservative refugee advocates.

[ . . . ]

There is little specialization in Indian district practice but this

---

[2] L.W. Hazlehurst (1966).

by itself does not seem a sufficient explanation for the poor development of partnerships. Sets or small cliques sometimes solidify into formal law partnerships but such firms are very rare at the district level where the joint family provides the basis for what little cooperative enterprise there is, inside and outside the courts. District lawyers often express the opinion that nonrelatives are not likely to trust one another sufficiently to permit the widespread development of a partnership system. It is significant that where nonkin based partnerships *do* exist at the district courts, income is usually divided between partners on a daily basis; where kinsmen are in partnership, professional fees usually go into a joint family purse.

The constant struggles of lawyers to prevent conflicting hearings from getting on their appointment books suggest that there is scope for some division of labor even if not amounting to formal specialization in fields of law. But for partnership as a business style to develop, client acceptance of the pattern would be necessary and interviews with litigants suggest that many of them would be unwilling to trust multiple counsel. Paradoxically, mistrust of the lawyer's ability to 'be there on the day' leads a number of litigants to retain a second string counsel, thus indirectly achieving one of the benefits that a partnership system might provide.

## LEADING LAWYERS

Despite its egalitarian ethic, the bar is, of course, stratified. A tiny handful of advocates are recognized as 'leading lawyers.' This title is conferred on only five or six of the lawyers described in this paper. Below the level of the leading lawyer, three other ranks are sometimes explicitly recognized. One advocate labeled these: below top, average, and below average. At the bottom are briefless lawyers, *e.g.*, struggling beginners or old, semiretired practitioners. In the third rank are established lawyers who have had more than ten years of practice. The second rank is a category of men with many years of practice and often with some more or less important position in the community at large outside the bar but who lack the district-wide professional reputation of the top practitioners.

Leading lawyers are relatively isolated or setless, in my limited use of that term. They are rarely seen chatting about nonlegal matters in small groups of advocates on the compound or in the library. In fact, one of the markers of the leading advocate status is infrequency of appearance in these locations. Unlike the majority of his colleagues, the leading advocate is found *in* court rather than *at* the courts. When he is not appearing before judges or magistrates he is usually to be found in his *baithak*-office dealing with a throng of clients. The difference between the size of a leading district lawyer's practice and that of the remainder of the bar is extreme and a day or two spent at the home of a leading lawyer leaves the visitor with the impression that half the litigants of the district must be in his hands.

Leading lawyers neither need nor can afford the time for minor informal interaction with colleagues. In the course of his career, a leading lawyer attracts a large number of juniors but these relationships tend to be perfunctory and not the basis of what I have called sets. Two of the leading lawyers of the bar were members of partnerships in the past but in both cases the other partner has died and not been replaced. Three of them have sons who are in practice with them. Although leading lawyers are relatively uninvolved in the formation of cliques, they are involved in the third kind of group I mentioned, the alliance. I conclude this paper with a brief study of a situation which illustrates the formation of alliances, the bar association annual election.

## THE BAR ELECTION: A CASE STUDY

Each year the members of the bar elect a president, vice president, secretary and members of a small committee. The president's duties include giving a tea party to the bar and, more formally, representing it in discussion with the judiciary and the High Court in matters affecting professional conduct. The post is not onerous but it is felt by lawyers and litigants to be a distinctly prestigious one. There is a belief among rural clients (not without some foundation) that office holders in the bar association have more and better extra-juridical access to the judiciary than do other lawyers. As lawyers tell it, the bar association, through its officers, has been able to discipline the judiciary. This has usually involved

getting discourteous magistrates transferred. Indifference to the
bar's self-esteem rather than judicial incompetence seems to have
been the issue that led to these transfers in the cases I know
about.

In the chatting and gossiping of the bar that I have said is an
important part of its ethos, the personalities and idiosyncracies of
fellow members are often brought under review or made the
subject of biting comment. The personalities of leading lawyers
tend to be the main issues at the time of bar elections. It is
appropriate here, therefore, to say something about the personalities involved in this election.

The retiring president was a leading lawyer of the refugee
section—an elderly, conservative, orthodox Sikh whose practice
is an equal mixture of civil and criminal work. His numerous
distant relatives include two or three other lawyers in practice at
the courts. One of these was the outgoing secretary, a young
non-Sikh refugee criminal lawyer whose aggressiveness was said
to have been helpful in getting his elder kinsman elected the year
before. . . .

The key figures in this election (A, B, and C) were three leading
local advocates. In the election of the previous year, B had been
an unsuccessful candidate for president. At first glance, the present
contests appeared to be a struggle between the topmost leading
civil practitioner (A) and one of the two leading criminal lawyers
of the district (C). Neither A nor C accepts any cases outside his
respective specialty, so the question of professional competition
did not on the surface appear to be a relevant issue in the contests.

The 'real' struggle, however, was an indirect one involving A
and B. Both A and B have risen to positions of undoubted regional
fame from similarly humble village backgrounds. The families of
both men were small moneylenders in the days before cooperative
banks, block development and land reform put an end to that
class. In terms of the local-refugee stereotypes discussed above,
both fall well within the local *bania* mold. It is difficult to find
anything markedly modern or unorthodox about their establishments, which are housed in unpretentious and rather cramped
*mohallas* in the center of the town.

Their styles of life contrast sharply with that of the other
candidate, C, one of the two leading criminal lawyers of the
district. He is a Kashmiri Brahmin and not a member of any

sizable local community. His family's large and rather ostentatious house on the outskirts of town is the location of memorable dinners and parties that are modern and rather unorthodox. It is rumored that even with his huge and prosperous practice, he lives beyond his means. His clients include several of the region's biggest businessmen and high government officers enmeshed in corruption proceedings and these people are often guests at his parties. The average practitioner does not play host to his clients in this way, but his is not an average clientele. . . .

In the preliminaries to the election itself—the announcing of candidates, the canvassing for support and the withdrawal (in the contests for lesser posts) of some candidates—there were no discussions of issues. As I have noted, the leaders themselves tended to be the issues. *A*'s rival, *B*, persuaded *C* to stand and then worked on securing support for him among the cliques of the local section.

During the years of rivalry between *A* and *B*, the former has cultivated ties with the refugee section. Occasional assistance to a junior, advice on some legal point, the loan of a lawbook, or accommodation with regard to dates for hearings are among the little acts on which a political alliance can be built among bar members. These favors are more readily dispensed to those who do not constitute a professional threat to the donor, *i.e.*, are not in a position to entice away clients. To cement such alliances it is not necessary or even desirable for two lawyers to spend much time openly chatting together in an informal clique. (And in *A*'s case, his interpretation or enactment of the lawyer identity is so intense that the term 'informal' seems inappropriate when applied to him.)

As *A*'s prestige has increased he has, inevitably, drawn clients away from other civil practitioners. As I have noted, there is a tendency for civil practice to be concentrated in the hands of local practitioners. It is not surprising, then, to find this preeminent local civil lawyer turning toward the refugee section for political support nor to find his rival, *B* (another local civil lawyer), working behind the scenes to seek out and support a prestigious criminal practitioner, *C*. Such an opposition would be least likely to appear based on professional jealousy. The concentration of leading lawyers on the local side of the compound rather limited *B*'s choice of 'pawns.'

Among the alliances that appeared to have been formed for the purposes of this election were those between *B* and *C*; between *A* and an unimportant new member of the bar (discussed below); between *A* and the outgoing president; and between *C* (or *B*) and the outgoing secretary. No doubt there were several others. In none of these alliances was there anything like a set or clique relationship. For example, *B* and *C* are both local, but beyond this have little in common and in the maintenance of their leading lawyer status remain normally somewhat aloof from one another.

On the day of the election, after the customary tea party, polling went quite smoothly until almost the end. Then there occurred an incident which set the bar into an uproar. Several lawyers, perhaps a large part of the bar, had guessed that something of this order would occur.

A young probationer lawyer's application for full membership of the bar had (either by chance or contrivance) come up for approval by the governing body on the morning of the polling day. This young advocate was an ally of *A* (his membership fee had been paid by a lawyer who was contesting for the post of vice president and who was also one of *A*'s allies, being associated with him as junior counsel in a number of cases).

The outgoing president and secretary, who were ex-officio members of the governing body, had developed strained relationships during their year in office. Possibly because of this, the secretary had become a warm supporter of *C* (to whom he felt indebted for help received at the beginning of his career) while the outgoing president had become an ally of *A*. The written minute of the handling of the probationer's application by the governing body was ambiguous. The secretary had wanted his membership approval to be postponed until after the election. The president had favoured giving him full membership before the election and thus the right to vote. When the probationer attempted to collect a ballot paper, he was challenged and the most undignified and seemingly unprofessional row involving a large part of the bar broke out. There was a great deal of vituperation and some threats of assault. There followed, on the spot, an ad hoc council meeting of the brotherhood in which the key figures seemed to be parodying their workaday selves. Just as villagers in their *panchayat* meetings can produce a rather distorted variation on the urban courtroom scene, so, apparently, can lawyers. Eventually the president ruled in favour of the probationer. The polling was completed. *A* beat *C* by only two votes.

## CONCLUSION

Undoubtedly the bar association election could be dismissed as what it certainly was—a storm in a tea cup. I have, however, endeavoured to see it as something more than this by using it to focus the foregoing discussion of the social relations that obtain among lawyers.

It is useful to compare what I have called 'alliances' with what Mayer calls 'action sets' in his analysis of a municipal election in Dewas.[3] Like the action set, the alliance is a purposive creation of an ego for the sole purpose of securing political support. In this respect, the alliance differs from the bar clique or set which need not be political and is often formed with no special end other than companionship in view. The section, of course, is not ego-centred and is an ascribed status group.

Unlike the linkages of an action set, the alliance does not have a variety of possible bases. All the ties that are used in alliances are those created by mutual involvement in the day to day working of the courts. This difference between action set and alliance is, I think, mainly one of complexity and context. Alliances are single relationships in a highly limited context. Action sets are complexes of linkage welded in the course of interaction in a large variety of contexts.

The bar election discussed above was followed a few weeks later by election to the State Legislative Assembly. Several district lawyers contested in various constituencies. When they did so, they enlisted the help of fellow lawyers to such an extent that a participant observed, 'Everyone in the bar is working for someone.' These helpers used their influence to secure votes for their favoured candidates and in doing so formed part of each candidate's action set. In contrast, in the bar association election there was little of this intermediary work: the context is already too small and too highly interactive for many intermediaries to

[3] A.C. Mayer 1966, 1967.

be necessary. Once an ally is made, of course, he is likely to bring his set with him in voting.

Lawyers, legal systems, and the legal profession can be usefully examined at a variety of levels and in several contexts. At the high level of grand theory there are such problems as why societies need lawyers (not all legal systems have them). In this paper I have looked at the other end of the continuum. I have attempted to see what can be said about the social relations that develop among lawyers in a particular legal system, given both the system and the lawyers.

# The Aborted Restoration of 'Indigenous' Law in India*

## MARC GALANTER

Traditional law—Hindu, Muslim and customary—has been almost entirely displaced from the modern Indian legal system. Today, the classical *dharmaśāstra* component of Hindu law is almost completely obliterated. It remains the original source of various rules of family law. But these rules are intermixed with rules from other sources and are administered in the common-law style, isolated from *śāstric* techniques of interpretation and procedure.[1] In other fields of law, *dharmaśāstra* is not employed as a source of precedent, analogy or inspiration. As a procedural—technical system of laws, a corpus of doctrines, techniques and institutions, *dharmaśāstra* is no longer functioning. This is equally true of Muslim law. The local customary component of traditional law is also a source of official rules at a few isolated points, but it too has been abandoned as a living source of law.[2]

'Legal system' and 'law' are employed here in a narrow (but familiar) sense to refer to that governmental complex of institutions, roles and rules which itself provides the authoritative and official definition of what is 'law'. In contemporary India, as in other complex societies, there are myriad agencies for making

* Excerpted from Marc Galanter, 'The Aborted Restoration of "Indigenous" Law in India', *Comparative Studies in Society and History* 1972, 14: 53–70.

[1] On the fate of *dharmaśāstra*, see Derrett (1961); Galanter (1968).

[2] On the role of custom in the courts, see Jain (1963); Kane (1950); Roy (1911).

rules and settling disputes which lie outside of the legal system as narrowly and authoritatively defined. Many matters are regulated by traditional legal norms; tribunals of the traditional type continue to function in many areas and among many groups, but without governmental force. The point here is that they have been displaced from the official system, powerfully influenced by it and in many cases entirely supplanted by it. The official legal system comprises laws, techniques, institutions and roles which are, with few exceptions, modifications of British or other western models.

The first part of this paper examines briefly the failure—or perhaps containment is more accurate—of post-Independence attempts to replace the present legal system with revived indigenous law. The second part attempts to explain this failure and to suggest its implications for the comparative study of legal systems.

## I

The dichotomy between the official law and popular legality[3] has been the theme of a continuing stream of criticism from administrators, nationalists and students of Indian society, who have emphasized the unsuitability of British-style law in India. . . . Administrators and observers have blamed the legal system for promoting a flood of interminable and wasteful litigation, for encouraging perjury and corruption, and generally exacerbating disputes by eroding traditional consensual methods of dispute-resolution. The indictment was familiar by the mid-nineteenth century:

> . . . in lieu of this simple and rational mode of dispensing justice, we have given the natives an obscure, complicated, pedantic system of English law, full of 'artificial technicalities', which . . . force them to have recourse to a swarm of attorneys . . . that is . . . *professional rogues* . . . by means of which we have taught an ingenious people to refine upon the quibbles and fictions of English lawyers . . . . The course of justice, civil as well as criminal, is utterly confounded in a maze of artifice and fraud, and the natives, both high and low, are becoming more and more demoralized. . . . [4]

[3] For analysis of the dissonance between British and Indian notions of legality, see Cohn (1959); Rudolph and Rudolph (1965).

[4] Dickinson (1853: 46).

In the nationalist movement, there were similar complaints, issuing in proposals for the restoration of indigenous justice. There was hostility to the courts as an agency of British control, and the civil disobedience movements of 1920–2 and 1931 included attempts to boycott the official courts and to organize truly Indian tribunals which would work by conciliation, relying on moral suasion rather than coercive sanctions. The misgivings of some nationalists about the legal system were succinctly expressed by a Gandhian publicist in 1946, who accused the British system of working havoc in India by replacing quick, cheap and efficient *panchayat* justice with expensive and slow courts which promote endless dishonesty and degrade public morality.[5] . . .

The Constituent Assembly (1947–9) contained no spokesmen for a restoration of *dharmaśāstra*, nor for a revival of local customary law as such. An attempt by Gandhians and 'traditionalists' to form a polity based on village autonomy and self-sufficiency was rejected by the Assembly, which opted for a federal and parliamentary republic with centralized bureaucratic administration.[6] The only concession to the Gandhians was a Directive Principle in favor of village *panchayats* as units of local self-government.[7] The existing legal system was retained intact, new powers granted to the judiciary and its independence enhanced by elaborate protections. All in all, Constitution amounted to an endorsement of the existing legal system.

In the early years of Independence there was much open discussion of the need for large-scale reform of the legal system. There was some outspoken criticism that the system was entirely unsuited to Indian conditions and should be radically altered or abandoned.[8] . . .

[5] Agarwal (1946: 97, 100, 131). (In his Foreword to this volume M.K. Gandhi said 'There is nothing in it which has jarred me as inconsistent with what I would like to stand for'.)

[6] On the rejection of the village alternative, see Austin (1966: chap. 2). . . .

[7] Art. 40 provides: The State shall take steps to organize village *panchayats* and endow them with such powers and authority as may be necessary to enable them to function as units of self-government.

[8] During this period the legal system was also under attack from another direction by those who regarded the courts as obstacles to rapid reform and development and saw lawyers as agents of delay and obfuscation in the service of narrow private interests. Such sentiments were present in the highest places. E.g., in the debate over the First Amendment, Prime Minister Nehru complained:

The most prominent and politically potent of these critics were Gandhians and socialists within the ruling Congress party, who supported a revival of *panchayat* justice. . . . Restoration of *panchayats* was proposed as one phase of the reconstruction of India's villages, in which faction and conflict, bred by colonial oppression, would be replaced by harmony and conciliation. Critical discussion focused almost exclusively on adjectival law—on court administration (delay, expense, corruption), complexity of procedure, unsuitability of rules of evidence, the adversarial rather than conciliatory character of the proceedings, and (occasionally) the nature of penalties. Although different personnel and procedures might be expected to entail different bases of decision, there was virtually no discussion of 'substantive law'.

This movement had little support among legal professionals.[9] Lawyers and judges agreed that the system displayed serious defects—perjury, delay, proliferation of appeals, expense. But they did not attribute its shortcomings to its foreignness. Except for a measure of decentralization for petty cases, they rejected the notion that the remedy lay in a return to indigenous forms. Almost without exception, the profession viewed the Anglo-Indian law as a most beneficent result of the British connection. . . . While many lawyers called for re-examination and even radical reformation of the legal system, almost none could perceive any advantage in reversion to pre-British models. . . .

Proposals for an indigenous system were among the many matters taken up by the Law Commission in its full-survey of the administration of justice in 1958. The Commission found that even a brief depiction of the ancient system

---

'Somehow . . . this magnificent Constitution that we have framed was later kidnapped and purloined by the lawyers.' Parliamentary Debates XII–XIII (Part II) Col. 8832 (May 16, 1951). Proposals that judicial processes be replaced by administrative tribunals from which lawyers were to be excluded were common and frequently acted upon. See Law Commission 1958: 671 ff. This 'left' criticism tended to share with the Gandhian its unflattering estimate of lawyers.

[9] The most prominent exception was the eminent advocate (later Home Minister and Governor) Dr K.N. Katju. See Katju (1948); Malaviya (1956: 781). Dr Katju was also a member of the Congress Village Panchayat Committee which proposed a cautious program of giving *panchayats* small-cause powers and emphasized their conciliatory aspects of settling disputes by persuasion and advice. All-India Congress Committee (1954: 40).

shows how unsound is the oft-repeated assertion that the present system is alien to our genius. . . . [It] is easy to see that in its essentials even the ancient Hindu system comprised those features which every reasonably minded person would acknowledge as essential features of any system of judicial administration, whether British or other. . . . We can even hazard the view that had the ancient system been allowed to develop normally, it would have assumed a form not very much different from the one that we follow today.[10]

The Commission notes that the attraction of the indigenous system lay not in the intricacies of classical textual law but in the simplicity and dispatch of popular tribunals that applied customary law. But it finds it unthinkable that such courts could be expected to cope with the complexities of the law in a modern welfare state:

No one can assert that in the conditions which govern us today the replacement of professional courts by courts of the kind that existed in the remote past can be thought of. . . . We cannot see how the noble aims enshrined in the Preamble to our Constitution can ever be realized unless we have a hierarchy of courts, a competent judiciary and well-defined rules of procedure.[11]

While rejecting any fundamental change in system, the Commission indicates that to a limited extent it might be possible to utilize some of the simple features of judicial administration that obtained in the past in the form of judicial *panchayats*. Reviving or establishing popular village tribunals had been recommended by many bodies throughout the British period and such tribunals had been established in some places. After surveying their accomplishments the Law Commission recommended the establishment of *panchayats* with simplified procedure and exclusive jurisdiction over petty matters.[12]

In the late 1950s the Government adopted the policy of community development, whereby elective village *panchayats* were established as instruments of village self-government in the hope that they would increase initiative and participation in economic development. The eager promotion of these administrative *panchayats* secured the acceptance of judicial *panchayats* in almost all states.[13] Either the administrative *panchayats* themselves

[10] Government of India, Ministry of Law (1958: I, 29–30).
[11] Ibid., 30–1.
[12] Ibid., chap. 43.
[13] The basic policy study is by Ministry of Law (Government of India, 1962).

or allied bodies, elected directly or indirectly, were given judicial responsibilities in specified categories of petty cases. Almost uniformly lawyers were barred from appearing before these tribunals.

The establishment of judicial *panchayats* was officially urged in the hope of resolving the alienation of the villager from the legal system. . . . Although the establishment of these judicial *panchayats* derived sentimental and symbolic support from the appeal to the virtues of the indigenous system, it should be clear that these new tribunals are quite a different sort of body than traditional *panchayats*. The new judicial panchayats are selected by popular election from clear territorial constituencies, they are fixed in membership, they decide by majority vote rather than a rule of unanimity; they are required to conform to and apply statutory law; they are supported by the government in the compulsory execution of their decrees; these decrees may be tested in the regular courts.[14]

As might be expected, judicial *panchayats* enjoy little favor with bar and bench. . . . In reviewing their work on appeal, courts have tolerated some departure from ordinary judicial procedures, but they have also restricted the powers and discretion of *panchayats*. In particular, the exclusion of lawyers in cases where a party has been arrested for a crime has been held unconstitutional by the Supreme Court.

The reception of judicial *panchayats* by villagers awaits systematic study. Little is known, e.g., about the kinds of cases *panchayats* are hearing, the classes that are using them, the law being applied, the impact of revisions by regular courts, the development of local expertise. It is often claimed that *panchayats* have reduced litigation in the countryside and it is clear that they have to some extent relocated it and probably made it less expensive. But it is not clear that the there has been any strong movement away from the courts in favor of *panchayats*.[15]

Like the traditional *panchayats*, the statutory ones seem to face

---

For a concise survey of developments, see Ministry of Food, etc. (Government of India, 1966).

[14] On the contrast of the new statutory *panchayats* with traditional village *panchayats*, see Retzlaff (1962: 23 ff.); Luschinsky (1963b: 73).

[15] E.g., in a survey of government officers in the field conducted by the Rajasthan Study Team, almost two-thirds did not believe *nyaya panchayats* had led to a reduction of litigation (Government of Rajasthan, 1964: 336).

severe problems of establishing their independence of personal ties with the parties,[16] of enforcing their decrees,[17] and acting as expeditiously as it was hoped they would.[18] A recent survey found it 'remarkable that rural respondents favoured a greater degree of supervision and control by the Government . . . over their functioning'.[19]

Judicial *panchayats* invite comparison with Paul Brass's findings about Indian medicine, which he sees undergoing a dual modernization, in which the growth of 'modern medicine' in the western style is accompanied by a 'revival' of the indigenous schools of medicine. He finds that this revival is really another stream of modernization which he calls 'traditionalization', i.e., a movement that uses traditional symbols and pursues traditional values, but engages in technological and organizational 'modernization'.[20] Village *panchayats* fit Brass's model of 'traditionalization': the traditional *panchayat* symbolism and values of harmonious reconciliation and local control and participation are combined with many organizational and technical features borrowed from the modern legal system—statutory rules, specified jurisdiction, fixed personnel, salaries, elections, written records, etc. The movement to *panchayats* then is not a restoration of traditional law, but its containment and absorption; not an abandonment of the modern legal system, but its extension in the guise of tradition.

## II

Why was the movement for indigenous justice so readily contained? Why did the proponents of indigenous law settle for what is hardly more than the marginal popularization of existing law? Let us look at the actors, goals and issues in the 'dispute'.

[16] Robins (1962: 245). Malaviya (1956: 432).

[17] Purwar (1960: 225).

[18] Purwar (1960: 220). . . . It should be noted that the expeditiousness (and cheapness) of indigenous justice are at least partly legendary. For example, under the Mahrattas, cases concerning land tenure might take from two to twelve years and perhaps half of the cases were never decided. See 'Lunsden's report on the Judicial Administration of the Peshwas' (1819), reprinted in Gune (1953: 373 ff.). As to expense, see Gune (1953: 86, 131).

[19] G.S. Sharma (1967: 19).

[20] Brass (1969).

First, the present legal system was supported by a numerous and influential class of lawyers . . . who were fully committed to the system, had a heavy personal stake in its continuance, and were genuinely convinced of its general virtue[21] and that re-vivalism was a threat to them as well as a mistake for the country.[22] On the other hand, there was no organized body of carriers of the proposed alternative, no educational institutions to produce them and no existing group whose occupational prospects might be advanced. (In all of these, traditional law stands in contrast to *ayurvedic* medicine). . . .

Second, the proponents of an indigenous system presented no vivid alternative. Contrast, for example, movements for replacing one language with another, where there is an alternative that is palpable to all and clearly promises advantage, symbolic if not tangible, to many. Here, the proponents themselves were not moved by a lively sense of what the alternative might be.

*Dharmaśāstra*, of course, was one alternative, an elaborate and sophisticated body of legal learning. But any proposal in this direction would run foul of some of Independent India's most central commitments. It would violate her commitment to a secular state, insuring equal participation to religious minorities. Furthermore, *dharmaśāstra's* emphasis on graded inequality would run counter to the principle of equality and would encounter widespread opposition to the privileged position of the higher castes. Indeed, the one area where *dharmaśāstra* retained some legal force, Hindu family law, was in the early 1950s being subjected to thoroughgoing reform which largely abandoned the *śāstra* in favour of a Hindu law built on modern notions.[23] Thus,

---

21 An eminent advocate (now Vice-President) who had been a member of the 1958 Law Commission recalled five years later that ' . . . after a comparative study of the various systems prevailing in other countries [we] reached the conclusion that the British system which we had adopted was the best. This system secured greater and more enduring justice than any other system'. He went on to warn that 'Ideas from the foreign countries may be borrowed and adopted in our system. But it will be dangerous to introduce innovations which will result in radical changes. They may not fit in with our system which had been a part of our national life for a long time' (G.S. Pathak in Sen *et al.*, 1964: 80–1).

22 On the size, eminence and influence of the legal profession, see Galanter (1968–9) and the various contributions to *Law and Society Review* (1968–9).

23 On these reforms, see Derrett (1958); on the crucial role of lawyers in producing them, see Levy (1968–9).

it is hardly surprising that none of the leading documents sup-porting *nyaya panchayats* even mentions *dharmaśāstra.* . . . It was not an available alternative for practical application.

Nor was the local customary component of traditional law a likely candidate. Customary law with its innovative, quasi-legisla-tive element restored would be a formidable counterweight to national unity, mutual intelligibility, free movement and inter-change. It had no evident capacity to contend with nationwide problems and projects. Although there were vestiges of such traditional law extant, there was no pronounced widespread admiration for its contemporary representatives. Indeed they were in at least as bad popular repute as the courts.[24]

Yet another alternative, a creative synthesis of Indian and Western, blending the best of both into a new system adapted to India's needs and aspirations, was easy to call for, but hard not only to produce, but to portray. Such a call was not without appeal to lawyers, but they were disinclined to abandon the existing system pending its arrival.[25]

Third, the revivalist cause was not attached to any concrete grievance that could mobilize popular support. Court delay and expense were not adequate issues for this purpose. It was hard to attach organized personal or political ambition to them. Ap-parently the symbolic gratifications to be had from restoration of indigenous law were not sufficiently appealing to any significant sections of the population. On the other hand, the interests that were threatened were concrete and tangible and defended by organized and articulate groups.

We may ask then why actors, goals and issues were in such short supply, compared, for example, to linguistic changeover movements or even the *ayurvedic* movement described by Brass. Ironically it appears that the answer is that the legal system was

---

[24] For example, Berreman (1963: 271–2, 281–2) reports that villagers have little faith in the objectivity of *panchayats* and avoid using them, especially in property disputes, on grounds that they would decide wholly in terms of self-interest. Contemporary *panchayats* seem to experience the same difficulties with tutored witnesses as do the official courts. . . .

[25] 'It would be folly to throw away what we have acquired and start a search for something which may prove elusive and which may result in atavistic retrogression. . . . We must retain the present system as long as we are unable to replace it . . . with a superior one . . . that is at the same time more acceptable to . . . our sense of justice . . . our common man' (Misra, 1954: 49).

so thoroughly domesticated. That is, indigenization on the ideological/programmatic level failed because the law had become 'indigenous' on the operational/adaptive level.

The law and the society had adapted to each other in several ways. The law itself underwent considerable adaptation. British institutions and rules were combined with structural features (e.g., a system of separate personal laws) and rules (e.g., *dharma-śāstra*, local custom) which accorded with indigenous understanding. The borrowed elements underwent more than a century and a half of pruning in which British localisms and anomalies were discarded and rules elaborated to deal with new kinds of persons, property and transactions.[26] By omission, substitution, simplification, elaboration, the law was modified to make it 'suitable to Indian conditions'.[27]

The numerous body of legal professionals were, almost without exception, so thoroughly committed to the existing system that it was difficult for them to visualize a very different kind of legal system. Its shortcomings were seen as remediable defects and blemishes, not as basic flaws which required fundamental change. To lawyers the system seemed fully Indian. . . .

The lawyers not only disseminated the official norms, but served as links or middlemen, putting the law in the service of a wide variety of groups in the society and providing new organizational forms for forwarding a variety of interests. The lawyers were the carriers of what we might call an all-India legal culture which provided personnel, techniques and standards for carrying on public business in a way that was nationally intelligible. Thus the legal system and the lawyer supplied much of the idiom of public life. To the lawyers and the nationally oriented educated class of whom they formed a significant part, the legal system was

[26] Special adaptations of common law to suit Indian conditions include, e.g., in the criminal law the elaborate protection of religious places and feelings, the different treatment of bigamy, adultery, false evidence and defamation; in contract law, treatment of duress and agreements in restraint of trade. See Lipstein (1957: 74–5); Acharyya (1914: Lecture III); Setalvad (1960: chaps. 2–3). Examples of distinctive 'Indian common law' may be found in Setalvad (1960: 59–60); Acharyya (1914: 38, 136).

[27] Derrett's (1969) provocative assessment of the carryover of traditional elements in contemporary Indian law includes a series of interesting examples of ways in which modern legislation (on, e.g., safety, welfare and employment) gives expression to traditional normative concerns.

the embodiment and instrument of the working principles of the new India—equality, freedom, secularism, national uniformity, modernity.

In a very different way, villagers are also at home in this legal system. At least, they are neither as radically isolated from the system nor as passive as they appear to some critics of the present system. Villagers . . . utilize both 'indigenous' and official law in accordance with their own calculations of propriety and advantage.[28]

[ . . . ]

The displacement of indigenous law from the official legal system does not mean the demise of traditional norms or concerns. The official system provides new opportunities for pursuing these, at the same time that it helps to transform them.[29] There is no automatic correspondence between the forum, the motive for using it and the effect of such use; both official courts and indigenous tribunals may be used for a variety of purposes. Official law can be used not only to evade traditional restrictions, but to enforce them.[30] Resort to official courts can be had in order to disrupt a traditional *panchayat*,[31] or to stimulate it into action. Official law can be used to vindicate traditional interests,[32] caste tribunals may be used to promote change.[33]

Not only are villagers capable of using the official courts for their own ends, but they have assimilated many elements of official law into the workings of indigenous tribunals. Nicholas and Mukhopadhyay, in their study of two Bengal villages, report that 'almost all persons have had some experience in . . . the government court, and the form of village legal proceedings is modelled after this experience. Stress is laid upon evidence such as eye-witness accounts, written documents, markings of injury, correct description of a stolen article'.[34]

---

[28] Srinivas (*c*. 1964). . . .

[29] On the role of law (and lawyers) in providing new modes of caste organization and activity, see McCormack (1966). More generally, Derrett (1968) argues that in spite of superficial discontinuities, modern legal concepts and institutions provide a vehicle for the authentic continuation of Hindu tradition.

[30] E.g., Srinivas (*c*. 1964: 90).

[31] E.g., Lynch (1967: 153).

[32] Derrett (1964); Ishwaran (1964: 243); Luschinsky (1963a).

[33] Cohn (1965: 98–9, 101).

[34] Nicholas and Mukhopadhyay (1962: 21).

Traditional law, either absorbed into the official system or displaced from it, has been transformed along the lines of the official model. As I have argued elsewhere, the attrition of traditional law resulted not from the normative superiority of British law, but from its technical, organizational and ideological characteristics, which accomplished the replacement and transformation of traditional law half inadvertently.[35]

The Indian experience suggests a set of counter-propositions. It suggests that neither an abrupt historical break nor the lack of historical roots prevents a borrowed system from becoming so securely established that its replacement by a revived indigenous system is very unlikely. It suggests that a legal system of the modern type may be sufficiently independent of other social and cultural systems that it may flourish for long periods while maintaining a high degree of dissonance with central cultural values. It suggests that a legal system may be disparate internally, embodying inconsistent norms and practices in different levels and agencies.

These counter-propositions point to the need for some refinement of familiar notions of what legal systems are normally like. Specifically, they point to the desirability of disaggregation: we need to find ways of asking how various parts of the legal system are related to different sectors of the society.

If a legal system need not be historically emergent from its society, what are the mechanisms by which it becomes 'rooted'? How does it secure acceptance and support from crucial sections of the population? If a legal system can persist without pervasive support from other social institutions (or global agreement with cultural norms), what are the specific links that connect it with other institutions and norms and what are the mechanisms that maintain its segregation from them? If a legal system is not itself a normative monolith, what are the mechanisms that permit a variety of norms and standards to flourish? How are widely

---

[35] Galanter (1966, 1968). The introduction of new opportunities into India's compartmented society generated numerous disputes that were not resolvable by the earlier decentralized dispute-settling mechanism, which relied on local power for enforcement and enjoyed only intermittent and remote external support. British law and courts fostered and filled a demand for near-at-hand authority that could draw upon power external to the immediate setting of the dispute.

disparate practices accommodated? It is submitted that the discontinuities observed in the Indian case should not be dismissed as exceptional or pathological, but should be taken as the basis for hypotheses for probing some of the general characteristics of legal systems that are often obscured in our view of societies closer to home.

# Courts and Conflict in an Indian City: A Study in Legal Impact*

## ROBERT L. KIDDER

The impact of legal norms has long been a central question in the sociology of law. Beyond the problem of describing the type of impact created by particular legal norms is the more fundamental question of whether those norms have any impact at all relative to their intended effect. The apparently simple question of impact directs the sociologist into some of the most basic questions concerning the relationship between legal norms and their implementing agencies, legal norms and cultural values, legal norms and normative change, and the functions of the specifically legal in a complex social system.

In the study of India's legal system the question of legal impact has been central because much evidence has been interpreted to show a significant hiatus between legal norms and the behaviour of both citizens and legal personnel, especially in the area of civil litigation. A frequently expressed popular explanation of this hiatus has been that the legal institutions are 'foreign' to Indians, that they were introduced by foreign administrators who could not comprehend Indian genius, that apparent 'deviance' of responses to legal norms is due to the inability of foreign institutions to adapt to local social conditions.

. . . Bernard Cohn has summarized this 'culture conflict' view as follows:

* Excerpted from Robert L. Kidder, 'Courts and Conflict in an Indian City: A Study in Legal Impact', *Journal of Commonwealth Political Studies*, 1973, 11: 121–39.

It is my thesis that the present attitude of the Indian peasant (a slot machine attitude towards litigation) was an inevitable consequence of the British decision to establish courts in India patterned on British procedural law. The way a people settles disputes is part of its social structure and value system. In attempting to introduce British procedural law into their Indian courts, the British confronted the Indians with a situation in which there was a direct clash of the values of the two societies; and the Indians in response thought only of manipulating the new situation and did not use the courts to settle disputes but only to further them.[1]

The 'direct clash' occurs specifically because, according to Cohn, Indian peasants value inequality in the eyes of authority, status as a basis of relationships, compromise as the object of dispute-settling mechanisms, and diffuse definitions of relevant relationships. His thesis is that British legal institutions based on values of equality, contract, decisiveness, and specificity directly violated local values and were therefore incapable of achieving the kind of legal impact he assumes was intended. At the heart of this analysis is the assertion that a society's legal norms must closely reflect its non-legal, 'cultural' norms in order to be effective in that society.

In this article I report on research which raises serious questions about the 'culture conflict' explanation for patterns of court use in India. I shall demonstrate that the behaviour of litigants can be understood in terms of situational and structural pressures and opportunities which can exert their influence specifically because litigants accept and value the courts as adjudicators of legal rights. I argue that, if formal legal provisions are not having their intended impact on the relations between litigants, the explanation lies in the relationship of those provisions to the social structure of the judicial system rather than in their incongruity with indigenous values.[2]

---

[1] B.S. Cohn 1959; also in this volume.

[2] The research reported here was conducted in 1969 and 1970 in the courts of Bangalore, Mysore, with supplementary observations made in lesser courts in outlying districts. The method was eclectic and inductive, consisting mainly of systematic field observation. I kept verbatim notes of a great variety of courtroom situations which I observed repeatedly. Similar notes were made of conversations with lawyers. Since my grasp of Tamil and Kannada was inadequate I employed a number of assistants and interviewers to gather different kinds of data. In

## LITIGATION AND CONFLICT RESOLUTION

One approach to the study of legal impact is to compare observed practices with intended results. Litigation in Bangalore is formally structured as a process of adjudication. Analysis of my data, however, indicates that the operation of formally adjudicative structures has the effect of fostering negotiated outcomes dependent on the strategies of the conflicting parties rather than the decisive actions of judicial authority.

### THE ADJUDICATIVE MODEL

Adjudication is a service theoretically provided in Bangalore by a hierarchically organised, nationally integrated court system which shares many common grounds with the conceptual framework upon which English law has developed. In ideal-typical terms, adjudication is conceived as a process of fact-sifting and law-interpreting designed to elicit a final truth which justifies a decision favouring only one of the conflicting positions. In this it

---

addition to my own interviews with English-speaking litigants I employed a multilingual law student with several years' experience as a court clerk to conduct partially structured interviews with non-English-speaking litigants whom he selected by casual contact at the court over a four-month period. He kept detailed notes of his conversations with these litigants and I kept my own notes of my conversations with him about his interviews. Additional notes come from conversations with law teachers and students who completed questionnaires for me. Local lawyers generally refused to reply to questionnaires in writing but many were stimulated by the questions to seek me out and try to give me a 'true picture' of their work. I also conducted extensive interviews with over thirty caste association leaders in Bangalore, in which I probed the extent and type of their involvement with courts, lawyers, and litigation. In the process I obtained much useful information about the inter-relationships between their positions as caste leaders and their leadership roles in several other groups. Further information came from off the cuff remarks recorded by seven interviewers during a sample survey of Bangalore designed to study the degree of people's involvement with litigation. This information is, like all the other data analysed here, used as a complementary means of understanding the actor's 'definition of the situation'. It is not used deductively as a statistical test of a hypothesis so it is not necessary to deal with the sampling technique, except to say that the notes were based on 1770 interviews with 'heads of households' in a representative cross-section of Bangalore's residential districts.

differs from a mediational model because in mediation facts and law are secondary to the expediency of achieving a common ground of settlement between conflicting interests. The assumption underlying adjudication is that only one side can have a correct legal claim.

As a model of conflict resolution, the adjudicative model tenders a hypothesis about the impact of its operations, namely that final judgements will have the following effects: (i) the winner receives the exact and full relief due him; (ii) the loser accepts his loss, willingly or otherwise, and creates no further trouble; (iii) the rest of society feels content that its values have been sustained; and (iv) social actors will no longer make the mistaken assumptions upon which the loser's cause was based.

This model is the *formal* context within which law is experienced by litigants. It provides the language and logical structure within which all actions concerning litigation must publicly be rationalised. One approach to the study of the impact of this legal apparatus would be to compare actual litigation against this model.

## LITIGATION AS NEGOTIATION

The research reported here indicates that actual procedures, attitudes, and responses to court-oriented activity and opportunity have produced a process better understood as negotiation—in fact, a process which in many ways contradicts the adjudicatory model. In brief the skills developed by the various specialists of legal administration and the interest structure which has evolved within and around the bureaucracies of legal administration have produced a maze of such intricate and unstable practices and relationships that the legal system cannot provide predictable, decisive, final outcomes through knowledge of, and appeal to, 'the law' in Bangalore. Instead, civil litigation has become a field of battle with great leeway for innovation and surprise. Strategies of conflict are constantly emerging as older ones become useless through over-exposure. Entrepreneurial attitudes and skills become recognised as assets, even perhaps qualities essential for success in the system.

The result is a system which satisfies the formal interests of the law as a separate institution dependent for survival on continual public reaffirmation of its values, while profoundly altering its actual social function. The social process of litigation has produced a mechanism for prolonged negotiations based on a utilitarian manipulation of every resource, both personal and organisational, made available by the court system. Compromise is the most predictable product of this process, even where, as is often the case, compromise is what actors are consciously trying to avoid.

By the term 'negotiation', I mean something more than the kind of self-conscious, face-to-face, or mediated search for common ground between conflicting interests which is involved in descriptions of union-management contract negotiations. 'Negotiation' as used here is more akin to the kind of implicit exchange meant by Scheff in his concept, the 'negotiation of reality'.[3] It does not always include explicit proposals or a search for common grounds. At certain stages there may be no recognition of the process as negotiation. But the inability of the judicial system independently to produce a conclusion in disputes is the essential ingredient in the pattern of negotiations.

The negotiation which occurs through the process of civil litigation in Bangalore is carried on by indirection. Litigants do not usually even recognise it as negotiation and for that reason they neither carry on direct discussions with opponents nor invoke mediational services from the great variety of actors (judges, lawyers, clerks, touts) who could act as mediators. Instead negotiation consists of continual tactical manoeuvres carried on by each litigant. Stances are adopted and legal manoeuvres selected, not only in view of their potential for 'success' in the legal sense, but with an expectation about the way in which the opponent will interpret the action. Each side is concerned with demonstrating to the other just how far he will go. The great variety of manoeuvres available through court procedures and social networks provide a complex repertoire of gestures for the gradual escalation of pressure. . . .

What distinguishes litigation as an arena of negotiation is that its formal rationale denies the grounds for the compromise which is its most predictable product. Further, most of the tactics obtain their bargaining credibility from their relationship to formally

[3] T.J. Scheff 1968: 3–17.

adjudicative provisions and practices. I shall argue that, contrary to the 'culture conflict' argument, the court system draws new customers specifically because of its ideology of legal-moral absolutes and that its actual functional impact arises from its failure to match this ideological stance. Specifically, while compromise may remain an important cultural value, novice litigants see litigation as their only alternative against an uncompromising opponent. But the apparatus of legal justice to which they appeal has become so differentiated and entwined with the contradictions of conflicting interests, that it is incapable of asserting an effective authoritative stance independent of the strategies of its constituent actors. . . .

## BASES OF NEGOTIATION

How can a litigant bargain with his opponent without direct or mediated contact? What are the devices of manipulation provided by the courts? What are the lessons of negotiation which a novice must learn? The room for manoeuvre is provided by relationships and procedures operating at several levels simultaneously. These can be grouped according to their relationship to the adversary process, procedural regulations, and the social network of actors involved in processing of cases.

### THE ADVERSARY PROCESS

Adversarial proceedings are justified by the theory that facts and relevant law concealed by one of the opponents will be aired by the other, thus aiding the search for truth on which to base a judgment. In practice this has created fertile grounds for a proliferation of techniques aimed at manipulating official definitions of reality and law. My data reveal over and over that one of the most salient features of litigation for novice litigants is the gap they experience between their subjective understandings about their cases and the steps they become convinced are necessary in order to achieve a satisfactory official definition of reality.

The more legitimate of these methods relates to the work of lawyers who become perceived by litigants as masters of mystification and contrivance. The litigant finds himself becoming a party to such practices as coaching, which means detailed instructions from the lawyer concerning what should and should not be said in testimony. Both lawyers and clients reported the critical importance of adhering to the agreed story in testimony. There are numerous stories which pass among litigants concerning the almost demonic skills of some lawyers whose cross-examinations can destroy even the most honest witness. The litigant must learn to lay aside his common sense intuition about what to say and instead follow the lawyer's reconstructed case unswervingly.

Related to this is the fact that the litigant finds himself following his lawyer down a path of fact reconstruction which violates his own common-sense understanding about sequences of events, factual relevance, and obvious conclusions. In one case, for example, a group of Muslim litigants were seeking compensation for farm lands taken by the government to expand Bangalore's suburbs. Their lawyer was tracing their claim on the lands back to grants which had been made just after Tippu Sultan's defeat by the British in the late eighteenth century. The litigants themselves knew nothing of this history. They knew only that they had been farming the land as far back as their oldest member could recall. But they were engaged in a joint effort with their lawyer to construct a story about their claim which far surpassed any of their expectations prior to their litigation. Of course, such a case also illustrates the tremendous scope of 'reality' which could serve rival theories about claims to the land.

Another source of scope for factual manipulation arises from the typically poor documentation of many claims. One lawyer for example described the considerable confusion he had encountered arising from the fact that Hindu marriages are not formally registered. Where cases depend on proof of completed marriage vows the trial can turn into a battle of witnesses since there is no documentation. Considering the intimate links between Indian family and property rights, one can begin to get a sense of the scope this situation provides for the pursuit of rival definitions of reality.

[ . . . ]

Supplementing their own lies, litigants and lawyers reported what they considered to be a widespread practice of hiring professional witnesses. In our survey we even discovered one respondent who explained his unusually frequent court appearances as being performances paid for by his local police headquarters to strengthen their cases. . . .

Documentary manipulation and the bribing of court functionaries were related processes described by many respondents. In one case a litigant and his lawyer succeeded in strengthening their case by having the courts declare as false eighteen years of tax records upon which their opponent was resting his case. Such adulteration was only one example of what many litigants and lawyers felt could be done with official records if the 'gift' to the record-keeper was adequate. In fact my interviewer kept verbatim records of conversations he overheard in which a village headman was carefully instructing six fellow villagers on ways to invent records and evidence and on which clerks were approachable for what purposes. These lessons included trial approaches to various offices, some of which the interviewer observed.

Since a whole host of clerks, peons, and administrators preside over the machinery of documentation, fee payments, filing procedures, scheduling and general court administration, they control the ease and accuracy by which definitions of reality are introduced into litigation. As one lawyer said:

> . . . you see, there are so many regulations just for these filings. For example, the margins must be two inches on either side and three inches from the top and like that there are so many things. And he will say 'Look here, this is only one and a half inches, you go do it again'. So like that, unless you give him something then you will not get the filing on the proper date and your client will be angry.

[ . . . ]

Related to the bribe is the exercise of 'influence'—that diffuse web of obligations built up over a long period of time between persons with repeated contact in a variety of social settings or role sets. Kinship and caste may be grounds for influence of this kind. Litigants develop a keen vigilance against it and there is evidence that they take action to protect themselves from it. For example, in interviewing members of one caste association which had litigation pending, I heard repeatedly that, although their own fellow caste members were practicing law, none of them could develop a clientele from within the caste because they were perceived as lacking adequate influence. Instead they all preferred Brahmin lawyers, not for their expertise, ritual purity, oratorical skill, or general superiority, but specifically because of their supposed influence. Checking this theory, I discovered that indeed in every case I observed involving members of this caste only Brahmin lawyers were used. The most extreme attempt I encountered at influencing reality definitions in litigation concerned a lawyer who was eventually convicted of murdering witnesses whose testimony was likely to damage his clients. He was known among Bangalore litigants as a powerful and fearsome lawyer and his techniques were treated as understandable, though extreme, in view of the demands and opportunities of judicial justice.

Courtroom justice, however, requires more from the litigant than mere control over reality definitions. These definitions must be constructed in such a way that they coincide with a favourable legal theory. The question of relevant law actually becomes another battleground which offers great scope for bargaining manoeuvres. Litigants, for example, showed high sensitivity to questions of precedent. A frequent claim of novice litigants was that they had 'all the cases' on their side. More experienced litigants, however, regarded such claims as foolishly naive because their experience had exposed them to the great battles of precedent that take place in court. A common sight in court is a lawyer standing behind a deep pile of law reports, laboriously reading case after case in support of his client's case. Disappointed clients frequently blamed their lawyer's laziness for their loss—they remain convinced that just a bit more search would have produced the decisive case in their favour. Many such clients were found actually switching lawyers on these grounds, so of course lawyers feel pressed to weight their performances with as many citations as the judge will tolerate.

[ . . . ]

To paraphrase Berger and Luckman,[4] the adversary process revolves around negotiations aimed at a 'legal construction of reality'. The great scope for manipulation within this constructive process creates the discretionary space upon which bargaining contingencies thrive.

---

[4] Berger and Luckmann 1966.

## PROCEDURAL REGULATIONS AND OPTIONS

Such theory manipulation represents only one level of opportunity in litigation for the development of bargaining positions. Regardless of the success or failure of any one theory, procedural provisions constitute a vast set of opportunities for the avoidance of adjudicative effects. The salience of these provisions is reflected in the great array of comments we received concerning delay in courts.

There is no absolute definition of delay in reference to litigation. It is a subjective term which reflects a contrast between expectations of swift, decisive justice and the actual experience of drawn-out manoeuvring. However, a variety of evidence from Bangalore lends rather convincing support to the laments of frustrated litigants. . . . Two factions of a caste association were contesting the propriety of the leading faction's use of funds for the construction of a memorial hall. The dispute arose in 1950 as an internal political battle and moved into the courts in 1954. The trial courts gave a ruling in 1960, one appeal was concluded in 1963, a second appeal in 1964, and another appeal in 1970 at which I was present. In a neighbouring town a well-known case involved two neighbours who had been fighting each other for twenty-five years over a strip of dirt three feet wide which ran between two houses. The only thing that surprised people about the case was that they would fight so tenaciously over such useless land. The twenty-five year figure alone did not seem unusual. . . .

These are just illustrations of the kinds of delay that are possible in the Bangalore courts. The variety and number of such cases which we discovered indicates that people do regularly avail themselves of the opportunity to prolong cases and avoid final official action. For at least some major forms of litigation, there is never a point at which it is possible to maintain that all legal remedies have been exhausted, that a 'loser' has been totally defeated.

Even more important than the absolute duration of cases, however, is the fact that litigants experience them as delay and regularly express either frustration or satisfaction (depending on whose advantage is served) over them. Most important, these expressions of frustration or satisfaction were a direct result of the respondent's interpretation of delay as being the intentional product of a shrewd litigant. That is, 'delay' always reflected a perceived gap between what the courts could do if allowed to act and what they were actually able to do as a result of a litigant's manoeuvres. The sense of frustration often became generalised to every aspect of court procedure, so that, for example, the nonappearance of a judge due to illness was even interpreted by some litigants as a manoeuvre directed at them alone by an unseen conspiracy allied with their opponents.

[ . . . ]

Many lawyers expressed annoyance at the waste of time caused by court procedures. In fact one cause of delay is that lawyers usually try to attend several cases on the same day, assuming that, given the normal level of procedural uncertainty and the options open to opponents, most of the cases will be postponed for one reason or another. The result is that many of the hearings that *do* come up must be postponed until the next opening a month later because at least one of the lawyers is already involved in another hearing.

On the positive side of delay were numerous statements in the following mould: 'Since we are rich, and we are having good income, we will be prepared to spend any amount of money to win'. To litigants with this point of view no event in litigation carried such serious weight that its effects could not be overcome by a man with means and patience. Even less wealthy litigants spoke of their use of delaying procedures simply to postpone probable formal outcomes. In some cases these were used simply to 'teach the other side a lesson', while in others the intention was to give the other side time to 'come to his senses' and agree to a compromise.

[ . . . ]

But for others, threat of delay constituted sufficient reason to alter their strategies significantly. Businessmen reported that they regularly abandon legitimate claims as business losses rather than incur further loss in the uncertain arena of litigation. Many such businessmen argued that they had as much chance of recovering such losses from the defaulter directly simply by waiting as by court action. And the cost would not include endless costly trips to court.

Altered strategies were reflected in an unusual statistic concerning the bars in two Munsiff's towns (i.e., towns having courts at the lowest level of original jurisdiction). Both towns had similar populations and court jurisdictions, but one (Town A) had only five lawyers while the other (Town B) had nearly thirty. Lawyers from Town A explained that their potential clientele preferred to take cases directly to the higher courts in Bangalore instead of going through the frustration of the local court first. In Town B, the higher courts at the district headquarters were much more distant, making it economically less feasible to bypass the local courts. In other words, Town A litigants were taking advantage of their proximity to district headquarters courts to eliminate the delay which was obvious to them in their own local courts.

Delay, as can be seen in this example, has its effect as a bargaining strategy not only in its frustration of adjudicative finality. It also works because of the economics of litigation. For many litigants delay and expense were synonymous. There is the expense of productive resources such as land or machinery idled by court order for the duration of the dispute. In one case, a quarrelling family had $400,000 worth of houses, factories, and warehouses tied up for over five years because they could not reach a satisfactory partition of joint family property.

Additional expenses are incurred for each hearing, regardless of whether it occurs or is postponed. These include the litigant's own travel and food expenses along with those of the five to fifteen witnesses he must bring to support his case. . . .

A variety of circumstances permit the development of delaying techniques. The courts are always 'overcrowded' because clerks schedule cases on the assumption that most will be postponed. Some lower courts begin the day with as many as two hundred cases scheduled. Given these loads, it is not difficult for a party in any one case to convince the judge that postponement is necessary—judicial resistance to these moves is lowered by the schedule he faces.

Beyond the original trial stage, a determined opponent can manipulate appeals procedures to produce even more delay. Of litigants interviewed at court, almost half (fifty out of one hundred and three) declared that they would definitely appeal should they lose in the lower courts. Only ten were sure they would not appeal. The remainder either refused to entertain the possibility that a judge would rule against them or were called away from the interview before that question could be asked.

Even when the process of adjudication has apparently run its course and one side has achieved 'final victory', the effect of the judgment may still be negotiated because the decree must still be executed. In effect the victor is often left responsible for stimulating the enforcement bureaucracy to execute his decree. Rules consciousness in the bureaucracy can prolong the process for years. One landlord spent five years getting an eviction decree against his tenant, only to have the 'defeated' tenant disappear with the key. He then learned from the police that the tenant could easily keep him out of the house for at least two more years just by manipulating police eviction procedures. Meanwhile the landlord could not even collect rent on the property.

## THE NEGOTIABILITY OF ALLIANCES AND SERVICES

Although the adjudicatory model is designed around the assumption of simple, bipolar lines of conflict, the specialisation of roles which has arisen from differentiation within and around the judicial apparatus has created numerous sources of conflicting interests. For the naive litigant these contradictions constitute both hazard and opportunity since they represent elements which he and his opponent must organise and integrate into reliable alliances. Litigation means learning a new set of roles in new social networks. These networks are the products of unstable, shifting arrangements in response to specific conflicts and opportunities. As such, they are not reliable 'givens' to which the litigant need only become socialised, rather they are the material out of which he must innovate and maintain his own strategic unit.

The question of bribery and influence among court clerks, for example, seems straightforward, if deplorable, to the novice litigant. He understands harassment and rudeness as being due either to his own lack of resources or to his opponent's superior resources. But in fact much of the favour-peddling reflects the [fact] that experienced litigants, 'court birds', have their own positions in [a] web of [reciprocal] obligations, symbolic gestures, and meanings. Novices cannot deal at this level unless and until they demonstrate clear evidence that they intend long-term involvement which will assure repayment for favours rendered. I observed numerous instances which support the view that even 'insiders' must continually update their credentials and contacts. Much of the lawyer's work, in fact, revolves around his efforts to develop and maintain 'contacts' for possible future use. . . .

That the social network of alliances is problematic and unstable for litigants becomes even more clear in my attempt to identify touts and their role in the process. Touts are supposed to be paid intermediaries who help lawyers and clients find each other. Though illegal, and publicly despised by lawyers, touting services were clearly in evidence in Bangalore. Not only did lawyers and clients describe their own use of touts' services but our survey produced some self-described touts (though they would not use that term to describe their services) along with some of their customers. Ten of the litigants interviewed at court also described their performance of this function. The identification problem comes from the fact that most of those who do this work are experienced litigants involved in a great variety of relationships, practices, transactions, and expectations, all of which find expression and fruition in the processes of their own and other persons' litigation. Touting, in other words, is only one of many entre-preneurially bizarre and changeable types of activities and inter-ests for these men. Because of this occupational marginality centred around the processes of litigation, the unwary litigant's alliance is often threatened by multi-directional conflicts of interest.

Village officials, such as the *patel* and the *shambogh*, who provide the most local link between government and villager, are natural potential touts. They have the advantages of education and experience and contacts with bureaucrats and lawyers. They also have access to detailed information about the financial invol-vements of their villagers. We discovered that many of the experienced litigants contacted at court turned out to be village officials. One had thirty different cases pending when interviewed. Most had at least three cases pending, usually land disputes involving fellow villagers. The striking thing, however, was the number of litigants who reported being introduced to their lawyers by such village officials. Acting as touts, they were helping one set of villagers. But acting as 'court birds' they were consolidating their wealth at the expense of another set. For the novice litigant this overlap can pose serious dangers because the information he must yield to the tout could be of value to a skilled opponent. The novice must guard against the danger that his tout might decide to become an opponent. In addition, since the official usually knows both parties in a village dispute, he may choose to play the double agent, stimulating conflict for the rewards both sides may give him. The accusations of litigants whose opponents were village officials indicated that these interest conflicts are a real danger to a tout's customers.

[ . . . ]

The point is that, in addition to the other sources of uncertainty which create room for negotiation in the litigation process, the social networks at court are a constantly changing source of threats and aids to a litigant's case. Control of alliances is a source of constant concern and commentary among all litigants. Mastery of them is one of the defining characteristics of the experienced litigant. Infiltration of an opponent's alliances can greatly increase the opponent's cost of resisting a reasonable settlement.

The effect of these various bases of negotiation is to undo the impact of adjudicative absolutes. The most predictable outcome of cases is some kind of compromise either willingly or fatalistically yielded. This outcome is apparent in the statistics on cases reaching final judgment in the formal legal sense. Over the last fifty years the average number of cases actually reaching the final decree stage ranged between 11 and 20 per cent. The rest were disposed of 'without trial' or 'without contest', meaning that some kind of arrangement was made between the contestants leading to withdrawal of the conflict from the court arena.

## CULTURE CONFLICT V. STRUCTURE AND PROCESS

On the whole then the most normal course of events in litigation consists of delay and compromise. The adjudicative ideal is rarely achieved. But to prove that this failure is a function of 'culture conflict' it would be necessary to show that this pattern is both expected and valued by court users and that it does not predominate as a pattern in other cultures. My data show that the former is definitely not the case and comparison of those data with various studies of American and British litigation suggests that cultural differences are apparently better explained by reference to the structure of adversarial relationships rather than to a unique Western respect for the judicial process.

## BANGALORE 'VALUES'

My interviews indicated overwhelmingly that novice litigants approach courts expecting 'justice'—i.e., a decisive, effective judgment in their favour. This expectation was apparent not only in direct statements but in a variety of actions and indirect attitudes. The behaviour of litigants in Town A, mentioned above (page 485), illustrates a more general phenomenon in action—that everyone interviewed believed that the courts above those they had directly experienced would be free of the complications they had found in their own experience. Town A litigants thought they would find purity in Bangalore. Those with Bangalore court experience knew it would be there in the High Court, while High Court veterans saw only the Supreme Court as a haven for the honest. . . .

Response of Mysoreans to the development of writ petition law also illustrates a valuation for swift justice. Writ petitions over constitutional guarantees take very little time or money because they are filed directly before the High or Supreme Court and cost only Rs 25. They became popular in Mysore after States reorganisation in 1956 when they were developed as a means of settling the employment problems created by Mysore's need to integrate five pre-reorganisation governmental jurisdictions. But they have since spread to other areas of dispute so that between 1962 and 1970 the number of writs filed annually increased from around two thousand to over eight thousand five hundred. Being a very new area of law and procedure, writ proceedings produce swift, uncomplicated, and relatively final 'victories'. There has been little time for the development of complex networks of 'specialists' who can complicate the process. And factual debate and the battle of witnesses is unnecessary because facts are stipulated at the outset—the only question concerns the individual's constitutionally guaranteed rights.

Actual responses such as these lend credibility to frustrated litigants' claims that their experiences violate their expectations in ordinary litigation. While they may value compromise (many paid at least lip service to it) as a general good, they are seeking something more final and absolute in court. The fact that they must settle for something less is due to the vast scope for innovative manipulation I have discussed.

[ . . . ]

## WESTERN 'VALUES'

The culture conflict hypothesis also suffers when Indian patterns of court use are compared to behaviour in Western courts. Multiplex relationships* such as those involved in most of the Indian data presented here hold much greater potential for obscuring the adjudicative process because they involve the consolidation of a variety of social roles within what the disputants consider to be issues relevant to the case. The grounds for dispute are much broader, as are the bases of negotiation, when compared to simplex relationships which are very narrowly defined and more characteristic of complex industrialised societies. The broader the range of issues and potential areas of agreement, the more problematic such agreement becomes. In games theory terms, the 'settlement range' is too broad to permit easy discovery of mutually acceptable terms.[5] . . . Ross' study of car accident claims cases, for example, deals with a relationship which is clearly of the simplex type—i.e., car accident victims. Ross shows that the average case is settled by compromise through the intervention of the insurance claims adjusters. Those few cases that do go to court are decisive, not prolonged.[6] This apparent difference from Indian behaviour can be explained by reference to the structure of relationships included in these negotiations. This structure is usually simplex in nature both during the events defined as creating the legal claim (the accident) and in the sequence of relationships culminating in settlement. For one thing, tort claims create much less factual ambiguity than other disputes such as those over land. The dispute usually has a clear starting point and the content of satisfactory outcomes is simple. There is less room for uncertainty and thus less miscalculation about the aims

---

* *Multiplex, or multi-stranded, relationships are illustrated by those between a villager and his headman, or patel, who will introduce the villager to a lawyer, coach him on dealing with court officials, and may also engage him later in an adversary court action. A simplex relationship would be illustrated by that between a customer and a previously unknown shopkeeper. [Eds]*

[5] T.C. Schelling 1963.

[6] H.L. Ross 1970.

and probable behaviour of the opponent. This is so because of the typical lack of contact between accident victims before their accident. In other words the apparent clarity of tort claims in these cases is due to the lack of multiplex relationships between litigants.

Furthermore, the presence of a hierarchically organised bureaucracy (the insurance company) as one of the actors means that (i) routine experience with such cases leads to much less miscalculation about the probable strategies of an opponent; (ii) the bureaucracy can absorb formally unjustifiable losses which an individual could not and can go to greater expense than an individual in fighting 'outrageous' claims or seeking to establish new precedents; (iii) bureaucratic actors are less wedded to their agency's best interests than to personal career considerations. This leads them to greater desire for swift settlement because speed is the professional criterion by which they are judged. Taking a case to court is more a means of diffusing responsibility for large claims than a strong action aimed at victory. For that reason Ross' data shows higher finality of judgments than we see in the Bangalore data; (iv) protracted conflict with any opponent is a distraction from the organisation's specialised purpose—profits. It is therefore more willing to ignore its strict legal rights than is a person whose entire status and well-being may be at stake in a dispute. The involvement of a bureaucracy as a party in car claims cases, in other words, maintains the court-located relationship on a simplex basis, countering any trend towards multiplex complications which lone legal actors might be tempted to import into such cases (e.g., pleas of poverty, pleas for empathy due to common status, or attempts to pressure an opponent with a countersuit).

## CONCLUSION

The concepts of adjudication and conflict resolution are both parts of a single way of interpreting the significance of the process of litigation. That interpretation treats man as an actor in a social system which tends always towards balance or equilibrium. Conflict is a source of imbalance in the system and law is treated as a means of resolving the conflict and restoring the balance. Adjudication by law is treated as a crucial step in this balancing act and its success or failure is thought to depend on its congruence with the values of the system's actors.

The results of this study support a quite different view of the significance of the litigation process. This view reflects an avoidance of what Wrong has called the 'Oversocialized Conception of Man in Modern Sociology'.[7] Adjudication emerges from this study as just one of many contingencies in what is essentially a process of negotiation within a changing social environment.

The product may not be 'conflict resolution', and perhaps it need not be. The American insurance company seeks, and gets, conflict resolution in courts because involvement in those conflicts is a distraction from its specialised *raison d'être*. For the company settlement of a dispute means termination of a temporary relationship. But the 'court birds', communities, and factions in Bangalore have no specialised *raison d'être*. Prolonged litigation arises out of on-going permanent relationships in which neither cooperation nor conflict can or will be permanently resolved by any single action. To an important degree, these communities and individuals find an element of self-definition in their conflicts and their litigation is therefore bound to stand in contrast to the actions of a bureaucracy conceived of as a profit-generating organisation.

To conclude that Indian court use is frivolous or misguided is to misjudge the importance of conflict as a constructive force in social interaction. It is also to ignore informal opportunity structures which are created by systems of formal adjudication. Those informal structures will receive form and content from the relational structure existing between litigants. Bangalore's courts appear as they do because of the predominance of multiplex relationships being brought before the courts.

---

[7] D. Wrong 1961: 183–93.

## FURTHER READINGS

Upendra Baxi, *The Crisis of the Indian Legal System*. New Delhi: Vikas, 1982.

Trenchent critique of the Indian complex of police, courts, prisons, and related issues during and after the colonial period. Reviews alternative channels for law and justice, especially for the poor.

Veena Das, Sociology of Law: A Trend Report. In *ICSSR Survey of Research in Sociology and Social Anthropology*. Bombay: Popular, 1974, pp. 367–400.

A useful, though somewhat dated, review of the literature and bibliography under the rubrics: processes of dispute settlement; judicial behaviour; the legal profession; and law and the wider society. Touches on the multiple sources of legal norms: *dharmashastras*, diverse caste and tribal traditions, Islamic law, the modern legal system.

J. Duncan M. Derrett, *Essays in Classical and Modern Hindu Law*, 4v. Leiden: E.J. Brill, 1976 on.

Important collection of wide-ranging papers, by a major authority, on long-term societal processes and ideologies in South Asia, especially the working of the *dharmashastras* and of modern law. Explores the implications of the historic conjoining of the Indian and the Western traditions of conflict resolution during the colonial period.

Marc Galanter, *Law and Society in Modern India*. Delhi: Oxford University Press, 1989.

Assembles over two decades of Galanter's scholarship around the themes: emergence of the modern legal system; legal conceptions of the social structure; assessment of India's policies and practices over 'compensatory discrimination for historically disadvantaged groups'; and judges, lawyers, and social reform.

Rajeev Dhavan, Introduction to Galanter, pp. xiii–c [88 pp.].

Magisterial review of the sociology of law in India, sketching the historic context in which Galanter's work is located.

Yash Ghai, Robin Luckham, and Francis Snyder, eds, *The Political Economy of Law: A Third World Reader*. Delhi: Oxford University Press, 1987.

Massive collection of readings in the political economy of law in Third World countries. Drawing on major theoretical writings and case studies, examines the emergence of law as a technique for expressing and regulating social relations; the interrelationships between law, state, economy, and ideology; and the nature and functioning of legal institutions.

# Epilogue

N. JAYARAM AND SATISH SABERWAL

Conflict is a comprehensive category. Studies of conflict cover a vast range of phenomena: resistance, revolutions, certain kinds of movements and legal processes, ethnocentrism, and much else. The Introduction presented a preliminary set of perspectives on these phenomena, drawing upon sociological and allied traditions. It sought to furnish the reader with a set of concepts for working through the case studies that followed. In this epilogue we wish to suggest further perspectives in which to consider questions of conflict.[1] We begin by outlining a set of dimensions along which the enormous variations in the phenomena, subsumed under the rubric of conflict, may be explored. The next section will list four axial arguments around which the subsequent parts of this chapter are cast.

## DIMENSIONS OF CONFLICT

It is possible to examine numerous dimensions along which the nature of conflicts can vary. We shall take notice of four such: the scale of conflict; its intensity; its mode; and the nature of symbolization in the conflict.[2]

[1] Need we add that our discussion here is nowhere near being exhaustive. For political conflict, the contributors to Gurr (1980) provide an important review of issues. (We thank Professor Karmeshu for calling Gurr's work to our attention).

[2] The Introduction and other parts of this Epilogue explore several other dimensions of this variation. Simmel (1955) covered yet others.

First, the simple difference of scale: from a brawl within a family to a world war. A sharp tongue may be effective at one end; something more lethal may be used at the other end of the scale. (While the scale of conflict is obviously important, yet there may be correspondences across differences of scale and levels of complexity. Illustratively, the proposition about a group closing ranks in the face of external threats, and the reservations on this proposition, may be tested equally on neighbourhood gangs and on international relations.)

There are more complex dimensions too. With reference to the intensity of conflict, we may draw on the work of political sociologists and anthropologists (e.g. Swartz *et al.* 1966: 11f, following David Easton). Political conflict may be joined at any of several possible levels.[3] In the following series of questions, there is a movement towards increasingly inclusive implications of contestation; the changes resulting from such contestation would cut successively deeper:

> who should head the government? The question may imply change of only one person, or of a small group close to him or her;
> which party should form the government? At issue here would be the replacement of many more persons—and possibly of operative policies;
> how should the legitimate right to govern be determined? This question takes us to the rules of the game, to the possibility of changing the operative Constitution; the situation at hand may be revolutionary. And finally:
> what should be the boundaries of the political community? At this level, the very territorial unit which is to constitute the political community is at stake. Implied here may be moves either towards enlarging the scale of the political unit, as in plans for a European Community, or towards reducing the scale, as in the recent fortunes of the former Soviet Union.

Two comments are in order. One, the earlier questions in the above series are closer to the 'competition' end, later ones to the

---

[3] The *intensity* of conflicts has other aspects too: its duration, its destructiveness, and the depth of partisan commitments in any episode (see Introduction).

'conflict' end. As we saw in the Introduction, the difference commonly turns on the vitality of the shared, operative rules of the game. The extent of such shared 'rules of the game'—and their substance—are important variables in shaping the intensity, and therefore the character, of the conflict at issue. Need we add that such shared rules become available in a society if these have been consciously instituted at some time, and sustained as part of ongoing arrangements; their existence, quality, and operational availability are not natural, invariable, parts of social existence.

Secondly, in a hierarchy of levels like the one outlined above, contestation at a lower level may well betoken commitment to the normative order operative at the higher level: to be competing for 'which party should form the government' implies affirmation, ordinarily, *(1)* of the Constitutional regime governing this competition and *(2)* of the boundaries of the political community governed under this regime.[4]

Conflicts vary, one from another, along other dimensions too. Consider the question of modes of conflict. Using force to impose one's will on others is, of course, a procedure common to many species. Force may be used in various ways: maybe in a riot, when superior force may intervene; or it may be directed at oneself, as in breastbeating or suicide. Abjuring force, the adversaries may struggle rather to gain greater public sympathy and support. Or, they may have to join explicit, articulated arguments, say in a court of law: an apparatus established specifically for mediating in, and settling, disputes within a framework of general rules.

Finally, the nature of symbolization.[5] Conflicts can arise in, or be pressed through, a counterposing of symbols. We have to remember that there is no intrinsic connection between a symbol and whatever it represents. Imagine the countless associations with the word 'Ram', the image of a 'cow', or with something like a national flag or an anthem. The arbitrariness of the relationship

---

[4] We recognize the possibility that a group may make a bid to form the government intending, if successful, to move then to re-cast the Constitution—or even the boundaries of political community. Real-life processes rarely fit into trim analytic categories without difficulty.

[5] The play of symbols in social life, and in the making of identities, has been an exceptionally fertile field of study in recent decades (e.g. several essays in Singer 1984). Questions of identity lie at the heart of numerous conflicts.

between the symbol and what it connotes, and suggests, is absolutely crucial.

We are, in principle, free to give a symbol whatever meaning(s) we wish. Symbols work rather in Humpty Dumpty's style: 'When I use a word,' he tells Alice in 'Through the looking glass', 'it means just what I choose it to mean—neither more nor less.' If ordinary communication does proceed in an orderly manner, it is only because the habits of routine social practice severely check this potential for arbitrariness of meaning. Such constraints are much weaker for symbols of the kind we are discussing.

It is this arbitrariness that gives symbols their virtually infinite capacity for absorbing, carrying, and conveying heavy charges of meaning and emotion. A symbol may carry a vast profusion of meanings. A word or a gesture may stand for one's identity, one's emotions, one's memories of the past, one's intentions for the future, and much else; hence, at times, the symbols' enormous capacity to command the loyalty of men and to drive them to activities of extraordinary magnitude, for good or for evil.

The profusion of meanings carried by a symbol includes those which are there but in fact remain unarticulated. Consequently there may be a high level of uncertainty in communication around charged symbols of this kind. This uncertainty yields the space for serious misunderstandings—and grounds for conflict. We comment on some aspects of these complex issues at some length in the Appendix.

In concluding this discussion of the dimensions of conflict we may note that the conflict over a particular issue may straddle several dimensions, levels, and media. A local tiff may be joined to a national issue (see Alm). A major confrontation, such as that in Ayodhya in the late eighties and the early nineties, may be directed so as to proceed simultaneously on many fronts: legal court cases, mass media campaigns, re-writing of history, legislative debates, and riots in the streets. No wonder the course, and the many faces, of a conflict at times leave us bewildered!

## AXIAL ARGUMENTS

The variety of sources from which conflict originates and the variety of courses that conflicts take are virtually infinite; yet we may try to bring some order to that diversity, and thereby advance our understanding of conflicts. To this end, we shall use a series of 'axial arguments'. The dictionary defines an 'axis' as 'the line about which a rotating body turns or may be supposed to turn'; subsidiary meanings include: 'a principal line of development, movement, etc.' By 'axial arguments' we mean the principal lines along which the arguments in this Epilogue are developed. We shall use four such axes:

a) Differentiation and integration: Every society is more or less differentiated, and therefore each carries differences of viewpoint such that their carriers could well pull their own social fabric apart. Yet, a great many societies have, historically, found the means to stay together: needless to say, those which could not do so succumbed to, or were absorbed by, others which were more resourceful. The resources for societal integration are as varied as those for conflict: force, ideology, everyday practices, institutions, and so forth. A society's integrative capacities are part of its resources for constituting, reconstituting, and ordering itself. While in this, as in other matters, there is a great deal of variation between societies, no society is integrated so completely that it leaves no room for conflict.

This, first, axis offers a perspective on society in general. The next two seek out the substance of conflicts.

b) Life cycle of conflicts: We may conceive of a conflict as if it has a 'life cycle', being 'born', growing in size, and coming to an end. Our long evolutionary heritage, and genetic endowment, probably contribute to our tendency to fight; and so do the man-made worlds of symbol, myth, language, ideology, and everyday social categories—whether or not we may be conscious of them. Feedback processes are active here as elsewhere: ongoing conflicts can grow by 'feeding on themselves'; Gregory Bateson called this process 'schismogenesis'. Most conflicts get restrained, however, before these have done too much damage: modulating processes work in nearly every society. Yet their working is not inevitable: conflicts in a society may get out of control, so much so that a general breakdown of orderly social processes follows—and the society loses control over its own fortunes.

c) Order and conflict: The mainstream western sociological tradition enquired after the nature of social integration, asking how it is possible for societies to function at all (functionalists), and then moved to explore the value of conflict in social processes. It is not difficult for a Marxist, such as Tom Bottomore, to urge that conflicts be accepted as normal to society (1975: Ch. 11); however, non-Marxists also have come to the view that certain kinds of conflict may well be functional in various ways. Even if this search for the uses of conflicts comes close, at times, to 'scraping the bottom of the barrel', it has led to interesting explorations.

Conflicts are good for giving salience to social identities, and oppositions, and to the corresponding social boundaries. Conflict can be cathartic 'letting off steam', releasing aggressive feelings and clearing the air, even if the relief be temporary. Conflict can be a means of communication: putting up resistance is a means of telling the other party how serious an issue is for oneself. Going on strike is one way to force an issue on to the day's agenda. Joining conflict may enable one to secure changes in prevailing social arrangements. We should notice that the relationship may operate in the reverse direction too: strong social identities, release of aggressive feelings, hostile communication, and certain kinds of change can lead to conflict as well.

The second axis, on the 'life cycle', will array a variety of elements in the courses commonly taken by social conflicts—and, the third, the functions of conflicts. Both these sets of issues concern societies generally, regardless of space or time. Our last axis concerns the 'mixing of cultural codes'. We consider this in relation to some encounters within South Asia, but the issues have wider appeal.

d) Mixing of cultural codes: The Introduction hinted at the importance, in our historical experience, of the mixing of cultural codes, resulting from the colonial, and earlier, cultural encounters. Our selections, especially on Conflict Resolution, illustrate some consequences of the multi-layered colonial encounter. This Epilogue will explore this encounter is some depth. The reader will recognize that the theme has been with us for a long time, though it has carried varied labels: social change, modernization, colonialism, development, and so forth. We focus here on the encounter between two complex civilizations which came to evolve very different forms in which to constitute themselves; and we consider especially its implications concerning the patterns, and the magnitudes, of conflict in contemporary India.

## DIFFERENTIATION AND INTEGRATION

A conflict originates in differences of perception between those who get drawn into the conflict. Differences from others may result from the societal division of labour—and associated differences in status, power, and the like. Differences can also result from the juxtaposing of diverse social traditions; or, despite shared traditions, from allegiance to diverse symbols which have come to mark contrasting identities—as is often the case in ethnic conflicts.

### Integrative Mechanisms

All societies are differentiated, more or less, if only into different lineages, clans, and the like. Indeed, social differentiation is an aspect of all division of labour. Consequently, every society has centrifugal pulls; yet it is unusual for societies to really fall apart, as happened in the former Soviet Union and eastern Europe in the early nineties. Societies endure much of the time because they have found ways to hold things together. Various integrative mechanisms are commonly at play. Societies need such mechanisms for containing potential conflicts—and for securing coordinated activity on any substantial scale.

Societal integration may take a variety of routes. The strategic application of force may serve to contain other conflicts as well as to secure the compliance needed for coordinated activity; yet, if adequate ideological support is lacking, the integration so achieved may be fragile and its continuation may depend on steady applications of fresh force to hold the parts together. Shared ideologies, including shared symbolic orders, may serve to promote integration within a group—though the ideology may promote hostilities with other groups. The ideology and the symbols may be embedded in the society's everyday practices.

## Ordering Devices

A crucial part of the body of concepts and ideas in a tradition serves to specify how one should act. Societal norms—rules, customary or otherwise—specify courses of action, of course; these specify too, implicitly or explicitly, the limits within which a particular norm applies. Alongside a norm of peaceableness there may be another that specifies when, to hold one's honour, one must fight. Such ordering principles or devices help pre-empt the possibility of a good deal of conflict. The caste order tended to separate groups firmly at one level; yet it was imperative to coordinate their specialized functions and to minimize conflicts between the groups: a variety of everyday rituals served to tie the different castes together at the local level (Harper 1964).

It is an aspect of a culture's integration that its varied concepts, ideas, and practices tend, over time, towards a measure of internal consistency. This straining to consistency acts in all societies. Concerning the sources of this pressure, it has been suggested that parents everywhere have to meet their children's demand for explaining, more or less consistently, the why and the wherefore of their society's prevailing ideas and institutions (Berger and Luckmann 1966: 79). This impulse to consistency in a society's ideas, however, is a variable: its strength would depend, say, on the calibre of its accessible apparata of logic, and the intensity of their application.

On the other hand, a society may be blessed with specialist institutions—say a Church or a bureaucracy—devoted to the promulgation of such integrative ideologies and practices. The quality and strength of such institutions—and, more generally, of social forms available for organization—is a crucial variable. How exactly a society is integrated can make all the difference to its long-term performance (Mann 1986; Saberwal 1991a). We wish to indicate here two lines of argument, both proceeding from a society's pattern of integration, or structuring: the first connects this integration with the patterns of conflict; the second, with societal resilience.

## Integration, Loose or Rigid

How a society is integrated crucially shapes the course of its conflicts (see Coser 1956: 154). Broadly, we may posit a continuum, with flexibility and rigidity at its two ends; the qualities of particular social units would lie at various points along this continuum. Flexibly integrated societies and groups allow freer expression of antagonistic claims and tolerate conflict in greater measure. Such societies would experience a multiplicity of conflicts. The release of the members' energies in various directions may help ensure the stability of the overarching social arrangements though, as our epigraph from Bohannon indicates, a society or social group with uncontrolled conflicts will come to grief.

Rigidly integrated societies, in contrast, inhibit the free expression of antagonistic claims and tend to suppress conflicts. Should conflict break out in such a society nevertheless, it may well become intense and radical, becoming concerned not merely with the immediate issues but also with the accumulated grievances which had earlier been denied room for expression. Such a conflict may result in the society's breakup or the dissenters' withdrawal from the particular social space. As Coser says, conflict is dysfunctional where structures are too rigid and do not allow contrary viewpoints to be expressed (1956: 152).

## Rank Differentiation and Integration

The integration of complex societies, we have suggested, is associated with certain kinds of differentiation. Differentiation—between superordinate and subordinate roles—is necessary, furthermore, for ensuring coordination in any complex undertaking. The larger, and more complex, a society, the greater its need for coordinated activity—and therefore for such differentiation. However, the Danish sociologist, Kaare Svalastoga, has pointed out that a society can have too much of this differentiation—and its associated inequalities—as well as too little.

A 'society desirous of maximizing its resilience', says Svalastoga (1965: 7), has to attend to two aspects. One aspect is social rank differentiation. Such a society, desiring to maximize resilience, has to seek rank differentiation of an order which is neither too high nor too low. That is to say, the society has to ensure that this differentiation is no more elaborate than needed for the tasks at hand; and that, yet, it is elaborate enough to facilitate both coordination of activity and the upward flow of talent.

A similar need for balance holds for the other aspect, social integration. This too has to be limited on both sides: not so high that it would subvert the demands of efficient functioning, nor so low that it would subvert the possibilities of cooperation.

Underlying this proposal, there are some strong assumptions: that the society in question has agencies which can choose a form for its future—and which have the stamina to work steadily towards achieving that form, over a long enough period. Such agencies, and the corresponding social visions and capabilities, are human creations: these are available only after a society has managed to set them up; their availability is not a 'given' of social existence.

The reader will notice that we have repeatedly stressed that all social mechanisms and institutions are human artefacts, that the quality of these social devices is variable, and that some work better than others. Their quality and their functioning can improve or these can deteriorate: it is the application of human vision, of human will, and of human skills that makes the difference. We wish to promote a 'provisional' conception of these institutions; and this applies as much to a society's integrative and ordering devices as it does to any other.

## LIFE CYCLE OF CONFLICTS

The familiar notion of a 'life cycle' will serve to shape the following discussion: that conflicts, like living organisms, have beginnings; these grow—'mature', if that is the word; and most conflicts do end. While all metaphors have traps, this general conception will allow us to consider several aspects of conflicts in an orderly manner.

## Elements in Conflicts

Societies, and human beings, have endemic qualities which may predispose them—more or less unconsciously—to continual conflicts. Over the generations, phenomena of social conflict have received concerted attention from an array of social sciences: evolutionary studies (including human evolution), conflict behaviour among animals, infants' and children's behaviour, and the full range of psychology, anthropology, sociology, political science, and much else. We take a wide-angled view of the sources of human conflict. For a start, we locate the phenomenon in the human condition itself. As our guide into these diverse, intricate matters, the Introduction (Part 5) relied on the excellent recent synthesis by Johan M.G. van der Dennen (1987). His focus is on ethnocentrism, an important element in a wide range of conflicts, and on the associated, widespread tendency to look upon outgroups with hostility.

There are elements in human conflict behaviour—such as suspicion of strangers, and fear—which may have come to us as part of our evolutionary heritage and genetic endowment; these we share with various non-human species. Furthermore, there are other, uniquely human elements too: especially the effects on us of our exceptional capacities for working with symbols, myths, ideologies, and the like. In reviewing the literature, van der Dennen keeps a fine balance between these different sets of elements; and the Introduction took note of his review at some length.

The Introduction recognized, too, that a good deal of conscious awareness, calculation, and mobilization goes into the shaping of most conflicts. A consideration of these issues continues in the following section.

## Mobilization and Struggle

Much conflict stays confined to small niches in space and time. Yet a more or less substantial class of persons may come to recognize an identity of interest in a particular issue; and they may proceed to mobilize themselves—and others—to mount a struggle to advance their Cause. A social movement may be born and flourish for a while; and at least some movements are vehicles for rather intense conflicts (see Guha, Oommen).

The Introduction noted (Part 6) that the range of arms and armour, not to mention ideology, summoned to battle may be limited only by the adversaries' ingenuity, resources, and judgement (see Swartz *et al.* 1966: 23–6, 32). Funds may be raised through voluntary contributions or extortion or from interested parties beyond the borders. Cadres may be recruited and trained for the struggle; and their commitment and motivation may be raised to a pitch where they are ready to give their lives for the Cause. Secrecy is essential to such movements, however; and therefore it is not easy to enforce accountability with them. Armed men, raising funds for the Cause at gunpoint, may well deploy these for their private purposes instead.

We may not underestimate the power of symbols and images, myths and lore, in rallying supporters to a Cause. These are part of culture, part of a society's consciousness of history. These are internalized from generation to generation—consciously or unconsciously—in the course of socialization, and are invocable in calls to action. Primordial groups are able to summon a much wider range of images and myths to their Cause than can other kinds of groups.

However, none of this should be seen as happening 'automatically'. The adversaries may, or may not, see a great deal at stake in any given engagement—and they may, or may not, throw all they have into a particular struggle. The complexity of conflicts echoes the complexity of social existence itself. Consequently, even within a narrow range of conflict situations—say between workers and employers in industry—the adversaries may have a wide variety of alternatives for shaping their conflicts, whether in particular episodes or in long-term campaigns. This applies to every phase of an encounter: initiating, conducting, continuing, and terminating the conflict (see Ramaswamy).

We wish to note, finally, that the occasion for conflict may also be precipitated by the actions, or policy initiatives, of the government or some other agency. Every action, or change of policy, means the allocation, or denial, of some opportunity, privilege, or resource to one party or another. Permission to worship at a disputed place, a proposal to amend the personal law of a community, a decision to make a particular language compulsory in schools, moves on caste-based reservations, amendments to labour legislation, moves on land reforms: all such actions have some beneficiaries; but others may, ipso facto, feel aggrieved—and be moved to resist or protest. Other conflicts may issue, directly or indirectly, from diverse other projects: say political yatras, or a political party inciting one group against another as part of the 'democratic' game of winning and retaining power.

## Modulations of Conflict

All in all, we hold 'conflict' to be doubled-edged. At one end, conflicts may sweep away the shackles of established practice, releasing fresh creative energy; conflict between generations often has this consequence. At the other end, conflicts can be hugely destructive: think of all the everyday riots in south Asian societies, or of a modern war. Every scuffle, however, does not lead to war. In most societies, the intensity and frequency of conflicts commonly get dampened, before these have done too much damage, by a varied lot of influences and mechanisms, and we may review their range. We distinguish, first, between two kinds of social conditions which help dampen hostilities and antagonisms: passive and active.

In the passive restriction of hostilities, social linkages are so distributed that conflicts in one group or locality do not easily spread to others. The world of the Indian village, for example, used to be small. To be sure, its mix of antagonisms, aggressions, habits of retaliation, and the like had consequences; but their spread would ordinarily stop at the edge of the village. The closer integration of local communities into larger social wholes, in recent generations, has changed the situation dramatically. The older, passive modes of containing conflicts work much less adequately now than formerly. Given the emergence of 'mega-categories' in society (see Alm), and today's modes of instant communication, these chains of consequences do at times spread contagions into and out of villages, far and wide, within hours and days.

Societies may also be organized as to actively dampen conflicts and their damaging consequences. This may happen through the working of mediators, countervailing pressures, and the like. That is to say, we might speak of a culture for managing conflicts, wherein a range of roles, ideas, and institutions is available, whose effect is to regulate and to modulate, conflicts.

The contending parties may realize that they have a shared interest in limiting the scale of conflict (see the studies in Haynes and Prakash 1991); one may choose to conserve one's resources to fight another day. Adversaries too frenzied to recognize the value of limiting the conflict may be made to realize it by others: by a common patron or mediator, interested in both parties, or by the pressure of public opinion.

A special word about the mediator is in order. Conflicts, interpersonal or inter-group, are generally marked by an inadequate understanding, or a misunderstanding, of the mutual expectations between contending parties. Issues extraneous to the crux of contention may muddy the scene further. Hence the significance of the mediator. His or her role may lie primarily in clearing misunderstandings, and eliminating extraneous issues, from negotiations concerning the conflict. Furthermore, the mediator may help establish new norms, or revive dormant ones, which have to govern the relation between the contending parties.

The more complex societies commonly institute specialized mechanisms for regulating conflict: this may be called the institutionalization of conflict.[6] Once the reality of conflict is socially accepted, its content and form may be legitimized, codes to regulate its methods, weapons and techniques formulated, and fora for pursuing the dispute established. Industrial courts and Election Commissions illustrate the possibilities. Issues would be joined in such settings less destructively, ordinarily, than in the case of disputes settled through force of arms. Yet it must always be remembered that these public mechanisms are human artefacts, instituted historically to cope with particular kinds of contingencies (see Oommen).[7]

Our readings also remind us, however, that the mere existence of such mechanisms does not ensure their effectiveness. Rigidly structured societies may resist the open processing of conflicts

---

[6] This expression was coined originally by Theodor Geiger in 1949 to designate an important change in class conflict since Marx's time (see Dahrendorf 1959: 64f).

[7] Patel (1987) sees Gandhi's influence in institutionalizing the management of conflict in Ahmedabad's textile industry during the 1920s and 30s.

even though institutions for the purpose are available; and even in loosely structured societies the regulative institutions may not be effective, or may have lost their credibility. An institution's effectiveness is contingent on various elements, among them the attitudes and the psychological drives necessary for making the mechanism work (see Ramaswamy).

Whether or not the requisite attitudes and drives have become part of the particular functionaries' personality would depend on their life experiences, before and during their location in their particular role. Yet the resolutions of conflicts, speedily and authoritatively, is important, especially for complex societies. Cumulating, unresolved conflicts may have ominous consequences: among them that of subverting wider confidence in the society's capacity for orderly functioning.

Where secular institutions of justice and authority are weak, a society may have devised procedures and resources for dampening conflicts. For example:

a setting like a panchayat allows issues to be aired, and possible responses explored, even if it lacks the power to enforce decisions (see Freed and Freed and Madsen);

oaths, ordeals, and the like, in whose working divine powers are believed to give the signs, even though these have to be interpreted by human agents (Roberts 1965);

the right of asylum, usually in a sacred place or with a sacred person. The tradition ensures protection to the person who takes such asylum. Among the Nuer of southern Sudan, 'As soon as a man slays another he hastens to the home of a leopard-skin chief . . . to seek sanctuary from the retaliation he has incurred (Evans-Pritchard 1940: 151).' The culprit safe at 'the chief's' home, the latter proceeds then to mediate between the parties, using his social and ritual influence to persuade the kinsmen of the slain to accept compensation for the dead man from the slayer's kin—which they do, while displaying all possible reluctance. (See also Hoebel 1954: 169.)

the play of cross-cutting ties. A conflict between two groups— say, two neighbouring families—is less likely to fester and grow if its members are affiliated with multiple, overlapping groups—say an active kindred, a political faction, and a

religious sect. On one hand, the prevailing social arrangements would be such that these bring into action mediators,
who may have the confidence of, have a stake in, and are
able to see the viewpoints of, both sides to the dispute. On
the other hand, one's identity is not tied exclusively to a
single boundary; nor need one commit oneself wholly to a
particular conflict.

The course of conflicts is shaped also by the values prevailing
in the society: peaceableness may, or may not, be thought to be
a worthy end; one may, or may not, have grown up learning that
it is possible, and important, to seek one's goals in ways that avoid
wasteful conflict.

With reference to such modulations of conflict, we wish to
repeat that the presence of such mechanisms, beliefs, and values
in a society is not inevitable, nor can their effectiveness be taken
for granted. Their presence, renewal, and decay—these are part
of, consequences of, particular historical processes. Like everything cultural, however, the culture for managing conflicts is also
a human artefact; and its quality varies—between societies and
over time. Whole societies may, over time, become more peaceable or more warlike, as human will and sustained effort are
applied one way or the other.

*Feedback in conflicts.* We may thank Gregory Bateson, the anthropologist, for bringing the 'systems' perspective into interpretations
of the growth, if not the origin, of conflicts.[8] The following
paragraphs seek to introduce the perspective to those unfamiliar
with it. The next section will consider its implications.

The idea of feedback is central to this view; but its use

---

[8] Bateson's initial discussion, and the concept of 'schismogenesis', appeared
in *Naven* (1936) in relation to his anthropological study of a society in New
Guinea. In developing the idea subsequently, he drew on cybernetics and the
theory of types (Bateson 1958, 1971).

The 'systems perspective' has been one of the most influential movements
of thought in the twentieth century. Norbert Wiener wrote an early classic in
the field (1950). Today it pervades everything from efforts at understanding
nature (e.g. Eigen and Winkler 1982) to artificial intelligence.

The discussion here offers no more than an introduction to a part of this
perspective. We thank Professor H.K. Das and Professor Karmeshu of Jawaharlal
Nehru University for advising us on the section.

in systems theory has to be distinguished from its everyday use. This everyday use refers to what Y learns from X about the latter's evaluation of Y's work actions, or ideas. In systems theory, however, feedback refers to a general process marking all self-regulating systems: whether it is a geyser maintaining hot water within a specified temperature range; the human body maintaining a 'normal' temperature; or a political system maintaining a relatively steady course, its managers modifying that course in the light of public opinion polls and the like, which gauge public responses to governmental initiatives (Easton 1965).

The general idea is that such self-regulating systems maintain themselves within relatively narrow limits of variation. These can do so because these are continuously regulated by a 'monitor', e.g. the thermostat in a geyser. The system is subject to change; the heating element in the thermostat raises the temperature of water. This change may be so large that it crosses a certain threshold: the temperature of water in the geyser may cross a certain pre-set level. The monitor, that is, the thermostat, intervenes and cuts off electric supply to the geyser's heating element.

Similarly, if the human body is exposed to high or low temperatures outside, the hypothalamus in the brain acts exactly like a thermostat, setting off processes which reduce or increase the heat being generated within the body. Or, if the prevailing rates of inflation spark growing opposition to current economic policies, reflected in political rallies, opinion polls, and the like, the government may move to curtail money supply in the system so as to check the inflation.

In the language of systems theory, in all these cases, the 'monitor' has intervened in response to information received—'feedback'—about the current condition of the system: and it has intervened so as to ensure that the system does not cross a set or acceptable threshold: that the water does not become hotter than the pre-set temperature, the body does not become too hot or cold, the public opposition does not cross managable limits. The feedback in each case has been 'negative', serving to ensure that the concerned system does not continue to move in its earlier direction: rather, by discontinuing or reversing movement in that direction, the system is able to maintain itself within relatively narrow limits of variation.

Feedback is negative, that is to say, when it serves to modify the system direction so as to keep it functioning within acceptable limits. We have considered earlier a range of mechanisms which serve to 'modulate', to restrain, a conflict—after it has taken off: mediatory roles, values supporting moderation, and the like. We noted then, however, that the availability of such mechanisms is a consequence of their having been instituted and maintained: their availability is not be taken easily for granted.

What happens when feedback is *positive*? In a system fitted with positive feedback, the monitor would intervene so as to ensure that the system continues to move in its earlier direction—only more vigorously than before: as water heats up in a geyser, the control system switches on another heating element for every rise of ten degrees; as the body temperature rises, the patient is surrounded not which icepacks but with more and more hot water bottles; every rally against rising prices persuades the government to print—and spend—money faster. Such a system, with unlimited positive feedbacks, will not last long: the geyser will explode, the patient will die, the government will fall. Unrelenting positive feedbacks are prescriptions for destroying any system.

A note of caution is necessary. We have indicated only a simple version of positive feedback. A complete system may undergo changes—involving positive feedbacks—along several parameters simultaneously. A phase of 'learning' and of social rearrangements may intervene. Processes of long term economic development illustrate this possibility (see Attwood); the system may come to be stabilized at another level.

## Breakdown and Termination

What does this mean for conflicts? It directs our attention to the fact that conflict situations may take a variety of courses. Negative feedback would serve to modulate the conflict, possibly bringing it to an end. Simmel 1955: 109ff has discussed the termination of conflicts at some length.

Alternatively, feedbacks may be positive, serving to exacerbate conflict further. While the modulating mechanisms commonly set limits to the magnitude of conflict in an episode, there may also be agencies which see their interests in *aggravating* the conflict (See Alm, Chakrabarty, and Das; Rastogi employs this perspective explicitly). With every fresh sign of growth of conflict, they may intervene more and more: inciting one or the other party, supplying destructive weaponry, spreading inflammatory rumours, and much else. Unless countered by other mechanisms, the system will rapidly reach a point where it is outside anyone's control. In extreme situations, this may precipitate a social breakdown, and major outside force may be needed for restoring order. In our experience of conflicts in South Asia over the decades, this has been an all-too-real possibility.

## ORDER AND CONFLICT

A key sociological insight, going back to Simmel (1908)[9] and Coser (1956), recognizes that all conflict and disorder are not necessarily 'bad'. Quite the contrary: these can under certain conditions be functional and, indeed, be a source of creativity. The introduction considered the element of catharsis in conflict, if it facilitates the release of pent-up hostile feelings, though we noted there that such catharsis may not be an unmixed blessing. We proceed now to other elements in this, counter-intuitional, insight.

### Identities and Boundaries

Coser follows Simmel in his central thesis: 'Conflict is a form of socialization' (Simmel 1955: 17f, passim; Coser 1956: 31). That is to say, situations of conflict may also be seen as settings for learning about, and growing up into, the social forms that constitute a society: in moments of conflict are displayed, more or less explicitly, ideas concerning 'who're our friends, who're with us' and 'who're our foes, who're against us'.[10] Conflict, thus,

---

[9] Simmel 1971: 70–95 carries excerpts from his *Conflict*, part of a larger work, 1908.

[10] Readers familiar with Evans-Pritchard's *The Nuer* (1940) would recall that what he calls 'structure' in their segmentary lineages is witnessed principally in

strengthens identities within the society. The 'we'-ness arises through mobilization against adversaries; 'hostilities' against an 'external' enemy may help overcome internal divisions (van der Dennen 1987: 36 summarizes the propositions concerning the underlying processes from the literature in psychology).[11]

Simultaneously, while strengthening the identities, conflicts reaffirm and renew the boundaries separating these entities. Patterned enmities, reciprocal antagonisms, and the like help maintain the divisions, and reaffirm the structure, including the pattern of stratification in the society. These boundaries are functionally important for members of the society; this is a crucial area of social orientation though, admittedly, such identities and boundaries may have their dysfunctions too.

To return to the familiar, however, let us recall that conflicts can indeed damage or destroy identities, boundaries, values, and much else also. The implications of conflict are thus variable, ranging all the way from reinforcing the social fabric to tearing it apart. The difference lies in how well conflicts in a society are regulated, mediated, modulated, and controlled; and we have

---

moments of conflict: mobilization takes place in terms of the boundaries in that system. It is through such enactments that the youngsters can learn what the society system of boundaries is, that they come to be 'socialized' into this aspect of the society.

[11] The issues are complex. On one side, one's identity—sense of the self—may of course be secured in other ways too: say, as an *individual*, though here, too, conflict may be important. One's affirming oneself, say in opposition to one's peers or authority figures or both, can be central to one's defining one's self.

On the other side, increased group cohesion is not a *necessary* consequence of conflict and crisis. For one thing, 'The corollary to the "search for the outer enemy" is the search for the inner enemy when . . . rigid [group] structures encounter defeat or an unexpected external danger'; hence, scapegoating (van der Dennen 1987: 33ff).

More generally, it has been suggested that:

Group integration decreases during a crisis if a likely solution to the crisis problem is unavailable. Group integration increases during a crisis if a likely cooperative solution to the crisis problem is present. Groups disintegrate during a crisis if a likely, competitive solution to the crisis problem is present. (Hamblin 1958 cited in ibid.: 35).

Clearly, under any of these conditions, the outcomes depend (1) on how the situation is perceived and interpreted by the participants, that is, how exactly they define the situation; and (2) on the quality of leadership in the group which persuades others to accept one, rather than another, definition of the situation.

reviewed several kinds of procedures and resources that may contribute to such regulation.

## Communication in Conflict

Certain kinds of conflict can aid in communication. The dramatic force of a conflict may help breach barriers which had served to impede such communication earlier. In a polity or an industrial organization, intermediary officials may have failed to convey relevant information accurately up and down the hierarchy; or, the adversaries' strong preconceptions may have prevented such prior communications from being appraised accurately (see Guha). Insofar as a conflict precipitates a crisis, major or minor, attempts to resolve the crisis may direct attention to the hitherto neglected information—or preconceptions.

## Conflict and Change

In particular socio-historical settings, 'conflict' and 'social change' may go together in a variety of ways. A conflict may be structurally significant, yielding radical changes in the relationships between the adversaries or even in the society as a whole as in India's freedom movement; or it may be structurally insignificant, without such effects, as in a street brawl. Between these poles, we may recognize several kinds of situations.

Conflict within a family may lead to changes, but these changes may only be cyclical: several social patterns alternate here by virtue of a longer-term internal logic. To illustrate such a cycle we may consider a society in which joint families of the patrilineal kind are valued and preferred.

Cyclical changes: The life cycle of such families takes them through several phases. If we begin with the phase when, structurally, it is at its simplest, we have the nuclear family of a couple and its children. Sons grow up, marry, and bring their brides to live in the parental home, making up a joint family. Prevailing norms may require these couples to continue to live together—at least as long as the parents are alive. With the parents' demise, we may have to redesignate the joint family as an extended one. At about that time, if the parents had more than one son, friction between the constituent families may grow, and pulls for them to separate may get stronger: a split in the joint family may yield several nuclear families again (see Madan and Rizvi).

The precise distribution of family types in the community would reflect the random play of contingent elements: the number of sons, the parents' age at death, the emotional tone of relationships within the family, and so forth. The family types' distribution would consequently vary from year to year; but the long-term pattern of changes would be cyclical, without a discernible direction to the changes. What we have illustrated with the simple case of the family can be seen also in other, more complex social settings (see, for a case of cyclical political systems, Leach 1954; and, for a model of cyclical changes in patterns of conflict, Attwood).[12]

Challenges to the old order: A range of conflicts may be implicated in any major structural change, as the older patterns of power and status are challenged by the bearers of a new order. Recent generations have witnessed enormous, cumulative enlargements of possible scales of activities and relationships, not to mention the changing political systems; consequently, there have inevitably been vast upheavals in matters of wealth, power, and status. The moment of conflict may then be part of ongoing processes of social restructuring; and 'conflict' and 'social change' may facilitate each other reciprocally (Coser 1967: Ch. 1). Similarly, as we shall see shortly, the counterposing of diverse cultural traditions may have large implications for the entrenched patterns of power and status; and therefore such juxtaposing may also release a battery of conflicts.

Shaping the social frameworks: Actors may take initiatives whose consequences, intended or otherwise, turn out to be large;

---

[12] Need we say that all changes are not cyclical in character. 'Social change' may have a purposive dimension, a direction, provided certain conditions are met. The matter is complex, and here we can only indicate its link with 'conflict'. Put briefly, for a society to realize directional changes, it needs roles, institutions, and the like which make choices in terms of a set of purposes, persistently, authoritatively (van Parijs 1981: Ch. 4; Saberwal 1987). Led by such roles and institutions, the society may be able to maintain continuity and a sense of direction, even amidst conflicts and disruptions.

so large indeed that these change the very frameworks for subsequent contestation. Prophet Mohammed's ability to establish
a state in the hitherto acephalous Arab society made a decisive
difference to the seventh century Arab patterns of conflict. Instead
of getting spent in internal feuds and fighting, their energies
were thenceforth directed outwards. Within a century of the
Prophet's death, the Arabs' writ ran from southern France in
the West and to the Indus in the East. Likewise, Gandhi's
injection of the technique of civil disobedience into the national
movement served to transform the framework of conflict between
Indian nationalists on one side and the colonial government on
the other.

## Mixing of Cultural Codes

The mention of Gandhi and the national movement brings
us to recent Indian historical experience, and the following
pages will explore this phase at some length. The epilogue
hitherto, as well as the Introduction, have sought to prepare
the ground by offering a diverse set of perspectives on the
phenomenon of conflict. These have been general considerations, applicable to different types of contestation across the
board. Yet both the form and the substance of a dispute are
shaped crucially by its social location: the protracted dispute
reported by Madsen would make little sense outside north
Indian Jat society. Conflicts within a family, a political party,
or an industry have their characteristic rhythms too, as our
selections for the different domains show.

We propose now that any society, in a particular epoch,
displays a characteristic pattern of conflicts. Their substance, their
form, their frequency, their distribution, and the modes of their
resolution—all these vary with the society's historical circumstances. The issues cannot be explored in their full complexity here.
Our purpose is modest: here we wish only to suggest some
relationships between the patterns of conflict in modern India—
and their complex historical settings. Encounters between diverse
cultures and traditions are inherently loaded with potentials for
conflict—especially since the parties to the encounter may not
be keen to avoid conflict; on the contrary! This potential arises

because a culture or tradition has, among its most distinctive marks, a characteristic repertoire of ordering devices, of condensed (and other) symbols, and of associated metaphysics. Such a repertoire arises, and is shaped, in course of the specific historical courses taken by the society.

Elements from different traditions may well, on occasion, blend with each other, like milk and water. How far this mingling goes, and how well, depends on the circumstances of the encounter: the intrinsic ideologies, orientations, and resilience of the traditions, the nature of the institutions representing the different traditions, the prevailing patterns of power and authority, and much else. The blending together of the traditions, in any case, would be a process in history, subject to all the vicissitudes of history. The completeness of the process cannot be taken for granted, a priori.

Difficulties arise partly from the circumstance that particular identities, associated with the distinctive traditions, may endure through the encounter—or may be revived (or, indeed, freshly aroused) on later occasions. Where the cultural encounter is framed by armed conquest, of one or another kind—say, the dominance of caste societies over adjacent tribal ones; the Saltanat, the Mughal, or successor regimes during the medieval period; or the colonial one subsequently—the diverse traditions in encounter may, when the dust settles, give the impression of co-existing harmoniously. Insofar as the separate identities associated with the different traditions have not dissolved themselves substantially, the harmonious co-existence may depend heavily on acquiescence to certain equations of power. Hence Dumont's terse comment, apropos the course of relations between Muslims and Hindus:

> Regarding the two communities, what we must understand is that the modus vivendi that they attained was, in relation to their respective values, a kind of compromise which depended for its maintenance on the continuance of Muslim power (1964: 55).

Remove the political equation that underwrites such harmony—and that harmony is in jeopardy.[13]

---

[13] There remains the strong possibility that seemingly minor elements out of the contrasting traditions become emblematic of larger differences of culture and (at least potential) identities (see Appendix). Indeed, in the consciousness of

Subsequent conflict, in such a situation, may well be attributed to the element which disturbed the political equation—say an intrusive colonial regime; yet conflicts of the same genre, if not the same details, may have existed before the previous political equation had come to be stabilized—and these may continue, full-bloodedly, even after the intrusive element has been ejected. In accounting for the course of these conflicts, a parsimonious explanation may not then fasten only on the transient, intrusive element. It must draw, rather, on our more general understandings of the devices requisite for undergirding durable social arrangements: that is, supportive ideologies, propagated and sustained by entrenched, credible institutions.

Indian historical experience over recent centuries invites these issues' exploration with reference to at least two sets of encounters: those between Islam and indigenous peoples in the first instance, and between the European tradition and institutions and the indigenous ones in the second.

## Pre-colonial India

In much of caste-organized, agrarian, village India, the caste order provided the societal integration needed for maintaining the agricultural cycle as well as a full round of ritual and social activities. Devices for internal regulation, operative within the jati and the locality ensured that these social spaces would be able to function autonomously. This sense of autonomous functioning was especially strong for the locally dominant groups.

The integrative devices, supralocally, had drawn on diverse sources and taken various trajectories: little on this score, by way either of symbols or of institutions, was shared between, say, the Rajputs, the Chola, and the Mughals. The Mughal imperial arrangements did accommodate the ideas and institutions of subordinate entities as subordinate layers; their relative ranks were not in doubt. Relationships of cultural subordination prevailed in the localities too: in eighteenth century northern

---

those who are immediately involved, the larger differences may be recognized but dimly.

India, the Hindu merchant castes held sway in, say, Benaras; while Muslim groups, who had operated the erstwhile arrangements of government, dominated the small towns (Bayly 1983: 176–82, 189–93).

Indeed the different traditions appeared to co-exist harmoniously. Yet, uniquely, the caste order can enable constituent groups to keep their distinctive identities, even in conditions of political adversity. Their harmonious, subordinate co-existence has to be seen as *pro tem*: it would last while the prevailing equations of power held, to be opened for fresh negotiation with a shift in political circumstances.

The larger political equations are important for the course of relationships between the relatively stable social groups which are, actually or potentially, in adversarial relationships. These are no less important for groups which may appear to be above the battle. For example, we may refer to the case of the sufis and the like: in eighteenth century Awadh, while the Nawabi regime lasted, the sufis preached a doctrine of love and brotherhood, drawing upon Hindu and Muslim myth and symbol indiscriminately. The doctrine of tolerance appeared to flourish, backed by the Nawabs who saw their own power as being crucially dependent on cordial relations between Hindus and Muslims (Alam 1994; 1989). With the Nawabs passing, this political support dwindled: the colonial regime's ideological bases, and administrative ethos, were different. In the emerging order, the sufi synthesis tended to succumb to strident, exclusivist assertiveness by the orthodox religious men on both sides, clearing the way for the endemic 'religious' contentiousness that has followed (Bayly 1983: 335–8, 346–68; Freitag 1989).

We have argued that an impression of harmonious co-existence between different traditions may be transient; its continuation may be contingent on the constituent groups' continuing acquiescence to certain equations of power. We argued this with illustrations from the centuries preceding colonial rule in India. This transience has been manifest again in the aftermath of that colonial rule. To make the latter point, we must first sketch in something of the distinctiveness of the Western repertoire of ordering devices—and the associated metaphysics: these necessarily entered the colonial arrangements of government, were imbibed deeply by some groups within Indian society, and

indeed pervade much of 'institution building' and the like in
post-colonial India too.

## Europe

Ordering devices, and the associated metaphysics, of west European provenance have been key strands in the making of
contemporary India—indeed of the contemporary world. Consequently, these strands invite attention in their own right. We
have space here to take only the barest notice of these complex
matters.[14]

In the settlement of disputes, it is possible in any society to
take recourse to force and violence. For regulating—and for
modulating—a vast range of conflicts, however, Western Europe
came to make quite unusual arrangements in the course of its
historical evolution. The distinctive mark of these arrangements
was their reliance on general rules. These bodies of general rules
were, commonly, organized into wide-ranging, impersonal legal
codes, and these were administered with the help of specialist
courts and the legal profession.[15]

The skills of working with general categories come down
from the ancient Greek philosophers (Lloyd 1990: Ch. 2).[16]
These went into the practice of formulating general laws. Such
law-making, and bringing the laws to bear on everyday disputes,
come down from the ancient Roman lawmakers. In the aftermath
of the waning of the Roman empire, the habits of working
with general rules and laws tended to decline in Europe. After
the eleventh century, however, complex, wide-ranging developments —in economies, in polities, in the growth of legal learning—contributed to the revival of legal institutions and practices
in western Europe.[17]

Among the most spectacular uses of general laws is that of

[14] For more extensive consideration, Saberwal 1991a, 1991b, 1991c.

[15] This development was the strongest within states, with their sovereign
authority; but international law has also been growing in recent generations.

[16] We thank Dr Majid Siddiqi for calling this work to our attention.

[17] Ramanujan 1989, in a litterateur's statement, sees this as a major facet of
the contrast between the Indian and the Western traditions, Saberwal 1991b
tracks the course of these interlinked developments in medieval Europe.

framing, and working with, formal Constitutions to regulate polities, large or small; and Italian city-states, like Florence, were writing—and re-writing—Constitutions for themselves from the twelfth century on. Working with general rules, impersonal laws, and formal Constitutions has contributed importantly to the long-term ordering of European societies.

This impulse has worked alongside the proliferation of a variety of institutions. The Church, the states, the Universities, and all manner of corporations, including industrial units in recent times, illustrate that profusion of institutions. These institutions, often of large scale, have commonly carried the mark of authority, and a capacity for sustained, imperative coordination, associated with bureaucracies. These have been crucial historic resources in managing conflicts within, and in ensuring the orderly functioning of, these complex societies.[18]

## Colonial India

The colonial ambience led to major shifts in the loci, and in the manner of exercising, power and authority. The locus of administrative authority shifted from indigenous to colonial hands; and the latter worked in a style drawing upon the European legal and administrative traditions. These shifts disturbed the received, older social hierarchies on one side and, on the other, altered the structure of opportunities: all together, these shifts served to make it possible for some hitherto subordinated groups to become more assertive. Their implications for conflict took the form that they did partly owing to the pre-existing patterns of Indian society.

As is commonly the case when political regimes change markedly, the structures of prevailing opportunities changed under the colonial regime also: political opportunities flowed out of the hands of entrenched groups, while unforeseen commercial and other opportunities came the way of new groups. This was partially linked with the nascent enlargement of scales—in production, in the physical movement of people, in governmental bureaucracy—associated with the new regime.

---

[18] The overall ordering role of such institutions remains even though these would themselves have, at times, been parties to conflicts at another level.

On the other side, the earlier rules of the game of government were being replaced. Groups which may have been unhappy over the earlier arrangements got the signal, then, to appeal to another authority, that swore by different rules. This presented a clear threat to the previous, indigenous social authorities, and to their dominance in the localities.

Neither formal arenas nor public deliberative styles were readily available for negotiating alternative pecking orders. Issues came to be joined around religious events, such as religious processions at the time of major festivals. Determined attempts at enlarging one's socio-ritual space, or at resisting its abridgment, would force a crisis; and negotiations would follow, wherein the local pecking order might be adjusted. (Freitag 1989: 127, passim).

## Contemporary India[19]

The passing of administrative authority from indigenous to colonial hands, we have suggested, had served to disturb both the pre- existing social hierarchies and the structures of available opportunities. The implications of these shifts led to much subsequent social turbulence. The reverse flow of authority, into indigenous hands in the post-colonial period, has made fresh ground for turbulence—and conflict.

A far-reaching, expansive enlargement of scales—part technical, as in production, transportation, and communication, and part social, as in the growth of cities, bureaucracies, and the resources for learning—had been associated with the colonial regime—and is indeed among the continuing hallmarks of our time. We have noted that these processes disturb the established hierarchies continually, necessitating adjustments that may seem to be threatening to many, and continuing to provide grounds for conflicts, regardless of the political regime which prevails.

The colonial regime had presided over a split level society in India. At one level, and ultimately in control, was the colonial bureaucracy whose authority rested upon European legal and administrative ideas: the state's monopoly over force; a legal order built on impersonal, general rules; and a body of social and

---

19 This summary rests on Saberwal 1993 which cites the supportive literature.

political theory including, for example, support for the 'individual' as against hereditary groups, collective social disabilities, and the like. Its characteristic devices for resolving disputes and maintaining social order leaned heavily on authoritative legislation and the formal courts of law.[20]

This bureaucracy presided over a society whose long-entrenched premises were often at variance with the foregoing. To try to make the Western ordering devices effective at much social depth would have required administrative resources so large—and evoked popular resistance so intense—that the attempt was never seriously made. The reach of the legislation and of the courts of law remained, by and large, limited to the operations of government itself, to issues of large-scale commerce and substantial property, and to the wider public domains including some limited kinds of social reform.[21]

This, then, was one level of the colonial society. Subordinate to it was another. At this second level, within the autonomous working of social spaces like those of the jati and locality, the older, familiar, indigenous devices for internal regulation, control, and conflict management had continued in good measure, commonly underwriting the older idioms of dominance. These relied on the ideology of caste hierarchy, the possibility of mobilizating caste groups, the use of force on private account, and related resources.

Substantial continuity marked the passage from the colonial to the post-colonial phase. Western devices for conflict management, through authoritative legislation and formal courts of law, continued at one level; framing the Constitution of free India was one of its triumphs. At the other level, however, the older idioms of dominance also continued. Yet the equation between the two levels changed subtly, but effectively: for the basis for determining who could govern legitimately had been shifting decisively.

[20] Needless to say, the armed might of the police and the army always stood behind these institutions, giving their writ credibility.

[21] Not always, though. In *Jeffrey*'s study of late nineteenth and early twentieth century Travancore, faced with the contrary premises of the European as well as other Indian ideas concerning correct family relationships, the moral basis for the matrilineal Nair joint family dissolved: it underwent a 'parameter collapse', to use a phrase from the British anthropologist Edwin Ardener (Ovesen 1991: 103). Noticeable collapses, or reversals, happened in other pockets too (e.g. Dirks 1987: 380).

In the heyday of the empire, the rulers' legitimacy derived ultimately from colonial authority; they did not have to seek fresh mandate periodically, from the ruled, for continuing to rule—principally in terms of Western ideas of governance. The post-colonial situation had been paradoxical: the new Constitution—set to Western keys—locates legitimacy in electoral support from below. Rulers, and potential rulers, at several levels must peri-odically seek mandate from the governed. All the massive social and political turbulence of recent decades notwithstanding, the ideas operative among the governed continue in good measure to echo indigenous idioms: idioms both of symbol and rhetoric to which they respond, and of the patterns of authority on the ground. Those who get elected in this ambience often lack an understanding of, let alone a full commitment to, the Western conceptions of law and government: conceptions which underline the Constitution, by whose authority they have been elected.

Put otherwise, contemporary Indian society and polity harbour two sets of ordering devices simultaneously, one indigenous, the other Western. No surprise, then, that the situation should spawn opportunities for conflicts. These opportunities stem from several sorts of contention. On one hand, there is the contention for dominance—relative strength, status, and privileges in the emerg-ing, changing order—as between the protagonists of these two sets of ordering devices, let alone the contention between groups on the same side of the fence. On the other hand, as indigenous ideas and devices grow more strident, difficulties arise because these devices have not been attuned to, these have not evolved historically in response to, the kind of social complexity which they now have to address.

Set to contrasting keys, the implications of the divergent order-ing devices can be mutually subversive. The core premises of the Western social, political, and legal traditions, in their Indian versions, have served to undermine the legitimacy of the caste order, fully backing the Ambedkarite and other, similar revolts. So widespread has the assault on the caste system been that, as an ordering device, it can be more or less written off. Indeed, key elements out of the caste system become agencies for con-flict—and therefore disorder (see Alm).

On the other hand, the ordering capacities of Western-inspired bureaucratic functioning, of formal legal institutions, and of the general conceptions of the legal order have also been declining. Of alien provenance, and able to claim but shallow roots in the contemporary Indian tradition, these work best with general rules, impersonally, with an unfamiliar conception of the 'individual', and so forth. As these domains succumb to the pressures of interests defined in caste, religious, and similar terms, their capacity to maintain their own consistency and integrity declines. With both sets of ordering devices getting eroded, a growing tendency towards anomie has long been evident.[22]

## CODA

In situations of conflict, as in other social situations, our perceptions of what there 'is' are always at risk from our wishes about what there 'ought to be'. This happens between those who stand across a fence in a particular moment of contestation. This happens also with scholars who study and write about conflicts. Reluctant to acknowledge the existence of a range of conflicts, for whatever reasons, we may be tempted to bury them under such concepts as 'false consciousness' or India's hallowed traditions of tolerance and community living.

This volume recognizes the paramount claims of what there 'is'—howsoever unpleasant it may be. Only by grasping 'what there is' accurately can we expect to be able to carry our notions of what there 'ought to be' into reality. It is our hope that the reader will find the materials assembled in this volume an aid to accurate appraisals of a major aspect of our social existence, namely conflicts.

---

[22] This stance finds support in *Cohn*. In contrast, *Galanter* and *Kidder* are struck by the extent to which these mechanisms have been domesticated in Indian society. Read carefully, however, the limited quality of *Kidder*'s optimism is obvious enough.

# Appendix

## SYMBOLS AND CONFLICT

We may explore some aspects of the play of symbols in conflict using categories advanced by Basil Bernstein, concerning how people use their language.[23] His framework has emerged from sociolinguistic research into the contrasts—between working- and middle-class children in England—in the patterns of using language. His argument is that it is characteristic of the subcultures associated with the English working and middle classes (and, more generally, with those in contemporary Western industrial societies) that their members should select and organize their 'speech events' in a particular way—marked respectively by what he calls the 'restricted code' and the 'elaborated code' though persons may switch their linguistic code under certain circumstances (1971: Ch. 9; p. 145). Children learn their habits of language use from several sources in their particular social milieu.

Put briefly, some social groups are tied rather closely to a limited set of social contexts and relationships, separated from other social groups by more or less unseen barriers. One communicates with others in the same, shared context ordinarily, so that the speaker and listener partake of a (relatively limited) common range of experiences and meanings. A large part of the communication is implicit, intuitive, without need to articulate the whys and wherefore of what one is trying to convey. Since the need for such articulation arises but seldom in this social stratum, its members do not acquire the practised skills of laying out the premises of their own experience or interpretations; they do not try routinely to uncover these preconscious springs of their own,

---

[23] This summary closely follows Saberwal 1991 c: 723f.

and of others', behaviour. They manage to go through their social rounds with only a restricted code of language use. Bernstein sees the English working class's pattern of language use as being limited by this restricted code since, historically, it has not had access to an elaborated code.

The elaborated code, in contrast, is the province of the middle class in an industrialized society. Its members learn to deploy actively a much larger lexical, and syntactical, repertoire. The speaker has acquired the linguistic capability to communicate far and wide, to persons who may not share one's experiences of the context at issue: a capability which is the mark of an 'educated' person. One's training in one's early years prepares one to handle a large variety of social contexts and relationships, having to communicate with a variety of people of diverse social backgrounds. Sometimes one communicates about shared experiences with kin and friends; and then a restricted code would do. These English middle class children are able to use both kinds of codes.

Where social encounters are wide ranging, one may not always take for granted that the other person is aware of, and can readily grasp, one's particular experiences and meanings. For what one is trying to convey to the other, one has to try to spell out the fine shadings of its context. Furthermore, in having to present to others the premises implicit in one's own, and in others', behaviour, one may oneself become more conscious of these premises. As a result, it becomes more probable that one would be inclined, reflexively, to act on–to work consciously at modifying–one's own behaviour. Communication here is between individuals in their distinctive roles, as in a highly differentiated, industrialized society.

A restricted code may serve adequately for communicational needs where the roles are less individualized–or more 'communalised', as Bernstein puts it, in the sense of being relatively undifferentiated, or relatively stable, standardized roles within the group (ibid.: 175–9; passim). The linguistic and other symbols employed in such a situation may be condensed, one's identity, intentions, emotions, and much else being carried in a word or a gesture (ibid.: 177; see also Gouldner 1985: 235–9).[24]

---

[24] Preston (1980: esp. Chs. IV and V) documents the use of condensed symbols in worship in a temple in Orissa. As part of a complex ritual during a

Lack of skill with using elaborated codes entails, too, difficulties in articulating one's cognitions, emotions, and intentions with much precision. We may take brief note of its wider social implications. The past century and more have witnessed the physical movement of vast numbers of people in India, one element in the pervasive enlargement of possible social scales in recent generations (Saberwal 1986: Ch. 2; Barth 1978). Large fractions of those on the move in fact function only in restricted codes. Their vernacular skills from their home area may have only limited use in their new linguistic milieu; and their proficiency in the language of their host area may barely suffice for elementary shopping and the like. Multilingual practice may relieve the constriction of their communicative range in only a minor way.

Groups from diverse religious, linguistic, and other social backgrounds come together in metropolitan, industrial, and other large centres. Each such group ordinarily carries its own body of more or less distinctive, heavily charged symbols. These symbols may have mutually exclusive meanings for corresponding groups (see Chakrabarty for the uses of 'cow' and 'pig' among jute mill workers in late 19th century). Their counterposing may come to stand for an opposition between the different groups:

> If two symbolic systems are confronted, they begin to form, even by their opposition, a single whole. In this totality each half may be represented to the other by a single element which is made to jump out of context to perform this role (Douglas 1973: 63).

The new neighbours may never have learned to articulate their fears, hopes, and intentions; indeed their social repertoire may lack the skills for communicating with strangers at any length at all. Consequently, they may not be able to articulate to themselves, and to others, the (partly unconscious) grounds for the opposition between them and their neighbours. The most routine of conflicts,

---

major festival, the principal priest at the temple strews flowers at the feet of the image of the goddess. Consider his testimony about their significance (1980: 55):

> What is a flower? It is my soul. It is my prayer. All of my Self is offered in the flowers. . . . the ideas in the mind are expressed to the goddess with the help of flowers. My mind, my body, my life, my soul—all these things are given through the flowers. It is a divine medium. They are *divine* flowers.

transformed into and expressed in condensed symbols, would thus acquire an 'ethnic' dimension.[25]

---

[25] Societies may be seen as being *flexible* or *rigid* (pp. 502f); we may note here that the symbolic order associated with a society or social group may also be flexible or rigid. One measure of the flexibility of a symbolic order would lie in its resources for reflexivity: that is, its resources permitting its own reconstitution in the light of ongoing experience, including the experience of contrary viewpoints. A rigid symbolic order, in contrast, is exclusivist. It does not encourage contrary viewpoints to be considered sympathetically, leave alone efforts at reconciling them or searching for compromises.

# Bibliography

ACHARYYA, BIJAY KISOR
1914        *Codification in British India*, Calcutta: S.K. Banerji & Sons.

AGARWAL, SHRIMAN NARAYAN
1946        *Gandhian Constitution for Free India*, Allahabad: Kitabistan.

AHMED, SUFIA
1974        *Muslim Community in Bengal, 1884–1912*, Dacca: Oxford University Press.

ALAM, MUZAFFAR
1989        Competition and Co-existence: Indo-Islam Interaction in Medieval North India, *Itinerario* 13: 37–59.

FORTHCOMING *Assimilation from a Distance: Renewal of a Tradition in Late Medieval Awadh* (to appear in *Festschrift* in honour of Romila Thapar).

ALL INDIA CONGRESS COMMITTEE
1954        *Report of the Congress Village Panchayat Committee*, New Delhi.

ANDERSON, B.
1983        *Imagined Communities: Reflections on the Origin and Spread of Nationalism*, London: Verso.

APPADURAI, A. AND C. BRECKENRIDGE
1976        The South Indian Temple: Authority, Honour, and Redistribution, *Contributions to Indian Sociology* n.s. 10: 187–211.

*Aside*
1988        *Aside: the Magazine of Madras* (fortnightly), 16–30 Novem-
1989        ber 1988 and 1–15 April 1989.

ASSMANN, JAN
1988        Kollektives Gedachtnis und Kulturelle Identitat, in Jan
            Assmann and Tonio Holchet (eds), *Kultur und
            Gedachtnis*, Suhrkamp Tasenbuch Wissenschaft 724.

ATHREYA, V.B., G. DJURFELDT, AND S. LINDBERG
1990        *Barriers Broken: Production Relations and Agrarian
            Change in Tamil Nadu*, New Delhi: Sage.

ATTWOOD, D.W.
1974        Patrons and Mobilizers: Political Entrepreneurs in an
            Agrarian State, *Journal of Anthropological Research* 30:
            225–41.

1977        Factions and Class Conflict in Rural Western India, in
            M. Silverman and R.F. Slisbury (eds), *A House Divided:
            Anthropological Studies of Factionalism*, St. John's, New-
            foundland: Memorial University, Institute of Social and
            Economic Research.

AUGUSTINE, JOHN S. (ed.)
1982        *The Indian Family in Transition*, New Delhi: Vikas.

AUSTIN, GRANVILLE
1966        *The Indian Constitution: Cornerstone of a Nation*, Oxford:
            Clarendon Press.

BAGAL, J.C.
1953        *History of the Indian Association, 1876–1951*, Calcutta.

BAILEY, F.G.
1963        Closed Social Stratification in India, *Archives Europeenes
            de Sociologie* 4: 107–24.

1965        Decisions by Consensus in Councils and Committees,
            in M. Banton (ed.), *Political Systems and the Distribution
            of Power*, New York: Praeger.

BAILEY, F.G.
1969        *Strategems and Spoils*, New York: Schocken.

BAKER, C.J.
1984        *An Indian Rural Economy, 1880–1955*, Delhi: Oxford
            University Press.

BAMFORD, P.C.
1925        *Histories of the Non-Co-operation and Khalifat Movements*,
            reprint, Delhi: Deep Publications, 1974.

BANAJI, JAIRUS
1985        Conflict and Bargaining in Bombay: Being a Prelim-
            inary Survey of Bargaining Relationships and the Sour-
            ces of Bargaining Power in the New Industries.
            Mimeographed.

BARNES, S.B.
1969        Paradigms—Scientific and Social, *Man* 4: 94–102.

BARTH, FREDRIK (ed.)
1969        *Ethnic Groups and Boundaries: The Social Organization
            of Cultural Difference*, London: Allen & Unwin.

1978        *Scale and Social Organization*, Oslo: Universitetsforlaget.

BATESON, GREGORY
1936        *Naven*, (2nd edition) Stanford: Stanford University Press,
            1958.

1971        *Steps to an Ecology of Mind*, London: Intertext.

BAYLY, C.A.
1983        *Rulers, Townsmen and Bazaars: North Indian Society in
            the Age of British Expansion, 1770–1870*, Cambridge:
            Cambridge University Press.

BEALS, ALAN R.
1974        *Village Life in South India*, Chicago: Aldine.

BEALS, ALAN R. AND B.J. SIEGEL
1967          *Divisiveness and Social Conflict: An Anthropological Approach*, Bombay: Oxford University Press.

BECK, BRENDA E.F.
1982          Indian Minstrels as Sociologists: Political Strategies Depicted in a Local Epic, *Contributions to Indian Sociology* 16: 35–57.

BERGER, P.L. AND T. LUCKMANN
1966          *The Social Construction of Reality*, Harmondsworth: Penguin.

BERNSTEIN, BASIL
1971          *Class, Codes and Control: Theoretical Studies Towards a Sociology of Language,* vol. 1, London: Routledge & Kegan Paul.

BERREMAN, GERALD D.
1963          *Hindus of the Himalayas*, Bombay: Oxford University Press.

BHARAT, SHALINI AND MURLI DESAI (eds)
1991          *Research on Families with Problems in India: Issues and Implications (2 vols)*, Bombay: Tata Institute of Social Sciences.

BINGLEY, A.H.
1978          *History, Caste, and Culture of Jats and Gujars* (1st edition 1899), New Delhi: Ess Ess Publications.

BINNS, DAVID
1977          *Beyond the Sociology of Conflict*, London: Macmillan.

BLOCH, MAURICE
1991          Language, Anthropology and Cognitive Science, *Man* n.s. 26: 183–98.

BOHANNAN, PAUL (ed.)
1967          *Law and Warfare: Studies in the Anthropology of Conflict*, Garden City, New York: Natural History Press.

BOTTOMORE, T.B.
1975 *Sociology as Social Criticism*, London: Allen and Unwin.

BRASS, PAUL R.
1965 *Factional Politics in an Indian State: The Congress Party in Uttar Pradesh*, Berkeley: University of California Press.

1972 The Politics of Ayurvedic Education, in L. Rudolph and S. Rudolph (eds), *Education and Politics in India*, Delhi: Oxford University Press, 342–71.

1990 *The Politics of India since Independence*, (The New Cambridge History of India, IV/1, Cambridge: Cambridge University Press.

BUCHANAN, D.H.
1934 *The Development of Capitalist Enterprise in India*, New York: Macmillan.

CARRAS, MARY C.
1972 *The Dynamics of Indian Political Factions: A Study of District Councils in the State of Maharashtra*, Cambridge: Cambridge University Press.

CARSTAIRS, ROBERT
1912 *The Little World of An Indian District Officer*, London.

CARTER, ANTHONY T.
1974 *Elite Politics in Rural India: Political Stratification and Political Alliances in Western Maharashtra*, Cambridge: Cambridge University Press.

CENSUS OF INDIA
1911 *Bengal, Bihar, and Orissa and Sikkim*, Vol. 5, Part 1, Report by L.S.S. O'Malley, Calcutta.

1911 *Baroda*, Vol. 16, Part 1, Report by Govindbhai H. Desai. Bombay.

1971 Social and Cultural Tables, Series I, Part II-C (1).

CERTEAU, M. DE
1984      *The Practice of Everyday Life*, Berkeley: University of
          California Press.

CHAMBLISS, WILLIAM J. (ed.)
1973      *Sociological Readings in the Conflict Perspective*, Reading,
          Massachusetts: Addison-Wesley.

COHEN, ABNER
1974      *Two Dimensional Man: An Essay on the Anthropology of
          Power and Symbolism in Complex Society*, London: Rout-
          ledge & Kegan Paul.

COHEN, ALLAN R.
1974      *Tradition, Change and Conflict in Indian Family Business*,
          The Hague: Mouton.

COHN, BERNARD S.
1959      Some Notes on Law and Change in North India,
          *Economic Development and Cultural Change* 8: 79–93.

1965      Anthropological Notes on Disputes and Law in India,
          in L. Nadar (ed.), *The Ethnography of Law, American
          Anthropologist*, Special Publication, vol. 67, no. 6, part 2,
          82–122.

COLLINS, RANDALL
1975      *Conflict Sociology: Toward an Explanatory Science*, New
          York: Academic Press.

COMAROFF, J.
1985      *Body of Power, Spirit of Resistance*, Chicago: University
          of Chicago Press.

COSER, LEWIS
1956      *The Functions of Social Conflict*, Glencoe: Free Press.

1967      *Continuities in the Study of Social Conflict*, New York:
          Free Press.

CROOKE, WILLIAM
1896        *The Tribes and Castes of the North Western Provinces and Oudh*, Calcutta.

DAHRENDORF, RALF
1959        *Class and Class Conflict in Industrial Society*, Stanford: Stanford University Press.

1969        Toward a Theory of Social Conflict, in Walter L. Wallace (ed.), *Sociological Theory: An Introduction*, London: Heinemann, 213–26.

DERRETT, J. AND M. DUNCAN
1958        Statutory Amendments of the Personal Law of the Hindus since Indian Independence, *American Journal of Comparative Law* 7: 380–93.

1961        The Administration of Hindu Law by the British, *Comparative Studies in Society and History* 4: 10–52.

1964        Aspects of Matrimonial Causes in Modern Hindu Law, *Revue du Sud-est Asiatique*, 203–41.

1968        *Religion, Law and the State in India*, London: Faber and Faber.

1969        Law, Paper presented to Study Conference on Tradition in Indian Politics and Society, 1–3 July 1969, University of London (School of Oriental and African Studies), mimeographed.

DESAI, A.R. (ed.)
1979        *Peasant Struggles in India*, Delhi: Oxford University Press.

1986        *Agrarian Struggles in India After Independence*, Delhi: Oxford University Press.

DESAI, I.P. *et al.*
1985        *Caste, Caste Conflict and Reservations*, Delhi: Ajanta.

DHANAGARE, D.N.
1983        *Peasant Movements in India, 1920–50*, Delhi: Oxford
            University Press.

DHARMPAL
1971        *Civil Disobedience and Indian Tradition*, Varanasi: Sarva
            Seva Sangh Prakashan.

DICKINSON, JOHN
1853        *Government of India Under a Bureaucracy*, London. [Re-
            printed and published by Major B.D. Basu, Allahabad,
            1925.]

DIRKS, NICHOLAS
1987        *The Hollow Crown: Ethnohistory of an Indian Kingdom*,
            Cambridge: Cambridge University Press.

DOUGLAS, MARY
[1973]      *Natural Symbols: Explorations in Cosmology* (1st edition
            1970) Harmondsworth: Penguin.

DUBE, LEELA
1974        Sociology of Kinship: A Trend Report, in *A Survey of
            Research in Sociology and Social Anthropology*, vol. 2,
            Bombay: Popular Prakashan.

DUMONT, L.
1959        A Structural Definition of a Folk Deity, *Contributions to
            Indian Sociology* 3: 75–87.

1964        Nationalism and Communalism, *Contributions to Indian
            Sociology* 7: 30–70.

1966        Marriage in India, The Present State of the Question;
            III: North India in Relation to South India, *Contributions
            to Indian Sociology* 9: 90–114.

1986        *A South Indian Subcaste*, Delhi: Oxford University Press.

1988        *Affinity as a Value* (1st edition 1983) Delhi: Oxford
            University Press.

DUNCAN, GRAEME
1973 *Marx and Mill: Two Views of Social Conflict and Social Harmony*, Cambridge: Cambridge University Press.

DUSHKIN, L.
1985 Backwards and Forwards, in R.E. Frykenberg and P. Kolenda (eds), *Studies of South India: An Anthology of Recent Research and Scholarship*, Madras: New Era Publications.

DUYKER, EDWARD
1987 *Tribal Guerrillas: The Santals of West Bengal and the Naxalite Movement*, Delhi: Oxford University Press.

EASTON, DAVID
1965 *A Systems Analysis of Political Life*, New York: John Wiley.

EIGEN, MANFRED AND RUTHILD WINKLER
1982 *Laws of the Game: How the Principles of Nature Govern Chance*, New York: Penguin.

ENGINEER, ASGHAR ALI (ed.)
1984 *Communal Riots in Post-independence India*, Hyderabad: Sangam Books.

1989 *Communalism and Communal Violence in India: An Analytical Approach to Hindu-Muslim Conflict*, Delhi: Ajanta.

EPSTEIN, T. SCARLETT
1962 *Economic Development and Social Change in South India*, Manchester: Manchester University Press.

1973 *South India: Yesterday, Today and Tomorrow*, New York: Holmes & Meier.

ERIKSON, ERIK
1958 *Young Man Luther*, New York.

EVANS-PRITCHARD, E.E.
1940        *The Nuer*, Oxford: Oxford University Press.

FAIRCHILD, HENRY PRATT
1970        *Dictionary of Sociology and Related Sciences*, Totowa,
            New Jersey: Little Field, Adams.

FANON, FRANTZ
1965        *The Wretched of the Earth*, London: Macgibbon & Kee.

FINK, CLINTON
1968        Some Conceptual Difficulties in the Theory of Social
            Conflict, *Journal of Conflict Resolution* 12: 412–60.

FRANCIS, W.
1906        *Madras District Gazetteers: Madura, Vol. 1*, Madras:
            Government Press.

FRANKEL, FRANCINE R. AND M.S A. RAO (eds)
1989        *Dominance and State Power in Modern India, 2 Vols*,
            Delhi: Oxford University Press.

FREIDRICH, PAUL
1989        Language, Ideology and Political Economy, *American
            Anthropologist* n.s. 1: 1–25.

FREITAG, SANDRIA B.
1989        *Collective Action and Community: Public Arenas and the
            Emergence of Communalism in North India*, Berkeley:
            University of California Press.

1990        *Collective Action and Community: Public Arenas and the
            Emergence of Communalism in North India*, Delhi: Ox-
            ford University Press.

FROMM, ERICH
1973        *The Anatomy of Human Destructiveness*, New York: Faw-
            cett Crest.

FULLER, C.J.
1976      *The Nayars Today*, Cambridge: Cambridge University Press.

GABORIEAU, MARC
1972      Muslims in the Hindu Kingdom of Nepal, *Contributions to Indian Sociology* n.s, 6: 84–105.

GALANTER, MARC
1966      The modernization of Law, in Myron Weiner (ed.), *Modernization*, New York: Basic Books.

1968      The Displacement of Traditional Law in Modern India, *Journal of Social Issues* 24: 65–91.

1968–9    The Study of the Indian Legal Profession, *Law and Society Review* 3: 201–17.

GEERTZ, C.
1983      *Local Knowledge*, New York: Basic Books.

GLUCKMAN, MAX
1955      *Custom and Conflict in Africa*, Glencoe, Illinois.

GOFFMAN, E.
1959      *The Presentation of Self in Everyday Life*, Garden City, New York: Doubleday.

GOPAL, S (ed.)
1991      *Anatomy of a Confrontation: The Babri Masjid–Ram Janmabhumi Issue*, New Delhi: Viking/Penguin.

GOSWAMI, B.B.
1979      *The Mizo Unrest: A Study of Politicization of Culture*, Jaipur: Aalekh.

GOUGH, E. KATHLEEN
1955      The Social Structure of a Tanjore Village, in McKim Marriott (ed.), *Village India*, Chicago: University of Chicago Press.

1960    Caste in a Tanjore Village, in E.R. Leach (ed.), *Aspects of Caste in South India, Ceylon and Northwest Pakistan,* Cambridge: Cambridge University Press.

GOULD, H.A.
1960    The Micro-demography of Marriages in a North Indian Area, *Southwestern Journal of Anthropology* 16: 476–91.

1961    A Further Note on Village Exogamy in North India, *Southwestern Journal of Anthropology* 17: 297–300.

GOULDNER, ALVIN W.
1985    *Against Fragmentation: The Origins of Marxism and the Sociology of Intellectuals,* New York: Oxford University Press.

GOVERNMENT OF INDIA, MINISTRY OF LAW
1958    *Law Commission of India, Fourteenth Report (Reform of Judicial Administration),* 2 vols, New Delhi: Manager of Publications.

1962    *Report of the Study Team on Nyaya Panchayats,* Delhi.

GOVERNMENT OF INDIA, MINISTRY OF FOOD, AGRICULTURE, COMMUNITY DEVELOPMENT AND COOPERATION (DEPARTMENT OF COMMUNITY DEVELOPMENT).
1966    *Panchayati Raj at a Glance* (as on 31 March 1966), New Delhi.

GOVERNMENT OF RAJASTHAN, PANCHAYAT AND DEVELOPMENT DEPARTMENT
1964    *Report of the Study Team on Panchayati Raj,* Jaipur.

GRAMSCI, ANTONIO
1985    *Selections from Cultural Writings,* London.

GREENBLATT, S.
1988    *Shakespearean Negotiations,* Berkeley: University of California Press.

GROSS, JAN T.
1986          Polish–Jewish Relations during the War: An Interpreta-
              tion, *Archives Europeenes de Sociologie*, 27: 199–214.

GUHA, RAMCHANDRA
1991          *Unquiet Woods*, Delhi: Oxford University Press.

GUHA, RANAJIT
1982–7        *Subaltern Studies: Writings on South Asian History and
              Society, Vols 1–5*, Delhi: Oxford University Press.

GUNE, V.T.
1953          *The Judicial System of the Marathas*, Poona: Deccan
              College Post-Graduate and Research Institute.

GUPTA, DIPANKAR (ed.)
1991          *Social Stratification*, Delhi: Oxford University Press.

HARDGRAVE, R.L. Jr.
1969          *The Nadars of Tamilnad*, Berkeley: University of Califor-
              nia Press.

1977          The Mapilla Rebellion 1921: Peasant Revolt in Malabar,
              *Modern Asian Studies* 2: 57–99.

HARDY, P.
1972          *The Muslims of British India*, London: Cambridge
              University Press.

HARPER, EDWARD B.
1964          Ritual Pollution as an Integrator of Caste and Religion,
              *Journal of Asian Studies* 23: 151–97.

HASAN, ZOYA, S.N. JHA AND RASHEEDUDDIN KHAN (eds)
1989          *The State, Political Processes and Identity: Reflections On
              Modern India*, New Delhi: Sage.

HAYNES, DOUGLAS AND GYAN PRAKASH
1991          *Contesting Power: Resistance and Everyday Social Rela-
              tions in South Asia*, Delhi: Oxford University Press.

HAZLEHURST, L.W.
1966        *Entrepreneurship and the Merchant Castes of a Punjabi City*, Durham, N.C.: Duke University Program in Comparative Studies on Southern Asia.

HERSCHMAN, PAUL
1981        *Punjab Kinship and Marriage*, ed. by Hilary Standing, Delhi: Hindustan Publishing Corporation.

HOEBEL, E. ADAMSON
1954        *The Law of Primitive Man*, Cambridge, Mass.: Harvard University Press.

HOLMSTROM, MARK
1985        *Industry and Inequality: The Social Anthropology of Indian Labour*, Cambridge: Cambridge University Press.

HUSSAIN, M. BASHEER
1972        *The Cauvery Water Dispute*, Mysore: Rao and Raghavan.

INDIA, CONSTITUENT ASSEMBLY
1947        *Proceedings of the North East Frontier (Assam) Tribal and Excluded Areas Sub-committee, Vol. II (Evidence) Part I*, New Delhi: Government Press.

INDIA, MINISTRY OF INFORMATION AND BROADCASTING
1986        *Mizoram Accord*, Delhi: Gowardhan Kapoor & Sons.

IRSCHICK, E.F.
1986        *Tamil Revivalism in the 1930s*, Madras: Cre-A: (sic).

ISHWARAN, K.
1964        Customary Law in Village India, *International Journal of Comparative Sociology* 5: 228–43.

IYER, RADHA
1980        The Datta Samant factor, *Business Standard* 15 Sept.

JACKSON, A.M.T.
1907        Note on the History of the Caste System, *Journal of the Asiatic Society of Bengal* n.s. 3: 509–15.

JAIN, M.P.
1963          Custom as a Source of Law in India, *Jaipur Law Journal*
              3: 96–130.

JAIN, S.N. *et al.*
1971          *Inter-state Water Disputes in India*, New Delhi: Indian
              Law Institute.

JANNUZI, F. TOMASSON
1990          *India in Transition: Issues of Political Economy in a Plural
              Society*, Hyderabad: Orient Longman.

JOHRI, SITA RAM
1970          *Dark Corner of India*, Lucknow: Himalaya Publications.

KAKAR, S.
1982          *Shamans, Mystics, and Doctors*, New York: Knopf.

1985          Myths as History, *Times of India* 30 April, Bombay.

KANE, P.V.
1946          *History of Dharmasastra*, vol. 3, Poona.

1950          *Hindu Customs and Modern Law*, Bombay: University
              of Bombay.

KANNAN, K.P.
1988          *Of Proletarian Struggles: Mobilization and Organization
              of Rural Workers in South-west India*, Delhi: Oxford
              University Press.

KAPUR, PROMILLA
1970          *Marriage and the Working Woman in India*, Delhi: Vikas.

KAPUR, RAJIV A.
1987          *Sikh Separatism: The Politics of Faith*, Delhi: Vikas.

KATJU, K.N.
1948          Speech reported in the *All India Reporter Journal* 1948:
              22.

KOHUT, H.

1972      Thoughts on Narcissim and Narcisstic rage, *Psychoanalytic Study of the Child*, New York: International University Press.

KUPER, ADAM

1973      Anthropologists and Anthropology: The British School 1922–72, Harmondsworth: Penguin.

*Law and Society Review*

1968–9      A special issue devoted to lawyers in developing societies with particular reference to India, 3: (2–3) Nov. 1968–Feb. 1969.

LEACH, E.R.

1954      *Political Systems of Highland Burma*, (1st edition 1964) Boston: Beacon Press.

LEONARD, KAREN

1978      Hyderabad: the Mulki–Non-Mulki Conflict, in Robin Jeffrey (ed.), *People, Princes and Paramount Power: Society and Politics in the Indian Princely States*, Delhi: Oxford University Press, 65–106.

LEVY, HAROLD L.

1968–9      Lawyer-scholars, Lawyer-politicians and the Hindu Code Bill, *Law and Society Review* 3: 303–16.

LIDDLE, JOANNA AND RAMA JOSHI

1986      *Daughters of Independence: Gender, Caste and Class in India*, New Delhi: Kali for Women.

LIPSTEIN, K.

1957      The Reception of Western Law in India, *International Social Science Bulletin* 85–95.

LLOYD, G.E.R.

1990      *Demystifying Mentalities*, Cambridge: Cambridge University Press.

LUDDEN, D.

1989      *Peasant History in South India*, Delhi: Oxford University Press.

LUSCHINSKY, MILDRED S.

1963      The Impact of Some Recent Indian Government Legislation on the Women of an Indian Village, *Asian Survey* 3: 573–83.

LYNCH, OWEN M.

1967      Rural Cities in India: Continuities and Discontinuities, in Philip Mason (ed.), *India and Ceylon*, New York: Oxford University Press, 142–58.

MACDONALD, NORMAN

1975      The Biological Factor in the Etiology of War: A Medical View, in M.A. Nettleship, R. Dalegivens and A. Nettleship (eds), *War, its Causes and Correlates*, The Hague: Mouton, 209–31.

MALAVIYA, H.D.

1956      *Village Panchayats in India*, New Delhi: Economic and Political Research Department, All-India Congress Committee.

MANN, MICHAEL

1986      *The Sources of Social Power. I: A History of Power from the Beginning to AD 1760*, Cambridge: Cambridge University Press.

MAPLE, TERRY AND DOUGLAS W. MATHESON (eds)

1973      *Aggression, Hostility, and Violence: Nature or Nurture?* New York: Holt, Rinehart and Winston.

MARTINDALE, DON

1961      *The Nature and Types of Sociological Theory*, London: Routledge and Kegan Paul.

MARX, KARL

1963      *Selected Writings in Sociology and Social Philosophy* (ed.

by T.B. Bottomore and M. Rubel), Harmondswsorth: Penguin.

MAYER, A.C.

1966      The Significance of Quasi-groups in the Study of Complex Societies, in M. Banton (ed.), *The Social Anthropology of Complex Societies*, New York: Praeger, 97–122.

1967      Caste and Local Politics in India, in P. Mason (ed.), *India and Ceylon*, London: Oxford University Press, 121–41.

McCORMACK, WILLIAM

1966      Caste and the British Administration of Hindu Law, *Journal of Asian and African Studies* 1: 25–32.

MILNER, MURRAY, Jr.

1988      Status Relations in South Asian Marriage Alliances: Toward a General Theory, *Contributions to Indian Sociology* 22: 145–69.

MISRA, L.S.

1954      Inaugural address, *All-India Reporter Journal* 1954: 48.

MITSCHERLICH, ALEXANDER

1969      Protest and Revolution, *International Journal of Psychoanalysis* vol. 50, pt. 1.

MOON, PENDEREL

1945      *Strangers in India*, London.

NARAYAN, HEMENDRA

1984a     Bitter Experience of Government-MNF talks, *Indian Express* 8 Oct.

1984b     The Rise of Laldenga and the MNF, *Indian Express* 10 Oct.

NELSON, J.H.

1868      *The Madura Country: A Manual*, New Delhi: Asian Educational Services, 1989 reprint.

NETTLESHIP, M.A., R. DALEGIVENS, AND A. NETTLESHIP (eds)
1975     *War, its Causes and Correlates*, The Hague: Mouton.


NIBEDON, NIRMAL
1980     *Mizoram: The Dagger Brigade*, Delhi: Lancer.


NICHOLAS, RALPH AND T. MUKHOPADHYAY
1962     Politics and Law in Two West Bengal Villages, *Bulletin of The Anthropological Survey of India* 11: 15–40.


OOMMEN, T.K.
1982     Foreigners, Refugees and Outsiders in the Indian Context, *Sociological Bulletin* 31: 41–64.


OVESEN, JAN
1991     The Voice of Prophecy: A Review Article, *Ethnos* 56: 101–5.


PANDEY, GYANENDRA
1990     *Construction of Communalism in Colonial North India*, Delhi: Oxford University Press.


PARASHAR, ARCHANA
1992     *Women and Family Law Reform in India*, New Delhi: Sage.


PARSONS, TALCOTT
1964     The Father Symbol: An Appraisal in the Light of Psychoanalytic and Sociological Theory, *Social Structure and Personality*, New York.


PATEL, SUJATA
1987     *The Making of Industrial Relations: The Ahmedabad Textile Industry, 1918–39*, Delhi: Oxford University Press.


PENDSE, SANDIP
1981     The Datta Samant Phenomenon, *Economic and Political Weekly* 16: 695–97; 745–9.

PETTIGREW, JOYCE
1975        *Robber Noblemen: A Study of the Political System of the Sikh Jats*, London: Routledge.

PHADNIS, URMILA
1989        *Ethnicity and Nation-building in South Asia*, New Delhi: Sage.

PRADHAN, M.C.
1966        *The Political System of the Jats of Northern India*, Bombay: Oxford University Press.

PRESTON, JAMES J.
1980        *Cult of the Goddess: Social and Religious Change in a Hindu Temple*, New Delhi: Vikas.

PUBBY, VIPIN
1987        Mizo Poll Results, *Indian Express* 19 Feb. 1987.

PURWAR, VIJAYA LAKSHMI
1960        *Panchayats in Uttar Pradesh*, Lucknow.

RAHEJA, GLORIA GOODWIN
1988        *The Poison in the Gift: Ritual, Prestation, and the Dominant Caste in a North Indian Village*, Chicago: University of Chicago Press.

RAMACHANDRAN, V.K.
1990        *Wage Labour and Unfreedom in Agriculture: An Indian Case Study*, Oxford: Clarendon Press.

RAMANUJAN, A.K.
1989        Is there an Indian Way of Thinking? An Informal Essay, *Contributions to Indian Sociology* 23: 41–58.

RAMASWAMY, E.A.
1984        *Power and Justice: The State in Industrial Relations*, Delhi: Oxford University Press.

RANGASWAMI, AMRITHA
1978      Mizoram: Tragedy of Our Own Making, *Economic and Political Weekly* 13: 653–62.


RAO, C. NARAYANA
1984      Crisis in Mizoram, in B.L. Abbi (ed.), *North East Region: Problems and Prospects of Development*, Chandigarh: Centre for Research in Rural and Industrial Development.


RAPAPORT, ANATOL
1960      *Fights, Games and Debates*, Ann Arbor: University of Michigan Press.


RASTOGI, P.N.
1975      *The Nature and Dynamics of Factional Conflict*, Delhi: Macmillan India.


RAY, RABINDRA
1988      *The Naxalites and Their Ideology*, Delhi: Oxford University Press.


RETZLAFF, RALPH H.
1962      *Village Government in India: A Case Study*, London: Asia.


REX, JOHN
1981      *Social Conflict: A Conceptual and Theoretical Analysis*, London: Longman.


REYNOLDS, V., V.S.E. FALGER, AND IAN VINE
1987      *The Sociobiology of Ethnocentrism (Evolutionary Dimensions of Xenophobia, Discrimination, Racism and Nationalism)*, London: Croom Helm.


ROBERTS, JOHN M.
1965      Oaths, Autonomic Ordeals, and Power, *American Anthropologist* 67, No. 6, Part ii (special issue on Ethnography of Law), 186–212.

ROBINS, ROBERT S.
1962            India: Judicial Panchayats in Uttar Pradesh, *American Journal of Comparative Law* 11: 239–46.

ROBINSON, FRANCIS
1974            *Separatism Among Indian Muslims*, London: Cambridge University Press.

ROSENTHAL, DONALD B.
1972            Sources of District Congress Factionalism in Maharashtra, *Economic and Political Weekly* 7: 1725–48.

ROSS, H.L.
1970            *Settled Out of Court*, Chicago.

ROY, ANIMESH
1982            *Mizoram: Dynamics of Change*, Calcutta: Pearl Publishers.

ROY, SRIPATI
1911            *Customs and Customary Law in British India*, Calcutta: Hare Press.

ROY BURMAN, B.K.
1970            *Demographic and Socio-economic Profiles of the Hill Areas of North-East India, Census of India 1961*, Delhi: Department of Publications.

RUDOLPH, L.I. AND S.H. RUDOLPH
1965            Barristers and Brahmins in India: legal cultures and social change, *Comparative Studies in Society and History* 8: 24–49.

1987            *Modernity of Tradition*, [Delhi: Orient Longmans, 1967 Original.]

SABERWAL, SATISH
1986            *India: The Roots of Crisis*, Delhi: Oxford University Press.

SABERWAL, SATISH
1987        A Comparative Study of Very Long-term Processes, *International Political Science Review* 8: 307–18.

1991a       Ideas, Institutions, and Experience, *Sociological Bulletin* 40: 1–19.

1991b       On the Rise of Institutions, or, the Church and Kingship in Medieval Europe, *Studies in History* 7: 107–34.

1991c       Segmentation and Literacy, *Economic and Political Weekly*, Annual number, 26: 723–38.

1994        Democratic Political Structures, in T.V. Sathyamurthy (ed.), *Social Change and Political Discourse in India: Structures of Power, Movements of Resistance, Vol. 1: State and Nation in the Context of Social Change*, Delhi: Oxford University Press, 174–97.

SARIN, V.I K.
1980        *India's Northeast in Flames*, New Delhi: Vikas.

SARKAR, JADUNATH
1920        *Mughal Administration*, Calcutta.

SARKAR, SUMIT
1973        *The Swadeshi Movement in Bengal, 1903–8*, Delhi: Orient Longman.

SCHEFF, T.J.
1968        Negotiating Reality: Notes on Power in the Assessment of Responsibility, *Social Problems* 16: 3–17.

SCHELLING, T.C.
1963        *The Strategy of Conflict*, London.

SCHWARTZBERG, J.E.
1965        The Distribution of Selected Castes in the North Indian Plain, *Geographical Review* 15: 477–95.

SEN, A.K., M.C. SETALVAD, G.S. PATHAK
1964        *Justice for the Common Man*, Lucknow: Eastern Book
            Co.

SEN, SUMANTA
1984        Remote Control, *India Today* 31 May 1984.

SETALVAD, M.C.
1960        *The Common Law in India*, London: Stevens & Sons.

SHAH, GHANSHYAM
1990        *Social Movements in India: A Review of the Literature*,
            New Delhi: Sage.

SHARMA, G.S.
1967        Changing Perceptions of Law in India, *Jaipur Law
            Journal* 7: 1–19.

SHARMA, M.P. AND K.D. GANGRADE
1971        *Inter-Generational Conflict in India*, Bombay: Nachiketa.

SHUKLA, R.L.
1972        *Britain, India, and the Turkish Empire 1853–82*, Delhi.

SIEGEL, BERNARD J. AND A.R. BEALS
1960        Pervasive Factionalism, *American Anthropologist* 62: 394–
            417.

SIMMEL, GEORG
1955        *Conflict* (tr. Kurt H. Wolff), New York: Free Press.

1971        *On Individuality and Social Forms*, Chicago: University
            of Chicago Press.

SINGER, MILTON
1968        The Indian Joint Family in Modern India, in Milton
            Singer and Bernard S. Cohn (eds), *Structure and Change
            in Indian Society*, Chicago: Aldine.

1984        *Man's Glassy Essence: Explorations in Semiotic Anthropol-
            ogy*, Bloomington: Indiana University Press.

SINHA, D.M.
1971a    *Meerut District, District Census Handbook, Primary Census Abstracts; ser. 21, pt. X-B*. Lucknow: Director of Census Operations.

1971b    *Muzaffarnagar District, District Census Handbook, Primary Census Abstracts; ser. 21, pt. X-B*, Lucknow: Director of Census Operations.

SPEAR, PERCIVAL
1951    *Twilight of the Mughals*, Calcutta.

SPODEK, HOWARD
1971    On the Origins of Gandhi's Political Methodology: The Heritage of Kathiawad and Gujarat, *Journal of Asian Studies* 30: 361–72.

SRINIVAS, M.N.
1963    A Study of Disputes, Delhi: University of Delhi (Delhi School of Economics, Dept. of Sociology), mimeographed.

SUMNER, WILLIAM GRAHAM
1911    *War and Other Essays*, New Haven: Yale University Press.

SVALASTOGA, KAARE
1965    *Social Differentiation*, New York: David McKay.

SWARTZ, MARC J., VICTOR W. TURNER, AND ARTHUR TUDEN
1966    Introduction, in their ed., *Political Anthropology*, Chicago: Aldine, 1–41.

THAPAR, ROMILA, HARBANS MUKHIA AND BIPAN CHANDRA
1969    *Communalism and the Writing of Indian History*, New Delhi: People's Publishing House.

*Transindia*
1978    *Transindia* 3:1, May 1978.

TURNER, V.
1969        *The Ritual Process*, Chicago: Aldine.

TURNER, VICTOR W.
1974        Religious Paradigms and Political Action: Thomas Be-
            cket at the Council of Northampton, in his *Dramas,
            Fields, and Metaphors*, Ithaca: Cornell University Press,
            60–97.

UBEROI, PATRICIA (ed.)
1993        *Family, Kinship and Marriage in India*, Delhi: Oxford
            University Press.

VAN DER DENNEN, JOHAN M.G.
1987        Ethnocentrism and In-group/Out-group Differentiation,
            A Review and Interpretation of the Literature, in V.
            Reynolds, V.S.E. Falger and Ian Vine (eds), *The
            Sociobiology of Ethnocentrism*, London: Croom Helm,
            1–47.

VAN GENNEP, A.
1960        *The Rites of Passage*, Chicago: University of Chicago
            Press.

VAN PARIJS, PHILIPPE
1981        *Evolutionary Explanation in the Social Sciences: An Emerg-
            ing Paradigm*, London: Tavistock.

VARMA, D.K.
1981        State Labour Front Disturbing, *Financial Express* 22 July
            1981.

VATUK, SYLVIA
1975        Gifts and Affines in North India, *Contributions to Indian
            Sociology* 9: 156–96.

VERGHESE, T.C.
1993        *Agrarian Change and Economic Consequences: Land
            Tenures in Kerala, 1850–1960*, New Delhi: Allied.

WALSH, CECIL
1912          *Indian Village Crimes*, London.

WASHBROOK, D.A.
1975          The Development of Caste Organization in South India,
              1880 to 1925, in C.J. Baker and D.A. Washbrook, *South
              India: Political Institutions and Political Change, 1880–
              1940*, Delhi: Macmillan.

WEBER, MAX
1964          *The Theory of Social and Economic Organization* (tr. A.M.
              Henderson and T. Parsons), New York: Free Press.

WEINER, MYRON
1978          *Sons of the Soil: Migration and Ethnic Conflict in India*,
              Delhi: Oxford University Press.

WIENER, NORBERT
[1950]        *The Human Use of Human Beings: Cybernetics and Society*,
              Garden City, N.Y.: Doubleday, 1954 Anchor edition.

WOODIS, JACK
1972          *New Theories of Revolution: A Commentary on the Views
              of Frantz Fanon, Regis Debray and Herbert Marcuse*, New
              York: International Publishers.

WRONG, D.
1961          The Oversocialized Conception of Man in Modern
              Sociology, *American Sociological Review* 26: 183–93.

# Index